Legal Practice in the Formative Stages of the Chinese Empire

Sinica Leidensia

Edited by

Barend J. ter Haar
Maghiel van Crevel

In co-operation with

P.K. Bol, D.R. Knechtges, E.S. Rawski,
W.L. Idema, H.T. Zurndorfer

VOLUME 130

The titles published in this series are listed at *brill.com/sinl*

Legal Practice in the Formative Stages of the Chinese Empire

An Annotated Translation of the Exemplary Qin Criminal Cases from the Yuelu Academy Collection

By

Ulrich Lau
Thies Staack

BRILL

LEIDEN | BOSTON

Cover illustration: Detail of slip 001 of the Yuelu Academy *Wei yu deng zhuang si zhong* with the key formula *gan yan zhi* 敢濡（讞）之 "(We, the responsible officials,) venture to submit (the following case) for decision." Courtesy of Yuelu Academy, Changsha (People's Republic of China).

Library of Congress Cataloging-in-Publication Data

Names: Staack, Thies, translator, writer of added commentary. | Lau, Ulrich, translator, writer of added commentary. | Yuelu shu yuan, owner.
Title: Legal practice in the formative stages of the Chinese empire : an annotated translation of the exemplary Qin criminal cases from the Yuelu Academy collection / By Ulrich Lau, Thies Staack.
Other titles: Wei yu deng zhuang si zhong. English
Description: Leiden ; Boston : Brill, 2016. | Series: Sinica Leidensia ; volume 130 | Includes bibliographical references and index.
Identifiers: LCCN 2016008887 (print) | LCCN 2016009214 (ebook) | ISBN 9789004315433 (hardback : alk. paper) | ISBN 9789004315655 (E-book)
Subjects: LCSH: Wei yu deng zhuang si zhong. | Criminal law--China--History-- To 1500--Early works to 1800. | China--History--Qin dynasty, 221-207 B.C--Early works to 1800. | Wei yu deng zhuang si zhong. Manuscripts.--Yuelu shu yuan. | Criminal law--China--History--To 1500--Manuscripts. | China-History--Qin dynasty, 221-207 B.C--Manuscripts.
Classification: LCC KNN265.A4 W45 2016 (print) | LCC KNN265.A4 (ebook) | DDC 345.31/07--dc23
LC record available at http://lccn.loc.gov/2016008887

Typeface for the Latin, Greek, and Cyrillic scripts: "Brill". See and download: brill.com/brill-typeface.

ISSN 0169-9563
ISBN 978-90-04-31543-3 (hardback)
ISBN 978-90-04-31565-5 (e-book)

This book is printed on acid-free paper and produced in a sustainable manner.

Contents

PART 2
Annotated Translation of the Wei yu deng zhuang

Preface

From 2010 until 2014, we were part of the research project "The Legal Manuscripts of the Qin (3rd century BC) held in the Collection of Yuelu Academy", which was directed by Prof. Michael Friedrich, conducted at the University of Hamburg and funded by the DFG (German Research Foundation). Since 2009 we had already been in close contact with the editorial team of the Yuelu Academy manuscripts, led by Prof. Chen Songchang 陳松長. Over the next few years we accepted several invitations to participate in conferences and reading sessions with the editorial team in Changsha; Prof. Chen likewise accepted invitations to Hamburg, where he stayed as a visiting scholar in the summers of 2013 and 2014. This close cooperation in the study of the Yuelu Academy legal manuscripts was extremely beneficial for our work. Prof. Chen provided our project with digital photographs of the material discussed in this book long before these were first published as part of an edition in 2013. Prof. Arnd Helmut Hafner, who was mainly responsible for that edition, likewise shared with us his transcriptions of the Yuelu Academy collection of criminal cases (as well as subsequent revisions) at multiple points in the editorial process. The Yuelu Academy editorial team also directly profited from some of the research results of our project.

The present book is the main result of the aforementioned Hamburg project. It consists of two parts. The first is conceived as an introduction to the extant sources on early Chinese law, the manuscripts in possession of Yuelu Academy, and especially the *Wei yu deng zhuang si zhong* 爲獄等狀四種, a collection of 15 criminal cases from pre-imperial Qin that is the subject of this study. This introductory part further outlines legal terminology, instances of jurisdiction, stages of criminal procedure and other critical points for the understanding of criminal procedure during the Qin and early Han period and situates the collection of Qin cases in the broader context of legal manuscripts from pre-imperial and early imperial China. The second larger part is a translation of the *Wei yu deng zhuang si zhong*, including brief introductions to each of the 15 cases, diplomatic and fully punctuated editions, and extensive philological notes.

At the time of this book's appearance, the long-expected study on the legal texts from Zhangjiashan tomb no. 247 by Anthony J. Barbieri-Low and Robin D. S. Yates (Sinica Leidensia 126) will have been published as well. We are certain that their seminal work could have greatly benefited this book, but unfortunately it was not available to us before we submitted the final manuscript. We therefore were unable to include adequate references to Barbieri-Low and

Yates' study, but we highly encourage readers of this book to consult it as well, as we assume that the two works will nicely complement one another.

The completion of this book would not have been possible without the help and support of many friends and colleagues. We owe a special debt of gratitude to Prof. Michael Friedrich (University of Hamburg, CSMC), Prof. Chen Songchang (Yuelu Academy) and Prof. Arnd Helmut Hafner (Tokyo University of Foreign Studies). Further, we would like to thank: Prof. Enno Giele (University of Heidelberg), Dr. Michael Lüdke (University of Erlangen), Prof. Constance A. Cook (Lehigh University), Prof. Christoph Harbsmeier (University of Oslo), Dr. Irina Wandrey (University of Hamburg, CSMC), Dr. Haeree Park (University of Hamburg, CSMC) and Dr. Paul Nicholas Vogt (University of Heidelberg). Dorit Staack kindly helped us create the maps in this volume. We would also like to express our gratitude to Patricia Radder and Gera van Bedaf (Koninklijke Brill NV) for their kind support and patience, the anonymous reviewers of this work for many helpful suggestions, and both the DFG and the Centre for the Study of Manuscript Cultures (CSMC) in Hamburg for funding this endeavour.

Last but certainly not least we would like to thank our families for their constant support and encouragement during the work on this book.

Ulrich Lau and Thies Staack
November 2015

Chinese Dynasties and Historical Periods (ca. 1000 BC–AD 200)

Zhou 周	**1045(?)–256 BC**
Western Zhou 西周	1045(?)–771 BC
Eastern Zhou 東周	770–256 BC
Spring and Autumn (Chunqiu 春秋)	722–481 BC
Warring States (Zhanguo 戰國)	475–221 BC
Qin 秦 (Empire)	**221–206 BC**
Han 漢	**206 BC–AD 220**
Western Han 西漢	206 BC–AD 8
Xin 新 (Wang Mang 王莽)	AD 9–23
Eastern Han 東漢	AD 23–220

Maps of the Qin Empire and the Provinces of the South

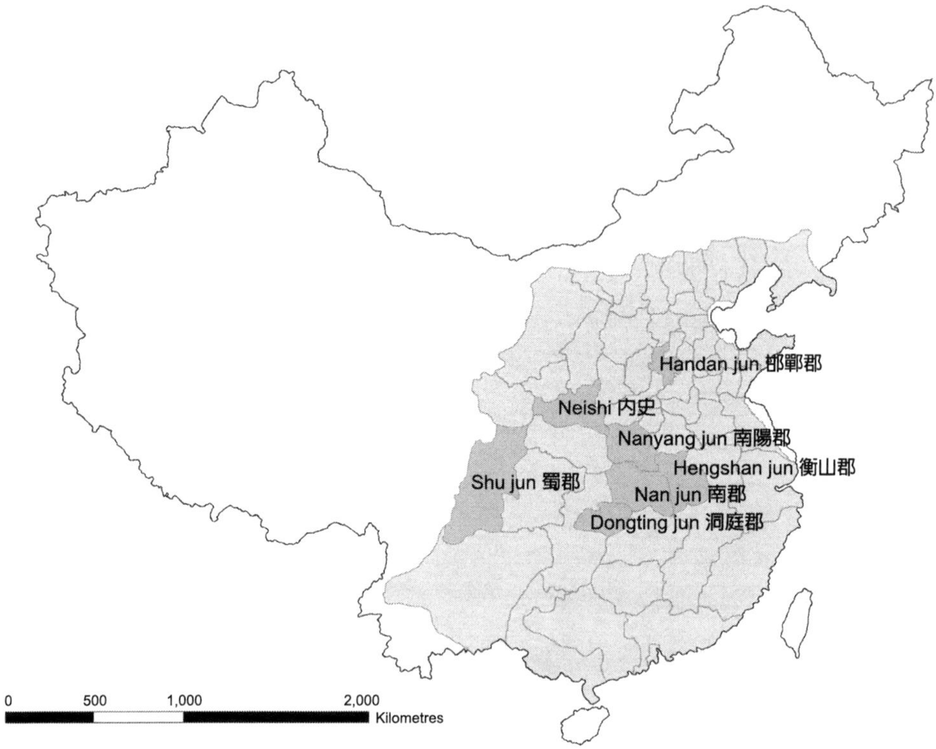

MAP 1 *The Qin Empire (221–206 BC)*[1]

1 This drawing is based on Hou Xiaorong 2009, 117. It shows the provinces (*jun* 郡) of the Qin Empire (marked in grey) inside the border of today's People's Republic of China. Provinces that are directly or indirectly (by the name of a prefecture that can be assigned to a certain province) mentioned in the Yuelu Academy *Wei yu deng zhuang si zhong*, and that therefore must have been established in the pre-imperial period of Qin, have been highlighted in dark grey.

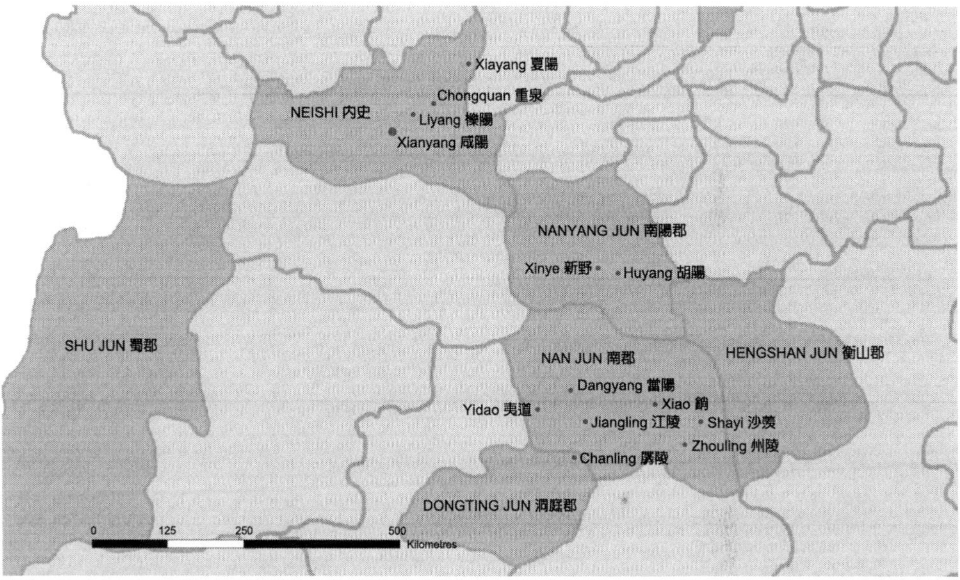

MAP 2 *The Qin provinces of the South*[2]

2 This drawing is based on Hou Xiaorong 2009, 185 and 441. It shows the provinces (*jun*) and prefectures (*xian* 縣, marked by dots) that are directly or indirectly (by the name of a prefecture that can be assigned to a certain province) mentioned in the Yuelu Academy *Wei yu deng zhuang si zhong*. Note that Xianyang 咸陽, the capital of the Qin Empire, was added to the map, whereas one prefecture, namely Liyang 醴陽, was not included, as its exact location is unclear. See footnote 678.

PART 1

Introduction

CHAPTER 1

Sources on Early Chinese Law before the Yuelu Academy Finds

1.1 Received Literature

Until the second half of the 20th century, the possibilities for research on early Chinese law were rather limited due to the scarcity of sources. Even though the beginnings of statute law can be traced back at least to the late Spring and Autumn period (722–481 BC), specific legal texts had not been handed down within the otherwise so abundant Chinese literary transmission until the 7th century AD. The oldest extant legal code can be dated to the Tang dynasty (AD 618–907).[3] From early historiographic sources we know that as early as during the late Spring and Autumn and the early Warring States period (6th and 5th centuries BC), in a time of political instability and permanent military conflicts, several attempts were made to stipulate laws in writing.[4] The first attempt was made by the chancellor of the state of Zheng 鄭, Zichan 子產 (d. 522 BC), who had so-called *Xingshu* 刑書 ("Documents on Punishment") compiled by him cast on bronze vessels in the year 536 BC.[5] Other states followed this example: In 513 BC "Documents on Punishment", compiled in 549 BC by chancellor Fan Gai 范匄 (also known as Fan Xuanzi 范宣子, d. 548 BC), were cast on bronze vessels in the state of Jin 晉.[6] In the state of Zheng, penal laws were also recorded on bamboo slips by Deng Xi 鄧析 (d. 501 BC) in the late 6th century BC.[7] Neither the exact wording nor any details on the content of these early examples of written law have been transmitted. According to an account in the "Treatise on Penal Law" of the *Jinshu* 晉書, which was compiled in the 7th century AD, the so-called "Canon of Law" (*Fajing* 法經) is said to have had the most significant influence. This canon of penal law, of which only the division into six chapters and their titles is known, was compiled by Li Kui 李悝 (455–395 BC) from the state of Wei 魏 and allegedly served as a blueprint for the penal laws introduced by the reformer Shang Yang 商鞅

3 See the *Tanglü shuyi* in the edition by Liu Junwen (1983). For an annotated translation see Johnson 1979, 1997.

4 On these early examples of written law see e.g. Caldwell 2014, 14–25.

5 *Zuo* Zhao 6,607,3.

6 *Zuo* Zhao 29,729,18.

7 *Zuo* Ding 9,771,5.

 | DOI 10.1163/9789004315655_002

(390–338 BC) in Qin 秦 around 356 BC.[8] After the conquest of all other kingdoms and the unification of 221 BC, these Qin laws became valid in the entire Qin Empire.

Although the first Chinese empire of the Qin dynasty (221–206 BC) only lasted for 15 years, this dynasty gained paramount importance because it set a long-lasting framework for the succeeding Chinese empires with regard to the law and administration of justice. Before the foundation of the empire, several ancient Chinese states had attempted to create written law, but in no other state had rule been based so strictly on statutory law as in Qin. The rulers of the following Han dynasty (206 BC–AD 220) and important representatives of classical learning were unanimous in disapproving of the overthrown dynasty, and influenced the historiography of Han times accordingly, which was the most important source on the history of the Qin dynasty until the 20th century. Therefore, the *Shiji* 史記 or the "Treatise on Penal Law" (*Xing fa zhi* 刑法志) of the *Hanshu* 漢書 hardly provide objective information on the legal system of the Qin. Texts of Qin statutes are not quoted in the *Shiji*. Insights into the jurisdiction can be gained from accounts of over a dozen criminal cases,[9] which, however, were intended to illustrate the despotism of legal authorities and the misuse of penal law. The sources name draconic criminal regulations which are said to have served as the most important instrument of Qin rule. Sima Qian 司馬遷 (145 or 135–86 BC) emphasises the importance of the penal reform (*bian fa* 變法) initiated by the legalist chancellor Shang Yang in Qin around 350 BC.[10] These reforms implemented a meritocratic system, in which military achievements led to social ascension. Punishments that "did not spare the mighty and powerful",[11] and were imposed without regard to the person, served to discipline a disordered society and to consolidate power. An innovation was the division of the population into units of five and ten households, the members of which were collectively liable (*lian zuo* 連坐) for each other and were facing the severest form of death penalty (being cut in two at the waist, *yao zhan* 腰斬) if they failed to report an offender from their own unit to the authorities.[12] However, the level of penalties mentioned seems to be a Han time exaggeration because in actual practice the collective punishment never

8 *Jinshu* 30, 922; *Tanglü shuyi* 1, 2. The titles of the six chapters of penal law were *Dao* 盜, *Zei* 賊, *Qiu* 囚, *Bu* 捕, *Za* 雜 and *Ju* 具.

9 Guo Chengwei 1992, 21–24; Xin Ziniu 1997, vol. 1, 88–101. Cf. the famous criminal proceedings against the former chancellor Li Si (*Shiji* 87, 2560–2562; translation in Bodde 1938, 48–52).

10 *Shiji* 68, 2229.

11 *Zhanguoce* 39/12/23.

12 *Shiji* 68, 2230.

exceeded that given to the actual offender, as proven by Qin and early Han manuscripts that were excavated during the second half of the 20th century.[13] Sima Qian conceded that Shang Yang's reforms had a positive effect in so far as robbers and bandits from the mountains no longer troubled the populace. Furthermore, the people reportedly put their bravery to test in campaigns for the sovereign instead of personal feuds, and "great order" (*da zhi* 大治) is said to have prevailed.[14] The "Treatise on Penal Law" expressly reproves the First Emperor of the Qin dynasty (Qin Shihuang 秦始皇, 259–210 BC) for his obsession with penal law:

> He solely relied on mutilation punishments and penalties and personally wielded textbook and ink; in the day-time he decided on lawsuits, during the night he put in order the documents. He himself measured the decisions, daily weighing off one picul. And yet villainy and evil arose side by side [so that] the red-clothed [felons] blocked the roads and the gaols became [as busy as] markets.[15]

A further aggravation of penal law under the Second Emperor Hu Hai 胡亥 (229–207 BC), which had been initiated by the influential eunuch Zhao Gao 趙高 (d. 207 BC),[16] is said to have contributed to the demise of the Qin dynasty. When the hired agricultural labourer Chen She 陳涉 (d. 208 BC), who in 209 BC was leading 900 conscripts during his military service, was not able to arrive at his destination in time due to heavy rain that had made the roads impassable, he was facing the death penalty for "failing to meet a deadline" (*shi qi* 失期).[17] Chen She did not see another way to escape his execution than to start a rebellion. Although he himself died during heavy battles with the Qin troops, his rebellion caused a civil war, which finally led to the dynasty's overthrow. The founder of the following Han dynasty, Liu Bang 劉邦 (256–195 BC), abrogated the laws of the odious Qin dynasty in the year of his takeover in 206 BC and issued a strongly simplified penal law with only three basic offences: homicide, bodily injury and theft.[18] But as this apparently could not fulfil its purpose, his chancellor Xiao He 蕭何 (257–193 BC) purportedly selected from among the

13 See section 4.4 below. Particularly sadistic forms of execution like tearing out ribs or boiling in a cauldron (*Hanshu* 23, 1096) likewise lack evidence from legal manuscripts of the time.

14 *Shiji* 68, 2231.

15 *Hanshu* 23, 1096; Hulsewé 1955, 332–333.

16 *Shiji* 87, 2552–2553.

17 *Shiji* 48, 1950.

18 *Hanshu* 1A, 23.

Qin laws those which he deemed suitable for use under the new circumstances and compiled them into a collection of statutes in nine chapters (*Lü jiu zhang* 律九章) in approximately 200 BC.[19] There is only one further reference confirming the title of this collection within the received literature of Han times;[20] the text of the statutes contained in it is not transmitted. A comparison with excavated legal manuscripts reveals that the information on the division of the *Lü jiu zhang* into chapters, as provided by the *Jinshu*,[21] is not reliable.[22]

This general outline of the development of early Chinese law is based on several slightly different versions of the same story that can be found in the dynastic histories.[23] Apart from such accounts, received literature also provides more scattered information on early Chinese law, e.g. in form of citations from statutes and ordinances. This information has been gathered and compiled by various scholars, first and foremost Shen Jiaben 沈家本 and Cheng Shude 程樹德, followed by Hulsewé.[24] However, even these commendable attempts at the reconstruction of the pre-imperial and early imperial legal system could not fill the huge gaps that remained due to the scarcity of sources.

1.2 Excavated Manuscripts

Since the 1970s, the number of sources has increased significantly with the excavation of legal manuscripts from ancient tombs, and more recently due to a growing number of finds from disused wells. The oldest examples excavated to date were found in 1987 in a tomb near Baoshan 包山, Hubei province. The tomb occupant had once been a high judicial official in the ancient state of Chu 楚 and died in 316 BC. In his tomb several examples of official

19 *Hanshu* 23, 1096.

20 *Lunheng* 12, 126.

21 *Jinshu* 30, 922.

22 For example, it is said that the statutes on levies (*Xing lü* 興律), on stables (*Jiu lü* 廄律), and on households (*Hu lü* 戶律) were newly established at the beginning of the Han dynasty. However, the Qin manuscripts excavated from Shuihudi tomb no. 11 contain administrative statutes on stables and parks (*Jiu yuan lü* 廄苑律) and there can be found Qin statutes on levies for military and civil service (*Xing lü*) in the manuscript collection of Yuelu Academy (Chen Songchang 2009a, 86).

23 Most prominently in *Hanshu* 23 and *Jinshu* 30. For an English translation of the former treatise see Hulsewé 1955, 321–350. The latter has been translated into German by Heuser (1987).

24 Shen Jiaben 1985, Cheng Shude 1955. Based on their work, Hulsewé (1955) later completed a compilation of scattered sources, which also drew on some early manuscript finds.

documents were found, e.g. a register of legal cases including entries on deadlines, names of accused persons and of officials investigating the cases, records on individual lawsuits with the names of the persons involved in the proceedings as well as the cases' subject-matter and several more detailed case records.[25]

In comparison to those found in Baoshan tomb no. 2, the legal manuscripts excavated from Shuihudi 睡虎地 tomb no. 11 in 1975 have been objects of extensive studies for a much longer time.[26] These manuscripts were placed in the tomb of a man named Xi 喜. According to a chronicle buried beside the legal manuscripts, Xi was appointed a scribe in 244 BC at the age of 19[27] and promoted to the responsible position of a *ling shi* 令史 "secretary of the prefect"[28] in Anlu 安陸 in 241 BC.[29] He held the same office in the prefecture of Yan 鄢, where he tried criminal cases for the first time in 235 BC at the age of 28[30] and remained in charge of the jurisdiction until his death, probably around 217 BC.

The legal manuscripts from Shuihudi can be distinguished into five groups according to varying form and content: a selection of 18 administrative statutes,[31] separate statutes for the control/supervision of granaries,[32] miscellaneous excerpts from statutes,[33] commentaries on different penal statutes,[34] as well as "models for sealing (the property of criminals) and for gathering evi-

25 Hubei sheng Jing Sha tielu kaogudui 1991; Chen Wei et al. 2009, 1–91; Zhu Xiaoxue 2013. For studies on the legal manuscripts see Chen Wei 1996, 21–66; Zhang Boyuan 2014a; Weld 1999 and 2003.

26 Shuihudi Qinmu zhujian zhengli xiaozu 1990; Chen Wei et al. 2014, vols. 1 to 3; Hulsewé 1985 (in the following *RCL*).

27 *Biannianji* 10.2.

28 For *ling shi* see footnote 1175.

29 *Biannianji* 13.2.

30 *Biannianji* 14.2, 19.2. Cf. Yates 2011, 357.

31 This manuscript was named *Qinlü shiba zhong* 秦律十八種 by the editors. It does not bear a comprehensive title, but the name of the respective statute is noted after each individual article.

32 The title of this manuscript, *Xiao* (*lü*) 效 (律), which can be equated with *jiao* 校 "to crosscheck" (Wang Hui 2008, 157; Bai Yulan 2012, 136; Feng and Deng 2006, 412; Schuessler 2007, 307), is written on the verso of the first slip according to the arrangement of the editors. For nine of the articles (*XL* 19–40=*RCL* B 8–16) there are (near) duplicates in the *Qinlü shiba zhong* manuscript (*QLSZ* 21–27, 162–178=*RCL* A 19, 82–89).

33 The name *Qinlü zachao* 秦律雜抄 was given by the editors as this manuscript lacks a comprehensive title. The title of the respective statute is only cited for some excerpts.

34 Just like *Qinlü shiba zhong* and *Qinlü zachao*, the title for this manuscript, *Falü dawen* 法律答問, was chosen by the editors.

dence by judicial inspection",[35] which also include several model records of investigation and interrogation during criminal proceedings.[36]

At the end of the year 1989, another major discovery of manuscripts from the Qin dynasty was made at Longgang 龍崗 tomb no. 6, not far from Shuihudi. The manuscripts contained administrative and penal regulations from the years 220 to 207 BC, which concern aspects like the forbidden hunting parks of the ruler, imperial speedways, cattle and horse breeding or crop yields. Furthermore, the finding of fact of a retrial that resulted in the acquittal of the defendant is recorded on a wood tablet also placed in the tomb.[37]

At the turn of 1983 and 1984, two remarkable manuscripts from the first years of the Han dynasty were discovered in tomb no. 247 at Zhangjiashan 張家山, Hubei province. The first was a selection of 27 statutes and several ordinances (*Ernian lüling* 二年律令),[38] probably from the second year of the reign of Empress Lü 呂 (186 BC), which at the time of excavation contained the earliest extant version of Chinese penal statutes;[39] the second was a collection of 22 criminal cases titled *Zou yan shu* 奏讞書.[40] According to a calendar that was also found in tomb no. 247, the tomb occupant was an official who from 202 BC onwards served the Han dynasty,[41] was relieved from his office due to illness in the first year of Emperor Hui 惠 (194 BC),[42] and probably died during the reign of Empress Lü (187–180 BC), or shortly afterwards.[43]

Eleven of the titles which are used for the administrative statutes from Zhangjiashan accord with statute titles occurring in the Shuihudi manuscripts.

35 This title (*Feng zhen shi* 封診式) is written on the verso of slip no. 98 of the manuscript.

36 On the *Feng zhen shi* see section 5.1 below.

37 Liu and Liang 1997; Zhongguo wenwu yanjiusuo and Hubei sheng wenwu kaogu yanjiusuo 2001; Chen Wei et al. 2014, vol. 4.

38 Zhangjiashan er si qi hao Hanmu zhujian zhengli xiaozu 2001; Peng Hao et al. 2007; cf. Zhu Honglin 2005; Tomiya 2006; Barbieri-Low and Yates 2015.

39 *Zei lü* 賊律 (*ENLL* 1–54), *Dao lü* 盜律 (*ENLL* 55–81), *Ju lü* 具律 (*ENLL* 82–125), *Gao lü* 告律 (*ENLL* 126–136), *Bu lü* 捕律 (*ENLL* 137–156), *Wang lü* 亡律 (*ENLL* 157–173), *Shou lü* 收律 (*ENLL* 174–181), *Za lü* 雜律 (*ENLL* 182–196).

40 Zhangjiashan er si qi hao Hanmu zhujian zhengli xiaozu 2001; Peng Hao et al. 2007; cf. Ikeda 2002 and 2015; Cai Wanjin 2006; Gao Heng 2008, 341–407; Lau and Lüdke 2012; Korolkov 2013; Barbieri-Low and Yates 2015.

41 *Lipu* 2.

42 *Lipu* 10.

43 The calendar from Zhangjiashan tomb no. 247 refers to the years 202–186 BC. The collection of statutes and ordinances is often dated to the second year of Empress Lü (186 BC).

However, the exact content of the respective texts is only partly identical. Both collections contain statutes on agriculture,[44] currency,[45] markets at border control points,[46] statute labour,[47] ranks granted for military achievements,[48] the appointment of officials,[49] control of granaries,[50] food rations for couriers at relay stations,[51] forwarding of documents,[52] and the enrolment for labour and military service.[53] Beside these, the administrative statutes from Zhangjiashan also contain statutes on coinage and circulation of cash,[54] financial aids for burial equipment and burial ceremonies,[55] households,[56] establishment of heirs (of rank holders),[57] salaries of officials,[58] as well as the training of scribes, diviners and invocators.[59]

Apart from these manuscripts further important finds are still awaiting publication. These include 372 bamboo slips with 15 penal and administrative statutes,[60] which were excavated from Zhangjiashan tomb no. 336 in 1988 and were dated to around 173–167 BC, the early years of the reign of Emperor Wen 文 of the Han.[61] Likewise, a collection of 306 bamboo slips with penal statutes and 544 slips with administrative statutes as well as other legal documents from the years 170–157 BC (reign of Emperor Wen), which were discovered during the year 2006 in Shuihudi tomb no. 77, remain unpublished.[62] In 2010, a

44 *Tian lü* 田律: QLSZ 1–12=RCL A 1–6; ENLL 239–257.
45 *Jin bu lü* 金布律: QLSZ 64–96=RCL A 36–50; ENLL 418–439.
46 *Guan shi lü* 關市律: QLSZ 97=RCL A 51; ENLL 258–263.
47 *Yao lü* 徭律: QLSZ 115–124=RCL A 64; ENLL 278–280, 407–417.
48 *Jun jue lü* 軍爵律: QLSZ 153–156=RCL A 90–91; ENLL 392–395.
49 *Zhi li lü* 置吏律: QLSZ 157–161=RCL A 79–81; ENLL 210–224.
50 *Xiao lü* 效律: QLSZ 162–178=RCL A 82–89; ENLL 347–353.
51 *Zhuan shi lü* 傳食律: QLSZ 179–182=RCL A 92–94; ENLL 228–238.
52 *Xing shu lü* 行書律: QLSZ 183–185=RCL A 95–96; ENLL 264–277.
53 *Fu lü* 傅律: QLZC 32–33=RCL C 20; ENLL 354–366.
54 *Qian lü* 錢律: ENLL 197–209.
55 *Ci lü* 賜律: ENLL 282–304.
56 *Hu lü* 戶律: ENLL 305–346.
57 *Zhi hou lü* 置後律: ENLL 367–391.
58 *Zhi lü* 秩律: ENLL 440–473.
59 *Shi lü* 史律: ENLL 474–487.
60 According to personal communication with Peng Hao 彭浩, the manuscripts contain a small selection of administrative statutes as well as all the penal statutes that were also found in Zhangjiashan tomb no. 247, apart from the *Shoulü*.
61 Jingzhou diqu bowuguan 1992. The tomb originally had the number 136.
62 Hubei sheng wenwu kaogu yanjiusuo and Yunmeng xian bowuguan 2008, 31–37, esp. 35.

collection of criminal cases from the Eastern Han period was discovered during construction works at "May 1st Square" (Wuyi guangchang 五一廣場) in Changsha 長沙, Hunan province. These manuscripts were dated to the years AD 90–112.[63] Fragments of legal texts and records of individual criminal cases also appear in the administrative manuscripts that were found at Liye 里耶, Juyan 居延, and Tuzishan 兔子山. To date, an annotated compilation of text passages relevant for legal history has been produced only for the Juyan manuscripts.[64]

---

63 Changsha shi wenwu kaogu yanjiusuo 2013 and Changsha shi wenwu kaogu yanjiusuo et al. 2015.

64 Li and Liu 1994; Li Junming 2005.

CHAPTER 2

The Yuelu Academy Manuscript Collection[65]

In December 2007 the Yuelu Academy at Changsha purchased more than 2,000 bamboo and wood slips on the antique market in Hong Kong. These slips originally constituted more than ten separate manuscript rolls dating from pre-imperial through imperial Qin times (late 3rd century BC). As the manuscripts did not derive from a scientific excavation, but were apparently looted from an ancient tomb by grave robbers, their provenance is unclear. It can therefore not be completely ruled out that the manuscripts might stem from more than one excavation site, but to this date there is no evidence that would support such a claim.[66] At the time of purchase, the manuscripts had been separated into eight bundles of unsorted individual slips, which first had to be cleaned, photographed and categorised.[67] A general introduction published by Chen Songchang 陳松長, one of the main editors of the Yuelu Academy manuscripts, provided first details about their form and content in 2009.[68] The slips had different measurements ranging between 23 and 30 cm in length, and 0.5 to 0.8 cm in width; some showed traces of two bindings, others of three. Moreover, an initial investigation revealed at least eight different styles of script, which strongly suggested that the manuscripts were written by more

65 The following chapters 2 to 6 of the introduction part contain material that was or is going to be published separately also in Lau 2013, 2014 and Lau (forthcoming) as well as Staack (forthcoming).

66 The fact that the Yuelu Academy manuscripts contain texts of diverse content, i.e. calendars, divinatory, mathematical and legal texts, is, as such, not extraordinary, if compared with the manuscript collections that were excavated from tombs such as Shuihudi tomb no. 11 or Zhangjiashan tomb no. 247. These exhibit a similar textual diversity and would in fact suggest that the Yuelu Academy manuscripts likewise derive from a tomb. Another interesting point, namely the occurrence of three separate calendars, which appear to contain entries on different persons, could likewise be seen as an indicator that these calendars did not derive from the same excavation site. However, it has recently been shown that the three calendars are indeed connected, not only by the calligraphic style of (parts of) the script, but also by the personal names that are recorded in them, see Chen Wei 2012b.

67 For photographs of the manuscripts in the condition shortly after purchase see Zhu and Chen 2010, 204–220. In addition to the eight bundles mentioned, an anonymous collector donated 76 slips, which had obviously at an earlier date been separated from the other slips, to Yuelu Academy in summer 2008.

68 Chen Songchang 2009a.

 | DOI 10.1163/9789004315655_003

than one person.[69] Besides three calendars (*Zhiri* 質日[70]) from the years 220, 213 and 212 BC, a guidebook for officials (*Wei li zhi guan ji qianshou* 爲吏治官及黔首), a divinatory manuscript (*Zhanmeng shu* 占夢書) and a mathematical manuscript (*Shu* 數), more than 75% of the material consists of legal manuscripts. The total number of complete and fragmentary slips or items is 2,176.[71] The non-legal material has already been published in two volumes. The first volume contains the calendars (160 items), the guidebook (80 items) and the divinatory manuscript (48 items); the second contains the mathematical manuscript (236 items).[72] This leaves overall 1,652 items for the legal manuscripts.

The legal material is not entirely published yet and can be divided into two types of texts according to content: the largest part of presumably up to 1,400 items is formed by statutes (*lü* 律) and ordinances (*ling* 令), and still awaits publication.[73] The other part of the legal material is contained in the already published third volume of the series: a collection of criminal case records comparable to the *Zou yan shu* 奏讞書 from Zhangjiashan tomb no. 247, which was named *Wei yu deng zhuang si zhong* 爲獄等狀四種 by the editors.

2.1 The Question of Authenticity

Since the provenance of the slips is unclear, doubts may be raised about their authenticity.[74] However, the following points should also be kept in mind. First, the verso of many slips from the Yuelu Academy collection exhibit two phenomena, namely ink-drawn or knife-cut diagonal lines as well as mirror-inverted imprints of writing. These phenomena not only provide

69 Chen Songchang 2009a, 75–76.

70 Note that the titles of some manuscripts provided in Chen Songchang 2009a were different from those in the final edition (e.g. *Guan zhen* 官箴 instead of the later *Wei li zhi guan ji qianshou* 爲吏治官及黔首 for the guidebook; *Rizhi* 日志 instead of *Zhiri* 質日 for the calendars). The reason for this is that some of the titles chosen by the editors could be replaced by original titles later discovered in the manuscripts. For the case of the *Wei li zhi guan ji qianshou* see Chen Songchang 2010a.

71 Zhu and Chen 2010, preface.

72 Zhu and Chen 2010 and 2011.

73 Some studies on these statutes and ordinances, which also include transcriptions and sometimes photos of selected slips, have been published by members of the editorial team. For these see Chen Songchang 2009b, 2009c, 2010b, 2012a, 2012b, 2014a, 2014b, 2015; Yu Zhenbo 2009, 2010, 2015; Ou Yang 2015.

74 Cf. Goldin 2013.

important evidence for the reconstruction of manuscripts,[75] but can also support a claim for the authenticity of the Yuelu Academy slips. As has been shown, lines similar to those occurring on most of the Yuelu Academy slips can also be found on many archaeologically excavated slips.[76] Although the verso line phenomenon was briefly mentioned in the edition of the Baoshan slips more than twenty years ago,[77] its significance was first discussed in 2011,[78] more than three years after the Yuelu Academy slips had been purchased. The case is similar for the verso imprints of writing. It has only recently been demonstrated that in some cases they reflect the three-dimensional structure of manuscript rolls.[79] This means that both phenomena were all but unknown before 2011, and it is therefore highly unlikely that a potential forger would have been aware of them or, for that matter, their significance. A second important point is that there are some semantic and syntactic peculiarities to be found in the Yuelu Academy collection of criminal cases, which is in fact the main focus of this study. These peculiarities also occur in some other manuscripts from the Qin and early Han period, but have never previously been the subject of scholarly analysis or discussion. One example is the usage of *suo* 所. In legal manuscripts from Qin and early Han times, *suo* is a postposition that marks the recipient or giver as the object after verbs of transmitting, which take two objects. In such cases, the word is used instead of a preposition such as *yu* 於.[80] A second example is the usage of *shi* 蝕, usually known in the meaning "to eclipse". In legal manuscripts *shi* occurs in the phrase *wei shi* 未蝕, which refers to a principle of determining punishment for certain offences that have not been carried out, above all to illicit sexual intercourse.[81]

2.2 Possible Origin of the Collection

A comparison with other corpora of Qin and early Han manuscripts with legal material, which were mostly excavated from tombs (most prominently Shuihudi tomb no. 11, Longgang tomb no. 6, Zhangjiashan tomb no. 247), suggests that the Yuelu Academy manuscripts were probably also looted from an

75 Sun Peiyang 2011; Staack 2013, 2014b; Yuelu shuyuan cang Qinjian zhengli xiaozu 2013.

76 Sun Peiyang 2011, 454.

77 Hubei sheng Jing Sha tielu kaogudui 1991, 4.

78 Sun Peiyang 2011.

79 Staack 2013, cf. Yuelu shuyuan cang Qinjian zhengli xiaozu 2013.

80 For *suo* see footnote 681.

81 See in detail footnotes 1155 and 1187.

ancient tomb. The occupant of that tomb might have been a scribe in charge of the administration of justice at the level of the prefecture (*xian* 縣).[82] The three calendars that were found among the Yuelu Academy manuscripts recorded important activities of the possible tomb occupant. On two slips, which were mentioned in connection with the calendars in the preliminary report, it is stated that an official, who might have kept this calendar, became the scribe of the controller of works (*si kong* 司空) in the 24th year of the reign of King Zheng 政 of Qin (i.e. 223 BC), and was transferred in the subsequent 25th year to the position of a *ling shi*.[83] The reason for the later exclusion of these two slips and two further ones from the three calendars in the final edition was probably the fact that the details mentioned about the possible tomb occupant's career in the previous years do not, at least at first sight, fit into any of these calendars, which refer to different periods in time. However, the information on the official activities of the possible tomb occupant relating to his scribal duties, including the conduct of criminal proceedings, would fit into the context of the *Wei yu deng zhuang* and the other legal manuscripts purchased by the Yuelu Academy.

---

82 For the status and training of hereditary scribes at lower authorities who were buried in tombs together with legal manuscripts see in detail Yates 2011, 345–360. Some words should be said on the translation of the words *xian* 縣 and *jun* 郡 in this work. The former has been rendered as "prefecture", the latter as "province". We are aware that there are more widely used alternative translations of these terms, namely "county" and "commandery". However, we decided to use the likewise conventional terms "prefecture" and "province" for the following reasons. First, the head of a prefecture and his deputy can conveniently be rendered as "prefect" and "vice prefect", respectively. Second, the term "commandery" carries military connotations which do not fit the *jun* as a civil institution – the military institution on the level of the *jun* was the *du wei* 都尉, which was often also spatially separated from the *jun*.

83 Slips no. 0687, 0625; Chen Songchang 2009a, 77. For the view that the tomb occupant was the father of the mentioned official – but likewise an official – see Chen Wei 2012b.

CHAPTER 3

The *Wei yu deng zhuang* Manuscripts[84]

The so-called *Wei yu deng zhuang si zhong* 爲獄等狀四種 "Four Types of Documents for Trying Criminal Cases and Other (Procedures)" (hereafter abbreviated as *Wei yu deng zhuang*) represents a collection of criminal cases from the pre-imperial period of Qin (between 246 BC and 222 BC). The following sections will introduce both the codicological features as well as the basic content of the four manuscripts compiled by the Yuelu Academy editors under this name.

3.1 Codicological Features

The *Wei yu deng zhuang* contains 257 slips with 15 different criminal case records (12 of them comparably well preserved) that, for various reasons, were submitted by local officials to the higher authorities for decision. Although all of these cases show similarities in structure and content to those contained in the *Zou yan shu* from Zhangjiashan tomb no. 247,[85] it is clear that they were not part of one and the same codicological unit, i.e. one roll, as is the case with the *Zou yan shu*.[86] Instead, the *Wei yu deng zhuang* appears to originally have consisted of four independent manuscript rolls that differed in terms of the writing support (bamboo vs. wood), the dimensions of the slips as well as the number and position of the bindings. These four manuscripts are referred to as first, second, third and fourth "category" (*lei* 類) in the edition. Figure 1 demonstrates the codicological differences.

An examination of the *Wei yu deng zhuang* slips further suggests that the writing on all of them actually belongs to the same type of script, although at

84 For general introductions see Zhu and Chen 2013, preface; Yuelu shuyuan cang Qinjian zhengli xiaozu 2013 as well as Zhang Boyuan 2014d.

85 See chapter 4 below.

86 For the following discussion of the codicological and palaeographical features of the *Wei yu deng zhuang* in comparison to the *Zou yan shu* see in detail Staack (forthcoming). Cf. Zhu and Chen 2013, preface. The fact that the *Zou yan shu* consisted of only one codicological unit becomes evident from the drawing of the position of the slips at the time of excavation, see Zhangjiashan er si qi hao Hanmu zhujian zhengli xiaozu 2001, appendix B.

 | DOI 10.1163/9789004315655_004

the same time considerable differences in the style of script are evident.[87] Table 1 shows some examples of frequently used characters in four different styles.

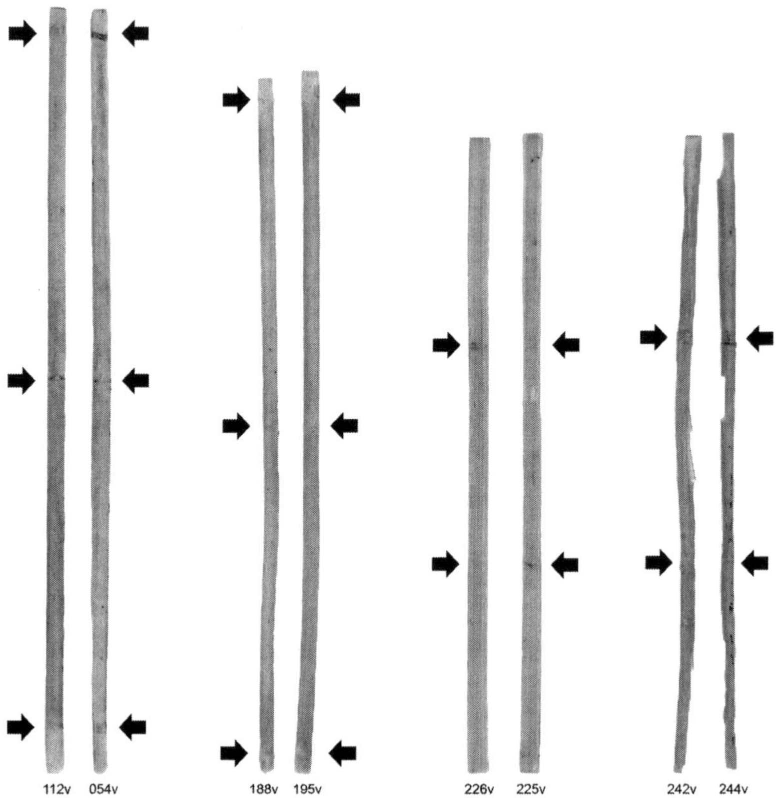

FIGURE 1 *Sample slips from* Wei yu deng zhuang *manuscripts I–IV* (*from left to right*).[88]

To sum up, codicological differences in material, the dimensions of the slips and the number and/or position of bindings, which are in fact always paralleled by palaeographical differences in style of script (see Table 2), were the

87 For some tentative criteria to distinguish the categories "type" and "style" of script as well as "hand" see Richter 2006.

88 Please note that these photos show the verso of all eight slips, because on the wood slips (225 and 226) traces of bindings (indicated by arrows) are barely visible on the recto. Also, the slips do not appear in their original size although the proportions are true to scale. Cf. Yuelu shuyuan cang Qinjian zhengli xiaozu 2013, 78, fig. 1.

reasons to conclude that the *Wei yu deng zhuang* originally consisted of four independent manuscript rolls.

As can already be seen from the quantity of slips in the four manuscripts, MS I is by far the largest codicological unit of the *Wei yu deng zhuang*. It comprises seven of the overall 15 case records; MS II contains six case records, whereas MS III and IV contain only one each. For the multiple-text manuscripts I and II, it was possible to reconstruct the sequence of the case records through an analysis of diagonal lines and mirror-inverted imprints of writing on the verso of the slips.[89]

TABLE 1 *Overview of different styles of script inside the* Wei yu deng zhuang.[90]

Style / Character	A	B	C	D
bu 不	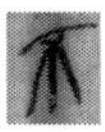 (099.26)	 (198.14)	 (230.4)	 (243.11)
zhi 之	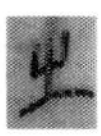 (048.1)	 (170.11)	 (217.11)	 (242.28)
wei 爲	 (055.7)	 (205.35)	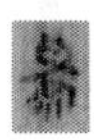 (226.7)	 (244.21)
gan 敢	 (023.5)	 (147.16)	 (210.15)	 (241.1)

89 The first comprehensive discussion of the verso line phenomenon is Sun Peiyang 2011. For a discussion of mirror-inverted imprints and the reconstruction of MS I see Staack 2013 as well as Staack (forthcoming) (cf. Zhu and Chen 2013, appendix C); for MS II see Zhu and Chen 2013, appendix C. The reconstruction of MS II, however, has to be considered as (partly) tentative, as stated by the editors (Zhu and Chen 2013, 176 with footnote 1 as well as 318).

90 Each character form is followed by a reference number in parentheses. This always comprises the number of the slip (according to the edition in Zhu and Chen 2013) as well as the number of the character on the respective slip, separated by a dot. For further examples of characters see Staack (forthcoming). Cf. the analysis of scribal hands in Chen and Zhang 2014.

TABLE 2 *Overview of codicological and palaeographical differences inside the* Wei yu deng zhuang.[91]

Category/MS	Material	Number of slips	Length	Number of bindings	Style of script
I	bamboo	137	27.5 cm	3	A
II	bamboo	73	25 cm	3	B
III	wood	27	23 cm	2	C
IV	bamboo	13	23 cm	2	D

3.2 Basic Content

The whole collection was named *Wei yu deng zhuang si zhong* by the editors to integrate different titles that had been found on the verso of three slips: 1. *Wei yu* [...] *zhuang* 爲獄□狀, 2. *Wei qi ju zou zhuang* 爲乞鞫奏狀, 3. *Wei fu zou zhuang* 爲覆奏狀. It is important to note that these titles were found on three slips that all belong to MS II (i.e. 137v, 139v, 140v), whereas no titles were found on the other three manuscripts. It is therefore uncertain exactly how – and if at all – the titles relate to the other three manuscripts and why there are three different titles on the same manuscript.[92] As far as content is concerned, there are obvious differences between the four *Wei yu deng zhuang* manuscripts. First of all, the cases recorded in the manuscripts were tried during different periods of time. Whereas all dated cases in MS I fall into the period between

91 For the data collected here see Zhu and Chen 2013, preface. The overall number of 257 slips is the sum of the 252 slips and fragments contained in Zhu and Chen 2013 plus five additional slips published as addenda in Hafner 2013a and 2014a.

92 The editors assume that the meaning of *wei fu* 爲覆 is actually the same as that of *wei qi ju* 爲乞鞫 as both refer to the retrial of a criminal case. Therefore, the two titles *Wei fu zou zhuang* and *Wei qi ju zou zhuang* refer to the same matter (for a different view see Su Junlin 2014b, 307). They further proposed that the case records contained in MS II had been circulated separately (with separate titles) before they were collected in one MS under the title *Wei yu* [...] *zhuang*, which the editors deemed to be a more general title for the whole MS II (Zhu and Chen 2013, preface). Apparently they considered this title appropriate to stand for all four manuscripts as a whole, so that it replaced the earlier title *Zou yan shu* 奏讞書, which had been chosen with regard to the *Zou yan shu* from Zhangjiashan (Chen Songchang 2009a, 85). For some criticism on the current title see Su Junlin 2014a.

229 and 222 BC, those in MS II are considerably older (246 and 242 BC).[93] The case in MS III can be dated to the same period as those in MS I (225 BC); the date of the one in MS IV is uncertain.[94]

All seven records in MS I reflect the so-called *yan* 讞-procedure of submitting criminal cases to the higher authorities for decision.[95] In all of the case records the phrase *gan yan zhi* 敢讞之 "we venture to submit this for decision", which typically occurs at the beginning and the end of these submissions, can be found at least once. In most cases of MS I the reasons for submission appear to have been certain doubts (*yi* 疑) of the officials at the prefecture-level. These doubts, which are formulated in five of the cases, could pertain to the correct punishment (cases I.1, I.5 and I.7), the correct amounts of rewards (for arresting criminals; case I.2) and apparently also to the correct method of judgement (leading to different punishments; case I.6). In two other cases of MS I (I.3 and I.4), the reason for submission was merely that approval by the higher authorities was required.

The cases in MS II clearly have a different focus, which is twofold. Two of the submissions (cases II.9 and II.10) are actually official letters, which served as recommendations of certain investigating officials for promotion. Although they are directed to the higher authorities, this is done with one of the standard formulas for submitting reports, *gan yan zhi* 敢言之 "we venture to report this", not *gan yan zhi* 敢讞之 as in the cases of MS I. As letters of recommendation, the two case reports are similar to case no. 22 of the *Zou yan shu*. Case records II.11 and II.12 represent the second type of submission in MS II, which can be compared with *Zou yan shu* case no. 17. They are accounts of retrials, which were each initiated by a "petition for a new finding of fact" (*qi ju* 乞鞫) filed by a convicted offender. In both cases the offender committed illicit

93 It should be noted that the dating of some cases in MS II suggested in this work differs from that postulated in Zhu and Chen 2013. This mainly concerns case II.10, where it can be argued that this case should be dated to 242 BC (see footnote 1089) instead of 227 BC, as proposed by the editors (Zhu and Chen 2013, 185 with footnote 1). Furthermore, the dating of case II.8 to the year 219 BC (Zhu and Chen 2013, 175 with footnote 2) is questionable as the case could likewise be dated to the year 246 BC. Note that individual case records of the *Wei yu deng zhuang* are always referred to by MS (I to IV) plus no. of the case record (1 through 15 according to the edition), so for example I.1 means case no. 1, which is part of MS I.

94 The tentative identification of the date on slip 237 as 221 BC (Zhu and Chen 2013, 239 with footnote 1) is not applied here because the character before *liu* 六 is hardly legible and its identification as *nian* 廿 might therefore be in doubt.

95 On the formal classification of the *Wei yu deng zhuang* cases see in detail section 4.6 below.

sexual intercourse, but considered his punishment to be unjustified. For the cases II.8 and II.13 it is difficult to decide which type of submission they can be assigned to due to their fragmentary state.

Case III.14 again is a typical *yan*-submission as can easily be gathered from the introductory/concluding formula *gan yan zhi* 敢讞之. Finally, case IV.15 does not allow a clear affiliation to a certain type of submission as none of the mentioned formulas occur. However, there are certain hints that point to a *yan*-submission.[96] For an overview of the *Wei yu deng zhuang* cases see the table in appendix III.

96 For these see footnote 1413 below.

CHAPTER 4

The *Wei yu deng zhuang* in Comparison with the *Zou yan shu* from Zhangjiashan Tomb No. 247

The newly acquired legal manuscripts of the Yuelu Academy give us the chance to compare a collection of criminal cases from pre-imperial Qin with the *Zou yan shu* from the beginning of the Han dynasty in order to examine continuity and historical change in the jurisdiction and to reconstruct the development of the legal system from the pre-imperial Qin period to the beginning of the Han dynasty.

4.1 Legal Terminology

One focus of interest during the investigation of the *Wei yu deng zhuang* was the analysis of legal terminology. The exploration of this terminology could not rely on definitions, which are the usual means to define terms in modern technical languages, as there are only very few contemporary definitions of legal terms from early imperial China. Instead, words were considered to be special legal terms, if they (1) have stable semantic relations to other terms, which can be described by the use of contrasting pairs, and (2) therefore occur in stable positions within the formal structure of legal texts, and (3) imply social and legal institutions that are not part of their immediate meaning. The degree of terminological fixation depends on the degree to which these three criteria are fulfilled.

There is a considerable degree of correspondence in terminology between the criminal case collections mentioned. In the dictionary of early Chinese legal terminology, which Ulrich Lau compiled in cooperation with Michael Lüdke, 125 legal terms used in the *Zou yan shu* are analysed.[97] At least 78 of these terms[98] (68%) can also be found in the *Wei yu deng zhuang*. There are eleven legal terms in the Yuelu Academy case collection, which do not occur in the *Zou yan shu*. Of these, four might have been Qin-specific. Beside the term *zhuang* 狀, which according to the editors refers to a type of document describ-

97 See Lau and Lüdke (forthcoming).

98 Cf. the list of legal terms occurring in the *Wei yu deng zhuang* in appendix IV.

 | DOI 10.1163/9789004315655_005

ing the facts of a criminal case[99] and in this meaning only occurs in the *Wei yu deng zhuang*, these are *hou* 候 "convict of *hou* (i.e. "watchman") category",[100] *lei lun* 纍/累論 "to pass judgement based on the accumulation (of punishments)"[101] and *wei shi* 未蝕 "to not have carried out (an offence)".[102] The other seven can likewise be found in Qin legal manuscripts from Shuihudi tomb no. 11 as well as in Han received literature or the *Ernian lüling* from early Han times: *dai* 紿 "to deceive sb. into doing sth.",[103] *fu* 服 "to confess (a criminal offence)",[104] *gou* 購 "reward (for arresting robbers and bandits)",[105] *jie* 劫 "to blackmail sb.",[106] *qiang* 強 "(to fornicate) by force",[107] *she* 赦 "to grant an amnesty, to pardon",[108] and *zheng* 爭 "to contest (someone's) claim to sth."[109] Therefore, it can be assumed that essential parts of the legal terminology used in the early Chinese empires were already evolved in pre-imperial Qin.

In the *Wei yu deng zhuang* there are even traces of Eastern Zhou legal language. The term *ci* 辭 for instance does not only mean "statement"[110] as in other legal manuscripts from Qin and Han times, but is also used as "to lodge a complaint", a meaning which is frequently associated with this word in received literature from the Eastern Zhou period.[111]

Some divergent legal terms between Qin and early Han manuscripts were already known from the Qin manuscripts excavated in Shuihudi. These manu-

---

99 Zhu and Chen 2013, 177, footnote 4. For a detailed explanation of this interpretation, which is mainly based on references to *zhuang* from the dynastic histories, see Su Junlin 2014b. Cf. Barbieri-Low (2011, 132), who interprets *zhuang* as "narration of the facts of the crime" in some official charges from Juyan, and Giele (2006, 170), who translates *zhuang* as it occurs in the dynastic histories as "circumstances of a crime" or loosely as "eyewitness report". See further footnote 1036, cf. also footnotes 741 and 1124.

100 *Yuelu* WYZ 024; *QLSZ* 193=*RCL* A 103; *QLZC* 4, 6=*RCL* C 3, 4; *FLDW* 117=*RCL* D 97.

101 *Yuelu* WYZ 095, 102, 106; *XL* 1=*RCL* B 1. See in detail footnote 876.

102 *Yuelu* WYZ 164, 171, 174, 176, 183–184, 186–187; *FLDW* 65=*RCL* D 52. See in detail footnote 1187.

103 *Yuelu* WYZ 015, 019, 020, 081–083; *ENLL* 261. See in detail footnote 555.

104 *Yuelu* WYZ 193, 199, 204, 206; *FZS* 4=*RCL* E 2.

105 *Yuelu* WYZ 003, 006–007, 009–011, 015–016, 019–022, 027–029, 036–037, 039, 042–043; *FLDW* 44, 53, 134–141=*RCL* D 36, 43, 112–119; *ENLL* 61, 95, 97, 137, 139, 148–150, 152, 154–155, 161, 172, 427, 430–432. See also footnote 502.

106 *Yuelu* WYZ 110–111, 122–123, 129–130, 133; *ENLL* 68–73. See in detail footnote 933.

107 *Yuelu* WYZ 171, 174, 176, 178, 183–184, 186; *ENLL* 191–193. See in detail footnote 1205.

108 *Yuelu* WYZ 046, 061, 203–204, 207; *FLDW* 37, 125, 153=*RCL* D 29, 105, 131; *FZS* 6, 13, 40=*RCL* E 4, 5, 15; *ENLL* 148, 190–193. See in detail footnote 670.

109 *Yuelu* WYZ 066, 068–071, 073; *FZS* 23–24=*RCL* E 11; *ENLL* 335, 380.

110 For *ci* see footnote 564.

111 *Yuelu* WYZ 068, 070. See in detail footnote 765.

scripts use *duan* 端[112] instead of the later common term *gu* 故 for "intentionally (committing an offence)" or *zi* 貲[113] instead of *fa* 罰 for "fine" in early Han manuscripts. Many terms for statutory offences are similar. Some did not have the exact same wording, but seem to refer to the same offence. For example, the Han time offence of *shou xing qiu wang fa* 受行賕枉法 "offering or accepting bribes (to the effect of) bending the law"[114] is quoted in case no. I.1 of the *Wei yu deng zhuang* as *shou ren huo cai yi wang lü ling* 受人貨材（財）以枉律令 "to accept valuables offered by sb. to the effect of bending the statutes and ordinances".[115] The identity of these offences, for which the same principles as for theft were applied, becomes evident from the punishments. These are always imposed according to the value of the misappropriated goods (*zang zhi* 臧值).[116] Some offences, for example *bang wang* 邦亡 "absconding from the state (of Qin)", were not adopted for the Han statutes due to historical transformations.[117] Moreover, some statutory offences mentioned in the criminal cases of the *Wei yu deng zhuang* neither occur in the early Han legal manuscripts *Zou yan shu* and *Ernian lüling* nor in the other legal manuscripts from the Qin dynasty excavated so far. These inlude *mou bang wang* 謀邦亡 "conspiring to abscond from the state (of Qin)" in case no. I.5[118] as well as *ni zi shui* 匿訾稅 "evading property tax" in case no. I.7 (classified as *dao* 盜 and punished according to the value of misappropriated goods),[119] *dao mai gong di* 盜賣公地 "illegally selling government land" in case no. I.4 (also classified as *dao* 盜)[120] or *wei wei si shu* 爲僞私書 "drawing up a forged private letter" in case no. III.14[121] of the same collection. Case no. I.6 deals with minor cases of misconduct in office that do not play any role in the *Zou yan shu*, but are mentioned in parts of the Shuihudi legal manuscripts. Of course, the lack of evidence does not mean that the above offences were no longer prosecuted from the beginning of the Han dynasty on.

---

112 *Yuelu* WYZ 102; *FLDW* 34, 36, 38, 43, 45, 93, 124=*RCL* D 27, 28, 30, 35, 38, 77, 104.

113 For *zi* see footnotes 558 and 594.

114 *ZYS* 52; *ENLL* 60.

115 *Yuelu* WYZ 029.

116 *Yuelu* WYZ 030.

117 For *bang wang* see footnote 512.

118 *Yuelu* WYZ 089, 092.

119 *Yuelu* WYZ 130, 132. Cf. *Longgang* 142, 147; *ENLL* 260.

120 Cf. *Yuelu* WYZ 087 with 082, 084–086.

121 *Yuelu* WYZ 234.

4.2 Instances of Jurisdiction

Records of criminal cases describe legal acts of institutions that belong to different levels of the administration. The first instance of jurisdiction was the prefecture (*xian* 縣) that was subordinate to the province (*jun* 郡) as the next instance. The highest agency of jurisdiction was the *ting wei* 廷尉 at the royal/imperial court, the highest legal authority was the ruler. From the records of criminal cases in the *Zou yan shu* and the *Wei yu deng zhuang*, it is not always exactly clear which instances are involved because only the officials of the prefectures are without doubt identifiable. In the *Zou yan shu*, prefects are not referred to by their official titles (*ling* 令 or *zhang* 長) but with the name of their prefecture and their personal name.[122] In the *Wei yu deng zhuang*, prefects are not only mentioned with their personal name, but additionally denoted as "officeholders" (*shou* 守)[123] in a certain prefecture that is likewise named; in official communication prefects are addressed as *se fu* 嗇夫 by their superiors.[124] Prefect and vice prefect (*cheng* 丞) are responsible for the submission of doubtful criminal cases to the superior authorities,[125] occasionally only the vice prefect.[126] In official communication regarding a judgement, the responsible prefect, his vice prefect and a secretary (*shi* 史) are named.[127] *Shi* probably referred to a "judicial secretary" (*yu shi* 獄史).[128] The translation in this volume will employ sub-headings to mark which part of a record in the opinion of the authors has to be attributed to which agency. The considerations that led to these identifications shall be described in the following.

At the lowest level of jurisdiction the prefecture was responsible for finding the facts in criminal cases. It had to conduct a first investigation even if it was not entitled to pass judgement on its own authority or if it had to obtain the approval of the higher authorities (e.g. the royal/imperial court) for it. While

---

122 *ZYS* 17, 36, 75, 80, 92, 97, 124 (Qin case). The only exception is *ZYS* 69.

123 *Yuelu WYZ* 001, 003, 004, 013, 025, 031, 040, 061.

124 *Yuelu WYZ* 186, 205; *ZYS* 26, 121 (Qin case).

125 *Yuelu WYZ* 001, 031; *ZYS* 1, 17, 36.

126 *Yuelu WYZ* 044, 210; *ZYS* 8, 28.

127 *Yuelu WYZ* 013, 061. Occasionally a judgement was only signed by the vice prefect (*Yuelu WYZ* 174).

128 See similar listings of the officials responsible for a criminal case, which use *yu shi* (*ZYS* 97; cf. *Liye* 8–406). In contrast, the prefect, the vice prefect and the "secretary of the prefect" (*ling shi* 令史) were held liable for contraventions of subordinates (*ENLL* 130, 488; *Yuelu Lüling* 1132 [yet unpublished], cf. *Yuelu Lüling* 1912 [yet unpublished] with *yu shi*). The authors thank Prof. Chen Songchang for the permission to quote these and other yet unpublished statutes (*lü*) and ordinances (*ling*) from the Yuelu Academy collection.

there is one example in the *Zou yan shu* in which criminal procedures against a delinquent prefect were initiated by his successor in office,[129] criminal acts of leading officials from the prefectural level are usually investigated by the province.[130] The *Wei yu deng zhuang* mentions the governor of a province (*jun shou* 郡守) in connection with the following activities: He gave responses (*bao* 報) to submissions of the prefectures, which contained a final ruling regarding the punishment[131] or the amount of the rewards for the arrest of bandits.[132] In other cases the governor – after inspection (*lu yu* 錄獄) – ordered a prefecture to submit the finding of fact of a case that had already been concluded for re-examination[133] or to initiate a retrial.[134] However, for some activities mentioned in the *Zou yan shu*, such as submission of doubtful cases by the governor,[135] criminal procedures of the provincial authorities against subordinate officials,[136] or retrials conducted by the provincial authorities by order of a chief prosecutor (*yu shi* 御史),[137] there is no evidence in the *Wei yu deng zhuang*.

Often the unspecific designation *li* 吏 is used to refer to certain officials. From the context it becomes clear that the term *li* in both collections of criminal cases neither refers to subordinate officials nor to any specific subaltern position, but to the representatives of state authority ("the Authority") and more generally officials[138] of different rank as an address or self-reference ("You, as official",[139] "I, as official"[140]). The sections of criminal case records that start with "*li*" have to be regarded as notes that were directly attached to a submission of the prefecture. From the institutional context the addressee of these documents had to be aware of who the "*li*" in question were and which role they played in the administrative apparatus. The notes usually contain two alternative proposals for the sentence, which start with the formulae *li yi*

129 The prefectures were even responsible for the investigation of capital crimes, but not entitled to pass judgement in these cases (*ENLL* 396).

130 *ZYS* 67, 74.

131 *Yuelu WYZ* 025.

132 *Yuelu WYZ* 040.

133 *Yuelu WYZ* 044–046. Cf. the same order in *Yuelu WYZ* 063–064.

134 *ZYS* 75–78.

135 *ZYS* 49, 51, 53, 54, 56, 58, 60, 61.

136 *ZYS* 67, 74.

137 *ZYS* 124, 131 (Qin case).

138 *ZYS* 184, 193, 228 (Qin cases); *Yuelu WYZ* 015, 034, 062, 064, 109, 144, 148, 149, 193, 220, 225, 230.

139 *ZYS* 5, 43; *Yuelu WYZ* 160, 184, 194.

140 *ZYS* 7, 15, 24, 33, 47; *Yuelu WYZ* 024, 039, 094, 107, 136, 202, 235.

吏議 "the officials deliver (the following) legal opinion"[141] (or *li dang* 吏當)[142] and *huo yue* 或曰, respectively. The former probably expressed the opinion of the majority, the latter that of the minority within the authority that forwarded these proposals for judgement. It is not made explicit to which instance the respective officials belong. Scholars who have analysed the first five cases of the *Zou yan shu* hold divergent views on this matter. The majority holds the opinion that the officials referred to by *li* in the formula *li yi*/*li dang* must belong to the higher authorities: Some argue that they were officials of the provincial authorities;[143] others identify them as *du li* 都吏, provincial investigators directly appointed by the central government,[144] or associate them with the agency *ting wei* within the central government.[145] In contrast, some scholars assume that the *li* in *li yi*/*li dang* were the relevant officials of the prefecture.[146] According to the editors' analysis of case I.1 of the *Wei yu deng zhuang*, the divergent proposals for a judgement must be attributed to the officials of the prefecture (*xian*) because the final ruling of Nan province (Nan jun 南郡) as the higher authority differed from both proposals.[147] This new evidence confirms the last of the views introduced above.

Another term of which the exact meaning is not immediately clear is *ting* 廷 "court", which could refer to different authorities in legal manuscripts: first, the prefecture *xian* 縣; second, the province *jun* 郡; third, the agency of the minister of trials (*ting wei*)[148] at the royal/imperial court and, fourth, to the royal/imperial court more generally. As part of the phrase *ting bao* 廷報 "response by the court (with a final ruling)"[149] *ting* refers especially to the *ting wei* and his office at the court. The minister of trials himself as well as other ministers of

---

141 ZYS 24–25, 33–34; *Yuelu* WYZ 024, 039, 094, 107, 136, 235.

142 ZYS 7, 15–16, 47. This formula does not occur in the *Wei yu deng zhuang*.

143 Cai Wanjin 2006, 142–143; Peng Hao et al. 2007, 340, footnote 15.

144 Zhou Haifeng 2014, 56–59. The *du li* was ordered by the respective "official with a salary of 2,000 *shi* 石" to conduct retrials initiated by the petition of an accused (ENLL 116), to review capital crimes as well as cases of homicide that had been unintentional or occurred during a contest (ENLL 396), and to check the official inventories, when the official responsible for this retired, was relocated or had held his office for three years (ENLL 347). A comparison of *Hanshu* 4, 113 and *Juyan* 213.15 shows that the "official with a salary of 2,000 *shi*" who was the superior of the *du li* actually was the governor of a province. The office of *du li* that was responsible for criminal procedures is also mentioned in legal manuscripts from the Qin dynasty (*Liye* 8–528r, 528v; *Yuelu Lüling* 1007, 1728).

145 Miyake 1998, 190–191.

146 Ikeda 2002, 142–143; Gao Heng 2008, 347.

147 Zhu and Chen 2013, 110, footnote 42. See also footnote 639.

148 For the duties of the *ting wei* see Hulsewé 1987 and Shen Gang 2004.

149 ZYS 50, 52–55, 57, 59–60, 62; *Yuelu* WYZ 177.

the government are only mentioned in the *Zou yan shu*,[150] not in the *Wei yu deng zhuang*. However, a "court secretary" (*ting shi* 廷史)[151] who can be assigned to the agency of *ting wei* occurs in that collection of criminal cases. The meaning of the standard formula *ting yi wen* 廷以聞 "the court brought this to (His Majesty's) attention"[152] was that a case had been directly submitted to the ruler as the highest legal authority by the *ting wei*. It only occurs in the *Zou yan shu*; legal decisions of the ruler are not mentioned in the *Wei yu deng zhuang*.

4.3 Rank Order of Punishments

From an investigation of Qin and Han legal manuscripts the following rank order of punishments, which is clearly graded according to severity, can be gathered:

1. Fines (*zi* 貲) in four degrees of one shield (*dun* 盾), one, two or three suits of armour (*jia* 甲) during the Qin dynasty, which were in Han times replaced by pecuniary fines (*fa* 罰) in three degrees of one, two and four ounces of gold (*liang jin* 兩金);
2. Redemption fees (*shu* 贖) in six degrees from eight to 40 ounces of gold;
3. Banishment (*qian* 遷);
4. *Nai* 耐-punishment (shaving off the beard as stigmatising mark) in connection with penal labour of the lightest category as watchman convict (*hou* 候) (only Qin); in connection with penal labour as robber guard convict (*si kou* 司寇); in connection with penal labour as bond servant convict (*li chen* 隸臣 or *li qie* 隸妾, for men and women, respectively);
5. Mitigated version of the most severe form of penal labour for privileged persons as firewood gatherer convict (*gui xin* 鬼薪) or rice sifter convict (*bai can* 白粲), for men and women, respectively;
6. Most severe form of penal labour as earth or grain pounder convict (*cheng dan* 城旦 or *chong* 舂, for men and women, respectively) without mutilation (*wan* 完);
7. Most severe form of penal labour as tattooed (*qing* 黥) earth or grain pounder convict;

150 *ZYS* 26, 121, 184, 189–196 (last three Qin cases).

151 *Yuelu WYZ* 175, 218; *ZYS* 189 (Qin case). See in detail footnote 1212.

152 *ZYS* 26, 47.

8. Death penalty in three degrees (*qi shi* 棄市 "casting away in the marketplace", *zhe* 磔 "quartering", and *yao zhan* 腰斬 "cutting in two at the waist").

This rank order,[153] which has to be taken into account, if a punishment has to be mitigated or increased by one or two degrees, is nearly identical in the *Zou yan shu* and the *Wei yu deng zhuang*. In the latter, the death penalty is only represented by the more severe form of *zhe* "quartering",[154] for which there is no evidence in the *Zou yan shu*, but only in the *Ernian lüling*[155] and the manuscripts from Shuihudi.[156] Furthermore, almost all categories of penal labour for life occur in both collections of criminal cases: In the *Wei yu deng zhuang* as well as the *Zou yan shu* offenders are sentenced to the most severe form of penal labour as earth pounder convicts (*cheng dan*). This was either combined with mutilation (*qing* "tattooing")[157] or the convict was left without mutilation (*wan*).[158] Moreover, in Qin as well as in early Han times the more lenient punishment *nai wei gui xin* 耐爲鬼薪 "being shaved and made a firewood gatherer convict" was automatically given to privileged holders of the second or a higher rank instead of the most severe form of penal labour as an earth pounder convict.[159] In both collections, offenders are also sentenced to the less severe form of the category *nai* 耐 as bond servant convicts (*li chen*).[160] The most lenient penal labour of the category *nai* as watchman convict (*hou*), which only occurs in one case of the *Wei yu deng zhuang*[161] and the Qin legal manuscripts from Shuihudi,[162] was probably abolished at the beginning of the Han dynasty.

In both collections we also find two types of regular pecuniary penalties: higher fees for redemption from being tattooed (*shu qing* 贖黥)[163] or shaved

153 Cf. Li Junming 2011, 30–50 and Lau and Lüdke 2012, 69–70. The rank order of punishments is almost completely listed in *ENLL* 127–130.

154 *Yuelu WYZ* 141, 147, 166.

155 *ENLL* 3, 66, 68.

156 *FLDW* 67=*RCL* D 54.

157 *ZYS* 27, 31, 47–48, 72–73, 122, 158, 182, 187, 192 (last five Qin cases); *Yuelu WYZ* 045, 060–061, 087, 094.

158 *ZYS* 181–182; 224 (Qin cases); *Yuelu WYZ* 136, 244.

159 *ZYS* 158–159 (Qin case); *Yuelu WYZ* 045, 061, 244. On this principle for determining punishment cf. *ENLL* 82.

160 *Yuelu WYZ* 174, 205–206, 235; *ZYS* 65–66, 182 (Qin case).

161 *Yuelu WYZ* 024.

162 *QLSZ* 193=*RCL* A 103, *QLZC* 4, 6=*RCL* C 2, 3; *FLDW* 117=*RCL* D 97.

163 *Yuelu WYZ* 013.

(*shu nai* 贖耐)[164] and smaller fines named *zi* in the *Wei yu deng zhuang*[165] and *fa* in the *Zou yan shu*[166] as in other legal manuscripts from the beginning of the Han dynasty.[167] A special kind of low penalty in Qin and early Han was temporary punitive military service imposed on offending officers and conscript soldiers.[168]

Sometimes the accused in both collections were exempted from punishment (*chu* 除).[169] In two cases of the *Wei yu deng zhuang*, the offenders were also granted amnesties (*she* 赦),[170] while in the *Zou yan shu* there is no evidence for amnesties.

Occasionally, the punishment for an offence in the *Wei yu deng zhuang* differs from that stipulated by early Han law, e.g. for *jie ren* 劫人 "extorting (money or valuables) from sb./blackmailing sb.", which is in case 1.7 classified as a case of theft (*dao* 盜) and therefore punished according to the value of the misappropriated goods (*zang zhi*)[171] instead of quartering (*zhe*) as stipulated in the *Ernian lüling*.[172]

4.4 Principles for Determining Punishment

Many principles, which according to the *Zou yan shu* provide the basis for determinig punishment at the beginning of the Han dynasty,[173] can also be observed in the cases of the *Wei yu deng zhuang*. In contrast to many modern legal systems, there was no discretionary scope in early imperial China. Instead, a certain criminal act on principal always entailed a specific punishment. Judgements with regard to the individual circumstances were not within the judge's discretion, but were only possible insofar as the law itself differentiated offences on the grounds of circumstances or severity of individual culpability. Such differentiation was made for offences such as homicide or bodily injury. The *lex talionis*, i.e. the principle of retributive justice, which can be found in

164 *Yuelu* WYZ 235; ZYS 53.

165 *Yuelu* WYZ 030, 107, 136, 236.

166 ZYS 62.

167 ENLL 4, 5, 7, 11–12, 15, 17, 28, 31, 42–43, etc.

168 *Zi shu* 貲戍 in *Yuelu* WYZ 015, 022; QLZC 12–13=RCL C 8; *fa shu bian* 罰戍邊 in ENLL 143. Cf. ZYS 147 (Qin case).

169 *Yuelu* WYZ 094, 198; ZYS 47, 122–123 (Qin case).

170 *Yuelu* WYZ 045, 061, 204, 207.

171 Cf. *Yuelu* WYZ 130 and 136.

172 ENLL 68.

173 Cf. Lau and Lüdke 2012, 70–80.

Babylonian and Old Testamentary law, although present in certain aspects,[174] was not the most important basis for the jurisdiction in cases of homicide or bodily injury during the Qin and early Han dynasties. The sentence was rather based on a sophisticated evaluation of the factual circumstances and the degree of criminal behaviour demonstrated by the crime the offender had committed.

For the classification of homicide and bodily injury, the dichotomous terms *zei* 賊 "with malice" and *guo shi* 過失 "inadvertently" as well as *dou* 鬥 "during a fight" and *xi* 戲 "during a contest" were available to the judicial officials at the beginning of the Han dynasty. Offences that were classified as *zei* were punished most severely. In such cases there had been no incidents that could have directly provoked the offender and would thus have given him cause for the assault. *Zei* rather implied an especially malicious and cold-blooded behaviour, which included both the planning of the offence as well as the surprise of an unsuspecting victim. In cases classified as *dou* the judicial officials assumed that the involved persons had become infuriated during an originally verbal argument and had allowed themselves to be provoked into assaulting each other. Therefore, the injuries had not been inflicted intentionally but in the heat of the moment, a fact that was viewed as a mitigating circumstance, provided that no weapons or metal tools had been used.[175] If weapons had been used, the delinquents were sentenced to the most severe form of penal labour, albeit without mutilation,[176] which would have been the case if the bodily injury had been inflicted with malice (*zei*).[177] If a bodily injury during a quarrel led to the death of one of the involved persons, then the death penalty was imposed.[178] This sentence was passed regardless of the actual circumstances or the behaviour of the delinquent, and without distinction from cases of homicide involving malice.[179] According to law, no punishment was to be imposed if a bodily injury had been inflicted inadvertently[180] (*guo shi*) or during a con-

174 殺人者死，傷人者刑 "Any person who kills somebody, is punished with death. Any person who injures somebody, is punished with mutilation." (*Hanshu* 83, 3395; cf. *Shiji* 8, 362). Punishments in some stipulations from 186 BC were also based on this principle (*ENLL* 21, 25), where mutilations can be interpreted as retaliation for bodily injury.

175 *FLDW* 83, 86=*RCL* D 68, 71; *ENLL* 27–28, 90.

176 *FLDW* 84–85=*RCL* D 69–70; *ENLL* 27; citation from "Han statutes" in *Hanshu* 83, 3395.

177 *ZYS* 42, 48; citation from "Han statutes" in *Hanshu* 83, 3395; *ENLL* 25.

178 *ENLL* 21, 24.

179 *ZYS* 93; *ENLL* 21.

180 *ENLL* 21.

test (*xi*).[181] Even if the victim was killed, the delinquent only had to pay the fee stipulated for redemption from the death penalty.[182]

In contrast to the *Zou yan shu*, the dichotomous terms described above do not occur in the *Wei yu deng zhuang* as well as in the yet unpublished collection of Qin statutes and ordinances acquired by Yuelu Academy. There is, however, clear evidence that these classificatory terms were already used by judicial officials during the Qin dynasty.[183] In the *Wei yu deng zhuang* there are examples of *dao sha ren* 盜殺人 "killing sb. in the act of committing a theft";[184] this however constituted a different statutory offence in Qin and early Han times and was punished by quartering (*zhe*).[185]

Outside the area of homicide and bodily injury, analogous terms were used for the classification of criminal behaviour. Both collections of criminal cases mention the offence "committing an error of judgement" (*lun shi zhi* 論失之)[186] where *shi* indicates that the error was committed without intent in contrast to intentionally (*gu* 故 or *duan* 端) committing "perversion of justice" (*bu zhi* 不直).[187] Officials who committed a judicial error only had to pay the fee for redemption from the punishment that had been erroneously applied.[188] In contrast, the punishment for intentionally passing a wrong judgement was significantly more severe. The responsible official received exactly the same punishment that he either misapplied or failed to apply to the original accused, except in the case of the death penalty, where the official was sentenced to the most severe form of penal labour as earth pounder convict, which according to statutory provisions from 186 BC was combined with cutting off the left foot.[189]

A similar dichotomy is also inherent in terms for other offences. When partners committed the statutory offence of illicit sexual intercourse (*jian* 奸), a basic distinction, which affected the level of punishment, was made between

---

181 *ENLL* 21, *Shiji* 95, 2664.

182 *ENLL* 21.

183 Cf. the distinction between the offences of homicide and causing bodily injury of the categories *zei* and *dou* in *FLDW* 66, 86, 119=*RCL* D 53, 71, 99.

184 *Yuelu WYZ* 002–004, 018–019, 141, 164, 166–167; cf. *Yuelu WYZ* 033, 035, 037–038.

185 Qin: *Yuelu WYZ* 141, 147, 166; early Han: *ENLL* 66, 68.

186 *Yuelu WYZ* 014; *ZYS* 120, 196; *Longgang mudu*; *ENLL* 107; *Liye* 8–1365; *Liye* 8–70 and *Yuelu 34 nian zhiri* 8.3, 29.3 (the ordinance mentioned may be the same as the one quoted in *Liye* 8–1832+8–1418+8–1133; cf. also *Liye* 8–70).

187 *ENLL* 93, 113, 118, 124.

188 *ENLL* 95–96. During the Western Han this was reduced to the half of the corresponding redemption fee (*Xuanquan* 12).

189 *ENLL* 93.

illicit sexual intercourse "by mutual consent" (*he* 和)[190] and "by force" (*qiang* 強).[191] The victim of a rape was always exempted from punishment,[192] whereas the perpetrator was punished more severely than for illicit sexual intercourse by mutual consent.[193]

In both collections, offences against property were mostly punished according to the value of misappropriated goods quoted in cash.[194] In correspondence to the amount (less than 22, 22 to 109, 110 to 219, 220 to 660, more than 660 cash), the statutes provided five graded punishments ranging from low fines to the most severe form of penal labour in combination with tattooing.[195] If property offences were committed under aggravating circumstances, the capital punishment of quartering (*zhe*) was applied irrespective of the value of the misappropriated goods. This was the case if the theft was committed by a gang of at least five robbers who had united for that purpose (*qun dao* 群盜),[196] or if a person was killed or injured during the theft (*dao sha shang ren* 盜殺傷人).[197]

The statutory offence of absconding (*wang* 亡) referred to the act of leaving, without authorisation, the place where the offender was registered by the authorities and where he was mandated to stay. By absconding, the persons concerned evaded the control exercised by their husbands, masters or superiors and, at the same time, the obligation to pay taxes and to perform military service and statute labour. Sometimes they also escaped prosecution. Absconding was punished depending on the legal status of the offender (officials and free men without office;[198] free women;[199] male and female slaves;[200] convicts[201]) and according to the duration of absence from the place of regis-

190 For *he* see footnote 1221.

191 For *qiang* see footnote 1205.

192 *ENLL* 191.

193 *ENLL* 193.

194 *Yuelu WYZ* 059–060, 086, 130–131; *ZYS* 51, 62, 71–72, 224 (Qin case).

195 *Longgang* 40, 41; *ENLL* 55–56; cf. *FLDW* 1–2, 33–36, 38–39, 42, 49=*RCL* D 1, 27, 28, 30, 33, 34.

196 *ENLL* 65, 66. For gang robbery see footnote 500. During Qin times, a more severe form of death penalty seems to have already been imposed on members of a robber gang who committed the offence of *dao sha ren* because the reward for arresting robbers who committed this offence was twice the amount of the reward given for arresting suspects who had committed an offence punishable by death (cf. *Yuelu WYZ* 016 and 021–022).

197 For *dao sha ren* see footnote 499.

198 *Yuelu WYZ* 051; *ENLL* 157.

199 *ENLL* 158, 88–89.

200 *ZYS* 8–16, 36–48, 51; *ENLL* 159–160.

201 *Yuelu WYZ* 158, 187; *ENLL* 164–165.

tration. The penal law of the Qin dynasty distinguished between the statutory offences of *lan wang* 闌亡 "unauthorised absconding"[202] and *jiang yang* 將陽 "vagrancy".[203] The distinction was based on the duration of absconding.[204] The same punishments for the same durations of absence were also imposed in early Han times on officials and free persons (*li min* 吏民) who had committed the offence of absconding.[205] *Bang wang* "absconding from the state" was a particular statutory offence during Qin times, which was not punished according to duration as was the case for other forms of absconding. Offenders who committed *bang wang* were always sentenced to being tattooed as well as to the most severe form of penal labour as earth pounder convicts.[206]

Certain forms of participation in a criminal offence, often without actually carrying out the offence, or of aiding and abetting an offender were punished in the same way as the offence itself. These include *mou* 謀 "conspiring with sb. (to commit an offence)"[207] or *zhi* 知 "knowing about (an offence without reporting it to the authorities)".[208] Conspiracy to commit an offence was only punishable, if the statutes decreed so.[209] The same rules (*tong fa* 同法) as for theft[210] or homicide/bodily injury[211] also applied for conspiring with sb. to commit these offences. This means that conspiracy had the same legal consequences as the actual crimes also with regard to secondary rules such as collective punishment of the offender's household members, ward heads and neighbours/members of his unit of five.[212] In case no. 16 of the *Zou yan shu*, a prefect conspired with his client to maliciously kill a judicial secretary (*mou zei sha ren* 謀賊殺人) and incited the client to commit the murder.[213] In Qin case no. 17 of the *Zou yan shu*, a musician was prosecuted for conspiring with a thief

202 *FLDW* 48, 139, 167=*RCL* D 93, 117, 146; *Liye* 8–1716; *Yuelu Lüling* 0185, cited according to Chen Songchang 2012a, 6.

203 *FLDW* 163=*RCL* D 143; *FZS* 97=*RCL* E 6; *ZYS* 212 (Qin case); *Liye* 8–1716.

204 See in detail footnote 612.

205 *ENLL* 157.

206 For *bang wang* see footnote 512.

207 For *mou* see footnote 829.

208 For *zhi* see footnote 659.

209 For several statutory offences during Qin and Han times where conspiracy was punishable see footnote 829.

210 *ENLL* 57.

211 *ENLL* 26; *ZYS* 94.

212 *FLDW* 20=*RCL* D 18.

213 *ZYS* 84. Cf. the statutory provisions concerning conspiration to commit murder (*ZYS* 94; *ENLL* 23, 26).

to steal a cow.[214] In case no. 1.5 of the *Wei yu deng zhuang*, conspiracy to abscond from the state (of Qin) (*mou bang wang*) was a punishable offence,[215] for which there is no evidence in early Han legal manuscripts. A person who as an accessory knew about an offence and had lent certain forms of support to it (e.g. by not reporting it) was liable to the same punishment (*tong zui* 同罪) as the principal perpetrator.[216] However, there probably was no collective punishment for the accessory's household members, etc.[217] In case no. 14 of the *Zou yan shu*, a judicial secretary knowingly harboured an unregistered man (*she ni wu ming shu zhe* 舍匿無名數者).[218] In case no. 1.3 of the *Wei yu deng zhuang*, two members of a gang of vagrant absconders received a share of looted goods from their accomplices in the knowledge that these had originated from a grave robbery.[219] Aiding and abetting an offender also included leaving a remand prisoner unpunished (*zong qiu* 縱囚), for which the responsible officials received the same punishment that the law prescribed for the prisoner who was left unpunished.[220] The statutes provided a different punishment only in cases where the death penalty was to be imposed. As early as in Qin times, an official who let a capital offender escape punishment was not executed himself, but tattooed and made an earth pounder convict.[221] Statutes from 186 BC ordered that in such cases the offending official's left foot should be cut off in addition to the most severe form of penal labour as an earth pounder convict.[222]

214 *ZYS* 99. Cf. the statutory provisions concerning conspiration to commit theft (*ENLL* 57).

215 Cf. *Yuelu WYZ* 092, 094.

216 Cf. examples for the imposition of the same punishment on accessories and principal perpetrators in cases of theft (*FLDW* 17, 18=*RCL* D 15, 16) and gang robbery (*ENLL* 63), illegal human trafficking (*ENLL* 67), blackmailing (*ENLL* 72–73), smuggling of gold (*ENLL* 76), illegal casting of cash (*ENLL* 203), relieving oneself or other people from punishment on the basis of a false rank (*ENLL* 394), illegal border crossing (*ENLL* 489), illegal export of horses (*ENLL* 510–511).

217 *FLDW* 20=*RCL* D 18.

218 *ZYS* 63–65.

219 *Yuelu WYZ* 045. Cf. the statutory provisions concerning the sharing of goods with another person in the knowledge that these had been stolen by him (*ENLL* 57) and the commentary on how to implement these provisions (*FLDW* 9=*RCL* D 8).

220 *ZYS* 95.

221 *ZYS* 158 (Qin case).

222 *ENLL* 93. However, there also is an example from the year 201 BC where Han judicial officials were punished with death for intentionally leaving capital offences unpunished (*ZYS* 95–96).

Inversion of the punishment (*fan zui* 反罪) was based on the same principle.[223] The phrase was used in the statutes to stipulate reciprocal punishment for certain offences, where the offender intentionally implicated a third person, e.g. by false incrimination (*wu gao* 誣告),[224] false testimony,[225] or fraudulent transcription of statements.[226] There are no examples for the imposition of reciprocal punishments for these offences in the collections of criminal cases under discussion.

If an offender committed two or more offences simultaneously, the punishment was not automatically increased (*jia* 加). Usually, only the most serious offence was punished.[227] On the other hand, certain situations required an increase of the punishment. According to Qin statutes law enforcement officers who committed theft while performing their duties were punished more severely than non-officials.[228] However, in both collections of criminal cases there are no examples for an increased punishment for property offences of officials. One might compare a reference to an ordinance according to which officials who by law are to be subjected to a mutilation punishment for theft shall not enjoy any privileges of rank (i.e. reduction, relief or redemption) with regard to the punishment.[229] In cases of perversion of justice, for which the law stipulated the inversion of punishment, the reciprocal punishment was increased by two degrees if a judicial official had acted on account of a bribe.[230] If a petition for retrial (*qi ji* 乞鞫)[231] filed by convicted persons who considered their conviction unjustified turned out to be unfounded (*bu shen* 不審), the original punishment was increased by one degree.[232] However, the statutes of Qin and early Han times did not expressly refer to all instances with a more severe punishment than usual as increased (*jia*) punishments. As previously mentioned, robbery committed as a gang was punished more severely, regardless of the value of the misappropriated goods. Furthermore, the statutes do

223 Cf. Lau and Lüdke 2012, 75–76.

224 *ENLL* 126.

225 *ENLL* 110; *Juyan xinjian* E.P.F22:1–2.

226 *ENLL* 111.

227 *ZYS* 25–27, 224 (Qin case); *ENLL* 99.

228 *FLDW* 1–3=*RCL* D 1, 2. In the course of the reforms of penal law in 167 BC, officials who had stolen from the funds supervised by them were sentenced to death (*Hanshu* 23, 1099).

229 *ZYS* 73. After the establishment of the Han reign, resigning one's rank or a reward in return for a relief from punishment was also excluded in cases where a person had failed to register properly (*ZYS* 66).

230 *ENLL* 93, 95.

231 *Yuelu WYZ* 139v; 172–187, 189–206; *ZYS* 99, 121; *FLDW* 115=*RCL* D 95; *ENLL* 114–117.

232 *Yuelu WYZ* 172, 176–177, 185–187, 204, 206–207; *ENLL* 114.

not refer to a more severe mutilation punishment by *jia* if this more severe punishment was imposed due to the fact that it was impossible to impose the less severe form a second time, e.g. cutting off the left foot.[233]

Active repentance by the offender was usually taken into account as a mitigating circumstance. An offender could be completely exempted from punishment if he assisted the authorities in arresting or reporting co-conspirators or accomplices.[234] The punishment was regularly reduced by one degree if an offender reported himself to the authorities before the offence was discovered (*xian zi gao* 先自告).[235] If absconders gave themselves up voluntarily, their punishment was likewise mitigated[236] or was converted to caning.[237] Beside members of the imperial family, holders of ranks (*jue* 爵) enjoyed an automatic reduction of certain severe sentences. Holders of the first rank and their wives escaped mutilation if by law they were to be sentenced to the most severe form of penal labour as tattooed earth or grain pounder convicts (*cheng dan chong*).[238] If an offender held the second or a higher rank, he even had the privilege to perform a more lenient form of penal labour as a firewood gatherer (*gui xin*) convict instead of the most severe form of penal labour.[239] Resigning of ranks and rewards also provided a basis for relief from (*mian* 免) or redemption of punishment (*shu* 贖).[240]

Children below the age of criminal responsibility were exempted from punishment.[241] For example, according to statutes from 186 BC, children below the age of 10 were exempted from punishment for all offences except homicide.[242] From some Qin legal manuscripts it can be gathered that criminal liability was connected to the body height an offender had reached at the time he committed an offence.[243] However, yet unpublished statutes and ordinances of Yuelu Academy suggest that the completed 14th year was the general age of

233 *ZYS* 32, 34; *ENLL* 88; *FLDW* 120=*RCL* D 100.

234 *ENLL* 2, 63, 64, 68–69, 71, 73, 206–207; *Longgang* 146.

235 For *xian zi gao* see footnote 921.

236 *ENLL* 166–167.

237 *ENLL* 157, 159, 165.

238 Cf. *Yuelu WYZ* 109–110 and 136; *ZYS* 182–183 and 188, 212 and 224 (Qin case); *ENLL* 83.

239 Cf. *Yuelu WYZ* 045 and 060–061; *ZYS* 158–159 (Qin case).

240 Cf. *ZYS* 66 and 73.

241 *Yuelu WYZ* 089, 091–092, 094.

242 *ENLL* 86.

243 It seems that male boys of at least six feet and five inches (approximately 1.50 m) were considered legal "majors" (*QLSZ* 51–52=*RCL* A 12; cf. *FLDW* 158=*RCL* D 138 and *FLDW* 6=*RCL* D 5). See in detail footnote 825.

criminal responsibility during the Qin dynasty.[244] At the beginning of the Han dynasty minors who had committed an offence normally punished with mutilation were spared mutilation up to the age of 17.[245] According to Qin statutes, minors – i.e. persons who had not yet been registered for military service and statute labour – were usually not sentenced to the most severe form of penal labour.[246]

Some principles for determining punishment which were applied in the *Wei yu deng zhuang* are not attested in the *Zou yan shu*. Offences such as *dao sha ren* "killing sb. in the act of committing a theft" in case no. II.10[247] or *jian* "illicit sexual intercourse" in case no. II.11[248] were categorised as less serious than defined by the statutes if the offender was unable to carry out his intended offence (*wei shi*). Obviously, the punishment had to be mitigated in such cases. A similar case was theft, if the offender did not appropriate the stolen goods (*dao wei you qu* 盜未有取), as in case no. I.1. The sentence stipulated by law was reduced, and the offender faced no more than the payment of the fee for redemption from the usual punishment.[249]

As mentioned above the institution of collective liability (*lian zuo*) commonly attributed to Shang Yang was a characteristic of early Chinese law. In manuscripts from Qin and early Han times, we find evidence for different forms of collective or organisational liability, applying to family members living in the same household (*tong ju* 同居),[250] or to neighbours who formed a unit of five households.[251] However, these persons received much more lenient punishment than the offender himself (only a fine in the case of an offender sentenced to tattooing and the most severe form of penal labour).[252] The principle of collective liablility was also applied to the head and the elders of the ward (*dian lao* 典老),[253] and to officials with a supervisory function, who were

244 Cf. *Yuelu Lüling* 0998, 1004, 1996, 0187, 2030 (yet unpublished); cf. *Yuelu* WYZ 092.

245 *Hanshu* 2, 85; *ENLL* 83, 91, 122. Cf. *FLDW* 6=*RCL* D 5.

246 *Yuelu* WYZ 233, 235; *Yuelu Lüling* 0187, 2030 (yet unpublished).

247 *Yuelu* WYZ 164.

248 *Yuelu* WYZ 171, 174, 176, 183. Cf. *FLDW* 65=*RCL* D 52.

249 *Yuelu* WYZ 013, 015, 022. For examples from the Qin dynasty where redemption fees were imposed on persons who did not carry out a planned theft see footnote 541.

250 For *tong ju* see footnote 940.

251 *ZYS* 123 (Qin case); *FLDW* 96–99=*RCL* D 80–81.

252 *ZYS* 123 (Qin case).

253 *Dian lao* 典老 (*FLDW* 98, 183=*RCL* D 81, 162). The editorial team of the Shuihudi manuscripts (Shuihudi Qinmu zhujian zhengli xiaozu 1978, 143, footnote 3 on *QLSZ* 33) identified *dian* (*FLDW* 20, 164=*RCL* D 20, 164; *FZS* 10, 73, 98=*RCL* E 3, 22, 6) as *li dian* 里典 "head of the ward" (*FLDW* 198=*RCL* D 177; *FZS* 52, 63=*RCL* E 19, 21; *Liye* 8–157r/v, 8–661) who was

prosecuted for offences committed by people they were responsible for.[254] Offenders who had been sentenced to death, castration or the most severe form of penal labour lost their property as a result of confiscation (*shou* 收) which extended to the wife and children. Additionally, these persons were made bond servant convicts (*li chen qie* 隸臣妾)[255] or sold into slavery.[256]

One of the specific measures that fell under *lian zuo* was known as *yi san zu* 夷三族 "execution of three generations of the clan (parents, wives, children and siblings)" of a person who had staged a rebellion against the ruling dynasty or had plotted to stage a rebellion (*mou fan* 謀反). The execution of the close relatives of rebels in three generations was first practised in Qin.[257]

4.5 Stages of Criminal Procedure

The different stages of criminal procedure during the Han dynasty, which had been investigated on the basis of received literature before the first legal manuscripts were excavated,[258] could be described in much more detail on the basis of the *Zou yan shu*.[259] Research on criminal procedure during the Qin dynasty

probably also named *li zheng* 里正 (*Hanfei* 35, 253; cf. *ENLL* 201, 329, 390). According to their opinion, *lao* refers to the *wu lao* 伍老 "elders of the unit of five" (Shuihudi Qinmu zhujian zhengli xiaozu 1978, 143, footnote 3 on *QLSZ* 33). A more likely other possibility is that *lao* in *dian lao* refers to the *fu lao* 父老 "elders of the ward" (*RCL* C 20, footnote 115 based on Moriya Mitsuo). In a list from Han times *fu lao* are mentioned after *xiang li, ting zhang, li zheng* and before the *wu ren* (*Hanshu* 90, 3673: 乃部戶曹掾吏與鄉吏、亭長、里正、父老、伍人) and there is evidence suggesting that during Han times the *fu lao* were in fact influential persons within a ward (*li*) (Tomiya 2015: *Juyan* 45.1A, 526.1A; Nishijima 1986, 575). The *Falü dawen* states that the *dian* as head of the ward is held liable for certain offences committed by members of his ward (*FLDW* 20=*RCL* D 18; cf. *dian lao* and *wu ren* as liable persons in *Yuelu Lüling* 1288, 1855, 1016, 1121 and *dian lao* and *si lin* 四鄰 "four neighbours" in *FLDW* 98=*RCL* D 81).

254 *Yuelu WYZ* 095, 099, 102, 105; *XL* 54–55=*RCL* B 26, 27; *ENLL* 105–106.

255 *ENLL* 435.

256 *ZYS* 122 (Qin case).

257 *Shiji* 5, 182; 87, 2561–2562. Cf. statutes from 186 BC according to which the parents, wives and children as well as siblings of a rebel were to be executed regardless of age (*ENLL* 2).

258 Hulsewé 1955, 71–81; cf. Zhang Ji 1999.

259 For a reconstruction of the different stages of criminal procedure in the *Zou yan shu* cf. Miyake 1998; Zhang Jianguo 1999, 294–314; Lau 2002; Li Junming 2011, 51–79; Yan Xiaojun 2012, 77–92; Gao Heng 2008, 408–468; Lau and Lüdke 2012, 80–89 and 351–352: Appendix I.

had to rely on the legal manuscripts from Shuihudi before the publication of the *Wei yu deng zhuang*.[260] The following summary includes new insights that can be drawn from this material.

The main precondition for the initiation of criminal proceedings was the disclosure of an offence that had to be reported to the authorities. Without such a report, which had to be recorded, the responsible authorities were not allowed to initiate procedures.[261] If the offender had not been detected yet, the officials handling the case had to collect evidence at the site of the crime and conduct a forensic investigation.[262]

There was a conceptual difference between *gao* 告[263] and *he* 劾.[264] The former term referred to a report filed by a non-official private person, the latter referred to an *ex-officio* charge against a delinquent official. A report (*gao*) was either filed by the victim as well as another person affected by the offence,[265] or by eyewitnesses.[266] It could also happen that a delinquent reported himself prior to the discovery of his offence.[267] On the local level a report could be filed with the *xiao zhang* 校長,[268] the head of the local police station (*ting* 亭), who in turn initiated a search (*qiu* 求) for the suspect together with his subordinate robber hunter (*qiu dao* 求盜)[269] or crossbow archer (*fa nu* 發弩) in order to arrest (*bu* 捕)[270] him or her. In pre-imperial Qin, a judicial secretary was responsible for the search for unknown suspects.[271]

Arrests could not only be executed by the above-mentioned law enforcement officers. Absconded private slaves were often caught by their owners.[272] In other cases, persons who had witnessed a crime such as bodily injury, illegal casting of cash or illicit sexual intercourse arrested an offender at the crime

260 On the reconstruction of criminal procedure during the Qin dynasty based on the legal manuscripts from Shuihudi tomb no. 11 cf. Momiyama 2006, 53–116; Liu Hainian 2006, 161–220; Li Jing 1985, 298–340.

261 *ENLL* 113.

262 *ZYS* 203–217 (Qin case); *Yuelu WYZ* 142–143; 151–157; *FZS* 52–54, 55–62, 63–72, 73–83, 84–90=*RCL* E 19, 20, 21, 22, 23. For the forensic methods applied by the Qin see Bodde 1982 and Yan Xiaojun 2012, 105–144.

263 For *gao* see footnote 498.

264 For *he* see footnote 545.

265 *Yuelu WYZ* 083, 111, 173; *ZYS* 28.

266 *FZS* 95=*RCL* E 25.

267 *Yuelu WYZ* 108, 111; *ZYS* 49.

268 *FZS* 25=*RCL* E 12; *ZYS* 36; cf. *ZYS* 76. For *xiao zhang* see also footnote 492.

269 *ZYS* 75–76. For *qiu dao* see also footnote 493.

270 For *bu* see footnote 505.

271 For the duties of the *yu shi* see footnote 539.

272 *ZYS* 9; *ENLL* 160.

scene or on the run.[273] For the arrest of offenders who had committed a crime punishable with penal labour a reward was paid in the same way as for military merits.[274] In some cases, reports that had led to the arrest of an offender were also rewarded.[275] Similarly, the cash (coins) an absconding offender carried with him were promised to the person who successfully arrested him.[276]

Although household members, neighbours and superiors of an offender were liable to punishment if they did not report his offence, not all forms of reports were accepted by the authorities. Anonymously submitted accusations (*tou shu* 投書) were not heard on principle.[277] Reports by children under the age of ten were also generally disregarded. The same is true for reports by offenders who had been sentenced to the most severe form of penal labour as well as remand prisoners who often incriminated others to save themselves, a fact that was considered as an aggravating circumstance and could lead to an increased punishment.[278] Judicial officials usually refrained from the initiation of criminal procedures for offences that had been discovered posthumously, especially those committed by a head of a household during his lifetime.[279] On principle, children were not allowed to report their parents for an offence; the same was true for a wife regarding offences of her parents-in-law as well as for slaves with regard to offences by their owner or his close relatives.[280] However, a wife was supposed to report offences of her husband (the head of the household).[281] Certain offences that were considered to be "family crimes" (*jia zui* 家罪) did not have to be reported to the authorities. This was the case for example if a head of the household had killed his children or slaves or inflicted bodily injury on them, or if a son had stolen from his father.[282]

Immediately after a delinquent who had been accused of an offence punishable by death, castration or the most severe form of penal labour was arrested, his complete property, estate, clothes and household effects were sealed

273 *FZS* 20, 95=*RCL* E 9, 25; cf. *FZS* 18=*RCL* E 8.

274 *FLDW* 135–141=*RCL* D 113–119; *Yuelu* WYZ 003, 006, 016, 021–022, 036–037; *ENLL* 137–138; cf. *Shiji* 68, 2230. See footnote 502.

275 *FLDW* 134=*RCL* D 112; *ENLL* 139.

276 *FLDW* 130=*RCL* D 108. If tax evasion was reported the reporting person was awarded half the amount of the evaded taxes (*Hanshu* 6, 183).

277 *FLDW* 53=*RCL* D 43; *ENLL* 118.

278 *ENLL* 134; *FLDW* 50, 111, 109, 117–120=*RCL* D 40, 91–92, 97–100.

279 *FLDW* 68, 106=*RCL* D 55, 88.

280 *FLDW* 104=*RCL* D 87; *ENLL* 133.

281 *FLDW* 170=*RCL* D 149.

282 *FLDW* 103, 106, 108=*RCL* D 86, 88–89. See also Lau 2005.

(*feng* 封) and put under supervision (*shou* 守) together with his wife and children, slaves and cattle.[283] An inventory of the sealed property had to be submitted to the prefectural authorities,[284] which liquidated it[285] in the event of a conviction and transferred the detained relatives into penal labour[286] or sold them into slavery.[287]

If the suspect of a crime was not located on the territory of the prefecture that had initiated criminal procedures, the authorities could request another prefecture to arrest and transfer (*dai* 逮) the suspect.[288] Suspects were placed under detention (*xi* 繫)[289] during criminal investigation and were usually forced to wear handcuffs (*xie* 械).[290] In the year 194 BC, the only remand prisoners (*qiu* 囚) who were not fettered were privileged groups such as officials with a salary of at least 600 *shi* 石, holders of the ninth or a higher rank, or servants of the emperor,[291] but also old persons above the age of 80, children below the age of 8, pregnant women, blind musicians and disabled persons.[292]

During Qin times, witnesses who were officials were seldom detained.[293] Only in the course of Western Han times did it become common practice to place a considerable number of witnesses under detention during trial.[294]

In both collections of criminal cases the trial at the prefecture (*xian*) as the court of first instance started with the first stage of interrogation, during which the accused and the witnesses made their statements without being interrupted by the interrogating officials.[295] The interrogated persons, some of whom were illiterate, made an oral statement, which was carefully recorded.[296]

283 FZS 8–12=RCL E 3; ENLL 174, 179.

284 ENLL 179.

285 ZYS 123 (Qin case).

286 ENLL 435.

287 ZYS 122 (Qin case).

288 ZYS 151, 156 (Qin case); *Hanshu* 23, 1097 with commentary by Yan Shigu; *Shiji* 118, 3075.

289 For *xi* see footnote 569.

290 FLDW 125=RCL D 105; *Liye* 8–532; *Juyan* 58.17+193.19, 118.18; *Shiji* 53, 2018; *Hanshu* 2, 85.

291 *Hanshu* 2, 85; holders of "royal staffs" were equal to these privileged groups (*Wangzhang shijian* cited according to *Sanjian* 24).

292 *Hanshu* 23, 1106 with commentary of Yan Shigu; *Juyan* 5.3; *Wangzhang zhuoling shu* cited according to *Sanjian* 145.

293 The governor of a province as well as its commander (*wei* 尉), an interim prefect and his vice prefect as well as a judicial secretary and the secretary of the prefect (ZYS 160). See Lau and Lüdke 2012, footnote 1338.

294 *Shiji* 122, 3153.

295 In early legal manuscripts statements are usually initiated by the verb *yue* 曰 and referred to by the noun *ci* 辭. For *ci* see footnote 564.

296 FZS 2=RCL E 2.

Witnesses were reminded in advance of the inversion of punishment as a possible consequence of an incorrect statement.[297] In the formalised protocol of the interrogation, parts that corresponded with the accusations or the statements of other persons were indicated by a short comment (*ta ru mou ren/he/shu* 它如某人/劾/書 "everything else corresponds to the statement of X/the *ex-officio* charge/document Y").[298] If the accused admitted his criminal liability (*zui* 罪) and could not offer any justification for his actions (*wu jie* 無解),[299] criminal proceedings were concluded.

If, at the end of the first stage of interrogation, there was no confession of guilt by the accused, the proceedings entered into their second stage (*jie* 詰).[300] At this stage, the accused was confronted with the offence he was accused of and the relevant statutes and/or ordinances,[301] with his own contradictory statements,[302] or with incriminating statements of accomplices and witnesses.[303] He was furthermore questioned about exculpatory evidence (*he jie* 何解).[304] At the second stage of interrogation, the judicial officials were obliged to consider objections of the accused to avoid a judicial error. Besides incriminatory statements, the accused could also be confronted with physical evidence from the scene of the crime (*zheng wu* 徵物)[305] or the results of the forensic inspection (*zhen* 診).[306] Only if the accused did not admit his criminal liablility in the face of overwhelming evidence, but instead still produced lies and prevarications, torture in form of blows with the stick (*chi* 笞)[307] on the back, bottom or thighs were permitted. However, this was considered to be a questionable means of obtaining a confession[308] because of the inherent danger

---

297 *Juyan xinjian* E.P.F22:1–2, 21, 330; commentary of Zhang Yan in *Shiji* 122, 3137; *ENLL* 110.

298 *Yuelu WYZ* 011, 016, 035, 048, 054–055, 067, 072, 089, 091, 099, 103, 119, 130–131, 174, 184–185, 191, 195, 215, 233; *ZYS* 3, 19, 71.

299 *Zui wu jie* 罪無解 "(I accept that) I am liable to punishment and cannot offer an explanation (justifying my actions)." (*Yuelu WYZ* 165, 241; *ZYS* 21, 22, 31, 87, 150). Cf. *zui wu ta jie* 罪無它解 in the same sense (*Yuelu WYZ* 084, 130) or in cases where it indicates that the person being interrogated insists on the validity of his or her explanation (*ZYS* 13, 45, 145, 148 [last two Qin cases]). See in detail footnote 800.

300 For the second stage of interrogation see the explanations in *FZS* 2–4=*RCL* E 2.

301 *Yuelu WYZ* 080–082, 102, 130; *ZYS* 4, 11, 19, 21, 30, 41, 139, 146 (last two Qin cases).

302 *Yuelu WYZ* 127–129, 184, *ZYS* 219 (Qin case).

303 *ZYS* 105, 217–218 (Qin case); *Yuelu WYZ* 202.

304 *Yuelu WYZ* 102, 129; *ZYS* 5, 12, 20, 22, 31, 42, 44, 87, 141, 147 (last two Qin cases).

305 *ZYS* 226 (Qin case); *Yuelu WYZ* 148; *FZS* 19, 21–22, 25=*RCL* E 9, 10, 12; cf. *ZYS* 216–217.

306 *FZS* 56, 86=*RCL* E 20, 23. See in detail footnote 1095.

307 *ZYS* 220 (Qin case), 107–108, 113–114; *Shiji* 95, 2664; 122, 3137 ; 122, 3153.

308 *FZS* 1=*RCL* E 1.

that the accused made a false confession just to end the torture.[309] Therefore, the use of torture always had to be recorded in the respective case file.[310]

As soon as the accused had admitted to his criminal liability,[311] the gathering of evidence was concluded with a note on the results of forensic examination (*zhen*) and of interagency enquiries on sentencing-relevant particulars (*wen* 問),[312] which were compared with the results of interrogation (*ru ci* 如辭).[313] The enquiries were made with the local authorities responsible for registration and criminal prosecution and were therefore independent from the statements of the persons involved in the trial. In this way the facts necessary to identify the accused, such as name, place of residence or affiliation to a certain office[314] were determined. The age[315] of the offender, which might have an influence on his criminal liability, as well as his criminal record[316] and his status,[317] which was important for determining the punishment, were established by the same procedure. In case of property crimes the authorities also enquired about the value of misappropriated goods, because this had a direct influence on the degree of punishment.[318]

Following this enquiry the results of the finding of fact were summarised (*ju* 鞫)[319] by the responsible officials and were probably also read out to the accused. If an earlier judgement had been revoked in the course of a retrial, a summary of the new finding of fact with a note on the unlawful sentence had to be drawn up.[320] At the end of the summary the officials gave the assurance that all described facts had been firmly established (*shen* 審).[321]

The written finding of fact was the basis for the judgement (*lun* 論) by the prefecture (*xian*). At the beginning of Han times, the officials of the first instance were allowed to impose all kinds of sentences except the death

309 *ZYS* 120 (Qin case); *Shiji* 87, 2560; *Hanshu* 51, 2370.

310 *FZS* 4–5=*RCL* E 2.

311 For *zui wu jie* see footnote 800; for *zui* as admission of criminal liability without *wu jie* see footnote 985.

312 For *wen* see footnote 562.

313 *Yuelu WYZ* 017, 035, 060, 085, 091, 104, 131, 166, 185, 187, 203, 233, 242; *ZYS* 5, 14, 22, 32, 45, 64, 71, 90, 120, 154–155, 224 (last three Qin cases).

314 *FZS* 6, 13, 96–97=*RCL* E 4–6; *ZYS* 64, 88.

315 *Yuelu WYZ* 091, 233; *ZYS* 13, 45; *ENLL* 83, 86.

316 *ZYS* 32; *FZS* 6, 13, 96=*RCL* E 4–6; *ENLL* 88.

317 *Yuelu WYZ* 091, 233; *ZYS* 45, 64, 88; *ENLL* 82–83.

318 *Yuelu WYZ* 130–131, 166; *ZYS* 71, 224 (Qin case); *ENLL* 55–56.

319 For *ju* see footnote 565.

320 *Longgang mudu*; *ZYS* 120; cf. *Yuelu WYZ* 176, 186, 204.

321 For *shen* see footnote 633.

penalty.[322] Only if high dignitaries, e.g. prefects[323] or holders of the ninth or a higher rank,[324] were to be sentenced, the authorities had to obtain approval by the court, even if the statutory offence was undebatable.[325] In the *Zou yan shu*, most of these cases were tried by provincial authorities, which submitted a proposal for judgement (*dang* 當) to the imperial court for approval.[326]

In several exemplary criminal cases, a prefecture voiced doubts about the appropriate legal decision (*yi* 疑)[327] and submitted the case to the higher authority for decision. In both criminal case collections the response by the higher authority (*bao* 報) contained a decision.[328]

From the evidence provided by the two collections of criminal cases, it can be concluded that the stages and many details of criminal procedure remained largely unchanged from the pre-imperial period of Qin until early Han times.

---

322 In cases of inadvertent killing or killing during a contest as well as cases where the offence was punishable with death, the finding of fact summarised by the prefecture always had to be submitted to the province for decision (ENLL 396–397). In two cases of the *Wei yu deng zhuang*, the death penalty against offenders who had committed murder during a theft (*dao sha ren*) and were to be quartered (*zhe*), was apparently imposed by the prefecture that had also conducted criminal procedures (*Yuelu* WYZ 147, 166).

323 ZYS 72 (salary of 600 *shi*), 96, 159. The *Wei yu deng zhuang* does not contain any cases of delinquent prefects. However, case no. 18 of the *Zou yan shu*, in which a prefect is convicted for an unauthorised remission of penalty, can be dated to the years 220/219 BC, *viz.* the imperial Qin period (for a discussion of the dating see Lau and Lüdke 2012, 16). The judgement proposed by Nan province had to be submitted to the emperor for approval, as can be gathered from the use of *dang* (ZYS 159). This proves that during Qin times the conviction of prefects and high dignitaries required the approval of the sovereign.

324 ZYS 64 (ninth rank), 96 (18th rank). The *Wei yu deng zhuang* does not contain cases of delinquent holders of the ninth or a higher rank. It can therefore not be decided whether their conviction required the approval of the sovereign during Qin times.

325 The dynastic histories describe that requests for approval by the emperor only had to be made in later periods if lower instances tried cases of high dignitaries. From 173 BC on the arrest of dignitaries with a salary of 2,000 *shi* or more was only allowed with approval of the emperor (*Hanshu* 4, 122). From 49 BC onwards the lower authorities also had to request the emperor's consent for judgements on officeholders with a salary of at least 600 *shi* (*Hanshu* 8, 274).

326 ZYS 65, 72, 159 (Qin case). In case no. 16 of the *Zou yan shu*, the case of a delinquent prefect is investigated by the newly appointed prefectural auhorities. In this case, a proposal for judgement is also formulated by the provincial authorities (ZYS 96).

327 For this category of cases see section 4.6.1 below.

328 For *bao* see footnote 581.

This is clear evidence for the continuity of procedural practice during this time.

4.6 Formal Classification of Criminal Cases

The following classification of criminal cases draws upon previous research results. The categories of cases that have been proposed by Lau and Lüdke[329] for the formal classification of the *Zou yan shu* are based on criteria which were inherent to the sequence of cases in the manuscript. The order of these cases is not only determined by the date of the judicial proceedings (early Han: cases no. 1–16; Qin: cases no. 17, 18, 21, 22, interrupted by the two cases no. 19 and no. 20 from the Spring and Autumn period), but also by their category:

- The first 13 cases of the *Zou yan shu* and case no. 21 belong to the category "doubtful punishment" (*yi zui* 疑罪).
- They are followed by the cases no. 14–16 and 18 of the category "proposed sentences" (*dang* 當). These were sentences against certain groups of privileged people (senior officials appointed by the emperor; holders of the ninth or a higher rank) that required imperial approval.
- The case no. 17 (Qin) was a "petition for retrial" (*qi ju*) filed by a convict who considered his punishment to be unjustified.
- The cases no. 19 and 20 were "fictitious cases from another time" (*yi shi* 異時), giving account of lawsuits from the Spring and Autumn period.
- The case no. 22 was a criminal case which was submitted to the higher authorities as a "recommendation of competent investigators for promotion".

The following three categories of cases can also be identified in the *Wei yu deng zhuang*:

329 In the first classification of the cases within the *Zou yan shu* (Lau and Lüdke 2012, 39–55) these were divided into four categories (*yi zui, dang, yi shi, lun* 論). Petitions for retrial and recommendations of competent investigating officials for promotion were still subsumed under the category *lun*. The revision of this classification results from a comparison with the *Wei yu deng zhuang*.

- Five of seven cases of manuscript I as well as the unique case of manuscript III can be assigned to the category "doubtful legal decisions (*yi*)";[330]
- Two of the six cases of manuscript II can be assigned to the category "petitions for retrial (*qi ju*)";
- Two other cases of manuscript II can be assigned to the category "recommendations of competent investigators for promotion".

Two further cases of manuscript I of the *Wei yu deng zhuang* that cannot be subsumed under the categories determined according to the *Zou yan shu* will be separately discussed below.[331]

4.6.1 *Doubtful Legal Decisions*

4.6.1.1 Procedure and Formal Characteristics of Submission

The cases in this category constitute the largest group of cases in the *Wei yu deng zhuang*. They are extremely instructive because they illustrate the regularised procedure of review over several administrative levels, which is called *yan* 讞 "to submit (a doubtful case) for decision (to the higher authorities)." According to this procedure, the officials at the court of the first instance (*xian*) were obliged to submit criminal cases to the head of the provincial authority (*jun*), to whom they were subordinated, if they were in doubt about the matters of law in the case concerned. The agency of the province, in turn, was to carry out a legal examination, name the applicable sentence and return its decision to the lower authorities. If the judicial officials at the province level were not able to arrive at a decision, they had to pass the case on to the agency of the minister of trials (*ting wei*) at the royal/imperial court. Again, the minister of trials had to either decide the case himself and, in a response to the prefecture's submission, name the applicable sentence, or, if also in doubt, compile a memorandum (*zou* 奏) for the ruler to which all relevant precedents (*bi* 比), statutes (*lü* 律), and ordinances (*ling* 令) were to be attached. Until the discovery of the Yuelu Academy manuscripts, legal historians thought that

330 In contrast to the *Zou yan shu*, doubts (*yi* 疑) are not restricted to the correct punishment in the *Wei yu deng zhuang*, but are also raised with regard to the amount of rewards or the legal status of an accused. Therefore, the more general label "doubtful legal decisions" appears more suitable to describe both collections.

331 The cases II.8 and II.13 have not been assigned to one of the mentioned categories because their highly fragmentary state did not allow any conclusions regarding this question. Case IV.15 is a special case also difficult to categorise as it might have been compiled together with a draft ordinance that was concluded by the formula of approval by the ruler (*zhi yue ke* 制曰可). See footnote 1416, cf. Hafner 2014a.

successive stages of appeal were first regulated in 200 BC by an edict of Emperor Gaozu 高祖.[332] Now, the *Wei yu deng zhuang* manuscripts prove that the *yan*-procedure of submitting criminal cases to the higher authorities for decision already existed in pre-imperial Qin. It is quite likely that corresponding provisions formed the legal basis for this procedure in this period, although there is no evidence for the key formula "*yi* (*zui*)" in the collection of statutes and ordinances purchased by the Yuelu Academy.[333]

These cases were mostly submitted to the higher authorities because of legal doubts about the appropriate punishment or the punishability of an offence, which could not be resolved at the lowest level of jurisdiction (prefecture/*xian*). The reasons for these doubts will be analysed in detail below.

One of the formal characteristics of cases concerning doubtful legal decisions in the *Zou yan shu* is that the judicial officials of the prefecture only provide the summarised finding of fact (*ju*) for the case in question[334] and voice their doubts about the punishment with the formula *yi* (*mou ren*) *zui* 疑(某人)罪. The exact same formula *yi zui* is only used in three of the six cases of this category in the *Wei yu deng zhuang*, i.e. cases no. I.1, I.5 and I.7.[335] In two other cases, the formula is modified; the doubts concerned the stipulated amount of rewards for arresting two different categories of robbers (no. I.2)[336] and the question of whether a senior official should be punished for each of his eight misdemeanours[337] or only for the most serious one (no. I.6). Another case (no. III.14) without mention of *yi zui* nor *yi* can also be classified as belonging to this category because the competent authority was not able to

---

332 *Hanshu* 23, 1106. Cf. the translations of this ordinance by Hulsewé (1955, 343), Lüdke (2003, 36) as well as by Lau and Lüdke (2012, 8–9).

333 Cf. an imperial decision instructing the chief prosecutor (*zhi zhao yu shi* 制詔御史) and quoted in *Yuelu Lüling* 1125/0968/1781 (yet unpublished), according to which delayed criminal proceedings where no decision had been made for several years were to be submitted to the chief prosecutor.

334 Cf. *Yuelu Lüling* 1707/1712 (yet unpublished): 其獄奏毆，各約爲鞫審，具傳其律令，令各與其當比編而署律令下曰，以此當某某及具署辠（罪）人毄（繫）不毄（繫）。"As far as the submission of the criminal cases in question is concerned, in each case summarise the finding of fact and assure that [the facts] have been firmly established, compile and append the relevant statutes and ordinances, let each of them be put together with the applicable precedents, then record the following note below the [quotations from] statutes and ordinances: 'This is applicable to XYZ' and also completely record whether the offenders are kept under detention or not."

335 *Yuelu WYZ* 028, 092, 134–135.

336 *Yi mou ren gou* 疑某人購 "we are in doubt about the (lawful) reward for X" (*Yuelu WYZ* 039).

337 *Yi mou ren bu dang lei lun* 疑某人不當纍論 "we are in doubt whether X should by law not be convicted based on the accumulation (of sentences)" (*Yuelu WYZ* 105–106).

reach a consensus on the legitimate sentence. It thus made two different proposals for the appropriate punishment.[338]

The formula *yi zui* can be followed by certain fixed phrases containing official communication: *xi* 繫 "X is placed under detention" (awaiting a decision by the higher authority)[339] and *ta xian lun* 它縣論 "in all other matters the prefecture has passed judgement" (a decision by the higher authority is not necessary for these matters).[340] Statutes, ordinances and/or precedents that were consulted while the officials tried to reach a verdict, are first quoted in full, followed by a statement or discussion on their applicability in the actual case.[341]

The judicial officials submitted all six cases to the higher authority for decision with the formula *gan yan zhi* 敢讞之. Subsequently, the competent authorities usually made two proposals. According to analysis of case I.1 of the *Wei yu deng zhuang*, the divergent proposals for judgement must be attributed to the officials of the prefecture (*xian*).[342] The first proposal, introduced with the formula *li yi*,[343] may be the proposal of the majority; the second one, introduced with the formula *huo yue*,[344] could be an alternative proposal of the minority within the agency of the prefecture.

4.6.1.2 Doubtful Legal Decisions in the *Wei yu deng zhuang*

Legal doubts always concerned matters that were material to the judgement. For example, it could be debatable if an action that had been factually determined under the law in force actually constituted a statutory offence. In case no. I.1 of the *Wei yu deng zhuang*, it is unclear if the punishments imposed on law enforcement officers and conscripts by the responsible prefecture because of an illegal deal with rewards for arrested bandits were in accordance with the

338 *Yuelu* WYZ 235.

339 *Yuelu* WYZ 023, 092, 135, 235, 245; cf. ZYS 23, 33.

340 *Yuelu* WYZ 039, 093, 135, 245; cf. ZYS 6, 15, 23, 33.

341 These citations of legal provisions occur in case records before the alternative proposals for judgement submitted by the prefecture for decision (ZYS 23–24), before a judgement submitted for approval by the province (ZYS 65–67; 72–73; 158 [Qin case]) or the new prefectural office (ZYS 93–95), before the legal reasoning of the *ting wei* at the court (ZYS 180–183 [Qin case]), before the interpretation of legal provisions as part of the second stage of interrogation (ZYS 4, 31), before the summarised finding of fact (*Yuelu* WYZ 36–37) or before the recommendation of investigating officials for a promotion (*Yuelu* WYZ 147).

342 Cf. section 4.2 above.

343 For *li yi* see footnote 572.

344 For *huo yue* see footnote 573.

applicable provisions.[345] It depended on the answer to this question, whether the leading prefectural officials who had passed the judgement were to be prosecuted for an error of judgement by imposing punishments that were too lenient, or whether they were to be exempted from punishment.[346]

Doubts often occurred if the accused had brought forward arguments for his justification that did not seem unreasonable at first sight and suggested that his actions were legally justified by some reason that might prevent punishment. Such arguments forwarded by the accused obviously also raised doubts in the first five cases of the *Zou yan shu*.[347] In case no. 1.5 of the *Wei yu deng zhuang*, the investigating officials of the prefecture arrived at different conclusions with regard to the question whether a young man had reached the age of criminal responsibility at the time he absconded together with his mother. If that was the case, he would have to be prosecuted for conspiracy to abscond from the state.[348] The man had originally fled from Qin when he was still a minor and had later gone into Qin captivity when his place of exile was conquered. He therefore denied having been able to conspire together with his mother to abscond from the state at that time.[349] Enquiries showed that the young man had absconded from Qin at the age of 12.[350] Apparently, it was

345 *Yuelu* WYZ 013–014. The legal basis of the verdict is explained in Lau 2014, 158–159.

346 *Yuelu* WYZ 24, 28, 30. Cf. Lau 2014, 160.

347 In case no. 1, a male member of the Manyi, who had not followed conscription for military service, argued that he was entitled to deny conscription because of a substituting monetary payment, which he had made according to law (ZYS 2, 5; Lau and Lüdke 2012, 92). In case no. 2, a female private slave justified her escape from her master's household stating that she had submitted to the Han dynasty during civil war, had accordingly gained the status of a free person and had only afterwards illegally been enslaved anew by her former master (ZYS 9–10, 13; Lau and Lüdke 2012, 107). In case no. 4, a released convict who had married an absconded maidservant asserted not to have known about her status as absconder at the time of the marriage (ZYS 29–30; Lau and Lüdke 2012, 1129). In case no. 5, a former private slave who had submitted to the Han during the civil war and therefore had been registered as a free man, justified the bodily injury he inflicted on a law enforcement officer by stating that he got infuriated by his unlawful arrest and had only defended himself, but had not acted with malicious aforethought (ZYS 38, 43; Lau and Lüdke 2012, 135–136). In case no. 3, the accused judicial secretary had confessed to having married another accused from the royal house of Qi, who had been relocated to the centre of the empire, thereby violating an explicit ban on marriage. He further confessed to have hidden her during the attempted escape to her home. However, he denied to have enticed the woman away by order of the king of Qi (ZYS 20–21; Lau and Lüdke 2012, 117).

348 Cf. *Yuelu* WYZ 092 and 094.

349 *Yuelu* WYZ 089.

350 *Yuelu* WYZ 091.

debatable whether the age at the time of absconding or the age at the time the accused was caught (22 years) were decisive; the former was below the age of criminal responsibility in Qin (probably 14 years), the latter above. The judicial officials were in doubt whether the accused, who had not voluntarily returned to Qin at the age of majority and who had furthermore already been deprived of his rank, had to be allowed mitigating circumstances.[351] In case no. I.7 of the *Wei yu deng zhuang*, a former menial had been reported because he had tried to extort a market stall and a guesthouse from a manumitted former female slave. The market stall and the guesthouse were part of her former master's heritage, and the former menial threatened to report the woman for her evasion of taxes if she did not follow his request.[352] In his statement, the menial reinforced his legal claim to this property and denied the reported extortion. He pointed out that his master had promised the market stall and the guesthouse to him before his death. And although there was no written will which could substantiate this claim, and the menial had furthermore received other property that might have been intended as a substitute for the originally promised property,[353] the officials had doubts as to whether the menial might still be the legitimate heir to the claimed market stall and guesthouse. In this case, his actions could not be considered extortion.[354] The background for this was probably that oral contracts were in some cases legally binding, even if there was no written will, and that said oral promise by the deceased had been confirmed by several witnesses.[355]

In other cases doubts arose if an offence had been committed in a situation that could not be properly subsumed under one of the existing statutory provisions. In two cases of the *Zou yan shu*, the competent official made a false entry in an authentic document. Apparently none of the existing regulations was applicable to this fraudulent activity, since the statutory offence of *wei wei shu* 爲僞書 usually covered the forgery of a document. The imperial court decided that making a false entry was also to be treated as a case of *wei wei shu*.[356] In case III.14 of the *Wei yu deng zhuang*, the judicial officials encountered similar

351 Lau 2014, 156–157.

352 *Yuelu* WYZ 109–111.

353 *Yuelu* WYZ 127–28.

354 Lau 2014, 151–154.

355 Lau 2014, 152, footnote 57.

356 ZYS 54–57; Lau and Lüdke 2012, 161–168. Cf. two other cases from the *Zou yan shu* where an offender who had instigated another person to make a false entry in the horse passport of a third person and a post official who had put a wrong date for the forwarding of a military dispatch on the accompanying letter, were punished for forging documents (ZYS 58–60; Lau and Lüdke 2012, 168–173).

problems. A scribal student had pretended to be the son of a famous general and had written in his name a private letter addressed to the head of the treasury of the neighbouring prefecture in order to gain a loan. The accused had intended to use this loan to abscond from the state of Qin. As only forgery of official documents – but not of private letters – was legally considered as forgery of documents, the judicial officials were indecisive as to which legal stipulations had to be applied in this case. The young age of the offender apparently served as a mitigating circumstance.[357] Moreover, the accused had not successfully implemented his plan and had neither received the loan nor had he actually absconded from the state of Qin. In case no. 1.1 of the *Wei yu deng zhuang*, the prefectural authorities were in doubt how they should judge an illegal deal with rewards for the arrest of bandits. The law enforcement officers ordered to arrest a gang of robbers had agreed to this deal with conscripts from the neighbouring prefecture, who had already successfully arrested these bandits. The officers had persuaded the conscripts to transfer the bandits and wanted to present them to the authorities. They had therefore paid the conscripts a small amount of money in advance and agreed to hand over the rest of the reward after they had received it from the authorities. This illegal deal with rewards was first classified as a case of theft by the prefectural authorities. As the rewards had not yet been given, they allowed the officers and conscripts to pay the fee for redemption from the punishment that was to be imposed for theft.[358] However, the higher authorities of the province considered the payment of money that had been made in advance as a case of bribery, for which the stipulations on the statutory offence of *shou ren huo cai yi wang lü ling* 受人貨材（財）以枉律令 "to accept valuables offered by sb. to the effect of bending the statutes and ordinances" were applicable.[359] This was an analogous application of a norm to a situation not directly covered by existing legal requirements, since the applicable statutes imply that corrupt officials were the addressees of bribes. As in case no. 7 of the *Zou yan shu*,[360] such a stipulation was applied to the bribery of non-officials, the purpose of which was the obstruction of the course of justice.

In some cases, the legal status of the accused was unclear. In the previously mentioned case no. 1.7 of the *Wei yu deng zhuang*, doubts concerned the status of a former private slave who had reported herself for evasion of property

357 Lau 2014, 161.

358 Lau 2014, 158–159.

359 *Yuelu WYZ* 029–030.

360 In this case, a woman was bribed by her absconded slaves in order to prevent her from reporting them to the authorities (*ZYS* 51–52; Lau and Lüdke 2012, 153).

taxes.[361] The status of the accused had an immediate effect on the punishment. The judicial officials were unable to decide whether the former slave was to be considered a released person – as noted in the district household register[362] – or the wife of a holder of the fifth rank, as which she had been treated by neighbours and the members of the ancestral lineage of the deceased merchant.[363] A similar question arose in case no. 6 of the *Zou yan shu*. Here, it had to be decided, whether a slave owner, by killing a slave he was legally required to manumit, had committed the capital offence of killing a free man, or the far less serious offence of chastising a slave resulting in death. Matters were complicated by the fact that the slave had formerly waived the manumission that had been ordered by the state, and instead had agreed with his master to continue his service as a slave. As the legal status of the killed person was therefore unclear, the judicial officials could not decide whether a report on lack of piety, which the slave owner had filed after the killing and which assumedly served as an excuse, had to be considered in reaching the verdict.[364]

Issues of status also figured prominently in case no. 1.2 of the *Wei yu deng zhuang*. The responsible officials were in doubt about the amount of rewards, which were to be given to law enforcement officers for the arrest of offenders who had killed or injured people in the act of committing theft. Four of the robbers were from Qin, the other ten had come as refugees from a region in the south of the state of Chu which had meanwhile been occupied by Qin. The officials of the responsible prefectural authority were not able to reach a consensus on the category of robbers to which these offenders belonged. The amount of the rewards for the arrest of the robbers of course depended on this decision.[365] While the majority of the officials in the prefectural authority held that all delinquents had to be indiscriminately regarded as members of a robber gang and the law enforcement officers had to be rewarded accordingly, some other officials assumedly pointed out that the reward for the arrest of robbers who had come from outside the state of Qin was considerably lower.[366]

361 *Yuelu WYZ* 134–135.

362 *Yuelu WYZ* 126.

363 *Yuelu WYZ* 114–115. See Lau 2014, 149–150.

364 *ZYS* 49–50; cf. *ENLL* 21, 24 and 39; Lau and Lüdke 2012, 145.

365 Cf. the two relevant quotations from the statutes in *Yuelu WYZ* 036–037. Unfortunately, the wording of the second statutory provision that was cited is not completely preserved.

366 *Yuelu WYZ* 039. Slip 039 only carries the beginning of the alternative second proposal for judgement. The assumption that this proposal referred to the second of the statutory provisions quoted above is based on the occurrence of the term *ta bang ren* 它邦人 "people from another state" in both passages.

In case no. 1.6 of the *Wei yu deng zhuang*, the method according to which the overall punishment for several misconducts in office by a leading official of the prefecture (probably the vice prefect) had to be calculated was contested. The judicial officials who tried the case were in doubt as to whether an accumulation of the sentences for every single misconduct (violations of ordinances, a major mistake, misdemeanours of subordinates) as stipulated in the ordinances[367] was justified or whether the official only had to be punished for the most severe offence, a principle that was usually applied in other cases. The accused official argumented that violations, mistakes and lapses had occurred during his official duties and that he also might have sometimes neglected his duty of supervision but that none of these misdemeanours should be classified as an intentional breach of duty for his private interest.[368] This hints towards the possibility that Qin law stipulated an accumulation of sentences only in cases where misdemeanours in office had been intentional, although there is no direct evidence for this yet.

In contrast to the *Zou yan shu*,[369] there is no case to be found in the *Wei yu deng zhuang*, in which judicial officials were in doubt as to which of two conflicting provisions that each stipulated a different punishment had to be applied. The *Wei yu deng zhuang* also does not provide direct evidence for cases in which judicial officials were reluctant to pass a judgement according to the letter of law if it seemed contrary to the generally accepted principles for determining punishment.[370]

367 *Yuelu* WYZ 102.

368 *Yuelu* WYZ 102–103.

369 Cf. the sentence against a border guard who failed to catch an absconder who was illegally crossing the border in case no. 8 of the *Zou yan shu* (ZYS 53) as well as the conflicting regulations in *ENLL* 404 (fining X ounces of gold for not noticing that an absconded person leaves or enters the country through the area of one's post) and in *ENLL* 488 (redeeming penal labour of the category *nai* for not arresting people who climb over the frontier fortifications). See Lau and Lüdke 2012, 158–160, especially footnote 828.

370 A judgement strictly conforming to the letter of law would apparently have contradicted accepted principles for determining punishment in cases no. 4 and 5 of the *Zou yan shu* (ZYS 30–34, 41–47). In case no. 4, a mutilated ex-convict married a maidservant without knowing that she had previously absconded. Although the ex-convict did not know about the absconding, law provided for judgement to be passed on him for the statutory offence of taking an absconder as wife. The insistence on full punishment even with the fact of a lack of knowledge was unusual in Qin and Han law, as in other cases the lack of knowledge led to a reduced punishment (*ENLL* 63, 74, 76, 170; cf. Lau and Lüdke 2012, footnote 732). In case no. 5, a former slave was to be punished for the statutory offence of *zei sha ren* "killing sb. with malice", because he injured the officer who attempted to arrest him as absconded slave. Although this punishment was in accordance with the existing law, the

4.6.1.3 Further Development and Function

Criminal cases of the category "doubtful legal decisions" were considered to be particularly difficult. Only under narrowly defined conditions was it allowed to submit criminal cases to the higher authorities for decision. Officials of a prefecture who forwarded criminal cases to their superior authorities because of doubts about the appropriate punishment, although the existing statutory provisions were clear (*bai* 白),[371] were censured by their superiors and could be prosecuted for making an erroneous legal interpretation. Many officials obviously shied away from the risk of being reprimanded. Therefore, they often did not dare to trouble their superiors with doubtful cases. In 143 BC, Emperor Jing 景 issued an edict prohibiting the further prosecution of officials for the unwarranted submission of criminal cases[372] in order to remedy this situation.

Difficult legal issues are dealt with in all six criminal cases from the *Wei yu deng zhuang* discussed above. Judicial uncertainty concerned the application of statutory provisions and principles for determining punishment, the question of legal status or criminal liability, as well as the validity of a verbal last will. In two of these doubtful cases (cases I.1, III.14), ingenious techniques of legal reasoning were demonstrated, i.e. the analogous application of a regulation to a situation not directly covered by existing regulations.[373] A further purpose of compiling cases that were in doubt was to provide models for the *yan*-procedure. Lower judicial officials or candidates for the corresponding offices could learn from these models which type of legal problems required a decision by the higher authorities and how such submissions were to be drawn up in a formally correct way. The doubtful cases from the *Wei yu deng zhuang* emphasised that any statement of the accused potentially exonerating him must be fully considered, and that the case has to be submitted to the higher authorities for a decision if there is any doubt about the validity of the accused person's arguments.[374]

---

competent officials were reluctant to apply the letter of the relevant provisions when it turned out that the arrest was not legitimate because the accused managed to be entered into the household registers as a free man after having submitted to the Han rule during the Chu-Han civil war.

371 ZYS 35; cf. *Yuelu* WYZ 030: 有律不當瀐（讞） "There is a statute on this, the case should not have been submitted."

372 *Hanshu* 5, 150.

373 Cf. Lüdke 2003, 59.

374 Cf. Lüdke 2003, 58–59.

4.6.2 *Cases Requiring Approval of the Higher Authorities*

Two cases in the first manuscript of the *Wei yu deng zhuang* cannot be subsumed under the category of "doubtful legal decisions" or any other category found in the *Zou yan shu* although both use the introductory and concluding formulae *gan yan zhi* 敢讞之.[375] These formulae indicate that both criminal cases were also submitted to the higher authorities for decision, but not because of doubts about the punishment or other matters.

In the criminal case no. 1.4 of the *Wei yu deng zhuang*, a conflict was caused when several merchants asserted claims to the same plot of commercially usable land. One of these merchants named Rui, whose request for the plot of land concerned had been rejected, used criminal means to achieve his objectives. Together with a rival he erected a market stall for selling coffins on the vacant site, even though the competent authority had refused to grant the plot for the stall to any of the competing merchants. Due to the unfavourable legal situation, Rui finally did not risk occupying this market stall, but instead sold his share to his brother-in-law Duo for the total price of 1,400 cash and led Duo to believe that he had received the plot for the market stall with the authorities' permission. For selling his share of the market stall, Rui was charged with the offence of illegal sale of government land for market stalls. This offence was classified as theft (*dao*) and sanctioned accordingly. As the value of the misappropriated land exceeded 660 cash, the commoner (*gong zu* 公卒) Rui had to be sentenced to the maximum punishment for offences against property, i.e. he had to be tattooed and made an earth pounder convict (*qing wei cheng dan* 黥爲城旦).[376] The officials of the prefecture of Jiangling 江陵 who passed this sentence were not in doubt about the punishment.

However, after the governor of Nan province, the immediate superior of the prefecture, read the prefecture's report, he complained that the report on the criminal proceedings against Rui did not clarify whether the price for the misappropriated land that was the basis of the judgement had been separately fixed by the offender during the illegal sale or was derived from separate evaluations carried out by the competent officials. The governor reminded the subordinate officials how to proceed if different items that had been sold together were separated in the course of an official evaluation:

> 問芮買（賣）與朵別賈（價）地，且吏自別直（值）。別直（值）以論，狀何如？勿庸報。鞫審，讞（讞）。3[377]

375 *Yuelu* WYZ 044, 061, 062, 087.

376 Cf. *ENLL* 55.

377 *Yuelu* WYZ 063–064.

> Enquire whether Rui, in selling [the market stall], separately negotiated the price of the land with Duo or whether the officials of their own accord separately evaluated [the land and the stall]. How should one behave[378] correctly, if a judgement is based[379] on separate evaluations? Do not give a response [with a decision]. Find the facts, [assure] that they are established, and submit the case [to us, the higher authorities, for decision].

In all cases of theft, the judicial officials were obliged to evaluate the misappropriated goods immediately after the thief's capture without regard to the value declared by the accused.[380] In the present case, the combined price of the land and the stall declared by Rui (1,400 cash) and the price reported by the prefecture after the official evaluation (1,000+269=1,269 cash) differed by 131 cash.[381] As the value of the land already exceeded 660 cash, this difference had no effect on the level of sentence. But it becomes clear that the value of the land, upon which the judgement is based, was in fact determined by the officials, for the accused had sold the land together with the stall for a total price of 1,400 cash. Rui was punished for the 1,000 cash he had actually misapproppriated through the sale and which, according to official evaluation, corresponded to the value of the land. The prefecture of Jiangling therefore complied with the request of its governor and provided the complete documentation of the criminal proceedings against the merchant Rui, including the formal criminal investigation and the judicial decision. This decision, which was mainly based on the official evaluation, apparently had to be approved by the higher authorities.

This case is comparable to the case no. 1.3, where the prefecture of Jiangling again was ordered to submit the finding of fact to the governor's province agency, together with the assurance that this had been firmly established (*ju shen* 鞫審).[382] Here, two individuals were prosecuted for participating in a grave robbery (*dao chu zhong* 盜埱冢).[383] Both of the accused, who had joined a band of vagrant absconders, neither committed the grave robbery nor did they conspire with the perpetrators. The robbers, however, informed both accomplices about the grave robbery and finally gave them a share of the grave

378 For the meaning of *zhuang* in the question *zhuang he ru* 狀何如 see footnote 741.

379 Compare similarly constructed phrases described in footnote 741.

380 *FLDW* 33, 35=*RCL* D 27, 28.

381 Cf. *Yuelu WYZ* 063 with *Yuelu WYZ* 075, 086.

382 *Yuelu WYZ* 045–046. The same procedure was stipulated if persons delivered anonymous letters (*tou shu*) to the authorities for which they were to be subjected to a formal criminal investigation (*FLDW* 53–54=*RCL* D 43).

383 *Yuelu WYZ* 044–045.

clothes and bronze vessels excavated from the grave in order to prevent them from revealing their knowledge.[384] According to Qin and Han law, anyone who had knowledge of a theft or even only received a tiny fraction of the loot for himself was punished like the thief for the full stolen amount.[385] Since the value of the misappropriated goods exceeded 660 cash, the offenders by law were to be sentenced to the most severe form of penal labour as tattooed earth pounder convicts (*qing wei cheng dan*). When the two accused were to be convicted for participating in a grave robbery, their offence was covered by an amnesty (*she* 赦). The offenders, therefore, needed to be exempted from punishment and made into released persons (*shu ren* 庶人).[386] The officials of the prefecture, however, were apparently not authorised to pardon them without the approval of the higher authorities.

The cases no. I.4 and I.3 form a category that is not found in the *Zou yan shu*. They are, however, to some degree, similar to cases of the category "proposed sentences" (*dang*),[387] in which the lower authorities had to submit a request for the imperial approval of a punishment. Imperial approval was necessary for passing sentence on members of certain privileged groups[388] and for punishing certain serious offences.[389] From these submissions, lower judicial officials or candidates could learn which types of sentences required the higher authorities' approval and which rules were to be observed for the corresponding proceedings.

384 *Yuelu* WYZ 055, 058, 060.

385 Cf. footnotes 659 and 663.

386 *Yuelu* WYZ 045, 061.

387 According to the formal classification of the *Zou yan shu* by Lau and Lüdke (2012, 45–51), cases of this category all use *dang* 當 "proposed sentences" instead of *lun* 論 "judgement" in reaching a decision (ZYS 65, 69, 96, 159).

388 The accused officials were appointed as prefects by the emperor in cases no. 18 from 220 BC (ZYS 124), no. 16 from 201 BC (ZYS 86, 92 [in addition holder of the 18th rank]) and no. 15 from 200 BC (ZYS 69, [in addition holder of the ninth rank]). In case no. 14 from 199 BC, the criminal official is holder of the ninth rank (ZYS 64). In case no. I.3 of the *Wei yu deng zhuang*, the term *dang* is used for the proposed judgements as well (*Yuelu* WYZ 060).

389 These included the offences of killing somebody with malice (*zei sha ren*), of conspiring to maliciously kill sb. (*mou zei sha ren*) and of leaving a suspected murderer unpunished (*zong qiu*) (ZYS 93–96); cf. the stipulation that offences punished with the death penalty as well as all offences of homicide were to be submitted to the province authorities for decision (*ENLL* 396).

4.6.3 *Petitions for Retrial*

4.6.3.1 Legal Basis

Cases with "petitions for retrial" (*qi ju*) form another comparable category. *Qi ju* referred to a procedure by which a convicted person could request a retrial of his case if he considered his conviction unjust. This right of appeal against a verdict had already been incorporated in the statutes from the pre-imperial period of the Qin dynasty.[390] A convicted person could only petition for a new finding of fact on the condition that he had been informed earlier of the contents of the original finding of fact. That this was indeed the case can be seen in at least three examples from pre-imperial Qin, which are analysed below. It is likely that at this time the finding of fact was already read out to the accused at the end of the trial (*du ju* 讀鞫), although the earliest explicit mention of this procedural step is only found in the commentary of Zheng Zhong 鄭眾 (as commentator known by the name Zheng Sinong 鄭司農, d. AD 83) to the *Zhouli* 周禮.[391] If the petition was granted, it resulted in a review (*fu* 覆)[392] connected with a second criminal investigation and was concluded by a new finding of fact, which, if substantially different, would require a different sentence. At the beginning of Han times, the procedure of *qi ju* was based on the following statutory provisions:

> 罪人獄已決，自以罪不當，欲气（乞）鞫者，許之。气（乞）鞫不審，駕（加）罪一等。其欲復气（乞）鞫，當刑者刑，乃聽之。死罪不得自气（乞）鞫，其父、母、兄、姊、弟、夫、妻、子爲气（乞）鞫，許之。其不審，黥爲城旦舂。年未盈十歲爲气（乞）鞫，勿聽。獄已決一歲不得气（乞）鞫。气（乞）鞫者各辭在所縣道，縣道官令、長、丞謹聽，書其气（乞）鞫，上獄屬所二千石官，二千石官令都吏覆之。都吏所覆治，廷及郡各移旁近郡；御史，丞相所治移廷。[393]

> If a person liable to punishment wishes to petition for a [new] finding of fact after his case has already been decided, because he considers his

390 Cf. the commentary of *FLDW* 115=*RCL* D 95: 以乞鞫及爲人乞鞫者，獄已斷乃聽，且未斷猶聽殹（也）？獄斷乃聽之。"Is a petition for a [new] finding of fact as well as a petition on behalf of another person only accepted when the case has already been decided, or is it [also] accepted when the case has not been decided yet? It is only accepted after the case has been decided." See also further evidence for this right of appeal during Qin times (*Liye* 8–114; *ZYS* 99, 121; *Yuelu WYZ* 139v, 175–176, 178, 184–187; *Yuelu Lüling* 1059 [yet unpublished]).

391 *Zhouli* 35, 873b.

392 For *fu* see footnote 1039.

393 *ENLL* 114–117.

punishment to be unjustified, this is granted. However, if the petition for a [new] finding of fact is unfounded, then his punishment is increased by one degree. If the same person [after having been sentenced for making an unfounded petition] wishes to yet again petition for a [new] finding of fact, then, in the event that he is by law to be subjected to a mutilation punishment, the petition is only heard after he has been mutilated. [Persons liable to] the death penalty are not permitted to petition for a [new] finding of fact themselves. However, if their father, mother, elder brother, elder sister, younger brother, husband, wife or child wishes to petition for a [new] finding of fact on their behalf, then this is granted. If a petition [by any of these relatives] is unfounded, then [the relative in question] is tattooed and made an earth or grain pounder convict. Petitions for a new finding of fact made on behalf [of a relative] by persons not yet fully ten years of age shall not be heard. If the case in question has already been decided for one full year, then it is not permitted to petition for a [new] finding of fact. In every case, the person who petitions for a [new] finding of fact makes his statement at the prefecture or march where he resides. The prefecture's or march's prefect or vice prefect carefully hears and writes down his petition for a [new] finding of fact. The official then submits the case to the superior province-level office; the province-level office orders provincial investigators to review the case. The imperial court and the provinces, respectively, transfer cases to neighbouring provinces that had been [originally] tried in a review by provincial investigators. Cases [originally] tried by the chief prosecutor or by the chancellor are transferred to the imperial court.

4.6.3.2 The Case No. 17 from Pre-imperial Qin and Its Consequences

In one case of the *Zou yan shu* (no. 17), a musician who could not resist torture had falsely incriminated himself of being the accomplice of a cattle thief.[394] The musician became a victim of judicial error under the following circumstances: The actual thief, who had likewise been subjected to torture for the purpose of forcing him to reveal his accomplices, felt that he had no choice but to falsely accuse the innocent musician of conspiring to steal a cow with him.[395] For conspiring to steal something, the same legal rules as for actually committing theft were to be applied.[396] As the value of the misappropriated cattle

394 *ZYS* 99–123, especially *ZYS* 109.

395 *ZYS* 113–114.

396 Cf. the applicable statutory provisions on complicity in footnote 663.

obviously exceeded 660 cash, the musician accused of conspiring was to be sentenced to the most severe form of penal labour as a tattooed earth pounder convict.[397] Instead of verifying the musician's alibi with independent witnesses (a step which exonerates him during the retrial), the investigating officials resorted to torture to extort a confession. This contrasts with the positive example of case no. 22, where the accused is only threatened with torture as a means to extract a confession after his explanations become unjustifiable in the view of both hard physical evidence and mutually consistent statements of multiple independent witnesses.[398] As a result of the criminal proceedings, the musician was innocently subjected to a mutilation punishment due to a judicial error. After the execution of the sentence, the musician continued to protest his innocence and petitioned for a retrial. This petition was granted and resulted in a second criminal investigation, which was concluded by a substantially different finding of fact. The musician repudiated the accusation of having conspired to steal the cattle and stated that he was forced to give a false confession under the threat of further torture. The interrogation of the witnesses confirmed that the convicted musician had been absent when the theft had been committed and when he was alleged to have attempted to rob the cattle for the first time. The traces of torture were closely inspected. The agency of the minister of trials, which probably also conducted the retrial, found that the competent officials committed a judicial error, reversed the judgement, and undertook measures for an acquittal as well as the complete rehabilitation of the accused, including the return of family members and compensation for the confiscated goods.[399] As the accused had suffered an irreversible mutilation, after his acquittal he was placed in a hidden government institution (*yin guan* 隱官)[400] in order to remove him from the public eye and safeguard him

397 Cf. *ENLL* 55.

398 *ZYS* 220. Cf. Lüdke 2003, 55.

399 *ZYS* 122–123.

400 *Yin guan* 隱官 "hidden office" or "hidden place of work" refers to the place where people were employed who had received a mutilation punishment, but whose sentence was later cancelled retroactively (*FLDW* 125–126=*RCL* D 105) or to the people themselves who were employed in this situation (*ZYS* 29). There were different circumstances under which people became *yin guan*: First, convicts who wrongly received a mutilation punishment because they were victims of a judicial error (*shi*) or even because of an intentional perversion of justice (*bu zhi*) were employed in/as *yin guan* (*ENLL* 124) when the wrongful conviction was discovered, for example as a result of a retrial requested by the mutilated convict (*qi ju*) (*ZYS* 122). Second, in Qin at least mutilated convicts who worked as artisans in government workshops could be relieved from their punishment if they themselves, or somebody else on their behalf, acquired military merits (*QLSZ* 156=*RCL* A 91); they were

against the ridicule and disdain he would have met in his former community where people used to keep their distance to *xing ren* 刑人 "people marked/stigmatised by mutilation".[401]

This case can be read as a warning not to use torture before all other means have been exhausted and when the statements of the suspect are not contradicted by hard evidence.[402] It illustrates the great danger to pass a wrong judgement as a result of forced confessions and of making the judicial officials liable to prosecution for an error of judgement (*lun shi zhi*)[403] when torture is applied too early and indiscriminately, and not all of the clues have been investigated. The case thus implies that judicial authorities should instead endeavour to protect suspects from false incrimination. The application of torture to extract confessions was accordingly restricted. In the *Feng zhen shi* 封診式, a Qin guide for correct procedure in criminal cases of the late third century BC, it is emphasised that finding out the truth about a suspect without the use of torture by caning is considered superior, while using torture by caning is, on the other hand, deemed inferior.[404] In this guide, detailed instructions concerning the use of torture are given:

then employed as artisan *yin guan* because they had been mutilated. Third, if members of a robber gang who had been amnestied and made released persons allowed manacled remand prisoners they were leading to abscond during transportation, the sentence formerly suspended was enforced and the members of a robber gang were punished with having their left foot cut off. If they could make amends by arresting (*bu* 捕) the absconders the mutilated robbers were employed as *yin guan* (*FLDW* 125–126=*RCL* D 105). Fourth, slaves (*nu* 奴) who were relieved from slavery by their owner on account of their good conduct were obliged to continue to work for their owner as "personal dependants" (*si shu* 私屬) for the time being; they became *yin guan* if they had previously been mutilated (*ENLL* 163). After the excavation of the Shuihudi manuscripts, the term *yin guan* has been identified by some scholars with *yin gong* 隱宮, which in the *Shiji* in all likelihood refers to convicts who have been subjected to castration (commentaries to *Shiji* 88, 2566; 6, 256). For a survey of the different interpretations including *yin gong*, see Jiang Feifei 2004 and Li Chao 2009. Where the mutilation of *yin guan* ex-convicts is mentioned in the legal manuscripts from Shuihudi and Zhangjiashan, they were not castrated, but had been tattooed (*ZYS* 32, 99, 122) and had had their nose or their left foot cut off (*ZYS* 32, 34; *FLDW* 126=*RCL* D 105). Therefore, it is doubtful whether *yin guan* can be identified with *yin gong*.

401 Cf. *Gongyang* 21, 2313a.

402 Lüdke 2003, 55.

403 For inadvertently committing an error of judgement and its legal consequence see footnote 186.

404 *FZS* 1=*RCL* E 1. Cf. McLeod and Yates 1981, 130–131.

訊獄　凡訊獄，必先盡聽其言而書之，各展其辭，雖智（知）其訑，勿庸輒詰。其辭已盡書而毋（無）解，乃以詰者詰之。詰之有（又）盡聽書其解辭，有（又）視其它毋（無）解者以復詰之。詰之極而數訑，更言不服，其律當治（笞）諒（掠）者，乃治（笞）諒（掠）。治（笞）諒（掠）之必書曰：爰書：以某數更言，毋（無）解辭，治（笞）訊某。[405]

Interrogation in a criminal case. – As general rule for conducting interrogations in criminal cases, you have to first hear fully the statements of those concerned and record their statements in writing, [letting] each of the persons [interrogated] to make his statement [without interruption]. Even if you know that the person concerned lies, there is no need to confront him immediately [with other evidence or inconsistencies]. If someone's statement has been completely recorded in writing, and there is still no [full] explanation, confront him with confronting issues. When confronting him, again fully hear and write down the statements he offers in explanation. Then look again at further points for which he has no [full] explanation and again confront him with these points. If he has been confronted [with inconsistencies] to the utmost and still repeatedly lies, changes his statements and does not confess, then, where the respective statutes warrant torture, use torture. If you torture him by caning, it is mandatory to write down: "Protocol: Because X repeatedly has changed his statement and has not offered a statement which would provide a [full] explanation, I interrogated X with the application of the cane."

4.6.3.3 Petitions for Retrial in the *Wei yu deng zhuang*

In the two cases of the *Wei yu deng zhuang* that belong to the category of petitions for retrial, both accused were charged with the statutory offence of illicit sexual intercourse (*jian* 奸), for which an offender according to Qin law had to be shaved and made a bond servant convict (*nai wei li chen qie*).[406]

405 *FZS* 2–5=*RCL* E 2. Cf. McLeod and Yates 1981, 131–133; Lüdke 2003, 117, 127; Barbieri-Low 2011, 127.

406 See the quotation from Qin statutes (*ZYS* 182) translated in footnote 1208. According to Han statutory provisions, the conditions for a criminal offence were only fulfilled if a male person had illicit sexual intercourse by mutual consent with the wife of another person (*yu ren qi he jian* 與人妻和奸). In such cases, the offender was punished with the most severe penal labour as an unmutilated earth or grain pounder convict (*ENLL* 192; *Xuanquan* 7).

In the first case (no. II.11), the convicted man protested that he had not carried out (*wei shi*) the illicit sexual intercourse with his repudiated wife.[407] In Qin, an abortive attempt seems to have been punished less severely than the completed offence.[408] Therefore, the convicted considered the first conviction by the prefecture of Dangyang,[409] as well as the second sentence[410] passed by the agency of the minister of trials as a result of the retrial, to be unjustified. The second retrial started with the review of the records of the original proceedings. The investigation had established that the convicted man attempted to have sexual intercourse with his former wife by force without being able to implement his plan. Because his attempt was not successful, the prefecture did not sentence the offender to the more severe punishment for illicit sexual intercourse by force.[411] Since he contradicted the statement of the victim during the first retrial conducted by a secretary of the minister of trials (*ting shi* 廷史), the convicted man had no choice but to confess that he attempted to rape his former wife. The secretary subsequently concluded that the petition for retrial was unfounded (*bu shen*).[412] Accordingly, the agency of the minister of trials decided to place the convicted under detention among the earth pounder convicts for six years (*xi cheng dan liu sui* 繫城旦六歲).[413] This punishment was evidently imposed on him for filing an unfounded petition for a retrial. Bond servant convicts who committed an offence punishable by penal labour of the category *nai* were by law to be sentenced to the same penalty.[414] During the second retrial, it again turned out that the objections of the convicted, who this time even absconded from the detention place, were not substantiated. The interrogation proved that the offender used force and was only interrupted when an outsider saw he was attempting to rape his former wife. As a result of the second retrial, the convicted man was sentenced to further twelve years of detention among the earth pounder convicts. This cumulative sentence consisted of six years for absconding as a bond servant convict[415] and six years for filing an unfounded petition for a retrial. The convicted man was to first serve these twelve years of detention previous to the remainig six years of his first conviction.

407 *Yuelu* WYZ 186.

408 Cf. *FLDW* 65=*RCL* D 52 with the explanations in footnote 1187.

409 *Yuelu* WYZ 174.

410 *Yuelu* WYZ 177.

411 Cf. a stipulation from 186 BC (*ENLL* 193) translated in footnote 1205.

412 *Yuelu* WYZ 176.

413 *Yuelu* WYZ 177.

414 Cf. a stipulation from 186 BC (*ENLL* 90) translated in footnote 1218.

415 Cf. a stipulation from 186 BC (*ENLL* 165) translated in footnote 1237.

In the second case exemplifying a petition for retrial (II.12), a bond servant convict (*li chen*) was likewise charged with the offence of illicit sexual intercourse. This time the accused was prosecuted for having illicit sexual intercourse by mutual consent with a woman interned at a government workshop for working off a payment obligation towards the government. He had first acknowledged the offence directly after being caught *in flagrante* by a convict guard without being subjected to torture. In his petition, however, he argued that he had not been arrested on the spot when he was alleged to have had illicit sexual intercourse (*bu bu jiao shang* 不捕校上). The convicted man obviously knew that the guard had to observe a special provision for the arrest of offenders suspected of illicit sexual intercourse.[416] He appears to have hoped that the guard, as an eyewitness who had been offered bribes by the woman's relatives, would amend his former statement to the extent that he did not actually arrest the couple *in flagrante*. During the first stage of interrogation of the retrial, the guard admitted that he had initially accepted the bribes, but returned them later. When the convicted man was confronted with statements of his sexual partner and witnesses, which were contradictory to his own, he was unable to explain the discrepancies. Consequently, the judicial officials inferred that the petition for retrial was unfounded. Although the original punishment for the illicit sexual intercourse (six years of detention among the earth pounder convicts for an offence punishable with penal labour of the category *nai* committed by a bond servant convict) was supposed to be increased by further six years of detention among the earth pounder convicts (for filing an unsubstantiated petition), the offence was covered by an amnesty, with the result that the convicted remained a bond servant.

4.6.3.4 Formal Characteristics and Function

The officials of the prefecture had to record the petition for a retrial and had to forward it to the higher authorities. All three retrials mentioned above seem to have been conducted by the agency of the minister of trials (*ting wei*).[417] The final section of the petitions for retrial also differs from that of the submitted doubtful cases. First, the agency of the minister of trials notifies (*wei* 謂) the head of the prefecture, where the petitioner was held under detention, of the

416 Cf. the translations of a relevant stipulation (ZYS 182–183) and a model for investigation (FZS 95=RCL E 25) from the Qin dynasty in footnote 1256.

417 In one case, the minister of trials notified the competent prefecture that his agency had reviewed the decision of the lower authority (ZYS 121); in another case, a secretary of the minister (*ting shi*) conducted the retrial and notified the competent prefecture of his decision (*Yuelu* WYZ 175, 186; cf. *Yuelu* WYZ 205).

results of the retrial (*fu zhi* 覆之).[418] Afterwards, a copy of the notification was to be forwarded (*teng* 騰) to those prefectures which were also dealing with the case.[419]

The two cases of the *Wei yu deng zhuang* fulfilled a specific function other than that of the *Zou yan shu*: They served as a warning against lodging an unfounded appeal. In this way, judicial officials were instructed on how to proceed in such cases.

4.6.4 *Recommendations of Competent Investigators for Promotion*

4.6.4.1 Legal Basis

The fourth category concerns recommendations for promoting competent investigating officials. One case in the *Zou yan shu* (no. 22)[420] from pre-imperial Qin as well as the cases no. II.9[421] and no. II.10[422] in the *Wei yu deng zhuang* belong to this category. A special ordinance enacted by the Qin ruler formed the legal basis for positive testimonials:

> 令曰：獄史能得微難獄，上。
>
> The ordinances read: "Whenever a judicial secretary is able to solve an obscure and difficult case, this is to be reported to the higher authorities."[423]

The letters of recommendation to the superior authorities were framed *pro forma* by the introductory and concluding formulae *gan yan zhi* 敢言之 "we venture to report this".[424]

4.6.4.2 Similarities in the Content

The contents of the three cases are rather similar. In each case, the offender committed armed robbery (robbery and bodily injury[425] or robbery and murder[426]) on a deserted road or in a secluded field hut. It was very difficult to

---

418 ZYS 121–122; *Yuelu* WYZ 186–187, 205–206.

419 ZYS 123; *Yuelu* WYZ 207.

420 ZYS 197–228.

421 *Yuelu* WYZ 142–149. This case is only preserved in fragments.

422 *Yuelu* WYZ 150–170.

423 ZYS 227–228; cf. *Yuelu* WYZ 147.

424 *Yuelu* WYZ 147, 149, 170. Cf. ZYS 227, 228 as well as two submissions of cases concerning criminal officials in ZYS 68, 92, 98.

425 ZYS 224.

426 *Yuelu* WYZ 142, 166.

solve the crime because the offenders actively diverted suspicion away from themselves. One of the accused put a tally for traders next to the injured woman to cast suspicion on the local merchants;[427] another left behind the clothes of a penal labour convict at the scene of the crime in order to make the officials believe that the murderer was a convict.[428] At first, the responsible officials were unable to gather usable evidence related to the crime.[429] All three offenders were described as perpetrators who represented a serious threat to common people[430] because they had no scruple about killing their victims[431] and were ingenious in covering up all their traces.

These cases did not pose any problem for the legal assessment. The detailed description of the investigation was rather intended as a textbook example for solving criminal cases which at first sight seemed to be hopeless. The responsible officials used resourceful investigation methods including the confidential questioning of the victims' neighbours,[432] using undercover informers to scope out the suspect's living conditions and economic circumstances,[433] and meticulous first-hand inspection of pieces of evidence.[434] In one case, the officials posted guards along the roads in order to intercept suspect persons and check up on them.[435] The various measures that were applied finally enabled the officials to discover the offender. During the first stage of interrogation, the suspect did not confess to the crime. At that point, the investigating officials confronted the accused with evidence contradicting his account, forcing him to amend his former statements.[436] In the course of this cross-examination, the officials, partially by threatening to carry out torture,[437] succeeded in obtaining the suspect's confession of guilt.[438]

427 ZYS 221–222.

428 *Yuelu* WYZ 161.

429 ZYS 225–226; cf. *Yuelu* WYZ 148.

430 ZYS 225; cf. *Yuelu* WYZ 148 and *Yuelu* WYZ 167.

431 ZYS 223; cf. WYZ 163–164.

432 *Yuelu* WYZ 154.

433 ZYS 206–211, WYZ 143.

434 ZYS 215–216.

435 *Yuelu* WYZ 155.

436 ZYS 217–220; *Yuelu* WYZ 158–159.

437 ZYS 220.

438 ZYS 224, *Yuelu* WYZ 164.

4.6.4.3 The Formula of the Letter of Recommendation

At the end of the letter of recommendation, the specific ethical standards of a judicial official were emphasised which make him suitable for the task as clerk-in-chief (*zu shi* 卒史)[439] within the provincial agency:

> 皆請（清）絜（潔）毋（無）害，敦殼（愨）守吏，心平端禮。[440]
>
> They all are officeholders who have integrity and moral purity, are impeccable[441] and dutiful.[442] In their hearts, they are impartial, upright and in accordance with the rites.

The wording of this recommendation of an official for promotion corresponds, to a large extent, to that in the *Zou yan shu* and in case no. II.9 of the *Wei yu deng zhuang*.[443] These similarities are hardly coincidental. They rather suggest that there were common models for this type of recommendation letter and that related exemplary criminal cases circulated among the judicial officials.

---

439 *Zu shi* 卒史 were secretaries of the governor of a province (*tai shou* 太守), the provincial commander (*du wei* 都尉) and the heads of different offices at the imperial court (*ENLL* 476; *Xuanquan* 95, 103, 188). The *zu shi* also tried criminal cases on the provincial level (Qin: *Liye* 8–78, 8–135, 8–224; *ZYS* 124; *Shiji* 53, 2014; 96, 2676; Han: *ZYS* 67, 74; cf. *tai shou zu shi* 太守族史 in *Hanshu* 63, 2769; 76, 3216, 88, 3594; 89, 3635; Shen Gang 2008, 148–149; Kyôto daigaku jinbun kagaku kenkyûjo kandoku kenkyûhan 2015, 354). There are differing indications on their actual number (*Shiji* 121, 3119; commentary of Ru Chun in *Shiji* 120, 3106). Towards the end of the Western Han period the governor of the province of Donghai had nine *zu shi* (*Yinwan mudu* M6D2r; Xie Guihua 1997, 47; Loewe 2004, 60). Cf. Lau and Lüdke 2012, 190 footnote 923.

440 *Yuelu WYZ* 169.

441 *Wu hai* 無害 is a term that refers to the professional competence of officials. The classification of an official such as *wu hai* was a precondition for recommending somebody to office (*Mo* 90, 358 with commentary by Sun Yirang; *Shiji* 122, 3152=*Hanshu* 90, 3661; *Hanshu* 39, 2005). The qualification *wu hai* was required from officials assuming responsible tasks, such as reviewing trials in cases involving serious offences that could result in death verdicts (*ENLL* 396).

442 *Jie* 潔 and *dun que* 敦愨 were required character traits of a good official in the Qin administration (*Yushu* 9: 凡良吏明法律令，事無不能殹（也）；有（又）廉絜（潔）敦愨而好佐上。"In general, good officials understand the law, the statutes and ordinances, and there is no official business where they are incompetent. Furthermore, they have integrity and moral purity, are honest and faithful and like to assist their superiors."). Cf. Yates 1995, 333–335 for the interpretation of this passage and the topos of the purity and pollution of officials in the Qin manuscripts from Shuihudi.

443 Cf. *ZYS* 228 and *Yuelu WYZ* 148.

Officials of the prefecture concluded their letter of recommendation with the formula:

> 任謁以補卒史，勸它吏。[444]
>
> I/we recommend and guarantee for [445] [the investigating official] and request that he is to fill the ranks of the clerks-in-chief [of the province] so that his example may be an encouragement for other officials.

In this way, they expressed the hope that other officials would follow their colleague's example. The function of presenting these three criminal cases was to train local judicial officials in techniques for conducting an effective investigation[446] and to provide models for submitting such recommendations.

All criminal cases compiled in the *Wei yu deng zhuang* were submitted to the higher authorities, which clearly demonstrates their significance. As can be seen from the above classification, however, there were different reasons for their submission.

---

444 *Yuelu* WYZ 149; cf. the variants of this concluding formula in ZYS 228 (謁以補卒史，勸它吏) and *Yuelu* WYZ 169–170 (任謁課以補卒史，勸它吏).

445 For *ren* see footnote 1086.

446 Cf. Lüdke 2003, 54–55.

CHAPTER 5

The *Wei yu deng zhuang* in Comparison with Other Legal Texts

5.1 Functional Comparison with the *Feng zhen shi*

The specific function of the collection *Wei yu deng zhuang* can also be illustrated by way of comparison with other legal manuscripts from tombs of Qin officials that overlap in certain respects. Especially the *Feng zhen shi* 封診式 "Models for Sealing and Investigating" from Shuihudi are worth close consideration.[447]

Although the title of the *Feng zhen shi* suggests otherwise, this manuscript not only provides examples and instructions on how to seize and seal (*feng* 封) the property of an accused charged with serious offences, and to secure evidence at the scene of a crime by forensic inspection (*zhen* 診). It also contains a number of model records of investigation and interrogation which might be used for conducting correct criminal proceedings.[448] The information from the *Feng zhen shi* gives researchers a better understanding of the *Wei yu deng zhuang*. The *Feng zhen shi* explains under which conditions the second stage of interrogation (*jie*) is to be initiated and how and by what means the accused is to be cross-examined in order to obtain a confession from him.[449] It provides a concrete example of the procedural requirements, which are mentioned in case no. II.12 of the *Wei yu deng zhuang*,[450] for arresting a fornicating couple.[451] Case no. II.10 of the *Wei yu deng zhuang*, which describes in detail the measures for investigating armed robbery,[452] bears similarities to a model presented in the *Feng zhen shi*, which documents the steps taken during the investigation

447 For a comparison between the *Feng zhen shi* and the *Zou yan shu* and the differences in content, see the discussion in Lüdke 2003, 40–42. In an analysis of the genre *shi* 式 in Han manuscripts, Gao Heng (2008, 230–238) also dealt with the different types of *shi* in the *Feng zhen shi*. This research has been continued by Barbieri-Low who compares the model forms of the *Feng zhen shi* with corresponding documents from the Han (2011, 126–130).

448 FZS 13–14, 15–16, 17–18, 19–20, 21–22, 23–24, 42–45, 46–49, 50–51, 95, 96–97=RCL E 5, 7, 8, 9, 10, 11, 16, 17, 18, 25, 6.

449 FZS 2–4=RCL E 2. Cf. *Yuelu* WYZ 080, 102, 127, 184, 201.

450 *Yuelu* WYZ 198, 204. Cf. ZYS 183, 188, 194, 195.

451 FZS 95=RCL E 25.

452 *Yuelu* WYZ 151–159. Cf. ZYS 203–213.

 | DOI 10.1163/9789004315655_006

of a burglary.[453] In both cases, the investigating officers first tried to gather evidence at the scene of the crime. All traces, such as a tunnel used for the burglary or the wounds of the killed persons and the clothes of a convict left behind at the scene, were carefully inspected. Afterwards, the neighbours or other witnesses who could provide information about the stolen clothes or about an unknown female corpse were interrogated.

Nevertheless, there are significant differences between both types of legal texts, which have been summarised by Lüdke.[454] The conclusions he derived from a comparison of the *Zou yan shu* and the *Feng zhen shi* appear to be valid for the *Wei yu deng zhuang* as well. The *Feng zhen shi* only deals with the procedure, not with the legal issues in question. This is illustrated by the fact that it largely ignores the judicial decision. In contrast, difficult legal issues are the main focus of the *Wei yu deng zhuang*. For this purpose, it was necessary to document the entire criminal proceedings, including the sentence. Unlike the *Wei yu deng zhuang*, the *Feng zhen shi* does not deal with individual cases. For all persons involved, it generally uses cyclical characters of the *tian gan* 天干 "heavenly stems" as blank names or *mou* 某, which mostly refers to names of places or officials. In this way, the *Feng zhen shi* provides a formula that needs to be filled in by replacing the cyclical characters and *mou* with the actual information from the case. As model documents, the *Feng zhen shi* standardised the written communication between officials, minimised the number of exceptions to be handled and contributed to the smooth functioning of the bureaucracy.[455]

5.2 Comparison with Official Court Precedents

On the basis of the sources available at present, it is difficult to answer the question of exactly how the *Wei yu deng zhuang* as well as the *Zou yan shu*, as collections of criminal cases, related to official court precedents, which had already been used for determining punishment in the formation of the early Chinese empire.

5.2.1 *The Early Han Precedent of the Absconded Private Slave Woman*

An early example for such a precedent is mentioned in case no. 3 of the *Zou yan shu*. In this case, Lan 闌, a judicial official in Qi 齊, accompanied a woman

453 *FZS* 73–83=*RCL* E 22. Cf. McLeod and Yates 1981, 157–159.

454 Lüdke 2003, 42.

455 Barbieri-Low 2011, 125–126, 153.

from the former ruling house of Qi on her forced resettlement to the capital area of Chang'an 長安. There, he fell in love with her, took her as his wife without permission and attempted to return with her to Qi. The couple was caught before they had crossed the border control station of the empire's central region within the passes.[456] The judicial official was prosecuted for the statutory offence of "coming from the feudal lords in order to lure sb. (to their territory)" (*cong zhu hou lai you* 從諸侯來誘)[457] although he had not talked the woman into absconding and returning home for the purpose of persuading her to go over to the feudal lords, but rather for the personal reason of living together. Since they were uncertain whether Lan's illegal activity actually constituted the offence of *cong zhu hou lai you*, the competent judicial officials submitted the case to the higher authorities for decision.[458] They further attached a precedent according to which a private slave woman, who had been put to work at a city wall of the state of Zhao 趙 and had absconded after having finished her employment for the personal reason of joining her older brother in Zhao, was sentenced for the offence of "absconding to the feudal lords" (*wang zhi zhu hou* 亡之諸侯).[459] The majority of the judicial officials argued that the case of the absconded slave woman was of "the same category" (*tong lei* 同類) as that of Lan.[460] Therefore, they argued for sentencing the judicial official in the same way, since the consequences of Lan's illegal activity and the intentional luring of a person to convert to the feudal lords were in fact the same. The record of the precedent only provides the results of the finding of fact and the decision. In contrast to the *Zou yan shu* or the *Wei yu deng zhuang*, no details are provided of the investigation or interrogation.

5.2.2 *The Qin Precedents of the Court*

During the Qin dynasty, a similar support in adjudication was denoted as *ting xing shi* 廷行事 "precedents of the court".[461] As a second important pillar of legal practice besides the statutes (*lü*) and ordinances (*ling*), they were also

456 *ZYS* 18–19.

457 *ZYS* 19–22.

458 *ZYS* 23.

459 *ZYS* 23–24.

460 *ZYS* 24.

461 *FLDW* 38, 42, 56, 59, 60, 66, 142, 148–152=*RCL* D 30, 33, 45, 47, 48, 53, 120, 126–130. There are alternative translations of the term *ting xing shi*, such as "practice of the court" (Hulsewé 1985, 131) or "matters administered by the court" (Lüdke 2003, 46). For the controversy over the meaning of *xing shi* see Lau and Lüdke 2012, 27.

called *bi xing shi* 比行事 “analogous cases and precedents”.[462] The function of the *ting xing shi* shall be demonstrated with the following example:

> 告人盜百一十，問盜百，告者可（何）論？當貲二甲。盜百，即端盜駕（加）十錢，問告者可（何）論？當貲一盾。貲一盾應律，雖然，廷行事以不審論，貲二甲。[463]

> A person is reported for having stolen 110 [cash]; the [interagency] enquiries [show] that he stole 100 cash. How is the reporting person to be sentenced? He is by law to be fined two suits of armour. [Now] the theft was 100 cash, [but] this is intentionally increased by adding 10 cash, the question is: How is the reporting person to be sentenced? He is by law to be fined one shield; the fine of one shield corresponds to the statutes. However, according to the precedents of the court, he is to be sentenced for [a report] that does not correspond to the facts and to be fined two suits of armour.

To understand this example, it is helpful to recapitulate the hierarchy of punishments for offences against property during the Qin dynasty. The offender was to be punished according to the value of misappropriated goods: For theft to the amount of 1 to 21 cash he was fined one shield (*yi dun*), and to the amount of 22 to 109 cash, he was fined two suits of armour (*er jia*). For theft amounting to 110 cash or more, the offender was to be punished with penal labour of the category *nai* as a bond servant convict (*li chen qie*). In this example, the reporting person is first punished for a report which does not correspond to the facts (*gao bu shen* 告不審). This implied that the reporting person did not mean to increase the value of the misappropriated goods. Reporting which does not correspond to the facts was punished with a sentence that was one degree less severe than the sentence that was carried out due to the inaccurately reported offence. In the present case, the reporting person was fined two suits of armour, which ranked directly behind the penal labour of the category *nai* as a bond servant convict, the punishment that was applied for theft amounting to the

462 *Yuelu Lüling* 1009 (yet unpublished): 制詔御史：吏上奏當者，具傳所以當者律令、比行事。“Imperial decision instructing the chief prosecutor: Officials who submit what they consider to be justified to their superiors, compile and attach those statutes, ordinances and analogous cases and precedents because of which they consider [their proposal for a judgement] to be justified.” *Yuelu Lüling* 1008 (yet unpublished): 以其律令、某比行事當之。 “According to these relevant statutes, ordinances and the analogous case or precedent X, we consider it to be justified [in case of the offender].”

463 *FLDW* 38–39=*RCL* D 30.

value of 110 cash. In the second case, the judicial officials assumed that the reporting person had intentionally increased the value of the misappropriated goods by ten cash. The report was now classified as false incrimination (*wu gao* 誣告), which according to the inversion-principle, was to be punished in the same way as the alleged theft. Therefore, the reporting person was fined one shield as stipulated by law for theft with a value of 10 cash. In the last case, the intentionally committed offence would be punished more leniently than the one committed without intent. As this apparently contradicted the accepted principles for determining punishment in Qin law, the supreme judicial authority decided as a rule to impose the more severe sentence for *gao bu shen* in such cases. *Ting xing shi* like these were judicial decisions made in a specific case that were neither covered by the relevant legal provisions nor conformed to the wording of the statutes. They could nonetheless be included in the statutes at a later point. This is exemplified by the case of an offender who killed officials while resisting his arrest. This actually constituted the statutory offence of *dou sha ren* 鬥殺人 "killing during a fight", because no premeditation was involved. In any case, the *ting xing shi* classified the killing of an arresting law enforcement officer as the more serious offence of *zei sha ren* 賊殺人 "killing somebody with malice",[464] although the sentence for either offences did not seem to differ. This legal interpretation was probably incorporated into the statutes from 186 BC.[465]

The decisions of *ting xing shi* did not always conflict with the statutes. Sometimes they treated illegal actions not covered by existing rules in analogy with other statutory offences, which were applied because the effects of both crimes were the same.[466] Other *ting xing shi* stipulated a measure be imposed for a certain group of persons in addition to a regular punishment: Officials who committed fraud and forgery, for which they were to be fined one or more shields, were also permanently dismissed from office (*fei* 廢).[467] Family members who stood as surety (*bao* 包) for the arrival of their banished relative at the place of banishment were to go to the place of banishment in his stead if the offender himself died or absconded.[468] On the basis of *ting xing shi*, victims of crimes such as *shan qiang zhi* 擅強質 "on one's own authority taking

464 *FLDW* 66=*RCL* D 53. Cf. the case of the former slave mentioned in footnotes 347 and 370. This manumitted slave injured the arresting robber hunter in a fight (*dou shang ren* 鬥傷人), but was nevertheless punished for the statutory offence of *zei shang ren* 賊傷人 "injuring somebody with malice".

465 *ENLL* 152.

466 *FLDW* 56=*RCL* D 45. Cf. Lüdke 2003, 45–46.

467 *FLDW* 59=*RCL* D 47.

468 *FLDW* 60=*RCL* D 48.

pledges by force" could be exempted from punishment. According to the statutes, those who took pledges from debtors under coercion and those who accepted pledges by mutual consent were fined in the same way. The *ting xing shi*, however, stipulated that persons who were forced to give pledges were not to be sentenced, while both those who accepted or gave pledges by mutual consent were to be sentenced.[469] In other instances, the *ting xing shi* simplified statutes by combining comparable statutory offences[470] or made amendments to the existing legal provisions.[471]

In contrast to the *Wei yu deng zhuang*, the *ting xing shi* from Shuihudi only concisely mention alternative decisions in particular cases, but provide no details of investigation or interrogation. It is not clear whether they directly refer to precedents in regard to which more detailed records were kept in the archives or only to an established practice to settle particular cases.

469 *FLDW* 148=*RCL* D 126. Victims of rape were likewise exempted from punishment (*ENLL* 191).

470 *FLDW* 142=*RCL* D 120.

471 *FLDW* 149–152=*RCL* D 127–130.

CHAPTER 6

Conclusions

6.1 Authentic Documents or Fictitious Cases? The Genre of Text

According to the available sources, it is difficult to decide whether the individual cases were based on authentic documents which were more or less adapted or were merely fictitious cases. Three cases of the *Zou yan shu*, which have obvious features of narrative texts, suggest that they were fictitious. These include the cases no. 19 and 20 from the Spring and Autumn period. Their formal structure is revealing. First, legal provisions from a different time or former statutes are quoted. Then, the finding of fact introduced by *jin* 今 "in the present case" is summarised. A dialogue follows between the judge, who is a well-known sage of the Spring and Autumn period, and the sovereign. The judge next reports his decision to the sovereign, whereupon the sovereign expresses deep consternation and reacts unfavourably. The judge gives a detailed, sophisticated account of the reasons for his decision, and finally the sovereign has no choice but to approve the proposed judgement. The climax is used as a rhetorical device: Suspense is built up by first indicating the decision and the disapproval of the sovereign; it is further intensified when the judge gives an account of his investigation. The decisive argument is made at the very end. In these two cases from the Spring and Autumn period, the original sequential order of legal reasoning and decision is reversed for the sake of narrative impact.[472] In its structure, the *Zou yan shu* case no. 21 from Qin times corresponds to a certain extent to the narrative cases no. 19 and 20.[473]

6.2 Used Formulae and Basic Structure

Narrative texts such as those in the *Zou yan shu* are not included in the *Wei yu deng zhuang*. The different case records of this collection follow the example of excavated official documents from Qin and Han times. An introductory cover letter mainly provides the exact date of the submission, the place of the submitting office as well as the position and the name of the prefectural

472 For an analysis of the narrative cases no. 19 and 20, see Lüdke 2003, 27–31.

473 There are also arguments for subsuming this case under the category of doubtful legal decisions, see Lau and Lüdke 2012, 44–45.

 | DOI 10.1163/9789004315655_007

officials responsible for conducting the criminal proceedings. At the beginning and the end of the submissions, the subordinate agency used polite formulae when it addressed its superiors: *gan yan zhi* 敢讞之, *gan yan zhi* 敢言之 or *ye* 謁.[474] These are commonplace in official communication, but not in narrative texts. A note that a copy of the present document should be forwarded to another prefecture for its information,[475] a note to whom the response of the higher authority was to be addressed,[476] or a reference to the number of the submitted bamboo slips,[477] which permitted control of the delivery, were typical of official correspondence. In two cases, the submission concludes with a dated letter in which the governor of the province evaluates the prefecture's submission and notifies the prefect of his decision.[478] The form of this notification is also indicative of the administrative practice.

In their basic structure, the case records of the *Wei yu deng zh*uang follow the typical sequence for administrative documents.[479] First, a person is reported to the authorities for having committed an offence. A report or an *ex-officio* charge is used by law as a precondition for initiating criminal proceedings. When the suspect and the witnesses are questioned, the correspondence between the statements is recorded. If required, the suspect is subjected to cross-examination in compliance with the relevant directives. After the confession, the results of the forensic inspection and of interagency enquiries on particulars relevant to sentencing are added and compared with the results of the interrogation. In conclusion, the finding of fact is summarised by the competent officials who assure that the facts are firmly established. The introductory and concluding terms *ju* 鞫 and *shen* 審 occur in the summarised finding of fact in the *Wei yu deng zhuang* and in excavated administrative documents

---

474 *Yuelu* WYZ 095, 149, 169. Cf. *ye bao* 謁報 "we request response (containing a decision from the higher authorities)" (ZYS 7, 15, 47, 98).

475 *Yuelu* WYZ 207; ZYS 123 (Qin case).

476 *Shu mou guan mou ren fa* 署某官某人發 "write (on the response): to be opened by person X of office Y" (ZYS 7, 15, 47; cf. *Liye* 8–61+8–293+8–2012, 8–64v, 8–155, 8–197, 8–2029).

477 That such notes were obligatory for certain types of submissions can be gathered from a Qin ordinance (*Yuelu Lüling* 1737 [yet unpublished]). For example, the formula *wei zou mou die* 爲奏某牒 "draw up a submission on X slips" was used in recommendations of investigators for promotion (*Yuelu* WYZ 148, 169; ZYS 228 [Qin case]) or in submissions of proposals for judgement which required the approval of the emperor (ZYS 68, 98).

478 *Yuelu* WYZ 028–029, 030; *Yuelu* WYZ 042.

479 See in detail the stages of criminal procedure in section 4.5.

from the Qin dynasty[480] as well as from the last years of the Western Han dynasty.[481] In some cases which were submitted to higher authorities for decision the applicable legal provisions are attached or it is noted whether the accused remains under detention. Although the purpose of the submission is to arrive at a decision, it does not anticipate this decision as in other official documents.

6.3 Possible Function of the *Wei yu deng zhuang*

Even if the cases were invented by an author who was versed in the law, they follow in their sequence and the frequent repetitions the model of authentic administrative documents. This structure suggests that the cases of the *Wei yu deng zhuang* were not simply designed for the amusement of an official audience. It is more likely that they provided precedents or procedural model records for the advanced legal training of candidates who would be given jurisdiction at lower administrative levels. In studying these models, future judicial officials were apt to insist on due process. The *Wei yu deng zhuang* was possibly compiled as a kind of private manual, but of course this does not rule out the possibility that it followed the example of case collections issued by government agencies.

Several problems concerning the function of legal manuscripts as burial offerings have still not been convincingly solved. It is not easy to distinguish between manuscripts which served as a status symbol, insofar as they showed that the deceased was a literate official, and manuscripts that were entombed because of the departed official's professional interests.[482] The question remains as to whether the tomb occupant had also used the manuscripts during his lifetime, or whether the manuscripts were exclusively compiled for the sake of the funeral. On the basis of the limited information on the ancient Chinese beliefs currently available from the sources, it is hard to say exactly how and for which purpose the deceased official might use exemplary criminal cases in his afterlife.

---

480 Cf. the file note on a case of officials who privately ordered convicts or conscripts to work as paid labourers where *ju* (*zhi*) and *shen* are used at the beginning and the end of the summarised finding of fact (*Liye* 8–1743v+8–2015v).

481 Cf. the file note on a case of an official who misappropriated public funds where *ju* and *shen* are also used as introductory and concluding terms (Tuzishan 兔子山 slip no. J3⑤: 1 quoted in Hunan sheng wenwu kaogu yanjiusuo 2013).

482 Giele 2010, 125; Giele 2003, 428–431.

PART 2

Annotated Translation of the Wei yu deng zhuang

Notes on the Translation

What follows is an annotated translation of the overall 15 case records contained in the *Wei yu deng zhuang*.[483] The annotations mainly contain philological discussions, which explain the translation of certain words by comparison with other occurrences of this word in excavated manuscripts and received literature, and provide a semantic, phonological[484] and/or syntactic analysis. Furthermore, they deliver references to important secondary literature, and also touch upon the historical and social background of the respective case. Legal problems and developments are mostly discussed in the short introductions preceding the translation of each case record.

The introductions are followed by two complementary editions, which represent the basis for the translation: one diplomatic and one fully punctuated edition. Comparing them with the excellent edition presented in Zhu and Chen 2013 (including the corrections provided in Hafner 2013a and 2014a), the reader will notice that they conform in large part with the latter. However, we have carefully checked every single character with the help of the original colour photographs as well as infrared images, and apart from proposing some different identifications or interpretations of characters and a slightly different placement of slip 095, we also took a more conservative approach to the identification of unclear characters. In such cases we preferred to put a square ("□") rather than base our translation on a highly tentative identification. Although the diplomatic edition uses modern character forms, these reflect the structure of the original characters written in the manuscripts. This means that characters have not been altered to comply with the modern standard forms to write the respective words (e.g. *shu* 鼠 is maintained instead of *yu* 予 "to give"). Also, no punctuation has been added so only the marks that are contained in the manuscripts – reduplication or ligature marks as well as hook-shaped and round segmentation marks – are displayed. Where the last part of a slip was left blank in the manuscript, a paragraph has been inserted.

483 The order of the cases follows the official publication Zhu and Chen 2013.

484 The Old Chinese (OC) reconstructions – marked with an asterisk – are based on Baxter and Sagart 2014b, the most recent version of the reconstruction described in Baxter and Sagart 2014a. In addition, other recent reconstructions proposed by Starostin (2006), Pan Wuyun 潘悟云 (cited according to TLS) and Zhengzhang Shangfang 鄭張尚方 (2003) have been consulted. Furthermore, a few reconstructions were slightly modified by the authors where additional loan writings or cognates are postulated.

 | DOI 10.1163/9789004315655_008

The second edition, which is immediately followed by the English translation, always provides the modern standard character forms for the words (supposedly) written in parentheses. The original segmentation marks have been substituted and supplemented by modern punctuation; paragraphs have also been inserted wherever suitable for clarification. Furthermore, subheadings in italics help to distinguish between procedural steps.

The notation conventions in the editions are as follows:

Diplomatic edition only:

＝	reduplication/ligature mark: indicates that the preceding character has to be reduplicated or interpreted as a ligature of two characters
∟	hook-shaped segmentation mark: separates different meaningful units or items/names in lists (scarcely used in the same way as a round segmentation mark)
•	round segmentation mark: indicates the beginning of a new case record or a new procedural step within the same case record
字	character form not complete, but legible with regard to context and/or extant strokes

Fully punctuated edition only:

（字）	modern standard character form of the word written (following the original character form)
〈字〉	modern standard character form of the word intended to be written (following a supposed scribal mistake)
【字】	character emended (to replace □ or ▨) according to the context and/or parallel text in the same manuscript

Both editions:

□	one character illegible
▨	slip broken (and one or more characters lost)
123	slip no. according to the edition in Zhu and Chen 2013 (always following the respective slip)

Note on capitalisation:

Throughout the translation – as in the whole book – we opted for minimal capitalisation of titles and ranks due to their frequent occurrence. Only "duke", "king" and "emperor" are capitalised if these titles are directly followed by a name, e.g. "King Zheng of Qin".

Case I.1

In this case from the year 222 BC subordinate law enforcement officers fraudulently laid claim to rewards for arresting bandits. The officers pursued a gang of bandits by order of the prefecture of Zhouling. As it turned out, these bandits had already been arrested by conscripts from the neighbouring prefecture of Shayi while they were on patrol in the mountains. Promising the conscripts that they would later receive the rewards, the officers talked the conscripts into handing the bandits over to them and gave them a partial payment of 2,000 cash in advance. Before the rewards were issued by the authorites, the illegal deal was discovered – probably by the leading officials of the prefecture of Shayi. This prefecture then brought an *ex-officio* charge of fraud against the officers from Zhouling prefecture and forced the neighbouring prefecture to initiate criminal proceedings against its subordinates.

In its verdict, the prefecture of Zhouling based the sentence on various statutes and ordinances, the exact wording of which is yet unknown. It can, however, be gathered that an illegal deal with rewards was obviously classified as a property offence; the same would have been the case in early Han times. For such offences the law required that the accused had to be punished according to the value of misappropriated goods, which in the present case exceeded 660 cash. Therefore, the offenders would have to be punished by being tattooed and being made earth pounder convicts. This form of penal labour was apparently considered to be too severe by the competent officials because the offenders had not yet received the rewards. Therefore, they imposed a more lenient punishment, letting the offenders instead pay the fee for redemption from being tattooed. Here a principle for determining punishment in property offences, which has not yet been found in statutes from early Han times, becomes apparent. According to legal provisions of the Qin dynasty, offenders who did not carry out a planned theft were allowed to pay the fee for redemption from the punishment that would normally have been applied for this offence. In addition, the officers of Zhouling prefecture were sentenced to three years of additional military service in the neighbouring province for misconduct in office. According to statutes from early Han times, this was a typical disciplinary penalty for officers and soldiers on a military campaign aimed at combatting banditry.

Before this sentence had been executed, it was reviewed by the supervisory prosecutor in charge of inspecting Nan province. He considered the judgement to be unlawful and gave orders to pass judgement anew. It is not expressly mentioned which agency conducted the retrial. However, the following

 | DOI 10.1163/9789004315655_009

decision of the province shows that the official who submitted the case to the higher authorities for decision was in fact again the prefect of Zhouling. In his submission, he made clear that the prefecture as the court of the first instance could not reach a consensus on the legitimate punishment for the officers and conscripts or on the question of its own criminal liability.

The two alternative votes for the sentence that are attached to the submission start with the formulae *li yi* and *huo yue* and probably express the votes of the majority and the minority within the competent authority. The majority approved the sentence of the prefecture of Zhouling as lawful and pleaded for acquitting the leading officials of any criminal liability. A minority suggested punishing the accused officers and conscripts more severely with penal labour of the category *nai* as watchmen. The legal basis for the latter vote is still unknown. The part of the manuscript documenting the sentence of the prefectural officials proposed by the minority is unfortunately missing. At least an acquittal would be out of the question since the leading officials were to be prosecuted for an erroneous judgement. The institutional affiliation of the officials who forwarded the two proposals is not made explicit. The same problem occurs in the first four cases of the *Zou yan shu*. The fact that, in the present case, the final ruling of Nan province as the higher authority differs from both proposals allows the conclusion that the proposals for judgement must be attributed to the officials of the prefecture of Zhouling. This further suggests that the prefecture of Zhouling also carried out the review that was initiated by an *ex-officio* charge of the supervisory prosecutor.

In the final decision, the higher authorities of Nan province found fault with the submission of their subordinate prefecture. They took the view that it was not necessary to submit the case for decision. The legal rules referred to were considered to be irrelevant for the case in question. On the contrary, the higher authorities thought that the statutory offence "bribing sb. or accepting sb.'s valuables for the purpose of bending the statutes and ordinances" was applicable to the case. For this offence the same principles as for theft had to be applied. This apparently constitutes the analogous application of a norm to a situation not directly covered by an existing legal requirement since the applicable statutes assumed that judicial officials were the addressees of bribes being offered for the purpose of bending the law. The sentence finally passed by the provincial authorities was not based on the illegal claim of rewards, which the offenders had not yet received, but on the partial payment of 2,000 cash, which had been paid by the officers and was considered to be a bribe used for the purpose of bending the law. Therefore, no mitigating circumstances for theft, which had not been carried out, were to be taken into account, with the result that the delinquent officers and conscripts had to be punished much more severely. Because the value of the offered bribes as well as those accepted exceeded 660 cash, they were by law to be tattooed and made earth pounder convicts.

The responsible officials of the prefecture of Zhouling were also considered to be liable to punishment, because they had imposed too lenient punishments on the offenders. They were fined one shield for committing an error of judgement. This was the minimum penalty during Qin times.

Diplomatic Edition

•廿五年六月丙辰朔癸未州陵守綰丞越敢讞之廼四月辛酉校長癸求$_{001}$盜上造柳士五轎沃詣男子治等八人女子二人告群盜=殺人⌞治等曰群盜=$_{002}$殺人⌞辟未斷未致購⌞到其甲子沙羨守驩曰士五瑣等捕□□□□癸等•癸□$_{003}$⧄□等群盜=殺人校長果部州陵守綰令癸與令佐士五行將柳等追⧄$_{004}$迹行到沙羨界中瑣等巳捕⌞瑣等言治等四人邦亡不智它人何辠⌞癸等智⌞利$_{005}$得群盜=殺人購⌞癸行請告瑣等曰瑣等弗能詣告移鼠癸=等=詣州陵盡鼠瑣等$_{006}$ **[Missing slip]** 鼠瑣等以爲購錢數⌞得公購備鼠瑣等⌞行弗詣告皆謀分購⌞未致購得它如沙羨書$_{007}$•□⌞柳⌞轎⌞沃⌞言如癸•士五瑣渠⌞樂曰與士五得⌞潘⌞沛戍之山材見治等共捕治等四$_{008}$人言秦人邦亡其它人不言所坐⌞得⌞潘⌞沛令瑣等將詣沙羨⌞沛等居亭約得購分$_{009}$購錢⌞未到沙羨實不智治等何辠弗能告有不智群盜購多⌞利癸等約死辠購聽$_{010}$請券付死辠購先受錢二千未受公購錢得沛等不智瑣等弗詣相移受錢它如癸$_{011}$等⌞沛⌞潘⌞得言如瑣等$_{012}$

五月甲辰州陵守綰丞越史獲論令癸瑣等各贖黥癸⌞行戍衡山郡各三歲以當灋先備$_{013}$贖不論沛等⌞監御史康劾以爲不當錢不處當更=論=及論失者言夬•綰等曰治等發興吏$_{014}$徒追⌞癸等弗身捕瑣等捕弗能告請相移紿以求購=未致得⌞綰等以盜未有取吏貲灋戍律$_{015}$令論癸瑣等口令瑣等環癸等錢它如癸等及劾•診問死辠購四萬三百廿⌞群盜=殺人購八$_{016}$⧄□它如告辤治等別⧄$_{017}$•鞫之癸⌞行⌞柳⌞轎⌞沃⌞群盜治等盜殺人⌞癸等追⌞瑣⌞渠⌞樂⌞得⌞潘⌞沛巳共捕⌞沛等令$_{018}$瑣等詣約分購未詣⌞癸等智治等群盜=殺人利得其購紿瑣等約死辠購⌞瑣等$_{019}$弗能告利得死辠購聽請相移紿券付死辠購先受私錢二千以爲購⌞得公購備⌞行弗$_{020}$⧄告約分購⌞沛等弗詣約分購不智弗詣相移受錢⌞獄未斷未致購得⌞死辠購四$_{021}$萬三百廿⌞群盜=殺人購八萬六百卌錢⌞綰等以盜未有取吏貲灋戍律令論癸瑣等不論$_{022}$ **[Missing slip]** 及它不毄敢□讞 之$_{023}$

•吏議曰癸瑣等論當毆沛綰等不當論⌞或曰癸瑣等當耐爲侯令瑣等環癸等錢綰等$_{024}$ **[Missing slip]**

□□年七月丙戌朔乙未南郡叚守賈報州陵守綰丞越子讞校長癸等詣男子治等告群盜$_{025}$⧄□鼠癸等癸曰治等殺人癸與佐行將□追瑣等巳捕治⧄$_{026}$人曰邦亡⌞不智它人辠癸等利得群盜購請瑣等鼠癸=等=詣盡鼠瑣等死辠購瑣等$_{027}$

鼠⌞癸先以私錢二千鼠以爲購數⌞行弗詣告皆謀分購未致購得疑癸⌞瑣⌞綰等皋⌞讞固有$_{028}$審癸等其審請瑣等所出購以死皋購備鼠瑣等有券⌞受人貨材以枉律令其所枉當$_{029}$貲以上受者貨者皆坐臧爲盜有律不當讞獲手其貲綰越獲各一盾它有律令$_{030}$

Edition and Translation

Submission by Zhouling Prefecture – Introductory Formula

廿五年六月丙辰朔癸未，州陵守綰、丞越敢瀧（讞）之：

In the 25th year on day *guiwei*[485] of the sixth month with the first day *bingchen*, Wan, incumbent[486] [prefect] of Zhouling,[487] and vice prefect[488] Yue venture to submit[489] [the following case] for decision:

---

485 This probably was the 25th year of King Zheng of Qin because *bingchen* occurs as the first day of the sixth month (Zhang Peiyu 2007, 73; Li Zhonglin 2012, 65). The day *guiwei* was the 28th day of the sixth month, i.e. 01/08/222 BC (Xu Xiqi 1997, 1240).

486 The almost exclusive usage of *shou* 守 for the prefect in the cases from the Yuelu Academy collection (*Yuelu* WYZ 001, 003, 004, 013, 025, 031, 040, 061, 068), in the documents from Liye (e.g. *Liye* 9–1v; cf. *shou cheng* 守丞 "vice prefect", e.g. in *Liye* 5–1r, 8–133v, 8–135r, 8–154r, 8–155, 9–2r or in combination with the office of *shao nei* 少内 in *Liye* 8–152r, of *si kong* 司空 in *Liye* 8–135r and of *tian guan* 田官 in *Liye* 9–981r) and the compound *shou li* 守吏 – obviously meaning "officeholder" (*Yuelu* WYZ 148, 169) – suggest that during Qin times every holding of an office was called *shou*, hence the translation "incumbent". Cf. Hubei sheng wenwu kaogu yanjiusuo and Xiangxi Tujiazu Miaozu zizhi zhou wenwu chu 2003, 10 and 24; Chen Songchang 2004, 19; Yang Zongbing 2004 and Sun Wenbo 2014. *Shou* could also mean "to hold an office temporarily" (*QLSZ* 161=*RCL* A 81: 官嗇夫節（即）不存，令君子毋（無）害者若令史守官。"If the overseer is absent, a master who is impeccable or the secretary of the prefect is ordered to hold the office temporarily."). So, for instance, a certain Yao temporarily performed the duties of the prefect of You until the arrival of Tui, the regular holder of this office, in one case of the *Zou yan shu* (ZYS 134). In Han times *shou* could designate an official who was on probation during the first year of his duty and only after this received the full status and salary (*Hanshu* 76, 3208; *ENLL* 102; *QLZC* 1=*RCL* C 1), An and Xiong 2007, 854–855.

487 Zhouling 州陵 is the name of a prefecture within Nan province (*Hanshu* 28A, 1566; *ENLL* 456; *Songbai mudu* 35r.1/3, 35v.1), which already existed in Qin times (cf. *Yuelu* WYZ 040; Hou Xiaorong 2009, 403–404). The administrative seat of Zhouling was located to the northeast of present Honghu in southern Hubei (*Lishi dituji* vol. II, 22/23, 7⑤). Cf. Chen Wei 2011.

488 For the function of the *cheng* 丞 "vice prefect" in the context of criminal procedure see Lau and Lüdke 2012, footnote 571.

489 In manuscripts from Qin and early Han times, 瀧 is the standard character (*Yuelu* WYZ 001, 025, 028, 030, 031, 039, 040, 042, 044, 046, 062, 064, 093, 095, 135, 235, 236; *QLSZ* 121=*RCL*

Original Case – Initiation of Criminal Proceedings

廼四月辛酉，校長癸、求$_{001}$盜上造柳、士五（伍）轎、沃詣男子治等八人、女子二人，告群盜盜殺人。
治等曰：
群盜盜$_{002}$殺人。
辟未斷，未致購。到其甲子沙羨守驩曰：
士五（伍）瑣等捕【治等，移鼠（予）】癸等。

On day *xinyou*[490] of the last[491] fourth month, *xiao zhang*[492] Gui and robber

---

A 64; *FLDW* 53, 72=*RCL* D 43, 58; *ZYS* 1, 8, 17, 23, 26, 28, 35, 49, 51, 53, 54, 56, 58, 60, 61, 228v; *ENLL* 102; *Shuowen* 11A, 566a; *Wangzhang shi jian* cited according to *Sanjian* 22) used to write the word *yan* 讞 (*Hanshu* 5, 150; 23, 1108; 58, 2682–2683; *Shiji* 122, 3139), which is the technical term for a procedure by which a judicial authority of the lower (*xian* 縣) or middle level (*jun* 郡) of the administration submitted criminal cases to the next-higher level for decision. The requirement for such a submission was that the submitting authority, after it had exhaustively investigated all points of fact, was still in doubt about the appropriate punishment, the punishability of the offence at stake in the case or other matters, such as the appropriate amount of rewards; this was signalled by the use of the term *yi* 疑. The legal manuscripts from the Yuelu Academy collection prove that the *yan*-procedure of submitting doubtful criminal cases to the higher authorities for decision already existed in pre-imperial Qin. This procedure was renewed in 200 BC by an edict of Emperor Gaozu (*Hanshu* 23, 1106). For an explanation of this edict see Lau and Lüdke 2012, 8–9. The submission had to correspond to a given form, which was usually introduced by the exact date, the rank and names of the submitting officials, and the initial formula *gan yan zhi* 敢灋（讞）之 (*Yuelu WYZ* 001, 031, 044, 062, 210; *ZYS* 1, 8, 17, 28, 36) as in the present case. This formula had to be repeated at the end of the submission (*Yuelu WYZ* 023, 093, 106, 135, 235; *ZYS* 6–7, 15, 23, 33, 47), see footnote 570.

490 This was the fifth day of the fourth month in the 25th year of King Zheng of Qin (cf. Zhang Peiyu 2007, 73; Li Zhonglin 2012, 65), i.e. 11/05/222 BC (Xu Xiqi 1997, 1240).

491 In excavated manuscripts and received texts from Qin and Han times, *nai* 廼/迺 "last, past" in front of months (*FZS* 17, 81, 96=*RCL* E 8, 22, 6; *Yuelu WYZ* 001, 031, 099; *Liye* 8–140r, 8–2085, 8–2161r; *ZYS* 9, 36; *Juyan* 13.6, 82.2; in combination with *wang* 往 in *Yuelu WYZ* 068; *nai* 乃 in *Shiji* 10, 422 and *Hanshu* 9, 281; 25B, 1262; 72, 3092; 81, 3359), feast days (*ZYS* 100, 102) or *gan zhi* characters designating days (*Liye* 9–981; *Juyan* 49.18, 306.12, 311.9; *nai* 乃 in *Hanshu* 99B, 4159) refers to the month or day immediately prior to the time of the speech, as has convincingly been demonstrated in Wang Huanlin 2007, 97. Cf. Chen Wei 2012a, 80–81, footnote 4 to *Liye* 8–140; Zhu and Chen 2013, 95 with footnote 3.

492 *Xiao zhang* 校長. For the function of this law enforcement officer, who in some cases from Qin and early Han times was identical to the head of a *ting* 亭 (*FZS* 25=*RCL* E 12; *ZYS* 36–37, 76), see Lau and Lüdke 2012, footnote 748. According to a list of the officials of the prefecture of Qianling from Qin times, there were six positions for *xiao zhang* in this prefecture, of which only two were occupied (*Liye* 7–67+9–631, cited according to Liye Qin jiandu jiaoshi xiaozu 2014). The number of *ting* in the prefecture of Qianling was probably significantly higher (cf. the number of *ting zhang* in the prefectures of the

hunter[493] Liu, holder of the second rank,[494] as well as the rank-and-file men[495] Jiao and Wo presented[496] the men Zhi and seven accomplices[497] as well as two women to the authorities and reported[498] them for killing people in the act of

---

province of Donghai during the late Western Han period according to Xie Guihua 1997, table 3, 47).

493 *Qiu dao* 求盜. For the function of this constable at a *ting* (FZS 21, 25, 55=RCL E 10, 12, 20; *Yuelu* WYZ 032, 040; *Liye* 8–167, 8–1252, 8–2027) see Lau and Lüdke 2012, footnote 753.

494 *Shang zao* 上造 was the title of the second within the hierarchy of twenty ranks (*jue* 爵) during Qin and Han times (e.g. *Yuelu* WYZ 044, 113; ZYS 158; ENLL 82; *Hanshu* 19A, 739). Holders of the second rank enjoyed certain legal privileges: If they committed an offence regularly punishable by the most severe form of penal labour, i.e. penal labour as tattooed earth pounder convicts (*qing wei cheng dan* 黥爲城旦), they were never mutilated, but their sentence was automatically reduced to penal labour as firewood gatherer convicts (*gui xin* 鬼薪, see ZYS 158: 篡遂縱囚，死罪囚，黥爲城旦；上造以上耐爲鬼薪。"For seizing by force a remand prisoner, letting him break out of prison or leaving him unpunished one is tattooed and made an earth pounder convict, if the prisoner [who goes unpunished] is liable to the death penalty. Holders of the second rank or higher are shaved and made firewood gatherer convicts instead."; ENLL 82: 上造、上造妻以上[...]有罪，其當刑及當爲城旦舂者，耐以爲鬼薪白粲。"If holders of the second or a higher rank or their wives [...] commit an offence which by law is to be punished with mutilation and penal labour as an earth or grain pounder convict they are [instead] to be shaved and to be made firewood gatherer or rice sifter convicts."). For the system of ranks see Lau and Lüdke 2012, footnote 626.

495 *Shi wu* 士五（伍）"rank-and-file man" (*Yuelu* WYZ 002–004, 008, 044, 047, 049, 051, 062–063, 074, 091, 092, 109, 137, 150, 208; *Liye* 5–1v, 8–19, 8–63v, 8–66v, 8–69, 8–71 etc.; FLDW 29, 33, 35, 71, 84, 163=RCL D 24, 27–28, 57, 69, 143; FZS 6, 8, 13, 15, 17, 19, 23, 28–29, 31, 34, 37, 40, 47, 50, 52, 61, 63, 73, 82, 84, 91, 95–96=RCL E 4, 3, 7–9, 11–15, 17–25, 6; ZYS 8, 36, 45, 70, 99–101, 212; ENLL 354–355, 357, 364) refers to persons without rank. Sons of holders of the first rank (*gong shi* 公士), of *gong zu* 公卒, *shi wu*, *si kou* 司寇 convicts and of released mutilated convicts (*yin guan* 隱官) were all made *shi wu* (ENLL 364–365). *Shi wu* were equal in terms of farm and land allocation to other groups having a similarly low legal status, like *gong zu* 公卒 and *shu ren* 庶人 (ENLL 312, 316). For *shi wu* see Lau and Lüdke 2012, footnote 630 with further references. Cf. Yates 1987.

496 *Yi* 詣 "to bring sb. before (the authorities), to present sb./oneself (to the authorities)" (e.g. *Yuelu* WYZ 006–007, 009, 034, 038, 047, 051, 141, 193, 200, 207; *Liye* 8–512, 8–1252, 8–1456r; ZYS 1, 28, 215; QLSZ 18=RCL A 9; FLDW 139=RCL D 117; FZS 19, 23,25, 37, 42, 48, 61, 68, 85, 96=RCL E 9, 11, 12, 15, 16, 17, 20, 21, 23, 6; ENLL 160) meant to present a suspected offender who had been arrested beforehand or pieces of physical evidence for an offence to the competent authorities. The authorities were then obliged to initiate judicial proceedings.

497 For the meaning of *deng* 等 in different contexts see Lau and Lüdke 2012, footnote 1296.

498 *Gao* 告 "to report an offence/offender to the judicial authorities" (e.g. *Yuelu* WYZ 031, 033, 083, 108, 111, 141, 142, 173; *Liye* 8–439; FLDW 38, 41, 44, 68, 96=RCL D 30, 32, 36, 55, 80; ZYS 1, 28, 36–37, 39–41, 44, 46, 49–50, 75, 84, 184, 197; ENLL 126–128, 132–134). Such a report was filed by private persons and not by officials who had jurisdiction in a respective area.

committing theft[499] as members of a robber gang.[500]
Zhi and his accomplices stated:
"We robbed and killed people as members of a robber gang."
Since a decision upon the punishment had not been made,[501] the reward [for arresting members of a robber gang who committed robbery and homicide][502]

Upon receiving a report, the responsible officials had the duty to initiate a formal inquest into the alleged offence. For the term *he* 劾, which is only used if a charge against an offender is brought by officials, see footnote 545.

499 *Dao sha ren* 盜殺人 "killing sb. in the act of committing theft" (e.g. *Yuelu* WYZ 141, 164, 166–167; *FLDW* 67=*RCL* D 54) is a particular statutory offence, which according to statutory provisions from 186 BC was punished by quartering (*zhe* 磔) (*ENLL* 66: 盜殺傷人[...]皆磔。"Those who kill or injure sb. in the act of committing theft [...] will all be quartered.") and much more severely as homicide committed out of other motifs.

500 *Qun* 群 in *qun dao* refers to a criminal organisation which, according to statutory provisions from 186 BC, is defined as a gang of five or more robbers (*ENLL* 62). The number of five men appears to have already been the distinguishing feature of a gang in legal texts from Qin times (cf. *FLDW* 1–2=*RCL* D 1 with *FZS* 25–30=*RCL* E 12). At the beginning of the Han dynasty, gang robbery was punished with quartering (*zhe* 磔), which was much more severe than the sentence for ordinary theft (*ENLL* 65–66: 群盜及亡從群盜[...]磔。"Members of a robber gang as well as absconders who follow members of a robber gang [...] will all be quartered."). During Qin times the statutory offence gang robbery must likewise have been punished with the death penalty because the reward for arresting one member of a robber gang was twice the amount of the reward for arresting an offender who was to be punished by death, but in the legal texts there is no evidence that quartering was imposed on members of a robber gang.

501 In the received literature of Zhou times, *bi* 辟 could refer to punishment (*Shu* Lüxing §18; *Zuo* Xiang 25,512,10) as a tool of the ruler to exercise authority. In legal manuscripts from Qin and early Han times, the synonymous *zui* 罪 is usually used to express the same meaning. The verb *duan* 斷 "to decide", which in the present context follows *bi* and is used in the passive voice, is used in two Han texts with *bi* as object in the meaning "to decide upon a punishment" (*Chunqiu fanlu* 8.4/40/6: 其堅足以斷辟 "his severity was sufficient to decide upon punishments"; *Hanguan liu zhong* 2.95/16/16: 決訟斷辟 "to adjudicate a legal dispute and decide upon a punishment"). Although *duan* usually occurs in combination with *yu* 獄 "criminal case" (*FLDW* 50, 111, 115=*RCL* D 40, 91, 95; *Yuelu* WYZ 021, 087; *Yuelu Lüling* 0589; *Liye* 8–1874; *ENLL* 102; *Zuo* Zhao 14,654,16; *Juyan* 101.8, 239.13, 482.19), it is also used in connection with two synonyms of *bi* in the meaning "punishment", *viz. zui* (*FLDW* 60, 122=*RCL* D 48, 102; *Yuelu Lüling* 1380, 1036; *Zuo* Xiang 25,512,10; *Mo* 68, 340; *Jinshu* 30, 923; 30, 938) as well as *xing* 刑 (*Shu* Lüxing §12; *Lü* 4, 35; 7, 66; *Shiji* 79, 2404; *Chunqiu fanlu* 13.6/63/14; *Hanguan liu zhong* 7.1239/102/11). In the same way as *zui*, *bi* could also occur as part of the phrase *you bi* 有辟, with the meaning "to be liable to punishment" (*Guoyu* 5, 147; *Zuo* Xi 24,184,7). For a different interpretation of *bi* in the present passage see Chen Wei 2013c.

502 In Qin and Han times persons who were able to arrest offenders who had committed serious offences punishable with penal labour of the category *nai* and more severe forms

was not given yet. When the day *jiazi*[503] of that [fourth month] came, Huan, incumbent [prefect] of Shayi,[504] stated:
"[Actually] the rank-and-file men Suo and his colleagues had arrested[505] [Zhi and his accomplices, but later transferred the robbers to] Gui and his colleagues."

of penal labour or the death penalty were entitled to receive a reward (*gou* 購, *FLDW* 140=*RCL* D 118: 其耐罪以上，購如捕它罪人；貲罪，不購。"If it is an offence punishable by [penal labour of the category] *nai* or a more severe [penalty], the reward is equal to that for arresting men being punished for other offences; if the punishment is a fine, there is no reward."). The amount of these rewards was stipulated in ounces (*liang* 兩) of gold or cash (*qian* 錢), and in many cases depended on the level of the penalty (*Yuelu WYZ* 16, 21–22, 36–37; *Yuelu Lüling* 1027, 1026, 1012, 1738, cited according to Chen Songchang 2014a, 8; *ENLL* 137–138). For the temporarily fixed exchange rate between ounces (of gold) and cash during the Qin dynasty see footnote 626. According to the statutory provisions of Qin and early Han times excavated so far, the determined reward for arresting a person who committed a particular offence varied (cf. Chen Songchang 2014a). This may be explained by the fact that the price of gold fluctuated or that the prosecution of certain offences probably had varying priority at different times.

503 This is likely to be the day *jiazi* (the eighth day) of the fourth month, i.e. 14/05/222 BC (three days after Gui and his colleagues presented the robbers to the authorities, see footnote 490) because *qi* 其 refers back to the month that was mentioned above (*Yuelu WYZ* 001).

504 Shayi 沙羨 was the name of a prefecture in the Qin dynasty (*Longgang mudu*) and at the beginning of the Han dynasty (*ENLL* 456). Shayi is said to have belonged to Jiangxia province during the Western Han dynasty (*Hanshu* 28A, 1568 with the commentary by Jin Zhuo according to which 羨 is to be pronounced like 夷; *Lishi dituji* vol. II, 22/23, 8⑤), but is attested as prefecture of Nan province in Qin times (Hou Xiaorong 2009, 399–400) and continued to be a prefecture of this province until the first decade of the reign of Emperor Wu (*Songbai mudu* 35r.1/3, 35v.1). The administrative seat of Shayi was located to the west of present Wuchang in southeast Hubei.

505 *Bu* 捕 refers to the regular arrest of suspects (*QLZC* 38=*RCL* C 24, *FLDW* 66, 140=*RCL* D 53, 118; *Yuelu WYZ* 005, 036–037, 145, 193–194; *Liye* 8–512, 8–992, 8–1008; *Longgang* 19; *ZYS* 37, 78, 81, 130, 177, 182; *ENLL* 137–156), which was often officially ordered. In that case, the arrest had to be carried out by the officer in charge of the responsible police station *ting* 亭 (*xiao zhang* 校長) or his subordinate, the robber hunter (*qiu dao* 求盜) (*FLDW* 66=*RCL* D 53, *FZS* 22, 30=*RCL* E 10, 12; *Yuelu WYZ* 032, 040; *ZYS* 37, 76, 81) as in the present case (cf. *Yuelu WYZ* 001–002). Sometimes suspects were arrested by other appropriate officials (*FLDW* 139=*RCL* D 117; *ZYS* 132, 153). The persons whose interests were infringed upon were probably also allowed to arrest the offender (*ZYS* 9). Even private persons could undertake an arrest; this at least applied to situations of imminent danger or where there otherwise would have been little chance to apprehend an offender (*FZS* 18, 20, 95=*RCL* E 8, 9, 25).

Original Case – First Stage of Interrogation

癸【曰】：$_{003}$
□□【治】等群盜盜殺人校長果部。州陵守綰令癸與令佐士五（伍）行將柳等追□$_{004}$迹。行到沙羨界中，瑣等巳（已）捕。瑣等言：治等四人邦亡。不智（知）它人何辠（罪）。癸等智（知），利$_{005}$得群盜盜殺人購。癸、行請告瑣等曰：瑣等弗能詣告。移鼠（予）癸等。癸等詣州陵，盡鼠（予）瑣等$_{006}$**[Missing slip]**[506]鼠（予）瑣等，以爲購錢數。得公購，備鼠（予）瑣等。行弗詣告，皆謀分購。未致購得。
它如沙羨書。$_{007}$

Gui [stated]:
"[...Zhi] and his accomplices killed people in the act of committing theft as members of a robber gang [within] the section[507] of *xiao zhang* Guo. Wan, incumbent [prefect] of Zhouling, ordered me, Gui, and Xing, prefectural assistant[508] and rank-and-file man, to lead[509] Liu and his colleagues to pursue[510] [...

---

506 For a tentative emendation of the missing text see Zhu and Chen 2013, 97.

507 For *bu* 部 "section kept under surveillance by the head of a *ting*" (ZYS 80–81: 蒼即與求盜大夫布、舍人簪裹餘共賊殺武于校長丙部中。 "Thereupon I, Cang, together with the robber hunter Bu, holder of the fifth rank, and the client Yu, holder of the third rank, together killed Wu with malice in the section of *xiao zhang* C."). Sometimes other constables like *shi li* 士吏 and *qiu dao* 求盜 were responsible for discovering that bandits in their section staged a raid (*ENLL* 144). Often, *bu* also refers to a section of the local administrative unit *xiang* 鄉 (*Liye* 8–1600; *ENLL* 5, 201, 247, 318, 322, 328, 334, 450, 464).

508 *Ling zuo* 令佐 does not occur in other manuscripts from Qin or early Han times with the exception of the administrative documents from Liye (e.g. *Liye* 6–5, 8–149, 8–197r, 8–433, 8–460, 8–647r, 8–919, 8–967, 8–1532, 8–1583).

509 *Jiang* 將, originally meaning "to take along, to take so.'s hand/to escort, take in hand", here in the sense "to lead/command (conscripts/soldiers forming a military unit)" (*Yuelu* WYZ 004, 026; ZYS 207; *Liye* 8–207, 8–439; *QLZC* 13=*RCL* C 8; *FZS* 26=*RCL* E 12; *ENLL* 140–141, 143; *jiang zhang* 將長 in *Yuelu* WYZ 037, *FLDW* 208=*RCL* D 188; *jiang jun* 將軍 in *Yuelu* WYZ 211, 213, 218, etc.; *FLDW* 52=*RCL* D 42; *Liye* 8–532; *ENLL* 440; *jiang li* 將吏 in *ENLL* 495–496).

510 *Zhui* 追 in a legal context means to pursue a fugitive suspect in order to arrest him, in most cases on the basis of some specific information (identity, whereabouts, clues found on the scene of the crime) that seem sufficient to track him down. Usually it was the duty of the personnel stationed at the local police station (*ting* 亭), including its head (*xiao zhang* 校長) and the robber hunter (*qiu dao* 求盜), to pursue the suspects as soon as the report of a criminal offence was received (ZYS 36–37; *FLDW* 66=*RCL* D 53; *Yuelu* WYZ 032). In the present case, *xiao zhang* Gui as well as the assistant of the prefect Xing were ordered to command the robber hunter Liu and two rank-and-file soldiers to pursue the members of a robber gang. These five persons were considered sufficient to arrest eight robbers and two women. According to statutes from 186 BC, when members of a robber gang commit homicide, bodily injury, or robbery by force, the prefecture or march authorities had to send out a sufficient number of local forces, even under the command

their] trail. When we on our march reached [the territory] inside the borders[511] of Shayi [prefecture], Suo and his colleagues had already arrested [the criminals]. Suo and his colleagues reported: 'Zhi and three of his accomplices absconded from the state.[512] We do not know which offences the other persons[513] have committed.'[514] My colleagues and I knew it and were

---

of the prefecture commander (*wei* 尉) and/or prefect (*ling* 令), to both the places where the criminals had become active and where they had disappeared in order to pursue and arrest them (*ENLL* 140). In this case and another one from the Yuelu Academy collection the legal term *zhui* appears alone (*Yuelu WYZ* 015, 018, 032; cf. *Longgang* 18; *ENLL* 19, 143), in most references, however, it occurs in the combination *zhui bu* 追捕 (*FLDW* 66=*RCL* D 53; *Longgang* 19; *ZYS* 37, 39; *ENLL* 140, 183; *Juyan* 71.61; *Shiji* 18, 3096; *Hanshu* 76, 3219).

511 *Jie zhong* 界中 literally "within the boundaries of" by synecdoche refers to an "area enclosed by the border", especially to the "(area of responsibility:) territory of a prefecture or march" (*Yuelu WYZ* 052; *ENLL* 234, 518). Cf. Giele 2003, 11–12, 15, 16.

512 *Bang wang* 邦亡 was a particular statutory offence during Qin times, which was not punished according to the duration of the escape as other forms of absconding. Offenders who committed *bang wang* were sentenced to being tattooed as well as to the most severe form of penal labour as earth pounder convicts (*FLDW* 48=*RCL* D 93: 告人曰邦亡，未出徼闌亡，告不審，論可（何）殹（也）？爲告黥城旦不審。 "To report somebody saying that he has absconded from the state, when he did not yet cross the border and did not abscond without permission, constitutes 'unfounded reporting'. How should this be sentenced? This is a case of 'unfounded reporting' [of an offence punishable by] being tattooed and made an earth pounder convict."; *FLDW* 5=*RCL* D 4: 人臣甲謀遣人妾乙盜主牛，買（賣），把錢偕邦亡，出徼，得，論各可（何）殹（也）？當城旦黥之，各畀主。"A private slave A plots to send the private slave woman B to steal their master's ox; they sell it and taking the money together abscond from the state. When crossing the border they are caught. How should each of them be sentenced? By law they are to be [made] earth pounder convicts and to be tattooed. Each is to be given back to his or her owner." See also *FLDW* 181=*RCL* D 160 as well as *Yuelu WYZ* 033, 089, 092 and 228). In Han times this offence was replaced by the capital crime *wang zhi zhu hou* 亡之諸侯 "absconding to the feudal lords" (*ENLL* 3; *ZYS* 20, 24).

513 *Ta ren* 它人 "other persons" probably are the six remaining offenders (of altogether eight men and two women according to *Yuelu WYZ* 002) who were not from Qin.

514 *Zui* 辠 is the original character form for the word *zui* 罪 "punishment". This form first appeared in bronze inscriptions (*Jinwen* 6.9735) and bamboo or wood manuscripts from the Warring States period (e.g. *Qinghua Baoxun* 8, *Huangmen* 8; *Guodian Lao* A 5, *Wuxing* 35, *Tang Yu zhi dao* 12; *Shanghai bowuguan Rongchengshi* 48) and also is the standard form in Qin manuscripts, e.g. the Yuelu Academy collection of criminal cases (*Yuelu WYZ* 010–011, 019–021, 027–029, 034, 076; 092; 130, 135, 164, 168, 198, 200, 241, etc.) and the Shuihudi legal manuscripts (Zhang Shouzhong 1994, 122). After the foundation of the Qin Empire in 221 BC it is said to have been replaced by *zui* 罪 on account of the graphic similarity to *huang* 皇 used in the emperor's title (*Shuowen* 14B, 741b). Indeed, the Qin manuscripts of Longgang, Fangmatan and Liye, which were most probably written after 221 BC use this new character form almost exclusively (*Longgang* 4, 22, 27, 42, 44–45, 73,

eager[515] to get the reward for [arresting criminals who had] killed people in the act of committing theft as members of a robber gang. I, Gui, and Xing asked Suo and his colleagues' consent[516] to the following: 'You are not able to present

96, 114, 122, 135, 145, 146, 148, 199, etc.; *Fangmatan Rishu* A 14; *Liye* 8–220, 8–533, 8–691, 8–755r, 8–811, 8–884, 8–1418, 8–1461, 8–1569, 8–2270, with the old form occurring only twice on *Liye* 8–144r and 8–2030r). *Zui* as a technical legal term refers to persons, not actions. The best rendering of its core sense is "liability to punishment". Liability to punishment was determined by statutes and ordinances, which stipulated a specific punishment for a certain culpable action, and by judicial proceedings, which found the stipulation applicable for a concrete case. As the degree of liability to punishment corresponded with the specific punishment, *zui* as a noun is usually best translated as "punishment". This is most evident from such common technical expressions as *jia zui* 加罪 "to increase the punishment" (*FLDW* 1=*RCL* D 1; *Longgang* 44; *ENLL* 114), *jian zui* 減罪 "to decrease the punishment" (*Longgang* 148; *ENLL* 127, 166–167), *chu zui* 除罪 "to exempt from punishment" (*Longgang* 146; *ENLL* 2, 63, 64, 69, 71, 72) or *yi zui* 疑罪 "to be in doubt about the punishment" (*Yuelu WYZ* 028, 092, 134–135; *ZYS* 6, 15, 23, 32–33, 47, 50, 52–54, 57, 59, 60, 62), in which *zui* takes the role of an object. Often, *zui* is an object of *you* 有 or *wu* 無: *you zui* 有罪, said of a person, means that the person "is liable to punishment" (for an offence committed by that person) (*Yuelu WYZ* 034, 076, 200; *FLDW* 177=*RCL* D 157; *ZYS* 215; *Longgang* 199; *ENLL* 35, 70, 82), while *wu zui* 無罪 means that the person "is not liable to punishment" (*Yuelu WYZ* 198; *Longgang* 32; *ZYS* 43, 191; *ENLL* 32). *Zui* also occurs as a stative verb with the same meaning "to be liable to punishment" (*Yuelu WYZ* 130, 164–165; *ZYS* 21–22, 31, 64, 71, 85, 87, 118, 150, 224). Verbal *zui* can likewise be used putatively as transitive verb and then means "to hold someone liable to punishment" (*Yuelu WYZ* 084, 130; *ZYS* 143). For *zui* found in first-person statements when an accused assumes criminal responsibility for a culpable action see footnote 985.

515 *Li* 利 "to be eager for/to, to desire" (*Zuo* Zhao 27,720,11: 宋、衛皆利納公，固請之。 "The states of Song and Wei were eager to restore the duke [of Lu], and strongly urged it."; *Shiji* 8, 356 [cf. Nienhauser II (2002), 30]: 諸將莫利先入關。"None of the [Chu] generals was eager to be first to enter the passes [of Guanzhong]."; *Xun* 22, 282 [cf. Knoblock III (1994), 133]: 不利傳辟者之辭。"He takes no pleasure in the proposals of flatterers and favourites."; *Li* 51, 1621c [cf. Couvreur 1950, vol. II, 420]: 先財而後禮，則民利。 "If one puts the valuables first and the courtesy last, then the people become greedy."; *Shiji* 38, 1623 [cf. Nienhauser V.1 (2006), 279–280]: 督利孔父妻[...]十年，華督攻殺孔父，取其妻。 "[Hua] Du desired the wife of Kong Fu [...] In the tenth year (i.e. 701 BC) he attacked and killed Kong Fu and took his spouse as wife."; cf. *Yuelu WYZ* 010, 019, 074).

516 *Gu* 告 *kʰˤuk (according to *Jiyun*, cited by Wang Li 2000) "to take one's leave of sb."="to ask sb. for permission to leave/go away" as in *Li* 1, 1233c (cf. Couvreur 1950, vol. I, 12): 夫爲人子者，出必告，反必面。 "When the son sets off, he must take his leave [of his parents]; when he returns, he must pay his parents a courtesy visit."; *Odes* 56,3: 永矢弗告。 "Forever, he swears, he will not say goodbye to me/leave me." *Gu* also occurs in the special sense "to ask for leave/furlough (of an official)" (*Hanshu* 90, 3670: 取告至長安。 "He took leave/furlough and arrived at Chang'an.") or "to ask for retirement (on account of age)" (*Zuo* Xiang 7,430,7: 晉韓獻子告老。 "Han Xianzi from Jin asked for retirement

[the robbers] to the authorities and report them [personally].[517] Transfer[518] them to us.[519] We [will] present them to the authorities at Zhouling and give you the complete [reward for arresting criminals who are liable to the death penalty].' [...] gave [...] to Suo and his colleagues and regarded this as the amount (i.e. a partial payment) of the reward in cash.[520] After receiving the

---

on account of age."). In connection with *qing* 請 *gu* means "to ask sb.'s permission/leave to take furlough/to retire" (*Shiji* 120, 3107=*Hanshu* 50, 2317: 黯多病[...]上常賜告者數，終不愈。最後病，莊助爲請告。 "[Ji] An repeatedly was ill [...] The emperor frequently granted him leave, but in the end he did not convalesce. When he was last ill, Zhuang Zhu asked for him the emperor's permission to retire."; cf. *Hanshu* 1A, 5: 告歸。 "[Gaozu] asked for permission to return home."). Here *qing gu* denotes "to ask sb.'s leave/consent".

517 Suo and his colleagues were apparently not informed about the actual offences committed by the gang of Zhi.

518 *Yi shu* 移鼠 with *shu* 鼠 (GSR 92a *hlaʔ) as common Qin graphic variant of *yu* 與 (GSR 89b *laʔ) or *yu* 予 (GSR 83a *laʔ) "to give, to turn/hand over" (QLSZ 42, 73–74, 154=RCL A 30, 37, 90; FLDW 140, 148=RCL D 118, 126; *Wei li zhi dao* 19.5, 27.5; *Yuelu* WYZ 026–029, 062, 066, 068–69, 071, 110, 117–118, 120–122, 127–129, 133–134, etc.); cf. Wang Hui 2008, 107; Bai Yulan 2012, 217–218.

519 Transferring arrested offenders for whom rewards or ranks were given to other people (who did not take part in the arrest) was prohibited by law (QLZC 38=RCL C 24: 捕盜律曰：捕人相移以受爵者，耐。 "The statute concerning the arrest of robbers says: Those who transfer arrested persons to another in order to receive a rank will be [punished by lenient penal labour of the category] *nai*."; ENLL 154–155: 捕罪人弗當以得購賞而移予它人，及詐（詐）僞，皆以取購賞者坐臧（贓）爲盜。 "All those who arrest an offender but are not entitled to get pecuniary or other rewards for him and therefore transfer him to other people as well as those who commit fraud and forgery [for the same purpose] will be prosecuted for the accepted pecuniary or other rewards as misappropriated goods [in the same way] as in a case of theft."). The same was true for officials who tried to get a reward through the use of a straw man (FLDW 139=RCL D 117: 有秩吏捕闌亡者，以畀乙，令詣，約分購，問：吏及乙論可（何）殹（也）？當貲各二甲，勿購。"A rank-holding official arrests a person who has unauthorisedly absconded and handed him over to B, ordering B to present him [to the authorities] agreeing with him to share the reward. Question: How are the official and B to be sentenced? They are by law to be fined two suits of armour each; they shall not be rewarded."). An exception to these rules was only made for people who had arrested offenders together. They could request to transfer their share of the reward to other people who took part in the arrest (ENLL 150–151: 數人共捕罪人而當購賞，欲相移者，許之。"If several people who are entitled to be awarded a pecuniary or other reward because they together arrested an offender wish to transfer these [rewards] to each other, this is granted to them."). However, if somebody falsely attributed a successful arrest to himself alone in a written report, he should not be rewarded (ENLL 154). Cf. Mizuma 2014, 22–23.

520 *Qian shu* 錢數 "amount of cash" (ENLL 403, 430; *Suanshushu* 32, 33, 46, 63, 65=Cullen 2004

governmental reward we would completely[521] give it to Suo and his colleagues. Xing did not present [the criminals] and report them, [but] we all (i.e. Gui, Xing and their colleagues) conspired[522] to share the reward.[523] We were caught[524] before the reward was given."

Everything else corresponded to the letter[525] from [the prefecture of] Shayi.

44–45, 51, 57–58 "number of cash"; *Jiuzhang suanshu* 1.18, 2.33, 2.37, 2.43, 3.3, 3.10, 3.11, 3.12, 3.13, 3.14, 3.19, 3.20, 6.24, 8.8=Chemla and Guo 2004, 167, 247, 251, 287, etc. "quantité de sapèques"). Here *shu* refers to a partial payment.

521 *Bei* 備 is sometimes synonymous with *jin* 盡 (cf. *Yuelu* WYZ 006) in the sense "to be complete" (*QLZC* 10=*RCL* C 6: 馬備 "when [the number] of horses is complete"; *Xun* 21, 260 [cf. Knoblock III (1994), 101]: 目視備色耳聽備聲。"Their eyes beheld all colours; their ears heard all sounds."). As in the present case, it is also used adverbially (*Zuo* Xi 28,204,4: 險阻艱難備嘗之矣。 "As for dangers, hardships, troubles and reverses, he has completely experienced them."). As a verb *bei* could also mean "to compensate, to make good (a deficiency)" (*QLSZ* 19=*RCL* A 9: 即入其筋、革、角及索入其賈（價）錢。錢少律者，令其人備之而告官。 "[The prefecture] immediately collects the sinews, hides and horns, as well as fully collects its value in cash. In case the money is less than [the sum stipulated by] the statutes, orders are given to the person(s) concerned to make good the deficiency, meanwhile informing the office.").

522 For the different meanings and implications of *mou* 謀, the joint planning/conspiracy to commit an offence, which was punishable in connection with certain offences, see footnote 829. In the present context *mou* is a kind of participation in offences which had not yet been carried out.

523 For the offence of sharing the rewards for arresting offenders see footnote 519 above.

524 *De* 得 means to catch someone who has been involved in a criminal offence. The word normally has either of the following implications: 1) When used on its own, *de* can imply that an offender has been caught in the act of committing an offence, as opposed to being arrested later (*ZYS* 184: 吏捕之弗得校上。 "The officials who arrested her failed to catch her in the sexual act [of fornication]."), or that a previously unknown offence has been discovered, as in the present case. In this technical use *de* can in a sense be regarded as the opposite of *zi chu* 自出 "to come out/give up oneself" (*FLDW* 4, 5, 12, 23, 30, 37, 53, 65, 76, 131, 167=*RCL* D 3, 4, 11, 20, 25, 29, 43, 52, 60, 109, 146; *Yuelu* WYZ 048, 050, 059–060; *ZYS* 18, 53, 105, 133, 203, 207, 209). 2) Less emphatically, *de* often implies that the suspect in a crime who is already known is caught after a search or manhunt. In this case, *de* is usually preceded by *qiu* 求 "to search", *zhui* 追 "to pursue" or *bu* 捕 "to arrest" and thus marks the success (or lack of success, if negated) of these actions (*Liye* 8–1463r; *ZYS* 61, 205; *ENLL* 139). Within the compound verbs *qiu de* 求得 and *bu de* 捕得, *de* can be explained as a complement of result. For the usage of *de* at the end of a finding of fact (*ju* 鞫) see footnote 714.

525 This letter obviously contained the charge of fraud against the subordinate officers from the prefecture of Zhouling by the leading officials of the prefecture of Shayi who probably discovered the illegal deal with rewards. In the comparable case no. 15 from the *Zou yan shu* where a neighbouring prefecture brings charges against a criminal prefect, this is called *yan* 言 "to report" (*ZYS* 69–71: 江陵言：[...]它如書。). This use of language

【行】、柳、轎、沃言如癸。
The statements of [Xing], Liu, Jiao and Wo corresponded to [the statement of] Gui.

士五（伍）瑣、渠、樂曰：
與士五（伍）得、潘、沛戍，之山材（裁）。見治等，共捕治等。四$_{008}$人言秦人邦亡，其它人不言所坐。得、潘、沛令瑣等將詣沙羡。沛等居亭，約得購分$_{009}$購錢。未到沙羡，實不智（知）治等何辠（罪），弗能告。有（又）不智（知）群盜購多。利癸等約死辠（罪）購，聽$_{010}$請券付死辠（罪）購，先受錢二千。未受公購錢，得。沛等不智（知）瑣等弗詣相移受錢。 它如癸$_{011}$等。

The rank-and-file men Suo, Qu and Le stated:
"We were performing military service with the rank-and-file men De, Pan and Pei[526] and went to the mountain on patrol.[527] There we saw Zhi and his accomplices and together arrested them. Four [of the arrested] persons said they were men from Qin who had absconded from the state. The others concerned (i.e. four men and two women) did not say for which offences they were to be prosecuted.[528] De, Pan and Pei ordered us to transfer them under guard[529]

---

might indicate that Zhouling was not subordinate to the prefecture of Shayi and the offences of the officers did not fall within its jurisdiction. Nevertheless, this report forced the neighbouring prefecture to initiate criminal proceedings against its subordinates.

526 The military unit of Suo originally comprised six men.

527 Here *cai* 材 (*GSR* 943g) possibly writes the homophonous *cai* 裁 (*GSR* 943c'; cf. Feng and Deng 2006, 336) with the meaning "to control" (*Xun* 10, 117 [cf. Knoblock II (1990), 125]: 治萬變，材萬物 "for putting the myriad transformations in good order, controlling the myriad things"; compare *Lü* 20, 255 [cf. Knoblock and Riegel 2000, 511]: 然且猶裁萬物，制禽獸。 "Despite all of this, humans are able to control the myriad things and subdue birds and beasts." and *Xun* 9, 105: 裁萬物 "control the myriad things"; see also *Guoyu* 4.50/72/3: 官師之所材也。 "That is what is controlled by the heads of the offices." and *Hanfei* 51, 361 [cf. Harbsmeier]: 治內以裁外而已矣。 "They governed well internally in order to control other states, that is all."). The editors interpret *cai* as a verb with the meaning "fell trees, cut timber"; however, without supporting evidence (Zhu and Chen 2013, 97 with footnote 22).

528 *Zuo* 坐 referred to the criminal prosecution of a person by the authorities, either for offences committed by the person himself/herself (*Yuelu WYZ* 009, 030, 145; *FLDW* 12=*RCL* D 11; *FZS* 92=*RCL* E 24; *ZYS* 214; *ENLL* 2, 14, 60, 155, 158, 174–175, 260–261), or for offences committed by other people such as closest relatives, neighbours, or subordinates (*Yuelu WYZ* 095, 099, 102, 105; *QLSZ* 80, 82, 167=*RCL* A 40–41, 82; *XL* 17=*RCL* B 7; *FLDW* 22, 155, 201=*RCL* D 19, 133, 181; *ZYS* 76, 123; *ENLL* 68–69, 106, 348, 350) if collective liability for the offences of these groups of persons was stipulated.

529 *Jiang* 將 "to take sb.'s hand/to escort sb." is used in the special sense "to guard convicts during transportation; to function as convict warden". With this meaning the word often

and present them to [the authorities at] Shayi. Pei and his colleagues,[530] who stayed at our *ting*,[531] made an agreement[532] with us to share the reward after we received it. Since we had not yet come to Shayi, we did in fact[533] not know

---

occurs as part of the compound *jiang si* 將司 "to lead and supervise (convicts)" (*Longgang* 43; QLSZ 134–135, 145–146, 147=RCL A 68, 69, 70; FLDW 125=RCL D 105) or in conjunction with *yi* 詣 "to bring sb. before (the authorities), to present sb./oneself (to the authorities)" (*Liye* 8–57, 8–1252, 8–1456r, 8–1552; FZS 48=RCL E 17) as in the present case. See QLSZ 146=RCL A 69: 城旦舂當將司者，廿人，城旦司寇一人將。司寇不足，免城旦勞三歲以上者，以爲城旦司寇。 "As regards earth and grain pounder convicts who have to be led and supervised, 20 persons are led by one robber guard of earth pounder convicts. If the number of robber guards is insufficient, relieve earth pounder convicts who have laboured for three years or more and make them robber guards of earth pounder convicts."; FZS 48=RCL E 17: 今鋈丙足，令吏徒將傳。 "Now we have fettered C's feet and an order has been given to officials and conscripts to lead and transfer him."; FLDW 125=RCL D 105: 群盜赦爲庶人，將盜戒（械）囚刑罪以上，亡[...]。"When members of a robber gang who have been amnestied and made released persons, lead manacled remand prisoners who have been robbers and who have committed an offence punishable by mutilation and more, and these abscond [...]." and ENLL 107: 守將奴婢而亡之 "guard and lead male and female slaves and let them abscond". Some of these quotations and other references (*Yuelu* WYZ 155; FLDW 116=RCL D 96) clearly demonstrate that convicts of the less severe categories robber guard (*si kou*) and bond servant (*li chen*) and even earth pounder (*cheng dan*) convicts who have already laboured as convicts for at least three years could serve as convict wardens.

530 In addition to Pei, the conscripts De and Pan, i.e. half of the unit, stayed at the police station where the squad was obviously stationed.

531 For *ting* as "police station" see footnote 753.

532 *Yue* 約 "to reach a verbal or written agreement" (FLDW 139=RCL D 117: 約分購。 "He agrees [with B] to share the reward."; ZYS 49–50: 昌與相如約弗免。 "Chang agreed with Xiangru to refrain from manumitting him (the private slave Xiangru)."; *Hanshu* 1A, 19 [cf. Dubs I (1938), 53]: 足下約先入咸陽者王之。 "Your honour has made an agreement that the one who first enters Xianyang shall be king over it."). An agreement on payments was normally to be recorded on a tally in the presence of witnesses (*Juyan* 262.29; cf. Li and Liu 1994, 387). Cf. the witnesses in contracts for the sale of burial land from Western and Eastern Han times who were all recorded by name as *zhi yue quan* 知約券 "cognisants of the tally concerning the agreement" (*Lidai qiyue* nos. 29, 30, 33, 37, 41 and 42).

533 *Shi* 實 "in fact" in legal manuscripts of Qin and Han times indicated that an assertion corresponded to the facts (*Yuelu* WYZ 130, 191, 229; ZYS 22, 145, 147), often in contrast to a contradicting assertion. *Shi* was mainly used adverbially (*Yuelu* WYZ 191: 其實未奸。 "He (Tian) in fact had not yet committed fornication."; ZYS 30: 符雖有名數明所，而實亡人也。 "Even though Fu had a [household] registration with Ming, she was in fact an absconded person."; ZYS 107–108: 講謂實不盜牛。 "I, Jiang, said to him that I in fact did not steal the cow." and FLDW=RCL D 185: 欲令乙爲盜之，而實弗盜。"He wishes to cause that B will be considered as having stolen them (the clothes), whereas in fact [B] did not steal them.").

which offence Zhi and his accomplices had [really] committed [and therefore] were not able to report them. Furthermore, we did not know, that the reward for [arresting] members of a robber gang was higher [than that for arresting suspects who committed a death-penalty crime].[534] [Accordingly] we were eager to reach an agreement with Gui and his colleagues on the death-penalty reward, and we accepted their request to agree on a tally[535] to be handed over[536] the [expected] death-penalty reward and to receive 2,000 cash in advance [as a partial payment]. Before we received the governmental reward [from Gui and his colleagues], we were caught. Pei and and his colleagues did not know[537]

534 The law enforcement officer Gui and his colleagues were only willing to give the reward for arresting suspects who committed a death-penalty crime and not the reward for arresting members of a robber gang (*qun dao* 群盜), which was twice the amount of the first (*Yuelu* WYZ 021–022) and amounted to 14 ounces of gold (*Yuelu* WYZ 036) or 8,064 cash for each of the ten arrested members of a robber gang. Probably the conscript Suo and his colleagues either did not know about the different amounts or about the offences Zhi and his accomplices had really committed and therefore accepted this smaller amount of rewards. Cf. Mizuma 2014, 22.

535 For the appearance and function of *quan* 券 "tally with notches", which could be used as a certificate of debts and was split in two or three parts, see in detail Lau and Lüdke 2012, footnote 1548. The existence of tallies that substantiated a respective claim is documented in legal documents from Qin and Han times (e.g. *Yuelu* WYZ 029, 109). With their aid, creditors could demand the payment of outstanding debts (*Yuelu* WYZ 111, 124–125), as in *Liye* 8–1008+8–1461+8–1532 (cf. Chen Wei 2012a, 261): 養大隸臣豎負華補錢五百，有約券。 "Shu, an adult bond servant convict who serves as cook, still owes me, Hua, 500 cash. There is a tally concerning the agreement." *Quan* can also be used verbally (cf. *Yuelu* WYZ 020: 聽請相移，紿券付死辠（罪）購。先受私錢二千。 "[Suo and his colleagues] accepted the request to transfer [the criminals to Gui and his colleagues] and were deceived into making a [contract on a] tally to be handed over the death-penalty reward. They received 2,000 cash of private money in advance as [part of the] reward."; ENLL 429: 官爲作務、市及受租、質錢，皆爲缿，封以令、丞印而入與參辨券之，輒入錢缿中，上中辨其廷。 "After coin receptacles for all the cash from official engagement in workshops and trade as well as from collecting taxes or redeeming pledges have been made, they are sealed by the prefect's and vice prefect's seal, and the persons concerned are given the third part of a tripartite tally to certify [the amount of money paid in]. The cash [coins] are to be put into the coin receptacle immediately. The middle part of the tally bond is submitted to the court of the prefecture concerned.").

536 *Fu* 付, which already occurs in the sense "to hand over, make over" (FZS 12=RCL E 3) in early Zhou bronze inscriptions, is an antonym to *shou* 受 "to receive" (ENLL 276: 郡縣官相付受財物 "valuables which the agencies of the province and the prefectures have handed over to or received from each other").

537 *Zhi* 智 is frequently used in manuscripts of Qin and early Han times to write the verb *zhi* 知, which in a legal context indicated that somebody knew about an offence. If the person

that we had transferred [the robbers to Gui and his colleagues] and received money [for this], without having presented [Zhi and his accomplices] to the authorities ourselves."
Everything else corresponded to [the statements of] Gui and his colleagues.

沛、潘、得言如瑣等。$_{012}$

The statements of Pei, Pan and De corresponded to [the statements of] Suo and his colleagues.

Original Case – Judgement

五月甲辰，州陵守綰、丞越、史獲論令癸、瑣等各贖黥。癸、行戍衡山郡，各三歲，以當灋（法），先備$_{013}$贖。不論沛等。

On day *jiachen*[538] of the fifth month the incumbent [prefect] of Zhouling, Wan, vice prefect Yue and secretary[539] Huo passed judgement[540] ordering

concerned did not report this offence to the authorities, he or she was liable to punishment. In the present case Pei's lack of knowledge resulted in his acquittal (*bu dang lun* 不當論, *Yuelu* WYZ 024). For *zhi* 知 as a kind of aid given to the offence cf. footnote 659.

538 This was the 19th day of the fifth month in the 25th year of King Zheng of Qin (cf. Zhang Peiyu 2007, 73; Li Zhonglin 2012, 65), i.e. 23/06/222 BC (Xu Xiqi 1997, 1240).

539 *Shi* 史 "scribe, clerk" probably refers to *yu shi* 獄史 "judicial secretary" because in the present context he is part of the competent decision-making body together with the prefect and the vice prefect as in ZYS 97. During Qin times *yu shi* dealt with investigations and interrogations in criminal cases at the level of prefectures (*Yuelu* WYZ 047, 051, 084, 142, 151, 154; *Liye* 8–133r, 8–186, 8–683r, 8–940, 8–987, 8–1007, 8–1058, 8–1232, 8–1441r, 8–1448r; ZYS 130, 197–198, 203, 227). At the beginning of the Han dynasty, the same tasks were entrusted to their successors in office (ZYS 61, 75; *Hanshu* 31, 1796; 51, 2367; 71, 3041–3042). The *yu shi* also took part in sealing the confiscated property of offenders (*ENLL* 179), issued arrest warrants (*Xuanquan* 17), immediately conducted the hearing, recorded the transcript and were responsible for accepting the decision of higher authorities in cases they had submitted for decision (ZYS 7, 47). During the Qin dynasty up to five *yu shi* were employed in a prefecture (ZYS 197–198, 203). At the end of Western Han times, one to five *yu shi* were registered in the official lists of the province of Donghai (*Yinwan mudu* M6D2r/v; cf. Xie Guihua 1997, 47–48). Cf. Lau and Lüdke 2012, footnote 615. It is noteworthy that only *ling shi* 令史 but no *yu shi* are mentioned in a list of the officials of the prefecture of Qianling from Qin times (*Liye* 7–67+9–631, cited according to Liye Qin jiandu jiaoshi xiaozu 2014), whereas the lists from the province of Donghai contain both *ling shi* as well as *yu shi* (*Yinwan mudu* M6D2r/v; Cf. Xie Guihua 1997, 47, table 3). In other Qin manuscripts there is evidence for *ling shi* (around 120 examples in the documents from layer 8 of Liye well no. 1; around 70 in the yet unpublished *Yuelu Lüling*) as well as *yu shi*

Gui, Suo and their colleagues to each pay the fee for redemption from tattooing.[541] Gui and Xing have to perform [additional] military

---

(around 80 examples in documents from Liye layer 8; more than ten in the yet unpublished *Yuelu Lüling*).

540 *Lun* 論, in legal terminology, refers to the passing of a specific judgement (*ZYS* 7, 23, 25, 78, 90, 126, 176; *Longgang mudu*; *QLSZ* 173, 177=*RCL* A 86, 88; *Yuelu WYZ* 022, 024, 039, 061, 063–064, 082; 093, 095, 135, 140, 147, 166, 171, 193, 199, 236, etc.; *FLDW* 26, 97, 144=*RCL* D 21, 80, 122; *ENLL* 93, 113, 396–397; *Juyan xinjian* E.P.T52:280A, E.P.T53:177; *Juyan* 118.13, 227.8; *Xuanquan* 12; *Wangzhang zhaoshuling* cited according to *Sanjian* 149; *Shiji* 10, 418). *Lun* involved subsuming the action subject to criminal investigation, as determined in the finding of fact (*ju* 鞫), to one of the offences listed in the statutes. This resulted in the imposition of the punishment stipulated in the statutes for that offence or, if no such subsumption was possible, in the acquittal of the accused. The judgement concluded the trial (*zhi* 治).

541 Below, the respective offence is classified as a case of *dao* 盜 "theft", which should be punished with being tattooed and the most severe form of penal labour as earth or grain pounder convict because the value of the misappropriated goods (*zang* 贓) exceeded 660 cash (*ENLL* 55). Since the illegally claimed rewards had not yet been given, the offenders were only sentenced to pay the fee for redemption from tattooing (*shu qing* 贖黥). As shown by the present example and occurrences of this sentence in other legal manuscripts, cases in which a theft could not be carried out were punished with *shu qing* during Qin times (*FLDW* 4=*RCL* D 3: 甲謀遣乙盜，一日，乙且往盜，未到，得，皆贖黥 "A plots to send B out to steal. On the same day, B is about to go and steal, but, before he arrives, he is caught. Both pay the fee for redemption from tattooing."; *FLDW* 30–31=*RCL* D 25: 且未啟亦爲抉？抉之弗能啟即去，一日而得，論皆可（何）殹（也）？抉之且欲有盜，弗能啟即去，若未啟而得，當贖黥。 "Furthermore, when [the lock] has not yet been opened, is this also 'forcing'? If by forcing one is unable to open it (the lock) and leaves to be caught on the same day, which [sentences are to be imposed] for both [these cases]? If one forced it with the desire to steal, [but] one is unable to open it and then leaves, or one is caught before having opened it, one by law is to pay the fee for redemption from tattooing."). In early Han times this fee amounted to one catty (*jin* 斤) of gold (*ENLL* 119), which was equivalent to 9,216 cash in Qin times. The payment of redemption fees can be found in the statutes of 186 BC as regular punishment for offences committed without intent, such as passing a wrong judgement (*ENLL* 95–96), killing sb. inadvertently or in a contest (*ENLL* 21) or as regular mitigation for certain privileged groups (*ENLL* 39: killing children and own slaves by parents as result of chastisement, 48: killing convicts by officials as result of chastisement; *FLDW* 113=*RCL* D 94: gang robbery or rape committed by princes and chiefs of barbarian vassal states). There are only few examples where redemption fees were imposed on persons who did not carry out a plotted offence, and in contrast to Qin times the respective offences were not property crimes (*ENLL* 496). In comparable cases of plotting to kill sb. with malice or illegally casting coins, the punishment for offenders who had not carried out these offences was

service[542] [as punishment] in Hengshan province,[543] each of them for three years, in order to comply with the law. They shall first make up the fee for redemption. No judgement has been passed on Pei and his colleagues.

Retrial – Initiation of Criminal Proceedings

監御史康劾以爲不當。錢不處，當更論。更論及論失者言夬（決）。

The supervisory prosecutor[544] Kang brought forward an *ex-officio* charge,[545]

only reduced by one degree (*ENLL* 23, 208). In other cases, the same punishment as for the offence actually committed had to be imposed (*ENLL* 68).

542 In early Han stipulations *shu* 戍 "military service" (*ENLL* 96–97) was imposed as punishment on officers and soldiers who had been drafted to combat banditry for failing to arrest bandits who killed or injured the commander or other members of their own military unit (*ENLL* 141), for not daring to attack out of cowardice (*ENLL* 143), and for not detecting a bandit raid (*ENLL* 144) or for failing to discover contraband gold while on border guard (*ENLL* 76, cf. *ENLL* 226). Additional examples can be found for punishing illegal issue of rations in the army (*QLZC* 11–13=*RCL* C 8), gambling (*ENLL* 186), recommending unqualified persons for office (*ENLL* 210), or unauthorised possession of land as a result of false entries in the household registers (*ENLL* 323). This punitive military service, which often had to be performed in the border regions, was imposed for one to four years.

543 Hengshan 衡山 was a province neighbouring Nan province during the Qin dynasty until 206 BC (*Shiji* 6, 248). In 202 BC it was restored as a province by Emperor Gaozu (*Hanshu* 34, 1886; cf. *Hanshu* 28A, 1567; 28B, 1638; *Lishi dituji* vol. II, 11–12, 5②) with its administrative seat near present Huanggang, Hubei. For the prefectures belonging to the province of Hengshan during Qin times see Hou Xiaorong 2009, 411–413.

544 *Jian yu shi* 監御史 in Qin times were prosecutors appointed to inspect a specified number of provinces who were directly responsible to the central government (*Hanshu* 19A, 741; according to the commentary of Jin Zhuo on *Hanshu* 39, 2013). They were charged with prosecuting provincial officials who had committed an offence or malfeasance. The *jian yu shi* were predecessors of the later regional inspector *ci shi* 刺史 in the Han dynasty (*Shiji* 53, 2014 with commentary of Su Lin; An and Xiong 2007, 57–58). The *jian yu shi* named Kang in the present case was obviously responsible for inspecting Nan province to which Zhouling belonged. Cf. analogical judicial review of pending criminal cases by a governor of a province in footnote 1194.

545 *He* 劾 refers to a criminal charge brought by a judicial official against persons under his jurisdiction. This *ex-officio* charge initiated formal criminal proceedings. In all case records of the *Zou yan shu* and most other early Chinese legal texts that contain *he*, the *ex-officio* charge is brought against persons serving in an official capacity (*ZYS* 17, 19, 63, 64, 77, 81, 134, 154, 163; *XL* 54–55=*RCL* B 26–27; *Yuelu WYZ* 014, 064, 067, 097–099, 105).

[because] he considered this [judgement] to be unlawful.[546] [As] the money [for the redemption fees] has not been paid(?)[547] [yet], judgement by law has to be passed anew.[548] The persons who pass judgement anew as well as the persons who committed a judicial error in passing [the first] judgement[549] shall report on the decision.[550]

---

546 *Bu dang* 不當 without a following verb is to be understood as a stative verb in the sense "to be unlawful/unjustified" (*Yuelu WYZ* 186–187, 205–206; *ZYS* 42: 武宜聽視而後與吏辯是不當狀。 "It would have been proper for you, Wu, to obey Shi and only later together with us, the officials, get straight whether your conduct was correct or unlawful."; *ZYS* 122: 雍以講爲盜，論黥爲城旦，不當。 "The prefecture of Yong considered me, Jiang, to be a thief and sentenced me to penal labour as tattooed earth pounder convict; this was unlawful/unjustified."; *ENLL* 105 [cf. Giele 2006, 22]: 其[...]論有不當者 "if among the judgement passed [...] there is something which is not justified/lawful"; *ENLL* 114: 罪人獄已決，自以罪不當，欲气（乞）鞫者，許之。 "If a criminal offender/person liable to punishment wishes to petition for a [new] finding of fact after his case has already been decided, because he considers his punishment as not justified, then this is granted."; *Hanshu* 5, 150: 有令讞而後不當，讞者不爲失。 "When [an official] ordered that a case is submitted to the higher authorities for decision and later it turns out that the submission is unjustified, the official who submitted the case has not committed a judicial error."; *Hanshu* 23, 1102; 23, 1106.

547 The editors' identification of the character as *chu* 處 is tentative. *Chu* does not occur in combination with *qian* 錢 or *shu* 贖 anywhere else in received literature or manuscripts from pre-Han and Han times.

548 *Geng lun* 更論 "pass judgement anew" only occurs once in *Zhanguoce* 222/119/14 (cf. Crump 1970, 304: "reconsider") where it is however not used in a legal context. Cf. *geng zhi* 更治 "to try anew" (*Liye* 8–1832+8–1418+8–1133 [cf. Chen Wei 2012a, 281]) in footnote 1252.

549 *Lun shi* 論失 refers to committing judicial errors when passing judgement (*ZYS* 120; *Longgang mudu*; *ENLL* 107). This was punished with payment of the redemption fee for the punishment erroneously imposed (*ENLL* 95–96). *Shi* indicates that the punishable action was done without intent.

550 According to Chen Wei (2013c) *guai* 夬 (*GSR* 312a) is used here to write *jue* 決 (*GSR* 312b) in the meaning "to decide (a criminal case)" as in other Qin manuscripts (*Wei li zhi dao* 44.3; *Longgang* 204; cf. Wang Hui 2008, 617; Bai Yulan 2012, 516–517). In the sequence of criminal procedure *jue* was situated after the trial of a case and before the report of a decision (*Dunhuang* 77). *Yan jue* 言決 "report on a decision" repeatedly occurs in manuscripts, often in connection with *lun* 論, as in the case under discussion (*Liye* 16–5r: 縣亟以律令具論當坐者，言名夬（決）泰（太）守府。 "The prefecture should immediately compile [the records] and pass judgement according to the statutes and ordinances on those who by law are prosecuted for a criminal offence and should [then] report their names and the decisions to the office of the governor of the province."; *Liye* 8–473, 8–859, 8–1016, 8–1405, 8–1516r, 8–2012 [cf. Chen Wei 2013c]; cf. *Longgang* 202: 未夬（決）而言者; *Xuanquan* 228: 已言決). The combination *lun yan jue* however does not occur in received classical literature. With regard to the similarity of the characters *shi* 史

Retrial – First Stage of Interrogation

綰等曰：
治等發，興吏$_{014}$徒追。癸等弗身捕，瑣等捕。弗能告，請相移，給以求購。購未致，得。綰等以盜未有取、吏貲灋（發）戍律$_{015}$令論癸、瑣等。口令瑣等環（還）癸等錢。
它如癸等及劾。

Wan and his colleagues stated:[551]
"When Zhi and his accomplices set out,[552] we levied officers and conscripts[553] to pursue them. Gui and his colleagues did not arrest [the crimi-

and *guai* 夬 in manuscripts from the Qin and early Han periods (cf. Zhang Shouzhong 1994, 41 and 43 with Chen Songchang 2001a, 114 and 119), the possibility of a scribal error for *shi* 史 (*GSR* 975a) *s-rəʔ, which could be used to write *shi* 事 (*GSR* 917a) *m-s-rəʔ-s (*Jinwen* 18.1208 from late pre-imperial Qin according to Huang Dekuan 2007, 251), is also given. Furthermore, there are many references to *yan shi* 言事 "to report an affair/matter" in the dynastic histories (*Shiji* 101, 2746; 107, 2843; cf. *Hanshu* 70, 3021; *Liye* 8–970).

551 This is the statement of the prefect of Zhouling, who conducted the first trial and is now interrogated during the retrial ordered by the prosecutor of the province. Probably the very same prefect also conducted the retrial because it was he who submitted this case to the higher authorities as mentioned in the decision of Nan province below (see *Yuelu WYZ* 025).

552 *Fa* 發 "to set out" (*ENLL* 144: 盜賊發，士吏、求盜部者，及令、丞、尉弗覺智（知），士吏、求盜皆以卒戍邊二歲，令、丞、尉罰金各四兩。"When robbers and bandits set out and the military officers and robber hunters [responsible] for the respective section, or the prefect, vice prefect or [prefecture] commander do not detect this, then the military officers and robber hunters have to perform [additional] military service at the frontier for two years, while the prefect, vice prefect and [prefecture] commander are each fined four ounces of gold."; *ENLL* 146: 群盜、盜賊發，告吏，吏匿弗言其縣廷，言之而留盈一日，以其故不得，皆以鞫獄故縱論之。"When it is reported to an official that members of a robber gang or bandits have set out, but the official conceals the fact and does not report it to his prefectural court, or reports it only after he has kept [the news] back for one full day, and if the robbers or bandits for this reason are not caught, then judgement is to be passed in both of these cases for [the statutory offence of] 'intentionally leaving [an offender] unpunished when finding facts in a criminal case'."; *Yuelu WYZ* 149). *Dao zei fa* 盜賊發 furthermore occurs in *Shiji* 127, 3218; *Hanshu* 71, 3042; 76, 3208 (cf. *dao fa* 盜發 in *Hanshu* 99C, 4171).

553 From the statement of Gui (*Yuelu WYZ* 004) and from the response of Nan province (*Yuelu WYZ* 026), it becomes clear that *xiao zhang* Gui and *ling zuo* Xing are obviously commanding troops and therefore have to be identified as the *li* 吏 "officers", whereas the robber hunter Liu and the two rank-and-file men Jiao and Wo have to be considered as *tu* 徒 "conscript soldiers". For *tu* in the meaning "conscript" cf. *FZS* 48–49=*RCL* E 17; *Liye* 8–207r, 8–439; *ENLL* 76, 140–141, 143.

nals] themselves; Suo and his colleagues arrested them. [Because Suo and his colleagues] were not able to report [the criminals], they were requested to transfer them[554] [to Gui and his colleagues] and were deceived[555] [by Gui and his colleagues] in order to claim the reward. Before the reward was given, they were [all] caught. We passed judgement on Gui, Suo and their colleagues according to the statutes and ordinances[556]

554 The pronominal adverb *xiang* 相 does not only mean "each other", but sometimes also "the others" or "them", see Unger 1987–97, vol. I, 269 and He Leshi 2006, 444.

555 *Dai* 紿 means "to deceive sb. into doing sth." and is especially used in the context of trade (ENLL 261: 諸詐（詐）紿人以有取，及有販賣貿買而詐（詐）紿人，皆坐贓與盜同灋。"All those who defraud or deceive somebody in order to make profit as well as defraud or deceive somebody while selling and buying in a trade transaction will all be prosecuted for the misappropriated goods to which the same legal rules as for theft apply."). In the Yuelu Academy collection of criminal cases *dai* occurs in the sense "deceive sb. into buying sth." (*Yuelu* WYZ 081–082), "deceive sb. into agreeing on sth./making a deal" (*Yuelu* WYZ 019–020), "deceive sb. into believing sth." (*Yuelu* WYZ 015) or is used adverbially in the sense "under false pretences" (*Yuelu* WYZ 083).

556 *Lü* 律 "statutes" and *ling* 令 "ordinances" were the two main sources of written law from the Qin dynasty onwards. Both terms were often used together in the compound *lü ling* (*Yuelu* WYZ 029–030; *Liye* 5–1r, 5–6r, 5–17, 6–4, 8–157v, 8–173r, 8–222, 8–644v, 8–759, 8–1560r, etc.; QLSZ 26=RCL A 19; ZYS 27; ENLL 1, 107; *Shiji* 122, 3138; *Juyan* 3.32, etc.; *Juyan xinjian* E.P.T5:64, etc.). At regular intervals, the secretaries of the prefect were ordered to appear before higher authorities to collate their copies of the statutes and ordinances (*Liye* 6–4, 8–173r; cf. QLSZ 199=RCL A 108). Formerly, legal historians emphasised that ordinances can sometimes hardly be distinguished from statutes (Hulsewé 1955, 31–32; Shen Jiaben 1985, 1366; Cheng Shude 1955, 11). On the other hand, two cases of the *Zou yan shu*, in which both the statutes and ordinances relevant for a particular case are quoted (ZYS 72–73, 157–158), rather suggest that the former contained the basic, most general provisions, while the latter contained more specific regulations, which clarified the application of the statutes to specific situations, made exceptions from the statutes for special circumstances or decreed how to implement a statute. This corresponds to a document from 227 BC, where the governor of Nan province states that the enactment of ordinances is necessary because otherwise the statutes would not suffice to prevent the people in their craftiness to exploit the statutes' loopholes (*Yushu* 2: 灋（法）律未足，民多詐巧，故後有閒令下者。"Laws and statutes were not yet sufficient and many people were fraudulent and tricky; therefore later, whenever there was a loophole [in the legal system not covered by *fa* or *lü*], ordinances were enacted."). According to a statement of Du Zhou, minister of trials since 109 BC, the statutes were understood as received from the past (*Shiji* 122, 3153 [cf. Watson 1993, vol. II, 405]: 前主所是著爲律，後主所是疏爲令。"Whatever the earlier rulers thought right they wrote down as statutes, and whatever the later rulers thought right they elaborated on as ordinances."). Later sources, which are however not sufficiently reliable, claim that *lü* as a technical term was first used around 350 BC when the Qin chancellor Shang Yang adopted the *Fajing* 法經 of Li Kui for his state

on theft without having appropriated [haul][557] and on officers who as

(*Jinshu* 30, 922; *Tanglü shuyi* 1, 8); from then on, the written statutes were simply called *lü*. According to the official history, when Liu Bang in 206 BC seized power he immediately revoked the Qin law and replaced it with a very much simplified penal law that only consisted of provisions on homicide, bodily injury and theft (*Hanshu* 1A, 23). This proved to be insufficient, and thus chancellor Xiao He was commissioned to select those provisions from Qin law that seemed appropriate for the new circumstances, and from these he compiled the *Lü jiu zhang* 律九章 (*Hanshu* 23, 1096). Leaving aside these accounts in later sources, whose reliability can be doubted, some facts can definitely be gathered from the actual examples of *lü* that are cited in received literature or have been found in excavated manuscripts. There were different *lü* containing legal rules on several penal and administrative matters. They were organised into separate *zhang* 章 "articles" (cf. ZYS 188). Within the Yuelu Academy collection at least 16 different statutes from the Qin dynasty were found (Chen Songchang 2009a, 86). Further quotations from the *lü* occur in the collection of criminal cases (*Yuelu* WYZ 036–037) and Qin administrative documents (*Liye* 8–463, 8–1198). The legal manuscripts unearthed in 1975 in tomb no. 11 at Shuihudi quote extensive passages of the Qin statutes, while statutes from the early years of the Han era entitled *Ernian lüling* have been discovered in tomb no. 247 in Zhangjiashan. The *Zou yan shu* from the same tomb also contains several quotations from statutes, cf. Lau and Lüdke 2012, appendix III. The wording of some Han statutes has earlier been reconstructed using quotations in the dynastic histories (Shen Jiaben 1985, 1363–1779; Cheng Shude 1955, 52–92). To this, compilations of quotations from statutes in further palaeographic sources were recently added (see Li and Liu 1994, 92–119; Lian Shaoming 1988; Gao Heng 2008, 147–162). *Ling*, on the other hand, appear to have been enacted by the ruler as the situation required. As term for the ruler's edict *ling* is first found in pre-imperial and imperial Qin (*QLSZ* 12, 57, 97, 189, 191, 196=*RCL* A 6, 16, 51, 99, 101, 106; *FLDW* 142–143=*RCL* D 120–121; *Yuelu* WYZ 029–030, 043, 102–103, 147; ZYS 149, 157, 227; *Liye* 8–41, 8–61r, 8–62r, 8–64r, 8–70r, 8–154r, 8–163r, 8–756, 8–767r, 8–1832, etc.; cf. *wang ling* 王令 "royal order" in *Liye* 8–461r and *ling* "orders" of higher officials as in *Liye* 8–159r, 8–1514r). It continued to be used after the beginning of the Han era (ZYS 27, 65, 73). Compilations of Han *ling* mentioned in the dynastic histories can be found in Cheng Shude 1955, 21–23, Shen Jiaben 1985, 1719–1721 and Hulsewé 1955, 42–44. A collection of *ling* mentioned or quoted in the legal manuscripts is provided in Li and Liu 1994, 119–167.

557 The illegal deal with the rewards was obviously classified as a property offence (*dao* 盜, cf. ENLL 154–155); for the relevant stipulations see footnote 519. The punishment for *dao* was graded according to the value of the misappropriated goods (*zang* 贓) (*Longgang* 40–41; ENLL 55–56). Because the offenders did not appropriate the stolen goods (*wei you qu* 未有取), the sentence was reduced and the offenders got away with paying the redemption fee for the punishment normally imposed for theft of an amount exceeding 660 cash. This principle for determining punishment in the field of theft has not been found in other legal texts from the Qin and Han dynasties. For payment of redemption fees as regular punishment for offences committed without intent see footnote 541.

penalty[558] are mobilised[559] to [additional] military service. Suo and his col-

558 For *zi* 貲 "fine" in conjunction with additional military service see *QLZC* 11–12=*RCL* C 8: 不當稟軍中而稟者，皆貲二甲，法（廢）；非吏殹（也），戍二歲；徒食、敦（屯）長、僕射弗告，貲戍一歲。"Where the issue of rations [to certain persons] in the army is not justified, to still issue these entails a fine of two suits of armour for both; they are [permanently] dismissed. If they are not officers, [the fine is] two years of military service. If messmates, corporals or sergeants do not report [the previously described offences], they are fined one year of military service." The term *fa* 罰 *bat, which replaced *zi* in Han law, is used in the same context (*ENLL* 142–143: 逗留畏耎（愞）弗敢就，奪其將爵一絡〈級〉，免之，毋爵者戍邊二歲；而罰其所將吏徒以卒戍邊各一歲。"For those who halt out of cowardice and do not dare to advance, the commander is deprived of one degree of his rank and relieved from his command; those without a rank have to perform two years of [additional] military service at the frontier; the officers and conscripts commanded by him are each fined one year of [additional] military service at the frontier as [normal] soldiers."). See also *fa shu* 罰戍 as designation for a type of temporary convicts in Qin administrative documents (*Liye* 8–429, 8–761, 8–781, 8–2246). Cf. also *ZYS* 147: 聞等上論奪爵令戍。"I have heard that my colleagues submitted a [proposed] sentence [to the emperor that the offenders] should be deprived of their ranks and be ordered to perform military service." Therefore, the original segmentation of the present passage by the editors should be changed in the following way: 以盜未有取、吏貲灋（發）戍律令論癸、瑣等。

559 *Fa* 灋 (*GSR* 642 l), the original character form of *fa* 法 (*GSR* 642k) *pap, occurs in legal manuscripts in adverbial usage with the meaning "as prescribed by law/according to law" (*QLSZ* 153=*RCL* A 90 [cf. Kroll 1990, 66]: 從軍當以勞論及賜，未拜而死、有罪灋（法）耐䙴（遷）；其後及灋（法）耐䙴（遷）者，皆不得受其爵及賜。"When sb. who had joined the army by law is to be awarded [a rank] or rewarded because of his merits, but before this is conferred he dies [or] commits an offence for which he, according to the law, is to be punished with being shaved and/or banished, his heir and he who, according to the law, is to be punished with being shaved and/or banished, both are not entitled to receive the rank or the reward."; *Shiji* 88, 2566 [cf. Bodde 1940, 55]: 秦王令蒙毅法治之。"The king of Qin ordered Meng Yi to try [him] according to the law."). However, as attribute in conjunction with *shu* 戍 or synonymous words *fa* cannot be found at all. Sometimes *fa* 灋 was used to write *fa* 發 (*GSR* 275c) *pat "set out" (*ENLL* 64: 群盜灋（發）"members of a robber gang set out") or "to dispatch, mobilise, levy (conscripts)" (*Hanshu* 85, 3462: 徵法（發）如雨。"The levies raised were [frequent] as rain."). In the present context, *fa* appears in the combination *fa shu* 發戍 "mobilise conscripts (for military service)" (*ENLL* 415; *Hanshu* 99, 4125 [cf. Dubs III (1955), 313]; *Hanshu* 61, 2700; *Juyan* 506.9B; *Juyan xinjian* E.P.T51:15). Chen Wei (2013a) regards *fa* 灋 as loan character for *fei* 廢 (*GSR* 275f) *pat-s<**pap-s (*Jinwen* 2.2836, 2.2837, 6.9735; *Baoshan* 16, 18; *Guodian Ziyi* 9; *Shanghai bowuguan Xizhe junlao* 3, *Hengxian* 5, 11, 13; *Yushu* 3; Wang Hui 2008, 643–644; Bai Yulan 2012, 598) in the sense "to dismiss from office" (*QLZC* 10, 11–12, 21=*RCL* C 6, 8, 13).

leagues were ordered verbally[560] to give back[561] the money to Gui and his colleagues."
Everything else corresponded to [the statements of] Gui and and his colleagues as well as to the *ex-officio* charge.

Retrial – Forensic Examination and Interagency Enquiries

診、問：
死辠（罪）購四萬三百廿。群盜盜殺人購八$_{016}$【萬六百卌錢…】□。
它如告、辤（辭）。
治等別☐$_{017}$

[Results of the] forensic examination and the interagency enquiries:[562] The reward for [arresting 10 persons who committed] a death-penalty crime is 40,320 [cash]. The reward for [arresting 10 persons who] killed people in the act of committing theft as members of a robber gang is 8[0,640 cash.[563] …].

---

560 For *kou ling* 口令 "verbal order" see *Jinwen lu* no. 198 (page 263.112).

561 *Huan* 環 (*GSR* 256n) as loan graph for *huan* 還 (*GSR* 256k) here in the sense "to repay" (*ZYS* 123: 除坐者貲；貲已入環（還）之。 "Exempt the persons [collectively] liable for his offence from fines; if the fines have already been paid, they are to be repaid."). Cf. Lau and Lüdke 2012, footnote 1183.

562 The combination *zhen wen* 診問 is also found in *Yuelu WYZ* 035, 140r and 241 as well as *ZYS* 88. This expression combines two different entries of the record of criminal proceedings. See Lau and Lüdke 2012, footnote 1033, 1034. The entry for the forensic investigation *zhen* 診 "to inspect first-hand" remains empty; for *zhen* see footnote 1095. The second entry *wen* 問 "interagency enquiries" (*Yuelu WYZ* 035, 091, 104, 130, 140–141, 166, 203, 209, 232, 241; *ZYS* 5, 13, 22, 32, 45, 64, 71, 88, 120, 151, 224) refers to enquiries made by the judicial officials during trial on matters that were potentially important for the outcome of the trial. These enquiries were mostly directed to other government agencies, but never to the accused or the witnesses. Among the matters on which information was sought are age of the accused, previous convictions, status (rank), place of residence/registration, emolument and affiliation to a government agency (if the accused was an official), the value of misappropriated goods – as in the present case – and duration of absconding.

563 The reward for arresting ten persons who committed a death-penalty crime (40,320 cash) was equivalent to seven ounces (*liang* 兩) of gold for one person (*Yuelu Lüling* 1889 cited according to Chen Songchang 2014a, 8; cf. *Yuelu WYZ* 043). At the beginning of the Han dynasty, the reward for arresting a capital offender was much higher (*ENLL* 137: 亡人、略妻、略賣人、強奸、僞寫印者棄市罪一人，購金十兩。 "For [each arrest of] anyone who has committed an offence punishable by death, [like …] absconders [or those who] abducted the wife [of another], abducted and sold a person, fornicated by force or forged an official seal, ten ounces of gold are to be rewarded per person [arrested]."). Cf. the higher rewards to the amounts of 70,000, 50,000 or 30,000 cash for arresting one capital offender who was to be executed in a more severe way than *qi shi* 棄

Everything else corresponded to the report and the statements.[564] Zhi and his accomplices have been [...] separately.

Retrial – Finding of Fact

鞫之：
癸、行、柳、轎、沃，群盜治等盜殺人，癸等追。瑣、渠、樂、得、潘、沛巳（已）共捕。沛等令$_{018}$瑣等詣，約分購，未詣。癸等智（知）治等群盜盜殺人。利得其購，紿瑣等約死辠（罪）購。瑣等$_{019}$弗能告，利得死辠（罪）購。聽請相移，紿券付死辠（罪）購。先受私錢二千，以爲購，得公購備。行弗$_{020}$【詣】告，約分購。沛等弗詣，約分購，不智（知）弗詣、相移受錢。獄未斷，未致購，得。
死辠（罪）購四$_{021}$萬三百廿；群盜盜殺人購八萬六百卌錢。

Finding of fact:[565]
[As far as] Gui, Xing, Liu, Jiao and Wo[566] [are concerned], when the members of a robber gang Zhi and his accomplices killed people in the act of committing theft, Gui and his colleagues pursued [them]. [Meanwhile], Suo, Qu, Le,

---

市 (in Qin: *Yuelu Lüling* 1849 cited according to Chen Songchang 2014a, 8; in early Han: *ENLL* 71, 150). According to *Yuelu WYZ* 022, the reward for arresting ten members of a robber gang who robbed and killed persons amounted to 80,640 cash. This was equivalent to 14 *liang* for one person (*Yuelu WYZ* 036).

564 *Ci* 辭 "statement" was usually written with the character *ci* 辤 in Qin and early Han manuscripts. In criminal procedure the word refers to statements made by the accused or witnesses during interrogation (*FZS* 2–5=*RCL* E 2; *ZYS* 5, 105; *Shiji* 57, 2072), which took place after the authorities received the report of an offence or an *ex-officio* charge and before they arrived at a finding of fact. *Ci* is in almost every case used as a noun (*Yuelu WYZ* 035, 060, 085, 091, 104, 131, 141, 166, 185, 187, 203, 233, 242; *Liye* 8–209r, 8–314, 8–2015v, etc.; *ZYS* 5, 14, 22, 32, 45, 64, 71, 90, 105, 120, 155, 224). For the verbal meaning "to state" *yue* 曰 is normally used in the legal manuscripts.

565 *Ju* (*zhi*) 鞫(之) is the standard formula introducing the summary of the finding of fact (*ZYS* 5, 14, 22, 32, 45, 64, 71, 90, 105, 120, 155; *Liye* 8–209v, 8–1743v+8–2015r, 8–2191v; *Yuelu WYZ* 037, 060, 085, 092, 105, 131, 140r, 141, 174, 176, 186, 204, 234, 242). In the present case, *ju zhi* assumingly is the finding of fact of the retrial ordered by the prosecutor (see *Yuelu WYZ* 014).

566 Jiao und Wo, who were also questioned during the interrogation procedure (*Yuelu WYZ* 008), belong to the group of Gui (*Yuelu WYZ* 001–002). There is apparently no verb in the first sentence of the finding of fact, which is a mere enumeration of names. It might be the case that the names function as an exposed subject, but there is no particle to be found, which would usually be expected to mark such an exposure (Pulleyblank 1995, 71–75).

De, Pan and Pei had already arrested [the members of a robber gang] together. Pei and his accomplices ordered Suo and his colleagues to present [the robbers to the authorities at Shayi] and made an agreement to share the reward, [however, Suo and his colleagues] did not yet present [the robbers to the authorities at Shayi]. Gui and his colleagues knew that Zhi and his accomplices had killed people in the act of committing theft as members of a robber gang. They were eager to get the reward for them and deceived Suo and his colleagues into making an agreement on the reward for [arresting offenders liable to the] death penalty. Suo and his colleagues were not able to report [the criminals] and were eager to get the reward for [arresting offenders liable to the] death penalty. So they accepted the request to transfer [the criminals to Gui and his colleagues] and were deceived into making a [contract on a] tally to be handed over the death-penalty reward. They received 2,000 cash of private money[567] in advance as [part of the] reward. After [Gui and his colleagues] received the governmental reward, they would make up the deficiency. Xing did not present and report [the robbers to the authorities, but] made an agreement to share the reward. Pei and his colleagues did not present [the robbers to the authorities either, but also] made an agreement to share the reward. They did not know that [Suo and his colleagues] did not present [the robbers] to the authorities but transferred them and received money [for it from Gui and his colleagues]. The case had not been decided,[568] and the reward had not yet

567 *Si qian* 私錢 "private money" (*Liye* 8–1264) in contrast to the governmental (*gong* 公) rewards (*gou* 購). This private money, which was a partial payment of the complete reward, was considered as a form of bribery in the final decision of the superior province (*Yuelu* WYZ 029–030).

568 *Yu wei duan* 獄未斷 "the case has not been decided yet" (FLDW 115=RCL D 95: 以乞鞫及爲人乞鞫者，獄已斷乃聽，且未斷猶聽毆（也）？獄斷乃聽之。"Is a petition for a [new] finding of fact as well as a petition on behalf of another person only accepted when the case has already been decided, or is it [also] accepted when the case has not been decided yet? It is only accepted after the case has been decided."; FLDW 50=RCL D 40; *Hanshu* 8, 651: 太始四年，坐教人誣告衆利侯當時棄市罪，獄未斷病死。"In the fourth year of the *taishi* reign he was prosecuted for instructing a person to falsely report Dangshi, the lord of Zhongli, for an offence punished with the death penalty. He died from illness before the criminal case had been decided."; *Hanshu* 75, 3192: 下獄治服，未斷病死。"He was put into prison and confessed during trial/torture, he died from illness before [the case] had been decided."). Cf. the synonymous expression *yu wei jue* 獄未決 (*Longgang* 204; ENLL 178). In Qin and Han legal terminology *yu* 獄 mostly referred to a case as being subject to a formal criminal investigation (*Yuelu* WYZ 044, 064, 087, 137v, 168, 173, 175, 199, 213; *Liye* 8–133r, 8–135r, 8–136r, 8–141r, 8–164r, 8–273, 8–314, 8–1556r; ZYS 75, 153–154; ENLL 93, 110, 113, 116, 118, 396; FLDW 33, 93, 109=RCL D 27, 77, 92; FZS 1–2=RCL E

been given, when they were caught. The reward for [arresting 10 persons who committed] a death-penalty crime is 40,320 [cash]. The reward for [arresting 10 persons who] killed people in the act of committing theft as members of a robber gang is 80,640 cash.

Retrial – Decision of Zhouling Prefecture

綰等以盜未有取、吏貲灋（發）戍律令論癸、瑣等。不論$_{022}$**[Missing slip]** 及它不毄（繫）。

Wan and his colleagues passed judgement on Gui, Suo and their colleagues according to the statutes and ordinances on theft without having appropriated [the haul] and on officers who as a penalty are mobilised to [additional] military service. They did not pass judgement on [...] as well as the others are not held under detention.[569]

Submission by Zhouling Prefecture – Concluding Formula

敢瀻（讞）之。$_{023}$

We venture to submit [this case] for decision.[570]

1–2). For *yu* in the sense "remand prison" as the place where the trial took place see footnote 1306.

569 *Ji* 毄 was regularly used to write the word *xi* 繫 "place under detention, remand in custody". Suspects of more serious offences were usually placed under detention after they had been arrested (*Yuelu* WYZ 023, 092, 135, 144, 194, 206, 212, 228, 235; *Liye* 8–144r; *FLDW* 6, 53=*RCL* D 5, 43; *ZYS* 23, 33, 61, 76, 96, 122, 159; *ENLL* 118, 134) until they were either released or a punishment was executed on them. Important witnesses were sometimes also placed under detention during judicial proceedings (*ZYS* 160).

570 For *yan* and the phrase *gan yan zhi* see footnote 489. The present extract from the case record does not mention which agency was charged to conduct the retrial. In three comparable cases from the *Zou yan shu*, in which prefects committed a criminal offence, the competent agency of the province (*ZYS* 74) or, if this agency was also involved, that of the neighbouring province (*ZYS* 131) as well as newly appointed leading officials of the same prefecture brought proceedings against the respective prefect (*ZYS* 97). But from the subsequent response of Nan province it can be concluded that in the present case the prefect of Zhouling was the official who finally submitted the case to the higher authorities for decision (*Yuelu* WYZ 025) after he had newly summarised the finding of fact. However, in contrast to the cases of the *Zou yan shu*, the offence of the prefect of Zhouling was not the main reason for the retrial. Rather, it should be clarified whether the judgement passed on the law enforcement officers and the conscripts was legitimate. It depended on this decision whether the prefect would be prosecuted for an error of judgement (*lun shi zhi* 論失之). In their submission to the higher authorities, the judicial officials of the prefecture of Zhouling pointed out that they did not arrive at an unanimous opinion on which sentence would be justified.

Alternative Votes for Judgement

吏議曰：
癸、瑣等論當毆（也）。沛、綰等不當論。
或曰：
癸、瑣等當耐爲侯（候）。令瑣等環（還）癸等錢。綰等$_{024}$

The [responsible] officials[571] deliver [the following] legal opinion:[572]
"The judgement on Gui, Suo and their colleagues is lawful. Pei, Wan and their colleagues by law are not to be sentenced."
Some say:[573]
"Gui, Suo and their colleagues by law are to be shaved and made convincts of *hou* category.[574] Order Suo and his colleagues to return the money to Gui and his colleagues. Wan and his colleagues [...]."[575]

---

571 It is not mentioned to which instance these officials belong. For the previous discussion on their affiliation see section 4.2 of the introduction. From the fact that, in the present case, the final decision of Nan province as the higher authority (*Yuelu* WYZ 029–030) differs from both alternative proposals (*Yuelu* WYZ 024), the editors draw the convincing conclusion that the proposals for a judgement must be attributed to the officials of the prefecture of Zhouling (Zhu and Chen 2013, 102 with footnote 42).

572 *Li yi* 吏議 "the (responsible) officials deliver (the following) legal opinion" (cf. Giele 2006, 186–188) (ZYS 24, 33; *Yuelu* WYZ 024, 039, 094, 107, 136, 235; cf. FLDW 83=RCL D 68; ZYS 184, 189, 194) refers to the first of two divergent judicial opinions on the sentence, which are attached to the submission. This first option, which approved the sentence of the prefecture of Zhouling as lawful and pleaded for acquittal of the leading officials, seems to express the prevailing opinion within the competent authority. In the *Zou yan shu*, *li dang* 吏當 is sometimes used instead of *li yi* (ZYS 7, 15, 47). Schuessler (2007, 566) interprets *yi* 議 as a putative derivation from the stative verb *yi* 義 "to be right/just", hence "consider to be right".

573 *Huo yue* 或曰 (ZYS 7, 16, 25, 33; *Yuelu* WYZ 039, 094, 136, 235) probably refers to a dissenting opinion, which suggested punishing the accused officers and conscripts more severely with penal labour as watchmen. The legal basis for this proposal is unknown.

574 *Nai wei hou* 耐爲侯（候） was the most lenient form of penal labour during the Qin dynasty (QLSZ 193=RCL A 103; QLZC 4, 6=RCL C 2, 4; FLDW 117=RCL D 97). It was later abolished by the Han. *Nai* 耐 denotes a humiliating marking of a convict, which consisted in shaving off the offender's beard. During Qin times *nai* was also accompanied by less severe penal labour of the categories *si kou* 司寇 (FLDW 117=RCL D 97; *Liye* 8–756) and *li chen qie* 隸臣妾 (*Longgang* 40, FLDW 8, 35=RCL D 7, 28; ZYS 182; *Yuelu* WYZ 171–172, 174, 205–206, 235) as well as the privileged category *gui xin* 鬼薪. For *nai wei gui xin* see footnote 666.

575 Because the following slip is missing, the proposal put forward by the minority for sentencing the responsible leading officials is not preserved. At least an acquittal can be ruled out, because the leading officials were to be prosecuted for a judicial errror.

[Missing slip]

Response to the Submission by Nan Province (Decision)

【廿五】年七月丙戌朔乙未，南郡叚（假）守賈報州陵守綰、丞越。
子讞（讞）：
校長癸等詣男子治等，告群盜盜$_{025}$【殺人。沙羨曰：士五（伍）瑣等捕治等移】[576]鼠（予）癸等。癸曰：治等殺人，癸與佐行將【徒】追。瑣等巳（已）捕治【等。四】$_{026}$人曰邦亡，不智（知）它人辠（罪）。癸等利得群盜購，請瑣等鼠（予）癸等，癸等詣盡鼠（予）瑣等死辠（罪）購。瑣等$_{027}$鼠（予）；癸先以私錢二千鼠（予）以爲購數；行弗詣告，皆謀分購。未致購得。
疑癸、瑣、綰等辠（罪）。

In the [25th] year on day *yiwei*[577] of the seventh month with the first day *bingxu*, Jia, the temporary[578] governor[579] of Nan province,[580] gave a response[581] to the incumbent prefect of Zhouling, Wan, and vice prefect Yue. You submitted [for decision]:

---

576 For this emendation and the according explanation see Zhu and Chen 2013, 103 with footnote 46.

577 This probably was the 25th year of King Zheng of Qin, because *bingxu* occurs as first day of the seventh month of the 25th year (cf. Zhang Peiyu 2007, 73; Li Zhonglin 2012, 65). *Yiwei* was the 11th day of the seventh month, i.e. 13/08/222 BC (Xu Xiqi 1997, 1240).

578 *Jia* 叚 (GSR 33a) for *jia* 假 (GSR 33c) "temporarily acting". *Jia* was a designation for an official who temporarily held the office of another (An and Xiong 2007, 856–857; Bielenstein 1980, 92) as in ENLL 102: 相國、御史及二千石官所置守、假吏 "probationary or temporarily acting officials appointed by the chancellor, by the chief prosecutor or by a two-thousand-bushel office". The temporary governor of Nan province mentioned here occurs again in *Yuelu* WYZ 040. Cf. the temporary governors of Nan province (*Liye* 8–974) as well as the provinces of Langye (*Liye* 8–657r), Dongting (*Liye* 8–759, 8–1523r/v, 8–2115), Nanyang (*Shiji* 6, 232), Kuaiji (*Chu Han chunqiu* quoted according to the commentaries on *Shiji* 7, 297) as well as the temporary deputy governor of the province of Ba (*Liye* 8–61+8–293+8–2012, cf. Chen Wei 2012a, 46) during Qin times. Qin manuscripts also mention temporary provincial secretaries (*Liye* 8–78r, 16–5r; ZYS 124), temporary provincial commanders (*Liye* 9–10v), temporary provincial prosecutors (*Liye* 8–528r), temporary secretaries of the prefect (*Liye* 8–802) and temporary assistants (QLZC 1=RCL C 1; *Liye* 8–1231). In 207 BC Xiang Yu also acted as temporary commander-in-chief (*Shiji* 7, 305).

579 During the Qin dynasty *shou* 守 resp. *tai shou* 泰/大（太）守 was the title of the governor of a province (*jun* 郡) (*Liye* 5–23, 8–61r, 8–62r, 8–67r, 8–101, 8–228, 8–410, 8–657r, 8–672r, 8–755r, 8–759, 8–772r/v, 8–974, 8–1155, 8–1225, 8–1234, 8–1404, 8–1481r, 8–1523r/v, 8–1586, 8–1829, 8–2115, 16–5r, etc.; *Yuelu* WYZ 040, 063; FLDW 95=RCL D 79; FZS 52=RCL E 17), which as an administrative unit was placed below the central government and above its subordinate prefectures (*xian* 縣). At the beginning of Han times and probably also during the Qin dynasty the governor as head of the provincial administration – including

"The *xiao zhang* Gui and his colleagues presented the man Zhi and his accomplices and reported them for [killing people] in the act of committing theft as members of a robber gang. [In a written report the prefecture of Shayi notified us that Suo and his colleagues had actually arrested the robbers and transferred them] to Gui and his colleagues. Gui and his colleagues stated: 'When Zhi and his accomplices killed people, I, Gui, and the assistant Xing led conscripts to pursue [them]. [Meanwhile] Suo and his colleagues had already arrested Zhi and his accomplices. Four men [from the gang of Zhi] stated that they had absconded from the state, [but Suo and his colleagues] did not know which offence the others had committed. My colleagues and I were eager to get the reward for members of a robber gang, [so] we requested Suo and his colleagues to hand over [the robbers] to us. After having presented [the robbers to the authorities] my colleagues and I would completely give Suo and his colleagues the death-penalty reward. Suo and his colleagues [accordingly] gave [us the robbers]. I gave [them] 2,000 cash of my private money in advance, which was regarded as the amount of the reward (i.e. a partial payment). Xing did not present and report [the robbers to the authorities], [but] we all conspired to share the reward. Before the reward was given we got caught.' We are in doubt about the [correct] punishment[582]

the jurisdiction – received a salary of 2,000 *shi* 石 (ENLL 440–441). Cf. Bielenstein 1980, 93; An and Xiong 2007, 544–569.

580 Nan jun 南郡, "Nan province" or the "southern province", to which the prefecture of Zhouling was subordinate, was established by Qin in 278 BC after the conquest of Ying. Its administrative seat was located on the site of this former capital of Chu (*Shiji* 5, 213; Hou Xiaorong 2009, 396–405) near present Jingzhou, Hubei (*Lishi dituji* vol. II, 11–12, 4/5②).

581 *Bao* 報 refers to different types of responses. In some cases a response merely contained a note on the receipt of a certain document, in others, as in the present case, it contained a decision (*Yuelu* WYZ 040, 177, 236; *Liye* 8–135r; ZYS 7, 15, 34, 47, 50, 52, 53, 55, 57, 59, 60, 62, 98; ENLL 93, 205; *Hanshu* 23, 1106). Cf. Giele 2006, 155–157; Zhu Xiangrong 2012, 186–187.

582 *Yi zui* 疑罪 "to be in doubt about the punishment" (ZYS 6, 15, 23, 32–33, 47, 50, 52, 53, 54, 57, 59, 60, 62, 184; *Yuelu* WYZ 092, 134–135) is one of the main reasons for the submission of legal cases to the higher authorities for decision (*yan* 讞). The majority of cases found in the *Zou yan shu* from Zhangjiashan belongs to this category of criminal cases (Lau and Lüdke 2012, 39–45). In several cases from the Yuelu Academy collection of criminal cases, the reasons for submission likewise appear to have been certain doubts of the local officials. However, these doubts, which are formulated with *yi* 疑 in six of the cases, were not merely raised with regard to the correct punishment (*Yuelu* WYZ 028, 092 and 134–135), but also with regard to the right amount of rewards (formulated as *yi gou* 疑購 "to be in doubt about the [right amount of the] reward", *Yuelu* WYZ 042), the legal status of the accused (*Yuelu* WYZ 134–135) and the correct method of judgement (leading to different punishments; *Yuelu* WYZ 105–106). Until the discovery of the Yuelu Academy manuscripts, legal historians thought that the procedure of review over successsive administrative

for Gui, Suo, Wan and their colleagues."[583]

⿰氵獻（讞）固有028審。癸等，其審請瑣等。所出購，以死辠（罪）購備鼠（予）瑣等，有券。受人貨材（財）以枉律令，其所枉當029貲以上，受者、貨者皆坐臧（贓）爲盜。有律不當⿰氵獻（讞）。獲手，其貲綰、越、獲各一盾。
它有律令。030

What you submit is indeed unambiguous.[584] As far as Gui and his colleagues are concerned they in fact made a request to Suo and his colleagues. There is a tally contract [being testimony to the fact that] of the reward to be disbursed[585] [by the authorities] the death-penalty reward should be completely given to Suo and his colleagues. [In cases of] "accepting valuables offered by sb.[586] to

levels was first regulated in 200 BC by an edict of Emperor Gaozu (*Hanshu* 23, 1106). Now it has become clear that the *yan*-procedure of submitting criminal cases to the higher authorities for decisison already existed in pre-imperial Qin.

583 The preceding part is a quotation from the submission of the prefecture.

584 For an evaluation of a submission by the higher authorities cf. ZYS 26: 大（太）僕不害行廷尉事，謂胡嗇夫：⿰氵獻（讞）獄史闌，⿰氵獻（讞）固有審。 "The *taipu* Buhai who was acting as minister of trials notified the overseer of the prefecture of Hu [of the following]: As for the submitted [case of the] judicial secretary Lan, what you submit is indeed unambiguous." In that as well as the present case, the higher authorities criticise a submission as unnecessary because the points on which doubts are raised in fact appear to be "unambiguous" (*shen* 審) facts. On *yi* 疑 "to be doubtful" as the antonym of *shen* see footnote 633. Instead of understanding *gu* 固 as an adverb in the present passage, a second possibility would be to read *you* 有 as *you* 又 and interpret *gu* and *shen* as two stative verbs (*Hanfei* 45, 315; *Guoyu* 1.15/9/17). For *gu* 固 as a stative verb see also *Hanfei* 49, 343 (cf. Harbsmeier): 罰莫如重而必，使民畏之，法莫如一而固，使民知之。 "If nothing is as severe and inevitable as the penalty, this makes the people fear it; if nothing is as consistent and steady as the law, this makes the people take note of it."

585 For *chu* 出 cf. *chu qian* 出錢 which could mean "to disburse" (QLSZ 64–65=RCL A 42: 出錢，獻封丞、令，乃發用之。 "When cash [coins] are to be disbursed, the seal impression is presented to the vice prefect and prefect and thereupon [the basket] is opened and [the cash] are used."; QLSZ 67=RCL A 44: 錢十一當一布。其出入錢以當金、布，以律。 "Eleven cash are eqivalent to one 'cloth'. When cash are disbursed or entered to serve as equivalent for gold or cloth, this is to be done in accordance with the statutes.").

586 *Huo* 貨, literally "movable goods", here with the special meaning "bribes" (*Hanfei* 15, 78 [cf. Harbsmeier]: 爵祿可以貨得者。 "Ranks and salaries can be attained through bribes.") as in *qu huo yu mou ren* 取貨於某人 "to accept bribes from sb." (*Zuo* Cheng 16,393,8; Xiang 26,520,2–3; Zhao 21,687,12; Zhao 27,720,11) or *qiu huo yu mou ren* 求貨於某人 "to demand bribes from sb." (*Zuo* Zhao 1,570,1–2; Zhao 13,645,6; Zhao 23,696,2–3; Ding 4,749,2–3); for explanations see Lau 1999, 308. *Huo cai* 貨財, which sometimes occurs as

the effect of bending the statutes and ordinances",[587] if the respective [statutes and ordinances], which shall be bent, warrant[588] the imposition of a fine or more, the one who accepted the bribes[589] as well as the one who offered[590]

---

nominal compound in the sense "possessions" (*FLDW* 209=*RCL* D 189) or "bribes" (*Hanfei* 14, 74), is interpreted in the present passage as verb-object construction meaning "to offer valuables/bribes". For the verbal usage of *huo* see footnote 590.

587 Cf. the similar statutory offence *shou xing qiu wangfa* 受行賕枉法 with different wording in Han law (*ENLL* 60: 受賕以枉灋（法），及行賕者，皆坐其臧（贓）爲盜。罪重於盜者，以重者論之。"Those who accept bribes in order to bend the law as well as those who offer bribes are all prosecuted for what they have thereby misappropriated as in a case of theft. In cases where the punishment [which should be evaded by offering bribes] is more severe than that for theft [of the respective amount of money], [the offering persons as well as the accepting persons] are sentenced to the most severe one."; *ZYS* 52; *Dunhuang* 1875). In the present case, the application of this statutory offence is an example for an analogous application of a norm to a situation not directly covered by an existing norm since the usual targets of bribes offered in order to bend the law would be corrupt judicial officials. In their final decision (*bao* 報), the authorities of Nan province found fault with the submission of Zhouling prefecture. They pointed out that it was not necessary to submit the case in question, and that, moreover, the legal rules referred to (*Yuelu WYZ* 022) were irrelevant. On the contrary, the higher authorities held that the statutory offence "bribing sb. or accepting sb.'s valuables for the purpose of bending the statutes and ordinances" was applicable to the case. The same principles as those applied for theft were applied to this offence. This decision is obviously based on the amount of 2,000 cash, which had evidentially been exchanged between Gui, Suo and their colleagues – they even made a tally contract for this – and must have been considered as a kind of bribe. In contrast to common theft, no mitigating circumstances for theft which had not been carried out were recognised, with the result that the imposed punishments must have been much more severe. For the punishment resulting from this classification see footnote 592.

588 In legal texts, the subject of *dang* 當 and the following punishment is usually the offender (e.g. A當X "Offender A by law is to be punished with X."). For the rarely occurring construction with statutes as subject cf. *FZS* 4=*RCL* E 2: 詰之極而數訑，更言不服，其律當治（笞）諒（掠）者，乃治（笞）諒（掠）。"If he has been confronted [with inconsistencies] to the utmost and still repeatedly lies, changes his statements and does not confess, then, where the respective statutes warrant torture, use torture."

589 *Shou zhe* 受者. Cf. *shou qiu* 受賕 "to accept bribes" (*ENLL* 95; *Jijiupian* 4, 312) and *shou xing qiu* 受行賕 "to accept or offer bribes" (*ZYS* 52; *Shiji* 126, 3201; *Hanshu* 23, 1099; 23, 1112; 83, 3390; 90, 3673).

590 *Huo zhe* 貨者. *Huo* here used verbally "to bribe sb." (*Zuo* Xi 28,206,14; Xi 13,214,7; Zhao 26,712,12; *Meng* 4, 156). Cf. *xing qiu* 行賕 "to offer bribes" (*ENLL* 60; *Hanfei* 48, 338; *Shiji* 18, 896; 95, 2673; *Hanshu* 16, 549).

them are both prosecuted[591] for the misappropriated goods[592] as in a case of theft. There is a statute governing this, the case should not have been submitted. Huo was the one who handled[593] [the records that were submitted; accordingly,] Wan, Yue and Huo will each be fined one shield.[594] For everything else there are statutes and ordinances.

591 For *zuo* see footnote 528 above.

592 In manuscripts from Qin and early Han times, *zang* 臧 (GSR 727f') is the standard character used to write *zang* 贓 (GSR 727h'), which is the word for any kind of misappropriation, i.e. illicit gain derived from property offences (*dao* 盜), as well as for the goods thus misappropriated (FLDW 1, 6, 9, 12–13, 16–18, 25, 45–46, 49, 131, 182=RCL D 1, 7–8, 11–12, 14–16, 21, 38, 43, 109, 161; *Yuelu* WYZ 045, 059–060, 086, 130, 146, 166; *Longgang* 133, 137, 147, 148, 151, 201; ZYS 51, 62, 71, 224; ENLL 14, 20, 55, 58–59, 60, 72, 91, 95, 155, 199, 226, 230, 260–261). The punishment of most of the property offences was determined by the value (*zhi* 值) of the goods misappropriated by carrying out the offence. In Qin and early Han times, the statutes stipulated five successive punishments for theft and other property offences in correlation to the value of the misappropriated goods (*Longgang* 40–41; ENLL 55–56). If this value exceeded 660 cash, as in the present case, the maximum sentence for property offences could be imposed: The delinquent was to be tattooed and made an earth or grain pounder convict (ENLL 55; ZYS 72–73; cf. FLDW 33, 35=RCL D 27–28).

593 *Shou* 手, which frequently occurs after names in the Qin documents from Liye (*Liye* 5–1r, 6–6, 8–4, 8–48, 8–60v, 8–62v, 8–63r/v, 8–748v, 8–2012r, etc.), probably refers to the official who personally handled the document or wrote it with his own hand and seems to have been responsible for the correct recording. Cf. Giele 2005, 364–365, footnote 35; footnote 12 to *Liye* 5–1r in Chen Wei 2012a, 5; Zhu Xiangrong 2012, 171–175; Wu Xu 2014, 187.

594 The responsible officials of the prefecture of Zhouling were also considered to be liable to punishment because the punishment they had imposed on the offenders was too lenient. Therefore, the leading officials were fined one shield (*zi yi dun* 貲一盾) for committing an error of judgement (*lun shi zhi* 論失之). *Zi* 貲 "fine" was a light form of punishment, which was widely used to punish a large variety of smaller offences often committed in office (*Yuelu* WYZ 107; XL 51=RCL B 25; FLDW 139, 147, 175=RCL D 117, 125, 155) or in situations involving a lack of oversight by supervising officials (XL 23=RCL B 9; *Yuelu* WYZ 236) as in the present case. Commoners being liable for offences committed by a member of their unit or household were punished in the same way (*Yuelu* WYZ 136; ZYS 123; QLZC 36=RCL C 22). A *zi* was not calculated in currency, but in armour; four degrees existed: one shield (*dun* 盾), one suit of leather armour (*jia* 甲; *Yuelu* WYZ 107; *Longgang* 120; *Liye* 8–11; QLSZ 115=RCL A 64; XL 14, 51=RCL B 6, 25; QLZC 36=RCL C 22), two suits of leather armour (*Yuelu* WYZ 136; *Longgang* 41, 53; *Liye* 8–209v, 8–1783; QLSZ 115=RCL A 64; XL 51= RCL B 25; FLDW 8, 139, 147, 175=RCL D 7, 117, 125, 155) and three suits of leather armour (*Liye* 8–60r, 8–754r). One shield (equivalent to 384 cash, see *Yuelu Shu* 82–83 as well as Yu Zhenbo 2010, 38) was the minimum penalty during Qin times. A similarly low fine to the amount of two ounces of gold (*fa jin er liang* 罰金二兩) had to be paid for committing a judicial error when passing judgement according to legal provisions from early Han times (ENLL 95–97: 其非

故也，而失不審，各以其贖論之。[…] 贖城旦舂[…]、贖劓黥、戍不盈四歲 […] 罰金二兩。"In case [the offending official] did not act intentionally, but committed an error [when passing judgement] or did not establish the facts [during inspection, in a response or in a notification], judgement is to be passed that [the offending official] has to pay a fee for redemption from the respective punishment [he has erroneously passed]. […] If the accused erroneously is sentenced to pay the fee for redemption from penal labour as an earth pounder convict […] or from having the nose cut off and being tattooed or from having to perform [punitive] military service for less than four years, [… the responsible official] is fined two ounces of gold.").

Case I.2

In this case from the year 222 BC, rewards for arresting robbers again played an important role. A military unit from the prefecture of Zhouling under the command of a robber hunter was ordered to arrest bandits who had been reported for committing armed robbery, thereby killing and injuring people. After the successful arrest, the senior official of Zhouling initiated proceedings against the robbers. During their interrogation it was found that the accused belonged to two different groups. The first consisted of offenders who originally came from Qin, but had then absconded to Chu. The second consisted of fugitives from Chu who had failed to submit to the king of Qin. Interagency enquiries showed that the hometown of these fugitives had already been conquered and had become part of the Qin territory before they committed armed robbery. This meant that the fugitives should be considered as subjects of Qin.

Two statutory provisions concerning the rewards for arresting robbers are quoted, in which the amount of rewards depends on the classification of the offenders (members of a robber gang vs. robbers from abroad). Unfortunately, the wording of the second provision is not completely preserved.

The judicial officials of the prefecture were in doubt about the appropriate reward for arresting the two different categories of robbers. Therefore, they submitted this case to the higher authorities for decision, admitting that they were unable to reach a consensus. Two alternative votes based on the two statutory provisions were attached to this submission.

In their final decision, the superior officials of Nan province evaluated the submission. They supported the proposed differentiation between robbers who had absconded from the state of Qin and those who had come as fugitives from Chu. Accordingly, robber hunter Shi and his colleagues should receive different rewards for arresting the offenders from Qin and from Chu. From the amount of the rewards determined by the province, we can draw the conclusion that the offenders from Qin were not classified as members of a robber gang due to their small number, but as offenders liable to the death penalty. This was not the only aspect in which the decision of the province deviated from both votes of the prefecture. The reasons why the agency of the province did not apply the statutory provisions on the rewards for arresting criminal fugitives from abroad, which were apparently cited in this case, but instead a slightly higher amount are left to conjecture.

 | DOI 10.1163/9789004315655_010

Diplomatic Edition

廿五年五月丁亥朔壬寅州陵守綰丞越敢潚之廼二月甲戌走馬達告曰盜=殺傷走馬$_{031}$好□□□□□□□□□□求盜尸等十六人追⌞尸等□捕詣秦□□□□$_{032}$四人荊男子閬等十人告群盜=殺傷好等•治等曰秦人邦亡荊⌞閬等曰荊邦人皆居$_{033}$京州相與亡來入秦地欲歸義行到州陵界中未詣吏悔謀言曰治等已有辠秦=不$_{034}$□□□□居山谷以攻盜即攻盜=殺傷好等它如尸等•診問如告辤京州後降爲=$_{035}$秦=之後治閬等乃群盜殺傷好等⌞律曰產捕群盜一人購金十四兩⌞有曰它邦人$_{036}$□□□□□□所興毋什伍將長者捕之購金二兩•鞫之尸等產捕治閬等告群盜=殺傷$_{037}$好等治等秦人邦亡荊⌞閬等荊人亡來入秦地欲歸義悔不詣吏以京州降爲秦後群$_{038}$▨皆審疑尸等購它縣論敢潚之•吏議以捕群盜律購尸等⌞或曰以捕它邦人$_{039}$

[Missing slip]

廿五年六月丙辰朔己卯南郡叚守賈報州陵守綰丞越子潚求盜尸等捕秦男子治等四人$_{040}$荊男子閬等十人告群盜殺傷好等⌞治等秦人邦亡⌞閬等荊人來歸義行到州陵悔$_{041}$▨□□□□□京州降爲秦乃殺好等疑尺等購•潚固有審矣治等審秦人毆尸$_{042}$等當購金七兩閬等其荊人毆尸等當購金三兩它有令$_{043}$

Edition and Translation

Submission by Zhouling Prefecture – Introductory Formula

廿五年五月丁亥朔壬寅，州陵守綰、丞越敢潚（讞）之：

In the 25th year on day *renyin*[595] of the fifth month with the first day *dinghai*, the incumbent[596] prefect of Zhouling,[597] Wan, and vice prefect[598] Yue venture to submit[599] [the following case] for decision:

Initiation of Criminal Proceedings

廼二月甲戌，走馬達告曰：
盜盜殺傷走馬$_{031}$好□□□□□□□□□□求盜尸等十六人追。尸等【產】捕詣秦【男子治等】$_{032}$四人、荊男子閬等十人，告群盜盜殺傷好等。

595 This was the 16th day in the fifth month of the 25th year of King Zheng of Qin (cf. Zhang Peiyu 2007, 73; Li Zhonglin 2012, 65), i.e. 21/06/222 BC (Xu Xiqi 1997, 1240).

596 For *shou* in combination with a particular office see footnote 486.

597 For Zhouling see footnote 487.

598 For *cheng* see footnote 488.

599 For *yan* and the phrase *gan yan zhi* see footnote 489.

On day *jiaxu*[600] of the last second month Da, holder of the third rank,[601] reported:[602]
"Robbers[603] injured or killed Hao, holder of the third rank, [...] in the act of committing theft."
[...We ordered] the robber hunter[604] Shi and his colleagues – overall 16 men – to pursue[605] them. Shi and his colleagues arrested[606] [alive] and presented[607] to the authorities [the man Zhi and] three accomplices from Qin and the man Lang and nine accomplices from Jing (i.e. Chu),[608] and reported them for injuring or killing Hao and others in the act of committing theft as members of a robber gang.[609]

First Stage of Interrogation

治等曰：
秦人。邦亡荊。
閬等曰：

600 This was the 17th day of the second month in the 25th year of King Zheng of Qin (cf. Zhang Peiyu 2007, 73; Li Zhonglin 2012, 65), i.e. 25/03/222 BC (Xu Xiqi 1997, 1239).

601 Qin or Han received sources do not mention the rank *zou ma* 走馬 (ZYS 111, 215; *Yuelu* WYZ 068, 089, 108, 113, 193). In the Qin manuscripts of Yuelu Academy *zou ma* signifies the third of twenty ranks (*jue* 爵), which in documents of the Qin Empire excavated in Liye and in Han times is called *zan niao* 簪裊 (*Hanshu* 19A, 739; 簪褭 in *Liye* 8–26+8–752 [dated to the 32nd year of Qin Shihuang=215 BC, cf. Chen Wei 2012a, 35], 8–781+8–1102 [dated to the 31st year of Qin Shihuang=216 BC, cf. Chen Wei 2012a, 226], 16–5v [dated to the 27th year of Qin Shihuang=220 BC, cf. Wang Huanlin 2007, 104–105]) and ranked between *bu geng* 不更 and *shang zao* 上造 (cf. Wang and Tang 2010, based on *Yuelu Shu* 122–123). The Qin rank *zou ma* needs to be distinguished from the two Zhou titles *zou ma* 走馬 (*Jinwen* 2.2807; 3.4174) or *cou ma* 趣馬 "horse driver" (*Odes* 193,4; 258,7; *Shu* Lizheng §8; *Zhouli* 33, 861a) used for officials.

602 For *gao* see footnote 498.

603 For *dao* see footnotes 541, 557 and 795.

604 For *qiu dao* see footnote 493.

605 For *zhui* see footnote 510.

606 For *bu* see footnote 505.

607 For *yi* see footnote 496.

608 *Jing* 荊 is the old name of the southern state Chu 楚, which was already used during the Western Zhou period (*Jinwen* 3.3907; 7.10175; *Odes* 178,4; 300,5; *Chunqiu* Zhuang 10th year). The usage of Jing in quoted ordinances (ZYS 157) and the official annals of the Qin dynasty (*Shiji* 6, 234) has been explained by Gao You (ca. AD 168–212, commentary to *Lü* 6, 58) and in an 8th century AD commentary as being caused by avoidance of the tabooed personal name Zi Chu 子楚 of King Zhuang Xiang 莊襄王 (*zheng yi* commentary to *Shiji* 6, 234), who reigned from 249–247 BC. The name Jing is also mentioned in regulations for official designations in Qin (*Liye* 8–461r).

609 For *qun dao* see footnote 500.

荊邦人。皆居$_{033}$京州，相與亡。來入秦地，欲歸義。行到州陵界中，未詣吏，悔。謀言曰：治等巳（已）有辠（罪）秦。秦不$_{034}$□□□□居山谷以攻盜。即攻盜盜殺傷好等。
它如尸等。

Zhi and his accomplices stated:
"[We are] men from Qin. We absconded from the state[610] to Jing (i.e. Chu)."
Lang and his accomplices stated:
"[We are] men from the state of Jing. We all lived at Jingzhou[611] and absconded[612] together. We came here, entered the territory of Qin and wished to take refuge [under the Qin rule].[613] On our march we reached [the territory] inside the

610 For *bang wang* see footnote 512.

611 The place name Jingzhou 京州 is otherwise unknown for the territory of Jing/Chu in the third century BC. A seal inscription from Han times mentions this name in the combination 京州韓聶 "Han Nie [of] Jingzhou" (cf. Luo Fuyi 1978, 5.14 [京] and 11.15 [州]).

612 *Wang* 亡 referred to the offence of leaving, without authorisation, the place in which one was mandated to stay or not reporting to the place to which one was mandated to go. The penal law of the Qin dynasty distinguished between the statutory offences of *bang wang* 邦亡 "absconding from the state" (cf. footnote 512), *lan wang* 闌亡 "unauthorised absconding" (*FLDW* 48, 139, 167=*RCL* D 93, 117, 146; *Liye* 8–1716) and *jiang yang* 將陽 "vagrancy" (footnote 858). As elaborated on by Chen Songchang (2012a, 6), the difference between *lan wang* and *jiang yang* lay in the duration of absconding (*Yuelu Lüling* 0185: 闌亡，盈十二月而得，耐。不盈十二月爲將陽，毄（繫）城旦舂。"Who unauthorisedly absconds and is caught only after 12 months, is to be punished [with penal labour of the category] *nai*. [Absconding for] less than 12 months constitutes 'vagrancy' and is to be punished with detention among the earth and grain pounder convicts."). The same punishments for an absence of fully or less than 12 months were imposed on officials and free persons (*li min* 吏民) who committed absconding at the beginning of the Han dynasty (*ENLL* 157). The absconder Da in the present case was a rank-and-file man without rank and therefore unconditionally subjected to penal labour. Holders of the first or a higher rank were entitled to compensate for their days of absconding by working for government workshops (*zuo guan fu* 作官府). In this case and in other cases, the status of the absconding person was taken into account for sentencing purposes. Different punishments were stipulated for officials or free men, for slaves and for convicts.

613 The term *gui yi* 歸義 was used when non-Chinese tribes surrendered to the ruling dynasty. *Gui* 歸 occurs in the sense "to turn towards, find shelter" as well as "place of refuge" (*Guoyu* 1.27/17/26–27: 藪，物之歸也。 "Marshland is the refuge of living beings."; *Zuo* Zhao 7,613,12: 鬼有所歸乃不爲厲，吾爲之歸也。 "If a ghost has a place to find shelter, it does not become an evil spirit. I have made such a refuge for the ghost."). *Yi* 義 (*GSR* 2r) *ŋraj-s "be right, righteous, lawful, correct, proper, seemly" as self-designation of Qin and of the Chinese empire during Han times was traced by Benedict to *wo* 我 (*GSR* 2a) *ŋˤajʔ (Schuessler 2007, 566), which originally meant "we (also as *pluralis majestatis*), our" (Serruys according to Schuessler 1987, 643). Cf. *xia* 夏 as Chinese oecumene in contrast to

borders[614] of Zhouling [prefecture], but before we appeared before the officials, we had reservations[615] [about this]. We consulted[616] on the [following] proposal:[617] 'Zhi and his accomplices have already committed crimes[618] in Qin. Qin will/does not [… Let us, instead of taking refuge under Qin rule,] dwell in a mountain valley to do hold-ups.'[619] In doing [such a] hold-up, we killed or injured Hao and others in the act of committing theft."
Everything else corresponded to [the statements of] Shi and his colleagues.

---

the Qin dependencies/vassal states *Qin shu*/*chen bang* 秦屬/臣邦 (*FLDW* 176=*RCL* D 156). Therefore *gui yi*, which should literally be translated as "to find shelter/refuge among the legitimate/righteous ones (i.e. submit to Us, the dynasty of Qin/Han)" is used for foreign tribes and states (*Shiji* 126, 3207; 19, 977; *Hanshu* 8, 266; 69, 2973; 79, 3295; 94B, 3816; *Dunhuang* 98, 2201; *Xuanquan* 211, 240; see also Luo Fuyi 1987, no. 1206).

614 For *jie zhong* see footnote 511.

615 Although there is sufficient evidence for *hui* 悔 (*GSR* 947s) *hmʕə-s in the meaning "to repent, regret" (*Odes* 22,1; 88,1; *Chuci* 1/1/15, 1/1/24; *Zuo* Yin 1,2,9; *Wei li zhi dao* 14.1; 41.1; *Yuelu WYZ* 075–076), this meaning does not make sense in the present context, because it is unlikely that Lang and his accomplices felt regret for something they had not done or omitted. *Hui* also occurs in the sense "fault" (*Odes* 245,8; 256,12; 241,4 according to Gao Heng 1980, 391, 404, 438 and Xiang Xi 1986, 178) and for this reason it seems to be etymologically related to *you* 尤 (*GSR* 996a) *Gʷə "fault", in *ZYS* 29 written with *hui* 恢 (GSR 950b), so that the verbal usage of *hui* could be understood as "to regard sth. as fault/mistake". *Hui* could also have the related verbal meaning "to have reservations" (*Lunyu* 7, 140 [cf. Harbsmeier]: 子曰暴虎馮河死而無悔者吾不與也。"The master said: 'Those who would die without reservations going at a tiger barehanded or walking across the Yellow River – I would not take them [as commanders].'").

616 For *mou* see footnotes 522 and 829.

617 *Yan* 言 in the special sense "proposal, advice" (*Hanfei* 5, 20 [cf. Harbsmeier]: 故群臣陳其言君以其言授其事。"Thus when the various ministers put forward their proposals, the ruler assigns the tasks according to these proposals."; *Hanfei* 32, 209 [cf. Harbsmeier]: 王登爲中牟令上言於襄主。"When Wang Deng was prefect of Zhongmou, he submitted [the following] proposal to Xiang Zhu."; *Li* 54, 1642 [cf. Couvreur 1950, vol. II, 502–503]: 事君大言入則望大利[…]君子不以小言受大祿。"Those who serve a ruler expect great appanages for great advice. […] The gentleman does not accept a high salary for little advice.").

618 For *zui* see footnote 514.

619 *Gong dao* 攻盜 "to raid, do hold-ups" (*Zuo* Xiang 10,444,9; *Hanshu* 94A, 3787; *ENLL* 62: 盜五人以上相與功（攻）盜，爲群盜。"If five or more robbers do hold-ups together, this is a case of gang robbery."; *ENLL* 1: 守乘城亭障，諸侯人來攻盜，不堅守而棄去之若降之[…]。"If those being charged with the defence of a walled city, a station or a border post do not staunchly defend it when the men of the feudal lords come to raid it, but instead give it up and run away or surrender it […].").

Forensic Examination and Interagency Enquiries

診、問如告、辤（辭）。
京州後降爲$_{035}$秦。爲秦之後，治、閬等乃群盜殺傷好等。

The [results of the] forensic examination and the interagency enquiries[620] corresponded to the report and the statements.[621]
Jingzhou afterwards submitted and became [part of the territory of] Qin.[622] After it had become [a part of] Qin, Zhi, Lang and their accomplices killed or injured Hao and others in the act of committing theft as members of a robber gang.

Citation of Relevant Statutory Provisions

律曰：
產捕群盜一人，購金十四兩。
有（又）曰：
它邦人$_{036}$□□□□□□所興，毋（無）什伍將長者捕之，購金二兩。

[In the] statutes[623] it is said:
"Someone who arrests one member of a robber gang alive[624] shall be rewarded[625] with 14 ounces[626] of gold."[627]

---

620 For *zhen* and *wen* see footnote 562. The exact wording of the results of the forensic examination as well as the interagency enquiries is not recorded because they apparently did not provide information that was not already known from the statements.

621 For *ci* see footnote 564.

622 *Xiang* 降 "to submit, to surrender" (*Lipu* 2: 新降爲漢。"Xin submitted and became subject to the Han."; *QLZC* 38=*RCL* B 23: 寇降，以爲隸臣。"Enemies who surrender are made bond servant convicts." and *ZYS* 9: 楚時去亡，降爲漢。"At the time [of the rule] of Chu I ran away and absconded, submitted and became subject to the Han.").

623 For *lü* see footnote 556.

624 *Chan* 產 "alive" (*ENLL* 148: 能產捕群盜一人若斬二人，捧（拜）爵一級。"If someone is able to arrest one member of a gang of robbers or kill two of them, his rank is increased by one degree."; *ENLL* 430: 不幸流，或能產拯一人，購金二兩；拯死者，購一兩。"When unfortunately [there are persons] drowning and someone is able to pull one person out of the water alive, he is rewarded with two ounces [of gold]. If someone [is able to] pull a dead [person out of the water], he is rewarded with one ounce [of gold].").

625 For *gou* see footnote 502.

626 14 *liang* 兩 "ounces" (one *liang* was equivalent to 15.6 g according to Qiu Guangming 1992, 394–397) of gold corresponded to 8,064 cash during the Qin dynasty (one *liang*=576 cash). This calculation is based on two pieces of evidence from administrative records (*Liye* 8–60r: 貲三甲，爲錢四千三十二。"A fine of three suits of armour is [equal to]

It is furthermore said:
"[If] a person from another state [...] and someone arrests him, who was not levied[628] by [...] and is [also/therefore?] not member of a military unit of five or ten[629] commanded by lower or higher military leaders,[630] [the arresting

---

4,032 cash.") and a Qin mathematical manual (*Yuelu Shu* 082: 貲一甲，直（值）錢千三百卌四，直（值）金二兩一錘。"A fine of one suit of armour is worth 1,344 cash or two ounces (*liang*) and one *chui* of gold."; quoted and explained in Yu Zhenbo 2010, 36–38). This calculation accords with the total amount of 80,640 cash as reward for arresting ten members of a robber gang who robbed and killed people in the preceding case (cf. *Yuelu* WYZ 002 and 022).

627 For *jin* 金 referring to *huang jin* 黃金 "gold" as a means of payment during the Qin and Han dynasties see Lau and Lüdke 2012, footnote 893.

628 For a passage in Han statutes similar to the context of this case see *ENLL* 61: 徼外人來入爲盜者，要（腰）斬。吏所興能捕若斬一人，搴（拜）爵一級。不欲搴（拜）爵及非吏所興，購如律。"If people coming from outside the border enter [the Han territory] to commit robbery, they are to be cut in half at the waist. If [conscripts] levied by the officials accomplish to arrest or kill one [such] person, they are conferred one degree of rank. Those who do not wish to be conferred a rank and those who were not levied by the officials are to be rewarded according to the statutes." Cf. *Yuelu* WYZ 014–015.

629 *Shi* 什 and *wu* 伍 were the basic military units of ten and five soldiers in the Qin and Western Han army. These basic military units were probably connected with the local administrative units of five (*ENLL* 305) and ten neighbouring families, which had been established by chancellor Shang Yang in the course of his reforms in the mid-4th century BC (*Shiji* 68, 2230). The families of the same unit were mutually liable for any offences committed by their members; they also had to report them to the authorities under penalty (*ENLL* 201, 260). Likewise, the members of the military units for example had to report soldiers in their ranks who did not return from their deployment beyond the borders (*ENLL* 495). Soldiers had also to be grouped into units of five when put into action against bandits (*ENLL* 141: 吏將徒，追求盜賊，必伍之，盜賊以短兵殺傷其將及伍人，而弗能捕得，皆戍邊二歲。"Officials leading conscripts to pursue and search for bandits must organise them into units of five. When they (the units) are not able to arrest the bandits, although these killed or injured their commander or a member of their unit with short-range weapons (i.e. daggers, swords or pikes), they are all to perform two years of [additional] military service at the frontier.").

630 *Jiang zhang* 將長 "higher and lower commanders" (*FLDW* 208=*RCL* D 188: 可（何）如爲大痍？大痍者，支（肢）或未斷，及將長令二人扶出之，爲大痍。"What is a 'serious wound'? A serious wound is when a limb has perhaps not been completely severed, [but the injury] goes so far that the higher and lower commanders have to order two men to support him out [of the fray] – that is a serious wound." with note 5 and 6, where *jiang* and *zhang* are explained as commanders of military units of 100 resp. 5 men according to *Shangjunshu* 19, 34 [cf. Duyvendak 1928, 296]: 五人一屯長，百人一將。"For every five men is there a corporal, *tunzhang*, and for every hundred men a centurion, *jiang*."). For *jiang* in the sense "to lead/command" see footnote 509 above.

person] shall be rewarded with two ounces of gold."[631]

Finding of Fact

鞫之：
尸等產捕治、閬等告群盜盜殺傷$_{037}$好等。治等秦人，邦亡荊；閬等荊人。亡來入秦地，欲歸義。悔，不詣吏。以京州降爲秦後群$_{038}$☐皆審。

Finding of fact:[632]
Shi and his colleagues arrested Zhi, Lang and their accomplices alive and reported them for killing or injuring Hao and others in the act of committing theft as members of a robber gang. Zhi and his accomplices are men from Qin who absconded from the state to Jing. Lang and his accomplices are men from Jing. They absconded, came and entered the territory of Qin and wished to take refuge [under the Qin rule]. [Because] they had reservations, they did not appear before the officials. After Jingzhou had submitted and become [part of the territory of] Qin [...]. These are all established facts.[633]

Submission by Zhouling Prefecture – Concluding Formula

疑尸等購。它縣論。敢瀌（讞）之。

631 Two *liang* of gold corresponded to 1,152 cash during the Qin dynasty, cf. footnote 626 above. According to other statutory provisions from Qin and early Han times a reward of two *liang* was offered for arresting one offender who was to be punished with penal labour as mutilated or unmutilated earth or grain pounder convict (*FLDW* 135–137=*RCL* D 113–115; *ENLL* 137–138) or even more lenient penal labour or banishment (*Yuelu Lüling* 1738, 1928 cited according to Chen Songchang 2014a, 8). These punishments were normally stipulated for theft, but not for robbing and killing as members of a robber gang, the offences for which Lang and his accomplices in the present case were prosecuted (*Yuelu WYZ* 037–038). Unfortunately, the wording of the quoted statute is fragmentary and it is therefore not entirely clear what kind of offenders had to be arrested to receive the reward of two *liang*. At least the statute appears to refer to people from states other than Qin.

632 For *ju* see footnote 565.

633 The term *shen* 審 "to be factually correct/an established fact" usually concludes the summarised finding of fact (*ju* 鞫) in records of criminal proceedings and represents the responsible officials' assurance that the facts summarised by them are true (*Yuelu WYZ* 046, 061, 092, 105, 134, 140r, 141, 174, 176, 186, 205, 235; *Liye* 8–2015v, etc.; *FLDW* 53=*RCL* D 43; *ZYS* 6, 15, 23, 32, 47, 65, 72, 91, 106, 121, 157). *Shen* appears to be the antonym of *yi* 疑 "to be doubtful", see *Yuelu WYZ* 140: 鞫：譊刑審，妘殺疑。 "Finding of fact: That Nao injured [sb.] is an established fact; if Yun killed [sb.] is doubtful."

[However,] we are in doubt[634] about the [lawful] reward for Shi and his colleagues. In all other matters the prefecture has passed judgement.[635] We venture to submit [this case] for decision.[636]

Alternative Votes for Judgement

吏議：
以捕群盜律購尸等。
或曰：
以捕它邦人$_{039}$

[Missing slip]

The [responsible] officials deliver [the following] legal opinion:[637]
"Reward Shi and his colleagues according to the statutes on arresting members of a robber gang."
Some say:[638]
"[Reward them] according to the [statutes on] arresting men from other states [...]."[639]

634 Here the leading officials voice doubts about the appropriate reward, not about the punishment stipulated by law. For the comparable *yi zui* see footnote 582.

635 In a submission to the higher authorities, the phrase *ta xian lun* 它縣論 (ZYS 6, 15, 23, 33; *Yuelu* WYZ 093, 106, 135) usually followed the voicing of certain doubts by the prefectural office. It means that a decision by the higher authorities was only requested with regard to a certain doubtful aspect and that everything else (e.g. the punishment for other offenders brought to trial in the course of the investigation, see ZYS 90) had been or would be decided by the prefectural office itself. In this way the prefecture pointed out that it had fulfilled its official duties. See Zhang Jianguo 1999, 313; Ikeda 2002, 32 and 37, footnote 16; Momiyama 2006, 276 and 279, footnote 1 (referring to Gakushûin daigaku Kankan kenkyûkai 2002, 113); Lau and Lüdke 2012, footnote 610 as well as Zhou Minhua 2012, 87.

636 For *yan* and the phrase *gan yan zhi* see footnote 489.

637 For *li yi* see footnote 572.

638 For *huo yue* see footnote 573.

639 In the light of the first case, it is plausible that *li yi* 吏議 describes a proposal by the same authority that also has submitted the case, i.e. the prefecture, because the following *bao* 報 is done by provincial officials, not the highest authority (see *Yuelu* WYZ 040), cf. footnote 571. Here too, it seems unreasonable to assume that the provincial officials are responsible for both, the proposals for decision (*li yi*) as well as the final decision (*bao*) itself.

Response to the Submission by Nan Province (Decision)

廿五年六月丙辰朔己卯，南郡叚（假）守賈報州陵守綰、丞越。
子瀟（讞）：
求盜尸等捕秦男子治等四人、$_{040}$荊男子閬等十人，告群盜【盜】殺傷好等。治等秦人邦亡；閬等荊人。來歸義，行到州陵，悔$_{041}$☐□□□□□京州降爲秦，乃殺好等。疑尺〈尸〉等購。

In the 25th year on day *jimao*[640] of the sixth month with the first day *bingchen*, Jia, the temporary[641] governor[642] of Nan province,[643] gave a response[644] to the incumbent prefect of Zhouling, Wan, and vice prefect Yue.
You submitted [for decision]:
"The robber hunter Shi and his colleagues arrested Zhi and three other men from Qin as well as Lang and nine other men from Jing and reported them for injuring or killing Hao and others in the act of committing theft as members of a robber gang. Zhi and his accomplices are men from Qin who absconded from the state; Lang and his accomplices are men from Jing. They came to seek refuge [under the Qin rule], but when on their march they reached Zhouling, they had reservations [...] Jingzhou submitted and became [part of the territory of] Qin. Only then did they kill Hao and others. We are in doubt about the [lawful] reward for Shi and his colleagues."

瀟固有審矣。治等審秦人殹（也）；尸$_{042}$等當購金七兩。閬等，其荊人殹（也）；尸等當購金三兩。
它有令。$_{043}$

Your submission is reliable and unambiguous.[645] Zhi and his accomplices in fact are men from Qin; Shi and his colleagues are to be rewarded with seven ounces of gold[646] [for arresting them]. Lang and his accomplices are men from

---

640 This was the 24th day of the sixth month in the 25th year of King Zheng of Qin (cf. Zhang Peiyu 2007, 73; Li Zhonglin 2012, 65), i.e. 28/7/222 BC (Xu Xiqi 1997, 1240).

641 For *jia* in combination with a particular office see footnote 578.

642 The governor Gu/Jia already appeared in the first case (see *Yuelu* WYZ 025). For *shou* see footnote 579.

643 For Nan jun see footnote 580.

644 For *bao* see footnote 581.

645 For the phrase *yan gu you shen* see footnote 584.

646 Seven *liang* corresponded to 4,032 cash during the Qin dynasty, cf. footnote 626. This amount does not correspond to the statutory reward of 14 *liang* for arresting a member of a robber gang (cited in *Yuelu* WYZ 036), but it is equivalent to the reward for arresting offenders liable to the death penalty (see *Yuelu* WYZ 016, 021–022). Possibly Zhi and his

Jing; Shi and his colleagues are to be rewarded with three ounces of gold[647] [for arresting them]. For everything else there are ordinances.[648]

accomplices could not be classified as members of a robber gang, because their gang only consisted of four men (*Yuelu* WYZ 040, cf. the stipulations in *ENLL* 62, cf. *FLDW* 1–2=*RCL* D 1).

647 Three *liang* corresponded to 1,728 cash during the Qin dynasty, cf. footnote 626. This amount does not correspond to the statutory reward of two *liang* cited in *Yuelu* WYZ 036–037. The legal basis for granting a reward to the amount of three *liang* is still unknown. Chen Wei (2013b) reads *er liang* "two ounces" instead of *san liang*. This interpretation corresponds with *FLDW* 134–137=*RCL* D 112–115.

648 For *ling* see footnote 556.

Case I.3

In this case from 224 BC, two persons were prosecuted for participating in a grave robbery. Since the value of the misappropriated goods exceeded 660 cash, the offenders by law were to be sentenced to the most severe form of penal labour as tattooed earth pounder convicts. One of them, as holder of the second rank, was entitled to perform the mitigated version of this form of penal labour as a firewood gatherer convict. However, this case of participation in grave robbery was covered by an amnesty. Therefore, the offenders were exempted from punishment and became released persons (*shu ren*). It seems that such a pardon regularly had to be approved by the higher authorities. As this had apparently not been observed by the prefecture that had conducted the criminal proceedings, the governor, as its immediate superior, gave order to summarise the established facts and to submit the case to the governor's province agency for decision.

Complying with the governor's order, the prefecture inspected the records of the case in question. The convicted persons who had joined a band of vagrant absconders had neither originally committed grave robbery themselves nor conspired with the perpetrators: One of them remained in the hideout of the robbers as their cook, and the second only joined the gang long after they had dug up the grave mound. However, the gang afterwards informed the two about the grave robbery and gave them a share of the excavated clothes and bronze vessels, probably in order to prevent them from disclosing the robbery to the authorities. Three prefectures (Jiangling, Chanling and Liyang) cooperated in the investigation. One participant in the robbery was discovered when he tried to illegally sell bronze vessels that originated from the grave robbery. After the case was solved, the competent judicial officials were in no doubt about the punishment for the two accused participants. According to Qin law, anyone who had known about a theft and had received even a small part of the loot for himself was punished in the same way as the original thief – for the full amount stolen. The reason for submitting the case to the higher authorities apparently was the fact that the officials were not authorised to make a decision about exemption from punishment through amnesty.

Diplomatic Edition

•廿三年四月江陵丞文敢潚之廿三年九月庚子令下劾掾江陵獄上造敞士五$_{044}$
猩智人盜埱冢分臧得敞當耐鬼薪猩黥城旦遝戊午赦爲庶人鞫$_{045}$審潚$_{046}$

 | DOI 10.1163/9789004315655_011

•今視故獄廿一年五月丁未獄史窣詣士五去疾⌞號曰載銅•去疾⌞號曰號乘軺$_{047}$之醴陽與去疾買銅錫冗募樂一男子所載欲買得它如窣$_{048}$
•執一男=子=士五定名猩$_{049}$
□□□□□□□樂爲庸取銅草中得它如號等$_{050}$
•孱陵獄史民詣士五達與猩同獄將從猩•達曰亡與猩等獵漁不利負責$_{051}$冗募上造祿等從達等漁謂達⌞祿等亡居荑道界中有廬舍⌞欲毆從祿⌞達$_{052}$等從祿⌞猩獨居舍爲養達與僕徒時等謀埱冢不告猩冢已斲分器乃告$_{053}$猩⌞蒔等不分猩⌞達獨分猩它如猩•猩曰達等埱冢不與猩謀分器蒔等不分$_{054}$猩⌞達獨私分猩=爲樂等庸取銅草中它如達及前•醴陽丞悝曰冗募上造敞$_{055}$**[Missing slip]**埱冢者錫到舍達已分錫⌞達謂敞已到前不得錫今冢中尚有器=已出買敞所⌞時$_{056}$告達請與敞出餘器分敞達曰發冢一歲矣今斲敞乃來不可與敞⌞達等相將之水旁$_{057}$有頃來告敞曰與敞=來後前者爲二面敞爲一面敞曰若皆行到冢得錫敞買及受分覺$_{058}$亡得它如達等•達言如敞•達等埱冢不與猩敞謀得衣器告猩敞受分臧過六百六十錢$_{059}$⧄如辤•鞫之達等埱冢不與猩敞謀⧄衣器告猩敞受分臧過六百六十錢得猩當黥$_{060}$城旦敞耐鬼薪遝戊午赦審⌞江陵守感丞暨史同論赦猩敞爲庶人⌞達等令別論敢潚之$_{061}$

Edition and Translation

Submission by Jiangling Prefecture – Introductory Formula

廿三年四月，江陵丞文敢潚（讞）之：

In the fourth month[649] of the 23rd year, vice prefect[650] Wen of Jiangling[651] [prefecture] ventures to submit[652] [the following case] for decision:

Order by the Superior Governor to Submit the Original Case for Decision

廿三〈二〉年九月庚子，令下劾：
掾（錄）江陵獄：上造敞、士五（伍）猩智（知）人盜埱冢，分臧（贓）。得。敞當耐鬼薪，猩黥城旦。遝戊午赦，爲庶人。
鞫$_{045}$審，潚（讞）。$_{046}$

---

649 The fourth month in the 23rd year of the reign of King Zheng of Qin lasted from April 29th to May 27th 224 BC (Xu Xiqi 1997, 1236; cf. Zhang Peiyu 2007, 73 and Li Zhonglin 2012, 65).

650 For *cheng* see footnote 488.

651 Jiangling 江陵 was a prefecture (*xian* 縣), which had been established by the Qin after the conquest of the Chu 楚 capital Ying 郢 in 278 BC on the territory of the seized residence of the Chu kings (*Shiji* 129, 3267; 5, 213; *Yuelu* WYZ 044, 061–062, 097; *Liye* 8–1328, 8–1444r/v, 16–52; *Yushu* 8; ENLL 449; Hou Xiaorong 2009, 397). Its administrative seat was located near present Jingzhou, Hubei (*Lishi dituji* vol. II, 11–12, 5②).

652 For *yan* and the phrase *gan yan zhi* see footnote 489.

It was the 22nd year, the ninth month, the day *gengzi*,[653] when an order was given to send down[654] the [following] *ex-officio* charge:
"[I, the governor,] inspected[655] the [following] criminal case[656] from Jiangling:

---

653 This was the 29th day of the ninth month in the 22nd year of King Zheng of Qin, i.e. 01/11/225 BC (Xu Xiqi 1997, 1234; cf. Zhang Peiyu 2007, 73 and Li Zhonglin 2012, 65). The year *nian san* 廿三 in the manuscript is likely to be a scribal error because in the ninth month of the 23rd year of the reign of King Zheng there was no day *gengzi* (Xu Xiqi 1997, 1236; cf. Zhang Peiyu 2007, 73 and Li Zhonglin 2012, 65) and the *ex-officio* charge which initiated the criminal proceedings must have predated the submission of the case to the higher authorities for submission. Therefore most probably the 22nd year was meant here.

654 For *xia he* 下劾 cf. ZYS 134–135: 氏曰：刻（劾）下，與脩（攸）守媱、丞魁治。"Shi stated: 'When the *ex-officio* charge [of the province] was handed down, I tried [the case] together with the incumbent prefect of You, Yao, and vice prefect Kui.'" In administrative documents of the early imperial period *xia* 下 (in MC *qu sheng*) is always used for "handing down documents" from superiors to subordinate agencies (ZYS 125, 129 [*yu shi da fu* to province]; ENLL 502 [*xiang guo* to *nei shi*]; 8–155 [vice prefect to *shao nei*]; probably also in 16–5v). It is unlikely that *ling xia* here occurs in the sense "to issue a decree/ordinance (by the ruler)" (*Shiji* 5, 202; 6, 255; 30, 1433; 121, 3119; *Yushu* 2 [cf. translation in footnote 556]; *Hanshu* 22, 1032; 94B, 3803). Likewise, *xia* 下 in the meaning "to hand sb. over (to the relevant/competent officials) for sentencing" (Cang Xiuliang 1996, 27: *Hanshu* 86, 3489; *xia li* 下吏 in *Hanshu* 31, 1823) or "to hand sb. over to prison in order to investigate his offence" (*xia yu* 下獄 in *Hanshu* 72, 3062) does not make sense in this context. *Ling* was also not used to refer to a prefect in legal documents addressed to the superior authorities, especially not without mentioning his name and place of office. For this reason, *ling* in connection with *xia he* should be translated impersonally as "order was given to send down an *ex-officio* charge". For *he* see footnote 545. The present case was apparently submitted to the higher authorities by order of the province agency.

655 The usage of *yuan* 掾, which could be identified as an orthographic variant of *lu* 錄 "to inspect (documents such as case-files, accounts, proposals for a judgement)" (Gao Heng 2008, 369), suggests that the authorities at the province level of administration, e.g. the governor, inspected cases in the course of routine checks as in ZYS 75: 淮陽守行縣掾（錄）新郪獄。"The governor of the province of Huaiyang on a tour around the prefectures inspected criminal cases from Xinqi/the remand prison in Xinqi." In the *Zou yan shu* case the governor ordered a retrial (*fu* 覆/復). The same appears to be the case in the present passage. In legal manuscripts of Qin and early Han times, *lu* usually takes the objects *yu* 獄 "criminal case/remand prison?" (*lu yu* 掾獄 in ZYS 75, 144, 146; identical with *lu yu* 錄獄 in *Hanshu* 81, 3353), *ji* 計 "accounts" (for examples see foonote 863) or *dang* 當 "proposal for judgement" (ENLL 396–397: 二千石官丞謹掾當論，乃告縣道官以從事。"The vice governor carefully inspects the proposal, passes judgement and accordingly informs the offices of prefectures and marches how to deal with the matter."). For a detailed palaeographic and semantic analysis of *lu* and the institution *lu qiu tu* 錄囚徒 "inspect the remand prisoners" the beginnings of which reach back to Western Han times

Chang, holder of the second rank,[657] and rank-and-file man[658] Xing knew[659] that someone had dug up[660] a tomb[661] in order to steal,[662] and shared[663] the misappropriated goods.[664] They were caught.[665] Chang was by law to be shaved[666]

(*Hanshu* 71, 3036 [86 BC] with commentary by Yan Shigu; 81, 3353 [32 BC]; 86, 3482) see Lau and Lüdke 2012, footnote 972.

656 For the term *yu* see footnote 568.

657 For the rank *shang zao* see footnote 494.

658 For *shi wu* see footnote 495.

659 *Zhi* 智 for *zhi* 知. This word indicated that somebody knew about an offence. If the person concerned did not report this offence to the authorities, he or she was liable to punishment. The support of an offence could be treated in the same way as the offence itself; it was, however, not a general rule that support to commit an offence resulted in the same punishment. For each offence, separate rules determined if, and to which degree, aid given with or without knowledge was culpable. It is remarkable that most of the rules that also discussed knowledge were concerned with theft (*dao* 盜). Sharing illegal proceeds with knowledge of the offence resulted in punishment for theft. The whole amount stolen was taken into account for the sentence for each party involved, even if the amount received by one party did not amount to one cash, the minimim amount necessary for regular punishment (*FLDW* 9=*RCL* D 8: 甲盜，臧（贓）直（值）千錢，乙智（知）其盜，受分臧（贓）不盈一錢，問乙可（何）論？同論。 "A committed theft; the value of the misappropriated goods is 1,000 cash. B, knowing that A has stolen them, accepts a share of the misappropriated goods [to the value of] less than one cash. Question: How is B to be sentenced? He is to be sentenced in the same way as A.").

660 *Chu* 埱 "to dig up, excavate" (*FLDW* 28=*RCL* D 23; *FZS* 76=*RCL* E 22). *Chu* was synonymous with *fa* 發 (see *dao fa zhong* 盜發冢 in *ENLL* 66) and *jue* 掘 (*Shiji* 129, 3282 [cf. Watson 1993, vol. II, 453]: 掘冢，姦事也。 "Excavating graves is a criminal offence."), two terms that were later used for the offence of grave robbery.

661 *Zhong* 冢 "burial mound" as in *ENLL* 66: 盜發冢[...]皆磔。 "Opening graves for the purpose of theft [...] is, in all cases, punished with execution by quartering."

662 For *dao* see footnotes 541, 557 and 795.

663 *Fen* 分 "to share" (*FLDW* 9=*RCL* D 8; *ENLL* 57: 謀遣人盜，若教人可盜所，人即以其言□□□□□及智（知）人盜與分，皆與盜同灋。 "For plotting theft and for dispatching another person to commit theft, or for instructing another person about a place where [sth.] can be stolen and also for this [other] person who then according to this advice [...] shares [misappropriated goods] with another person, knowing that this person had stolen [them], without exception the same legal rules as for theft apply."). According to Qin law, someone who had knowledge about a theft and received even only a small part of the loot for himself was punished in the same way as the thief for the full amount stolen (*FLDW* 9=*RCL* D 8; *FLDW* 17, 18=*RCL* D 15, 16).

664 For *zang* see footnote 592.

665 For *de* see footnote 524.

666 For *nai* see also footnote 574. In the present case, *nai* is a characteristic of the privileged *gui xin* 鬼薪 convicts (*FLDW* 110=*RCL* D 92; *Yuelu WYZ* 061; *Liye* 8–805; *ZYS* 158–159).

and made a firewood gatherer convict;[667] Xing was by law to be tattooed and made an earth pounder convict.[668] [However] they were [instead] included[669] in the amnesty[670] of [day?] *wuwu* and were made released persons.[671] [I, the

667 *Gui xin* 鬼薪 "firewood gatherer" is a term for male convicts (*QLZC* 5=*RCL* C 3; *ZYS* 158; *Yuelu WYZ* 061, 244; *Liye* 8–533, 8–683r, 8–805, 8–1279, 8–1434r, 8–1515r, 8–1566v, 8–1631, 8–2034r, 8–2156, 8–2423; *Hanshu* 2, 85; cf. *FLDW* 113=*RCL* D 94) who, as holders of the second or a higher rank, have committed an offence punishable by the most severe form of penal labour as tattooed earth pounder convicts (*qing cheng dan* 黥城旦). Holders of the respective ranks belonged to a group of privileged persons who were automatically granted a mitigated version of the most severe form of penal labour (*ENLL* 82: 上造、上造妻以上[...]有罪，其當刑及當爲城旦舂者，耐以爲鬼薪白粲。 "If holders of the second or a higher rank or their wives [...] commit an offence which by law is to be punished with mutilation and penal labour as an earth or grain pounder convict, they are [instead] to be shaved and to be made firewood gatherer or rice sifter convicts."). Chang who held the second rank (*shang zao* 上造) (*Yuelu WYZ* 044) was therefore entitled to perform the mitigated version of penal labour as a firewood gatherer.

668 *Qing cheng dan* 黥城旦. *Qing* 黥 was a mutilation punishment which consisted in tattooing the convict's forehead with black ink. During Qin times, this mutilation was always combined with the most severe form of penal labour as a male earth pounder or female grain pounder convict (*cheng dan chong* 城旦舂) (*Longgang* 108, 70; *FLDW* 1, 33, 35, 37, 48, 86, 119, 167=*RCL* D 1, 27, 28, 59, 71, 93, 99, 146; *Yuelu WYZ* 060–061, 087, 094; *ZYS* 99, 158, 182; *Shiji* 8, 255). This punishment was retained in early Han times (*ZYS* 27, 31, 47–48) until the abolishment of mutilation in 167 BC (*Hanshu* 23, 1099). For consciously accepting a share of stolen goods, the same rules as for theft itself applied (*ENLL* 57). Therefore, the punishment in the present case must be based on the value of the stolen burial objects, which exceeded 660 cash (*ENLL* 55: 盜臧（贓）直（值）過六百六十錢，黥爲城旦舂。 "If, in cases of theft, the value of the misappropriated goods exceeds 660 cash, [the offender] is tattooed and made an earth or grain pounder convict.").

669 *Ta she* 遝赦. *Ta* 遝 (*GSR* 678e) *(g-)lˤəp, an older variant of *dai* 逮 (*GSR* 509c) *(g-)lət-s<**(g-)lˤəp-s, was frequently used in manuscripts from Qin and early Han times and either stands for a verb meaning "come to, reach, include, cover", a preposition (e.g. *dai ye* 夜 in *Zuo* Ai 6,809,2; *dai ri* 日 in *Li* 8, 1293a; *dai an* 闇 in *Li* 24, 1442c), or a conjunction derived from the verb with the meaning "when/then it came to the time of" (*Zuo* Cheng 13,379,18–19; Ding 4,752,14; *Shiji* 72, 2326; 101, 2742). *Ta* in the compound *ta she*, however, is not used impersonally (*Yuelu WYZ* 203–204, 207). The subject is the person who is granted amnesty, as in the synonymous phrases *hui she* 會赦 (*Shiji* 120, 3110; 122, 3135; *Hanshu* 1B, 54; 7, 230; 50, 2321; 51, 2366; 53, 2414; 53, 2431; 60, 2662; 67, 2914; 74, 3134; 76, 3204; 76, 3229; 83, 3397; 86, 3491; 90, 3650; 90, 3667; *FLDW* 153=*RCL* D 131; *ENLL* 148–149) and *yu she* 遇赦 (*Hanshu* 45, 2176; 49, 2287). For *ta* 遝 cf. footnote 881.

670 *She* 赦. For amnesties during the Qin period see Sun Kai 2004, 347–348 (in 286 BC acc. to *Shiji* 5, 212; in 281, 280 and 279 BC acc. to *Shiji* 5, 213). Whereas his two predecessors declared a general amnesty ([*da*] *she zui ren* [大]赦罪人) on the occasion of their enthronement in 250 and 249 BC (*Shiji* 5, 219), and at least two amnesties are attested for his successor, the Second Emperor in 209 BC (Xu Kuang cited in a commentary to *Shiji* 6,

governor, hereby ask the responsible officials to] find the facts, [assure] that they are established and submit the case [to the higher authorities for decision]."[672]

Original Case – Initiation of Criminal Proceedings

今視故獄：
廿一年五月丁未，獄史窣詣士五（伍）去疾、號曰：
載銅。

Now[673] [we] inspected the former criminal case:[674]

---

266) and 208 BC (*Shiji* 6, 270), there is no evidence of a general amnesty during the reign of King Zheng of Qin, the later Qin Shihuang. As emperor he apparently only granted amnesties to individuals such as Zhao Gao, whom Meng Yi found guilty of an offence punishable by death (*Shiji* 88, 2566). See also *FLDW* 37, 125–126, 153=*RCL* D 29, 105, 131; *FZS* 6–7, 13, 40–41=*RCL* E 4, 5, 15; *Wei li zhi dao* 3.1; *ENLL* 148–149; *Xuanquan* 11: 赦前有罪，後發覺勿治。"If an offence is committed before an amnesty and only afterwards discovered, the offence shall not be tried." For amnesties during Han times in the garrisons at Edsin Gol cf. Shen Gang 2008, 224. Nothing is known about the mentioned *wuwu*-amnesty or about amnesties marked by cyclical signs designating days, months or years during the Qin rule before and after the unification of the Chinese empire.

671 *Shu ren* 庶人 refers to persons who were released from bondage. This status was granted to manumitted male (*ENLL* 382; *Hanshu* 4, 130) and female slaves (*ENLL* 162, 385), mostly after the death of their master, or to released penal labour convicts (*Hanshu* 23, 1099; *Longgang mudu*; *QLSZ* 151, 156=*RCL* A 72, 91; *ENLL* 205, 436), *viz.* offenders who were exempted from punishment with simultaneous loss of their rank (*Shiji* 18, 919; 20, 1062; *Hanshu* 65, 2852; 74, 3144; 83, 3396) and those who were included in an amnesty (*FLDW* 125=*RCL* D 105; *Juyan xinjian* E.P.T5:105). With regard to land allocation, *shu ren* were treated in the same way as *gong zu* 公卒 and *shi wu* 士伍 (*ENLL* 312, 316). Offspring of a female *shu ren* and a male slave retain the status of *shu ren* (*ENLL* 189). Cf. Lau and Lüdke 2012, footnote 656 as well as Hafner 2012.

672 The same sequence of finding the facts (*ju* 鞫), assuring that they are established (*shen* 審) and submitting the case in question to the higher authorities (*yan* 讞) is also used in *Yuelu WYZ* 064 and *FLDW* 53=*RCL* D 43. Cf. also the abbreviated version *ju shen* (*Liye* 8–1344; *Yuelu WYZ* 141). For the three terms *ju*, *shen* and *yan*, see in detail footnotes 565, 633 and 489.

673 *Jin* 今 introduces the actual proceedings (*Yuelu WYZ* 177, 190, 202; *ZYS* 18, 37, 69, 106, 129, 162, 175, 183, 189) in contrast to former criminal proceedings regarding the same case or precedents. See Lau and Lüdke 2012, footnotes 672 and 1343.

674 *Shi gu yu* 視故獄 indicates the review of former criminal proceedings, cf. *shi yu* 視獄 (*Yuelu WYZ* 064), *fu shi qi yu* 覆視其獄 (*Yuelu WYZ* 173) and *fu shi qi gu yu* 覆視其故獄 (*ZYS* 99).

In the 21st year, in the fifth month, on day *dingwei*,[675] the judicial secretary[676] Su presented[677] the rank-and-file men Qu Ji and Hao [to the authorities] and stated:
"They transported bronze [vessels] on a carriage."

Original Case – First Stage of Interrogation

去疾、號曰：
號乘軺$_{047}$之醴陽。與去疾買銅錫（賜）冗募樂一男子所。載欲買（賣），得。
它如䇞。$_{048}$

Qu Ji and Hao stated:
"Hao went to Liyang[678] driving a small carriage.[679] Together with Qu Ji he bought bronze vessels[680]

675 This was the 28th day of the fifth month in the 21st year of the reign of King Zheng of Qin with the first day *gengchen* (cf. Zhang Peiyu 2007, 73 and Li Zhonglin 2012, 65), i.e. 17/07/226 BC (Xu Xiqi 1997, 1232).

676 For (*yu*) *shi* see footnote 539.

677 For *yi* see footnote 496.

678 Liyang 醴陽. The name of this prefecture is not found in Han dynastic histories or in a list of prefectures contained among early Han statutes (*ENLL* 443, 447–460). However, it also appears in other Qin (*Liye* 8–761, 8–2319) and Western Han manuscripts (*ZYS* 69–70 and *Hedijian* 222, where Liyang is mentioned as being located between the prefectures of Yicheng 宜成 und Jingling 竟陵 in the Changjiang river basin). On a wood tablet dated to the early years of the reign of Emperor Wu (around 140–129 BC), Liyang is referred to as a prefecture of Nan province (*Songbai mudu* 35r.1/3, 35v.1). For the controversial discussion on the location of Liyang see Lau and Lüdke 2012, footnote 935. Hou Xiaorong (2009, 428–429) assigns Liyang to the province of Dongting.

679 *Yao* 軺 (*Guan* 73, 359), also *yao che* 軺車 (*Shiji* 100, 2729; *Longgang* 54; manuscripts from the Fenghuangshan tombs no. 8, 167 and 168 cited according to *Sanjian* 641, 929 and 927), referred to a small two-wheeled carriage to which one horse was harnessed (Shen Gang 2008, 171: *Juyan* 25.2 and 341.25; Sun Ji 2011, 113 with illustration 24–1). Cf. a quotation from statutes according to the commentary of Ru Chun to *Shiji* 1B, 57, where *yao che* is said to be drawn by one or two horses.

680 *Yang* 錫 occurs with the meaning "horse's (engraved) bronze frontlet" in texts from the Western Zhou and Spring and Autumn period (*Odes* 261,2; *Zuo* Huan 2,38,2). Here, it is used in a compound together with a word signifying a kind of metal, *tong* 銅 "copper". For the following reasons, *yang* 錫 can be interpreted as a writing error or graphic variant of *xi* 錫 "tin". First, in the Qin manuscripts from Shuihudi the phonophoric components *yi* 易 and *yang* 昜 sometimes cannot be differentiated clearly or were confused (cf. Zhang Shouzhong 1994, 151 [易], 95 [賜] and 212 [陽]). Second, there is evidence for the occurrence of the compound *tong xi* 銅錫 in received literature from Han times (*Shiji* 10, 433;

from[681] one temporarily recruited[682] man [named] Le.[683] We loaded them

---

Hanshu 24B, 1153 [cf. Swann 1950, 233]; *Lunheng* 35, 123). As it is obvious that the copper (*tong* 銅) and tin (written as *yang* 鍚) mentioned in the present case come from a tomb robbery, the haul of which is later referred to collectively either as *yang* 鍚 (*Yuelu* WYZ 056, 058) or *qi* 器 "vessels" (*Yuelu* WYZ 053, 056–057, 059–060), *yang* probably does not only refer to tin, but more generally to the burial offerings (made of metal). For *xi* 錫 (GSR 850n) as a common loan graph for *ci* 賜 (GSR 850t) in the sense "to bestow; gift" see footnote 705 below.

681 In legal manuscripts from Qin and early Han times *suo* 所 is a postposition that marks the recipient or giver as object after those verbs of transmitting which take two objects. It is used instead of a preposition like *yu* 於 in the following way:

1) Verbs meaning "to buy" or "to sell", respectively "to loan/borrow"
Yuelu WYZ 163: 去買（賣）行道者所。 "[I, Tong,] went off to sell [the stolen clothes and tools] to people travelling on the road."
Yuelu WYZ 048: 與去疾買銅鍚（賜）冗募樂一男子所。 "Together with Qu Ji he bought bronze vessels from one temporarily recruited man [named] Le."
Yuelu WYZ 056: 器巳（已）出，買（賣）敞所。 "After these [vessels] were taken out, he would sell them to me, Chang."
ZYS 8: 買婢媚士五（伍）點所。 "[I, Lu,] bought the female slave Mei from the rank-and-file man Dian."
ZYS 10: 賣祿（祿）所。 "[Dian] sold [me, Mei,] to Lu."
ZYS 51: 順等自贖甑所。"Shun and the other [slaves] redeemed themselves from Zeng."
QLSZ 126=RCL A 74: 官府叚（假）公車牛者□□□叚（假）人所。 "Government workshops, which loan government carts and oxen, [...] and loan [them] to somebody."

2) Verbs meaning "to say" or "to report"
ZYS 40–41: 即告池所。 "Then [I, Jun,] reported [my former slave] to Chi [for having absconded]."

3) Verbs meaning "to hand over"
Yuelu WYZ 210–211: 君子子癸詣私書矰所。"Gui, the son of a *jun zi*, presented a private letter to me, Zeng."

4) Verb *you* 有 "to have"
Yuelu WYZ 114: 沛有子媛所四人。 "I, Pei, have four children with Wan."
ZYS 29: 符有名數明所。 "Fu had a [household] registration with Ming."

5) Verb *bu xiao* 不孝 "to be unfilial/behave unfilialy"
FZS 51=RCL E 18: 辭曰：甲親子，誠不孝甲所。 "His statement ran: 'I am A's son, I have been truly unfilial towards A.'"

682 *Rong mu* 冗募 "to be recruited for a temporary task" (QLZC 35=RCL C 22: 冗募歸，辭曰日已備，致未來、不如辭，貲日四月居邊。 "When those who were recruited for a temporary task return home and the statement is made: 'The days have been completed', whereas the documents have not yet come or do not agree with the statement, the fine is four months station at the frontier per day."). The meaning of *rong* 冗 is disputed, cf. footnote 6 to RCL A 7 and footnote 3 to *Liye* 8–60 in Chen Wei 2012a, 43–44. *Rong* seems to refer to temporary employment or casual work if there is need for such (*Hanshu* 24B, 1180

[on the carriage] and wanted to sell them. [Then] we were caught."
Everything else corresponded to [the statement of] Su.

執一男子，男子士五（伍），定名猩。049

We arrested[684] one man, he is a rank-and-file man. His officially registered[685] name is "Xing".

[cf. Swann 1950, 339]: 民浮游無事，出夫布一匹。其不能出布者，宂作，縣官衣食之。"Unsettled people wandering from place to place without [permanent] employment paid as tax for one square holding, one roll of cloth. Those unable to offer cloth were temporarily assigned to work, and were dressed and fed by the government."; *QLSZ* 50=*RCL* A 12: 雖有母而與其母宂居公者，亦稟之。"[As to infants] although they have a mother and they are with her while she is temporarily assigned to work for the government, they are also given rations."; *QLSZ* 151=*RCL* A 72: 百姓有母及同牲（生）爲隸妾，非適（謫）罪也而欲爲宂邊五歲[...]以免一人爲庶人，許之。"If commoners have a mother or a sister who is a bond woman, and they are not liable to punishment and wish to be assigned to the frontier for five years [...] in order to free one person to become a released person, this is permitted."). In connection with officials *rong* refers to (non-permanent?) auxiliaries in contrast to the head of a department (*QLSZ* 14, 80, 165=*RCL* A 7, 40, 83; *XL* 2, 52=*RCL* B 2, 25). *Mu* 募 means "to recruit/enlist volunteers with the promise of rewards, exemption from punishment, release from penal labour or manumission" (*Shiji* 5, 212 [cf. Nienhauser I (1994), 117]: 秦出其人，募徙河東賜爵，赦罪人遷之。"Qin expelled [Henei's] people, recruited people [of Qin] to move to Hedong with awards of rank, or pardoned convicts and sent them there."; *Shiji* 11, 443 [cf. Nienhauser II (2002), 204]: 募徙陽陵，予錢二十萬。"[The emperor] recruited [people] to move to Yangling, providing 200,000 cash [for the move]."; *Shiji* 30, 1419 [cf. Watson 1993, vol. II, 62]: 於是募民能輸及轉粟於邊者拜爵，爵得至大庶長。"[The government] then recruited people [to supply grain], conferring ranks to those who were prepared to send grain to the frontier. The ranks [varied with the amount of grain] but could reach as high as the eighteenth rank, called *da shu zhang*."; *Hanshu* 7, 221 [cf. Dubs II (1944), 157]: 募民徙雲陵，賜錢田宅。"Common people were recruited to move to Yunling, and [those who did so] were granted money, fields, and residences."; *Hanshu* 12, 353 [cf. Dubs III (1955), 73]: 募徙貧民，縣次給食。至徙所，賜田宅什器[...]。"Poor people were recruited to move [there]. In the prefectures where they lodged [as they were moving], they were given food, and when they reached the places to which they were supposed to move, they were granted fields, residences, tools [...].").

683 *Le/yue* 樂 is most likely a personal name because it later occurs in the phrase *Le deng* 樂等 "Le and others" (*Yuelu WYZ* 055). As a suffix *deng* only occurs after personal names in Qin and Han legal manuscripts (*Liye*, *FZS*, *ZYS*). *Yue* 樂 could also refer to musicians (*Zuo* Zhao 17,665,11; otherwise *nü yue* 女樂 "female musician" as in *Zuo* Xiang 11,450,17; Zhao 28,725,16; *Hanfei* 10, 40) who were also called *yue ren* 樂人 (*ZYS* 99).

684 *Zhi* 執 "to arrest" (*FLDW* 96=*RCL* D 80; *FZS* 16, 50–51, 85=*RCL* E 7, 18, 23), later replaced by the term *bu* 捕, cf. footnote 505.

685 *Ding* 定 "to determine, record (name, occupation/status, place of residence, etc. of a person)" (*FZS* 6, 13, 40, 44=*RCL* E 4, 5, 15, 16 [cf. footnote 28 to *RCL* A 19]; *Liye* 8–198r; cf. *FZS*

【猩曰】：
□□□□□樂，爲庸。取（聚）銅草（皂）中。得。
它如號等。050

[Xing stated]:
"[...] Le, by whom I was hired as labourer.[686] I stored[687] the bronze [vessels] in the pen.[688] [Later] I was caught."
Everything else corresponded to [the statements of] Hao and the others.

孱陵獄史民詣士五（伍）達。與猩同獄，將從猩。

The judicial secretary of Chanling[689] [prefecture], Min, presented the rank-and-file man Da [to the authorities]. [Da] is put on trial together[690] with Xing.

96–97=*RCL* E 6; *Liye* 8–136r). For this purpose, the entries in the relevant household registers were to be checked and/or changed, if necessary, see *ENLL* 322: 代戶，貿賣田宅，鄉部、田嗇夫、吏留弗爲定籍，盈一日，罰金各二兩。 "When [the head of] the household is replaced and fields and residence are sold, but the overseer of the district sector and the fields and [further] officials delay and fail to record [the change] in the registers for a whole day, each of them is fined two ounces of gold." Therefore, *ding ming* 定名 with the attributive *ding* used in the introduction of an accused (*Yuelu WYZ* 158, 223) should be translated as "officially registered name".

686 *Yong* 庸 (*GSR* 1185x) as well as its graphic variant *yong* 傭 (*GSR* 1185y) referred to "hired labourers" (*Shiji* 48, 1949; 100, 2733; *Hanfei* 49, 340; *Yuelu WYZ* 159; *Liye* 8–2015r). The phrase *wei ren yong* 爲人庸 (*Yuelu WYZ* 143–144) should be translated either as "become sb.'s/a private hired labourer" or "be hired by sb." (cf. *Yuelu WYZ* 055; *ZYS* 111). Cf. also Lao Gan 1951, 77–87.

687 *Qu* 取 (*GSR* 131a) writes the homeophonous *ju* 聚 (*GSR* 131k) (cf. Feng and Deng 2006, 153; Gao and Dong 1997, 362). *Ju* occurred in combination with different kinds of valuables in the meaning "to pile up, amass" (*Zuo* Xiang 24,505,7; *Hanshu* 24A, 1117; *Guan* 15, 80) or as "to collect, bring together; store" (*Kongjiapo Rishu* 109; *Zuo* Zhao 20,680,6).

688 *Cao* 草 (*GSR* 1049b) probably represents the homeophonous *zao* 皂 (*GSR* 1054a) (cf. *zao* 早 for *zao* 皂 in *QLSZ* 5=*RCL* A 2 and *Wuwei yijian* 71 [Bai Yulan 2012, 106]). *Zao* could mean "pen, fold" (*Guan* 81, 406) or "manger, trough" (*Zhuang* 9, 56–57; *Shiji* 83, 2477). Xing was obviously hired as a groom and, at his workplace, used either an empty pen or a manger for hiding the stolen bronze vessels.

689 Chanling 孱陵 is a prefecture, which belonged to the province of Dongting during the Qin dynasty (*Liye* 16–52; Hou Xiaorong 2009, 427). Its administrative seat was located to the west of present Gong'an, Hubei. According to Han sources, Chanling was situated in the province of Wuling 武陵 (*Hanshu* 28A, 1594; *Lishi dituji* vol II, 22/23, 6⑤) or in Nan province (*Songbai mudu* 35r.1/3, 35v.1 [dated to around 140–129 BC]) during the Western Han period.

690 In *tong yu* 同獄, *tong* seems to be used as adverb "together" and *yu* verbally in the sense "to put on trial" (*FLDW* 107=*RCL* D 90), cf. *yu* in the meaning "to litigate" (*Zhouli* 34, 870c; *Guoyu* 1.18/11/4). *Tong yu* could also be interpreted as a verb-object construction "[person

He shall join[691] Xing [as accused].

達曰：
亡，與猩等獵漁。不利，負責（債）。$_{051}$冗募上造祿等從達等漁，謂達：祿等亡居荑（夷）道界中，有廬舍。欲毆（驅）從祿。達$_{052}$等從祿。猩獨居舍爲養。達與僕徒時（蒔）等謀埱冢，不告猩。冢巳（已）勶（徹），分器，乃告$_{053}$猩。蒔等不分猩，達獨分猩。
它如猩。

Da stated:
"I absconded[692] and went hunting and fishing with Xing and others. It did not yield profit,[693] and I owed debts.[694] Lu, holder of the second rank, who was temporarily recruited, and his accomplices followed us to go fishing and said to me: 'We absconded [from our assignment, and now] live inside the borders[695] of Yidao[696] [march] and we have a field cottage[697] [to stay at]. We wish that

---

A]與[person B]同[object]". In legal texts, *fa* 法, *zui* 罪, *lei* 類, *lun* 論 and *ju* 居 occur as objects. In such cases, *yu* is used as a noun in the same way as *che* 車, *zhou* 舟, *yuan* 轅, *gong* 功 or *yi* 意 in other examples of this construction from received literature. *Tong* is then used as a verb with the meaning "to share" followed by a noun or adverbially in front of a stative verb (*Zuo* Xiang 11,450,11: 載書曰：凡我同盟，毋蘊年，毋壅利，毋保姦，毋留慝，救災患，恤禍亂，同好惡，奬王室。 "The words of the covenant were: 'All we who covenant together agree not to hoard up the produce of good years, not to shut one another out from advantages, not to protect traitors, not to shelter criminals. [We agree to] aid one another in disasters and calamities, have compassion on one another in seasons of misfortune and disorder, to share [the same] likes and dislikes, and to support the royal house.'").

691 *Jiang cong* 將從 "to join sb." (*Hanshi waizhuan* 2.1/7/11: 吾將從子而歸。 "I will join you and return home.").

692 For *wang* see footnote 612.

693 *Li* 利 here in the sense "to yield (financial) profit" (*Hanshu* 78, 3275). For *li* as "to be eager for/to, to desire" see footnote 515.

694 *Fu ze* (*zhai*) 負責（債） "to owe debts" (QLSZ 84=RCL A 41, QLSZ 136=RCL A 68: 作務及賈而負責（債）者，不得代。 "Owners of workshops as well as traders who owe debts are not allowed replacement."). Cf. footnote 971.

695 For *jie zhong* see footnote 511.

696 Yidao 荑道, later written 夷道, was a march (*dao* 道) within Nan province (*Hanshu* 28A, 1566; ZYS 1; ENLL 457; *Songbai mudu* 35r.1/3, 35v.1 [dated to around 140–129 BC]; *Lishi dituji* vol. II, 22/23, 5⑤; Hou Xiaorong 2009, 402) near present Yidu, Hubei.

697 *Lu she* 廬舍 "field cottage" (*Hanshu* 24A, 1119 [cf. Swann 1950, 117]: 餘二十畮以爲廬舍。 "The remaining twenty acres [of the royal domain] was reserved for cottages in which dwelt [the eight families while they worked the land during spring and summer]."; ENLL 4: 賊燔民室屋廬舍、積取（聚），黥爲城旦舂。 "For setting fire to people's

you go on a raid[698] with us.' [So] we (Da, Xing and others) followed Lu. Xing stayed at the cottage alone as cook.[699] I together with the groom[700] Shi and others conspired[701] to dig up a grave mound, [but] did not inform Xing about this. When the grave mound had already been penetrated into[702] [by a tunnel], we shared the vessels [we had found in it]. [Only] then did I inform Xing. Shi and others did not share with Xing. I alone shared with Xing."
Everything else corresponded to [the statement of] Xing.

猩曰：
達等埱冢，不與猩謀。分器，蒔等不分$_{054}$猩。達獨私分猩。猩爲樂等庸，
取（聚）銅草（皂）中。
它如達及前。

Xing stated:
"Da and others dug up a grave mound, [but] they [previously] did not conspire with me. [So when it came to] sharing the vessels, Shi and others did not share with me. Da alone shared with me privately.[703] When I was hired by

houses, field cottages and barns with malice, one is to be tattooed and made an earth or grain pounder convict.").

698 *Ou* 毆 (*GSR* 122j) *qʕo for *qu* 敺 (*GSR* 122d) resp. *qu* 驅 (*GSR* 122c) *kʰo (Gao and Dong 1997, 335–336) in the figurative sense "to chase after" (*Hanfei* 42, 302) or "to attack, raid" (*Shiji* 43, 1821: 取東胡歐代地。 "[Zhao] occupied the land of Dai raided by the Eastern Hu."; *Mawangdui Zhanguo zongheng jiashu* 161: 有（又）長敺（驅）粱（梁）北。"[Qin] raided the north of Liang again."; *Hanshu* 49, 2278: 胡虜數入邊地[...]毆略畜產。 "The Hu invaded the frontier areas several times [...] drove away and plundered the livestock."). Cf. Wang Hui 2008, 133 with the entry *qu* 區 for "chase and campaign using ambush" and Bai Yulan 2012, 173.

699 *Yang* 養 "to cook; cook" (*QLSZ* 72=*RCL* A 37; *QLSZ* 113=*RCL* A 62: 隸臣有巧可以爲工者，勿以爲人僕、養。 "When bond servant convicts are skilful and could be made artisans, they must not be made servants or cooks."; *ZYS* 56: 爲徒養 "to cook for the convicts").

700 *Pu tu* 僕徒 otherwise only occurs in Jia Putu 家僕徒, the name of the spearman on the right in the chariot of the duke of Jin during the Spring and Autumn period (*Zuo* Xi 15,164,14). This name was possibly derived from the function of this warrior (originally a groom?).

701 For *mou* see footnotes 522 and 829.

702 *Che* 鐅 for *che* 徹 "to penetrate into" (*FZS* 74=*RCL* E 22: 人已穴房內，鐅（徹）內中。 "Others had already tunnelled into the side room, penetrating into the room."; *FZS* 76=*RCL* E 22: 內中央有新穴，穴鐅（徹）內中。 "In the centre of the room there was a fresh hole; the hole penetrated into the room."). Further examples from Qin and early Han manuscripts are quoted in Bai Yulan 2012, 507–508. Cf. *xue che* 穴徹 (*Mo* 62, 333 [Johnston 2010, 817] "the tunnels communicate").

703 *Si* 私 "secretly, stealthy" or "privately"; cf. *Yuelu WYZ* 069.

Le and others[704] as labourer, I stored the bronze [vessels] in a pen."
Everything else corresponded to [the statement of] Da and the previous [statement of Xing].

醴陽丞悝曰：
冗募上造敞$_{055}$

[Missing slip]

The vice prefect Kui of Liyang [prefecture] stated:
"Chang, holder of the second rank, who was temporarily recruited, [...]."

【敞曰：
…】堀冢者錫（賜）。到舍，達巳（已）分錫（賜）。達謂敞：巳（已）到前，不得錫（賜）。今冢中尚有器。器巳（已）出，買（賣）敞所。時（蒔）$_{056}$告達請與敞出餘器，分敞。達曰：發冢一歲矣！今嬫（徹），敞乃來，不可與敞。達等相將之水旁，$_{057}$有頃，來告敞曰：與敞。敞來後，前者爲二面，敞爲一面。敞曰：若（諾）。皆行，到冢，得錫（賜）。敞買及受分。覺，$_{058}$亡，得。
它如達等。

[Chang stated:
"...] burial offerings[705] of the tomb raiders. When [I, Chang,] arrived at their cottage, Da had already divided the burial offerings [among the robbers]. Da said to me that I would not get [a share] of any of the burial offerings [captured during the time] before I had arrived. Now there were, however, still vessels in the grave mound. After these were taken out, he would sell them to me.[706] Shi

704 For *Le deng* see footnote 683.

705 For the reasons why *yang* 錫 should be interpreted as *xi* 錫 (*GSR* 850n) in this manuscript see footnote 680. Here *xi* is used as loan for the homeophoneous *ci* 賜 (*GSR* 850t), usually meaning "to bestow" (*Yi* 2, 25a; 2, 25b; *Odes* 176,3 and 261,1; *Zuo* Wen 1,228,1; *Shiji* 12, 457; cf. Feng and Deng 2006, 1016). However, *ci* also occurs as noun "gift, donation" (*QLSZ* 153=*RCL* A 90; *ENLL* 14, 392). With regard to a Han statute on donations (*ENLL* 282–304), which inter alia deals with several governmental contributions to the funeral of officials, e.g. coffins for the deceased (*ENLL* 283–284, 289), *ci* can also be interpreted as "burial offerings/objects".

706 It would be implausible here to read *chu mai* 出賣 as binominal verb "to sell" because of the following text passage (*Yuelu WYZ* 058: 敞買及受分。"Chang bought [a part] and received as share [another part of the vessels]."; cf. Zhu and Chen 2013, 123 with footnote 27). Furthermore, the first reference for *chu mai* 出賣 as binominal verb is given in sources from the third century AD (*Jinshu* 30, 924).

asked Da's consent[707] to get out the remaining vessels [together] with me and to give me a share. Da said: 'It has been a year since we opened the grave mound! Only now that we have penetrated into it [through a tunnel] does Chang come. It is not acceptable to give him [a share].' A short while after Da and the others had sauntered along[708] the riverside, they came to inform me: 'We will give you [a share]. [But as] you came later, [we as those who came] first shall receive two parts and you one part.' I said: 'I agree.' We all set off, came to the burial mound and got the burial offerings. I bought [a part] and received as share [another part of the vessels]. [Then the grave robbery] was discovered,[709] I absconded and was caught."
Everything else corresponded to [the statements of] Da and his accomplices.

達言如敞。

The statement of Da [concerning the involvement of Chang] corresponded to that of Chang.

Original Case – Interagency Enquiries

達等埱冢，不與猩、敞謀。得衣、器，告。猩、敞受分，臧（贓）過六百六十錢。059
【它】如舜（辭）。

Da and his accomplices dug up a grave mound [but previously] did not conspire with Xing and Chang. [After] they had got clothes and vessels[710] [out of

707 For *gu* in combination with *qing* see footnote 516.

708 *Xiang jiang* 相將 seems to be one variant of a rhyming binome (*die yun* type) meaning "to stroll/roam around", which is also written *xiang yang* 相羊 (*Chuci* 1/2/26) or *xiang xiang* 相翔 (*Zhouli* 36, 884b: 有相翔者誅之。"If there are vagrants they will be punished."). Cf. Zhu Qifeng 1934, 0867–0868 for further variants in received literature. In Qin legal manuscripts this binome is usually written *jiang yang* 將陽. For the legal term *jiang yang* see footnote 858.

709 *Jue* 覺 "discover/disclose (an offence)" (*FLDW* 68=*RCL* D 55: 甲殺人，不覺，今甲病死已葬，人乃後告甲[...]。"A kills a person, but this is not discovered. Now, if only after A has died of an illness and already been buried somebody posthumously reports A [...].").

710 The compound *yi qi* 衣器 refers to sb.'s personal effects excluding the valuables (*FLDW* 170=*RCL* D 149: 妻賸（媵）臣妾、衣器當收不當？不當收。"Are the slaves and personal effects of her dowry by law to be confiscated from a wife [of an offender, if she reported her husband for this offence]? No."; *FZS* 8=*RCL* E 3: 封有鞫者某里士五（伍）甲家室、妻、子、臣妾、衣器、畜產。"I have sealed the house, the wife

the grave mound], they informed [them]. [However,] Xing and Chang [later also] received a share. [The value of] the misappropriated goods exceeded 660 cash.
[Everything else] corresponded to the statements.[711]

Original Case – Finding of Fact

鞫之：
達等堀冢，不與猩、敞謀。【得】衣、器，告。猩、敞受分，臧（贓）過六百六十錢。得。猩當黥$_{060}$城旦，敞耐鬼薪。遝戊午赦。審。

Finding of fact:[712]
Da and his accomplices dug up a grave mound [but previously] did not conspire with Xing and Chang. [After] they [had got] clothes and vessels [out of the grave mound], they informed [them]. [However,] Xing and Chang [later also] received a share.[713] The value of the misappropriated goods exceeded 660 cash. They were caught.[714] Xing is by law to be tattooed and made an earth pounder convict, Chang is to be shaved and made a firewood gatherer convict.

---

and children, slaves, personal effects and cattle of A, rank-and-file man from quarter X, who is under formal criminal investigation."; ZYS 214–215: 有受孔衣器、錢財，弗詣吏，有罪。 "If there is someone who accepts personal effects or valuables from Kong without presenting them to the authorities, he or she will have committed an offence."). Accordingly, the personal effects described here appear to be those of the deceased buried in the grave mound that was robbed.

711 The preceding passage probably contains the results of interagency enquiries (*wen* 問), which were also used in other cases to gather information about the value of stolen goods (ZYS 71, 224; *Yuelu* WYZ 016, 130, 166) as basis for determining punishment. Although the term *wen* 問, usually used to mark the beginning of this part, is missing, the last two characters of the phrase *ta ru ci* 它如舜（辭）, usually marking the end of it, can be found on *Yuelu* WYZ 060. This suggests that the preceding passage in fact describes the results of interagency enquiries. For *wen* see footnote 562.

712 For *ju* see footnote 565.

713 In the first passage of the finding of fact, the judicial officials made it quite clear that the offence committed by Xing and Chang did not meet the requirements of conspiring to commit theft, but fulfilled the criteria for consciously sharing stolen goods with the same legal consequences as for the offenders (ENLL 57). Therefore, both accused were to be punished with the maximum penalty for property offences (ENLL 55). Cf. footnotes 663 and 668.

714 At the end of a finding of fact, *de* 得 is often followed by *shen* 審 (*Yuelu* WYZ 092, 134, 235; *Liye* 8–2015r; ZYS 6, 15, 23, 157). For other implications of the term *de* see footnote 524.

They were included in the amnesty of [day?] *wuwu*. [All these] are established facts.[715]

Original Case – Judgement

江陵守感、丞暨、史同論赦猩、敞爲庶人。達等令別論。

The incumbent prefect[716] of Jiangling, Gan, vice prefect Ji and secretary[717] Tong passed judgement[718] to grant amnesty to Xing and Chang and make them released persons. [As far as] Da and the others [are concerned] order was given to pass judgement on them separately.

Submission by Jiangling Prefecture – Concluding Formula

敢瀐（讞）之。061

We venture to submit [this case] for decision.[719]

715 For *shen* see footnote 633.

716 For *shou* in combination with a particular office see footnote 486.

717 For (*yu*) *shi* see footnote 539.

718 For *lun* see footnote 540.

719 For *yan* and the phrase *gan yan zhi* see footnote 489. The reason for this submission is asking the higher authorities' approval for the amnesty granted to the offenders.

Case 1.4

In this case, several merchants asserted claims to the same plot of commercially usable land, which caused a conflict. One of the merchants named Rui, whose request for the plot of land had been rejected, used criminal methods to achieve his objective. Together with his brother-in-law Duo he first won the bond servant convict Geng's support for a project of commercial participation. Geng was employed as a clerk within the market administration and was therefore suitable as a straw man. In response to an approved request the vacant plot was handed over to Geng, but the development of a market stall could not be carried out because in the meantime another merchant named Cai asserted his claims to the plot, and the vice prefect brought charges against Geng for his illegal acquisition.

Cai originally owned the contested plot and the market stall on it. The royal house had deprived Cai of his market stall to make a storehouse out of it, and assigned him a less profitable stall. When the government storehouse was later closed, Cai tried to take over the plot of his former stall again, but without success. In reply to his objection against the decision of the competent market station, the prefect gave order to reassign the market stall to Cai as long as no other person contested his claims. Because another merchant named Xi vied with him for the stall, Cai's claim for reassignment was unsuccessful. So he tried to make a private agreement on commercial participation with his rival Xi, and, in return, offered to develop and build up the plot at his own expense. Finally, Rui got in touch with both merchants and threatened to lodge a complaint if they did not share the stall with him. As the conflict escalated, the three rivals were brought before the authorities by the head of the market station, who gave a report to the prefect that the three disputants (Cai, Rui and Xi) had developed and built on government land without authorisation and contested each other's claims to the market stall. Thereupon the prefect decided that the plot on which the market stall was to be constructed should not be assigned to any of them.

Market stalls and the associated land were assigned to merchants by the competent market station with the rights of inheritance and sale; however, the plots could be confiscated from the owners by the government if it needed the immovable property for its own enterprises. Former claims could be asserted with the authorities, and objections against administrative decisions could be raised, but it was left to the decision of the appropriate authorities to grant or refuse such requests. Merchants registered in the market places were obviously

 | DOI 10.1163/9789004315655_012

only entitled to receive one stall. If this stall was confiscated due to governmental interests, they had to accept another one in exchange.

Due to the unfavourable legal situation after the decision of the prefect, Rui did not dare to occupy the market stall, which he had already built together with Cai, but sold his share to his brother-in-law Duo and led him to believe that he, Rui, had received the plot for the market stall with the authorities' permission. Fang, the son of Duo, paid Rui 1,000 cash in advance, which the latter completely spent. Later Rui feared that the authorities would discover that he had illegally sold the land and had tried to rescind the sale, but he was unable to repay the money.

It is interesting to note that Rui was not prosecuted for deceiving his partner, but for the illegal sale of government land for market stalls. Rui, by selling his share of the market stall, was charged with the offence of "illegally/for the purpose of theft deceiving a person into buying government land for market stalls", to which the officials referred during the confrontation, or with the offence of "illegal sale of government land", as mentioned in the reply of the accused. Both were classified as statutory offences of theft (*dao*). As the value of the misappropriated land exceeded 660 cash, the commoner Rui had to be sentenced to the maximum punishment for property offences, i.e. he had to be tattooed and made an earth pounder convict. Officials of the prefecture of Jiangling passed this sentence without hesitation because they were in no doubt about the punishment.

However, after having read the report of the prefecture, the governor of Nan province as the immediate superior complained that the report on the criminal proceedings against Rui did not clarify whether the price of the misappropriated land on which the judgement was based had been determined by the offender during the illegal sale or derived from separate evaluations of the land and market stall carried out by the competent officials. The governor reminded the subordinate officials of correct procedure in the event that different items that had been sold together were separated in the course of an official evaluation of misappropriated goods. The officials of the prefecture were not to give a response with the decision, but were only to summarise the established facts and to submit the case to the higher authorities for approval.

In all cases of theft, the judicial officials were obliged to evaluate the misappropriated goods immediately after the capture of a thief without regard to the value declared by the accused. In the present case the combined price of the land and the building stated by Rui (1,400 cash) and the one reported by the prefecture after the official evaluation (1,000+269=1,269 cash) differed by 131 cash. This shows that the value of the land, which served as the basis for Rui's sentence, was in fact determined by the officials, because the accused had sold the land together with the building for a total price of 1,400 cash. Rui was punished for the 1,000 cash he had actually received through the sale and which, according to the official evaluation, matched the value of the land. Therefore, the prefecture of Jiangling complied with the request of its governor and provided the complete documentation of the criminal proceedings against the merchant Rui, including the formal criminal investigation and the judicial decision. Apparently this decision, which was mainly based on the official evaluation, had to be approved by the higher authorities.

Diplomatic Edition

•敢潚之江陵言公卒芮與夫=材共蓋受棺列吏後弗鼠⌞芮買其分肆士$_{062}$五朵地直千蓋二百六十九錢以論芮⌞二月辛未大守令曰問芮買與朵別賈地且$_{063}$吏自別=直=以論狀何如勿庸報鞫審潚•視獄十一月己丑丞暨劾曰聞主市曹$_{064}$臣史隸臣更不當受列受棺列買問論•更曰芮朵謂更棺列旁有公空列可受欲受$_{065}$亭佐駕不許芮朵⌞更能受共更曰若更即自言駕=鼠更=等欲治蓋相移⌞材爭$_{066}$弗得聞材後受它如劾•材曰巳有棺列不利⌞空列故材列⌞十餘歲時王室置市$_{067}$府奪材以爲府=罷欲復受弗得迺往九月辤守感=令亭賀曰毋爭者鼠材走馬喜$_{068}$爭賀即不鼠材=私與喜謀喜故有棺列勿爭材巳治蓋喜欲與喜　　貿喜$_{069}$曰可材弗言賀即擅竊治蓋以爲肆未歓芮謂材與芮共不共且辤爭材詑$_{070}$**[Missing slip]**辤賀=不鼠材芮將材芮喜言感曰皆故有棺肆弗鼠擅治蓋相爭感曰勿鼠⌞材$_{071}$□□□□□□□□□□□□□□□居材曰不可須芮來朵即弗敢居它如更$_{072}$•芮曰空列地便利=與材共喜爭芮乃智材弗得弗敢居迺十一月欲與人共漁毋⧄$_{073}$朵子士五方販棺其列下芮利□所共蓋公地卒又蓋□□□□與材共⧄$_{074}$芮分方曰欲即并賈地蓋千四百方前顧芮千巳盡用錢買漁具後念悔恐發$_{075}$覺有辠欲益賈令方勿取即往謂方賤令二千弗取環方錢方曰貴弗取芮$_{076}$毋錢環居三日朵責與期五日備賞錢不賞朵以故賈取肆朵曰若即弗環錢去往$_{077}$•漁得它如材更•方曰朵不存買芮肆芮後益賈弗取責錢不=得=居肆芮母索$_{078}$後環二百錢未備八百它及朵言如芮材•駕言如更•賀曰材喜⌞芮妻佞皆巳受$_{079}$棺列不當重受它及喜言如材芮•索言如方•詰芮=後智材不得受列弗敢居是公$_{080}$列地毆可故紿方曰巳受盜買于方巳盡用錢後撓益賈欲令勿取方弗取有弗$_{081}$環錢去往漁是即盜紿人買公列地非今且以盜論芮=可以解⌞芮曰誠弗受朵姊$_{082}$孫故爲兄妻有子⌞兄死孫尚存以方朵終不告芮=即紿買方巳用錢毋以賞上即以$_{083}$芮爲盜買公地辠芮=毋以壁毋它解它如前•獄史豬曰芮方并賈豬以芮不$_{084}$**[Missing slip]**九錢買分四百卅五尺直千錢它如辤•鞫之芮不得受列擅蓋治公地費六百九$_{085}$□□□□□□□地積四百卅□□□□□□四百巳受千錢盡用後環二百⌞地臧直千$_{086}$錢得獄巳斷令黥芮爲城旦未□□□□□□□$_{087}$

Edition and Translation

Submission by Jiangling Prefecture – Introductory Formula

敢瀐（讞）之。

We venture to submit[720] [the following case] for decision:

Report by the Prefecture on the Judgement Passed in the Original Case

江陵言：
公卒芮與大夫材共蓋受棺列。吏後弗鼠（予）。芮買（賣）其分隷（肆）士$_{062}$五（伍）朵。地直（值）千，蓋二百六十九錢。以論芮。

[The prefect of] Jiangling[721] [prefecture] reported:[722]
"The *gong zu*[723] Rui and Cai, holder of the fifth rank,[724] together built[725] and

720 For *yan* and the phrase *gan yan zhi* see footnote 489.

721 For Jiangling see footnote 651.

722 In this report, the prefecture of Jiangling notifies its superior authority of a criminal procedure which had already been completed.

723 *Gong zu* 公卒 was a designation for a special group of free men without any rank (*Liye* 8–113, 8–430, 8–445, 8–1563, 8–2246; *ZYS* 211) being placed between holders of the first rank and penal labour convicts of the most lenient form or released convicts who had suffered mutilation. *Gong zu* were of equal status as *shi wu* 士伍 and *shuren* 庶人 as far as the allotment of land and residence (*ENLL* 312, 316), the welfare for the elderly (*ENLL* 354–357) and their hereditary status are concerned. While *shu ren* seem to be people released from penal labour or slavery, *gong zu* were sons of holders of the fourth and third rank (with the exception of the heirs) and all sons of holders of the second rank (*ENLL* 360). Sons of *gong zu* as well as of *shi wu* were made *shi wu* (*ENLL* 364–365).

724 *Da fu* 大夫 was the fifth within the hierarchy of twenty ranks (*jue* 爵) in Qin and Han times (*Yuelu WYZ* 062, 108, 112–113, 131, 135, 193; *QLSZ* 179=*RCL* A 92; *QLZC* 7=*RCL* C 5; *FLDW* 127, 156=*RCL* D 106, 134; *Liye* 6–16, 8–19, 8–231, 8–232, 8–834, 8–1236, 8–1765; *ZYS* 204). For the system of ranks in Qin and Han times see Loewe 1960, Nishijima 1961, Zhu Shaohou 2008 as well as Lau and Lüdke 2012, footnote 626.

725 *Gai* 蓋 verbally "to cover", here actually meaning "to cover a roof with reed, to thatch a roof" (*QLSZ* 195=*RCL* A 106: 獨高其置芻廥及倉茅蓋者。"Only [the walls] of stores where grain is placed and granaries covered with reed (*imperata cylindrica*) should be made high."; *Dadai liji* 8.3/49/28: 以茅蓋屋 "to thatch the roof with reed"; *Shiji* 118, 3079 [cf. Watson 1993, vol. II, 326]: 縣爲築蓋家室。"The prefecture built and roofed a house for him."). *Gai* also occurred in the more general meaning "to erect, build" already in *Tongyue* 僮約, cited according to *Quan Hanwen* 42, 359b: 治舍蓋屋 "renovate lodgings and build houses". Cf. Zhu Xiangrong 2012, 167–170.

took over[726] a coffin market stall.[727] The officials later refused[728] to allot[729] [the market stall] to them. Rui sold his share of the stall[730] to the rank-and-file man[731]

---

726 *Shou* 受 "to receive, accept", in the context of land allocation also meaning "to take over (as inheritance, etc.), to be assigned" (*ENLL* 321: 受田宅，予人若賣宅，不得更受。 "Those who took over fields and residences, but handed them over to other people or sold residences, are not allowed to take over [fields or residences] again."; *ENLL* 239, 313, 314, 318). Cf. *Guoyu* 6.10/106/3 and *Zuo* Xuan 12,313,7. Maybe *shou* is used attributively here and *shou lie* 受列 could be translated as "stall that had been taken over" (cf. *QLSZ* 8=*RCL* A 3: 入頃芻稾，以其受田之數。 "The delivery of hay and straw per *qing* is to be done according to the number of fields taken over.").

727 *Lie* 列 "market stall" (*QLSZ* 68=*RCL* A 45: 賈市居列者及官府之吏，毋敢擇行錢、布；擇行錢、布者，列伍長弗告，吏循之不謹，皆有罪。 "Traders who occupy stalls as well as officials of government workshops should not venture to circulate cash or cloth [currency] selectively. When in case of selective circulation of cash or cloth the elder [and the members] of the group of five [neighbouring] stalls do not report this [to the authorities], and the officials are not careful when making their rounds, they all are liable to punishment."; *ENLL* 260: 市販匿不自占租，坐所匿租臧（贓）爲盜，沒入其所販賣及賈錢縣官，奪之列。 "When engaging in a trade transaction, evading the sales tax by not declaring one's own proceeds is prosecuted according to the provisions applicable to theft of the amount misappropriated by evading the tax; [in addition,] the [goods] sold in the transaction as well as the proceeds are to be seized into the government coffers and the market stall is to be taken away from the trader in question.").

728 *Fu* 弗, an emphatic negation (ant. *yu* 欲 "be willing to"), regularly refers to what the agent "will not do" or "refuses to do" (Harbsmeier 1993). Gassmann (1997, 257–258) interprets its meaning likewise as "sich nicht veranlasst sehen/sich weigern". Cf. Schuessler 1987, 175 where *fu* is interpreted as an indicative-volitional negative meaning "cannot, does not want to".

729 For *shu* 鼠 as common Qin graphic variant of *yu* 與 or *yu* 予 in the sense "to give" see footnote 518. *Yu* is often used in the context of land allocation (*Wei li zhi dao* 19.5=*RCL* F 1; *Zuo* Zhuang 21,100,12; Xi 25,194,8; Wen 1,228,13; Wen 18,279,17; Cheng 17,401,7; Xiang 27,529,13–14; *Hanfei* 22, 127; 32, 209).

730 *Si* 肆 "store, stall" (*Zhuang* 26, 177: 枯魚之肆 "dried fish store"; *Zuo* Xiang 30,553,18: 羊肆 "sheep store"; *Hanshu* 24A, 1127 [cf. Swann 1950, 150]: 山川園池市肆租稅之入 "revenues from taxes on [products of] mountains and rivers, gardens and ponds and market stalls"; *Lü* 15, 160 [cf. Knoblock and Riegel 2000, 339]: 商不變肆 "merchants do not change their store"; *Huai* 15, 254 [cf. Major et al. 2010, 586]: 賈不去肆 "merchants do not forsake their store"; *Hanshu* 24A, 1117 [cf. Swann 1950, 115]: 是以聖王[...]開市肆以通之。 "Therefore, the shrewd kings [...] opened stalls at the market in order to make contact with each other."; *Shiji* 127, 3216 [cf. Watson 1993, vol. II, 426]: 二人卽同輿而之市游於卜肆中。"The two men then sharing a carriage drove to the market, where they strolled among the diviners' stalls.").

731 For *shi wu* see footnote 495.

Duo. The land was worth[732] 1,000 [cash], the building 269 cash. For this [amount of misappropriated goods] judgement is passed[733] on Rui."

Order by the Superior Governor to Submit the Original Case for Decision

二月辛未，大（太）守令曰：
問芮買（賣）與朵別賈（價）地，且$_{063}$吏自別直（值）。別直（值）以論，狀何如？勿庸報。鞫審，瓛（讞）。

On day *xinwei* of the second month[734] the governor[735] gave an order saying: "Enquire[736] whether Rui, in selling [the market stall], separately[737] negotiated the price[738] of the land with Duo or[739] whether the officials of their own accord

732 *Zhi* 直 (*GSR* 918a) *drək was often used as a loan graph for the homeophonous *zhi* 値 (*GSR* 918h) *drək-s "to be worth/equivalent to", which indicates the "value" in received literature (*Li* 58, 1666b; *Shiji* 10, 433; 30, 1426; 58, 2087; Feng and Deng 2006, 20–21) and manuscripts (*QLSZ* 16, 80, 91, 148=*RCL* A 9, 40, 49, 70). *Zhi* often refers to the value of misappropriated goods (*zang* 贓) (*FLDW* 9, 12, 17–18=*RCL* D 8, 11, 15–16; *Longgang* 137; *Liye* 8–1287, 8–2015r; *ZYS* 72; *ENLL* 55, 58).

733 For *lun* see footnote 540.

734 It is difficult to date this case exactly on the basis of two dates only designating the month and the day, but not the year and the first day of the month. With regard to the other dates mentioned in manuscript I of the collection of criminal cases *xinwei* could be the 22nd day of the second month in the 21st year of King Zheng of Qin, i.e. 12/04/226 BC (Xu Xiqi 1997, 1231; cf. Zhang Peiyu 2007, 73; Li Zhonglin 2012, 65) or the 26th day of the second month in the 22nd year of King Zheng of Qin, i.e. 06/04/225 BC (Xu Xiqi 1997, 1233; cf. Zhang Peiyu 2007, 73; Li Zhonglin 2012, 65).

735 This must be the governor of Nan province who was the direct superior to the prefect of Jiangling. For the *tai shou* see footnote 579.

736 For *wen* see footnote 562. The enquiries of the governor here do not aim at establishing particulars relevant for the sentence before passing judgement, but at resolving open questions concerning the criminal case reported by the subordinate prefecture, i.e. questions concerning separate selling of land and building as well as the criminal prosecution of other persons involved.

737 *Bie* 別 (*GSR* 292a) "separately" in contrast to *bing* 并 "combined, together" (*Yuelu WYZ* 084). Cf. footnote 779.

738 *Gu* 賈 (*GSR* 38b) *krʕaʔ/s "to trade, sell" often writes its nominal derivation *jia* 價 (*GSR* 38c) *kra-s "price" (*QLSZ* 17–18, 69=*RCL* A 9, 46; *XL* 1, 12, 58=*RCL* B 1, 6, 29; *FLDW* 153=*RCL* D 131; *FZS* 39, 83=*RCL* E 15, 22; *Yuelu WYZ* 076–078, 081, 116; *Longgang* 37; *ZYS* 8, 123; *ENLL* 80, 230, 242, 290, 427–428, 433, 510; *Suanshushu* 46, 61–63; *Mawangdui Zhanguo zongheng jiashu* 20; *Xuanquan* 147; *Meng* 5, 234–235; *Shiji* 30, 1440; *Hanshu* 8, 252; 24A, 1125, 1145; cf. "proceeds" in *FZS* 38=*RCL* E 15; *ENLL* 260), for which a separate character was probably only created in Eastern Han times. Cf. Feng and Deng 2006, 875. Here *gu/jia* seems to be

separately evaluated[740] [the land and the stall]. How should one behave[741] correctly, if a judgement is based on separate evaluations?[742] Do not give a response[743] [with a decision]. Find the facts, [assure] that they are

used verbally in the sense "to negotiate/fix a price" (*FZS* 39=*RCL* E 15: 令少內某、佐某以市正賈（價）賈丙丞某前，丙中人，賈（價）若干錢。 "An order was given to the treasurer X and his assistant Y to fix a price for C according to the correct market price before the vice prefect Z; C is an average man; the price [for him] was so and so many cash [coins].").

739 *Qie* 且 is used as disjunctive conjunction between two interrogative sentences (*FLDW* 49, 57–58, 64, 66, 97, 115, 141, 171, 197=*RCL* D 46, 136, 52, 80, 95, 119, 150, 179); see e.g. *FLDW* 20–21=*RCL* D 18: 人奴妾盜其主之父母，爲盜主，且不爲？ "When a private slave or slave-woman rob their master's parents, is this 'robbing one's master', or is it not?" Cf. He Leshi 2006, 314; Yang Shuda cited according to Yu and Xie 1993, 144; Pei Xuehai cited according to Yu and Xie 1993, 142.

740 For *zhi* 直 as a loan graph for the homeophonous *zhi* 值 "to be worth/equivalent to" see footnote 732. Here it is used putatively in the meaning "to evaluate" (*XL* 1=*RCL* B 1; *FLDW* 33=*RCL* D 27: 士五（伍）甲盜，以得時直（值）臧（贓）。 "Rank-and-file man A commits a theft. At the moment of capture, the misappropriated goods are evaluated.") or "to estimate" (*QLSZ* 177=*RCL* A 88: 毋齎者乃直（值）之。 "In case [a tool] is not listed as equipment, then its value is to be estimated."; *XL* 12=*RCL* B 6: 直（值）其賈（價） "the value is to be estimated"), which fits the context above. Judicial officials who failed to evaluate the misappropriated goods straight after the capture of a thief were liable to punishment (*FLDW* 33, 35=*RCL* D 27, 28).

741 The question *zhuang he ru* 狀何如 is in the present and other cases followed by an instruction (cf. *Liye* 8–1564: 弗應而云當坐之狀何如？其謹案致，更上。 "How to behave in case [an action] does not correspond [to the ordinances], but [the provisions] say that it is by law to be prosecuted? You may examine it diligently and submit the case to the higher authorities again."). *Zhuang* was used in the sense "behaviour" (*ZYS* 42: 武宜聽視而後與吏辯是不當狀。 "It would have been proper for you, Wu, to obey Shi and only later together with us, the officials, get straight whether your conduct was correct or unlawful."; *Yuelu WYZ* 155: 苛視不犾（狀）者 "cross-examine and check up on [persons with] irregular behaviour"), but could also refer to "circumstances" (*ZYS* 107: 復謂講盜牛狀何如。 "[He] asked me, Jiang, again under which circumstances I had robbed the cattle."; *FLDW* 162=*RCL* D 142: 履錦履之狀可（何）如？ "Under which circumstances is one 'wearing brocade shoes'?").

742 Cf. the similar phrases *bing zhi qi zang yi lun* 并直（值）其臧（贓）以論 "to pass judgement according to the combined value of the misappropriated goods" (*ENLL* 58) and *dang bing zang yi lun* 當并臧（贓）以論 "by law judgement is to be passed according to the combined (value of the) misappropriated goods" (*FLDW* 12=*RCL* D 11; *FLDW* 49=*RCL* D 39). For *lun* see footnote 540.

743 The usage of *wu yong bao* 勿庸報 implies that no final judgement is to be passed, which accords with the institution of submitting doubtful criminal cases. Compare all cases of manslaughter and homicide where the lower-level authority was not allowed to pass a

established and submit the case [to us, the higher authorities, for decision]."[744]

Original Case – Initiation of Criminal Proceedings

視獄：
十一月己丑，丞暨劾曰：
聞主市曹$_{064}$臣史、隸臣更不當受列，受棺列，買（賣）。問論。

We inspected the criminal case:[745]
On the day *jichou* of the eleventh month[746] the vice prefect Ji[747] brought the following *ex-officio* charge:[748]
"I heard that Geng, unfree clerk[749] at the department[750] of the market superintendent and a bond servant,[751] was by law not entitled to take over a market

final judgement on its own, but was obliged to fully document the trial (ENLL 396: 縣道官所治死罪及過失、戲而殺人，獄已具，勿庸論，上獄屬所二千石官。"In cases of offences punishable with death, as well as in cases involving the killing of a person inadvertently or in a contest, which are tried by prefecture or march offices, no judgement shall be passed after the trial documents have been fully compiled; [instead], the case is to be submitted to the two thousand bushel official (i.e. the governor of the province) to which [the respective prefecture or march] is subordinated."). Cf. footnote 581.

744 Cf. the same formula on *Yuelu* WYZ 046 above as well as the explanations in footnote 672.

745 For *shiyu* see footnote 674. The following contains a review of former criminal proceedings.

746 This day could be the seventh day of the 11th month in the 21st year of King Zheng of Qin, i.e. 31/12/226 BC (Xu Xiqi 1997, 1231; cf. Zhang Peiyu 2007, 73; Li Zhonglin 2012, 65) or the 13th day of the 11th month in the 22nd year of King Zheng, i.e. 26/12/225 BC (Xu Xiqi 1997, 1233; cf. Zhang Peiyu 2007, 73; Li Zhonglin 2012, 65). Cf. footnote 734.

747 Cf. the official Ji 暨 in case I.6 (*Yuelu* WYZ 094[2], 095, 099, 101–102).

748 For *he* see footnote 545.

749 The expression *chen shi* 臣史 is otherwise unknown and therefore tentatively translated here as "unfree clerk". It is clear from the following that Geng definitely (also) was a bond servant convict. Possibly he had to work as a kind of unfree clerk.

750 *Cao* 曹 "department (within an authority)" is frequently mentioned in official communication (ZYS 7; *Liye* 8–778, 8–1874).

751 *Li chen* 隸臣 "bond servant convict" refers to male convicts performing a moderate form of penal labour (*Yuelu* WYZ 141, 158, 186, 205–207, 235). They were ranked between the most severe form of penal labour as earth pounder (*cheng dan* 城旦) and the more lenient form as robber guard (*si kou* 司寇) during the Qin and early Han dynasties. *Li chen* belonged to the category *nai* 耐, which meant that they were not mutilated but shaved. Offenders who committed less serious offences were often punished with penal labour as *li chen qie* (ENLL 55=*Longgang* 40; ENLL 16, 31, 33, 41, 158, 190, 251, 398; ZYS 66, 182). During Qin times it was common that invaders from outside who surrendered were made *li chen* convicts (QLZC 38=RCL C 23b). The same applied to missing conscripts who were assumed

stall, [but] he took over a coffin market stall and sold it. Make enquiries whether judgement has been passed."

Original Case – First Stage of Interrogation

更曰：
芮、朵謂更：棺列旁有公空列，可受。欲受，065亭佐駕不許芮、朵。更能受，共。更曰：若（諾）。更即自言駕，駕鼠（予）更。更等欲治蓋相移，材爭，066弗得。聞材後受。它如劾。

Geng stated:
"Rui and Duo said to me: 'Next to [your] coffin market stall there is a vacant government[752] market stall, which could be taken over. We wanted to take it over, [but] the assistant of the head of the *ting*[753] Jia did not grant [the request

---

to have died in battle, but were later discovered in their home community (QLZC 37=RCL C 23a). Wives and children of offenders who were sentenced to the most severe form of penal labour as intact earth pounder or prosecuted for rape were subjected to confiscation (*shou* 收) with the implication that they became *li chen* and *li qie* convicts (ENLL 435).

752 *Gong* 公 "government(al), public". Later in this case the plot for the market stall or the market stall itself are referred to as *gong lie di* 公列地 "government land for market stalls" or "government stall and land" (*Yuelu* WYZ 080–082), *gong kong lie* 公空列 "empty government market stall" (*Yuelu* WYZ 065) or *gong di* 公地 "government land" (074, 084–085). *Gong*, probably an abbreviation of *gong shi* 公室 "the house of the (Qin) duke" (later *wang shi* 王室 "the royal house [of Qin]") that was replaced by the official designation *xian guan* 縣官 (*Liye* 8–461r) after the foundation of the Qin Empire, referred to the government in legal manuscripts (QLSZ 7, 48–49, 76=RCL A 2, 11–12, 38; FLDW 90=RCL D 75; FZS 37=RCL E 15; *Yuelu* WYZ 216) or was used as an attribute for government/public property (QLSZ 16, 77, 84, 102, 126=RCL A 9, 39, 46, 56, 74; *Liye* 8–135r; in combination with buildings as in the present case in QLSZ 121=RCL A 64 and FLDW 159=RCL D 139). The antonym of *gong* was *si* 私 "private". All persons who privately used state property had to observe strict rules (QLSZ 126=RCL A 74; FLDW 175=RCL D 155). For the difference between privately cultivated fields and *gong tian* 公田 "government fields" during the Zhou dynasty see footnote 1336.

753 *Ting* 亭 "stations" were multi-storey buildings positioned at the city gates (ENLL 266, 491) and, at intervals of about 10 *li* 里 (ca. 4.2 km), along major thoroughfares inside and outside of towns (*Hanshu* 19A, 742). Administrative records from the end of the Western Han report that the prefectures of Donghai province employed, depending on their size, between four and 54 *ting zhang* 亭長 "station heads" in each prefecture, amounting to a total of 689 *ting zhang* in the whole province with a population of 1.4 million (Xie Guihua 1997, table 3, 47–48). The number of *ting zhang* reported should correspond to the number of *ting*. The *ting* played an important role in local administration, serving as police stations and as watchtowers, and offering accommodation and food to officials and

to take over the stall]. You are able to take it over and [could] share[754] it [with us].' I said: 'I agree.' Thereupon I myself submitted a request[755] to Jia [to permit

---

other authorised personnel passing through (*Hanshu* 99B, 4122). For the latter purpose, they were equipped with a kitchen and a *ting chu* 亭廚 "station cook" in charge (*ENLL* 471). Postal and relais stations for the courier service were normally placed in their proximity. In dangerous areas as well as close to the border, armed guards from the *ting* would transport the mail instead of the regular courier service (*ENLL* 266, 491). A *ting* was commanded by a *xiao zhang* 校長 (also called *ting zhang*); other constables stationed at a *ting* included the *qiu dao* 求盜 "robber hunter" and perhaps the *mentingzu* 門亭卒 "gate station officer" (*ENLL* 266). A *ting zuo* 亭佐 otherwise not mentioned in the legal manuscripts of Qin and early Han times also occurs in an Eastern Han source (*Dongguan Hanji* 7, 227). The *xiao zhang* and *qiu dao* were responsible for the maintenance of law and order in their sector and for tracking down offenders such as fugitive slaves, murderers, horse thieves, and members of a robber gang (*ZYS* 37, 75–76, 100; *FZS* 21–22, 25–26, 55=*RCL* E 10, 12, 20). Their superior was the *xian wei* 縣尉 "prefecture commander". A *ting* building was also used to detain people (*ZYS* 61). For *ting*, see also Chen Pan 1975, 42b-44b; Lao Gan 1982; Gao Min 1981; Yang Hongnian 1985, 399–408; Yu Haoliang 1985, 136; Gao Heng 1994, 106–112; Zhang Jinguang 2004, 587–594. For the controversial relationship between *ting* and *you* 郵 "postal station" see Ji Annuo 1997, 11–13; Gao Min 1998, 213–215; and Tomiya 2003.

754 *Gong* 共 is used here as a transitive verb in the sense of "to share" (*FZS* 93=*RCL* E 24: 皆莫肯與丙共桮（杯）器。"Nobody is willing to share a cup or a dish with me."; *Hanfei* 34, 235 [cf. Harbsmeier]: 與天下共其所有 "to share what one has with the world"; *Lunyu* 5, 109 [cf. Harbsmeier]: 與朋友共 "to share with friends"). On *gong* as a form of commercial participation see also Zhu Degui 2014, 158–159.

755 *Zi yan* 自言 implies that the agent makes representations to the authorities on his own behalf and of his own accord, which means that the authorities are addressed about a matter that concerns the agent. As *zi yan* is a general term for representations to the authorities, the content and aim of such a representation can vary in different situations, which also leads to different translations. In the present case, *zi yan* appears to refer to a request for permission. Similar cases show requests containing an appeal or complaint (*Yuelu WYZ* 104v/094[2]r: 暨自言曰：[...]。"Ji himself submitted a request [containing an appeal to the authorities] stating: [...]."; *Yuelu WYZ* 229: 有（又）撟（矯）爲私書，自言胡陽固所。"I again drew up a private letter under false pretences, in which I myself submitted a request to [prefect] Gu of Huyang."). Cf. complaints about outstanding debts found in documents from the border area at Edsin Gol (*zi yan ze* 自言責 in *Juyan* 3.6, 35.6, 44.22, 58.15A, 143.8, 158.3, 185.27A, 217.15, 261.42, 285.12, 506.9A; *Juyan xinjian* E.P.T4:92, 5:189, 51:8, 52:128, 52:247, 52:348, 52:487, 52:506, 61:4; 65:351; see also Shen Gang 2008, 88).

In other cases, *zi yan* refers to a report about an incident, which could have legal implications (*ENLL* 508: 諸乘私馬出，馬當復入而死亡，自言在縣官。"All persons who leave [Guanzhong] using private horses, which are to be brought in again, shall themselves report this to the authorities of the prefecture where they are staying if [these horses] die or disappear."; *ENLL* 78–79: 其叚（假）別在它所，有物故毋道歸，

me to take over the stall] and Jia assigned me [the market stall]. [When I,] Geng, and my accomplices (Duo and Rui) wanted to develop[756] and to build on [the land for the market stall], and transfer it to each other, Cai contested our claims to it, and we did not succeed[757] [with our plan]. I heard that Cai later took it over."
Everything else corresponded to the *ex-officio* charge.[758]

材曰：
巳（已）有棺列，不利。空列故材列。十餘歲時，王室置市$_{067}$府，奪材以爲府。府罷，欲復受，弗得。迺往九月辤（辭）守感。感令亭賀曰：毋（無）爭者鼠（予）材。走馬喜$_{068}$爭。賀即不鼠（予）材。材私與喜謀：喜故有棺列，勿爭。材巳（已）治蓋，喜欲，與喜貿。喜$_{069}$曰：可。材弗言賀，即擅竊治蓋，以爲肆（肆）。未歡（就），芮謂材：與芮共。不共，且辤（辭）爭。材詑$_{070}$**[Missing slip]**辤（辭）賀，賀不鼠（予）材、芮，將材、芮、喜言感曰：皆故有棺肆（肆）。弗鼠（予），擅治蓋相爭。感曰：勿鼠（予）。材$_{071}$□□□□□□□□□□□□□□□居。材曰：不可。須芮來。朵即弗敢居。
它如更。$_{072}$

叚（假）者自言在所縣道官。 "In case sth. that has been borrowed is at another place [with the one who borrowed it], but due to a bereavement [of close relatives] there is no way to return [the borrowed implements], the person who borrowed them shall himself report this to the authorities of the prefecture or march where he is staying."; *Yuelu* WYZ 193–194: 毋智【□】受錢，恐吏智（知），不敢自言。 "After I, Wuzhi, [...] had received the cash, I was afraid that the officials could get to know about this, [but] I did not dare to report it myself."). According to Bu Xianqun and Liu Yang (2013, 81) *zi yan* originally meant *zi jian* 自荐 "to recommend oneself/offer one's services" (*Hanfei* 46, 324: 夫欲得力士而聽其自言，雖傭人與烏獲不可別也。"Now if one wants to find a strong man and only listens to his self-recommendation, then even an ordinary person and Wu Huo could not be distinguished.").

756 *Zhi* 治 occurs three times in this case together with *gai* 蓋 without a further object (*Yuelu* WYZ 069–071) and once in reverse order with *gong di* 公地 "government land" as object (*Yuelu* WYZ 085). Because of the reverse order *zhi* and *gai* should be regarded as two paratactic verbs, and not as verb and noun in the sense of "to repair the roof". In the context of construction, *zhi* could mean "to repair, to put up" (ZYS 54; *Wei li zhi dao* 24.5; *Hanshu* 24A, 1132; 99, 4132 [together with the synonym *shan* 繕]; *Lunheng* 35, 123; *Gulienüzhuan* 1.1/1/12 [instead of the synonymous *wan* 完]) or "to build, to erect" (*Shiji* 87, 2558). In the context of agriculture, *zhi* has the meanings "to cultivate fields, to till the soil" (*zhi tian* 治田 in *Xun* 9, 107; *Hanshu* 24A, 1124–1125; *Guan* 76, 369; 78, 385) or "to develop land" (*zhi di* 治地 in *Meng* 5, 199). In the present case, a vacant plot was supposed to be developed into a market stall.

757 Cf. *bu de* 不得 in *Wei li zhi dao* 37.1: 強良不得 "the rigid ones will not succeed".

758 *He* 劾 "*ex-officio* charge" (cf. footnote 545) here refers to the charge brought by Ji (see *Yuelu* WYZ 064 above).

Cai stated:
"I already own a [second] coffin market stall which does not yield profit.[759] The vacant market stall originally was my market stall. More than ten years ago the royal house[760] set up a market storehouse and deprived[761] me [of my market stall] to make a storehouse[762] out of it. [When] the storehouse was [later] closed,[763] I wanted to take over [the place for the market stall] again, but I did not succeed. In the last[764] ninth month I lodged a complaint[765] [against the

759 For *li* in the sense "to yield (financial) profit" see footnote 693.

760 *Wang shi* 王室 "royal house" referred to the government/state authorities before it was replaced by the official designation *xian guan* 縣官 after the foundation of the Qin Empire (*Liye* 8–461r). Cf. footnote 752.

761 *Duo* 奪 "to take away, to snatch (money)" (*ZYS* 197; *ENLL* 186) and "to deprive sb." of his rank (*ZYS* 147; *QLZC* 37=*RCL* C 23a; *ENLL* 143, 186, 483; *Juyan* 250.23) or of his market stall, as in the present case (*ENLL* 260: 市販匿不自占租，坐所匿租臧（贓）爲盜，沒入其所販賣及賈錢縣官，奪之列。 "When engaging in a trade transaction, evading the sales tax by not declaring one's own proceeds is prosecuted according to the provisions applicable to theft of the amount misappropriated by evading the tax; [in addition,] the [goods] sold in the transaction as well as the proceeds are to be seized into the government coffers and the market stall is to be taken away from the trader in question.").

762 According to the explanation by Hulsewé (*RCL* "addenda et corrigenda" to A 41; footnote 13), *fu* 府 is not a general term for government buildings, but refers to "government storehouses", which were engaged in commercial dealings and deposited money (*QLSZ* 64, 68, 97=*RCL* A 42, 45, 51) that could be borrowed (*FLDW* 32=*RCL* D 26), stored hides (*XL* 42=*RCL* B 18) and loaned government carts and oxen (*QLSZ* 126=*RCL* A 74), or to "workshops" where people could work off debts to the government (*QLSZ* 84, 133=*RCL* A 41, 68; *FLDW* 63, 127=*RCL* D 51, 106). Such workshops (*guan fu* 官府) were occasionally referred to as *xi suo* 繫所 "detention places" because people who had to work off debts were probably held in custody there (cf. *Yuelu WYZ* 194 and 201).

763 *Ba* 罷 as in *Hanfei* 32, 209 (cf. Harbsmeier): 市罷 "the market was closed/given up".

764 There is no other reference for *nai wang* 迺往 in combination with a date. For *nai* meaning "last" see footnote 491. Here, it must refer to the last ninth month before the time of the statement.

765 For *ci* 辤 as the graph conventionally used for *ci* 辭 see footnote 564. In legal texts of Qin and Han times *ci* usually occurs as a neutral term meaning "statement (during interrogation)", but the word could also have the character of a defence or accusation. For the meaning "to indict, to accuse, to lodge a complaint" see *Shu* Lüxing §7: 鰥寡有辭于苗。 "Widowers and widows made their indictments against Miao."; *Zuo* Xiang 21,488,17: 西周鄙掠之，辭於行人。 "[The people in] Zhou's western borders plundered him, on which he complained to a messenger [from the king]." or *Zuo* Zhao 9,624,4: 周甘人與晉閻嘉爭閻田[...]王使詹桓伯辭於晉：[...]。 "The commandant of Gan in Zhou had a quarrel with Jia, the commandant of Yan in Jin, about the lands of Yan [...], the king sent Zhan Huan Bo to lodge the following complaint before Jin: [...]."
In the present context, *ci* also makes sense in the meaning "to lodge a complaint (against sth./sb.)" (*Yuelu WYZ* 191: 辤（辭）丞詔謁更治，詔不許。 "I lodged a complaint

decision before] the incumbent[766] [prefect] Gan. He gave orders to [the head of] the *ting*,[767] He, saying: '[If] nobody contests [Cai's] claims [to the market stall], assign it to Cai.' Xi, holder of the third rank,[768] contested my claims to it. So He did not assign [the market stall] to me. I privately consulted with Xi about the matter: '[Although] you formerly possessed the coffin market stall, you should not contest my claims [to it]. If you are willing, after I have [finished] developing and building on [the land for the market stall], I can make a deal with you.' Xi said: 'Agreed.' I did not report this to He, so I, without authorisation[769] and stealthily,[770] developed and built on [the land] to make a market stall out of it. Before I completed[771] this, Rui said to me: 'Share [the market stall] with me. If you do not, I will lodge a complaint and contest [your claims

---

[against the unjustified sentence] to vice prefect Shao and requested a retrial, but Shao did not grant [my request]."; ZYS 8: 大夫禒（祿）辤（辭）曰：六年二月中買婢媚士五（伍）點所，賈（價）錢萬六千。迺三月丁巳亡。求得媚，媚曰：不當爲婢。 "Lu, holder of the fifth rank, lodged the following complaint stating: 'In the second month of the sixth year I bought the female slave Mei from the rank-and-file man Dian, the price was 16,000 cash. On the day *dingsi* of the last third month she absconded. I searched for her and caught her. [But] she said: "It is not justified that I am enslaved."'"; see also *Yuelu* WYZ 070–071).

766 At the end of the preceding case I.3 Gan 感 appears as "incumbent prefect of Jiangling" (*Yuelu* WYZ 061). For *shou* in combination with a particular office see footnote 486.

767 The same construction, where *zhang* 長 "head" is also omitted, occurs in ZYS 100: 亭慶以書言雍廷曰：[…]。 "Qing, [the head of a] *ting*, in a note (letter?) reported [the case] to the [prefectural] court of Yong, stating: […]." On the tasks of a *ting zhang* see Yan Gengwang 1961, 240–242; Chen Zhi 1986, 69–75; Zhang Jinguang 2004, 587–588; An and Xiong 2007, 694–704. The *ting* in the present case apparently was a *shi ting* 市亭 "police station at the market" (cf. ZYS 100), at which the sale and purchase of slaves, horses and cattle had to be certified for a fee of 22 cash (*Yuelu Lüling* 1300–01 [yet unpublished]).

768 For *zou ma* see footnote 601.

769 *Shan* 擅 denotes that an action is done on someone's own authority. This implies that the person in question arrogated powers that he was not allowed to exercise. So *shan* could refer to the unauthorised killing of sb. (ZYS 87; FLDW 69=RCL D 56), extorting pledges (FLDW 148=RCL D 126), levying taxes (ENLL 185), calling up conscripts to labour service (*Hanshu* 8, 255), trying a case for revision (ENLL 113), loaning government tools (QLSZ 106=RCL A 57), or demolishing and changing government buildings, storehouses and prefectural courts (QLSZ 121=RCL A 64).

770 *Qie* 竊 "privily, stealthily" (*Zuo* Xiang 14,460,2: 秦人竊與鄭盟。 "The people of Qin stealthily made a covenant with Zheng."; *Zuo* Xiang 28,538,4: 饔人竊更之以鶩。 "The cook stealthily changed them (i.e. the fowls) for ducks.").

771 *Zu* 蹴 *dzʕuk (*Shuowen* 8B, 411b) for *jiu* 就 (GSR 1093a) *dzuk-s "accomplish, complete" (*Yantielun* 28, 32: 車器難就而易敗。 "Carriages, vessels and tools are difficult to complete, but easy to break.").

to it].' I lied[772] to [...] and lodged a complaint before He. [So] He did not give [the market stall] to me and Rui [but instead] brought[773] me, Rui and Xi [before the authorities] reporting the following to [prefect] Gan: 'They all formerly owned the coffin market stall [in question]. [When] I refused to assign it to them [again], they, without authorisation, developed and built [a new stall on the land] and contested each others' claims to [it].' Gan said: '[The market stall] shall not be assigned [to any of them].' I [... Duo said that Rui had sold him his share of the market stall and therefore he wanted to] occupy[774] [it]. I said: 'This is not acceptable. We will wait for Rui to come [and solve the matter].' Duo accordingly did not dare to occupy [the market stall]." Everything else corresponded to [the statement of] Geng.

芮曰：
空列地便利，利與材共。喜爭，芮乃智（知）材弗得，弗敢居。廼十一月欲與人共漁，毋【錢】。$_{073}$朵子士五（伍）方販棺其列下。芮利【買（賣）】所共蓋公地。卒又蓋□□□□與材共$_{074}$芮分方曰：欲即并賈（價）地蓋千四百。方前顧（雇）芮千，巳（已）盡用錢買漁具。後念悔，恐發$_{075}$覺有辠（罪）。欲益賈（價）令方勿取。即往（誑）謂方：賤。令二千。弗取，環（還）方錢。方曰：貴。弗取。芮$_{076}$毋錢環（還）。居三日，朵責。與期：五日備賞（償）錢；不賞（償），朵以故賈（價）取肆（肆）。朵曰：若（諾）。即弗環（還）錢，去往$_{077}$漁。得。
它如材、更。

Rui stated:

772 *Tuo* 詑 *(h)lˤaj "to lie" (*Liye* 8–461r: 更詑曰謾。 "Change ['lying', which was until now called] *tuo* to be called *man*."; *ZYS* 175: 諸以縣官事詑其上者 "all those who during their service in a government office lie to their superiors"; *Yuelu WYZ* 144, 229; *Shuowen* 3A, 96a). Cf. its graphic variant *tuo* 訑 (*GSR* 4q; *FZS* 2–4=*RCL* E 2: 詰之極而數訑，更言不服 [...]。 "If he has been confronted [with inconsistencies] to the utmost and still repeatly lies, changes his statements and does not confess, [...]."; *Zhanguoce* 421/203/18; *Yantielun* 29, 34).

773 For *jiang* 將 in the sense "to guard convicts during transportation; to function as convict warden" see footnote 529. Here, it means "to bring suspects before the authorities (under guard?)" or simply "bring sb. before" (*ENLL* 474 [cf. Yates 2011, 349]: 史、卜、祝學童學三歲，學佴將詣大（太）史、大（太）卜、大（太）祝。 "When the students of scribes, diviners, and invocators have studied for three years, their tutors bring them before the court scribe, court diviner and court invocator [respectively]."). The word could therefore be interpreted as a synonym of *yi* 詣 (cf. footnote 496).

774 The following part is most likely the second half of the statement of Cai.

"The land at the vacant market stall is convenient and advantageous[775] [for profit], I was eager[776] to share it with Cai. [When] Xi contested [Cai's claim], I realised that Cai would not get [the market stall and so] I did not dare to occupy it. In the last eleventh month I wanted to go fishing together with others and did not have [money to buy fishing equipment]. The son of Duo, the rank-and-file man Fang, deals with coffins below (i.e. down the row from) this market stall. I was eager [to sell] the government land, which I had built on together [with Cai]. Finally,[777] I again built on [...] together with Cai [... I [offered] my share to Fang saying: 'If[778] you want, I will fix the total price[779] of the land and the building to be 1,400 [cash].' Fang paid[780] me 1,000 [cash] in

775 *Bian li* 便利 "conveniently located" (*Shiji* 8, 382; 81, 2447). Cf. *li tian* 利田 "productive fields" (*Yuelu* WYZ 216; *QLSZ* 38=*RCL* A 27; *Hanshu* 1B, 66).

776 For *li* as "to be eager for/to, to desire" see footnote 515.

777 *Zu* 卒 "in the end, finally" (*Shiji* 81, 2441 [cf. Nienhauser VII (1994), 265]: 卒廷見相如，畢禮而歸之。 "In the end he (the king of Qin) granted Xiangru an audience in his court, completed the ceremonies, and sent him back.").

778 *Ji* 即 (*GSR* 923a) *tsək (Baxter and Sagart reconstruct *tsik because of rhymes with words of the rhyme class *zhi* 質 *-it/-ik in *Odes* 89,2; 99,1 and 250,6) has been convincingly interpreted as a late classical variant of the accentuating particle resp. consecutive conjunction *ze* 則 (*GSR* 906a) *tsʕək (Unger 1987–97, vol. II, 94; vol. VIII, 82–83) or as a loan graph for *ze* (Wang Hui 2008, 246; Feng and Deng 2006, 129; Bai Yulan 2012, 537; cf. Wang Shumin 1990, 342, 353). The current passage can be compared with *Yuelu* WYZ 069: 喜欲，與喜貿。 "If you, Xi, are willing, I can make a deal with you."

779 *Bing jia* 并賈（價） "total price" (*Suanshushu* 37) or "to fix a total price" (*Yuelu* WYZ 084). For *gu* 賈 (*GSR* 38b) as the character form commonly used to write *jia* 價 (*GSR* 38c) "price" see footnote 738.

780 *Gu* 顧 (*GSR* 53g) *kʕa-s here for the homophonous *gu* 雇 (*GSR* 53d) "spend money to buy labour/hire" (e.g. a farm-labourer in *Houhanshu* 3, 145; a ploughing ox in *Houhanshu* 4, 192) or "to rent (a lodging)" (*Houhanshu* 3, 132). Here *gu* occurs in its basic sense "give as a price for sth., remunerate sb. for sth., pay" (*Houhanshu* 7, 300: [...]以見錢雇直。 "[...] were remunerated for the value [of the grain they had provided] in cash"). For the same use of *gu* 顧 see Feng and Deng 2006, 1043–1044 with many examples (e.g. *Hanfei* 33, 201 [according to Zhang Jue 2010, 719, footnote 3; cf. Harbsmeier]: 則顧白馬之賦 。"Then he paid the tax for the white horse."; *Hanshu* 49, 2294: 斂民財以顧其功。"We tax the valuables of the people in order to remunerate their merits."; see also *Shiji* 100, 2731 [cf. Nienhauser VIII (2008), 311]: 楚人曹丘生，辯士，數招權顧金錢。"Cao Qiusheng from Chu was a rhetorician and several times sought an advantageous moment to be remunerated with money [for hired labour]."). Wang Li (1982, 124–125) assumed that *gu* 顧 (*GSR* 53g) *kʕa-s belongs to the same word family as *gu* 賈 (*GSR* 38b) *krʕaʔ "to buy" (*Zuo* Xiang 4, 422,14; Zhao 29,728,12; 沽 [*GSR* 49k] *kʕa in *Lunyu* 10, 222; 酤 [*GSR* 49b'] *kʕa-s in *Odes* 165,3; cf. Lau 1999, 304).

advance,[781] which I have already completely used up to buy fishing equipment. Afterwards, I intensively thought about [the deal] and had reservations[782] because I was afraid that it would be revealed that I committed an offence.[783] I wanted to make Fang not accept it by raising the price. So I insincerely[784] said to Fang: '[The price for the market stall] was too cheap. Let [the price be] 2,000 [cash]. If you do not accept [this new price of] 2,000 [cash], I will give you back the money [you already paid].' Fang said: '[This is too] expensive.' And he did not accept it. I had no money to repay [him]. After[785] three days, when Duo claimed [the money back], I set a deadline:[786] 'In five days I will completely[787] repay the money. If I do not repay it, you shall receive the market stall for the old price.' Duo said: 'I agree.' Then I failed to repay the money and went away [to go] fishing. [Then] I got caught."[788]
Everything else corresponded to [the statements of] Cai and Geng.

方曰：
朵不存，買芮肆（肆）。芮後益賈（價），弗取。責錢，不得。不得居肆（肆）。芮母索$_{078}$後環（還）二百錢，未備八百。
它及朵言如芮、材。

Fang stated:
"When Duo was not present, I bought the market stall from Rui. When Rui later raised the price I did not accept it. I claimed[789] back the money [I had already paid] but did not get it. I [also] did not get [the chance] to occupy the market

781 *Qian* 前 rarely also means "in advance" (*Li* 52, 1630b).

782 For *hui* see footnote 615.

783 For *you zui* see footnote 514.

784 *Wang* 往 (GSR 739k) *Gʷaŋʔ here for *kuang* 誑 (GSR 739x) *kʷaŋ-s "to deceive, to tell lies to sb.; liar" (*Hanfei* 13,66). Cf. *kuang* 狂 (GSR 739o) *gʷaŋ according to Zhang Jue (2010, 1253) for *kuang* 誑 (*Hanfei* 50, 355) or for *wang* 枉 (GSR 739q) "to bend/pervert (the law)" (ZYS 52).

785 *Ju* 居 is used here as a preposition determining a length of time (cf. ZYS 83, 107, 112; *Yuelu* WYZ 112–113, 115–116; FLDW 167=D 146). Unger interprets *ju* verbally and translates it as "es dauerte" or "nach soundso langer Zeit" (Unger 1987–97, vol. VI, 43–44). Yang Bojun and He Leshi (2001, 392) translate "after ...".

786 *Yu qi* 與期 "to set a deadline" (*Shiji* 39, 1656; 90, 2591).

787 For *bei* in adverbial usage see footnote 521.

788 For *de* see footnote 524.

789 *Ze* 責 "to demand a refund; to charge sb. debts" (QLSZ 83–85=RCL A 41: 其已分而死[...]毋責妻、同居。"When the share [of the repayment an official has been charged with for misdemeanours in his office] has already been alloted and he dies, [...] [these debts] must not be charged to his wife or to household members."; *Yuelu* WYZ 110–111).

stall. The mother of Rui, Suo, later paid back 200 cash [to me, but] 800 cash have not yet been provided."[790]
Everything else as well as the statement of Duo corresponded to [the statements of] Rui and Cai.

駕言如更。

The statement of [the *ting* assistant] Jia corresponded to [the statement of] Geng.

賀曰：
材、喜、芮妻佞皆巳（已）受$_{079}$棺列，不當重受。
它及喜言如材、芮。

[The head of the *ting*] He stated:
"Cai, Xi and the wife of Rui, Ning, have all already taken over a coffin market stall [in the past], they are not entitled to take over [a market stall] again."[791]
Everything else as well as the statement of Xi corresponded to [the statements of] Cai and Rui.

索言如方。

The statement of Suo (the mother of Rui) corresponded to [the statement of] Fang.

Original Case – Second Stage of Interrogation (Confrontation)

詰芮：
芮後智（知）材不得受列，弗敢居，是公$_{080}$列地殹（也）。可（何）故紿方曰巳（已）受，盜買（賣）于方？巳（已），盡用錢，後撓（嬈）益賈

790 In legal manuscripts, *wei bei* 未備 otherwise appears in the meaning "not yet completed" for the number of days of labour service, etc. (*QLSZ* 138, 142=*RCL* 68, 65). Here it should be identified with *bu bei* 不備 "shortage, deficiency" (*QLSZ* 23, 25, 29, 31–32, 83, 162, 167, 173, 177=*RCL* A 19, 21, 22, 41, 82, 84, 86, 88; *XL* 2=*RCL* B 2) as in *QLSZ* 174=*RCL* A 87: 者（諸）移贏以賞（償）不備 "all cases of transferring a surplus to repay a shortage".

791 Cf. analogous stipulations concerning land allocation (*ENLL* 321: 受田宅，予人若賣宅，不得更受。 "Those who took over fields and residences, but handed them over to other people or sold the residences, are not allowed to take over [fields and residences] again.").

（價），欲令勿取。方弗取，有（又）弗$_{081}$環（還）錢，去往漁。是即盜紿人買公列地，非？今且以盜論芮，芮可（何）以解？

We confronted[792] Rui:
"You later knew that Cai was not allowed to take over the market stall and [therefore you] did not dare to occupy it, [because] this is land for government market stalls. Why did you deceive[793] Fang saying that you had already taken over [the market stall and then] illegally sold it to him? Afterwards, you completely used up the money, later excessively[794] raised the price and wanted to make [Fang] not accept it. When Fang did not accept it, you nevertheless did not pay back the money [he had already given you] and went away to go fishing. This is illegally[795] deceiving a person into buying government land for market stalls, isn't it?[796] Now what if[797] we sentence[798] you

792 *Jie* 詰 "to confront (an accused)" as a legal term refers to the second stage of interrogation by the authorities, implying the systematic confrontation of the accused (*FZS* 2=*RCL* E 2; *ZYS* 4, 11, 19, 21, 30, 41, 44, 86, 105, 146, 149, 217, 218, 219; *Yuelu WYZ* 080, 102, 127, 184, 202) or of witnesses (*ZYS* 116, 117, 139; *Yuelu WYZ* 201) with matters of fact or of law that contradict their earlier statements. It was the responsibility of the judicial officials to be skilful in *jie* in order to prove criminal liability of an offender and to avoid miscarriages of justice against the innocent; for this, a judicial official had to realise where an interrogated person might be inconsistent or untruthful, to have the necessary counter-evidence at hand, and to be well versed in the law to prove the culpability of a suspect against denial. The accused, for his part, during the *jie* acquired full knowledge of the accusation and the evidence against him for the first time; at the same time, *jie* provided him with the opportunity to defend himself against the charge. Cf. Lau 2002, 361–362; Lau and Lüdke 2012, 85; Korolkov 2011.

793 For *dai* see footnote 555.

794 *Nao* 撓 (*GSR* 1164s) is used instead of the homeophonous *rao* 饒 (*GSR* 1164o) "to be abundant/plentiful". Accordingly, *nao yi* 撓益 could be identified with *rao yi* 饒益 "rich" (*Shiji* 129, 3258 [cf. Watson 1993, vol. II, 438]) or *yi rao* 益饒 (*Shiji* 56, 2052 [cf. Watson 1993, vol. I, 116]: 齎用益饒。"The resources were in increasing/plentiful supply."; 30, 1435 [cf. Watson 1993, vol. II, 77]: 用益饒矣。"[The government officials, for their part,] found themselves with increasing resources at their disposal."). *Nao* 撓 could also write the homophonous *nao* 橈 (*GSR* 1164p) "bent, crooked, unjust" (*Li* 16, 1373c; *Shiji* 53, 2016).

795 When *dao* 盜 is used adverbially to qualify an action, it means either "in the act of committing theft" (*ENLL* 66) or "illegally" (*ENLL* 74, 201; *FLDW* 64=*RCL* D 136).

796 *Fei* 非 according to He Leshi (2006, 120), Wang Shumin (1990, 556) and Yang Shuda (quoted in Yu and Xie 1993, 336) occurs in the final part of alternative questions (*Shiji* 61, 2124: 若伯夷、叔齊，可謂善人者非邪？ "[Persons] such as Bo Yi and Shu Qi, can they be called good men, or not?"; *Lao* 39 quoted in *Zhanguoce* 136B/68/6 [punctuation according to Wang Shumin]: 是其賤之本與？非夫？, cf. *Mawangdui Lao* B 177: 此其賤之本與? 非也? "Is this the root of the inferior [status of a person] or not?"; *Hanshu*

for theft,[799] how do you explain[800] [yourself]?"

64B, 2818: 此言與實反者非？ "These words contradict the truth, don't they?"). Cf. *qie bu* 且不 "or not" as another form of alternative question (*Yuelu* WYZ 230–231). For a similar construction containing an official accusation in other legal manuscripts from the Qin dynasty see ZYS 150: 是庢欲繹（釋）縱罪人明矣。吏以論庢，庢何以解之？ "From this it is clear that you, Tui, indeed intended to release and leave offenders unpunished. If we, the officials, are going to pass judgement on you for this, how do you explain this?" Cf. the combination of *shi* 是 referring to a statutory offence, which the accused committed according to the judicial officials' judgement, and the final question *he jie* 何解 (*Yuelu* WYZ 129; ZYS 20, 42, 147; for the combination of *he jie* and *yi mou zui lun* 以某罪論 cf. ZYS 31).

797 In contrast to the identification of this character as *ling* 令 by the editors and the according interpretation of *fei ling* 非令 as "not in accord with the legal stipulations" (Zhu and Chen 2013, 135 and 140 with footnote 28), the character in the manuscript should rather be identified as *jin* 今 "now". When comparing the forms of the characters *ling* and *jin* in Qin manuscripts (Zhang Shouzhong 1994, 143 and 77; Fang Yong 2012, 272 and 148–149), it becomes clear that in most cases the horizontal stroke of the hook-shaped bottom part of *jin* is connected with the right stroke of the roof-shaped top part, whereas in the character *ling* this can normally not be observed. In the present passage, *jin* can therefore be connected with the following word to form the introductory phrase *jin qie* 今且. In the passage *Mo* 19, 98: 今且天下之王公大人士君子, *jin qie* is, according to Wang Yinzhi (quoted in Yu and Xie 1993, 139), to be interpreted as *jin fu* 今夫, which introduces a supposed case in contrast to the preceding one. According to Wang Shumin (1990, 387; who quoted *Zhuang* 2; 12: 今且有言於此) *jin qie* is synonymous to *jin* 今 in the sense "supposing". On *jin* as initial particle see Unger 1987–97, vol. VII, 165–168. Cf. *Yushu* 7: 今且令人案行之，舉劾不從令者。"Now I will order people to examine them on an inspection tour, and trace and charge those who did not follow the ordinances."

798 For *lun* see footnote 540.

799 For *dao* see footnotes 541, 557 and 795. "Illegally deceiving a person into buying government land for market stalls" is evidently classified as statutory offence of *dao* "theft" by the officials.

800 In a legal context, *jie* 解 refers to the explanations offered by an accused to resolve factual inconsistencies or discrepancies between statements, or to defend himself against a legal assessment of his action as a criminal offence. In criminal procedure, such explanations were sought during the second stage of interrogation, usually by means of a confrontation (*jie* 詰) of the person being interrogated with unresolved matters of fact or of law. The following formulas are used in the case records in the context of a confrontation: 1) *he jie* 何解 (*Yuelu* WYZ 102, 129, 201–202; *Liye* 8–43, 8–314, 8–691r, 8–874, 8–1792; ZYS 5, 12, 20, 22, 31, 42, 44, 87, 141, 147) or the synonymous variant *he yi jie* (*zhi*) 何以解 (之) (*Yuelu* WYZ 082; ZYS 150) concluded the interrogating official's confrontation and thus served to demand a defence against a charge or an explanation for an inconsistency. 2) *wu jie* 無解 or *wu yi jie zhi* 無以解之: If used in the statement of an accused (*Yuelu* WYZ 241; ZYS 5, 22, 31, 87, 150), it means "I cannot offer a (full) explanation" and is often preceded or followed

芮曰：
誠弗受。朵姊$_{082}$孫故爲兄妻，有子。兄死，孫尚存。以方、朵終不告芮。芮即紿買（賣）方，巳（已），用錢，毋（無）以賞（償）。上即以$_{083}$芮爲盜買（賣）公地，辠（罪）芮，芮毋（無）以壁（避）。毋（無）它解。
它如前。

Rui stated:
"I in fact[801] did not take over [the market stall]. Duo's elder sister Sun[802] was formerly the wife of my elder brother,[803] and they have children. When my elder brother died, Sun was still alive. [Because of her] I assumed[804] that Fang

---

by *zui* 罪 "I am liable to punishment"; this indicates that the accused admits criminal liability. If used from the perspective of a judicial official (FZS 3=RCL E 2; ZYS 220), it means "(the accused) has no (full) explanation" and indicates that the defence or explanation offered was deemed insufficient, and that further interrogation, often under torture (FZS 4–5=RCL E 2; ZYS 220), was considered necessary. Sometimes the formula *wu yi jie mou ren yan* 無以解某人言 "to have no means to explain the statements (of codefendants and witnesses)" is used instead (*Yuelu* WYZ 202, 204, 206). 3) In some cases, *wu ta jie* 無它解 "I cannot offer any other explanation" seems to indicate that the person being interrogated insists on the validity of his or her explanation (ZYS 13, 45, 145, 148). In one of the cases of the Yuelu Academy, the accused who pleads not guilty uses this formula (*Yuelu* WYZ 103), but, in two other cases, the accused admits his criminal liability immediately after this formula (*Yuelu* WYZ 084, 130). Cf. the use of *wu ta jie* in the statement of an official who justified the arrest of an accused (*Yuelu* WYZ 201) as well as Zhu Xiangrong 2012, 166–167.

801 *Cheng* 誠 is used when an accused or a witness confirms the correctness of a charge or a statement during interrogation (*Yuelu* WYZ 082, 129, 161, 241; FZS 38, 51=RCL E 15, 18; *Liye* 8–1354; ZYS 28, 38, 39, 41, 43, 45, 63, 85, 112, cf. ZYS 196). For the synonymous term *shi* 實 see footnote 533.

802 Sun 孫 occurred as given name (*ming* 名) in other Qin manuscripts as well (*Liye* 8–1538, cf. the name Yisun 壹孫 on *Liye* 8–663r and 8–2101). For examples of Sun as second part of given names in Han manuscripts see Ôba 1995, 94–181.

803 This means that Rui and Duo, who previously cooperated to take possession of the stall and for this purpose employed the strawperson Geng (*Yuelu* WYZ 065–066), were related by marriage. Duo was the younger brother of Rui's sister-in-law Sun.

804 The editors (Zhu and Chen 2013, 136 with footnote 29) interpret *yi* 以 as an abbreviated form of *yi wei* 以爲 (Unger 1987–97, vol. V, 218–219; cf. ZYS 43: 自以非軍亡奴，毋罪。"I am of the opinion that I am not [to be regarded as] Jun's absconded slave, and [therefore] not liable to punishment.", ZYS 151–152: 義死，自以有罪，棄籍去亡。"Because Yi had died, I assumed that I myself had become liable to punishment, discarded the registers and absconded." and ZYS 194: 廷尉、史議皆以欺死父罪輕於侵欺生父。"You, minister of trials, as well as you secretaries in your legal arguments all hold that the punishment for treating one's father with disrespect after his death is less serious

and Duo would never[805] report[806] me [to the authorities]. So I sold [the market stall] to Fang under false pretences, afterwards used up the money and had no means to repay [him]. If you, the authorities, therefore regard me as someone who illegally sold government land and consider me liable to punishment, I have no means[807] to avoid this. I do not have any other explanation." Everything else corresponded to his previous [statement].

獄史豬曰：
芮、方并賈（價）。豬以芮不$_{084}$

[Missing slip]

The judicial secretary[808] Zhu stated:
"Rui and Fang fixed a total price [for the land and the building of the market stall]. Because Rui did not [...] I [...].

Original Case – Interagency Enquiries

九錢，買（賣）分四百卌五尺，直（值）千錢。
它如舜（辭）。

[... Rui ...]9 cash, sold [his] part [of the market stall with a space of] 435 feet[809] that was worth 1,000 cash.[810]

---

than [the punishment for] wronging and treating one's father with disrespect when he is still alive.").

805 *Zhong* 終 "all the time, constantly" in combination with the negative *bu* 不 means "never" (*Zuo* Xiang 29,544,9–10: 公冶致其邑於季氏而終不入焉。 "Gong Ye resigned his city to Ji [Wuzi], [but afterwards] never entered his house."; *Zuo* Wen 14,266,13: 元不順懿公之爲政也，終不曰公，曰夫己氏。 "[Duke Yi's brother] Yuan, dissatisfied with Yi's administration of the government, never spoke of him as 'duke', but as 'so and so no. 6'.").

806 For *gao* see footnote 498.

807 Different interpretations, and therefore different translations, of the indefinite substitution *wu yi* 無以 can be found (cf. *Yuelu* WYZ 083, 130, 202, 204, 206, 231; *QLSZ* 82=*RCL* A 41; *Shiji* 33, 1518 [cf. Nienhauser V.1 (2006), 134]) in secondary literature, e.g. "have no means/way to" (Cikoski 2011, 601, 607; He Leshi 2006, 427), "have no way of doing" or "lack the means to/whereby" (TLS), or "durch nichts, auf keine Weise, hat nichts wodurch, hat keine Möglichkeit=kann nicht, weiß nicht" (Unger 1987–97, vol. V, 210–211).

808 For (*yu*) *shi* see footnote 539.

809 One *chi* 尺 "foot" corresponded to about 23–24 cm in late Warring States, Qin and early Han times (Qiu Guangming 1992, 10–11, 54–56).

810 The preceding passage probably contains the results of interagency enquiries (*wen* 問), which were also used in other cases to gather information about the value of stolen goods (*ZYS* 71, 224; *Yuelu* WYZ 016, 130, 166) as the basis for determining punishment. Although

Everything else corresponded to the statements.[811]

Original case – Finding of Fact

鞫之：
芮不得受列。擅蓋治公地，費六百九$_{085}$□□□□□□□地積四百卅□□□□□□四百。巳（已）受千錢，盡用。後環（還）二百。地臧（贓）直（值）千$_{086}$錢，得。

Finding of fact:[812]
Rui was not allowed to take over a market stall. Without authorisation, he built on and developed[813] government land, for which he spent[814] 609(?) [cash ...] land accumulated to 43[5 feet ... the agreed total price was 1,]400 [cash]. After he had received 1,000 cash, he used it up completely. Later he paid back 200 [cash]. As to the land, the value of the misappropriated goods[815] is 1,000 cash. [Rui] got caught.

Original Case – Judgement

獄巳（已）斷，令黥芮爲城旦，未□□□□□□□$_{087}$

After the case had been decided,[816] order was given to tattoo Rui and make him an earth pounder convict.[817] [...].

---

the term *wen* 問, usually used to mark the beginning of this part, is missing, the phrase *ta ru ci* 它如舜（辭）, normally marking the end of it, can be found on *Yuelu* WYZ 085. This suggests that the preceding passage, in fact, describes the results of interagency enquiries. For *wen* see footnote 562. It remains unclear because of the lacunae whether and how the statement of the judicial secretary Zhu was connected to these enquiries.

811 For *ci* see footnote 564.

812 For *ju* see footnote 565.

813 For *zhi* with the meaning "to till, develop (land)" see footnote 756.

814 *Fei* 費 "to spend, to expend (money, valuables)" (*Zuo* Xi 33,223,16) or as noun "expenses" (*QLSZ* 37=*RCL* A 26; *QLZC* 22=*RCL* C 14; *ENLL* 410).

815 For *zang* see footnote 592. The usage of *zang* suggests that the offence committed by Rui was classified as a case of *dao* "theft". When the authorities responsible for the retrial determined punishment, they apparently only took into account the value of the misappropriated land and ignored the value of the building, which is mentioned with divergent amounts in the report of the prefecture (269 cash, *Yuelu* WYZ 063) and in the first offer of Rui (400 cash, cf. *Yuelu* WYZ 075).

816 Cf. the explanation of the phrase *yu wei duan* in footnote 568.

817 For the convicts of the *qing cheng dan* category see foonote 668. According to Qin and early Han statutes, this most severe form of penal labour was to be imposed for theft to the value of 660 cash or more (*FLDW* 33–36=*RCL* D 27, 28; *ZYS* 72–73; *ENLL* 55).

Case 1.5

In this case, a fugitive from Qin was arrested by Qin soldiers after the conquest of his place of exile in the former state of Chu. The criminal proceedings were initiated by a written report of the arresting Qin officer, in which the fugitive was apparently charged for conspiring to abscond from the state of Qin. Conspiracy was a kind of punishable participation in an offence, which the accused had not necessarily carried out himself. Conspiracy to commit an offence was punished in the same way as actually committing the offence.

During the interrogation, the accused first furnished particulars about his status relevant to his sentence. According to his statement, he was a minor holder of the third rank, which implied that he had not yet been registered for military and labour service. The fugitive admitted that together with his mother he had absconded from the state of Qin to Chu ten years ago, but held that at that time he was not yet able to conspire to commit the offence he was charged with because of his young age. Since the mother had died in the meantime, she could not be interrogated.

According to the results of interagency enquiries, the fugitive was 12 years old when he absconded, and since then had reached the age of 22 years. In Qin, holders of the third rank had to be registered for military and labour service at this age. As the fugitive had already been deprived of his rank and had been made a rank-and-file man shortly after his arrest, he would have had to have been registered at an even earlier age, which meant that he was definitely to be considered an adult at the time of the trial.

In the summary of the finding of fact, the competent officials of a prefecture, the name of which is not mentioned in the manuscript, affirm the facts established before, but express doubts about the appropriate punishment. The point of controversy most probably was the question of whether the fugitive had already reached the age of criminal liability at the time when the offence he was charged with had been committed. The age of criminal liability during the Qin dynasty is not mentioned in the legal texts currently available to us. Some manuscripts show that physical height also was an important criterion. Judging by the evidence of this case, it seems likely that minors of the age of 12 were not yet liable for criminal offences during the Qin dynasty.

The majority of officials within the competent authority voted for exemption of the fugitive from punishment. A minority suggested punishing the accused for absconding from the state since the accused had reached the age of full criminal liability since then. Therefore, no mitigating circumstances were to be taken into account.

 | DOI 10.1163/9789004315655_013

Diplomatic Edition

□讞之十二月戊午軍巫閒曰攻荊廬谿□故秦人邦亡荊者男子多$_{088}$
多曰小走馬以十年時與母兒邦亡荊亡時小未能與兒謀它如軍巫書$_{089}$
兒死不訊$_{090}$
問多初亡時年十二歲今廿二歲巳削爵爲士五它如辤$_{091}$
鞫之多與兒邦亡荊年十二歲小未能謀今年廿二歲巳削爵爲士五得審疑多辠
毄$_{092}$它縣論敢讞之$_{093}$
•吏議曰除多或曰黥爲城旦$_{094}$

Edition and Translation

Submission by the Prefecture – Introductory Formula

【敢】讞（讞）之：

[We venture to] submit [the following case] for decision:[818]

Initiation of Criminal Proceedings

十二月戊午，軍巫閒曰：
攻荊廬谿□故秦人邦亡荊者男子多。$_{088}$

It was the 12th month, the day *wuwu*,[819] when the *jun wu*[820] Jian stated:[821]

---

818 For *yan* and the phrase *gan yan zhi* see footnote 489.

819 Without information about the year and/or the first day of the twelfth month it is difficult to determine the exact date of the report. According to the proposal of the editors (Zhu and Chen 2013, 141 with footnote 1), *wuwu* could be the 13th day of the twelfth month in the 22nd year of King Zheng of Qin (cf. Zhang Peiyu 2007, 73; Li Zhonglin 2012, 65), i.e. 24/01/225 BC (Xu Xiqi 1997, 1233). The fact that Chu forces suffered a serious defeat in 226 BC (*Shiji* 15, 756) also speaks in favour of this dating because the accused (Duo) was apparently arrested during a Qin attack on Jing (i.e. Chu). Another point of reference could be the pacification of the Chu territory south of the Changjiang by general Wang Jian in 222 BC (*Shiji* 6, 234). Then, *wuwu* would be the sixth day of the twelfth month in the 26th year of King Zheng of Qin, i.e. 03/01/221 BC (Xu Xiqi 1997, 1241).

820 Legal documents of Qin and Han times usually provide personal information about persons who report an offence or an offender to the authorities, e.g. their rank (*Yuelu WYZ* 031, etc.; *FZS* 31, 34, 37, 42, 46, 50, 73, 84, 91=*RCL* E 13–18, 22–24; *ZYS* 8, 28, 36, 49), their official position (*Yuelu WYZ* 210, etc.; *FZS* 52, 55, 63=*RCL* E 19–21; *ZYS* 1, 75, 197) as well as their given name. There is, however, no other evidence for an office with the title *jun wu* 軍巫 "army shaman", and there is only one other example for shamans in the army (*Mo*

"[When] we attacked Luxi[822] in Jing[823] [... we arrested] the male Duo, originally a man from Qin, who had absconded from the state (i.e. Qin)[824] to Jing (i.e. Chu)."

First Stage of Interrogation

多曰：
小走馬。以十年時，與母兒邦亡荊。亡時小，未能與兒謀。
它如軍巫書。089

Duo stated:
"[I am] a minor[825] holder of the third rank.[826] Ten years ago[827] I absconded

---

68, 340 [cf. Johnston 2010, 839]). On military divination see Yates 2005. For Jian 閒 as given name see *Liye* 8–1743v.

821 This statement in the written form probably substitutes a report (*gao* 告) or an *ex-officio* charge (*he* 劾), which usually initiated criminal proceedings.

822 The place name Luxi 廬谿, which also occurs in the variant 盧谿 in one of the calendars from the Yuelu Academy collection (*Yuelu 27 nian zhiri* 32.4), is not known from received literature of Qin and Han times. It is uncertain whether this place on former Chu territory can be identified with the post-Han prefectural sites in the environment of modern Luxi xian 瀘谿縣 in Hunan, which belonged to the province of Wuqian 巫黔 during the Qin dynasty (Hou Xiaorong 2009, 424). The fugitive Duo must have been arrested by Qin troops during the conquest of this area of Chu.

823 For Jing as old name for Chu see footnote 608.

824 For *bang wang* see footnote 512.

825 On *xiao* 小 see Lau and Lüdke 2012, footnote 1012: According to early Han statutes, all sons, except the direct successor, gained a rank only after they had been registered (*fu* 傅) for military and labour service. The successor, however, inherited a rank immediately after his father's death, regardless of his own age. The registration obviously marked a point in time from which a person was no longer regarded as a minor (*xiao* 小), but as an adult (*da* 大). The judicial official Xi, who is mentioned in the manuscripts found at Shuihudi, was born in 262 BC and already registered in 246 BC (*Biannianji* 54.1, 8.2), i.e. when he was barely 17 years old. As far as the time of registration is concerned, early Han statutes not only distinguish between different ranks, but also between sons with the status *xiao jue* 小爵, who were entitled to immediately inherit a rank as successors, and other sons. According to these stipulations, a minor successor of a holder of the fifth rank inherited the third rank *zan niao* 簪裹 (ENLL 368), which corresponded to *zou ma* 走馬 during Qin times, after his father's death. A *xiao zou ma* should be registered for military and labour service at the age of 22 years according to Han law (ENLL 364). However, during Qin times a certain height of males (perhaps six feet and five inches, which corresponds to approximately 1.50 m) seemed to serve as the criterion for reaching the age of majority and being registered for military and labour service; cf. Gao Heng 2008,

from the state to Jing with my mother Er. At the time of our escape I was a minor[828] and [therefore] not capable of conspiring[829] with Er."

118–121 and Zhang Jinguang 2004, 218–224. It is yet unknown whether the rank of the father was also taken into account in determining the age of registration during Qin times.

826 For *zou ma* see footnote 601.

827 *Yi shi nian shi* 以十年時 with *yi* 以 as preposition before a specification of time (*QLSZ* 13, 71, 86, 90, 133=*RCL* A 7, 36, 47, 49, 68; *FZS* 15, 28, 52, 81, 92, 96–97=*RCL* E 7, 12, 19, 22, 24, 6; *Liye* 6–10, 8–140r, 8–154r, etc.; *ZYS* 75, 103, 108, 125). In the cited passages, *yi* 以 was generally interpreted with the meaning "at, in", sometimes as "from … onwards" (*QLSZ* 46, 51, 53, 77, 157=*RCL* A 33, 12, 13, 39, 79); cf. He Leshi 2006, 493; Unger 1987–97, vol. VI, 37–38. For *yi mou nian/sui shi* 以某年/歲時 in this passage the translation "X years ago" appears more suitable. For the same use see *Yuelu WYZ* 112: 沛妻危以十歲時死。"Wei, the wife of Pei, died ten years ago."; 115–116: 沛以三歲時爲識取妻。"Three years ago Pei arranged a marriage for Shi."; 161: 以旬餘時 "more than ten days ago" (cf. *Yuelu WYZ* 067–068: 十餘歲時，王室置市府，奪材以爲府。"More than ten years ago the royal house set up a market storehouse and deprived me, Cai, [of my market stall] to make a storehouse out of it.") and possibly *FZS* 52=*RCL* E 19: 以三歲時病疕，麋（眉）突。"At the time I was three years old/three years ago, I suffered from boils and my eyebrows fell out."; *FZS* 92=*RCL* E 24: 以卅餘歲時遷。"When she was over 30 years old/more than 30 years ago, she was banished."

828 During Qin times, criminal responsibility or possible exemption from mutilation depended on the height of the person who had committed an offence (*FLDW* 158=*RCL* D 138: 甲小未盈六尺，有馬一匹自牧之，今馬爲人敗，食人稼一石，問當論不當？不當論及賞（償）稼。"A is a minor and not fully six feet [tall]. He has a horse that he personally takes to graze. Now the horse is frightened by another person and eats one bushel of another person's grain. Question: Is he (A) by law to be sentenced or not? He is by law not to be sentenced nor to compensate for the grain."; *FLDW* 6=*RCL* D 5: 甲盜牛，盜牛時高六尺，毄（繫）一歲，復丈，高六尺七寸，問甲可（何）論？當完城旦。"A stole an ox; at the time he stole the ox he was six feet tall. Having been held under detention for one year, he was measured again; he was six feet and seven inches tall. Question: How is A to be sentenced? He by law is to be made an intact earth pounder convict."; *QLSZ* 51–52=*RCL* A 12; *FLDW* 67=*RCL* D 54).

829 On *mou* 謀 see Lau and Lüdke 2012, footnote 862: *mou* 謀 "to conspire, plot" usually refers to the joint planning/conspiracy to commit an offence as in *yu mou ren mou* 與某人謀 (*ZYS* 84, 99, 106; *ENLL* 23, 71; *Yuelu WYZ* 007, 028, 053–054, 069, 089, 092). Because in the present case the offence has been committed, it is impossible that *mou* only refers to the planning of an offence which has not yet been carried out (*ENLL* 22, 208; *mu* 牧 in *FLDW* 67=*RCL* D 60; cf. *ENLL* 35, 38; *Longgang* 114). For the different meanings of *mou* see in detail Sueyasu 2009, 421–424, footnote 66. As a kind of participation, *mou* was punishable with regard to several offences, which have not personally or not yet been carried out,

Everything else corresponded to the [reporting] letter of the *jun wu*.

兒死不訊。090

Er has already died and could not be interrogated.[830]

Interagency Enquiries

問：
多初亡時，年十二歲，今廿二歲。巳（已）削爵爲士五（伍）。
它如辤（辭）。091

[Results of the] interagency enquiries:[831]
At the time Duo originally[832] absconded, he was 12 years old; now he is 22 years

---

such as "staging a rebellion against the imperial dynasty" (*fan* 反) (ENLL 1–2; *Shiji* 90, 2594; *Hanshu* 4, 128; 84, 3436; *Juyan xinjian* E.P.T53:140), "killing somebody with malice" (*zei sha ren* 賊殺人) (ZYS 94), "injuring somebody with malice" (*zei shang ren* 賊傷人) (ENLL 22, 26; *Hanshu* 83, 3395), "stealing" (*dao* 盜) (ZYS 99–101), "illegally casting cash" (*dao zhu qian* 盜鑄錢) (ENLL 208), "blackmailing sb. in order to extort money or valuables" (*jie ren qiu qian cai* 劫人求錢財) (ENLL 68, 71; *Hanshu* 54, 2460; 94B, 3823) and "freeing (a remand prisoner) by force (and letting him break out of jail)" (*cuan qiu* 篡囚) (*Hanshu* 47, 2218; 81, 3345); cf. Hafner 2014c. However, according to early Han statutes, conspiracy was not punishable with regard to "absconding" (*wang* 亡 in ENLL 157–173). Therefore, *bang wang* must be a separate, more serious offence.

830 *Xun* 訊 "to interrogate" is the general term for the interrogation of suspects (FZS 5=RCL E 2; ZYS 76, 105, 107, 112; *Yuelu* WYZ 144, 157–159, 177, 190, 202; *Liye* 8–141r, 8–209r, 8–691r, 8–2015v, etc.), witnesses (FZS 86=RCL E 23; *Yuelu* WYZ 125; ZYS 140, 160, 200–202) and other persons who might provide information to help solve a crime (FZS 10, 64–65, 85–86, 89=RCL E 3, 20, 22, 23; ZYS 205, 212; *Yuelu* WYZ 143, 153–154). *Xun* is mostly followed by the name of a person as the object; in exceptional cases, it is used with the matter of the criminal investigation (ENLL 508) or *yu* 獄 "criminal case" (FZS 2=RCL E 2) as object. The absence of certain suspects or witnesses due to death as in the present and in another case (*Yuelu* WYZ 125) or due to absconding (ZYS 71) was to be recorded (ZYS 161). The same is true for persons who were not interrogated because they were still minors (*Yuelu* WYZ 125).

831 For *wen* see footnote 562. The age of the accused at the time of his absconding and at present as well as the loss of his rank are relevant for the determination of punishment.

832 For *chu* 初 He Leshi (2006, 53–54) distinguished the meanings "initially, originally, at that time" (*Shiji* 7, 295), "for the first time" (*Zuo* Yin 5,18,8) and "previously, formerly, once" at the beginning of a sentence (*Zuo* Yin 1,1,15).

old. He has already been deprived[833] of his rank,[834] and has been made a rank-and-file man.[835]
Everything else corresponded to the statements.[836]

Finding of Fact

鞫之：
多與兒邦亡荊，年十二歲，小未能謀。今年廿二歲。巳（已）削爵為士五（伍）。得。審。

Finding of fact:[837]
In the year that Duo absconded from the state to Jing with Er, he was 12 years old [and, therefore,] a minor not capable of conspiracy. This year he is 22 years old. He has already been deprived of his rank, and has been made a rank-and-file man. He was caught.[838] [All these] are established facts.[839]

Submission by the Prefecture – Concluding Formula

疑多辠（罪）。毄（繫）。$_{092}$它縣論。敢潚（讞）之。$_{093}$

We are in doubt about Duo's punishment.[840] He is held under detention.[841]

833 *Xue* 削 "cut (off); scrape off; reduce" in combination with *jue* 爵 means "to reduce the rank, to deprive sb. of his rank" (*Hanshu* 44, 2152: 皆當免、削爵為士伍，毋得官為吏。 "They were all, by law, to be dismissed from office, to be deprived of their rank and be made rank-and-file men and not to be permitted to become officials in the administration."; *Hanshu* 15B, 496; 36, 1924; 50, 2314; 72, 3077; 73, 3110; 74, 3142; 74, 3148). Cf. *duo jue* 奪爵 (*Yuelu* WYZ 244[2]: 其餘皆奪爵以為士五（伍）。"The remaining [conscripts] are to be deprived of their ranks and made rank-and-file men."; QLZC 37=RCL C 23a; ZYS 147, 149; ENLL 143, 186, 483).

834 *Jue* 爵 "rank". For the system of ranks in Qin and Han times see Loewe 1960, Nishijima 1961, Zhu Shaohou 2008 as well as Lau and Lüdke 2012, footnote 626.

835 For *shi wu* see footnote 495.

836 For *ci* see footnote 564.

837 For *ju* see footnote 565.

838 For *de* see footnote 524.

839 For *shen* see footnote 633.

840 For *yi* (*mou ren*) *zui* see footnote 582. The doubtful point was most probably whether or not the fugitive was below the age of criminal liability at the time when the offence was committed. According to statutes from early Han times, a minor was exempted from punishment for all offences except for homicide until he reached the age of 10 (ENLL 86), and was not subjected to mutilation until the age of 17 (ENLL 83). For the height of the offender as criterion for criminal responsibility cf. footnote 828. From the evidence of this case, it seems likely that minors of the age of 12 were not yet liable for criminal offences during the Qin dynasty.

In all other matters the prefecture has passed judgement.[842] We venture to submit [this case] for decision.[843]

Alternative Votes for Judgement

吏議曰：
除多。
或曰：
黥爲城旦。094

The [responsible] officials deliver [the following] legal opinion:[844]
"Duo is to be exempted."[845]
Some say:[846]
"[Duo] is to be tattooed and made an earth pounder convict."[847]

---

841 For *ji/xi* see footnote 569. Here, as in some other cases (*Yuelu* WYZ 135, 235; ZYS 23, 33, 159–160; cf. *Yuelu* WYZ 023), the word indicates that the suspect whose statutory offence/punishment is uncertain will be held under detention until the higher authorities have reached a decision.

842 For *ta xian lun* see footnote 635.

843 For *yan* and the phrase *gan yan zhi* see footnote 489.

844 For *li yi* see footnote 572.

845 *Chu* 除 "to exempt sb. from punishment", often used with a direct object, indicates the exemption of a person from punishment on the grounds of mitigating circumstances which were based on a specific regulation (with the grammatical patient in object position in *Yuelu* WYZ 207; QLZC 37=RCL C 23; ZYS 48; ENLL 145, 191; passive use with the grammatical patient in subject position in *Yuelu* WYZ 198; *Mo* 70, 350; XL 18, 43=RCL B 7, 19; FLDW 65, 125=RCL D 52, 105; ENLL 21, 110; for active use with *zui* 罪 "punishment" as object see footnote 514). There were a variety of situations for which an exemption from punishment could be decreed. Among them are: proven innocence (ZYS 122; QLZC 37=RCL C 23); committing only a very minor irregularity (XL 43=RCL B 19); voluntarily denouncing a planned rebellion to the authorities, at least if the co-conspirators were revealed (*Shiji* 118, 3097); personally catching convicts for whose escape one was responsible (FLDW 125=RCL D 105); co-operation with the authorities during the investigation and in the arrest of possible accomplices (ENLL 2, 63–64, 68–69, 73, 176) as well as age (ENLL 86). In the present case, the legal basis for this alternative vote may be the young age of the offender. For *chu* as "to appoint" see footnote 867.

846 For *huo yue* see footnote 573.

847 For *qing cheng dan* see footnote 668. According to Qin law, this is the normal punishment for persons who committed the statutory offence of *bang wang* (FLDW 5, 48=RCL D 4, 93), cf. footnote 512. The preceding loss of rank forms the legal basis for this judgement, as Duo would not be subjected to mutilation as a holder of a rank (ENLL 83).

Case I.6

The agency of a prefecture, possibly Jiangling, submitted this case from 226 BC to the higher authorities of the province for decision.

The submission was initiated by a request of a senior official (probably the vice prefect of the submitting prefecture) who had earlier been charged for several violations of ordinances, a major mistake and was additionally held liable for undetected misdemeanours of subordinate officials under his direct authority. A total of eight charges had accumulated. As, according to his view, the respective misdemeanours were all connected with each other (i.e. the administration of the senior official), the senior official considered a judgement based on the accumulation of sentences to be unlawful and thus made a request to submit his case to the higher authorities for decision.

The following documentation of the original case illuminates the background of this request. A brief list notes the eight different charges that were brought against the senior official. A note at the end of this list clarifies that the prefecture that conducted the former proceedings considered all these charges to be connected with each other, in which case the senior official would only have to be punished for the most serious offence and a judgement based on the accumulation of sentences was not justified. However, in contrast to this decision, the attached rejection considered these misdemeanours as not connected with each other. It is not mentioned to which agency this rejection should be attributed. However, a comparison with other criminal cases from Qin or early Han times indicates that either the superior province or a neighbouring prefecture could have rejected the prefecture's decision.

In the course of the retrial, which had been initiated upon the request of the senior official, his statement was consistent with his previous statements. In the second stage of interrogation, he was thus confronted with the fact that an ordinance actually provided the legal basis for the judgement to be based on the accumulation of sentences. The senior official stated in his response that he had never meant to violate the law or to abuse his authority for private purposes, and that his misdemeanours should not be classified as an intentional breach of duty.

In the finding of fact, the judicial officials of the prefecture again stated that all the misdemeanours were indeed connected. Still, the officials had doubts as to whether a judgement based on the accumulation of sentences was lawful. Therefore, they submitted the case to the superior agency of the province for decision and attached one proposal to this submission. According to this proposal, the senior official was to be fined one suit of armour, which in fact

 | DOI 10.1163/9789004315655_014

constituted the fine for the most severe of all the eight misdemeanours. As this fine had already been imposed on the accused after the initial proceedings, he was not to receive any further punishment. This was also in accordance with his request.

Diplomatic Edition

•□灋□□暨自言曰邦尉一□□戍令□□弗傳邦侯⌞女子蓄馬一匹買卿遣$_{094(2)}$[848][Missing slip]權⌞□谿卿倉天窻容鳥⌞公士豕田橘將陽未㾌自出當復田橘官令戍掾弗得⌞走$_{096}$偃未當傳官傳弗得⌞除銷史丹爲江陵史〼未定與從事廿一年庫計劾繆弩百凡八劾$_{097}$以贏論暨此過誤失及坐官毆相遝贏論重謁灋$_{095}$
□□□□□□□未劾不傳戍令其□□□亥劾幹其八月癸丑劾非轂其辛未劾窻$_{098}$豕其丁丑劾偃廼十月己酉暨坐丹論一甲其乙亥劾弩言夬相遝不贏它如暨$_{099}$言⌞卻曰不當相遝$_{100}$
⌞暨言如前$_{101}$
⌞詰暨贏論有令可故曰贏重可解⌞暨曰不䍧過誤失坐官弗得非敢端犯$_{102}$灋令赴隧以成私毆此以曰贏重毋它解它如前$_{103}$
⌞問如辤$_{104}$
•鞫之暨坐八劾小犯令二大誤一坐官小誤五巳論一甲餘未論皆相遝審疑暨不當$_{105}$贏論它縣論敢灋之$_{106}$
吏議貲暨一甲勿贏$_{107}$

Edition and Translation

Submission by the Prefecture – Introductory Formula

【敢】灋（讞）【之】：

[We venture] to submit [the following case] for decision:

848 Slip J15/094(2) was recently discovered by one of the authors of this volume among the yet unpublished statutes and ordincances from the Yuelu Academy collection; this slip can therefore not be found in Zhu and Chen 2013. The structure of the first part of the present case report only became clear after this new slip had been taken into consideration (Staack 2014a; cf. Hafner 2014a). In fact, a slight reordering of the following slips appears not only reasonable but necessary: Slip 095 of the edition should better be placed between slips 097 and 098.

Request to Submit the Case to the Higher Authorities for Decision

【丞】暨自言曰：
邦尉一□□戍令□□弗傳邦侯。
女子蓄馬一匹，買（賣）卿（鄉）遣$_{094(2)}$
[Missing slip]
權。
□谿卿（鄉）倉天窻（窗）容鳥。
公士豕田橘將陽，未㡿自出，當復田橘，官令戍，掾（錄）弗得。
走$_{096}$偃未當傳，官傳弗得。
除銷史丹爲江陵史，【簿】未定與從事。
廿一年庫計，劾繆（謬）弩百。
凡八劾。$_{097}$以羸（纍）論暨。此過誤失及坐官毆（也）。相遝，羸（纍）論重。謁瀳（讞）。$_{095}$

[Vice prefect] Ji[849] himself submitted a request[850] [containing an appeal to the authorities] stating:
"When the *bang wei*[851] [sent out] an order for military service [...] failed to forward it to the *bang hou*.[852]

849 Ji 暨 who appears as *cheng* 丞 below can probably be identified with the vice prefect of Jiangling also mentioned in case 1.3 (*Yuelu* WYZ 061).

850 For *zi yan* see footnote 755.

851 *Bang wei* 邦尉 was a title for a military commander during the Qin dynasty (*Liye* 8–649r). It is not clear whether this office is a forerunner of the *shu guo du wei* 屬國都尉 "commander in the dependent states" of Han times (*Hanshu* 19A, 742), or if it can be identified with the *jun bang wei* 郡邦尉, which was renamed to *jun wei* 郡尉 at the beginning of the Qin Empire (*Liye* 8–461r). The latter was often combined with the name of a province and in this case abbreviated as *wei* (ZYS 129). Since early Han times, the title of the commander of military forces in a province (*jun* 郡) was also *du wei* 都尉 (ZYS 1; cf. *Hanshu* 19A, 742). This official, who was appointed by the central government, was responsible for routine military affairs (Loewe 1967 vol. I, 60–61); if the governor (*tai shou* 太守) was absent, the *du wei* assumed the latter's role as commander-in-chief of the provincial forces (Li Yufu 2002, 322–324). The *du wei* was also responsible for the conscription and military training of recruits as well as for the military exercises held each year during the eighth month. The inspection of fortifications and the fight against criminal gangs were among his further duties. See Bielenstein 1980, 94; Loewe 1967 vol. I, 61, 74, 76; An and Xiong 2007, 574–581; Li Yufu 2002, 323–324.

852 *Bang hou* 邦侯 does not occur in other manuscripts from the Qin dynasty, and there is only one reference in received literature (*Shu* Kang Wang zhi gao=Guming xu § 33). Probably *bang hou* can be identified with *zhu hou* 者（諸）侯 (FLDW 179, 180, 203=RCL D 158–159, 183), who appear to have lived outside of Qin, because their messengers called *ke* 客 "strangers" had to "enter" the state of Qin (FLDW 203=RCL D 183). On the other hand, *zhu hou* were apparently distinguished from *wai chen bang* 外臣邦 "outer dependent/

A woman raised one horse and sold it to the district[853] [...].
[...] power.
The skylights[854] of the storehouses in [...]xi district were wide enough[855] to let birds through.
Shi, holder of the first rank,[856] who cultivated[857] mandarin

---

vassal states" (*FLDW* 180=*RCL* D 159). The dependent states of Qin were called *chen bang* (*FLDW* 72, 113, 177=*RCL* D 58, 94, 157) or *shu bang* 屬邦 (*QLSZ* 201=*RCL* A 110), which could be abbreviated to *bang* (*FLDW* 90=*RCL* D 75). Cf. *bang* as designation for the state of Qin in footnote 512.

853 *Qing* 卿 (*GSR* 714o), whose archaic graph shows two persons who kneel facing each other around a food vessel, was probably invented for the homeophonous *xiang* 饗 (*GSR* 714j) "banquet". From the earliest oracle-bone and bronze inscriptions right down to Qin manuscripts, 卿 served to write *xiang* 鄉 (*GSR* 714c) and its derivates (Huang Dekuan 2007, 1714–1716; Teng Rensheng 2008, 813; Li et al. 2007, 437). In the legal manuscripts from Shuihudi as well as in *Yuelu WYZ* 096 and 126, the graph 卿 was likewise used to write *xiang* 鄉 (Zhang and Zhang 1990, 491; Fang Yong 2012, 194 with *QLSZ* 21=*RCL* A 19; *XL* 28=*RCL* B 11 and *Yushu* 3). However, other forms of *xiang* with the double semantic determinative for "town" were also used in Qin manuscripts (Fang Yong 2012, 194 with *Yuelu 35 nian si zhiri* 13.4; *Longgang* 10; *Zhoujiatai* 14.3 and *Shuihudi Rishu* B 75.2; cf. Zhang Shouzhong 2012, 179 and 254).

A prefecture (*xian* 縣) was divided into several *xiang* 鄉 (cf. *Hanshu* 19A, 742; Bielenstein 1980, 103–104; Yan Gengwang 1961, 237–239; Zhang Jinguang 2004, 568–587). In Qin manuscripts, the head of the *xiang* and his assistant (*zuo* 佐) are sometimes mentioned together as the senior officials (*Yuelu WYZ* 126; *Liye* 8–39, 8–300, 8–938, 8–1241, 8–1710, 8–2247). According to documents excavated at Yinwan, there were 170 *xiang* in Donghai province at the end of the Western Han (*Yinwan mudu* M6D1r). With an overall population of 1,397,343 inhabitants in 266,290 registered households (*Yinwan mudu* M6D1r), one *xiang* would on average comprise 1,566 households with 8,220 inhabitants each. During the Han period, the most important dignitaries of a *xiang* were the *san lao* 三老, the *xiang you zhi* 鄉有秩, who were consulted in cases of legal dispute, the *xiang se fu* 鄉嗇夫, responsible for the levy of taxes, and the *you jiao* 游徼, who were entrusted with police work (cf. *Hanshu* 19A, 742; the list of *xiang you zhi*, *xiang se fu* and *you jiao* of Donghai province on *Yinwan mudu* M6D2r/v as well as table 3 in Xie Guihua 1997, 47–48). However, there is no evidence for *xiang you zhi* or *you jiao* in Qin sources.

854 *Tian chuang* 天窗 "skylight" (*Hanguan liu zhong* 7.2.11/112/9).

855 *Rong* 容 "to find room/space for, have enough space for, be large enough for" (*Hanfei* 10, 46 [cf. Harbsmeier]: 倉不容粟。"The granaries do not have enough room for the grain.") or "have enough space to enter" (*Zuo* Xiang 31,560,14: 門不容車。"The gate is not wide enough for carriages.").

856 *Gong shi* 公士, the first of twenty ranks (*Hanshu* 19A, 739). Their holders (as well as the holders' wives) enjoyed the privilege to be exempted from tattooing, when they were sentenced to the most severe form of penal labour as earth or grain pounder convicts (*ZYS* 182; *ENLL* 83).

orange trees, roamed around [as a vagrant],[858] but before he was accused [of having absconded],[859] he gave himself up[860] [to the authorities]. He, by law,

857 *Tian* 田 "to till/cultivate the soil" (*Odes* 210,1: 畇畇原隰，曾孫田之。"Cleared into even plots are the highlands and lowlands, his descendant cultivates them."; *Shiji* 8, 369 [Nienhauser II (2002), 48]: 諸故秦苑囿園池，皆令人得田之。"As regards all the former forbidden [game] parks, enclosures, gardens and ponds of Qin, [Gaozu] ordered the people be granted to cultivate them."; *Shiji* 30, 1436; *QLSZ* 51, 144=*RCL* A 12, 67; *ENLL* 239, 317; *ZYS* 56; *Longgang* 118; *Liye* 8–755r+8–756r+8–757r+8–758r+8–759r). *Tian ju* is probably identical with *shu ju* 樹橘 "to plant mandarin orange trees" (*Shiji* 129, 3272; *Hanfei* 33, 228). Mandarin orange trees were cultivated in gardens (*Shiji* 69, 2245 [cf. Nienhauser VII (1994), 99]: 楚必致橘柚之園。"Chu is sure to present gardens filled with tangerines and pomelos."). Cf. *sang lin* 桑林 "mulberry groves", which are sometimes also called *sang tian* 桑田 (*Odes* 50,3). Shi was probably obliged to do work on the mandarin orange plantation as a form of statute labour (*yao* 繇), and was thus not allowed to leave his workplace without authorisation.

858 *Jiang yang* 將陽 is a rhyming binome (*die yun* type) meaning "to stroll/roam around (as vagrant)". Apart from one single reference in received literature (*Shangshu dazhuan* 1.1/3/13), this graphic variant is only used in Qin legal manuscripts (*FLDW* 163=*RCL* D 143; *FZS* 97=*RCL* E 6; *ZYS* 212; *Liye* 8–1716). As demonstrated by Chen Songchang (2012a), the binome *jiang yang* is used as a legal term for the statutory offence of absconding for a period of less than 12 months (*Yuelu Lüling* 0185, cited according to Chen Songchang 2012a, 6: 闌亡，盈十二月而得，耐。不盈十二月爲將陽，毄（繫）城旦舂。"Who unauthorisedly absconds and is caught only after 12 months, is to be punished [with penal labour of the category] *nai*. [Absconding for] less than 12 months constitutes 'vagrancy' and is to be punished with detention among the earth and grain pounder convicts."). Cf. the graphic variant *xiang xiang* 相翔 (*Zhouli* 36, 884b: 有相翔者誅之。"If there are vagrants they will be punished."). For the non-terminological usage of this binome in other graphic variants see footnote 708.

859 *Chi* 㡿/斥 (*GSR* 792a/b) *t-hŋʌk here either occurs in the sense "to spy out, reconnoitre" (*Zuo* Xiang 18,476,9: 斥山澤之險 "to spy out/reconnoitre the places in the hills and marshes that were difficult to occupy") or is used as loan graph for *su* 愬/訴 (*GSR* 769b/792j) *s-ŋʕak-s "to complain about sth." (*Yushu* 11: 是以善㡿（訴）事，喜爭書。"Therefore, [bad officials] are good at complaining about affairs and enjoy quarrelling about documents."). *Su* could also mean "to accuse/lodge a complaint against sb." (*Zuo* Cheng 5,356,12: 許靈公愬鄭伯于楚。"Duke Ling of Xu accused the earl of Zheng in Chu.") or "to unjustly accuse sb./discredit sb." (*Lunyu* 14, 322: 公伯寮愬子路於季孫 "Gongbo Liao discredited Zi Lu in the presence of Jisun.").

860 *Zi chu* 自出 "to give oneself up, hand oneself in" (*FLDW* 131–132=*RCL* D 109, 110: 隸臣妾毄（繫）城旦舂，去亡，已奔，未論而自出，當治（笞）五十。"Bond servant convicts detained among the earth and grain pounder convicts who abscond and have already run away, but give themselves up before having been sentenced, by law are to be caned with fifty strokes.", *FLDW* 166=*RCL* D 145; *FZS* 18, 96=*RCL* E 8, 6; *ENLL* 100, *ENLL* 157: 吏民亡，盈卒歲，耐；不盈卒歲，毄（繫）城旦舂；[…]其自出殹（也），

would have had to cultivate mandarin orange trees again, [but] the office[861] [instead] ordered him to perform [additional] military service.[862] When inspecting[863] [the records of the office, I] failed to detect[864] this.

Messenger[865] Yan should, by law, not have been registered[866] for labour and military service yet, [but] the [relevant] office registered him and the [illegal/ unjustified registration] was not detected [by me].

[When I] appointed[867] the scribe Dan from Xiao[868] [prefecture] as scribe of

---

笞五十。"Officials and common people who have absconded for a full year [are to be punished with penal labour of the category] *nai*; [those who have absconded] for less than a full year are to be detained among the earth and grain pounder convicts. [...] Those who give themselves up are caned with 50 strokes."; ENLL 159, 165–167). According to the above stipulations, Shi, in the present case, was to be caned, but not to be punished with detention among the earth pounder convicts.

861 The editors interpret this passage differently (Zhu and Chen 2013, 295) as they consider *ju guan* 橘官 to represent the name of the "mandarin orange office(?)" (Fu Jiayi 2007, 158; *Hanshu* 28B, 1603–1604). However, this neglects the fact that *tian ju* 田橘 also occurs without the following *guan* 官 in the preceding sentence. Therefore, the connection between *ju* and *guan* in this passage can be doubted.

862 For the punitive military service *shu* see footnotes 542 and 559.

863 For *yuan* 掾 as orthographic variant of *lu* 錄 "inspect (documents such as case-files, accounts, proposals for a judgement)" in legal and administrative manuscripts of Qin and early Han times see footnote 655. Here *lu* occurs in combination with *ji* 計 "accounts" (XL 52=RCL B 25: 其它冗吏、令史掾計者 "the other officials temporarily assigned to work there and the secretary of the prefect who inspects accounts", XL 55=RCL B 27: 司馬、令史掾苑計 "when the marshal and the secretary of the prefect inspect the accounts of the stud-farm"; cf. *ji lu* 計錄 in *Liye* 8–488, 8–493).

864 *Fu de* 弗得 "to fail to discover/catch an offence/offender" (ZYS 193–194, 205).

865 *Zou* 走 "messenger/runner" (*Liye* 8–133v, 8–135r/v, 8–373, 8–453, 8–652v, 8–657v, 8–742v, 8–756, etc.; *Yuelu 34 nian zhiri* 34.4, 53.6).

866 *Fu* 傅 "to register sb. for labour and military service" (QLSZ 190=RCL A 100; QLZC 8=RCL C 5; FLDW 165=RCL D 175; ZYS 153; ENLL 354–366, 412–413).

867 *Chu* 除 "to appoint" (QLSZ 157=RCL A 79: 縣、都官、十二郡免除吏及佐 "when prefectures, central government offices and the [offices] of the 12 provinces dismiss or appoint officials as well as assistants"; FLDW 144=RCL D 122: 郡縣除佐，事它郡縣而不視其事者，可（何）論？以小犯令論。 "How are assistants who have been appointed by a [certain] province or prefecture, but who [instead] serve in another province or prefecture, [and therefore] do not perform their tasks [in the province or prefecture that appointed them], to be sentenced? They are to be sentenced for minor violations of ordinances."; *Liye* 8–157r, 8–650r). For *chu* as "to exempt sb. from punishment" see footnote 845.

868 Xiao 銷 was a prefecture during Qin (*Yuelu 35 nian si zhiri* 3.4; *Zhoujiatai* 364; *Liye* 8–153) and early Han times (ENLL 456). During the Qin dynasty it was possibly located between

Jiangling [prefecture], Dan already participated in discharging official duties before [his appointment] was recorded [in the registers].[869]
In the 21st year,[870] when [checking] the accounts[871] of the arsenal, [I] was charged[872] for a difference[873] of 100 crossbows.
All in all I, Ji, was charged eight times.[874] Judgement was passed[875] on me

---

the prefectures of Yan and Jiangling in Nan province (*Liye* 16–52). Its administrative seat was located near present Tianmen, Hubei (Hou Xiaorong 2009, 401–402).

869 Cf. *Liye* 8–2022r: 未定薄（簿）"not yet recorded in the registers".

870 This must refer to the 21st year of King Zheng of Qin (25/11/227–13/11/226 BC; Xu Xiqi 1997, 1231–1232; cf. Zhang Peiyu 2007, 73; Li Zhonglin 2012, 65).

871 *Ji* 計 "to account; accounts" (*QLSZ* 34, 35, 37, 63, 70–71, 78, 80, 90, 99, 117, 124, 139–140, 194=*RCL* A 24, 25, 26, 34, 36, 39, 40, 49, 53, 64, 68, 104; *XL* 50, 52, 54, 55, 56, 58=*RCL* B 24, 25, 26, 27, 28, 29). For accounts of weapons see especially *XL* 52–53=*RCL* B 25: 其它冗吏、令史掾計者，及都倉、庫、田、亭嗇夫坐其離官屬於鄉者，如令、丞。"The other officials temporarily assigned to work there and the secretaries of the prefect who inspect accounts as well as overseers of the main granary, of arsenals, of fields and police stations who are prosecuted [for misdemeanours occurring] in the detached offices [under their control] which are subordinate to a *xiang* will be dealt with in the same manner as the prefect and the vice prefect."; cf. *Liye* 8–151, 8–493.

872 For *he* see footnote 545. *He* frequently occurs as an active verb taking two objects (the first referring to the person who is charged and the second to the offence this person is charged with as in *ZYS* 63; *Shiji* 87, 2562; 118, 3095; *Hanshu* 64B, 2818) or only one direct object (referring either to the offence as in *Shiji* 102, 2753; or to the offender as in *Shiji* 122, 3137). Here, however, it is used in the passive voice (*Hanshu* 7, 230 [Dubs II (1944), 171–172]: 太常及廟令丞郎吏皆劾大不敬。"The minister of ceremony, together with the director, the vice director, the gentlemen and [other] officials of the temple, were all charged with 'great lack of respect'."; *Hanshu* 21A, 978: 壽王[...]再劾死，更赦勿劾。"Shou Wang [...] had twice been charged with [offences punishable by] death, but he was granted an amnesty and not to be charged."); cf. *you he* 有劾 "there is an *ex-officio* charge against sb. with sth." (*XL* 54, 55=*RCL* B 26, 27).

873 *Miu* 繆, as well as its variant *miu* 謬, occur in the sense of "to be mistaken in sth.", but could also mean "to differ from" (*Shiji* 13, 504; *Hanshu* 62, 2717). See especially *QLSZ* 71=*RCL* A 36: 計毋相繆。"The accounts should not differ from each other." and *XL* 56=*RCL* B 28: 計校相繆（謬）殹（也）[...]過二千二百錢以上，貲一甲。"When the accounts and checks [of stock] differ from each other, [...] and the difference exceeds 2,200 cash, [the overseer of the office] is fined one suit of armour."

874 These eight *ex-officio* charges concerned the following categories of misconduct in office: 1) not forwarding an order to do military service; 2) (falsely checking or accounting?) arrow shafts; 3) the irregular arrest of a remand prisoner; 4) the width of the skylights of storehouses, which exceeded the limit; 5) failure to discover a judicial error with regard to punitive military service; 6) failure to discover an unlawful registration for labour and military service; 7) liability for a newly appointed subordinate who started to discharge his duty before his change in appointment was entered into the registers; 8) a difference of 100 crossbows as result of incorrect accounting of the arsenal.

based on the accumulation [of sentences].[876] These [offences] are violations,[877] mistakes[878] and lapses[879] as well as liabilities for [misdemeanours in my]

---

875 For *lun* see footnote 540.

876 *Lei* 羸 (*GSR* 14c) *roj as loan graph for *lei* 纍/累 (*GSR* 577 f/r) *rojʔ (Wang Hui 2008, 507; Bai Yulan 2012, 298 and Feng and Deng 2006, 558; cf. *lei* 絫 in *Shuowen* 14B, 737–738 and *Hanshu* 21A, 956). *Lei* also occurs in the sense "to add up, accumulate" (*XL* 1=*RCL* B 1: 其有羸、不備，物直（值）之，以其賈（價）多者罪之，勿羸（纍）。"When there is a surplus or a shortage, the goods are to be evaluated, and [the persons responsible] are to be punished for the highest price among them; [the individual sentences] are not to be accumulated." Does this regulation correspond to the early Han legal rule that a person who committed several criminal offences could only be punished for the offence for which the law stipulated the most severe punishment (*ENLL* 99)? Cf. Zhang Boyuan 2014b.

877 *Guo* 過 "exceed, pass, transgress" or "transgression, misdemeanour" (*Zuo* Xuan 2,288,9: 人誰無過，過而能改，善莫大焉。"Who is without error? But there is no excellence greater than that of somebody who commits an error but is able to correct it."; *Shangjunshu* 7, 17 [cf. Duyvendak 1928, 230]: 夫過有厚薄，則刑有輕重。"Depending on whether a transgression is serious or petty, the punishment is severe or lenient."). In legal texts, *guo* only occurs in combination with *shi* 失 for "inadvertently (injuring/killing sb.)" (*ENLL* 21, 396). However, in the summary of the finding of fact below only *fan ling* 犯令 "violations against ordinances" as well as *wu* 誤 "mistakes" and *zuo guan* 坐官 "liabilities for (misdemeanours in one's) office" are mentioned (*Yuelu WYZ* 105). Therefore, *guo* can probably be identified with *fan ling* in the present context, leading to the translation "violation".

878 *Wu* 誤 "mistake " (*XL* 58–60=*RCL* B 29: 計脫實及出實多於律程，及不當出而出之，直（值）其賈（價），不盈廿二錢，除；廿二錢以到六百六十錢，貲官嗇夫一盾；過六百六十錢以上，貲官嗇夫一甲，而復責其出毆（也）。人戶、馬牛一以上爲大誤。誤自重毆（也），減罪一等。"When stores are omitted in accounting, or when issuing stores one issues more than the norm [established by] the statutes, as well as when one issues what should not be issued, the value is to be estimated. If it is not fully 22 cash, it is excused; from 22 up to 660 cash, the overseer of the office is fined one shield. If it exceeds 660 cash, the overseer of the office is fined one suit of armour, and he is also charged with [the value of] what he has issued. [A mistake in accounting of] one household, horse or ox, or more is a major mistake; if [the official in charge] traces [the mistake] himself, the punishment is reduced by one degree."; *FLDW* 209=*RCL* D 189: 可（何）如爲大誤？人戶、馬牛及者（諸）貨材（財）直（值）過六百六十錢爲大誤，其它爲小。"What are 'major mistakes'? [Mistakes in accounting the number of] households, cattle as well as all goods whose values exceed 660 cash are major mistakes; the others are minor [mistakes]."; *FLDW* 207=*RCL* D 186; *XL* 44=*RCL* B 20; *ENLL* 12).

879 *Shi* 失 "erroneous, inadvertently", in contrast to *duan* 端 (*FLDW* 33–36=*RCL* D 27–28) or *gu* 故 "intentional, premeditated" (*ENLL* 95), as "to commit a judicial error" in passing judgement (*Longgang mudu*; *ZYS* 120, 196; *ENLL* 107), imposing a mutilation punishment (*FLDW* 33, 35=*RCL* D 27–28; *ENLL* 124), bringing an *ex-officio* charge against sb. (*ENLL* 112),

office.[880] [As they] are connected[881] with each other, a judgement based on the accumulation [of sentences] is too severe. [I therefore] request[882] to submit[883] [this case] to the higher authorities for decision."

"to inadvertently start a fire" (ENLL 4, 405) or *guo shi* 過失 "inadvertently (injuring/killing sb.)" (ENLL 21, 396). It seems that *wu* and *shi* constitute a compound because in the summary of the finding of fact below only *fan ling* 犯令 "violations against ordinances" as well as *wu* 誤 "mistakes" are mentioned instead of *guo wu shi*. There is, however, relatively little evidence for *wu shi* as a compound in received literature from pre-Han and Han times (*Hanshu* 47, 2216; *Guoyu* 4.4/47/6; *Liu tao* 4.9/35/20; cf. *shi wu* in *Hanshu* 47, 2217; *Lunheng* 17, 42; *Lunheng* 29, 97).

880 *Zuo guan* 坐官 "to be liable for (misdemeanours in one's) office" (QLSZ 83–84=RCL A 41: 官嗇夫免，效其官而有不備者，令與其稗官分，如其事。吏坐官以負賞（償），未而死，及有罪以收，抉出其分。 "When the overseer of an office is dismissed and on checking his office there are shortages, orders should be given that he is to share this with his subordinates according to their duties. When an official is liable for [misdemeanours in his] office for which he is charged with repayment, but before [his share has been alotted/repayment has been done] he dies, as well as when he has committed a crime and therefore is under arrest/confiscated/held under custody, his share is to be cancelled."; XL 55=RCL B 27: 計有劾，司馬令史坐之，如令史坐官計劾然。"If there is an *ex-officio* charge because of the accounts, the secretary of the prefect and the marshal are adjudicated for this, just like the secretaries of the prefect are liable for *ex-officio* charges concerning accounts of [their] office."; ENLL 349–350). In the present case, *zuo guan* appears twice, cf. 暨坐丹論一甲 (*Yuelu* WYZ 099) and 坐官弗得 (*Yuelu* WYZ 102).

881 *Ta* 遝 *(g-)lʕəp for *dai* 逮 *(g-)lʕət-s<**(g-)lʕəp-s "to reach (to)" (*Mo* 68, 341 [Johnston 2010, 841]: 城之外，矢之所遝 "beyond the wall, as far as the arrows can reach") as part of the expression *xiang ta* 相遝 means "to connect, have contact" (*Liye* 8–1770r: [...]各一甲，與此相遝，它如劾。 "[...] each of them [is fined] one suit of armour; [the misdemeanours in office?] are connected with each other. Everything else corresponds to the *ex-officio* charge."); cf. *xiang dai* 相逮 "get in touch/come into contact with each other" (*Shiji* 27, 1318) and "to connect with each other" (*Guoyu* 1.14/8/17; *Hanshu* 25B, 1268) or *xiang ji* 相及 *g[r]əp "come into contact with each other/couple (as cattle)" (*Zuo* Xi 4,139,2), "come into contact with each other/couple (as human beings)" (*Guoyu* 4.35/65/14) or "to blend in each other" (*Zuo* Zhao 1,573,15).
In connection with the conviction of Ji, the term *xiang ta* may refer to the fact that an official who committed several offences/misdemeanours in his administration was only punished for the most serious offence (cf. XL 1=RCL B 1, which stipulates that if on checking the accounts of individual items recorded on the inventory it is discovered that there is a surplus or deficit, then the official responsible for the accounts is not punished for every single surplus or deficit [in case there are several cases], but only for the highest surplus or deficit).

882 *Ye* 謁 "to request sth. (from sb.)" (*Zuo* Zhao 16,661,13; *Guoyu* 8.7/124/1; FLDW 102=RCL D 85; FZS 45, 53=RCL E 16, 19; *Yuelu* WYZ 149, 168–169, 191, 199, 219; ZYS 7, 47, 68, 98, 100, 228).

883 For *yan* and the phrase *gan yan zhi* see footnote 489.

Original Case – List of Charges and Decision

□□□□□【月】□未劾不傳戍令；
其□【月】□亥劾幹（笴）；
其八月癸丑劾非毄（繫）；
其辛未劾窓（窗）、098豕；
其丁丑劾偃；
廼十月己酉暨坐丹論一甲；
其乙亥劾弩。
言夬（決）：相遝，不羸（纍）。
它如暨099言。

[…] on day […]*wei* of the [… month Ji] was charged for not forwarding the order for military service;
on day […]*hai* of the [… month] he was charged for arrow shafts;[884]
on day *guichou* of the eighth month[885] he was charged for irregularly[886] arresting[887] [a remand prisoner];
on day *xinwei*[888] [of the eighth month] he was charged for the skylights and [the incident with] Shi;
on day *dingchou*[889] [of the eighth month] he was charged for [the incident with] Yan;
on day *jiyou*[890] of the last tenth month he was held liable[891] for [misdemeanours of his subordinate] Dan and sentenced to [pay a fine of] one suit of armour;
on day *yihai*[892] [of the same month] he was charged for the crossbows.

884 *Gan* 幹 (GSR 140d) here for the homeophonous *gan* 笴 (GSR 1e) "arrow shaft" (*Zhouli* 39, 906a; 41, 924a, b).

885 *Guichou* was the sixth day of the eighth month in the 21st year of King Zheng of Qin (cf. Zhang Peiyu 2007, 73; Li Zhonglin 2012, 65), i.e. 21/09/226 BC (Xu Xiqi 1997, 1232).

886 *Fei* 非 as stative verb "to be wrong/irregular" (*Yi* 8, 90b: 辯是與非 "distinguish between right and wrong"; *Shu* Pangeng § 14: 用非罰 "use irregular punishments"; *Shiji* 130, 3297=*Hanshu* 62, 2717; *Mo* 3, 6; *Lunheng* 84, 281; 85, 286).

887 For *ji*/*xi* see footnote 569.

888 *Xinwei* was the 24th day of the eighth month in the 21st year of King Zheng of Qin (cf. Zhang Peiyu 2007, 73; Li Zhonglin 2012, 65), i.e. 09/10/226 BC (Xu Xiqi 1997, 1232).

889 *Dingchou* was the 30th day of the eighth month in the 21st year of King Zheng of Qin (cf. Zhang Peiyu 2007, 73; Li Zhonglin 2012, 65), i.e. 15/10/226 BC (Xu Xiqi 1997, 1232).

890 *Jiyou* was the third day of the tenth month of the following 22nd year of King Zheng of Qin (cf. Zhang Peiyu 2007, 73; Li Zhonglin 2012, 65), i.e. 16/11/226 BC (Xu Xiqi 1997, 1233).

891 For *zuo* see footnote 528.

892 *Yihai* was the 29th day of the tenth month of the 22nd year of King Zheng of Qin (cf. Zhang Peiyu 2007, 73; Li Zhonglin 2012, 65), i.e. 12/12/226 BC (Xu Xiqi 1997, 1233). That means that the *ex-officio* charge for the difference in crossbows of the 21st year's

The report on the decision[893] was: "[The incidents] are connected with each other and therefore [the sentences] were not accumulated [at the time of judgement]."
Everything else corresponded to Ji's statement.

Original Case – Rejection by the Competent Authority

卻曰：
不當相遝。$_{100}$

[The letter of] rejection[894] read:
"[The incidents by law are] not connected with each other."

Retrial – First Stage of Interrogation

暨言如前。$_{101}$

Ji's statement corresponded to his previous [statement].

Retrial – Second Stage of Interrogation (Confrontation)

詰暨：
羸（纍）論有令。可（何）故曰羸（纍）重？可（何）解？

We confronted[895] Ji:
"There is an ordinance about judgement based on the accumulation [of sentences]. Why did you say: [A judgement based on] the accumulation [of sentences] is too severe? How do you explain[896] this?"

暨曰：
不紵（幸）過誤失，坐官弗得。非敢端犯$_{102}$灋（法）令，赴隧（遂）以成私毆（也）。此以曰羸（纍）重。毋（無）它解。
它如前。$_{103}$

---

accounting of the arsenal was only brought against Ji in the first month of the following year, probably after the usual checking (*jiao* 校, cf. *XL* 56=*RCL* B 28).

893 On *yan jue* see footnote 550.

894 *Que* 卻 "decline, refuse, reject" (*Meng* 10, 411; *Hanfei* 35, 258), in administrative language especially for declining a request (*ye* 謁), e.g. for appointment of a person to a vacant office (*Liye* 8–157v) or for enquiry about a lost boat (*Liye* 8–135r), a criminal case (*yu shi* 獄事) submitted for trial (*Shiji* 103, 2773) or an explanation (*jie* 解) of an accused by the prefectural court (*Juyan xinjian* E.P.F22:30). Cf. Zhu Xiangrong 2012, 191–192.

895 For *he jie* see footnote 792.

896 For *jie* see footnote 800.

Ji stated:
"I unfortunately[897] [committed] violations, mistakes and lapses. [Furthermore, I] am liable for the [misdemeanours of subordinates in my] office, which I did not detect. It is not the case that I ventured to intentionally[898] violate the laws and ordinances,[899] or that I was eager[900] for advancement[901] in order to achieve my private aims.[902] Therefore, I said: [A judgement based on] the accumulation [of sentences] is too severe. I do not have any other explanation."[903]
Everything else corresponded to his previous [statement].

897 *Yang* 羊 was the character form normally used to write *xing* 幸 in Qin and early Han times (Zhang Shouzhong 1994, 162; Chen Songchang 2001a, 417). Cf. *bu xing si* 不幸死 (*Yuelu* WYZ 115), *bu xing duan ming si* 不幸短命死 (*Lunyu* 6, 113) and *bu xing zao si* 不幸早死 (*Shiji* 60, 2115).

898 *Duan* 端 "intentionally, wilfully" (*FLDW* 43=*RCL* D 35: 端爲，爲誣人；不端，爲告不審。 "If he did it intentionally, it is a case of 'false incrimination of sb.'; if it was unintentional, it is a case of 'an unfounded report'."; *FLDW* 33–34=*RCL* D 27: 吏爲失刑罪，或端爲，爲不直。 "As regards the officials, it is a case of committing a judicial error in punishing sb. with mutilation; if they did it intentionally, it is a case of 'perversion of justice'."; *Yuelu* WYZ 166). In the early Han dynasty *duan* was replaced by the term *gu* 故.

899 *Fan fa ling* 犯灋（法）令 "to violate the laws and ordinances" (*Hanfei* 21, 104). Cf. *fan fa* 犯法 "violate the laws" (*Yushu* 5), *fan ling* 犯令 "violate the ordinances" (*QLSZ* 57, 191=*RCL* A 16, 101; *FLDW* 142=*RCL* D 120), *fei ling* 法（廢）令 "disregard the ordinances" (*FLDW* 142=*RCL* D 120), *fan fa fei ling* 犯法廢令 "violate the laws and disregard the ordinances" (*Hanfei* 34, 244).

900 *Fu* 赴 "to throw oneself into, to plunge into (water etc.)" is used figuratively in the sense of "to be anxious/eager to, to strive for", e.g. to strive for military success (*Shiji* 111, 2928 [cf. Nienhauser IX (2011), 326]), financial profit to support relatives (*Hanshu* 78, 3275) or achievements (*Hanshu* 58, 2513).

901 *Sui* 隧 "passage" here for the homophonous and etymologically related *sui* 遂 "to advance, proceed" (antonym of *tui* 退 in *Yi* 4, 49a) with the meaning "success" (*Hanfei* 42, 303 [cf. Harbsmeier]: 遂之道 "the way of success") or the "advancement/career" of an official.

902 *Cheng si* 成私 "to achieve private aims (as official)" (*Hanfei* 14, 68; 31, 180; 36, 267 [Harbsmeier]: 成私者也 "to achieve private aims" and *Hanfei* 17, 83: 以成其私 "to achieve their private aims").

903 For *wu ta jie* see footnote 800.

Retrial – Interagency Enquiries

問如舜（辭）。104

The [results of the] interagency enquiries[904] corresponded to the statements.[905]

Retrial – Finding of Fact

鞫之：
暨坐八劾：小犯令二，大誤一，坐官小誤五。巳（已）論一甲，餘未論，皆相遝。審。

Finding of fact:[906]
Ji is prosecuted for eight *ex-officio* charges: two minor violations of ordinances,[907] one major mistake,[908] five liabilities for [subordinates in his] office or [own] minor mistakes.[909] He has already been sentenced to [pay a fine of] one suit of armour[910] [because of the liability for his subordinate Dan]. For the rest,[911] he is not to be sentenced [as the misdemeanours] are all connected with each other. [All these] are established facts.[912]

---

904 For *wen* see footnote 562. The exact wording of the results of the interagency enquiries is not recorded, because they apparently did not provide information that was not already known from the statements.

905 For *ci* see footnote 564.

906 For *ju* see footnote 565.

907 *Xiao fan ling* 小犯令 "minor violations of ordinances" (*FLDW* 144=*RCL* D 122). For *ling* see footnote 556.

908 For *da wu* 大誤 "major mistakes" an official was sentenced to pay one suit of armour (*XL* 58–60=*RCL* B 29; *FLDW* 209=*RCL* D 189). It is not mentioned which of the eight misconducts in office charged above was regarded as a major mistake.

909 It is mentioned above that Ji was liable for the misconduct of his subordinate Dan (*Yuelu WYZ* 097, 099), and that he was further liable for two misdemeanours of subordinates (regarding the incidents with Shi as well as Yan) which he did not detect (*Yuelu WYZ* 096–097). Therefore, Ji's liabilities for subordinates apparently amount to three cases. Accordingly, a translation of the passage as "five liabilities for [subordinates in his] office or [own] minor mistakes" (where the number of five includes liabilities on the one hand and own mistakes on the other) appears more reasonable than "five liabilities for minor mistakes [of subordinates in his] office".

910 Ji had to pay this fine for the misconduct of his subordinate Dan (*Yuelu WYZ* 099).

911 That is, for everything else apart from the misconduct of his subordinate Dan.

912 For *shen* see footnote 633.

Submission by the Prefecture – Concluding Formula

疑暨不當$_{105}$贏（纍）論。它縣論。敢瀐（讞）之。$_{106}$

We are in doubt[913] whether Ji should by law not be convicted based on the accumulation [of sentences]. In all other matters the prefecture has passed judgement.[914] We venture to submit [this case] for decision.[915]

Vote for Judgement

吏議：
貲暨一甲，勿贏（纍）。$_{107}$

The [responsible] officials deliver [the following] legal opinion:[916]
"Ji is to be fined[917] one suit of armour. [The individual sentences] are not to be accumulated."

913 Cf. the formula *yi* (*mou ren*) *zui* explained in footnote 582.

914 For *ta xian lun* see footnote 635.

915 For *yan* and the phrase *gan yan zhi* see footnote 489.

916 For *li yi* see footnote 572.

917 For *zi* see footnotes 558 and 594. During the Qin dynasty one suit of armour (*jia* 甲) was equivalent to 1,344 cash (*Yuelu Shu* 82–83; Yu Zhenbo 2010, 38).

Case I.7

In this case from 229 BC, a dispute arose concerning two buildings (a market stall for selling cloth and a guesthouse) from the inheritance of the merchant Pei. The dispute was between Wan, a former female slave of the deceased merchant, and his former menial, Shi. The criminal procedures were initiated by a self-denunciation by Wan, who reported herself to the authorities prior to the discovery of her offence. In her report Wan admitted that she concealed 68,300 cash when she declared the family property for her minor son, Yi. Furthermore, Wan reported Shi for blackmailing her. Shi had threatened Wan to report her to the authorities for evading property tax if she did not assign him the stall for selling cloth and a guesthouse from the inheritance of the deceased merchant Pei.

As guardian for the successor of Pei, Wan had failed to declare the amount of outstanding monetary claims of the deceased merchant as taxable property. These claims had been recorded on tallies, which served as contracts between five junior partners of Pei as debtors and the merchant as creditor.

In her statement, the accused Wan explained how she acquired possession of the contested buildings. Formerly Wan was a private slave woman of the deceased merchant who had sexual relations with her. Wan gave birth to the boy Yi and a girl. When the spouse of Pei died, Pei did not take another wife, but manumitted Wan and treated her like a wife. Because the former wife of Pei died childless, the eldest son of Wan, fathered by Pei, was eligible to become the heir of the merchant. He took his father's place as head of the household, inherited his rank – reduced by two degrees – and took possession of the merchant's stall and guesthouse.

Whereas Pei had informed the authorities of the manumission of his slave woman, he had not registered her as his wife. However, he had asked the members of his ancestral lineage to admit her as his wife to this community. Wives joining the community had to provide financial aid to destitute members. In her statement, Wan argued that she had fulfilled this duty just like the other wives and cited this as evidence that she was accepted as the legitimate wife of the merchant Pei by the members of his ancestral community.

One of the doubts, which would affect the sentence and was expressed by the competent judicial officials of the prefecture in the finding of fact, concerned the legal status of the accused woman. The judicial officials were unable to decide whether Wan was to be considered a released person, as recorded in the household registers of the district, or as the wife of a holder of the fifth rank, as witnessed by members of Pei's ancestral lineage. It was undisputed that Wan committed the statutory offence of evading property taxes, for which

 | DOI 10.1163/9789004315655_015

she was to be punished according to the value of misappropriated goods in the same way as in a case of theft. As a released person she would have to be tattooed and made a grain pounder convict; as the wife of a holder of the fifth rank Wan would, however, be entitled to be made a rice sifter convict, the privileged form of this penal labour. In any case, the punishment would have to be reduced by one degree because Wan reported herself to the authorities prior to the discovery of her offence.

In his own statement, the menial Shi partly confirmed Wan's statement, and added relevant details. He formerly lived together with Wan in the household of the merchant Pei. Shi had served his master as a menial from an early age. He had apparently proven to be a good menial in the market business because the merchant Pei had arranged a marriage for him as he would for his own son and had bought a house for the couple. Furthermore, he gave him a draught horse and a rice field for additional support, which enabled his protégé to establish his own household.

The bride's father only consented to the marriage between his daughter and Shi because Pei had promised that he would bequeath the market stall and the guesthouse to Shi. This promise suggests that Pei might originally have planned that his menial should continue his business. A particular point of contention in this case was whether the merchant kept his promise until his death. Wan denied that her husband had ordered the bequeathal of the two buildings to his former menial before he died. Therefore, Shi was legally not entitled to take over these properties. The merchant Pei had obviously failed to register his last will on a tripartite tally (*quan*) with the district authorities. It is not clear whether the authorities only had to hear disputes if the claims could be substantiated by certificates on tallies. However, the existence of verbal agreements during Qin times which did not require the written form in order to be valid indicates that the claims of the former menial in the present case may not have been automatically rejected by the authorities despite the absence of a written will.

Because Shi did not admit to being guilty of the statutory offence of blackmailing during the first stage of interrogation, the judicial officials initiated the second stage of interrogation at which the accused was confronted with inconsistencies in his statement and contradictory evidence. The interrogating officials concluded that the house, the horse and the rice field from Pei were to be deemed substitutes (*geng*) for the buildings which had originally been promised. They based this conclusion on Shi's statement, in which he had confirmed that he had accepted these objects while not claiming the other buildings before Pei's death. Therefore, they regarded Shi's claim as unfounded.

At the end of the second stage of interrogation, Shi pleaded guilty to the charge of blackmail on condition that the legal premises presented to him by his interrogators, who considered his actions punishable, were valid. The fact that the accused expressed reservations about his guilt had two effects: Since the accused forwent any further defence, it was possible to conclude the interrogation and summarise the finding of fact; but, since there were doubts, the case would be submitted to the higher authorities for a review of the validity of the legal premises before a decision was made.

The judicial officials were in doubt as to whether Shi might be the legitimate heir of the two buildings since Pei's promise to bequeath the two buildings to his former menial had been attested by several witnesses. Likewise, the officials were uncertain whether Shi's actions constituted the statutory offence of blackmailing. These doubts were voiced after the finding of fact and also became obvious in the alternative proposals for the sentence: The majority proposed to refrain from punishing Shi severely for blackmailing and instead only imposed a fine of two suits of armour. This fine seems to have been imposed on persons who failed to report the offences of their neighbours or members of their household to the authorities. As Shi originally lived in the same household with Wan, he should have reported her to the authorities for evading property taxes. On the other hand, the minority proposed to sentence the former menial Shi to the most severe form of penal labour as earth pounder convict and to deport him to the province of Shu. However, as a holder of the first rank he remained unmutilated. According to the proposal of the minority, Shi should in fact be punished for blackmailing.

Diplomatic Edition

▨之十八年八月丙戌大女子婏自告曰七月爲子小走馬義占家訾義當□夫＝建公卒$_{108}$昌士五積⌞喜⌞遺錢六萬八千三百有券婏匿不占吏爲訾⌞婏有市布肆一⌞舍客室一⌞公士$_{109}$識劫婏曰以肆室鼠識不鼠識＝且告婏匿訾婏恐即以肆室鼠識爲建等折棄$_{110}$券弗責先自告＝識劫婏$_{111}$
婏曰與義同居故夫＝沛妾沛御婏＝產義女㛍⌞沛妻危以十歲時死沛不取妻居可二$_{112}$歲沛免婏爲庶人妻婏＝有產男必女若居二歲沛告宗人里人夫＝快⌞臣走馬拳上造嘉⌞頡曰$_{113}$沛有子婏所四人不取妻矣欲令婏入宗出里單賦與里人通飲食快等曰可婏即入宗⌞里$_{114}$人不㽃死者出單賦如它人妻居六歲沛死義代爲戶爵後有肆宅⌞識故爲沛隸同居沛$_{115}$以三歲時爲識取妻居一歲爲識買室賈五千錢分馬一匹稻田廿畝異識＝從軍沛死來歸$_{116}$□婏曰沛未死時言以肆舍客室鼠識＝欲得⌞婏謂沛死時不令鼠識＝弗當得識曰婏$_{117}$匿訾不鼠識＝且告婏＝以匿訾故即鼠肆室沛未死弗欲以肆舍客室鼠識不告婏不智戶$_{118}$籍不爲妻爲免妾故它如前•識曰自小爲沛隸沛令上造狗求上造羽子女齔爲識妻$_{119}$令狗告羽曰且以布肆舍客室鼠識⌞羽乃許沛＝已爲識取齔即爲識買室分識馬田$_{120}$異識而不

以隸舍客室鼠識=□□□識□受它軍歸沛巳死識以沛未死言謂$_{121}$婉=不以隸室鼠識=且告婉匿訾婉乃鼠識=即弗告識以沛言求隸室非劫婉不智$_{122}$婉曰劫之故它如婉•建⌞昌⌞積⌞喜⌞遺曰故爲沛舍人〼織建等錢以市販共分贏市$_{123}$折建負七百⌞昌三萬三千⌞積六千六百⌞喜二萬二千⌞遺六千券責建=等=未賞識欲告$_{124}$婉=即折券不責建它如婉•婡快臣拳嘉頡言如婉•狗羽齡言如識•義⌞若小不訊必死$_{125}$•卿唐佐更曰沛免婉爲庶人即書戶籍曰免妾沛後妻婉不告唐更今籍爲免妾不智它$_{126}$•詰識⌞沛未死雖告狗羽且以隸舍客室鼠識而後不鼠識=弗求巳爲識更買室分識田馬$_{127}$異識⌞沛死時有不令⌞義巳代爲戶後有隸宅識弗當得何故尚求隸室曰不鼠識=且告婉$_{128}$匿訾婉即以其故鼠識是劫婉而云非劫何解⌞識曰□欲得隸室婉不鼠識=誠恐謂且告婉=乃鼠$_{129}$識=實弗當得上以識爲劫婉辠識=毋以避毋它解辠它如前•問匿訾稅及室隸臧直$_{130}$各過六百六十錢它如辤•鞫之婉爲夫=沛妾沛御婉=產義⌞婡沛妻危死沛免婉爲庶人以$_{131}$爲妻有產必⌞若籍爲免妾⌞沛死義代爲戶後有隸宅婉匿訾稅直過六百六十錢先自告=$_{132}$識劫⌞識爲沛隸沛爲取妻欲以隸舍客室鼠識後弗鼠爲買室分馬一匹田廿畝異識⌞沛死$_{133}$識後求隸室婉弗鼠識恐謂婉且告婉匿訾婉以故鼠隸=室=直過六百六十錢得皆審疑$_{134}$婉爲夫=妻爲庶人及識辠毄它縣論敢潚之$_{135}$
•吏議婉爲□□□貲識二甲或曰婉爲庶人完識爲城旦纍足輸蜀$_{136}$

Edition and Translation

Submission by the Prefecture – Introductory Formula

【敢潚（讞）】之：

[We venture to submit the following case for decision:][918]

Initiation of Criminal Proceedings

十八年八月丙戌，大女子婉自告曰：
七月爲子小走馬義占家訾（貲）。義當【責】大夫建、公卒$_{108}$昌、士五（伍）積、喜、遺錢六萬八千三百，有券。婉匿不占吏爲訾（貲）。婉有市布隸（肆）一、舍客室一。公士$_{109}$識劫婉曰：
以隸（肆）、室鼠（予）識。不鼠（予）識，識且告婉匿訾（貲）。
婉恐，即以隸（肆）、室鼠（予）識。爲建等折棄$_{110}$券，弗責。先自告，告識劫婉。$_{111}$

918 *Zhi* 之 might well be the last part of the phrase *gan yan zhi*, the initial formula for the submission of a doubtful criminal case to the higher authorities for decision. Cf. footnote 489.

It was the 18th year, the 8th month, the day *bingxu*,[919] when the adult[920] woman Wan reported herself[921] [for having committed an offence], saying:
"In the 7th month [of this year] I declared[922] the family property[923] for my

---

919 This was the 21st day of the eight month with the first day *bingyin* in the 18th year of the reign of King Zheng of Qin (Zhang Peiyu 2007, 73 and Li Zhonglin 2012, 65), i.e. 09/09/229 BC (Xu Xiqi 1997, 1266).

920 *Da* 大 "adult" (*QLSZ* 53=*RCL* A 13; *FZS* 9=*RCL* E 3; *ZYS* 2, 63).

921 *Xian zi gao* 先自告 (*Yuelu WYZ* 132; *ZYS* 49; Lau and Lüdke 2012, footnote 791). According to early Han legal stipulations, an offender gained mitigation (*jian* 減) of punishment by one degree through voluntary admission of guilt before his offence was discovered (*ENLL* 127–128). As can be seen from the results of the interagency enquiries (*wen* 問) as well as from the summarised finding of fact (*ju* 鞫), the present case was classified as a property crime (*dao* 盜). Accordingly, the punishment is based on the value of the misappropriated goods. As the value exceeded the amount of 660 cash, the accused Wan was to be punished with the most severe form of penal labour as a tattooed grain pounder convict (*qing chong* 黥舂), the maximum penalty for property crimes (*ENLL* 55). In reporting herself, she hoped to gain a mitigation of punishment by one degree. She would still be sentenced to the most severe form of penal labour, but would not have to suffer mutilation (*ENLL* 127). However, as the wife of a holder of the fifth rank, Wan could only be punished with the privileged form (*bai can* 白粲) of penal labour (*ENLL* 82). In this case, Wan would have to be punished with even less severe penal labour of the category *nai* 耐 as *li qie* 隸妾 because she reported herself prior to the discovery of the offence (*ENLL* 128).

922 *Zhan* 占 "declare (for enlistment into the registers)". The subjects of the early Chinese empire were obliged to declare different personal data to be entered in different registers for taxation. For the registration in the household registers, the term *zhan shu* 占數 "to declare the number (of household members for registration)" is used (*Hanshu* 100A, 4198 with commentary of Yan Shigu). This term is an abbreviation of *zhan shu ming shu* 占書名數 "to declare and make an entry (in the registers) for the names and the number (of the members of the households)" (*ZYS* 28–29, 66; *zhan shu* 占書 in *FZS* 11=*RCL* E 3; *zhan zhu ming shu* 占著名數 in *Shiji* 104, 2779). See in detail Lau and Lüdke 2012, footnote 644. Cf. *zi zhan* 自占 (*Shiji* 30, 1430; *Hanshu* 8, 248; 44, 2139; *ZYS* 28–29, 66). The household registers enabled the authorities to impose poll taxes on the subjects.
Merchants like the husband of Wan had to declare the amount of their proceeds in market registers (*shi ji* 市籍) for the purpose of taxation (*shi zu* 市租 "sales tax") (*ENLL* 260: 市販匿不自占租，坐所匿租臧（贓）爲盜，沒入其所販賣及賈錢縣官，奪之列。 "When engaging in a trade transaction, evading the sales tax by not declaring one's own proceeds is prosecuted according to the provisions applicable to theft of the amount misappropriated by evading the tax; [in addition,] the [goods] sold in the transaction as well as the proceeds are to be seized into the government coffers and the market stall is to be taken away from the trader in question.").
Wealthy merchants were also obliged to declare their property in order to pay property tax. The declaration of Wan concerned the property of their household. In Qin times, this kind of tax was called *zi shui* 訾稅 (*Yuelu WYZ* 130, 132), later in Han times the term *zi suan*

son Yi, minor[924] holder of the third rank.[925] Yi was by law entitled to [claim debts from] Jian, holder of the fifth rank, the *gong zu* Chang and the rank-and-file men[926] Tui, Xi and Yi [amounting to overall] 68,300 cash. There were

---

訾算 was used (*Hanshu* 5, 152). For the special taxation of merchants in Han times see also the proposal of Kong Jin, assistant to the superintendent of agriculture, from the year 119 BC (*Shiji* 30, 1430=*Hanshu* 24B, 1166–1167 [cf. Swann 1950, 279–283]). Cf. the case of Prince Liu Yin of Pangguang who was sentenced in 116 BC for having lent money without declaring the interest rate, which furthermore exceeded the legal norms (*Hanshu* 15A, 447).

In Eastern Han times wealthy people had to declare their property in strings of cash and were punished when failing to do so (*Xuanquan* 8: 兵令十三：當占緡錢，匿不自占，【占】不以實，罰及家長戍邊一歲。 "Ordinances for soldiers no. 13: Those who by law have to declare their strings of cash, but conceal and do not declare them, or do not declare them according to the facts, will be punished with one year of [additional] military service on the border. [This punishment] will include the heads of the family.").

923 *Zi* 訾 (*ENLL* 411; *Shiji* 59, 2097; 122, 3154; 124, 3187; *Hanshu* 5, 152; 91, 3690) for *zi* 貲 "property" (Gao and Dong 1997, 584; Feng and Deng 2006, 943: compare *Shiji* 117, 2999 with *Shiji* 102, 2751; for *zi* 貲 "fine" see footnotes 558 and 594). The editors (Zhu and Chen 2013, 153 with footnote 3) provide the following example of a declaration of "family property" (*jia zi* 家訾; see *Hanshu* 70, 2661) for the purpose of taxation during late Western Han times from *Juyan* 37·35:

候長觻得廣昌里公乘禮忠，年卅。

小奴二人直三萬　　大婢一人二萬　　軺車二乘直萬

用馬五匹直二萬　　牛車二兩直四千　　服牛二六千

宅一區萬　　田五頃五萬　　•凡訾直十五萬

"*Houzhang* Li Zhong, holder of the eighth rank [registered in the prefecture of] Lude, quarter Guangchang; 30 years old:

minor slaves, two persons, value of 30,000 [cash]; adult female slaves, one person, value of 20,000 [cash]; small carts, two vehicles, value of 10,000 [cash];

harnessed horses, five, value of 20,000 [cash]; ox carts, two vehicles, value of 4,000 [cash]; yoked oxen, two, [value of] 6,000 [cash];

residence, one, [value of] 10,000 [cash]; fields, five *qing*, [value of] 50,000 [cash]; total property, value of 150,000 [cash]."

924 For *xiao* see footnote 825. According to early Han legal stipulations, a minor successor of a holder of the fifth rank inherited the third rank *zan niao* 簪褭 (*ENLL* 368), which corresponded to *zou ma* 走馬 during Qin times, after his father's death. A *xiao zou ma* was to be registered for military and labour service at the age of 22 years according to Han law (*ENLL* 364). In the present case, Yi as a minor holder of the third rank must be younger than 22 years. Therefore, he had not yet been registered for military and labour service.

925 For *zou ma* see footnote 601.

926 For *shi wu* see footnote 495.

tallies[927] for this. I concealed[928] and did not declare [this amount of money] to the officials as property. I possessed one stall[929] for selling cloth[930] and one house[931] for accommodating guests[932] [from outside]. Shi, holder of the first rank, blackmailed[933] me saying:
'Assign[934] me the stall and the house. If you do not assign [these buildings] to me, I shall report you [to the authorities] for concealing property.' I was afraid[935] and so assigned the stall and the house to Shi. In favour of[936]

---

927 For *quan* see footnote 535.

928 *Ni* 匿 "to conceal", see Lau and Lüdke 2012, footnote 902. *Ni* is used here in the context of evading taxes (cf. *ENLL* 260; *Shiji* 30, 1430; *Mo* 70, 359; *Longgang* 142, 147). In the present case, Wan had obviously concealed outstanding monetary claims of the deceased merchant Pei to the amount of 68,300 cash, which had not yet been repaid to her by the junior partners of Pei. The property tax rate for merchants in Qin times is unknown. On the tax system of Qin and Han times see Nishijima 1986; Ma Yi 2007, 647–699; Zhang Jinguang 2004, 199–205.

929 For *si* see footnote 730.

930 *Bu* 布 "cloth", made of hemp (*cannabis sativa*; *ma* 麻 [*Odes* 150,3] or *xi* 枲 [*Shu* Yugong §7]), sackcloth (*boehmeria nivea*; *zhu* 紵 [*Shu* Yugong §15; *Zuo* Xiang 29, 546,10]) or kudzu-vine (*pueraria thunbergiana*; *ge* 葛 [*Odes* 203,2]). On hemp see Kuhn 1988, 17–19 and 27, fig. 4; on kudzu-vine see Kuhn 1988, 39 and 40, fig. 9.

931 *Shi* 室 "house" (*Odes* 189,2; *Meng* 2, 87; *FLDW* 10=*RCL* D 9; *FZS* 8=*RCL* E 3).

932 *She ke* 舍客 "to accommodate guests" (*Guan* 81, 408: 請以令爲諸侯之商賈立客舍。"I request to give an order to establish guesthouses for the merchants of all feudal lords."; *Shiji* 68, 2236; cf. *Shiji* 105, 2785). Note that a guesthouse at a market was also called *ke she* 客舍 "guesthouse" (*Yuelu WYZ* 167). However, at some point during the Qin dynasty the official name for guesthouses was changed from *ke she* to *bin si she* 賓【飤】舍 (*Liye* 8–461r). *Ke* 客 "guests" probably also included external merchants who came to sell their goods.

933 The basic meaning of *jie* 劫 is "to coerce sb. into doing sth." In statutes from early Han times, it very likely refers to the statutory offence of hostage taking (*ENLL* 68: 劫人、謀劫人求錢財，雖未得若未劫，皆磔之。 "For taking sb. as a hostage or conspiring to take sb. as a hostage in order to extort money or valuables one is without exception executed by quartering, even if one has not yet gained [the money or valuables] or not yet taken [the person in question] as a hostage."; cf. *Hanshu* 76, 3202: 富人蘇回爲郎，二人劫之。 "The rich man Su Hui who was a gentleman was taken as a hostage by two men."). In the context of the present case, *jie* clearly refers to the offence of blackmailing.

934 For *shu* 鼠 as common Qin graphic variant of *yu* 與 or *yu* 予 in the sense "to give" see footnotes 518 and 729.

935 *Kong* 恐 "to be afraid, get scared" without object (*Yuelu WYZ* 179, 228; *ZYS* 131: 新黔首恐，操其叚（假）兵匿山中。"The new subjects got scared, seized their borrowed weapons and hid in the mountains.").

936 *Wei* 爲 *Gʷ(r)aj-s as preposition.

Jian and his partners I broke[937] and discarded the bond tallies and did not claim [the debts from them].[938] Prior to the discovery of the offence I [hereby] report myself [to the authorities for concealing property] and report[939] Shi for blackmailing me."

First Stage of Interrogation

媿曰：
與義同居，故大夫沛妾。沛御媿，媿產義、女妣。沛妻危以十歲時死。沛不取妻。居可二$_{112}$歲，沛免媿爲庶人，妻媿。媿有（又）產男必、女若。居二歲，沛告宗人、里人大夫快、臣、走馬拳、上造嘉、頡曰：$_{113}$
沛有子媿所四人。不取妻矣，欲令媿入宗，出里單（殫）賦（賻），與里人通飲食。快等曰：可。
媿即入宗，里$_{114}$人不祥（幸）死者，出單（殫）賦（賻），如它人妻。居六歲，沛死。義代爲戶、爵後，有肆（肆）宅。
識故爲沛隸，同居。沛$_{115}$以三歲時爲識取妻；居一歲爲識買室，賈（價）五千錢，分馬一匹、稻田廿畝，異識。識從軍，沛死。來歸，$_{116}$【謂】媿曰：沛未死時言以肆（肆）、舍客室鼠（予）識。識欲得。媿謂：沛死時不令鼠（予）識，識弗當得。識曰：媿$_{117}$匿訾（貲）。不鼠（予）識，識且告媿。媿以匿訾（貲）故，即鼠（予）肆（肆）、室。沛未死，弗欲以肆（肆）、舍客室鼠（予）識，不告媿。不智（知）戶$_{118}$籍不爲妻、爲免妾故。
它如前。

Wan stated:
"I am living together[940] with Yi in the same household. Formerly I was a female

937 *Zhe quan* 折券 "to break a bond tally (in order to cancel debts)" (*Shiji* 8, 343; *Guan* 83, 412; 74, 364; *Hanshu* 100A, 4211).

938 For *ze* see footnote 789.

939 For *gao* see footnote 498.

940 *Tong ju* 同居 "(those persons who) live together (in the same household)" (*FLDW* 22=*RCL* D 19: 可（何）謂同居？戶爲同居。"What is the meaning of '[those who] live together'? The household is [meant by] '[those who] live together'."; *QLSZ* 85=*RCL* A 41; *QLZC* 89=*RCL* C 25; *FLDW* 20=*RCL* D 18; *ENLL* 72, 160, 201, 342, 371, 378, 380, 387).
In a commentary to *Hanshu* 2, 85, however, Yan Shigu explains this term as "besides the father, mother, wives and children (of the head of the household, persons) like his older and younger brothers, the children of his older and younger brothers, etc.", i.e. all male relatives who have not yet established a separate household. After an in-depth analysis of the received literature Hiranaka (1967, 320–336, 341) arrived at the conclusion that *tong ju* refers to relatives living in the same household, including parents and children. The term therefore seems to exclude persons not related to the head of the household, such as

slave[941] of Pei, holder of the fifth rank.[942] Pei had sexual relations[943] with me,

---

servants and slaves (RCL A 41, footnote 15). Some references are in accordance with this explanation (*Hanshu* 50, 2307; QLZC 39=RCL C 25). It would also make sense in a second definition found in the *Falü dawen*, which distinguishes between *tong ju* and *shi ren* 室人 "people of the house" (FLDW 201=RCL D 181). Unfortunately, *du hu mu* 獨戶母 as the definition of *tong ju* in this passage seems to be corrupt. It might be possible that the character *mu* 母 is written incorrectly and should instead be transcribed as *guan* 毌 for 貫 so that the definition means "*tong ju* are persons solely (strung:) listed in one household (register)" as Satake Yasuhiko suggests (quoted after RCL D 181, footnote 3; for the similarity of both characters in Qin manuscripts see Fang Yong 2012, 207 and 352; cf. Huang Dekuan 2007, 316 and 2628). However, servants and slaves were at least sometimes included among the *tong ju*, because later on in the text of the present case the term is used for a menial who lived together with his master in the same household (*Yuelu* WYZ 115). Here, *tong ju* also implies that mother and son lived together in the same household after the death of the merchant Pei.

941 *Qie* 妾 refers to a female slave, in contrast to male slaves (*nu* 奴). At the beginning of the Han dynasty, the term *qie* was replaced by *bi* 婢. Sources of slavery in Qin and Han include poor people selling their children in times of hardship, the enslavement of prisoners of war as well as the slave trade, mainly with neighbouring peoples in the south. The price of female slaves during the Qin dynasty is unknown. In the year 201 BC, the value of an adult female slave was 16,000 cash (ZYS 9), around 150 years later 20,000 cash (*Juyan* 37.35). But the price during the Qin dynasty might have been much lower because the price of an adult male slave at this time only amounted to 4,300 cash (*Liye* 8–1287), while the lowest value of an adult male slave during Western Han times was between 15,000 (*Quan Hanwen* 42, 359a) and 20,000 cash (Li Konghuai 2007, 581). State and private slaves need to be distinguished although it is difficult in some sources to distinguish state slaves and convict labourers. The lack of evidence for state slaves (*guan nu* 官奴) in the manuscripts from Qin and early Han times led some scholars to assume that the convicts of the bond servant category (*li chen qie* 隸臣妾) constitute the state slaves of this period. Wives and children of serious offenders who suffered confiscation (*shou* 收) were in fact made bond servant convicts (ENLL 435, 174–175). Slaves could move from the status of private to state slave and vice versa by way of donation, confiscation and purchase. See Wilbur 1943, 65–66, 72–74; Ch'ü T'ung-tsu 1972, 135–137; Yates 2001, 302–304; Wang Yanhui 2004; Li Junming 2011, 237–246 and Yates 2014.

942 For *da fu* see footnote 724.

943 *Yu* 御 "to sleep/copulate with" (*Zuo* Xuan 3,292,12: 文公見之，與之蘭而御之。 "Duke Wen saw her, gave her an orchid and copulated with her."; cf. *Zuo* Xiang 26,520,13: 姬納諸御，嬖，生佐。 "[Gong] Ji, the mother of the duke, procured her for sexual intercourse, she was favoured and gave birth to Zuo."; *Hanfei* 34, 233 [cf. Harbsmeier]: 宮婦不御者出嫁之。 "Among the women in the harem, he married off those he did not personally sleep with."; *Hanfei* 35, 255 [cf. Harbsmeier]: 桓公被髮而御婦人。 "Duke Huan undid

and I gave birth to Yi and the girl Qie. Wei, the wife of Pei, died 10 years ago.[944] [Since then] Pei has not taken [another] wife. After[945] approximately[946] two years Pei manumitted[947] me, made me a released person[948] and made me his wife. I gave birth again to the boy Bi and the girl Ruo. After two years, Pei informed the members of his ancestral lineage[949] and quarter[950] Kuai and Chen, holders of the fifth rank, Quan, holder of the third rank, and Jia and Xie, holders of the second rank, saying:

'I, Pei, have four children with[951] Wan. As I did not marry anymore, I wish that you let Wan gain entry to our ancestral lineage, pay[952] the contribution to the

---

his hair bun and slept with his woman."; ENLL 385: 婢御其主而有子[...]。"If a female slave, who copulated with her master, has children with him [...].").

944 For *yi* as preposition before a specification of time see footnote 827.

945 For *ju* see footnote 785.

946 For *ke* 可 before a specification of time meaning "around, about" see ZYS 101, 110, 112; Pei Xuehai (cited from Yu and Xie 1993, 134) as well as Yang and He 2001, 347.

947 *Mian* 免 as legal term means either "to release (accused or convicts)" or "to manumit (slaves)" (FZS 38=RCL E 15; ENLL 382, 385; *Hanshu* 4, 130). According to early Han stipulations, owners of slaves had the right to freely decide whether they wished to give freedom to slaves on account of good conduct (ENLL 162–163: 奴婢爲善而主欲免者，許之。奴命曰私屬，婢爲庶人。"If the owner of a male or female slave wishes to manumit him/her on account of good conduct, this is to be granted. A [male] slave then is declared a 'personal dependant', a female slave is made a released person."). If a female slave bore her owner a child, she was entitled to be manumitted after her owner's death (ENLL 385: 婢御其主而有子，主死，免其婢爲庶人。"If a female slave had sexual intercourse with her owner and has children with him, she is manumitted after her owner's death and made a released person."). Cf. Lau and Lüdke 2012, footnote 793.

948 For *shu ren* see footnote 671.

949 *Zong ren* 宗人 "members of the same ancestral lineage" (*Shiji* 82, 2453; *Zuo* Xiang 22, 493, 14; *Dongguan Hanji* 16, 714: 宗人[...]會飲食宴。"Members of the ancestral lineage [...] meet for drinking and eating in a banquet.").

950 *Li ren* 里人 "inhabitants of the same quarter" (FZS 12, 52, 63, 84, 91=RCL E 3, 19, 21, 23, 24; ZYS 201). See especially FZS 93=RCL E 24: 里節（即）有祠，丙與里人及甲等會飲食，皆莫肯與丙共桮（杯）器。"When there are sacrifices in our quarter and I, C, together with the inhabitants of my quarter as well as A meet to drink and eat, nobody is willing to share a cup or a dish with me."

951 For *suo* 所 as postposition that marks the recipient or giver as the object after verbs of transmitting see footnote 681. Here the verb *you* 有 takes two objects, the second of which (marked by *suo*) is a person with whom the agent has children.

952 *Chu* 出 "to pay" is often used in the context of paying taxes (*chu fu* 出賦) (FLDW 165=RCL D 175; ENLL 255, 429; *Liye* 8–518).

funeral expenses[953] for the destitute[954] in our quarter[955] and drink and eat

953 *Fu* 賦 (GSR 104g) *p(r)a-s "contribution" (*Zuo* Xiang 31,560,9) or "tax" (FLDW 165=RCL D 175; ENLL 255, 429; *Liye* 8–518) probably stands for the homeophonous *fu* 賻 (GSR 102x') *b(r)a-s "money contribution to the costs of a funeral" (*Li* 3, 1249b [cf. Couvreur 1950, vol. I, 50]: 弔喪弗能賻。"He offers his condolences to sb. and does not manage to make a contribution to the funeral costs."); *Li* 7, 1283a: 使子貢說驂而賻之。"[Confucius] let his disciple Zi Gong unharness an outside horse [of a team of three] and present it [to the parents of the deceased] as contribution to the funeral costs."; *Xun* 27, 325 [cf. Knoblock III (1994), 212]: 貨財曰賻，輿馬曰賵，衣服曰襚，玩好曰贈，玉貝曰唅。賻、賵所以佐生也，贈、襚所以送死也。"Presents of money and valuables are called *fu* gifts. Presents of horses and carriages are called *feng* gifts. Presents of clothing and mourning garments are called *sui* gifts. Presents of valuable curiosities are called *zeng* gifts. Presents of jade and cowries are called *han* gifts. *Fu* and *feng* gifts are used to assist the living; *zeng* and *sui* gifts are used to send off the dead." and *Shiji* 83, 2463 [cf. Nienhauser VII (1994), 283]: 鄒、魯之臣，生則不得事養，死則不得賻襚。"The vassals of Zou and Lu did not obtain the largesse [of the king of Zhou] when they were alive, nor his funeral gifts when they died."). Cf. *fu* 傅 (GSR 102u') *b(r)a-s for *fu* 賦 (Bai Yulan 2012, 183). According to Wang Li (1982, 175), *fu* 賻 belongs to the same word family as *fu* 扶, *fu* 傅 and *fu* 輔 with the basic meaning "to support".

954 *Dan* 單 (GSR 147a) *tˤar is probably used here for the homophonous *dan* 殫 (GSR 147g) (Feng and Deng 2006, 223). *Dan*, usually in the sense "be exhausted", especially also means "to use up/exhaust the resources/funds" (*Mo* 6, 20 [cf. Johnston 2010, 43]: 單財 "to use up the means"; *Xun* 10, 129 [cf. Knoblock II (1990), 137]: 貨寶單 "movable goods and treasures will be exhausted"; *Hanshu* 67, 2908 [cf. Watson 1974, 108]: 單幣 "using up their money"; *Hanshu* 86, 3498: 單貨財 "to use up the means"). In the present passage *dan* 殫 seems to refer to people whose means were used up, i.e. "the destitute". The editors interpret *dan* as a basic dwelling unit within the *xiang* 鄉 and *li* 里 (Zhu and Chen 2013, 155 with footnote 14), but there is no convincing evidence for the existence of such units during the Qin dynasty.

955 In Qin and Han times, *li* 里 designated the smallest administrative unit in the cities (ZYS 197; *Yuelu* WYZ 143, 177, 179; ENLL 307, 390) and probably also in the countryside, cf. Nishijima 1986, 551–552; Zhang Jinguang 2004, 594–602; Hsing 2014, 184–185. They were surrounded by walls (FLDW 186=RCL D 165; ENLL 182) and accessible through one or two gates (FLDW 160=RCL D 140; *Yuelu* WYZ 177, 179; ENLL 306). In FZS 91–94=RCL E 24 one *li* appears to have comprised 21 *hu* 戶 "households" (Zhang Jinguang 2004, 599); according to other Qin manuscripts the head of a *li* was in charge of 27 households (*Liye* 8–157v). In a list from tomb no. 10 of Fenghuangshan (dated to the year 153 BC) used in the course of tax collection, one *Zheng li* 鄭里 comprised exactly 25 households (*Sanjian* 811–836). The Yinwan administrative documents from the year 10 BC provide us with interesting statistic details on the population of Donghai province at the end of the Western Han. According to these accounts, the province had 1,397,343 inhabitants, who lived in 266,290 households, which were assigned to 2,534 *li* (*Yinwan mudu* M6D1r). Therefore, on average every *li* comprised 551 inhabitants in 105 households. According to the system set up by Guan

together[956] with the inhabitants of our quarter [when there is a funeral meal].' Kuai and the others said: 'Agreed.'[957]

So I, Wan, gained entry to their ancestral lineage. [Whenever] an inhabitant of this quarter unfortunately[958] died, I paid the contribution to the funeral expenses for the destitute, just like another man's wife [would have done it]. After six years, Pei died. [My son] Yi took his place, became heir[959] of the

---

Zhong in Qi, a *li* is an organisation of 50 *jia* 家 "families" (*Yinqueshan Shoufa shouling* 937; cf. *Guoyu* 3.1/40/26 and *Guan* 20, 121). Other sources mention that one *li* comprised 25 families (*Zhouli* 15, 740b; Maozhuan on *Odes* 76,1) or 100 families (*Guan* 57, 303; *Houhanshu* 28, 3625). The *li*, headed by a *li dian* 里典, is mentioned as the smallest administrative unit in *QLSZ* 25=*RCL* A 19 and *FLDW* 63=*RCL* D 51. It is also frequently mentioned in connection with the data necessary to identify a person (*FZS* 6, 8, 13, 15, 17, 19, 21, 23, 25, 28, 31, 34, 37, 42, 46, 50, 52, 61, 63, 73, 84, 95 and 96=*RCL* E 3, 4, 5, 6, 7, 8, 9, 10, 11, 12, 13, 14, 15, 16, 17, 18, 19, 20, 21, 22 and 23).

956 *Tong* 通 in adverbial usage "in sb.'s company, together with" (*ENLL* 63: 智（知）人爲群盜而通歙（飲）食餽遺之，與同罪；弗智（知），黥爲城旦舂。 "For eating or drinking together with another person or supporting this person with food in the knowledge that the person is a member of a robber gang, one is punished in the same way [as the member of a robber gang himself]; without knowledge, one is tattooed and made an earth pounder convict."). Cf. the synonymous *yu gong* 與共 (*FLDW* 15=*RCL* D 14). Here, *yin shi* 飲食 obviously refers to celebrating a funeral meal together, cf. meals held on the occasion of common sacrifices of inhabitants of the same quarter (*FZS* 92–93=*RCL* E 24).

957 *Ke* 可 as main verb "to approve, consent, permit", used as an expression of approval (cf. the note of approval after imperial decisions, e.g. *Liye* 8–1668; *ENLL* 491, 497, 503, etc.).

958 For 羊 as the character form normally used to write *xing* 幸 in Qin and early Han times see footnote 897. *Bu xing si* 不幸死 "to die unfortunately/unexpectedly" (cf. *ENLL* 312–313, 377, 500–501) seems to be synonymous to *ji si* 疾死 "to die of a disease".

959 *Hou* 後 refers to the "heir" of a person's household and rank (*QLSZ* 153=*RCL* A 90; *QLZC* 37=*RCL* 23a; *FLDW* 71=*RCL* D 57; *ENLL* 367–391). For *ji si zhi hou* 疾死置後 "appointing the heir after death of disease" see especially *ENLL* 367–371. For the right of succession of private slaves see *ENLL* 382–383: 死毋後而有奴婢者，免奴婢以爲庶人。以庶人律予之其主田宅及餘財。奴婢多，代戶者毋（勿）過一人，先用勞久，有夫（?）子，若主所言吏者。 "If after death there is no heir but slaves or slave women, then the slaves or slave women are to be manumitted and made released persons; according to the statute on released persons, their master's fields and residences as well as the movable property [goods] left by him are to be [given to] them. Supposing the slaves and slave women are numerous, the one who takes the place of the head of the household should not be more than one person; one should give precedence [to slaves] due to merits and length of service, [to those] who have husbands(?) and children or who have been mentioned to the authorities by their owner."

household and the rank[960] and took possession[961] of the stall and the residence.[962]
Shi formerly was a menial[963] of Pei and lived together with him in the same household. Three years ago Pei arranged a marriage for Shi; one year later, he bought a house for Shi at a price of 5,000 cash, allotted[964] him a horse and a rice field of 20 *mu* and separated[965] him [from his household]. Shi was serving in the army when Pei died. When he returned home, he [said to] me: 'Before Pei died, he promised me that he would assign me the stall and the house for accommodating guests. I wish to obtain them.' I said to him: 'When he died Pei [in his last will] did not order us to assign [the buildings] to you and [therefore] you are not entitled to obtain them.' Shi said: 'You concealed property. If you do not assign me [the buildings], I will report you.' Because of the concealed property I then assigned the stall and the house to Shi. Before he died, Pei did not wish to assign Shi the stall and the house for accommodating guests; [at least] he did not inform me of this. I do not know the reason why I was not entered into the household registers as Pei's wife, but [just] as a manumitted female slave."

---

960 For *jue* see footnote 834.

961 *You* 有 here with the meaning "to take possession of" (*Odes* 264,2; 300,7).

962 *Zhai* 宅 "residence, house with courtyard" is often distinguished from the fields (*tian* 田) (ENLL 314–316). The compound *si zhai* 肆宅 occurs only rarely in received literature (*Weiliaozi* B8/22/17: 賈不離其肆宅。"Merchants do not leave their stall and residence.").

963 *Li* 隸 seems to be unspecific with regard to gender. Here it designates a male member of the private menial staff (cf. *li* as maidservant in *Liye huji* 9 [K4] and *ZYS* 29; gender uncertain in *FLDW* 22=*RCL* D 19; *si li* 私隸 in *Jijiupian* 3, 183) who had to be enlisted in the household register of his master. *Li* has to be distinguished from the so-called bond servant convicts (*li chen qie* 隸臣妾) sentenced to governmental penal labour. *Li* already existed in the Spring and Autumn period (*Zuo* Zhao 7,611,15; Huan 2,38,16; Ai 2,797,6). The exact distinction between *li* and private slaves (*ren nu bi* 人奴婢) is unclear. Cf. Lau and Lüdke 2012, footnote 723.

964 The use of *fen* 分 indicates that the horse and the rice field were originally owned by the merchant. It proves that during the Qin dynasty merchants were not forbidden to acquire and own farm land.

965 *Yi* 異 "to separate sb." (ENLL 342–343: 寡夫、寡婦毋子及同居，若有子，子年未盈十四，及寡子年未盈十八，及夫妻皆瘁（癃）病，及老年七十以上，毋異其子。"If widowers and widows have no children or [other] persons who live in the same household, or if they have children [but] these are [all] below the age of 14, or only one child [but] this is below the age of 18, or if a husband and his wife are both handicapped or more than 70 years old, [these persons] should not separate their children [from their household]."). Cf. *fen yi* 分異 "be separated/live apart" (*Guan* 40, 240; *Shiji* 68, 2230; *Hanshu* 82, 3369; *Houhanshu* 90, 2684).

Everything else corresponded to her previous [statement as part of the self-reporting].

識曰：
自小爲沛隸。沛令上造狗求上造羽子女㱩爲識妻。$_{119}$令狗告羽曰：
且以布肆（肆）、舍客室鼠（予）識。
羽乃許沛。沛巳（已）爲識取㱩，即爲識買室，分識馬、田$_{120}$，異識而不以肆（肆）、舍客室鼠（予）識。識【亦弗求】，識□受它。軍歸，沛巳（已）死。識以沛未死言謂$_{121}$媛：不以肆（肆）室鼠（予）識，識且告媛匿訾（貲）。媛乃鼠（予）識。識即弗告。識以沛言求肆（肆）室，非劫媛。不智（知）$_{122}$媛曰劫之故。
它如媛。

Shi stated:
"Since I was a child, I was a menial of Pei. Pei ordered Gou, holder of the second rank, to ask Yu, holder of the second rank, for the hand of his daughter Han to become my wife. [Pei] let Gou inform Yu of the following:
'I will give Shi the cloth stall and the house for accommodating guests.'
Thereupon Yu promised Pei to give [me] his daughter's hand in marriage.[966] After Pei had arranged the marriage with Han for me, he bought a house for me, allotted me a horse and a field and separated me [from his household], but he did not assign the stall and the house for accommodating guests to me. I, Shi, [for the time being refrained from demanding them, since] I had [...] received something else. When I returned home from the army, Pei had already died. Based on what Pei had said/promised[967] me before his death I told Wan: 'If you do not assign me the stall and the house, I will report you for concealing property.' Thereupon Wan assigned me [the buildings]. So I did not report her [to the authorities]. I demanded the stall and the house because of Pei's promise. It is not the case that I blackmailed Wan. I do not know the reason why she says that I blackmailed her."
Everything else corresponded to [the statement of] Wan.

966 *Xu* 許 is used here in the special sense "to promise to give so. one's daughter's hand in marriage" (*Shiji* 8, 344: 沛令[...]求之不與，何自妄許與劉季？ "The prefect of Pei [...] asked you for her hand, but you did not give him her hand. Why did you foolishly promise to give Liu Ji your daughter's hand?").

967 *Yan* 言 sometimes meant "to promise" (*Zuo* Xiang 2,415,8: 若背之，是棄力與言。 "If I turn my back on him, I cast away his efforts [on our behalf] and my own promise.").

建、昌、積、喜、遺曰：
故爲沛舍人。【沛】織（貸）建等錢，以市販，共分贏。市$_{123}$折，建負七百，昌三萬三千，積六千六百，喜二萬二千，遺六千。券責建等，建等未賞（償）。識欲告$_{124}$娩，娩即折券，不責建。
它如娩。

Jian, Chang, Tui, Xi and Yi stated:
"Formerly we were retainers[968] of Pei. [Pei] lent[969] us cash in order to do trade and to jointly share the profit. Because we made a loss on a deal,[970] Jian was charged[971] with 700 cash, Chang with 33,000 cash, Tui with 6,600 cash, Xi with

968 On *she ren* 舍人 "members of the suite of prominent persons, retainers, clients" (*QLSZ* 101=*RCL* A 55 with footnote 8; *FLDW* 180=*RCL* D 159; *Yuelu WYZ* 211, 223; *ZYS* 70, 80, 83, 206; *Hanshu* 1A, 19 with commentary by Yan Shigu) see Lau and Lüdke 2012, footnote 946 as well as Zhang Yanxiu 2011. In this case *she ren* were junior partners of a merchant. They did not have sufficient capital and therefore depended on the merchant's loans for the financing of transactions. In return, they gave their patron a share of the profits.

969 The editors identified this character as *zhi* 織 (*GSR* 920f) *tək-(s), which is doubtful as only the left part (semantic determinative "silk") is clearly visible and the right part appears to be the possibly phonophoric component 弋 (*GSR* 918a) *lək (cf. Zhang Shouzhong 1994, 193 and 69). Accordingly, a tentative identification as ⿰糹弋 (Teng Rensheng 2008, 110; Bai Yulan 2012, 385; used to write words with the Old Chinese initial l- as in *Guodian Ziyi* 3 [for *te* 忒 (*GSR* 918g) * hlˤək] and *Jiudian* 36 [for *shi* 飾 (*GSR* 921h) * hlək]) with an undecipherable additional component, would also be plausible. The character in question may indeed have been used as a loan for *dai* 貸 (*GSR* 918p) *hlˤək-s "to borrow, draw a loan; to grant a loan".

970 *Shi she* 市折. *She* 折 (*GSR* 287a) *det (Baxter and Sagart: N-tet) "suffer a loss, to lose sth." (*Xun* 2, 16 [cf. Knoblock I (1988), 154]: 良賈不爲折閱不市。"A good merchant will not refrain from making deals because he [sometimes] suffers losses and deficits [according to Yu Xingwu quoted by Feng and Deng 2006, 1029 *yue* 閱 is used to write *tuo* 脫]."; *Hanshu* 24B, 1181 [cf. Swann 1950, 342]: 用其本賈取之，毋令折錢。"Paying the original price would take them over without causing loss of money [to producers].").

971 *Fu* 負 "to carry on the back, load, to impose a charge/responsibility, to bear, to incur" in a legal context has the meaning "to be charged with payment/compensation (for deficiency, damage, loss, expenses)" (*QLSZ* 23, 166=*RCL* A 19, 83; *FLDW* 159, 202=*RCL* D 139, 182; *ENLL* 7, 95, 351–352, 410; *Hanfei* 23, 139 [cf. Harbsmeier]: 與人爭買百金之璞玉，因佯失而毀之，負其百金。"[A wealthy trader from Song] quarrelled with others about buying an unworked jade with a value of one hundred *jin*. Therefore he pretended to have damaged the jade inadvertently and was charged with one hundred *jin* [for the damage]."; *FLDW* 159=*RCL* D 139: 今舍公官（館），旞火燔其假乘車馬，當負不當？出之。"Now, when lodging in a government residence, if a [lighting] torch burns a carriage and horses that had been borrowed, are these by law to be charged [the user] or not? Cancel [the compensation].") or "to charge (deficiency, damage, loss) to the responsible person's account" (*QLSZ* 80=*RCL* A 40: 縣、都官坐效、計以負賞（償）者，已論，嗇夫即

22,000 cash and Yi with 6,000 cash.[972] We had not yet repaid the claims against us, which were certified by bond tallies. When Shi wanted to report Wan, she broke the tallies and did not claim [the debts from us]."
Everything else corresponded to [the statement of] Wan.

媄、快、臣、拳、嘉、頡言如婉。

The statements of Qie, Kuai, Chen, Quan, Jia and Xie corresponded to [the statements] of Wan.

狗、羽、齡言如識。

The statements of Gou, Yu and Han corresponded to [the statement of] Shi.

義、若小不訊。必死。125

Yi and Ruo are minors[973] and were not interrogated.[974] Bi has already died.

卿（鄉）唐、佐更曰：
沛免婉爲庶人。即書戶籍曰：免妾。沛後妻婉，不告唐、更。今籍爲免妾。
不智（知）它。126

以其直（值）錢分負其官長及冗吏，而人與參辨券，以效少內，少內以收責之。"When prefectures and government offices are prosecuted [for irregularities when] checking and accounting, and they have been charged with repayment, after sentence has been pronounced the overseer immediately proportionally charges [the irregularities] to the accounts of the chief of the office concerned as well as the assigned officials according to the value in cash, and the persons concerned are [each] given one part of a tripartite tally to be presented to the treasury. The treasury uses this to collect the money and to demand the payment of it."; ENLL 7). See also *fu zhai* 負債 "owe debts" (QLSZ 136=RCL A 68) with footnote 694, *fu chang* 負償 "to be charged with repayment" (QLSZ 174–175=RCL A 87; ENLL 14, 95, 97) and *fu fei* 負費 (QLZC 22=RCL C 14).

972 The sum of the debts of all five retainers is 68,300 cash, which accords with Wan's statement (*Yuelu* WYZ 109).

973 The age of the minor (*xiao* 小) Yi must have been between 10 (there were at least 10 years between the death of Pei's wife Wei and the trial) and 21 years because Yi would have been registered at the age of 22 and would thus not be regarded as a minor anymore. Cf. footnote 825 above. As Yi's sister Qie, who was probably born after Yi (*Yuelu* WYZ 112), is in contrast to her brother interrogated as a major (and therefore must be at least 17 years old, see *Yuelu* WYZ 125), Yi was most probably between 18 and 21 years old.

974 For *xun* see footnote 830.

The head of the district[975] Tang and his assistant Geng stated:
"Pei manumitted Wan and made her a released person. So we wrote [an entry in] the household registers,[976] which reads: 'manumitted female slave'. When Pei later took Wan as his wife, he did not inform us of this. In the present registers, Wan is [recorded as] a manumitted female slave.
We do not know of anything else."

Second Stage of Interrogation (*Confrontation*)

詰識：
沛未死雖告狗、羽且以肆、舍客室鼠（予）識，而後不鼠（予）識。識弗求，巳（已）爲識更買室，分識田、馬，$_{127}$異識。沛死時有（又）不令。義巳（已）代爲戶後，有肆（肆）宅。識弗當得。何故尚求肆（肆）室曰：不鼠（予）識，識且告媿$_{128}$匿訾（貲）。媿即以其故鼠（予）識。是劫媿而云非劫，何解？

975 For *qing* 卿 writing *xiang* 鄉 and the administrative unit of *xiang* see footnote 853. The head of a *xiang* is also mentioned together with his assistant (*zuo* 佐) in Qin administrative documents, either without his official title (*Liye* 8–39), as in the present case, or as *shou* 守 "officeholder" (*Liye* 8–300, 8–938, 8–1241, 8–2247), or also as *fu* 夫 (*Liye* 8–157, 8–1710). *Fu* appears to be an abbreviation of *se fu* 嗇夫, which during the Qin period was used by superiors to address the head of a *xiang* (*Liye* 8–770), but was also used in legal provisions (*Yuelu Lüling* 1241, 1397, 1597, 1889, 0525, 0672 [yet unpublished]). In Qin manuscripts, *xiang se fu* apparently did not refer to one of the leading officials of a *xiang* who had specific tasks, as was the case in the Han period (*Yinwan mudu* M6D2r/v as well as table 3 in Xie Guihua 1997, 47; *Hanshu* 19A, 742). Moreover, the head of a *xiang* was also referred to as *zhu* 主 in Qin documents (*Liye* 8–1548).

976 *Huji* 戶籍. See Lau and Lüdke 2012, footnote 644: The head of the household was obligated to inform the authorities of the number of persons living in his household and to enter them into the household register. Household registers of Qin times have already been excavated at Liye. In these registers, the names and ranks of the head of the household as well as those of his brothers living in the same household were noted. Beside this, the names of his wife, second wife, mother, maidservant(s), children, cousins and slaves living in the same household were also entered into the register (*Liye huji* 1–22 [K 27, 1/25/50, 43, 28/29, 17, 8/9/11/47, 42/46, 30/45, 4, 2/23, 13/48, 36, 3, 5, 38/39, 15, 18, 6, 7, 26, 31/37; 33]). For surveys on the household registers from Liye see Xing Yitian 2007, Zhang Rongqiang 2008 and Li Mingzhao 2009. The manuscripts found in tomb no. 10 of Fenghuangshan (Hubei) give an impression of the household and tax registers of Han times. In these, the name of the head of the household, the number of workers on the fields and members of the household as well as the size of the fields are noted (cf. *Sanjian* 808–811, 812–814). For a survey on these sources see Qiu Xigui 1992, 540–563 and Nagata 1989, 578–610. The system of household registers is treated extensively in Yang Jiping 2007.

We confronted[977] Shi:

"Although, before his death, Pei informed Gou and Yu that he would assign you the stall and the house for accommodating guests, he later did not do so. You refrained from demanding [these buildings, because Pei] had already bought a house for you instead[978] of this, alotted you a field and a horse and separated you [from his household]. Also, when Pei died, he did not order it[979] [in his last will]. Yi had already taken his place, become the heir of the household, and had taken possession of the stall and the residence. You were not entitled to obtain them. Why did you nevertheless demand the stall and the house saying: 'If you, Wan, do not assign me [the buildings], I will report you for concealing property.' If Wan gave you [the buildings] because of this, this would mean [because] you blackmailed her, but you say it is not a case of blackmailing. How do you explain this?"

---

977 For *jie* see footnote 792.

978 *Geng* 更 could mean "to substitute sth. with sth., replace sth. by sth." (*Zuo* Xiang 28,538,3–4; *Li* 15, 1362) or "to compensate" (*Shiji* 30, 1421). Here it is used adverbially. Except for the common meaning "again, anew" (cf. *geng zhi* 更治 "to retry/judge a case again" as in *Yuelu* WYZ 191, 199 and *Liye* 8–1832+8–1418+8–1133 [cf. Chen Wei 2012a, 281]), in adverbial use *geng* otherwise appears in the sense "in turns" (*QLSZ* 197=*RCL* A 105: 官嗇夫及吏夜更行官。"The overseer of the office as well as the officials take turns to inspect the office nightly."; *FZS* 12=*RCL* E 3: 與里人更守之。"X guards it (the property) in turns together with the people of the quarter."; *ENLL* 305: 田典更挾里門籥（鑰）。"The heads of the fields [and quarters] take turns to carry the keys of the quarter gates.").

979 *Ling* 令 "to order (as a last will/in a testament)" (*ENLL* 334: 民欲先令相分田宅、奴婢、財物，鄉部嗇夫身聽其令，皆參辨券書之，輒上如戶籍。"If common people wish to order by will that their fields and residence, their slaves and their belongings be distributed to others/among each other, the overseer of the district should personally hear the order [of the testator] concerned and without exception document it (the order) on a tripartite tally. [A part of] the tripartite tally is immediately submitted to the higher authorities in the same way as the household registers."). The merchant Pei obviously failed to register his last will on such a tripartite tally (*quan*) with the district authorities. Two yet unpublished ordinances contained among the Yuelu Academy's legal manuscripts show that the written form only became mandatory for agreements to be valid in the 13th year of the reign of King Zheng of Qin (i.e. 234 BC). This can at least be seen for certain types of agreements – for instance to lend money (*Yuelu Lüling* 0631/0608) or to marry (*Yuelu Lüling* 1099/1087).

識曰：
□欲得隷（肆）室。婉不鼠（予）識，識誠恐謂：且告婉。婉乃鼠（予）$_{129}$識。識實弗當得。上以識爲劫婉，辠（罪）識，識毋（無）以避，毋（無）它解。辠（罪）。
它如前。

Shi stated:
"I wanted to obtain the stall and the house. When Wan did not assign [the buildings] to me, I really [tried to] frighten[980] her by saying: 'I will report you [to the authorities].' Only then Wan assigned me [the buildings]. In fact,[981] I was not entitled to obtain [them]. If you, the authorities, regard me as[982] someone who blackmailed Wan and are [therefore] going to punish me, I have no means[983] to avoid[984] [this] and do not have any other explanation. I am liable to punishment."[985]
Everything else corresponded to his previous [statement].

Interagency Enquiries

問：
匿訾（貲）稅及室隷（肆），臧（贓）直（值）$_{130}$各過六百六十錢。
它如辤（辭）。

[Results of the] interagency enquiries:[986]

980 *Kong* 恐 here in the causative sense "to frighten/terrify/intimidate sb." (*Hanfei* 6, 24; 9, 37).

981 For *shi* see footnote 533.

982 *Yi ... wei* 以 ... 爲. Cf. ZYS 43–44: 吏以爲即賊傷人，存吏當，罪，毋解。 "If you, the officials, are of the opinion that this is a case of [the statutory offence of] 'injuring sb. with malice', then (abiding by:) under the premise that your [opinion] is lawful, I am liable to punishment. I do not have another explanation." Here, the accused also expresses reservations about his guilt.

983 On *wu yi* see footnote 807.

984 Cf. the same formulation in *Yuelu* WYZ 083–084.

985 *Zui* 罪 occurs in statements when an accused assumes criminal responsibility for a culpable action; then it means "I am liable to punishment" (*Yuelu* WYZ 164, 241; ZYS 64, 71, 85, 118, 224). However, *zui* is often found as part of the formula *zui wu jie* 罪無解 "I am liable to punishment and cannot offer an explanation" (ZYS 22, 31, 43–44, 87, 150; *Yuelu* WYZ 241) or in a similar combination with *wu ta jie* 無它解 as in the present case. For *zui* see also footnote 514.

986 For *wen* see footnote 562. The interagency enquiries here give information about the value of stolen goods as the basis for determining punishment. Cf. footnote 711.

The value of each misappropriated good[987] – the evaded property tax[988] and the house and the stall – exceeds 660 cash.[989]
Everything else corresponded to the statements.[990]

Finding of Fact

鞫之：
婉爲大夫沛妾。沛御婉，婉產義、姎。沛妻危死，沛免婉爲庶人，以$_{131}$爲妻。有（又）產必、若。籍爲免妾。沛死，義代爲戶後，有肆（肆）宅。婉匿訾（貲）稅，直（值）過六百六十錢。先自告，告$_{132}$識劫。
識爲沛隸。沛爲取妻，欲以肆（肆）、舍客室鼠（予）識。後弗鼠（予），爲買室，分馬一匹、田廿畝，異識。沛死，$_{133}$識後求肆（肆）室。婉弗鼠（予），識恐謂婉：且告婉匿訾（貲）。婉（婉）以故鼠（予）肆（肆）室，肆（肆）室直（值）過六百六十錢。得。皆審。

Finding of fact:[991]
Wan was a female slave of Pei, holder of the fifth rank. Pei had sexual relations with her, and she gave birth to Yi and Qie. After the death of Pei's wife Wei, Pei manumitted Wan, made her a released person and [later] regarded her as his wife. Wan gave birth again to Bi and Ruo. In the registers, Wan remained a manumitted female slave. When Pei died, Yi took his place, became the heir of the household and took possession of the stall and the residence. Wan evaded the property tax, its value exceeded 660 cash. Prior [to the discovery of the offence], she reported herself [to the authorities] and reported Shi for blackmailing her.
Shi was a menial of Pei. Pei arranged a marriage for him and wanted to assign him the stall and the house for accommodating guests. Later, he did not assign him [the buildings], but bought him a house, allotted a horse and a field of 20 *mu* to him and separated him [from his household]. After the death of Pei, Shi demanded the stall and the house. When Wan did not assign [the buildings] to him, Shi frightened her saying: "I am going to report you for concealing

---

987 For *zang* see footnote 592.

988 *Zi shui* 訾稅 "property tax". Cf. *ni shui* 匿稅 "to evade taxes" (*Longgang* 147) and *ni zu* 匿租 (*Longgang* 142) as well as footnote 928.

989 Here, it becomes clear that the offence is categorised as a case of theft (*dao* 盜). If the value of misappropriated goods amounted to at least 660 cash, the most severe punishment for property crimes was to be applied (*ENLL* 55: 盜臧（贓）直（值）過六百六十錢，黥爲城旦舂。"If, in cases of theft, the value of the misappropriated goods exceeds 660 cash, [the offender] is tattooed and made an earth or grain pounder convict.").

990 For *ci* see footnote 564.

991 For *ju* see footnote 565.

property." Because of this Wan assigned him the stall and the house, the value of which exceeds 660 cash. [Both] have been caught.[992] All these are established facts.[993]

Submission by the Prefecture – Concluding Formula

疑$_{134}$婏爲大夫妻，爲庶人，及識辠（罪）。毄（繫）。它縣論。敢潚（讞）之。$_{135}$

We are in doubt[994] as to whether Wan is [to be considered as] wife of a holder of the fifth rank or a released person. We are furthermore [in doubt] as to how Shi is to be punished. [Both] are held under detention.[995] In all other matters the prefecture has passed judgement.[996] We venture to submit [this case] for decision.[997]

Alternative Votes for Judgement

吏議：
婏爲【大夫後妻】；貲識二甲。
或曰：
婏爲庶人；完識爲城旦，纍（縲）足輸蜀。$_{136}$

The [responsible] officials deliver [the following] legal opinion:[998]
"Wan is [to be considered as second wife of a holder of the fifth rank];[999] Shi is to be fined[1000] two suits of armour."

992 For *de* see footnote 524.

993 For *shen* see footnote 633.

994 For *yi* see footnote 582. Here, it does not only refer to doubts about the appropriate punishment for one of the accused, but also to doubts about the actual status of the other accused. Both doubts are the reason for submitting the case to the higher authorities for decision.

995 For *ji*/*xi* see footnote 569.

996 For *ta xian lun* see footnote 635.

997 For *yan* and the phrase *gan yan zhi* see footnote 489.

998 For *li yi* see footnote 572.

999 The characters between *Wan wei* 婏爲 and *er jia* 二甲 on this slip are hardly legible. The two characters preceding *er jia* 二甲 can, with some certainty, be identified as *zi Shi* 貲識 from the context and the remaining strokes. With regard to the precisely formulated doubts of the prefectural authorities about the status of Wan (*Yuelu* WYZ 134–135), it also appears justifiable to emend *da fu qi* 大夫妻 after *Wan wei* 婏爲 because to regard Wan as "wife of a holder of the fifth rank" is the only reasonable alternative to regarding her as a released person (*shu ren* 庶人, cf. the following vote of the minority). Still, the editors correctly put an indicator for a completely undecipherable character between *da fu* 大夫

Some say:[1001]
"Wan is [to be considered as] released person;[1002] leave Shi without mutilation[1003] and make him an earth pounder convict.[1004] Shackle his feet and deport[1005] him to [the province of] Shu."

---

and *qi* 妻 as a comparison with this exact formulation on the preceding slip (*Yuelu WYZ* 135) suggests an additional character on *Yuelu WYZ* 136. Based on an interpretation of the remaining traces of ink, it has been proposed that this character might have been *hou* 後 (Zhang and Zhong 2014), which would suggest that Wan was regarded as Pei's later or second wife (*hou qi* 後妻, see *Shiji* 1, 32; *ENLL* 380–381). As wife of a holder of the fifth rank, Wan could not be tattooed and made a grain pounder convict for theft of an amount of more than 660 cash, but was instead to be shaved and made a rice sifter convict (*nai wei bai can* 耐爲白粲, cf. *ENLL* 82). This punishment would have to be further reduced by one degree because Wan reported herself to the authorities prior to the discovery of her offence (*ENLL* 127–128). In the end, she was to be sentenced to being shaved and made a bond servant convict (*nai wei li qie* 耐爲隸妾).

1000 For *zi* see footnotes 558 and 594. During the Qin dynasty, two suits of armour (*er jia* 二甲) were equivalent to 2,688 cash (*Yuelu Shu* 82–83; Yu Zhenbo 2010, 38). The legal basis for the lenient punishment of the former menial is unclear. Similar fines seem to have been imposed on persons who failed to report the offences of their neighbours (members of the unit of five, *wu* 伍) or members of their household (*tong ju* 同居) (cf. *ENLL* 201; *FLDW 20, 22=RCL* D 18–19). As Shi originally lived in the same household with Wan, he could have been held liable for not reporting her offence.

1001 For *huo yue* see footnote 573.

1002 This vote based on the official registers was probably in accordance with the law because Wan gave birth to her deceased master's children, cf. footnote 947. As a manumitted slave Wan would have to be tattooed and made a grain pounder convict for theft of an amount of more than 660 cash. Nevertheless, her punishment would have to be reduced by one degree because Wan reported herself to the authorities prior to the discovery of her offence, cf. footnote 999.

1003 *Wan* 完 "to leave sb. intact, not submit sb. to mutilation" was a distinguishing feature among convicts of the most severe category of penal labour *cheng dan chong* 城旦舂 (*Yuelu WYZ* 244; *FLDW* 6, 50, 81, 84, 112, 116, 119, 120, 122, 124, 135=*RCL* D 5, 40, 66, 69, 91, 96, 100, 102, 104, 113; *Longgang* 33, 42; *Liye* 8–291; *ZYS* 181–182, 188, 224; *ENLL* 10, 12, 27, 55, 86–87, 90–91, 100, 120, 123, 127, 165, 170, 174, 176, 192, 195, 252, 398–399) in contrast to mutilated convicts of this category. This penal labour seems to be the punishment for blackmailing (*jie* 劫), which during Qin times was apparently classified as property crime. For theft of more than 660 cash, Shi was to be sentenced to the maximum punishment for property crimes (*qing wei cheng dan* 黥爲城旦, cf. *ENLL* 55). However, as holder of the first rank (*gongshi* 公士) he was not subjected to mutilation (*ENLL* 83). A more severe punishment for blackmailing as under Han law (*ENLL* 68) was apparently not applied during Qin times.

1004 For *cheng dan* see footnotes 668 and 1003.

1005 *Shu* 輸 "to transport/deport (a prisoner)" (cf. *ZYS* 181: 敖（傲）悍，完爲城旦舂，鐵鬑其足，輸巴縣鹽。 "For insubordination, one is made an unmutilated earth or grain pounder convict; [the convict's] feet are shackled with iron [chains], and he is deported to the saltworks in the prefectures of Ba [province]."; *ENLL* 158; *Shiji* 91, 2597; *Lüshuo* quoted from the commentary of Ru Chun on *Shiji* 6, 255).

Case II.8

This case – just as case II.13 below – appears to be highly fragmentary. It is clear from statements and the finding of fact that the two accused, a man named Nao and a woman named Yun, were allegedly involved in injuring and/or killing a person or persons. However, the investigating officials could only verify that Nao injured somebody (either Yun or another person). If, or under which circumstances, Yun killed someone – this might be Nao, a person who was previously injured by Nao or yet another person – is doubtful and apparently was the reason for the submission of this case to the higher authorities. From the final judgement on Yun it seems probable that Yun reported herself prior to the discovery of the offence and was convicted for "killing sb. inadvertently or in a contest".

Another question is whether the text on slips 137 to 141 should really be considered as belonging to one and the same case, or not. The editors assume that slip 141 describes a separate judgement that was cited at the end of the record of the present case.[1006] That the text on slip 141 refers to a different case is obvious from the names of the accused (Xi vs. Nao and Yun). Although the description of the whole case apparently did not exceed a single slip, it is still possible that it was a case in its own right, which would mean that manuscript II did contain seven and not six cases. On the other hand, however, this case might be related to the former case and could have been cited as part of its case record. At least it was handled by the same officials (Xiang and Ru), and the dates of the respective judgements are only ten days apart.

Diplomatic Edition

•十月癸酉佐競曰士五譊刑人市舍□□▨$_{137}$▨□□□曰譊歙宗□□▨$_{138}$□□□□不可起怒以刀刑棄刀▨$_{139}$▨□得診問鞫譊刑審妘殺疑•九月丙寅丞相史如論令妘贖舂倉人▨$_{140}$九月丙辰隸臣哀詣隸臣喜告盜殺人問喜辤如告•鞫審己卯丞相史如論磔▨$_{141}$

爲獄□狀$_{137v}$
爲气鞫奏狀$_{139v}$
▨爲覆奏狀$_{140v}$

1006 Zhu and Chen 2013, 176, footnote 1.

 | DOI 10.1163/9789004315655_016

Edition and Translation

Initiation of Criminal Proceedings

十月癸酉佐競曰：
士五（伍）譊刑人市舍□□⍁$_{137}$⍁□□

On day *guiyou*[1007] of the tenth month the assistant Jing stated:
"The rank-and-file man[1008] Nao injured[1009] a person in a guesthouse at the market[1010] [...]."

First Stage of Interrogation

□曰：
譊歓（飲）宗□□⍁$_{138}$□□□□不可起，怒，以刀刑，棄刀⍁$_{139}$⍁□得。

[?] stated:
"Nao was drinking[1011] [...] could not stand up, got angry, injured [?] with a knife, discarded the knife [...] was caught."[1012]

Forensic Examination and Interagency Enquiries

診、問。

[Results of the] forensic examination and the interagency enquiries.[1013]

1007 The editors state that the only years during the reign of King Zheng of Qin that have both a day *guiyou* in the tenth month and a day *bingchen* in the ninth (see slip 140 of the same case) are the second and the 28th year of King Zheng of Qin/Qin Shihuang, of which they consider the latter possibility more likely (Zhu and Chen 2013, 177, footnote 2). However, a comparison with the dates mentioned in the other cases of the same manuscript (sixth year of King Zheng of Qin, *Yuelu* WYZ 150 with footnote 1089; fifth year of King Zheng of Qin, *Yuelu* WYZ 168; first year of King Zheng of Qin, *Yuelu* WYZ 175) rather suggests a year near the beginning of the reign of King Zheng of Qin. This is why the respective date is tentatively identified as the first day of the tenth month in the second year of King Zheng of Qin (cf. Zhang Peiyu 2007, 72; Li Zhonglin 2012, 65), i.e. 25/11/246 BC (Xu Xiqi 1997, 1193).

1008 For *shi wu* see footnote 495.

1009 Here *xing* 刑 is not used as the legal term meaning "to mutilate", but in the more general sense "to injure" or "injury" (cf. *shang* 傷).

1010 *Shi she* 市舍 (*Houhanshu* 56, 1832). Cf. *ke she* in footnote 932.

1011 Because the editors consider the character following *zong* 宗 to write the personal name Yun 妘, they translate *yin* 飲 transitively as "to give Yun to drink" and understand *zong* as *zong ren* 宗人 (Zhu and Chen 2013, 300; cf. *Yuelu* WYZ 113 with footnote 949 above).

1012 For *de* see footnote 524.

1013 For *zhen* and *wen* see footnote 562. Here, the two terms appear to merely mark the position where usually the results of the forensic examination as well as the interagency

Finding of Fact

鞫：
譊刑審，妘殺疑。

Finding of fact:[1014]
That Nao injured [sb.] is an established fact;[1015] if Yun killed [sb.] is doubtful.[1016]

Judgement

九月丙寅丞相、史如論令妘贖舂。倉人☐$_{140}$

On day *bingyin*[1017] of the ninth month vice prefect Xiang and secretary[1018] Ru passed judgement,[1019] ordering Yun to pay the fee for redemption[1020] from penal labour as a grain pounder convict. The head of the grain storehouse[1021] [where she will have to work?...]

---

enquiries would be recorded. Probably there were neither examination nor enquiries needed in the present case, or they did not provide information that was not already known from the statements (cf. *Yuelu* WYZ 035).

1014 For *ju* see footnote 565.

1015 For *shen* see footnote 633.

1016 For *yi* see footnote 582.

1017 Following the proposal described in footnote 1007 above, this day is tentatively identified as the 30th day of the ninth month in the second year of King Zheng of Qin (cf. Zhang Peiyu 2007, 72; Li Zhonglin 2012, 65), i.e. 12/11/245 BC (Xu Xiqi 1997, 1194); cf. the view of the editors (Zhu and Chen 2013, 177, footnote 8). Note that this would mean that the investigation of this case was initiated on the very first day of the second year of King Zheng of Qin (see *Yuelu* WYZ 137 above), and that judgement was passed on the very last day of the same year. It remains unclear whether this is just a curious coincidence, or whether these dates were carefully chosen.

1018 For (*yu*) *shi* see footnote 539.

1019 For *lun* see footnote 540.

1020 For *shu* see footnote 541. From the final judgement on Yun (*Yuelu* WYZ 140) it can be gathered that Yun was probably convicted for "killing sb. inadvertently or in a contest" because she had to pay the fee for redemption from penal labour as a grain pounder. In early Han times, the normal punishment in this case was the obligation to pay the fee for redemption from the death penalty (*ENLL* 21), which means that the punishment was probably reduced by one degree. If the legal stipulations in pre-imperial Qin are comparable to those in early Han times, a possible explanation for this would be that Yun reported herself prior to the discovery of the offence (cf. *ENLL* 127–130).

1021 *Cang ren* 倉人 were responsible for grain storehouses (*Zhouli* 9, 700c).

Related Case(?) – Initiation of Criminal Proceedings

九月丙辰隸臣哀詣隸臣喜告盜殺人。

On day *bingchen*[1022] of the ninth month, bond servant[1023] Ai presented[1024] the bond servant Xi to the authorities and reported[1025] him for killing people in the act of committing theft.[1026]

Related Case(?) – Interagency Enquiries

問：
喜辤（辭）如告。

[Results of the] interagency enquiries:[1027]
The statement[1028] of Xi corresponded to the report.

Related Case(?) – Finding of Fact

鞫：
審。

Finding of fact:[1029]
[The previously mentioned circumstances/matters] are established facts.[1030]

1022 Cf. footnotes 1007 and 1017. This day is tentatively identified as the 20th day of the ninth month in the second year of King Zheng of Qin (cf. Zhang Peiyu 2007, 72; Li Zhonglin 2012, 65), i.e. 02/11/245 BC (Xu Xiqi 1997, 1194); cf. the view of the editors (Zhu and Chen 2013, 178, footnote 11).

1023 For *li chen* convicts see footnote 751.

1024 For *yi* see footnote 496.

1025 For *gao* see footnote 498.

1026 For *dao sha ren* see footnote 499.

1027 For *wen* see footnote 562.

1028 For *ci* see footnote 564.

1029 For *ju* see footnote 565. In this case, the finding of fact does not contain any new information apart from a note that the correctness of the information contained in the report (*gao* 告) and retrieved through interagency enquiries (*wen* 問) has been established (*shen* 審).

1030 For *shen* see footnote 633.

Related Case(?) – Judgement

己卯丞相、史如論磔☐141

On day *jimao*[1031] vice prefect Xiang and secretary Ru passed judgement to quarter[1032] [...]

Titles on the Verso of the Slips[1033]

爲獄☐狀137v

Drawing up[1034] a "case [...]"[1035] document.[1036]

1031 The next day *jimao* following the previously mentioned 20th day of the ninth month in the second year of King Zheng of Qin (footnote 1022) is the thirteenth day of the tenth month in the third year of King Zheng of Qin (cf. Zhang Peiyu 2007, 72; Li Zhonglin 2012, 65), i.e. 25/11/245 BC (Xu Xiqi 1997, 1195); cf. the view of the editors (Zhu and Chen 2013, 178, footnote 12).

1032 *Zhe* 磔 "quartering/dismemberment", one of the most severe forms of death penalty (*ENLL* 3, 65–66, 68, 88; *Hanshu* 5, 145) for the statutory offence *dao sha* (*shang*) *ren* 盜殺（傷）人 "killing (or injuring) somebody in the act of committing theft" (*FLDW* 67=*RCL* D 64; *Yuelu WYZ* 141, 147; *ENLL* 66). See Zhu Xiangrong 2012, 147–151.

1033 The editors suggested that the title on *Yuelu WYZ* 137v might be the main title for all six cases gathered in manuscript II (cases II.8 to II.13), see Zhu and Chen 2013, 177, footnote 4. According to their view, the other two titles (on *Yuelu WYZ* 139v and 140v) were titles of one (or more?) individual cases contained in manuscript II, which might be remnants from an earlier separate circulation of the individual cases (Zhu and Chen 2013, 177, footnotes 7 and 10). However, at least two of the slips bearing titles (*Yuelu WYZ* 137 and 140) can quite certainly be assigned to the same case (II.8) because of the occurrence of the personal name Nao 譊, and it is equally possible that all three titles were written on the verso of the first slips of the whole manuscript for practical reasons. Although the respective slips apparently all belonged to the same case (for *Yuelu WYZ* 139 this is less clear, see Zhu and Chen 2013, 176, footnote 1), the three titles probably referred to different cases inside manuscript II or were supposed to indicate that manuscript II contained three different categories of cases. There was not necessarily a main title that encompassed all six cases of manuscript II.

1034 The editors interpret *wei* 爲 as "to handle/conduct (a criminal case)" (Zhu and Chen 2013, 177, footnote 4).

1035 The character between *yu* 獄 and *zhuang* 狀 is fragmented. On the left side, the component *yan* 言 is still visible. For different possibilities for the identification of this character see Lau 2014, 140, footnote 5; cf. Su Junlin 2014b, 307.

1036 The editors interpret *zhuang* 狀 as "a document stating an opinion or fact(s)" (陳述意見或事實的文書), see Zhu and Chen 2013, 177, footnote 4. That the term refers to a certain type of document in the three titles seems clear, but its exact meaning remains obscure. For the view that *zhuang* might refer to documents that were probably drawn up at

爲气（乞）鞫奏狀$_{139v}$

Drawing up a "submission[1037] with a petition for a [new] finding of fact"[1038] document.

爲覆奏狀☐$_{140v}$

Drawing up a "submission with a review"[1039] document.

---

different points and for different purposes during the process of submitting cases to the higher authorities for decision, but were not necessarily included in the final documents compiled in collections like the *Zou yan shu* or the *Wei yu deng zhuang* see Su Junlin 2014b, 308–310. For other meanings of *zhuang* cf. footnotes 741 and 1124.

1037 For the view that *zou* 奏 refers to submissions to the higher authorities more generally – not necessarily only to the king/emperor – see Hafner 2014b.

1038 *Qi ju* 乞鞫. For this appeal procedure in Qin times see footnote 390. Cf. the translation of the stipulations from 186 BC on the *qi ju* procedure in section 4.6.3.1 of the introduction.

1039 As a legal term *fu* 覆 (GSR 1034m) *pʰ(r)uk or its variant 復 (GSR 1034a) refers to the review of a legal decision or a finding of fact of the lower authorities by higher authorities. *Fu* takes *yu* 獄 "criminal case" (復獄 in ZYS 124; 覆獄 in *Liye* 8–135r, 8–136, 8–255, 8–492, 8–632, 8–1729; *Shiji* 15, 758; *Hanshu* 86, 3499; *Yuelu* WYZ 173; ZYS 99) or the pronoun *zhi* 之 as objects (覆之 in ZYS 122; *Yuelu* WYZ 175, 206; ENLL 116; 復之 in ZYS 78, 129). Often, *fu* is combined with the verbs *zhi* 治 (覆治 in ENLL 113, 116–117; *Hanshu* 60, 2662; 76, 3204; 86, 3489; 復治 in ZYS 138, 144), *an* 案 (復案 in ENLL 396; *Hanshu* 76, 3223; 覆案 in *Shiji* 87, 2554; 93, 2640; 122, 3138; 123, 3171; *Hanshu* 9, 296) or *wen* 問 (覆問 in FZS 7, 14, 40–41, 44, 98=RCL E 4, 5, 15, 6; *Liye* 8–2005r; *Hanshu* 97B, 3975).

In addition to reviews conducted following a petition for retrial (*qi ju* 乞鞫, for these see footnote 1194), criminal cases were regularly subjected to a review by provincial investigators (*du li* 都吏), representing higher authorities, if the cases related to an offence punishable with the death penalty, or to the offences of killing another person (*sha ren* 殺人) inadvertently (*guo shi* 過失) or in a contest (*xi* 戲) (ENLL 396). Those cases had to be submitted to the provincial agency by the prefecture authorities, after the trial documents had been completed (*yu yi ju* 獄已具), implying that a finding of fact (*ju* 鞫) had already been made, but before a judgement had been passed (ENLL 396). It is not clear whether the full formal criminal investigation had to be repeated during this review. However, it is likely that the provincial investigators could conduct their own interrogations. They then had to inform the office of the governor of the province of the result of the review. The governor or his deputy, in turn, inspected the proposed sentence and passed the appropriate judgement, of which the lower authority was notified, so that it could enforce it (ENLL 396–397).

Apart from these types of cases where the statutes required a mandatory review, higher authorities could order a review of any case in which they suspected that the lower authorities did not properly discharge of their judicial duties (cf. *Zou yan shu* cases no. 16 and 18).

In the Qin administrative documents from Qianling prefecture, *fu yu* 覆獄 is basically an administrative act by higher authorities conducted by either the prosecutor (*Liye* 8–255, 8–632) or the provincial secretaries *zu shi* 卒史 (*Liye* 8–135r). For a detailed investigation of the judicial review see Mizuma 2012.

Case 11.9

This case, which is only preserved in fragments, apparently served as a model for recommendations of competent investigating officials for a promotion.

The first part of the case record is an account of the offence and the subsequent criminal investigations. The offender tied up and killed a disowned wife in a secluded field hut and stole her clothes. The case was difficult to solve, because the offender disappeared without a trace, and there was no usable evidence. It is not documented how the judicial secretary of the prefecture who was charged with the investigation found the suspect, but it becomes clear that he applied ingenious investigating methods. First, the suspect and all his acquaintances were confidentially questioned. Afterwards, the investigating official confronted the accused with the results of this questioning and forced him to amend his former statements. The suspect's confession of guilt is missing in the preserved fragments, and the name of a second offender appears. It is furthermore stressed that both offenders, who were liable to the death penalty and executed by quartering, were a great danger to society.

The second part of the case record is the actual letter of recommendation for the promotion of the investigating official. At the beginning of this letter, the ordinances forming the legal basis for recommending competent judicial secretaries to the higher authorities for promotion are quoted. At the end of the letter the required ethical standards which predestine a judicial official for the office of a provincial secretary are emphasised. Additionally, the hope that other officials will follow his example is expressed.

Diplomatic Edition

⧄大女子嬰等告曰棄婦毋憂縛死其田舍衣襦亡•令獄史□□⧄[142]⧄狀及譖訊居處薄宿所讎• 同曰歸義就日未盡爲人庯除芝•譖訊同歸義狀及邑里居處狀改曰隸臣非歸義[143]訊同非歸義可故同曰爲吏僕内爲人庯恐吏毄辟同⧄及薄宿類詑[144]

□譖謂同_和不首一吏者而言毋坐毆同曰毋坐毆不智所□•□譖謂同_爲吏人見同巫從同畏不敢捕同而⧄[145]⧄如同•臧直⧄[146]敗傷洋毋得同_顯_　大害毆巳論磔同顯•敢言之　　　令曰獄史能得微難獄⧄得微難獄⧄[147]爲奏九牒上此黔首大害毆毋徵物難得洋以智治訮詗謙求而得之洋精絜毋害敦裳守吏心平□⧄[148]中令綏任謁以補卒史勸它吏卑盜賊不發敢言[149]

Edition and Translation

Initiation of Criminal Proceedings

☐大女子嬰等告曰：
棄婦毋憂縛死（屍）其田舍，衣襦亡。

[…] the adult[1040] woman Ying and others reported:[1041]
"[We found] the tied up[1042] corpse of the disowned[1043] wife Wuyou in her field hut.[1044] Her clothes[1045] were gone."

Report on Investigations

令獄史□□☐$_{142}$狀及譖（潛）訊居處、薄宿所讎。

We ordered the judicial secretary[1046] [Yang …] circumstances[1047] of […] and

1040 For *da* see footnote 920.

1041 For *gao* see footnote 498.

1042 *Fu* 縛 "to tie up/fetter" (*FLDW* 81=*RCL* D 66; *FZS* 17, 19, 21, 25, 31, 37, 42=*RCL* E 8, 9, 10, 12, 13, 15, 16).

1043 *Qi* 棄 (*GSR* 535a) "to discard/disown (one's wife), i.e. divorce" (*Hanfei* 14, 73 [cf. Harbsmeier]: 爲棄正妻。"For [her] sake he disowned his regular wife."; *Hanfei* 14, 73 [cf. Harbsmeier]: 故妻以妾餘之詐棄。"Therefore, his wife was disowned because of concubine Yu's fraud."; *FLDW* 167=*RCL* D 146: 女子甲去夫亡，男子乙亦闌亡，相夫妻，甲弗告請（情），居二歲，生子，乃告請（情），乙即弗棄而得，論可（何）殹（也）？"The woman A leaves her husband and absconds; the man B also unauthorisedly absconds. They become husband and wife. A fails to inform [B] about the truth; only after two years, when she has given birth to a child, she informs him about the truth. B thereupon does not disown her. They are caught. How are they to be sentenced?"; *FLDW* 169=*RCL* D 148: 棄妻不書，貲二甲。"Not to register disowning one's wife is fined two suits of armour."; *ENLL* 380–381: 棄妻子不得與後妻子爭後。後妻毋子男爲後，乃以棄妻子男。"The son of a disowned wife is not allowed to contest for succession with the son of the succeeding wife. If the succeeding wife has no son who becomes the heir, then the son of the disowned wife [shall be made] the heir.").

1044 *Tian she* 田舍 "field hut, cottage" (*QLSZ* 12=*RCL* A 6: 百姓居田舍者毋敢醢（酤）酉（酒）。"Commoners living in field huts should not venture to sell wine.").

1045 For *yi ru* 衣襦 cf. *Yuelu WYZ* 152: 宜、安有布衣、帬（裙）、襦、絝、履，皆亡不得殹（也）。"Yi and An had coarse clothes – lower garments, short jackets, trousers and shoes – which are all gone and have not been found [again]." In this passage *yi* is a generic term for clothes, whereas *ru* denoted a jacket with short or long sleeves (Sun Ji 2011, 275 with illustrations 60–3 und 60–4) as one part of these clothes.

1046 For (*yu*) *shi* see footnote 539.

1047 For *zhuang* see footnote 741.

confidentially[1048] interrogated[1049] those with whom [Tong] had associated[1050] at his place of residence[1051] and his [temporary] lodging in the immediate vicinity.[1052]

1048 *Zen* 譖 (*GSR* 660j) *tsrəm-s (Pan Wuyun: *skrums) is used as loan character for the homeophonous *qian* 潛 (*GSR* 660n) *dzom-s (Pan Wuyun: *sgams) "secretly, confidentially" (cf. Lau and Lüdke 2012, footnote 1317). For the same usage see the parallel passages on *Yuelu WYZ* 154 as well as *Yuelu WYZ* 145 and *ZYS* 153. For the meaning "(behind somebody's back:) secretly, covertly" see *Hanfei* 1, 7: 潛行而出。"He left the city by foot, secretly."; *Hanfei* 38, 290: 潛御群臣者也。 "He secretly steers the various ministers."; *Zuo* Zhao 17,667,4: 使長鬛者三人潛伏於舟側。"Then he sent three men with long beards to lie hidden by the side of the boat." The meaning "to survey, to probe" or "to fathom, get to the bottom of" postulated by the editors (Zhu and Chen 2013, 186 with footnote 6) and based on the explanation by Wang Yinzhi of *Zhuang* 21, 134: 下潛黃泉 – better translated as "to dive down to the yellow springs" – can be questioned.

1049 For *xun* see footnote 830.

1050 Here a segmentation that slightly differs from that of the editors is chosen because *suo* in *suo chou* 所讎 is understood as relative pronoun. In the present context, the verb *chou* 讎 (*GSR* 1091a) *du as a cognate of *chou* 儔/疇 (*GSR* 1090k/l) *dru "(counterpart/of the same category:) mate, companion" (Wang Li 1982, 232–233) most probably means "to join sb./to associate with sb.". *Suo chou* accordingly means "the one who joins sb./associates with sb." or "mate, associate, companion (of the same rank), partner" (*Hanshu* 28B, 1658: 嫁取無所讎 "for taking a husband or a wife there is no partner"; cf. Cang Xiuliang 1996, 1140). Furthermore, *suo chou* also occurs in the sense "a person to whom sb. is hostile/whom sb. regards as enemy" (*Lü* 7, 73 [cf. Knoblock and Riegel 2000, 186]: 若此者天之所誅也，人之所讎也。"Such [people] are those who are punished by Heaven and to whom other people are hostile."), which, however, does not make sense in this context.

1051 *Ju chu* 居處 occurs here in the sense "place of residence" (*Shiji* 75, 2354 [cf. Nienhauser VII (1994), 192]: 孟嘗君待客坐語，而屏風後常有侍史，主記君所與客語，問親戚居處。客去，孟嘗君已使使存問，獻遺其親戚。 "When the lord of Mengchang entertained his retainers and sat talking with them, there were always attendant scribes behind a screen, charged with recording their lord's conversations with his guests and his queries about their relatives' place of residence. When the retainers left, the lord of Mengchang had already sent messengers to present greetings and offer gifts to their relatives.").

In a legal context, *ju chu* otherwise often means "living/housing conditions" or "daily behaviour" (*ZYS* 207: 謙（廉）問其居處之狀。"He thoroughly enquired about their living conditions."; *ZYS* 211: 偏（徧）令人微隨視爲謂、出入、居處狀。"Everywhere [they] let people confidentially pursue and observe words and deeds, revenues and expenses as well as the living conditions [of suspicious persons]."; *ENLL* 305; cf. *Lunyu* 13, 19; 17, 21; *Xun* 2, 14).

1052 *Bo* 薄 and the related word *po* 迫 could mean "(drawing near/coming close to:) be contiguous/near/close to" (*Hanfei* 10, 54: 軍旅薄城。"The army is close to the city walls.";

First Stage of Interrogation

同曰：
歸義。就（就）日未盡，爲人庸，除芝（芃）。

Tong stated:
"I took refuge [under the Qin rule].[1053] Although the days of [?][1054] were not complete yet, I was hired[1055] by a private man to remove weeds."[1056]

Hanfei 15, 79: 侮所迫之國者 "treat states disrespectfully that one is a close neighbour to").

Another possible interpretation is to read *bo* 薄 as *bu* 簿 (cf. footnote 1107). *Bu su* 簿宿 could in that case be understood as either "registered lodgings" or "lodgings (noted) in a personal(?) register". It is known that at least officials kept records of their temporary lodgings while traveling (see e.g. *Yuelu 27 nian zhiri* 30.4–33.4; cf. also "private" or "personal" [*si* 私] records of this type in *Yuelu 35 nian si zhiri* 2.4–15.4).

1053 For *gui yi* see footnote 613.

1054 *Liang* 就 for *jiu* 就 (Zhang Shouzhong 1994, 80; *Shuowen* 5B, 229a), written with the component 旡 (cf. *ji* 既 in Zhang Shouzhong 1994, 75; *Shuowen* 8B, 405b). The compound *jiu ri* 就日 is not found in other sources and its meaning is therefore uncertain. The editors interpret *jiu* 就 (GSR 1093a) *dzuk-s as loan graph for the homeophonous *jiu* 僦 *tsuk-s and further assume that this was some kind of obligatory service, which had to be fulfilled by people who had taken refuge (*gui yi* 歸義) under Qin rule (Zhu and Chen 2013, 179 with footnote 5). However, the usage of the word in several sources rather suggests that *jiu* "to hire, rent (a cart/carter)" referred to hired labour in contrast to statute labour (XL 49=RCL B 23: 上節（即）發委輸，百姓或之縣就（僦）及移輸者，以律論之。 "When superiors mobilise [people] for transport, commoners who go to the prefecture to be hired, as well as those who transfer the [call to] transport to others will be sentenced according to the statutes."; Shen Gang 2008, 257–258: *Juyan* 213.11, 214.125, 254.5, 502.11, 506.27, 586.5; *Juyan xinjian* E.P.T49:53A, E.P.F22:6, E.P.F22:29; *Shangjunshu* 2, 4; *Shiji* 120, 3113; *Hanshu* 50, 2325; *Shiji* 30, 1441=*Hanshu* 24B, 1174; *Hanshu* 90, 3665).

Jiu 就 in the sense "to turn towards" (*Guoyu* 3.1/39/22; *Shiji* 7, 320) could also be synonymous to *gui* in *gui yi* 歸義.

Thirdly, *jiu ri* might be identified with *ji ri* 即日 "on this very day" (*Shiji* 10, 417) as *jiu* according to Karlgren (1933, 73 no. 572/573) belongs to the same word class as *ji*. Cf. *Fangyan* 12.59, 75.

1055 For *yong* see footnote 686.

1056 *Fan* 芝 *p^{h}rom-s (*Shuowen* 1B, 40b), a graphic variant of *fan* 泛 (GSR 641b), *fan* 汎 (GSR 625f) and *fan* 氾 (GSR 626c) in the sense "to float/drift along in the water" (on these etymologically closely related words see Wang Li 1982, 621–622), is used here as a loan graph for *peng* 芃 (GSR 625g) *b^ʕ(r)om meaning "(grain stalks/shoots, oak trunks) densely growing" (*Odes* 54,4; 153,4; 238,1) and probably also "rankly growing". For *chu* 除 in the context of weeding cf. *Zuo* Yin 1,2,3–4: 蔓草猶不可除 "when even rankly growing grass (weed) cannot be removed" and *Zuo* Xiang 14,460,1: 我諸戎除翦其荊棘。"We, the Rong, extirpated the briars and thorns from it."

譖（潛）訊同歸義狀及邑里居處狀，改曰：
隸臣，非歸義。143

[Yang] confidentially interrogated Tong about the circumstances of his submission [to Qin rule] as well as the circumstances under which he took up his residence in the quarter of the town. He changed[1057] his statement:
"I am a bond servant convict[1058] and did not take refuge [under Qin rule]."

訊同：
非歸義，可（何）故？

[Yang] interrogated Tong:
"Why didn't you take refuge [under Qin rule]?"

同曰：
爲吏僕，内爲人庸。恐吏毄（繫）辟同☐

Tong stated:
"I was a servant[1059] of an official who employed me [as a hired worker] in his

---

1057 In judicial contexts, *gai* 改 was used when an accused or a witness amended his or her statement (*ci* 辭) before the judicial authorities prior to the conclusion of proceedings (*ZYS* 105, 113, 217, 220; *Yuelu WYZ* 158, 176, 183). A synonymous, probably more technical expression found in statutes and model documents is *geng yan* 更言, also translatable as "to amend one's statement" (*ENLL* 110; *FZS* 4=*RCL* E 2; *Yuelu WYZ* 193). Witnesses (*zheng* 證) were exempted from punishment (*chu* 除) if they amended their statement so that it corresponded to the truth (*geng yan qing* 更言情) before the finding of fact (*ju* 鞫) was made in the case, according to rules probably applying only to penal cases (*ENLL* 110).

1058 Originally, Tong was probably a prisoner of war who had become a bond servant convict in the same way as the accused in the following case II.10 (*Yuelu WYZ* 158, cf. *QLZC* 38=*RCL* C 23b: 寇降，以爲隸臣。 "Enemies who surrender are made bond servant convicts."). For penal labour as *li chen* convict see footnote 751.

1059 *Pu* 僕 in early Zhou times referred to grooms. This meaning was later extended to servants, for the pre-Qin evidence see Lau and Lüdke 2012, footnote 1567. In Qin and early Han times such servants could be employed by officials (*ENLL* 267: 吏有縣官事而無僕者，郵爲炊，有僕者，叚（假）器。 "For officials who take care of government business without having servants, the post stations take care of the cooking. For those who have servants the cooking utensils are lent [to the servants]."). These servants were often recruited from among penal labour convicts (*Liye* 8–130+8–190+8–193: 諸徒隸當爲吏僕、養者皆屬倉。 "All convicts who by law are to become servants or cooks of officials are attached to the granary."). Sometimes even conscripts became official servants (*Liye* 8–106: 遷陵戍卒多爲吏僕。"Conscripts from Qianling prefecture performing military service frequently become servants of officials."). The private employment of some categories of penal labour convicts was prohibited under certain circumstances (*QLSZ* 113=*RCL* A 62: 隸臣有巧可以爲工者，勿以爲人僕、養。 "When bond servant convicts are skilful and could be made artisans, they must not be made servants or cooks.";

house.[1060] I was afraid that [other] officials would place me under detention[1061] and inflict punishment[1062] on me, Tong, [...]."

及薄宿，類訑。 144

[...] and [temporary] lodgings in the immediate vicinity, it seemed that he was lying.[1063]

□譖（潛）謂同：
同和不首一吏（事）者而言毋（無）坐毆（也）。

[Yang] confidentially said to Tong:
"In your response[1064] you do not confess[1065] one single incident[1066] but

QLSZ 150=RCL A 71: 司寇勿以爲僕、養。"Robber guard convicts should not be used as servants or cooks."). The cases nos. 9 and 10 of the *Zou yan shu* deal with the illegal private employment (*si shi* 私使) of earth and grain pounder convicts by officials (ZYS 54–56).

1060 For this usage of *nei* 內 cf. ZYS 56: 采鐵長山私使城旦田、舂女爲䭣（饘），令內作。"The head of the iron ore mine, Shan, privately employed an earth pounder convict for tilling the soil and a grain pounder convict for preparing millet gruel and ordered them to work in his house." See also ZYS 54: 佐啟主徒，令史冰私使城旦環爲家作。"When assistent Qi was in charge of the convicts, the secretary of the prefect, Bing, privately employed the earth pounder convict Huan for his family."

1061 For *ji*/*xi* see footnote 569.

1062 For *bi* 辟 in the sense of "punishment" see footnote 501. In this context, *bi* occurs as a verb with the meaning "to inflict punishment on sb." (*Shu* Jinteng §13: 我之弗辟 "if I cannot inflict punishment [on the slanderers]"; *Shu* Jicai §3: 監罔攸辟。"The inspectors had no occasion to inflict punishments.").

1063 For *tuo* see footnote 772.

1064 *He* 和 (GSR 8e) *gˤoj-s "to respond", usually in singing (*Odes* 85,1).

1065 *Shou* 首 "to confess/submit" (*Hanshu* 47, 2218: 王陽病抵讕，置辭驕嫚，不首主令與背畔亡異。[...]今王當受詔置辭，恐復不首實對。"The king pretended to be ill and denied all; in making his statement he was arrogant and scornful and did not confess that he had incited [actions] which were not different from treachery. [...] Now the king is by law to receive an order to make his statement, but I am afraid that he will again not confess and answer according to the facts."). Cf. *shou li* 首吏 "to submit to the officials" (*Hanshu* 79, 3302: 趙都案驗，得其主守盜十金罪，收捕。並不首吏，都格殺。"Investigating the evidence in the case [of the prefect Bing], Zhao Du found out that [Bing] had committed the offence of theft [of funds at a value] of 10 [pounds of] gold, which he, as the responsible official, had to keep, and he was going to arrest him. But Bing did not submit to the official so that Du killed him when [Bing] resisted arrest.")

1066 *Shi* 事 here as "matter, incident, offence" (FLDW 100=RCL D84: 有（又）以它事告之 "to again report him for another incident").

[instead] say that you have not [yet] been prosecuted[1067] [for any offence]."

同曰：
毋（無）坐毆（也），不智（知）所【問】。

Tong stated:
"I have not yet been prosecuted [for any offence], I do not know anything of [the things] that you [ask about]."

☐譖（潛）謂同：
同爲吏【僕】，人見同，巫從同，畏不敢捕同而☒$_{145}$

[Yang again] confidentially said to Tong:
"[When] you were an official [servant], someone saw you, [?][1068] followed you, but was afraid and did not dare to arrest[1069] you [...]."

☒如同。

[The statement of ...] corresponded to Tong's [statement].

Interagency Enquiries(?)

臧（贓）直（值）☒$_{146}$

The value of the misappropriated goods[1070] was [...].

Judgement

敗傷。洋毋（無）得同、顯。同、顯　大害毆（也）。
巳（已）論磔同、顯。

[...] suffered damage.[1071] Yang was not expected to catch[1072] Tong and Xian. Tong and Xian are a great harm [for the people].[1073]

1067 *Wu zuo* 毋（無）坐 "I have not (yet) been prosecuted for any offence" (*ZYS* 214; cf. *wu ta zuo* 毋（無）它坐 in *FZS* 15–16, 18, 30, 38, 43, 51, 53, 94,96=*RCL* E 7, 8, 12, 15, 16, 18, 19, 24, 6; *Liye* 8–754r, 8–1364, 8–1659, 8–2109, 8–2264). For *zuo* see footnote 528.

1068 The meaning of *wu* 巫 (*GSR* 105a) *m(r)o (Pan Wuyun: *ma) in this passage is uncertain.

1069 For *bu* see footnote 505.

1070 For *zang* see footnote 592.

1071 *Bai shang* 敗傷 "to be damaged" (*Hanfei* 20, 104).

1072 For *de* see footnote 524.

1073 It appears that one character was deleted between *xian* 顯 and *da* 大. The editors assume that *min* 民 was effaced to replace it with *qianshou* 黔首, as seen on slip 148 below (Zhu and Chen 2013, 180 with footnote 13).

Judgement has already been passed[1074] to quarter[1075] Tong and Xian.

Submission by the Prefecture – Introductory Formula

敢言之。

We venture to report this.

Letter of Recommendation for Investigating Officials

令曰：獄史能得微難獄，【上。今獄史洋】得微難獄$_{147}$爲奏九牒，上。此黔首大害殹（也）。毋（無）徵物，難得。洋以智治，訮（研）詗，謙（廉）求而得之。洋精絜（潔）毋（無）害，敦穀（慤）守吏，心平□▨$_{148}$中令。綏任謁以補卒史，勸它吏，卑（俾）盜賊不發。

The ordinances read: "Whenever a judicial secretary is able to solve an obscure and difficult case, [this is to be reported to the higher authorities."[1076] Now the judicial secretary Yang] solved an obscure and difficult case [...], drew up a submission on nine slips and submitted it [to the higher authorities]. This was a great harm for the people.[1077] There were no pieces of evidence[1078] and [the case] was difficult to solve. Yang with his cleverness tried[1079] [this difficult case], spied on [people], thoroughly[1080] sought out[1081] [the crimi-

1074 For *lun* see footnote 540.

1075 For *zhe* see footnote 1032.

1076 The same ordinance is quoted in full in *ZYS* 227–228, see section 4.6.4.1 of the introduction. For *wei* 微 in this context see Lau and Lüdke 2012, footnote 1643.

1077 Cf. *ZYS* 225: 若思（斯）甚大害也。 "[With the situation being] like this it is an extremely great harm [for the people]." and *Yuelu WYZ* 167.

1078 For *zheng wu* see footnote 305.

1079 *Zhi* 治 as a legal term means "to try" and takes as object the matter of the trial *yu* 獄 "criminal case" (*FZS* 1=*RCL* E 1; *ENLL* 113, 215; cf. *ZYS* 176; *ENLL* 396) or an interrogated suspect person (*ENLL* 118). In legal manuscripts, *zhi* is also often used without any object (*Yuelu WYZ* 191, 199, 213; *FLDW* 106–107=*RCL* D 88, 90; *ZYS* 50, 67, 74, 97, 126, 128, 135, 144, 163; *ENLL* 104–106, 116–117). Cf. two variants of this passage: 以智治鐵（纖）微，謙（廉）求得 (*Yuelu WYZ* 169) and 以智訮（研）詗求得 (*ZYS* 226).

1080 *Qian* 謙 is used to write *lian* 廉 "thorough, meticulous" (*ZYS* 78: 其謙（廉）求捕其賊。"You may thoroughly search for his murderer and arrest him."; *Yuelu WYZ* 156, 168). See also Lau and Lüdke 2012, footnotes 991, 1554.

1081 *Qiu* 求 in a legal context refers to the search for a person whose whereabouts are not known. A search would be undertaken by the responsible authorities if the report of a criminal offence had been received, but the perpetrators were not known or were at large (*ZYS* 205, 210, 222; *FZS* 74=*RCL* E 22). In some cases, *qiu* also refers to a search for a person that was reported missing (*ZYS* 76). As in the present case, a search was usually supervised by one of the judicial secretaries *yu shi* 獄史 (*ZYS* 61, 197, 203; *Yuelu WYZ* 148, 168)

nals] and caught [them]. Yang is an incumbent official[1082] who has integrity and moral purity, is impeccable and dutiful.[1083] In his heart he is impartial[1084] [...] meet the legal requirements.[1085] Sui recommends and guarantees for him[1086] (Yang) and requests that he is to fill the ranks of the clerks-in-chief [of the province][1087] so that his example may be an encouragement for other officials, and may cause robbers and bandits not to appear.[1088]

overseeing local law enforcement, and actually carried out by robber hunters (*qiu dao* 求盜, see ZYS 37, 75, 80; ENLL 144; QLZC 38=RCL C 24; FLDW 2, 3, 66=RCL D 1, 2, 53; FZS 21, 25, 55=RCL E 10, 12, 20; cf. *Zhoujiatai* 260), whose function is clearly indicated by their title. Private individuals might undertake a search for absconded slaves (ZYS 9; ENLL 160) instead of reporting them to the authorities; if successful, they had the option to not present their slaves to the authorities for judgement, thus sparing them from mutilation (ENLL 159).

1082 *Shou li* 守吏 "officeholder/incumbent holder of an office", for the meaning of *shou* see footnote 486.

1083 Cf. the very similar formulations in ZYS 228r: 毋害，謙（廉）絜（潔）敦愨（愨）守吏也 and *Yuelu* WYZ 169: 請（清）絜（潔）毋（無）害，敦殼（愨）守吏. For *wu hai* 毋害 as qualification for an official see footnote 441; for further references to *lian jie dun que* 廉潔敦愨 see footnote 442.

1084 Cf. *ping duan* 平端 (ZYS 228r) and *xin ping duan li* 心平端禮 (*Yuelu* WYZ 169).

1085 *Zhong ling* 中令 "to meet the legal requirements" (Zhu and Chen 2013, 191 with footnote 30) also occurs in *Yuelu* WYZ 169. *Zhong* 中 in the meaning "to conform/correspond to" does otherwise not occur with *ling* 令 as the object in legal manuscripts or in received literature of Qin and Han times. Cf. *zhong fa* 中法 "to correspond to the law" (*Shangjunshu* 23, 39).

1086 *Ren* 任 "to recommend and guarantee for a person who should be appointed, to stand surety for sb." (QLSZ 101=RCL A 55: 亦令其徒、舍人任其叚（假）。"Orders are likewise given to conscripts/convicts and retainers to stand surety for those borrowers."; QLSZ 196=RCL A 106: 官吏有重罪，大嗇夫、丞任之。"[...] the officials of the offices will have committed a serious offence and the great overseer and the assistant have to guarantee for them."; QLZC 1=RCL C 1: 任法（廢）官者爲吏，貲二甲。"[To recommend and] guarantee for [a person who] has been permanently removed from office is fined two suits of armour."; FLDW 145=RCL D 123: 任人爲丞 "to recommend and guarantee for a person [to be appointed] as vice prefect"). Cf. Yates (1995, 350) on guarantees of performance in the Qin bureaucracy.

1087 For the office of the provincial secretaries *zu shi* 卒史 (*Yuelu* WYZ 170) see Lau and Lüdke 2012, footnote 923.

1088 The preceding sentences concerning the promotion of the investigating officials are very similar to those in in *Yuelu* WYZ 169–170: 任謁課以補卒史，勸它吏 and ZYS 228: 謁以補卒史，勸它吏.

Submission by the Prefecture – Concluding Formula

敢言【之】。149

We venture to report [this].

Case II.10

In a similar way to the preceding one, this case from 242 BC served as a recommendation for the promotion of competent investigating officials. The offender in this case also committed armed robbery. He killed three persons in a cottage or field hut while they were sleeping, and stole their clothes and tools. The case was difficult to solve because the murderer tried to divert suspicion from himself. He placed the clothes of a penal labour convict at the crime scene in order to make the officials believe that the murderer was a convict. At first, the three judicial secretaries who were commissioned with the investigations examined the dead bodies in order to identify them and to determine the cause of death. Then, they inspected the crime scene in order to obtain clues about the murder. They found the convict clothes and therefore interrogated the convicts within their own and the neighbouring prefectures. They also checked the registers for convicts who had absconded. Then they confidentially questioned the people who owned the neighbouring fields and posted robber guard convicts along the field paths and thoroughfares in order to intercept suspect persons with irregular behaviour and to check up on them. For a long time, the offender could not be caught. Only after a thorough search in Liyang and the neighbouring prefecture did the law enforcement officers discover a man with a new sheath and knife at his belt, who was acting suspiciously. During the first stage of interrogation, the suspect did not confess to the murder, but managed to tangle himself in a knot of contradictions requiring amendation of his former statements. In the course of the cross-examination, the judicial officials finally succeeded in obtaining the suspect's confession of guilt. Ultimately, the suspect described the particulars of the crime and even admitted that he had planned a second armed robbery.

The value of the misappropriated goods was determined as a result of the interagency enquiries. Following a note on the execution of the murderer, it is stressed that the offender was extraordinarily violent and ingenious in covering up all his traces, which made him dangerous to society.

At the end of the actual letter recommending the promotion of the investigators, the ethical standards required of a judicial official for the office of a provincial secretary are emphasised. In addition, the hope that other officials would follow his example is expressed.

 | DOI 10.1163/9789004315655_018

Diplomatic Edition

六年十一月己未私屬喜曰□⍁□□妾宜士五安□□⍁$_{150}$•即令獄史彭沮⌞衷往診安宜及不智可一女子死皆在内中頭頸有伐刑痏不智殺者⍁$_{151}$赤帬襦類城旦衣•喜曰嘗見死女子與安等作不智可人•衜曰宜安有布衣帬襦絝履皆亡不得$_{152}$毄即各日夜别薄譖訊都官旁縣=中城旦及牒書其亡者□⍁$_{153}$不智盜及死女子可人毋音毄•即令獄史觸與彭沮衷求其盜•觸等盡别譖訊安旁田人皆曰不智$_{154}$可人即將司寇晦别居千佰嬍道徼迣苛視不狝者弗得•觸等音以爲安□⍁有赤衣殺安等者□⍁$_{155}$⍁人日夜謙求櫟陽及它縣五日聞⍁$_{156}$佩新大鞞刀其瞻視不壹如有惡狀即訊言曰□⍁$_{157}$•訊同=大官隸臣可故爲寺從公僕同言類不讎且覆□=官同改曰定名魏故燕城人降爲隸臣輸寺從去亡$_{158}$訊魏=亡安取錢以補袍及買鞞刀魏曰庸取錢$_{159}$

[Missing slip] 甚矣以人莫智今吏智之未可奈可請言請魏欲盜恐□□□□□⍁$_{160}$得者求城旦赤衣操巳殺人置死所令人以爲殺人者□□□□□□□=以旬餘時以二錢買不□$_{161}$可官城旦敝赤帬襦以勝盛佗行出高門視可盜者□食時到安等舍□寄□其内中有頃安等$_{162}$皆臥出魏伐刑殺安等置赤衣死所盜取衣器去買行道者所以錢買布補⍁$_{163}$有母妻子在魏即買大刀欲復以盜殺人得錢材以爲用亡之魏未蝕而得辠$_{164}$

⍁□可解魏曰辠毋解⍁$_{165}$

•問如辤臧四百一十六錢巳論磔魏•魏晉人材犺端買城旦赤衣以盜殺人巳殺置死所以□令吏⍁$_{166}$得⌞一人殺三人田壄去居邑中市客舍甚悍非恆人毄有買大刀欲復盜殺人以亡之魏民大害毄甚微難得$_{167}$觸等以智治鐵微謙求得⌞五年觸與史去疢□□⍁□□今獄史觸彭沮⌞衷得微難獄磔辠$_{168}$一人爲奏十六牒上觸爲令史廿二歲年卌三彭沮衷勞年中令皆請絜毋害敦殼守吏心平端禮任謁$_{169}$課以補卒史勸它吏敢言之$_{170}$

Edition and Translation

Initiation of Criminal Proceedings

六年十一月己未私屬喜曰：
□⍁□□妾宜、士五（伍）安□□⍁$_{150}$

In the sixth[1089] year on day *jiwei*[1090] of the eleventh month, the personal dependant[1091] Xi stated:

1089 When comparing the first character on this slip with other occurences of the character *nian* 廿 in the same manuscript (e.g. on *Yuelu* WYZ 169), it appears that it should not be identified as *nian*, as proposed by the editors (Zhu and Chen 2013, 185). Rather, it could be the character *liu* 六 (cf. the form on *Yuelu* WYZ 169), which would also better accord with the other dates mentioned in this and other cases of the same manuscript (fifth year of King Zheng of Qin, *Yuelu* WYZ 168; first year of King Zheng of Qin, *Yuelu* WYZ 175).

"[…*li*] *qie* convict(?)[1092] Yi and the rank-and-file man[1093] An […]."

Report on Investigations

即令獄史彭沮、衷往診安、宜及不智（知）可（何）一女子死（屍），皆在內中。頭頸有伐刑痏。不智（知）殺者☐$_{151}$赤帬（裙）襦，類城旦衣。

Thereupon we ordered the judicial secretaries[1094] Peng Ju and Zhong to go and inspect[1095] the corpses of An, Yi and one unknown

1090 This was the eleventh day of the eleventh month in the sixth year of King Zheng of Qin (cf. Zhang Peiyu 2007, 73; Li Zhonglin 2012, 65), i.e. 20/12/242 BC (Xu Xiqi 1997, 1201).

1091 *Si shu* 私屬 "personal dependant" was a special designation for male slaves who were manumitted by their owner due to good conduct (*ENLL* 162–163: 奴婢爲善而主欲免者，許之。奴命曰私屬，婢爲庶人，皆復使及筭，事之如奴婢。主死若有罪，以私屬爲庶人，刑者以爲隱官。 "If the owner of a male or female slave wishes to manumit him/her on account of good conduct, this is to be granted. A [male] slave then is declared a 'personal dependant', a female slave is made a released person, both are exempted from deployment [to statute labour] and from the poll tax, they are to be employed in the same way as male and female slaves. If their master dies or commits an offence, his personal dependants are made released persons; those [among them] who had [previously] been subjected to a mutilation punishment are employed in a hidden workshop.").

1092 The illegible character before *qie* 妾 was probably *li* 隸. *Li qie* 隸妾 (*QLSZ* 49, 110, 151, 155=*RCL* A 12, 60, 72, 91; *FLDW* 174=*RCL* D 154; *FZS* 86=*RCL* E 23; *ZYS* 210) were the female counterparts of the male convicts *li chen* 隸臣 performing a less severe category of penal labour. For *li chen* see footnote 751.

1093 For *shi wu* see footnote 495.

1094 For *yu shi* see footnote 539.

1095 *Zhen* 診 as a legal term refers to a, mostly visual, inspection of people, animals, things or scenes. In formal criminal procedure, *zhen* "inspection" is one of three possible ways of gathering evidence (*ZYS* 45, 109, 118, 165–167, 216), together with *xun* 訊 "interrogation" (footnote 830) and *wen* 問 "interagency enquiries" (footnote 562). Like *wen*, *zhen* immediately precedes the finding of fact (*ju* 鞫), which presupposed that all available evidence had been gathered. *Zhen* always involved a first-hand examination of concrete, physical evidence. A *zhen*-inspection during criminal investigation is conducted by the officials charged with conducting the investigation (*ZYS* 165–167), i.e. a judicial secretary (*yu shi* 獄史) in the present case and other Qin cases (*ZYS* 216). It was also possible for the responsible officials to send the secretary of the prefect (*ling shi* 令史) for inspections of the scene of an incident (*FZS* 56, 63, 74, 87=*RCL* E 20, 21, 22, 23), who in some cases was assisted by a bond servant convict (*li chen* 隸臣) or prison bond servant (*lao li chen* 牢隸臣) (*FZS* 56, 64, 75, 87=*RCL* E 20, 21, 22, 23). It was further possible to draw on people specially qualified for a certain type of inspection, such as a physician to diagnose a suspected case of leprosy (*FZS* 53=*RCL* E 19), an obviously specially trained secretary of

woman,[1096] which were all [laid down] inside a room.[1097] At the necks[1098] there

the prefect to perform a medical examination (FZS 39=RCL E 15), or a bond woman experienced in midwifery to examine a woman after a miscarriage (FZS 86, 89=RCL E 23). In particular, *zhen* referred to:

1) postmortem examination of a corpse (sometimes after exhumation) or a severed head in order to determine the cause of death or to identify the dead person (FZS 30, 32, 35=RCL E 12, 13, 14; *Yuelu* WYZ 151; *Hanshu* 93, 3739–3740) or to exclude the possibility of foul play in a case of suspected suicide (FZS 63, 64, 68=RCL E 21);

2) medical examination, e.g. of the victim of a possible offence in order to ascertain the nature and cause of his injuries (ZYS 45; FZS 32=RCL E 13) or of a miscarriage (FZS 86–87, 89=RCL E 23); of a convicted person to find out if he was tortured during trial (ZYS 109, 118); of a slave who is to be sold to the government for insubordination, probably to ascertain his value (FZS 39=RCL E 15); of a suspected bearer of an infectious disease such as leprosy, which, if confirmed, probably led to banishment to a segregated place (FZS 53=RCL E 19; cf. FLDW 122, 123=RCL D 102, 103);

3) inspection of a place or scene in order to obtain clues about an alleged offence (ZYS 165–167; FZS 74–75=RCL E 22);

4) inspection of implements that might have been used to carry out an offence (ZYS 216);

5) face-to-face confrontation of the accused with people knowing him for the purpose of identification; this is called *xiang zhen* 相診 "inspect (identify?) face-to-face" (FZS 98=RCL E 6).

In one case the inspection at the scene of crime was intended to measure distances that two groups of soldieres had run back during their retreat as well as to measure the height and width of fortifications (*Yuelu* WYZ 241–242).

1096 Cf. *bu zhi he ren* 不智（知）何人 "unknown person" (FZS 55=RCL E 20: 署中某所有賊死、結髮、不智（知）可（何）男子一人。"At the place X within [the area of] my post there is a corpse of one unknown male person with bound-up hair who was murdered."; ZYS 197; *Shiji* 87, 2562).

1097 *Nei* 内 "room (of a house)" (FZS 8–9=RCL E 3: 甲室、人：一宇二内，各有戶，內室皆瓦蓋。"As regards A's house and people, [these include] one house with two rooms, each with a door; the inner dwellings are all covered with tiles."; FZS 64, 75=RCL E 21, 22; *Hanshu* 49, 2288). Cf. Lau and Lüdke 2012, footnote 1474.

1098 *Tou jing* 頭頸 as a compound meaning "neck" (*Li* 30, 1485 [cf. Couvreur 1950, vol. 1, 722]: 頭頸必中。"[When bowing down,] the neck must be erect."). *Tou* 頭 (GSR 118e) sometimes writes the homeophonous *dou* 脰 (GSR 118d) "neck" (FZS 34–36=RCL E 14). Cf. footnote 9 to RCL E 14 by Hulsewé as well as Wang Hui (2008, 140) who also provides evidence for this loan writing in classical Chinese literature. In another passage, Hulsewé assumed the same loan writing and therefore translated *tou* as "neck" (FZS 56=RCL E 20 with note 10).

were injuries[1099] and wounds[1100] from cuts.[1101] We did not know the murderer [...but found a] red lower garment and short jacket,[1102] which seemed to be the clothes of an earth pounder convict.[1103]

喜曰：
嘗見死女子與安等作，不智（知）可（何）人。

Xi stated:
"Once I saw the woman who died working together with An and others, [but] I did not know who she was."

銜曰：
宜、安有布衣、帬（裙）、襦、絝、履，皆亡不得$_{152}$殹（也）。

Xian stated:
"Yi and An had coarse[1104] clothes – lower garments, short jackets, trousers[1105] and shoes[1106] – which are all gone and have not been found [again]."

即各日夜別薄（簿）譖（潛）訊都官旁縣、縣中城旦及牒書其亡者□☐$_{153}$
不智（知）盜及死女子可（何）人。毋（無）音（意）殹（也）。

1099 For *xing* see footnote 1009.

1100 *Wei* 痏 "wound" (*FZS* 35–36=*RCL* E 14: 診首[...]其右角痏一所，袤五寸，深到骨類劍迹。 "When inspecting the head [we found that ...] on the right temple there was a wound, five inches long and so deep that it entered into the bone, resembling the traces of a sword."; *FZS* 56=*RCL* E 20: 某頭左角刃痏一所，北（背）二所，皆從（縱）頭北（背），袤各四寸，相耎，廣各一寸，皆臽中類斧[...]。 "On the left corner of his neck, there was a wound from a blade and on the back two [wounds], all vertical to the neck and the back, each four inches long, stuck together and each one inch wide, all depressed, resembling [wounds made by] an axe [...]."). Cf. *wei* "bruise" in the compound *zhi wei* 疻痏 "swellings and bruises" (*ENLL* 28–29; *FLDW* 89=*RCL* D 74).

1101 Although only the component *ge* 戈 is visible, *fa* 伐 "to hit, cut" can be reconstructed in accordance with the parallel passage on *Yuelu WYZ* 163.

1102 *Qun* 帬 is a graphic variant of *qun* 裙 "lower garment; skirt". For *ru* 襦 cf. footnote 1045. *Qun ru* is also used as a compound for (upper and lower) outer garments (*Zhuang* 26, 177). The clothes of earth and grain pounder convicts were red (*QLSZ* 147=*RCL* A 70; cf. *QLSZ* 134–135=*RCL* A 68).

1103 For *cheng dan* see footnotes 668 and 1003.

1104 For *bu* see footnote 930.

1105 *Ku* 絝 is a graphic variant of *ku* 袴 "trousers (with long or short legs)" (Sun Ji 2011, 273–274 with illustrations 60–3 and 60–4). Sometimes *ru ku* 襦袴 was also used as a compound for outer garments (*Li* 28, 1471; *Lü* 18, 225).

1106 *Lü* 履 "shoes" (Sun Ji 2011, 295 with illustrations 65–1 and 65–2).

Thereupon, everyone [of the investigators] by day and night according to separate registers[1107] confidentially[1108] interrogated[1109] the earth pounder convicts within the prefecture and the prefectures adjoining the *du guan*, and noted on writing slips/tablets[1110] those who had absconded[1111] [...]. They [still] did not know who the robber[1112] and the dead woman were. They had no suspicions.[1113]

即令獄史觸與彭沮、衷求其盜。

Thereupon, we ordered the judicial secretary Chu to search for[1114] the respective robber together with Peng Ju and Zhong.

觸等盡別譖（潛）訊安旁田人，皆曰：不智（知）$_{154}$可（何）人。

Chu and his colleagues entirely separated and confidentially interrogated all of the people on the fields adjoining An['s field]. They all said: "We do not know who he is."

1107 *Bo* 薄 (GSR 771p) *bˤak for *bu* 簿 (GSR 771o) "register" (*Liye* 8–16, 8–62r, 8–142r, 8–686r, etc.; ZYS 54, 56), probably convict registers, which for example noted their tasks (ZYS 54, 56). *Bie bu* 別簿 probably means "according to separate registers" or "to separate registers" (cf. *bie ji* 別籍 in ZYS 145), which could imply that the investigating officials separated the tasks among themselves or that they compared separate registers. *Bo* could also be used as loan character for *po* 迫 (GSR 782k) *pˤrak "to press (on) sb., to come threateningly close to, to draw near" (*Hanshu* 62, 2726; *Zuo* Zhuang 11,87,3; Wen 12,260,12–13; according to Feng and Deng 2006, 804).

1108 For *zen* 譖 used to write *qian* see footnote 1048.

1109 For *xun* see footnote 830.

1110 *Die shu* 牒書 "to write down/note on a slip/tablet" (QLSZ 35=RCL A 25; *Liye* 8–317, 8–645r, 8–768r, 8–1043, 8–1514r; cf. FZS 91–92=RCL E 24: 即疏書甲等名事關諜（牒）北（背）。"Then we noted point for point the name, the status and the place of residence/birth of A and his accomplices on the back of a writing tablet." and ENLL 256).

1111 For *wang* see footnote 612.

1112 For *dao* see footnotes 541, 557 and 795.

1113 *Yin* 音 (GSR 653a) *q(r)əm is used here for *yi* 意 (GSR 957a) *ʔ(r)ək-s (Pan Wuyun: *qɯgs) (*Shanghai bowuguan Hengxian* 5–6; cf. Bai Yulan 2012, 913; Feng and Deng 2006, 1055) in the sense "suspicion; to suspect sb." (*Hanshu* 47, 2210: 賊未得也。於是天子意梁，逐賊，果梁使之。"The murderers had not been caught. Thereupon, the emperor suspected Liang, pursued the murderers and [found out that] indeed Liang had sent them."; FZS 82=RCL E 22: 不智（知）盜者可（何）人及蚤（早）莫（暮），毋（無）意毆（也）。"We do not know who the robbers were, or the time of the robbery. We have no suspicion.") or "to suspect sth., to assume" (*Hanshu* 37, 1975).

1114 For *qiu* see footnote 1081.

即將司寇晦別居千（阡）佰（陌）、敫（徹）道，徼（邀）迣，苛視不犳（狀）者。弗得。觸等音（意）以爲安□☒有赤衣，殺安等者□☒$_{155}$☒人日夜謙（廉）求櫟陽及它縣。五日聞☒$_{156}$佩新大鞞（鞞）刀。其瞻視不壹，如有惡狀。

Thereupon, they (Chu, Peng Ju and Zhong) commanded[1115] robber guard convicts[1116] at nightfall[1117] to position themselves separately along field paths[1118]

1115 For *jiang* see footnotes 509 and 529.

1116 *Si kou* 司寇 "overseer of the bandits/robber guard" in Qin and early Han times referred to convicts performing the most lenient or second most lenient form of penal labour. Penal labour as a *si kou* belonged to the category of *nai* 耐 "being shaved". If a free man committed an offence that was punishable by *nai*, but for which the statutes did not state with which concrete form of penal labour *nai* should be combined, he was made a *si kou* (*ENLL* 90). This may be the reason for the fact that being made a *si kou* is not found for any specific offence in Qin and early Han legal manuscripts. *Si kou*, as their name suggests, were above all employed as wardens of convicts sentenced for a more serious crime (*QLSZ* 146=*RCL* A 69: 城旦舂當將司者，廿人，城旦司寇一人將。"As regards earth and grain pounder convicts who have to be led and supervised, twenty persons are led by one robber guard of earth pounder convicts."). As in the present case, *si kou* were sometimes assigned to search for suspects (*ZYS* 207). *Si kou* were allowed to form their own households within the villages (*Liye* 8–19) and were entitled to receive the same plot of fields (50 *mu* 畝) and a yard half the size as those of the released convicts *yin guan* 隱官 (*ENLL* 312, 317).

1117 *Hui* 晦 does not occur as a personal name in the list of Qin names compiled by Liu Zhao (2010). Cf. the name Mei 每 for a woman in *ZYS* 210. Accordingly, *hui* 晦 most probably refers to "nightfall", i.e. the time when it is beginning to get dark (*Chuci* 3/7/25: 自明及晦，所行幾里？"From dawn to nightfall how many miles does he/it walk?"; *FZS* 73=*RCL* E 22: 乙獨與妻丙晦臥堂上。"I, B, alone with my wife C lay down in the main hall at nightfall."). Sometimes *hui* could also mean "darkness" (*ZYS* 101–102: 晦夜半時 "in the darkness at midnight").

1118 *Qian mo* 阡陌 refers to raised paths between fields, which at the same time marked field borders (*FLDW* 64=*RCL* D 136: 盜徙封，贖耐。可（何）如爲封？封即田千（阡）佰（陌）。"'To illegally shift border hills [is punished by paying the fee for] redemption from being shaved.' What are 'border hills'? Border hills are the field border paths."; *Qingchuan mudu* 2=*Sanjian* 604=*RCL* G: 正疆畔，及發千（阡）百（陌）之大草。"One corrects the borders and the field limits and cuts the tall grass on the border paths."; *Longgang* 120; *Shiji* 5, 203=*Hanshu* 24B, 1126; *Shiji* 68, 2232 [cf. Nienhauser VII (1994), 91]: 爲田開阡陌封疆，而賦稅平。"[Shang Yang] cultivated fields, opened up raised paths and boundary balks in the fields, and the taxes were levied equally."; *Shiji* 79, 2422; *Hanshu* 99B, 4129 [cf. Dubs III (1955), 324]: 故滅廬井而置阡陌。"Hence, the Qin [dynasty] eliminated the *jing* [system] of cottages and well-fields and established the raised border paths [between cultivated fields].").

and thoroughfares/clear the roads[1119] in order to intercept[1120] and block the way[1121] [as well as] cross-examine[1122] and check up on[1123] [persons with]

1119 *Che* 徹 in combination with *dao* 道 only occurs in *Longgang* 61: 僌（徹）弩道, where *che* is interpreted as "to clear (away)" (*qing chu* 清除) and *nu dao* as a special road to be used by crossbow archers, which crosses the speedway (Zhongguo wenwu yanjiusuo et al. 2001, 97). Accordingly, *che dao* could be translated as "to clear the road" or it might be interpreted as a compound in the sense of "through road/thoroughfare".

1120 *Jiao* 徼 (GSR 1162d) *kˤew could mean "to go on patrol" (*Hanshu* 19A, 732; FLDW 1=RCL D 1) but is also used as loan graph for *yao* 邀 (GSR 1162f) *qew "intercept sb., bar sb.'s way" (*Zuo* Xiang 16,471,12: 齊侯圍郕，孟孺子速徼之。 "The marquis of Qi laid siege to Cheng when Meng Ruzi Su barred his way.") or for *yao* 要 (GSR 1142a) *qew in the same meaning (Feng and Deng 2006, 708; e.g. *Meng* 4, 152 [cf. Lau 1984, 75]: 使數人要於路。"[Meng Zhongzi] sent several men to intercept [Mengzi] on the road."; *Meng* 9, 389 [cf. Lau 1984, 197]: 遭宋桓司馬將要而殺之。"There was the incident of Huan Sima of Song who was about to intercept and kill [Confucius].").

1121 *Zhi* 迣 (GSR 339) *t-hlet-s<**t-hlep-s is a Jin-Zhao dialect word for *lie* 迾 "to block sth./sb.'s way", which is pronounced in the same way as *zhi* 寘 (GSR 375x) *t-hlej-s (Baxter and Sagart: *ke-s, PanWuyun: *tjels) (*Shuowen* 2B, 74b). There is some evidence for *zhi* as loan graph for different words in the manuscripts from Mawangdui and Shuihudi (Feng and Deng 2006, 910; Wang Hui 2008, 639), but only one reference for the meaning "to block" (*Yuelu Wei li* 14.3), from which we can draw the conclusion that *jiao*/*yao* 徼/邀 (see footnote 1120) and *zhi* were probably synonyms. Cf. *zhe zhi* 遮迣 "bar the way" (*Hanshu* 72, 3088: 部落鼓鳴，男女遮迣。 "When the drums are sounding, men and women [have to go and] bar [the robbers'] way.").

1122 *Ke* 苛 (GSR 1i) *Gˤaj according to Feng and Deng (2006, 768) is used as a loan graph for *he* 呵/訶 (GSR 1j,k) *qʰˤaj meaning "to reproach, scold sb." (*Hanfei* 31, 185; *Hanshu* 24B, 1154) or "to cross-examine sb., take sb. to task, bother sb. with questions" (*Mo* 70, 348 [cf. Johnston 2010, 861]: 分里爲四部，部一長，以苛往來不以時行。 "They subdivided a quarter into four sections, each section one head, in order to take to task those travellers who did not travel at the right time."; *Hanshu* 99B, 4135 [cf. Dubs III (1955), 337]: 大司空士夜過奉常亭，亭長苛之[...]。 "An official of the chief prosecutor at night passed the police station [under the control of] of the minister of ceremonial. The station head cross-examined him."; ZYS 81 [cf. Lau and Lüdke 2012, footnote 1005]: 丙與發弩贅荷（苛）捕蒼。"C and the crossbowman Zhui cross-examined and arrested me, Cang."; *Yuelu* WYZ 220).

He and its graphic variants frequently appear in the context of border control in combination with other verbs such as *nan* 難 "cause difficulties" (*Hanfei* 32, 215: 關市呵難之 "to bother sb. and cause him difficulties at border inspection posts or marketplaces") or *liu* 留 "hold sb. up/delay sb." (*Hanshu* 10, 313 [cf. Dubs II (1944), 389]: 關東大水，流民欲入函谷、天井、壺口、五阮關者，勿苛留。"In the areas located east to [the land within] the passes there was a great inundation and those of the flood refugees who want to pass the four border checkpoints Hangu, Tianjing, Hukou or Wuyuan should not be cross-examined and held up."; *Hanshu* 99B, 4122 [cf. Dubs III (1955), 307]: 吏民出入，

irregular behaviour.[1124] [But the criminal] was not caught. Chu and his colleagues assumed that An [... Because ...] had been red clothes, the one who killed An and the others [was probably an earth pounder convict ... They let] men day and night start a thorough[1125] search in Liyang[1126] and other prefectures. After five days, they heard [... Tong] wore at his belt a new great sheath and a knife. His gaze[1127] (expression in the eyes) was devious;[1128] it was as if he had a bad appearance.[1129]

持布錢以副符傳，不持者，廚傳勿舍，關津苛留。"Officials and common people while travelling should carry with them a certificate or passport attesting their currency; if they do not carry this, the inns and relay stations should not accomodate them, and the border checkpoints at passes and fords should cross-examine them and hold them up."; *Wei li zhi dao* 39.3: 苛難留民 "cross-examine people, cause them difficulties and hold them up"). See also *Juyan xinjian* E.P.T13:3; *Juyan* 43.12A, 140.1A, 218.2, 495.12/506.20A.

1123 *Shi* 視 "to look closely at sb. (in order to appraise him), examine, inspect" (*Guoyu* 4.89/85/25: 叔魚生，其母視之。"When Shu Yu was born, his mother examined him."; *Zuo* Xi 15,164,16: 使韓簡視師。"He dispatched [his minister] Han Jian to inspect the troops."; *Shiji* 126, 3211: 巫行視小家女好者。"The shamanesses would go about looking at daughters from low-ranking families who were pretty."); here, especially in the sense "to check up on a suspect". For *shi* in the context of inspecting pieces of evidence see footnote 1310.

1124 犾 is a character variant of *zhuang* 狀. *Zhuang* referred to the external appearance, but also to the attitude, manners or behaviour of a person. *Bu zhuang* 不狀 can be equated with *wu zhuang* 無狀 "irregular behaviour", which not only implied misconduct in office (Xu Shihong 1998), but generally also offending behaviour (*Hanshu* 76, 3215–3216; 76, 3225; 80, 3318; 84, 3413; 94B, 3801; 97A, 3966; *Houhanshu* 3, 132).

1125 For *qian* 謙 used to write *lian* 廉 see footnote 1080.

1126 Liyang 櫟陽 had been walled as residence by Duke Xian of Qin in 383 BC (*Shiji* 5, 201; 15, 714) and became a prefecture in 374 BC (*Shiji* 15, 717; *Hanshu* 28A, 1545; ENLL 443), which was part of the Qin metropolitan province Neishi (*Hanshu* 28A). Its administrative seat was located at Wutunxiang 武屯鄉 to the northeast of present Xi'an in central Shaanxi (Hou Xiaorong 2009, 136–137, cf. *Lishi dituji* vol. II, 5/6, 6④).

1127 *Zhan shi* 瞻視 (TLS) "glance, expression in one's eyes" (*Lunyu* 20, 417; ZYS 213: 瞻視應對最奇。"The gaze and the reactions [of the suspect] were extremely odd.").

1128 *Bu yi* 不壹 "dishonest, insincere, devious" (*Zuo* Cheng 13,380,15: 不穀惡其無成德，是用宣之，以懲不壹。"I, hating such want of virtue, declare it to you, that such insincerity may be punished/chastised.").

1129 *E zhuang* 惡狀 "bad/rude manners/looks/appearance" (*Lü* 14, 154 [cf. Knoblock and Riegel 2000, 330]: 客進，狀有惡其名，言有惡狀。"When the retainer advanced, his appearance was uglier than his name [suggested] and his speech was even uglier [than his appearance].").

First Stage of Interrogation

即訊，言曰：□☑157

So they interrogated him and his statement was: "[...]."

訊同：
同大（太）官隸臣，可（何）故爲寺從公僕？同言類不讎，且覆□□官。

We (Chu, Peng Ju and Zhong) interrogated Tong:
"[If] you were a bond servant at the grand office,[1130] why were you [at the same time] a servant of the chief of Sicong [prefecture]?[1131] [Because] your statement seems to be inconsistent,[1132] we are going to check[1133] it [...] office."

1130 *Da guan* 大官 for *tai guan* 太官 (*QLZC* 23), an office that was subordinate to the *shao fu* 少府 and according to the commentary of Yan Shigu responsible for food rations (*Hanshu* 19A, 731). In early Han times, the salary of the head of a *tai guan* was 600 *shi* (*ENLL* 461). For the identification of the second character as *guan* instead of *gong* 宮, as proposed in Zhu and Chen 2013, see Wang Wei 2013.

1131 Cf. the second occurrence of *si cong* 寺從 below: 故燕城人，降爲隸臣，輸寺從. As *shu* 輸 in Qin legal and administrative texts is normally followed either by the thing or person that is transported/deported (e.g. *Liye* 8–82+8–129, 8–1618, 8–2008; *QLSZ* 201=*RCL* A 110) or the place (e.g. *Liye* 8–151) or office (e.g. *QLSZ* 86–87, 92=*RCL* A 47, 49; *Liye* 8–705, 8–1510) where something or somebody is transported/deported, *si cong* 寺從 is very likely a (yet unknown) place name (cf. Fu Jiayi 2007, 110–113; Luo Fuyi 1987, no. 8), probably a prefecture. Cf. the expression *Huyang gong* 胡陽公 "chief (i.e. prefect)/government of Huyang" (*Yuelu WYZ* 217–218, 219) according to which *si cong gong* 寺從公 could tentatively be interpreted as "chief of Sicong (prefecture)".

1132 *Bu chou* 不讎 means "to not correspond to the facts" (*Shiji* 107, 2853 [cf. Nienhauser IX (2011), 160]: 於是上使御史簿責魏其所言灌夫，頗不讎，欺謾。 "Thereupon the emperor ordered the chief prosecutor to charge the [marquis of] Weiqi by means of a written list of counts with what he had reported on Guan Fu. Because this report to a large extent did not correspond to the facts, [the marquis was charged with the statutory offence] deceiving and lying [to the emperor]."; *Shiji* 12, 471 [cf. Nienhauser II (2002), 239]: 五利妄言見其師，其方盡，多不讎。上乃誅五利。 "[The general of] the Five Benefits falsely stated that he had seen his teacher [of immortal ghosts]. The magician was at his wit's end, and his statement did mostly not correspond to the facts. The emperor then executed him.").

1133 *Fu* 覆 (*GSR* 1034m) *p^h(r)uk, sometimes written with the graphic variant *fu* 復 (*GSR* 1034a), in the administrative language of the Warring States period already meant "to inspect (the granaries based on inventories)" (*Hanfei* 31, 188) or "to re-examine (the text of a covenant stored in the royal archives)" (*Zuo* Ding 4,750,15: 載書[...]藏在周府，可覆視也。 "The writing of the covenant [...] was stored in the royal archives, and can be re-examined there."). In the present case, *fu* does not specifically refer to the review of legal decisions of lower authorities by the higher authorities (see footnote 1039), but

同改曰：
定名魏。故燕城人。降爲隸臣，輸寺從，去亡。158

Tong changed his statement:
"My registered name[1134] is Wei. I am originally from Yancheng.[1135] When I surrendered[1136] I was made a bond servant convict, got deported to Sicong [prefecture?], left and absconded."

訊魏：
魏亡，安取錢以補袍及買鞞刀？

We interrogated Wei:
"As you absconded, where did you take the money to have your coat[1137] patched and to buy a sheath and a knife?"

魏曰：
庸取錢。159

Wei stated:
"I earned the money from hired work."

Second Stage of Interrogation (*Confrontation*)

[Missing slip]

【詰魏：…】

[We confronted Wei: ...][1138]

【魏曰：…】
甚矣，以人莫智（知）。今吏智（知）之，未可奈可（何），請言請（情）：魏欲盜，恐□□□□□☐160得者求城旦赤衣，操，巳（已）殺

rather to the verification/examination of the suspect's statements by the lower authorities (e.g. a prefecture).

1134 For *ding ming* see footnote 685.

1135 Chen Jian (2013) identified this place name as Yancheng 燕城, a walled city in the state of Wei 魏 (*Shiji* 6, 224) to the northeast of present Yanjin in Henan (*Lishi dituji* vol. 11, 7–8, 5④; Hou Xiaorong 2009, 223).

1136 For *xiang* see footnote 622. Enemies who had surrended were made *li chen* convicts, see footnote 751 above.

1137 *Pao* 袍 "long robe" (Sun Ji 2011, 279 with illustration 61–6).

1138 The missing slip probably contained a confrontation (*jie* 詰) of Wei by the officials, cf. footnote 1139.

人，置死（屍）所，令人以爲殺人者城□□□□□□□誠以旬餘時，以二錢買不【智（知）】$_{161}$可（何）官城旦敝赤帬（裙）襦，以幐盛。佗行出高門，視可盜者。□食時到安等舍□寄□其内中。有頃，安等$_{162}$皆臥，出，魏伐刑殺安等，置赤衣死（屍）所，盜取衣器，去買（賣）行道者所。以錢買布補〼$_{163}$有母、妻、子在魏（魏）。即買大刀，欲復以盜殺人。得錢材（財），以爲用，亡之魏（魏）。未蝕而得。辠（罪）。$_{164}$

[Wei stated:[1139]
"…] because nobody knew [the truth about me]. Now that the officials got to know about it,[1140] I have no choice[1141] but to request to tell the truth:[1142] I wanted to steal[1143] [but] was afraid […] I sought for the red clothes of an earth pounder convict, which I [intended to] take and place by the corpses after having killed my victims,[1144] in order to make people believe that the murderer was an earth pounder convict. […] In fact,[1145] more than 10 days ago, I bought

---

1139 From the confession of guilt (*zui* 罪) at the end of this statement, it can be gathered that this is most probably a response to a preceding confrontation (*jie* 詰) by the officials.

1140 *Zhi* 知 with the object *zhi* 之 in the sense "to get to know about sth; to find sth. out; ascertain the facts about sth." (*Hanfei* 30, 177 [cf. Harbsmeier]: 乃僞謗樛豎以知之。"So he pretended to slander Jiao Shu in order to ascertain the facts."; *Lunyu* 7, 150 [cf. Harbsmeier]: 人必知之。"Somebody else is sure to find out."; *Zuo* Xi 32,220,11: 鄭必知之。"Zheng is bound to get to know about that.").

1141 *Wei ke nai he* 未可奈可（何） is a variant of *wu ke nai he* 無可奈何 "there is nothing one can do except/one has no choice but/there is no other way than" (*Hanshu* 94B, 3821: 單于知已無可奈何。"Shanyu knew that he had no other choice.").

1142 According to the orthographic conventions reflected by Qin and early Han legal manuscripts, *qing* 情 "truth" is always written with *qing* 請 (*FLDW* 167=*RCL* D 146; *FZS* 1=*RCL* E 1; *Yuelu WYZ* 184; *ZYS* 109, 112, 117, 145; *ENLL* 67, 121, 489, 496), which also appears to be the case here. Sometimes, especially "truth about a person/the real status of a person" is meant (*ZYS* 34: 解雖不智（知）其請（情）[…]。"Although Jie did not know the truth about her/her real status […]."; *ZYS* 113: 毛改言請（情）曰 […]。"I, Mao, amended [my statement] and told the truth saying […]."; *ENLL* 110: 證不言請 "witnesses who do not tell the truth"; *ENLL* 168, 172: 智（知）其請（情） "if they know the truth").

1143 For *dao* see footnotes 541, 557 and 795.

1144 *Sha ren* 殺人 here does not refer to the statutory offence of "killing sb./committing homicide", which in accordance with the legal regulations of 186 BC (*ENLL* 21) was to be punished with the death penalty of "casting away in the marketplace" (*qi shi* 棄市), but to the offence of *dao sha ren* 盜殺人 "killing sb. in the act of committing theft" because the offender Wei not only killed the sleeping persons, but also robbed the victims of their clothes and tools (*Yuelu WYZ* 152). Therefore, he was sentenced to the more severe death penalty of *zhe* 磔 "quartering" (*Yuelu WYZ* 166) as stipulated in early Han times (*ENLL* 66). Cf. footnote 499.

1145 For *cheng* see footnote 801.

the ragged red lower garment and short jacket of an earth pounder convict from an [unknown] office for two cash and put[1146] it into my bag.[1147] I shouldered[1148] it, went out the 'high gate' and looked for something to steal. At [...] mealtime[1149] I arrived at the field hut[1150] where An and the others had found accomodation[1151] [and hid] in one of the rooms. After a short while, when An and the others had all laid themselves down [to sleep],[1152] I came out [of my

---

1146 *Cheng* 盛 (*GSR* 818i) "to put sth. into (a container)" (*Odes* 15,2: 于以盛之，維筐及筥。"She goes to put them in vessels, there are baskets square and round."; *Shiji* 3, 104 [Nienhauser I (1994), 49]: 爲革囊盛血。"He made a leather sack, and filled blood into it."; *Hanfei* 10, 53 [cf. Harbsmeier]: 盛黃金於壺。"He put gold into a pitcher."; *Hanfei* 34, 241 [cf. Harbsmeier]: 可以盛水乎？"Can one put water into it?"; *Liye* 8–478: 盛錢木甲（匣）一。"One wooden box filled with cash.").

1147 *Teng* 縢 (*GSR* 893) "sack, bag" occurs very rarely (*Shuowen* 7B, 361a); cf. a list of clothes and household appliances in *Guan* 74, 364. It seems to be a derivation from the homophonous *teng* 縢 (*GSR* 893t) "to tie (up)" (*Odes* 128,3: 竹閉緄縢。"The bamboo laths [to which a bow is tied to keep it from warping] are tied to [the bows] with strings.").

1148 *Tuo* 佗 (*GSR* 4h) occurs in the sense "to put a burden on, load sth. on" in combination with pack animals (*Hanshu* 69, 2978) and in the figurative sense "to impose (a punishment) on sb./to burden sb. (with punishment)" (*Odes* 197,7). Cf. the semantic gloss *fu he* 負何 "carry on one's back" (*Shuowen* 8A, 371a).

1149 *Shi shi* 食時 (*Liye* 8–157v; early Han: *Mawangdui Wushier bingfang* 386; *Mawangdui Zaliaofang* 43; late Han: *Juyan xinjian* EPT43:40; *Juyan* 56.37; cf. Tomiya 2015, 136) referred to a time of day after sunrise in the early morning (Rao and Zeng 1993, 424–425 based on *Shuihudi Rishu* B 156; cf. *Zhoujiatai* 156–181, 367; *Shuihudi Rishu* B 233.1). Cf. the time schedule for officials in the Qin dynasty quoted by Yates 2012–13, 302. As the character before *shi* 食 could not be identified, it is also possible that some other period of time is meant. The time of the evening meal (*xi shi* 夕食 in *Zhoujiatai* 156–181), for example, would better fit the context where the victims soon afterwards laid themselves down to sleep.

1150 *She* 舍 "field hut, cottage" (*QLSZ* 12=*RCL* A 6: 百姓居田舍者毋敢醢（酤）酉（酒）。"Commoners living in field huts should not venture to sell wine.").

1151 *Ji* 寄 "to accomodate/lodge sb. (temporarily); to find accomodation (away from home)" (*Zuo* Xiang 14,461,17: 齊人以郲寄衛侯。"The people of Qi gave Lai to the marquis of Wei as his lodging."; *Zhanguoce* 133/64/20 [cf. Crump 1970, 189]: 願寄食門下。"He hoped that he would find accomodation and receive salary/board and lodging under his protection."; *Shiji* 92, 2609 [cf. Nienhauser VIII (2008), 69]: 常從人寄食飲。"He was constantly accomodated and fed by other people."; *FLDW* 200=*RCL* D 180: 可（何）謂旅人？寄及客，是謂旅人。"What is the meaning of 'travellers'? Lodgers as well as strangers – these are called 'travellers'.").

1152 If, in fact, *shi shi* 食時 (see footnote 1149 above) refers to some time in the evening, then *wo* 臥 is to be taken in its specific meaning "to lie down (to sleep)" (*FZS* 73=*RCL* E 22: 乙獨與妻丙晦臥堂上。"I, B, alone with my wife C lay down in the main hall at nightfall."; *Yuelu WYZ* 175).

hiding place], injured and [then] killed An and the others with cuts [of my knife], placed the red clothes [of an earth pounder convict] by the corpses, stole the clothes and tools [of An and the others] and went off to sell them to[1153] people travelling on the road. With the money I bought plain fabric to patch [my coat …] I have a mother, wife and children at Wei.[1154] Therefore I bought a big knife and wanted to use it to kill somebody in the act of committing theft again. After getting the valuables I would have used these means to abscond to Wei. Before I could carry out[1155] [this plot], I was caught. I am liable to punishment."[1156]

⧄□可（何）解？

[We confronted Wei:
"…] How do you explain[1157] this?"

魏曰：
辠（罪）。毋（無）解。165

1153 For *suo* 所 as postposition that marks the recipient or giver as object after verbs of transmitting see footnote 681 as well as Lau and Lüdke 2012, footnote 629.

1154 The kingdom of Wei 魏 was only conquered by Qin in 225 BC. According to a reference to the fifth year of King Zheng of Qin (*Yuelu WYZ* 168) – which would be the year 242 BC – the present case can probably be dated to the period before the conquest when Wei was still an independent state. A further hint towards this is that also the first year of King Zheng is mentioned in another case that was part of the same manuscript as the present case (i.e. group II, see *Yuelu WYZ* 175). It is not certain whether Wei, which was one of the three states that had emerged from the division of Jin 晉 and is therefore identified with Jin 晉 below (see *Yuelu WYZ* 166), referred to the second capital Daliang 大梁 (since 361 BC, near present Kaifeng in Henan, see *Lishi dituji* vol. I, 35–36, 7④) or to the town of the same name near present Ruicheng in southern Shanxi (*Lishi dituji* vol. I, 35–36, 3④). Cf. Cang Xiuliang 1991, 794.

1155 *Wei shi* 未蝕. *Shi* 蝕 (*GSR* 921d) *m-lək is usually known in the meaning "to eclipse" (literally "to swallow/consume the moon or the sun"). In legal manuscripts, *wei shi* refers to a principle of determining punishment for certain offences that have not been carried out, above all to illicit sexual intercourse. For the usage of *wei shi* in connection with the statutory offence of illicit sexual intercourse see footnote 1187. In this case, *wei shi* occurs in the context of robbing and killing. For attempted robbery and homicide which had not yet been carried out/completed, an offender probably was also punished less severely than for an offence that has been carried out. Cf. *dao wei you qu* 盜未有取 "theft without having appropriated [haul]" in case I.1 (*Yuelu WYZ* 015, 022).

1156 For *zui* as confession of the accused see footnotes 514 and 985.

1157 For the meaning of the concluding question *he jie* 何解 directed to the accused during the confrontation (*jie* 詰) as second stage of interrogation see footnote 800.

Wei stated:
"I am liable to punishment. I do not have [any other] explanation."[1158]

Interagency Enquiries

問如辤（辭）。臧（贓）四百一十六錢。

The [results of the] interagency enquiries[1159] corresponded to the statements.[1160] The [value of the] misappropriated goods[1161] is 416 cash.

Judgement

巳（已）論磔甕。

Judgement has already been passed[1162] to quarter[1163] Wei.

Letter of Recommendation for Investigating Officials

甕晉人，材犺（伉）。端買城旦赤衣，以盜殺人。巳（已）殺，置死（屍）所，以□令吏【弗】$_{166}$得。一人殺三人田壄（野），去居邑中市客舍，甚悍，非恆人殹（也）。有（又）買大刀，欲復盜殺人，以亡之甕（魏）。民大害殹（也）。甚微難得。$_{167}$觸等以智治韱（纖）微，謙（廉）求得。五年觸與史去疢□□⧄□□。

Wei is a man from Jin. He has an aggressive disposition.[1164] He intentionally[1165]

1158 For the implications of *wu jie* in the reply of the accused see footnote 800.

1159 For *wen* see footnote 562. The exact wording of the results of the interagency enquiries is not recorded because they apparently did not provide information that was not already known from the statements.

1160 For *ci* see footnote 564.

1161 For *zang* see footnote 592.

1162 For *lun* see footnote 540.

1163 For *zhe* see footnote 1032.

1164 *Kang* 犺 (GSR 698) *$k^{hʕ}$ang-s may stand for the homophonous *kang* 伉 (GSR 698c), which could refer to a physical condition or a character trait (*Hanshu* 8, 243 [Dubs II (1944), 211]: 選[...]伉健習騎射者，皆從軍。 "They selected [...] those who were belligerent, robust and trained on riding and [crossbow] archery to join the army."; *Hanshu* 83, 3398: 伉俠 "martial artists/fighters"; *Hanfei* 15, 80 [cf. Harbsmeier]: 太子輕而庶子伉 "when the heir apparent is a light-weight and the other potential heirs are powerful"; cf. Feng and Deng 2006, 46).
Kang is closely related to the homeophonous *gang* 剛 (GSR 697b) * $k^{ʕ}$ang "hard, strong", which also describes a character similar to the offender in the present case (*Hanfei* 10, 51 [cf. Harbsmeier]: 鮑叔牙爲人剛愎而上悍，剛則犯民以暴。 "Baoshu Ya is hard/aggressive, stubborn and overbearing. Hard/aggressive, he assaults the people with

bought the red clothes of an earth pounder convict and used them to kill people in the act of committing theft. After he had killed [the people], he placed [the red clothes] by the corpses to [...] and to cause the officials [not] to catch him/find out about him. One man who kills three people in the fields and then goes off to stay in a market guesthouse[1166] within the city is extremely impertinent.[1167] He is not a normal person. [He] furthermore bought a big knife and wanted to kill people in the act of committing theft again to abscond to Wei with [the haul]. This is a great harm for the people.[1168] [The case] was extremely obscure and difficult to solve.[1169] Chu and his colleagues with cleverness tried[1170] these obscurities,[1171] thoroughly sought for

violent force."; cf. *Hanfei* 47, 324 where *gang cai* 剛材 is defined in the following way: 交爭逆令謂之剛材。 "Being quarrelsome and disobeying orders is called '[carved from] hard timber'."; cf. also the traits *gang qiang* 剛彊 in *Xun* 3, 26 [cf. Knoblock I (1988), 175]: 剛彊猛毅。 "He is unyieldingly strong and fiercely resolute." and *Bohutong* 3/8/20 [cf. Tjan II (1952), 371]: 剛強理直謚曰武。"He who is strong, vigorous, principled and straightforward is posthumously called 'martial'." or *kang qiang* 亢強/*qiang kang* 強肮（伉）in *Guan* 84, 414 [cf. Rickett II (1998), 501]: 諸侯亢強 "the feudal lords are belligerent and strong" or *Yushu* 12).

1165 For *duan* see footnote 898.

1166 For *ke she* cf. footnote 932.

1167 *Han* 悍 "refractory, insubordinate" in legal manuscripts usually refers to the behaviour of wives or slaves. An insubordinate wife could be chastised by her husband (*FLDW* 79=*RCL* D 64). According to early Han legal stipulations, a husband who caused his insubordinate wife bodily harm was exempted from punishment under certain circumstances (*ENLL* 32: 妻悍而夫毆笞之，非以兵刃也，雖傷之，毋罪。 "If a wife is insubordinate and therefore her husband beats or canes her, then he does not commit an offence even if he injures her, unless he uses weapons or knife blades."). Male and female private slaves who were to be punished for insubordination were to be brought before the authorities by their master if he requested that they should suffer a mutilation punishment (*FZS* 42–43=*RCL* E 16; cf. *ENLL* 44), and afterwards sold (*FZS* 37–38=*RCL* E 15). See also Lau and Lüdke 2012, footnote 1455.

1168 Cf. *Yuelu WYZ* 148 and footnote 1077.

1169 Cf. *Yuelu WYZ* 147 and footnote 1076.

1170 For *zhi* see footnote 1079.

1171 *Qian wei* 鐵微 for *xian wei* 纖微 "inconspicuous, hardly visible", originally meaning "sheer fabric" (*Guan* 68, 350 [cf. Rickett II (1998), 362]: 女勤於纖微。"Women are diligent in producing sheer fabric.") is also used in a figurative sense (*Hanshi waizhuan* 9.19/69/11 [cf. Hightower 1952, 308]: 禍起於纖微。 "Disaster/misfortune starts with the inconspicuous."; *Xinshu* 8.3/57/17: 纖微皆審謂之察。"If the hardly visible is closely examined this is called 'scrutinise'."; *Bohutong* 12/32/24 [cf. Tjan II (1952), 469–470]: 纖微未見於外。"[The ruler's faults are] inconspicuous and not yet visible to the outside world."; cf. *Wei li zhi dao* 5.1).

[the criminal] and caught [him]. In the fifth year,[1172] Chu and the secretary Qu Chen[1173] [...]

今獄史觸、彭沮、衷得微難獄，磔辠（罪）$_{168}$一人。爲奏十六牒，上。觸爲令史廿二歲，年卌三。彭沮、衷勞年中令。皆請（清）絜（潔）毋（無）害，敦殼（愨）守吏，心平端禮。任謁$_{169}$課以補卒史，勸它吏。

Now the judicial secretaries Chu, Peng Ju and Zhong[1174] have solved an obscure and difficult case of one person who committed an offence being punished with quartering. They drew up a submission on 16 slips and submitted it [to the higher authorities]. Chu became secretary of the prefect[1175] when he was

---

1172 This is likely to be the fifth year of the reign of King Zheng of Qin, i.e. 242 BC. Cf. footnote 1154.

1173 A *yu shi* 獄史 "judicial secretary (of a prefecture)" named Qu Chen 去疢 also occurs in *ZYS* 197. However, as can be seen from the list of Qin names compiled by Liu Zhao (2012, 365), Qu Chen was a commonly used name in Qin times, and therefore the two texts do not necessarily refer to the same person.

1174 *Zhong* 衷 possibly is an orthographic variant of *zhong* 忠, which occurs as the personal name of a judicial secretary of a prefecture (*yu shi* 獄史) in *ZYS* 197.

1175 For *ling shi* 令史 see Takamura 2008, 11; Lau and Lüdke 2012, footnote 835; cf. Yates 2011, 347. The influential position of the *ling shi* is illustrated by the fact that they ranked third in the list of the prefecture's leading officials after the prefect and vice prefect who were held liable for undetected serious offences within their jurisdiction (*ENLL* 130, 488–489). According to a list of the officials of the prefecture of Qianling from Qin times, there were 28 *ling shi* in this prefecture. Of these, 10 had been ordered to do labour service outside their office (*Liye* 7–67+9–631, cited according to Liye Qin jiandu jiaoshi xiaozu 2014). The tomb occupant of Shuihudi tomb no. 11 was entrusted with the trial of criminal cases only six years after he had been appointed *ling shi* (*Biannianji* 13.2, 19.2). During the Qin period, the arrest of delinquents, the postmortem examination of the bodies of victims as well as investigations at the scene of crime were among the tasks of the *ling shi* (*FZS* 16, 24, 39, 48, 50, 56, 63, 74, 85=*RCL* E 7, 11, 15, 17, 18, 20, 21, 22, 23). They were also sent on punitive expeditions against rebels (*ZYS* 135). On the office of *ling shi* see also Hulsewé 1985, 39, footnote 4 on A 22. In Qin times there were also other officials besides the *ling shi*, who were especially responsible for the investigation of criminal cases, although these *yu shi* 獄史 do not occur in the above-mentioned list from the prefecture of Qianling. In lists of officials from the province of Donghai that can be dated to the late Western Han period, two to six *ling shi* and one to five *yu shi* are noted for each prefecture after the prefect (*ling* 令 or *zhang* 長), the vice prefect (*cheng* 丞) and the prefecture commander (*wei* 尉). In the salt and iron offices of the province of Donghai, there were one to three *ling shi* who were subordinates of the respective directors (*zhang* 長) and his deputy (*cheng* 丞) (*Yinwan mudu* M6D2r/v). See Xie Guihua 1997, 47–48 and Loewe 2004, 67–69. Cf. also footnotes 128 and 539.

22 years old;[1176] he is [now] 43 years old. Peng Ju and Zhong's seniority in office[1177] and age meet the legal requirements.[1178] They all are officeholders[1179] who have integrity and moral purity, are impeccable and dutiful.[1180] In their hearts, they are impartial, upright and in accordance with the rites.[1181] We recommend and guarantee for them[1182] and request evaluation [of their performance][1183] in

1176 Cf. the biography of Xi 喜, the occupant of Shuihudi tomb no. 11, who became secretary of the prefect of Anlu at the age of 21 (*Biannianji* 13.2).

1177 *Lao* 勞 "merits in office, seniority", which in the documents from Edsin Gol is given in years (usually *sui* 歲), months and sometimes even days (Shen Gang 2008, 51, 105–106). The count of years of seniority is mentioned in the *Zhong lao lü* 中勞律 from Shuihudi (*QLZC* 15–16=*RCL* C 9: 敢深益其勞歲數者，貲一甲，棄勞。 "Persons who venture to overly increase the number of their years of seniority are fined one suit of armour and their seniority is cancelled."). For the merit lists of Han-time frontier garrisons providing personal data such as official position, rank, name and seniority, knowledge and abilities, age, height or distance between place of residence and service, see the compilation of Li and Liu 1994, 551–560 and Lau and Lüdke 2012, footnote 1432. In some documents from Edsin Gol the length of *lao* and the age of officers are given together (*Juyan* 13.7, 37.57, 89.24, 179.4; *Juyan xinjian* E.P.T50:14, 52:36, 59:104). Cf. also the analyses by Chen Pan 1975; Li Zhenhong 1988; Ôba 1982, 556–563 and 1992, 137–143; Xing Yitian 1993 and Hu Pingsheng 1995.

1178 For *zhong ling* see footnote 1085.

1179 *Shou li* 守吏 "officeholder/incumbent holder of an office", for the meaning of *shou* see footnote 486.

1180 Cf. *Yuelu WYZ* 148 and footnote 1083.

1181 Cf. *Yuelu WYZ* 148 and footnote 1084.

1182 For *ren* see footnote 1086.

1183 *Ke* 課 means "to evaluate". In the manuscripts from Shuihudi, *ke* is only used for evaluating horses and cattle (*QLSZ* 13=*RCL* A 7) as well as for the amount of iron obtained from mining (*QLZC* 23=*RCL* C 14). In the context of evaluating officials *ke* can be found in early Han stipulations (*ENLL* 475–476: 有（又）以八體（體）試之，郡移其八體（體）課大（太）史，大（太）史誦課，取冣（最）一人以爲縣令史，殿者勿以爲史。三歲壹並課，取冣（最）一人以爲尚書卒史。 "Furthermore, examine them using the eight styles [of writing]. The provinces send the evaluation results on the eight styles to the grand scribe. The grand scribe reads aloud the evaluation results and selects one of the excellent candidates to become secretary of a prefect. Those with inferior [evaluation results] shall not become scribes. Once every three years combine/put together the evaluation results [of the annual examinations] and select one of the excellent candidates to become officer-scribe in the imperial secretariat."; cf. *Hanshu* 74, 3147 [Watson 1974, 192]: 歲竟丞相課其殿最，奏行賞罰而已。 All I, the chancellor, have to do is at the end of the year [determine] those who are inferior and excellent [by means of] evaluation and submit [the results] to the emperor to carry out rewards and punishments."). The result of an evaluation which qualified an official for promotion had to be *zui* 最 "excellent".

order to fill with them the ranks of the clerks-in-chief [of the province][1184] so that their example may be an encouragement for other officials.[1185]

Submission by the Prefecture – Concluding Formula

敢言之。170

We venture to report this.

1184 For *zu shi* see footnote 1087.

1185 Cf. *Yuelu* WYZ 149 and footnote 1088.

Case II.11

This case from 246 BC is the first of two cases belonging to the category of petitions for retrial (*qi ju*), which is a procedure by which a convicted person could request a retrial of his case if he considered his conviction unjustified. The present case record was apparently drawn up in the course of a second retrial, but it at least partly includes records of a first retrial as well as the original trial.

The offender had originally been charged with illicit sexual intercourse by force with his disowned wife. He was punished by Dangyang prefecture with penal labour of the category *nai* as a bond servant convict. According to Qin statutes, this was the punishment for illicit sexual intercourse, but it was apparently also applied in this case of illicit sexual intercourse by force, because the offender was caught before he could carry out the offence (*wei shi*).

As a convict, the man made a first petition for retrial, stating that the illicit sexual intercourse had been by mutual consent rather than by force. However, the agency of the minister of trials conducting the retrial came to the conclusion that his petition was unfounded and therefore sentenced him to detention among the earth pounder convicts for six years. This was the normal punishment for bond servant convicts who had committed an offence punishable by penal labour of the category *nai*.

During the second retrial, which was probably again conducted by the agency of the minister of trials at the royal court, it again became clear that objections raised by the offender against the preceding judgements were unfounded. The interrogation proved that the offender was using force when he attemped to have illicit sexual intercourse with his former wife, but was interrupted by a third person. So he was compelled to amend his statement and to confess to having attempted fornication by force. When the offender was asked for the reasons for filing a second unfounded petition, he replied that he had hoped the investigating officials would not find out the truth.

As a result of the second retrial, the offender was sentenced to a further six years of detention among the earth pounder convicts. As he had previously been sentenced to twelve years of detention (six years for his first unfounded petition for retrial and an additional six for absconding from this first detention), he was ultimately to be detained for a total of 18 years.

 | DOI 10.1163/9789004315655_019

Diplomatic Edition

▨□□□□□□□未蝕當陽論耐▨$_{171}$隸臣得之气鞫廷覆之以得之不審毄得之□□▨$_{172}$•覆視其獄尪[1186]告爲得之妻而棄晦逢得=之=捽偃尪欲與尪奸尪弗聽有□□□▨$_{173}$得之曰捽偃尪欲與奸它如尪•其鞫曰得之強與人奸未蝕審=丞□論耐得之爲隸臣$_{174}$

元年四月得之气鞫曰和與尪臥不奸•廷史賜等覆之•尪曰得之屛欲與尪奸尪弗聽捽搒毆尪它如故獄$_{175}$•得之改曰欲強與尪奸未蝕它如尪•其鞫曰得之毆屛尪欲強與奸未蝕气鞫不審=$_{176}$

•廷報之毄得之城旦六歲•今訊得=之=曰逢尪和與奸未巳聞人聲即起和與偕之尪里門宿得▨$_{177}$弗能與奸它如气鞫書•尪曰晦逢得=之=欲與尪奸 尪弗聽即捽倍屛尪欲強與尪奸尪與務$_{178}$毆搒尪=恐即逯謂得之迺之尪里門宿到□□▨與尪奸即去它如故獄$_{179}$

顛曰見得之牽尪=謂顛救吾得之言曰我□□□□□□毆顛弗救去不智它$_{180}$

雎曰尪言逢得=之=欲與尪奸尪弗聽即毆▨$_{181}$▨不智它▨$_{182}$

•得之改曰逢尪欲與奸尪不肎得之即捽屛尪揭帬欲強與奸尪與得之務未蝕奸尪謂得之迺之尪里□▨$_{183}$得之與偕欲與奸尪不肎有毆之它如尪•詰得=之=強與尪奸未蝕可故而气鞫得之曰狌吏不得=之請▨$_{184}$气=鞫=爲不審辠毆•問▨气鞫它如辤$_{185}$

•鞫之得之气鞫不審=•謂當陽嗇夫當陽隸臣得之气鞫曰□□不強與棄婦尪奸未蝕當陽論耐得$_{186}$之气鞫廷有論毄城旦皆不當•覆之得之去毄亡巳論毄十二歲而來气=鞫=不如辤以毄子縣其毄得之城$_{187}$旦六歲備前十二歲毄日$_{188}$

Edition and Translation

Second Retrial – Petition for a New Finding of Fact

▨□□□□□□□未蝕。當陽論耐【得之爲】$_{171}$隸臣。得之气（乞）鞫（鞫）。廷覆之，以得之不審毄（繫）得之【城旦六歲】。▨$_{172}$

[…] did not carry it out[1187] (the fornication with his disowned wife). Dangyang[1188]

1186 Due to typesetting issues the original character in the manuscript has in every case been replaced with *yu* 尪. For a discussion of this character see footnote 1198.

1187 *Wei shi* 未蝕 "to not have carried out (a planned criminal offence)" as a principle of determining punishment here refers to the unsuccessful attempt to commit the statutory offence of fornication/illicit sexual intercourse (*jian* 奸). It already occurs in this sense in the *Falü dawen* from Shuihudi (*FLDW* 65: 今内（納）人，人未蝕奸而得). The editors of the Shuihudi manuscripts misinterpreted this as "Supposing one lets a bad person enter, but people arrest him without letting his plot succeed […]." At the same time they explained *shi* 蝕 as *shou na* 受納 "to accept" (Shuihudi Qinmu zhujian zhengli xiaozu

[prefecture] sentenced[1189] me to be shaved[1190] [and made me] a bond servant convict.[1191] I petitioned for a [new] finding of fact.[1192] The court[1193] reviewed[1194]

1978, 179 footnote 1). However, in Qin and Han legal manuscripts *jian* 奸 does not mean "plot, conspiracy", but always refers to the statutory offence of illicit sexual intercourse, cf. footnote 1203. The exact meaning of *na* in this passage becomes clear by comparison with two passages from the *Zuozhuan* where *na* can be translated as "to introduce a girl to the ruler's bed" (*Zuo* Xiang 26,520,13: 姬納諸御，嬖。 "[Duchess mother Gong] Ji introduced her (a girl called Qi) to the [duke's] bed. [Qi] became a favourite with him."; *Zuo* Zhao 14,654,14–15: 韓宣子命斷舊獄。罪在雍子。雍子納其女於叔魚。叔魚蔽罪邢侯。 "Han Xuan Zi gave order [to Shu Yu] to settle an old criminal case. Yong Zi was guilty of the offence. He introduced his daughter [for sexual intercourse] to Shu Yu who [thereupon] pronounced [the innocent] Xing Hou guilty."). Therefore, the above passage from the *Falü dawen* (FLDW 65=RCL D 52: 內（納）奸，贖耐。今內（納）人，人未蝕奸而得，可（何）論？除。) should be translated as: "'Introducing [a girl to someone] for fornication [is punished by] paying the fee for redemption from being shaved.' Supposing [a procurer] introduces a girl to someone else, but the person in question is caught before he carried out the fornication. How is [the procurer] to be sentenced? He is to be exempted from punishment." It is obvious that this unsuccessful attempt is recognised as mitigating factor. For *wei shi* in the context of robbing and killing see *Yuelu* WYZ 164, cf. footnote 1155.

1188 Dangyang 當陽 was a prefecture within Nan province (*Hanshu* 28A, 1566; Hou Xiaorong 2009, 398–399) with its administrative seat south of present Jingmen, Hubei (*Lishi dituji* vol. II, 22–23, 6⑤). It twice occurs without any context in the Qin documents from Liye (8–2235, 8–2430r), but is not mentioned in a list of all prefectures from early Han times (ENLL 443–460).

1189 For *lun* see footnote 540.

1190 For *nai* "to be shaved" as characteristic of *li chen* 隸臣 (and *si kou* 司寇 or *hou* 候) convicts performing lenient forms of penal labour see footnote 574.

1191 For *li chen* convicts see footnote 751.

1192 For *qi ju* see footnote 390.

1193 *Ting* 廷 "court" could refer to different authorities at different levels of the administration, see section 4.2 of the introduction. Here *ting* must refer to higher authorities, either to the province or to the royal court.

1194 For *fu* see footnote 1039. In the present case, the convicted person petitioned for retrial (*qi ju* 乞鞫) because he considered his sentence to be unjustified. According to statutory provisions from early Han times, the prefecture as the lowest judicial authority had to give a full hearing to the petition, record it in writing, and pass the case on to the governor of the province, who in turn ordered provincial investigators (*du li* 都吏) to review the original sentence (ENLL 116). In pre-imperial Qin times, the investigators would first acquaint themselves with the records of the original trial and conduct a full formal criminal investigation, including a renewed interrogation of the accused and the witnesses, and a questioning of the officials who had been responsible for the original trial (ZYS 99, 106, 120–122). In the comparable case II.12 of the Yuelu Academy collection,

my case, considered [my petition] unfounded[1195] and placed me under detention [among the earth pounder convicts[1196] for six years. …]

Original Case – Initiation of Criminal Proceedings

覆視其獄：
尪告：
爲得之妻而棄。晦逢得之，得之捽偃尪，欲與尪奸。尪弗聽，有（又）□□□□$_{173}$

We inspected his case [in the course of] the review:[1197]
Yu[1198] reported:
"I [once] was the wife of Dezhi, [but] was disowned[1199] [by him]. At nightfall,[1200] I came upon Dezhi. He grabbed me by the hair,[1201] bent me down to the

the *li chen* convict Tian petitioned for retrial because he considered his conviction for fornication/illicit sexual intercourse unjustified. During the review, it became apparent that his petition was unfounded (*Yuelu* WYZ 205–206). For that reason, the sentence should be increased by one degree (*ENLL* 114). In three cases, which are recorded in the *Hanshu*, retrials were even requested posthumously after the wrongly accused had been driven to suicide (*Hanshu* 77, 3261; 76, 3223; 86, 3489; 86, 3499). There is also an example of a father who appealed to the authorities and submitted a countercharge because his son had unjustly been charged with a capital offence. This countercharge resulted in a review (*Hanshu* 76, 3204).

1195 *Bu shen* 不審 "unfounded" (*ZYS* 41, *Yuelu* WYZ 204; *ENLL* 12, 93, 112, 114, 132, 135; *QLSZ* 123–124=*RCL* A 64; *XL* 50=*RCL* B 24; *QLZC* 6, 32–33=*RCL* C 4, 20; *FLDW* 42=*RCL* D 33; *Xuanquan* 12) or "uncertain/unknown" (*ZYS* 114, *Juyan* 159.23; 229.1–2; *Dunhuang* 683; Shen Gang 2008, 26). For *shen* 審 at the end of the finding of fact (*ju* 鞫) see footnote 633.

1196 For *ji*/*xi* see footnote 569. Here *cheng dan liu sui* 城旦六歲 can be emended with regard to slip 177 below. *Xi cheng dan liu sui* 毄（繫）城旦六歲 "to be placed under detention among the earth pounder convicts for six years" is a punishment which by law was to be imposed on *li chen qie* convicts who committed an offence punishable by penal labour of the category *nai* 耐 (*Yuelu* WYZ 177, 187–188, 207; *FLDW* 109, 111, 118=*RCL* D 92, 91, 98; *ENLL* 90, 96, 97, 165). For minor offences, the detention only lasted three years (*ENLL* 97, 165), or the duration was not mentioned at all (*QLSZ* 141–142, 143=*RCL* A 65, 66; *FLDW* 132=*RCL* D 110; *ENLL* 93, 157).

1197 Cf. 覆視其故獄 "for the purpose of review we inspected his old criminal case" (*ZYS* 99).

1198 The character 㚬, consisting of the semantic determinative *jiao* 交 and the phonophoric *yu* 于 (*GSR* 97a) *Gʷ(r)a, is considered by the editors (Zhu and Chen 2013, 196 with footnote 2) to be a graphic variant of *yu* 尪 (*Shuowen* 10B, 495b) that according to the *Guangyun* (940) was read MC ʔju (OC *qʷ(r)a).

1199 For *qi* see footnote 1043.

1200 For this meaning of *hui* see footnote 1117.

1201 *Zuo* 捽 (*GSR* 490b) "to grab by the hair" (*Hanshu* 48, 2257: 不使捽抑 "does not let him be grabbed by the hair and pressed down to the ground" with the commentary by Yan Shigu;

ground[1202] and wanted to fornicate[1203] with me. I refused to obey him, [so] he also [...]."

Original Case – First Stage of Interrogation

得之曰：
捽偃尪，欲與奸。
它如尪。

Dezhi stated:
"I grabbed Yu by her hair, bent her down to the ground and wanted to fornicate with her."
Everything else corresponded to [the statement of] Yu.

Original Case – Finding of Fact

其鞫（鞫）曰：
得之強與人奸，未蝕。審。

In the finding of fact[1204] concerned (i.e. of the original case) it said:
"Dezhi [wanted to] fornicate with somebody by force,[1205] [but] he did not carry it out. [All these] are established facts."[1206]

FZS 84=RCL E 23: 甲與丙相捽。"[I], A, and B grabbed each other by the hair."; *Lü* 11, 108 [cf. Knoblock and Riegel 2000, 249]: 王子慶忌捽之投之於江。"Prince Qingji grabbed him by the hair and threw him into the river.").

1202 *Yan* 偃 "to lie down/on one's back" (*Odes* 205,5). In the meaning "to bend towards the ground" it is used for grain stalks (*Shu* Jinteng §16) or blades of grass (*Lunyu* 12, 275) bending down under the influence of heavy wind. Here, it appears to be used as a transitive verb "to bend sb. down/throw sb. to the ground".

1203 *Jian* 奸 refers to the statutory offence of fornication/illicit sexual intercourse (ZYS 20, 25, 182, 184, 186–188, 193, 195; FLDW 65, 75, 172–173=RCL D 52, 153, 151–152; FZS 95=RCL E 25; *Yuelu* WYZ 190–192; *Liye* 8–1391, 8–1675; ENLL 188–193). On *jian* 奸 see also Lau and Lüdke 2012 footnotes 679 and 1466.

1204 *Ju* 鞠 for the homophonous *ju* 鞫. For *ju* see footnote 565.

1205 *Qiang* 強 "by force" (FLDW 75=RCL D 153; *Yuelu* WYZ 176, 178, 183–184, 186; ENLL 192–193; *Xuanquan* 7) as adverbial qualifier for the statutory offence of illicit sexual intercourse/fornication in contrast to *he* 和 "by mutual consent", see footnote 1221 (cf. *he* and *qiang* in the context of taking pledges in FLDW 148=RCL D 126). Fornicators who used force were punished more severely than partners who had illicit sexual relations by mutual consent (ENLL 193: 強與人奸者，府（腐）以爲宮隸臣。"Those who fornicate with sb. by force are castrated and made bond servant convicts in the palace."). Victims of rape were not punished for illicit sexual intercourse (ENLL 190–191: 其強與奸，除所強。"If the person concerned commits fornication by force, the victim is exempted from punishment.").

1206 For *shen* see footnote 633.

Original Case – Judgement

丞□論耐得之爲隸臣。174

Vice prefect[1207] [...] sentenced[1208] Dezhi to be shaved and made him a bond servant convict.

First Retrial – Petition for a New Finding of Fact

元年四月得之气（乞）鞫曰:
和與尪臥，不奸。

In the fourth month of the first year[1209] Dezhi petitioned for a [new] finding of fact stating:
"I lay down[1210] together with Yu by mutual consent.[1211] We did not fornicate."

廷史賜等覆之。

Court secretary[1212] Ci[1213] and his colleagues reviewed [the case].

1207 *Cheng* 丞 here probably refers to the vice prefect of Dangyang because in the final notification of the higher authorities Dezhi is mentioned as a *li chen* convict of the prefecture of Dangyang. For the office of *cheng* see footnote 488.

1208 For *lun* see footnote 540. A citation from a Qin statute in ZYS 182 constitutes the legal basis for this judgement: 律曰：[...]奸者，耐爲隸（隸）臣妾。 "The statutes say: [...] Those who commit fornication/have illicit sexual relations are punished by being shaved and made *li chen qie* convicts." The use of force (*qiang jian* 強奸) was apparently not taken into account as aggravating circumstance when determining the punishment (cf. ENLL 193), probably because Dezhi could not carry out the intended offence.

1209 The fourth month of the first year of the reign of King Zheng of Qin lasted from the 3rd until the 31st of May 246 BC (cf. Xu Xiqi 1997, 1193 with Zhang Peiyu 2007, 72 and Li Zhonglin 2012, 65).

1210 *Wo* 臥 "to lie down to sleep" (ZYS 17; FZS 73=RCL E 22) does not necessarily have sexual connotations. Cf. footnote 1152.

1211 For *he* 和 "by mutual consent" see footnote 1221.

1212 *Ting shi* 廷史 appears in *Zou yan shu* case no. 21 as a member of the staff of the minister of trials (*ting wei* 廷尉) at the royal/imperial court who took part in discussing a case and reaching a verdict (ZYS 189). In the commentary on a reference in the *Hanshu*, this official is described as "secretary of the *ting wei*" (*Hanshu* 23, 1102 [cf. Hulsewé 1955, 338]: 今遣廷史與郡鞠獄。"At present there are sent out court secretaries to investigate criminal cases together with the [officials of the] province." with gloss by Ru Chun). For the position of *ting shi* see also An and Xiong 2007, 156 and Bielenstein 1980, 38. Cf. further references (ZYS 184 [cf. Nylan 2005–06, 30]: 廷尉、正始、監弘、廷史武等卅人議當之。"The minister of trials [Gou], trial judge Shi, inspector Hong, court secretary Wu, altogether 30 person, delivered a legal opinion and put forward a proposal for a judgement

First Retrial – First Stage of Interrogation

尪曰：
得之庰（屛），欲與尪奸，尪弗聽，捽搒毆尪。
它如故獄。175

Yu stated:
"Dezhi made me fall to the ground[1214] and wanted to fornicate with me, [but]

---

in the case."; *ZYS* 189: 今廷史申徭使而後來，非廷尉當。"Now court secretary Shen, who had only just returned from an assignment to work, considers the proposed judgement of the minister of trials as not justified."; *Xuanquan* 31: 給事廷史刑壽爲詔獄。"The court secretary on duty Xing Shou was ordered by the emperor to try criminal cases."; *Shiji* 122, 3147 [cf. Watson 1993, vol. II, 397–398]: 王温舒者[…]爲吏，以治獄至廷史。"Wang Wenshu […] became an official and on account of his trying of criminal cases he came to the position of court secretary."; *Shiji* 122, 3154: 杜周初徵爲廷史 "when Du Zhou was first appointed as court secretary"; *Hanshu* 23, 1102: 廷史路温舒上疏。"Lu Wenshu, the court secretary, presented an exposition."). The above evidence suggests that the *ting shi* can be assigned to the agency of the minister of trials at the royal/imperial court. This means that the revision proceedings as a result of the convicted man's petition in this case as well as in the comparable case no. 17 of the *Zou yan shu* were apparently initiated by the authorities of the minister of trials.

1213 A judicial secretary (*yu shi* 獄史) of the prefecture of Yong 雍 with the same name is mentioned in case no. 17 of the *Zou yan shu* (*ZYS* 106, 120), which can also be dated to the year 246 BC. It is, however, highly unlikely that the same person is referred to in both cases because the prefectures and the agency of the minister of trials at the court are authorities at different levels of the administration. Furthermore, Dangyang prefecture in the present case belongs to Nan province, whereas Yong prefecture in case no. 17 of the *Zou yan shu* is part of the metropolitan area (Neishi 内史), which means that the trials were conducted at different places.

1214 Elsewhere the character 庰 (Zhang Shouzhong 1994, 148) only occurs in the *Feng zhen shi* from Shuihudi (*FZS* 84=*RCL* E 23: 與同里大女子丙鬭，甲與丙相捽，丙債庰甲。"[I, A,] fought with the adult woman C from the same quarter. I and C grabbed each other by the hair. C threw me to the ground."). The editors (Shuihudi Qinmu zhujian zhengli xiaozu 1978, 275 with footnote 3) identified this character with *bing* 屛 (*Shuowen* 9B, 444a), probably a variant of *bing* 屏 (*GSR* 824f) *peŋʔ, but this identification is doubtful because *bing* 屛 has the phonophoric *bing* 幷 (*GSR* 824a) *peŋ (OC rhyme class *geng* 耕) and not the phonophoric *jian* 幵 (*GSR* 239a) *kˤen (OC rhyme class *yuan*$_2$ 元) as the character in question. According to the phonologists Karlgren (*GSR*), Pan Wuyun (TLS) and Zhengzhang Shangfang (2003, 280–281, 369–370) as well as the palaeographer Huang Dekuan (2007, 2620–2622), the two phonophorics constitute different *xie sheng* series (the contrary view was held by Shen Jianshi, cf. *xie sheng* series no. 27 in Shen Jianshi 1985, 43–47). Huang Dekuan (2007, 2622) identifies the character 庰 with *xi* 屛, which is not found in the sources of pre-Han and Han times, but only in the medieval dictionary *Yupian* (AD 548), where it is glossed as *dao di* 倒地 "to fall to the ground".

I refused to obey him, [so] he grabbed me by the hair, hit me with a stick[1215] and beat[1216] me [with his hand]."

According to the *Yupian*, *xi* has the same sound value (*yin* 音) as *qi* 溪 (*GSR* 876q) *khˤe, which belongs to the MC rhyme class *qi* 齊. Other phonological data is not provided (*xi* does not occur in the *Guangyun*). Some words from the *xie sheng* series *GSR* 239 (*jian* 幵, etc.) can actually be assigned to the MC rhyme class *qi*, as for instance *ji* 笄 (*GSR* 586a). Traditionally, *ji* 笄 is classified as belonging to the OC rhyme class *zhi* 脂 (Dong Tonghe 1948, 224) and therefore should be reconstructed as OC *kˤij, whereas Starostin sorted *ji* 笄 into the OC rhyme class *ge*$_2$ 歌 (OC *kēj) and Pan Wuyun or Zhengzhang Shangfang into the OC rhyme class *jia* 佳/*zhi* 支 (OC *kee or *k-ŋee). It is difficult to decide which reconstruction is correct, but the possible relationship to *qi* 稽 (*GSR* 552o) *kʰˤijʔ "bow (the head/forehead) to the ground" (*Odes* 209,6; 262,5; *Hanshu* 54, 2444) would come down in favour of the rhyme class *zhi* 脂. In *FZS* 84, *xi* 幵 seems to be a synonym of the preceding verb *fen* 僨 (*GSR* 437h) "to fall down, overturn" (*Zuo* Yin 3,11,14: 鄭伯之車僨於濟。"The carriage of the earl of Zheng was overturned into the [river] Ji."; *Hanshu* 49, 2284: 輸者僨於道。"Those who transported them/it fell/dropped [dead] on the roads."). This interpretation would then accord with the present case where *xi* must have a similar meaning as *yan* 偃, "to bend sb. down", which was used in the preceding report by Yu (cf. *Yuelu WYZ* 173 and footnote 1202).

1215 *Peng* 搒 (*Juyan* 4.9; *Gangu Hanjian* 7, 11=*Sanjian* 34, 38) for the homophonous *peng* 榜 (*GSR* 740p') *bˤraŋ "to cane, beat with a stick/cane" (*Shiji* 87, 2561 [cf. Bodde 1938, 51]: 輒使人復榜之。"[Zhao Gao] immediately ordered men to flog him anew."). *Peng* mostly occurs in the context of torture during interrogation in the compounds *peng lue* 榜掠 "to torture sb. with blows of a stick/cane" (*Hanshu* 77, 3262; *Shiji* 87, 2561 [cf. Bodde 1938, 50]: 趙高治斯，榜掠千餘，不勝痛，自誣服。"When Zhao Gao tried (caned?) [Li] Si, he gave him a flogging of more than one thousand strokes so that [the latter], unable to endure the pain, falsely confessed.") or *peng chi* 榜笞 "to cane, to beat with a stick/cane" (*Houhanshu* 3, 146; *Shiji* 89, 2584=*Hanshu* 32, 1840–1841; *Jijiupian* 4, 302; *Juyan xinjian* E.P.T59:123; cf. *Gangu Hanjian* 11=*Sanjian* 38). In connection with *ou* 毆, *peng* only occurs in the present case (cf. *Yuelu WYZ* 179).

1216 In a legal context, *ou* 毆 "to beat" referred to beating another person without causing physical injury, in contrast to *shang* 傷, which referred to any assault that resulted in bodily harm (*ENLL* 28). Beating was a punishable offence if directed towards certain classes of people to whom respect was owed due to their position in the family or the society in general. Punishments varied according to social status or position of the perpetrator and the victim. Punishments ranged from the death penalty to low pecuniary fines. The statutes distinguished between domestic beating, beating of commoners by slaves or convicts, beating of holders of ranks and beating incidents involving an official. In the present case no other family ties than the relationship between a husband and his former wife are relevant. According to early Han statutes, a husband was authorised to beat his refractory wife with a cane and could even injure her without being punished if he did not use weapons or knife blades (*ENLL* 32), whereas a wife who beat her husband was sentenced to being shaved (*nai* 耐) and made a *li qie* 隸妾 convict (*ENLL* 33). However, because, in the present case, the man Dezhi had disowned his wife and no

Everything else corresponded to the original case.

得之改曰：
欲強與尪奸，未蝕。
它如尪。

Dezhi changed his statement:
"I wanted to fornicate with Yu by force, [but] I did not carry it out."
Everything else corresponded to [the statement of] Yu.

First Retrial – Finding of Fact

其鞫曰：
得之毆庰（屏）尪。欲強與奸，未蝕。气（乞）鞫不審。審。176

In the finding of fact concerned (i.e. of the first review) it said:
"Dezhi beat Yu and made her fall to the ground. He wanted to fornicate with her by force, [but] he did not carry it out. His petition for a [new] finding of fact is unfounded. [All these] are established facts."

First Retrial – Judgement

廷報之：
毄（繫）得之城旦六歲。

The court gave [the following] response[1217] [to the submission]:
"Place Dezhi under detention among the earth pounder convicts for six years."[1218]

---

officials, slaves or convicts were involved, only the stipulations concerning beating outside the family could be applied. In these cases, the punishment depended on the ranks of the perpetrator and his victim: If a holder of a lower rank beat the holder of a higher rank, the perpetrator was fined four ounces of gold. If perpetrator and victim were of equal rank, the perpetrator was fined two ounces of gold (*ENLL* 28). Only the latter punishment should have been applicable in the present case.

1217 In eight out of ten references to *ting bao* 廷報 in the *Zou yan shu*, *ting* refers to the agency of the minister of trials (*ting wei*) because only this agency could have acted as a higher authority for a province that submitted a doubtful criminal case (*ZYS* 50, 52–55, 57, 59–60, 62; cf. *ZYS* 7, 34). In the present context, this administrative affiliation also makes sense since a court secretary (*ting shi* 廷史) as a member of the staff of the minister of trials is mentioned earlier (cf. *Yuelu WYZ* 175 and footnote 1212). For different identifications of *ting* see footnote 1193. For *bao* see footnote 581.

1218 For the possible legal basis of this judgement cf. *ENLL* 90: 隸臣妾及收人有耐罪，毄（繫）城旦舂六歲 。"Bond servant convicts as well as relatives of criminals held in custody who commit an offence [punished by penal labour] of the *nai* category are placed

Second Retrial – First Stage of Interrogation

今訊得之，得之曰：
逢尪，和與奸。未巳（已），聞人聲。即起，和與偕之尪里門宿。得【之】$_{177}$弗能與奸。
它如气（乞）鞫書。

Now,[1219] when we interrogated[1220] Dezhi [again in the course of the second review], he stated:
"I came upon Yu and fornicated with her by mutual consent.[1221] Before we had finished, I heard somebody's voice. I immediately rose [from the ground] and with [Yu's] consent went to a lodging[1222] [near the] gate of her quarter together with Yu.[1223] I was not able to fornicate with [Yu]."
Everything else corresponded to the document of the petition for a [new] finding of fact.

---

under detention among the earth pounder convicts for six years." For detention among the earth pounder convicts cf. footnote 1196.

1219 For *jin*, which introduces the actual case (in contrast to earlier proceedings), see footnote 673.

1220 For *xun* see footnote 830.

1221 *He* 和 "by mutual consent" (ZYS 184) occurs as an adverbial qualifier of illicit sexual intercourse/fornication (*jian* 奸). *He jian* was punished less severely than illicit sexual intercourse by force (*qiang* 強), see footnote 1208 (cf. *ENLL* 192: 諸與人妻和奸，及其所與皆完爲城旦舂。"All those who have illicit sexual intercourse/fornicate with another's wife by mutual consent as well as those [wives] who fornicate with [other men], will be made earth and grain pounder convicts without mutilation."; *Xuanquan* 7). See also footnote 1205.

1222 *Su* 宿 designated a lodging outside the city or at the city gates, which according to the systematising description of the *Zhouli* is said to have been erected every 30 *li* in contrast to the larger guesthouses (*hou guan* 候館) at the marketplaces (*Zhouli* 13, 728b: 凡國野之道，十里有廬，廬有飲食；三十里有宿，宿有路室，路室有委；五十里有市，市有候館，候館有積。"On the roads in the open country outside the towns every ten *li* there is a hut; in the hut, food and drink is provided; every 30 *li* there is a hostel; in the hostel there are guestrooms, in the guestrooms there are stocks [of food]; every 50 *li* there is a market; at the market there is a *hou guan*, in the *hou guan*, there are stocks [of food]."). *Su* is also used verbally in the sense "to spend the night" (*Odes* 188,2: 昏姻之故，言就爾宿。"With a view to [our] marriage, I went and lodged with you."; *Odes* 284,2: 有客宿宿。"There is a guest who stays overnight."; *Hanfei* 10, 42 [cf. Harbsmeier]: 設舍以宿。"Set up a hut to stay for the night."; *Lunyu* 18, 394 [cf. Harbsmeier]: 止子路宿。"[The old man] made Zilu stay for the night.").

1223 *Xie* 偕 "together" (cf. *yu mou xie* 與某偕 "together with person X", see *Liye* 8–1558r; *Yuelu* WYZ 238, 242; *Odes* 31,4; 82,2; 94,2; 133,2).

尪曰：
晦逢得之。得之欲與尪奸，尪弗聽，即捽倍（踣）庰（屏）尪。欲強與尪奸。尪與務$_{178}$毆搒尪。尪恐，即逯（遯/遁）謂得之：逎（遒）之尪里門宿。到□□☒與尪奸，即去。
它如故獄。$_{179}$

Yu stated:
"At night-time I came upon Dezhi. He wanted to fornicate with me, [but] I refused to obey him, [so] he grabbed me by the hair, bent me forward[1224] and made me fall to the ground. He wanted to fornicate with me by force. When I struggled[1225] with him, he beat and hit me with a stick. I was afraid, so I evasively(?)[1226] said to him: '[Let us] together[1227] go to a lodging [near the]

1224 With regard to the previously mentioned *xi* 庰 "to (make sb.) fall down to the ground" and *yan* 偃 "to bend sb. down", *bei* 倍 (GSR 999c') *bˤəʔ is probably used for the homeophonous *bo* 踣 (GSR 999e') *bˤək "knock sb. down to the ground/to floor sb." (*Zuo* Xiang 14,460,3: 與晉踣之。"Along with Jin, we laid it (the deer) prostrate on the ground.") or "to cause to stumble/fall; overthrow (a state)" (*Zuo* Xiang 11,450,12: 踣其國家。"His state be utterly overthrown.").

1225 *Wu* 務 (GSR 1109j), known in the figurative sense "to wrestle with, strive/struggle for" (*Hanfei* 6, 22 [cf. Harbsmeier]: 其群臣官吏皆務所以亂，而不務所以治也。"Many ministers and officials were all striving for sth. that would lead to disorder, but were not striving for sth. that would lead to order."). The term is obviously used here literally as "to struggle with/against sb., to wrestle(?)".

1226 The character was identified as *lu* 逯 (GSR 1208) *rok and interpreted as loan graph for *miu* 謬 (GSR 1069m) *m-riw-s (Pan Wuyun: *mGrus) in the meaning "sham, pretend, feign" by the editors (Zhu and Chen 2013, 198 with footnote 15) who cite a reference from the *Shiji* (79, 2420 [cf. Nienhauser VII (1994), 247]: 復謬曰：何爲不可？ "[The Marquis of Ying] replied hypocritically saying: 'What would be wrong with this ?'"). However, there is no evidence for the use of *lu* 逯 as loan for *miu* 謬. The reading of the character is rather uncertain, so it is also difficult to determine the degree of phonological similarity.
The character in question could also be identified as *dun* 逯, an older graphic variant of *dun* 遯 (GSR 428d) *lˤunʔ-s "to withdraw", euphemistic for "to flee" (*Odes* 258,5: 寧俾我遯? "Why does [Heaven] cause us to skulk off?"). The Mawangdui version of the *Yijing* has *yuan* 掾 (GSR 171) *lon-s (*Mawangdui Zhouyi* 3) from the same *xie sheng* series instead of *dun* 遯 in the received *Yijing* version (*Yi* 4, 48a/b); cf. Wang Hui 2008, 663; Bai Yulan 2012, 780. For the interchangeability of the two lower right phonophoric elements of *yuan* 掾 and *lu* 錄 in the manuscripts of the Qin and early Han period see Lau and Lüdke 2012, footnote 972. *Dun* 遁 (GSR 465e), another common variant of *dun* 遯 (cf. Wang Li 1982, 515) that is used in the compound *dun ci* 遁辭 "evasive words"(*Meng* 3, 123), would also make sense in the present context.

gate of my quarter.' [When] we arrived […] fornicate with me, then he left." Everything else corresponded to the original case.

顛曰：
見得之牽尪。尪謂顛：救吾！得之言曰：我□□□□□□毆（也）。顛弗救，去。不智（知）它。$_{180}$

Dian stated:
"I saw Dezhi dragging Yu along.[1228] She said to me: 'Rescue me!' Dezhi said: 'We […].' I, Dian, failed to rescue her and left. I do not know about anything else."

雎曰：
尪言：逢得之。得之欲與尪奸，尪弗聽，即毆▨$_{181}$▨不智（知）它。$_{182}$

Ju stated:
"Yu reported to me: 'I came upon Dezhi. He wanted to fornicate with me, [but] I refused to obey him, [so] he beat [me…].' I do not know about anything else."

得之改曰：
逢尪，欲與奸。尪不肎（肯），得之即捽庰（屏）尪，揭帬（裙）欲強與奸。尪與得之務。未蝕奸，尪謂得之：迺（遒）之尪里【門宿。】$_{183}$得之與偕，欲與奸。尪不肎（肯），有（又）毆之。
它如尪。

Dezhi changed his statement:

1227 The editors (Zhu and Chen 2013, 198 with footnote 16) interpret 迺 as graphic variant of *qiu* 遒 (GSR 1096o) *dzu/tsu (Pan Wuyun: *sklu/sglu). By comparison with the parallel passage 和與偕之尪里門宿 (*Yuelu* WYZ 177) they also draw the conclusion that *qiu* 遒 should be interpreted as a synonym of *xie* 偕, which as an adverb means "together". The editors refer to the similar clause 與[…]偤（遒）之國 (*Jianshui Jinguan Hanjian* 73EJT1:1), where this meaning also makes sense. The adverb *qiu* might derive from the verb meaning "to collect, to bring together" (*Odes* 157,3: 四國是遒。"The states of the realm, them he brought together."; *Odes* 304,4: 百祿是遒。"All the blessings, them he brought together.").

1228 *Qian* 牽 (GSR 366k) "to pull/drag cattle on a rope" (*Meng* 1, 47 [cf. Lau 1984, 13]: 有牽牛而過堂下者。"He saw someone passing below the hall, pulling an ox."; *Zuo* Xuan 12,311,6: 鄭伯肉袒牽羊。"The earl of Zheng exposed his shoulder and dragged a sheep on a rope [as a symbol of his surrender]."; ZYS 101–102: 毛牽黑牝牛來。"Mao came here dragging a black cow on a rope."). It could also be understood figuratively "to be pulled about (against one's will)" (*Hanfei* 14, 75 [cf. Harbsmeier]: 而不以牽於世俗之言。"And they were not pulled about by the fashionable proposals of their time.").

"I came upon Yu and wanted to fornicate with her. She was not willing,[1229] [so] I grabbed her by the hair and made her fall to the ground, lifted[1230] her skirt and wanted to fornicate with her by force. She struggled with me. [Before] I had carried out the fornication, she said to me: '[Let us] together go to [a lodging near the gate] of my quarter.' I [went] together with her and wanted to fornicate with her. Yu was [still] not willing, [so] I beat her again."
Everything else corresponded to [the statement of] Yu.

Second Retrial – Second Stage of Interrogation (*Confrontation*)

詰得之：
得之強與尪奸，未蝕。可（何）故而气（乞）鞫？

We confronted[1231] Dezhi:
"You [wanted to] fornicate with Yu by force, but did not carry this out. Why did you petition for a [new] finding of fact?"

得之曰：
㺘（幸）吏不得得之請（情）。【□】$_{184}$气（乞）鞫。气（乞）鞫不審，辠（罪）殹（也）。

Dezhi stated:
"I was hoping[1232] that you would not find out the truth[1233] about me. [...] petitioned for a [new] finding of fact. As this petition for a [new] finding of fact was unfounded, I am liable to punishment."

1229 *Ken* 肎 for *ken* 肯 as auxiliary verb "to be willing (to do sth.)" (*FZS* 93=*RCL* E 24; *Yuelu WYZ* 227).

1230 *Qi* 揭 "lift (the skirt when wading through a ford)" (*Odes* 34,1: 深則厲，淺則揭。"Where it is deep, they wet their dress; where it is shallow, they lift their skirts.").

1231 For *jie* see footnote 792.

1232 On this way to write *xing* 幸 see footnote 897. *Xing* also occurred in the meaning "to hope for (a fortunate turn of events), to gamble on sth." (*Shiji* 8, 392 [cf. Nienhauser II (2002), 87]: 盧綰[...]幸上病愈自入謝。"Lu Wan [...] hoped that the sovereign's illness would improve and he could personally come in to apologise."; *Hanfei* 19, 94 [cf. Harbsmeier]: 有罪而幸免。"They will gamble on being relieved from punishment when they have committed an offence."; *Hanfei* 26, 151 [cf. Harbsmeier]: 不幸亂臣之無詐也。"One does not nourish unrealistic hopes that rebellious ministers are without deceit."; *Shiji* 84, 2485 [cf. Nienhauser VII (1994), 298]: 冀幸君之一悟，俗之一改也。"He hoped that his lord would awaken completely and convention would be reformed completely.").

1233 For *qing* 請 as the normal character used to write *qing* 情 "truth" in Qin and early Han legal manuscripts see footnote 1142.

Second Retrial – Interagency Enquiries

問：
〼气（乞）鞫。
它如辤（辭）。$_{185}$

[Results of the] interagency enquiries:
[…] petition for a [new] finding of fact.
Everything else corresponded to the statements.

Second Retrial – Finding of Fact

鞫之：
得之气（乞）鞫不審。審。

Finding of fact:
Dezhi's petition for a [new] finding of fact was unfounded. This is an established fact.

Notification of Competent Officials by the Agency of the Minister of Trials (Judgement)

謂當陽嗇夫：
當陽隸臣得之气（乞）鞫曰：
□□[1234]，不強與棄婦尪奸，未蝕。當陽論耐，得$_{186}$之气（乞）鞫，廷有（又）論毄（繫）城旦。皆不當。
覆之：
得之去毄（繫）亡。巳（已）論毄（繫）十二歲，而來气（乞）鞫，气（乞）鞫不如辤（辭），以毄（繫）子縣。其毄（繫）得之城$_{187}$旦六歲，備前十二歲毄（繫）日。$_{188}$

Notification[1235] to the overseer[1236] of Dangyang [prefecture]:
The bond servant convict Dezhi from Dangyang [prefecture] petitioned for a [new] finding of fact stating: "[…] I did not fornicate with my disowned wife Yu

1234 These two characters, which look similar to the later *kaishu*-form of the character *wang* 亡, have not been deciphered yet. Seen from the context one might guess that they indicate parts of text, which were left out or already missing/undecipherable in the model that was probably copied.

1235 *Wei* 謂 sometimes referred to a written notification by the higher authorities (*ZYS* 26, 121; *Yuelu WYZ* 205; *Liye* 8–61r, 8–657r, 8–755r, 8–1560r, etc.).

1236 As is sometimes the case in other legal manuscripts, the head (*ling* 令 or *zhang* 長) of a *xian* 縣 (*Yuelu WYZ* 205; *Yushu* 1; *QLSZ* 21, 120=*RCL* A 19, 64; *QLZC* 19, 39= *RCL* C 12, 25; *ZYS* 26, 121) is here referrred to as *se fu* 嗇夫 (see Qiu Xigui 1981, 226–229 and Lau and Lüdke 2012, footnote 708).

by force [because] I did not carry it out. [The vice prefect of] Dangyang sentenced [me] to be shaved [and made me a bond servant convict]. I petitioned for a [new] finding of fact, [but] the court sentenced me [again] to be placed under detention among the earth pounder convicts. All these [judgements] are unjustified."

[We] reviewed [the case]:

Dezhi left detention and absconded. After judgement had already been passed to place him under detention for 12 years,[1237] he came here and petitioned for a [new] finding of fact [again]. His petition did not correspond to the statements [of the victim and witnesses].[1238] For this, he is to be placed under detention in your prefecture. [Before] Dezhi is to be placed under detention as an earth pounder convict for [another] six years, he must fulfil[1239]

1237 These twelve years of detention among the earth pounder convicts are justified as follows: First, Dezhi was sentenced to labour service as a bond servant convict (for attempted rape, see *Yuelu* WYZ 174 above with footnote 1208). Then he was sentenced to six years of detention among the earth pounder convicts (for his first unfounded petition for retrial, see *Yuelu* WYZ 186–187, cf. ENLL 114). Afterwards, he apparently absconded from this six-year-detention and for this was sentenced to another six years of detention among the earth pounder convicts, which resulted in overall twelve years of detention (*Yuelu* WYZ 187). Whereas in Qin times the period of detention was only extended, in early Han times a higher degree of punishment would have been applied (cf. ENLL 165: 隸臣妾、收人亡，[…]其去毄（繫）三歲亡，毄（繫）六歲；去毄（繫）六歲亡，完爲城旦舂。"Bond servant convicts and relatives of criminals held in custody who abscond […] if they abscond from a three-year-detention, they will be placed under detention for six years; if they abscond from a six-year-detention, they will be made intact earth pounder convicts.").

1238 *Bu ru ci* 不如辤（辭）"not corresponding to the statements" (QLZC 35=RCL C 22: 冗募歸，辭曰日已備，致未來、不如辭，貲日四月居邊。"When those who were recruited for a temporary task return home and the statement is made: 'The days have been completed', whereas the documents have not yet come or do not agree with the statement, the fine is four months station at the frontier per day."). Here *bu ru ci* can be identified with *qi ju bu shen* 乞鞫不審.

1239 For *bei* 備 in the context of periods of detention see FLDW 132=RCL D 110: 隸臣妾毄（繫）城旦舂，去亡，已奔，未論而自出，當治（笞）五十，備毄（繫）日。"Bond servant convicts detained among the earth pounder convicts who abscond and run away, but give themselves up before having been sentenced, are, by law, to be caned fifty strokes; they have to fulfil their days of detention." and ENLL 90–91: 隸臣妾及收人有耐罪，毄（繫）城旦舂六歲。毄（繫）日未備而復有耐罪，完爲城旦舂。"Bond servant convicts as well as relatives of criminals held in custody who commit an offence [punished by penal labour] of the *nai* category are placed under detention among the earth pounder convicts for six years. If they commit an offence [punished by penal labour] of the *nai* category again before their days of detention have been fulfilled, they are made earth pounder convicts, but are left unmutilated." Cf. also the expressions

the days of the previous[1240] 12 years of detention [he was sentenced to].

---

qi ri wei bei 其日未備 "before their time/term has been completed" (QLSZ 138, 142=RCL A 68, 65), and *ri yi bei* 日已備 "the (number of) days has been completed" (QLZC 35=RCL C 22).

1240 *Qian* 前 is used here as an attribute in the sense of "previous, former, earlier" as in *qian yan* 前言 "first proposals" (*Hanfei* 18, 86) or "earlier statement" (*Lunyu* 17, 369), *qian gong* 前功 "previous merit" (*Zhanguoce* 27/9/25–26) or *qian hao* 前好 "former ties of friendship" (*Zuo* Xuan 12,311,10).

Case II.12

Like the preceding case, this one involves a petition for retrial. The offender, a bond servant convict, was charged with the statutory offence of fornicating by mutual consent with a woman interned in a government workshop. According to Qin statutes, an offender was to be punished with penal labour of the category *nai* for fornication. On this legal basis, the competent judicial officials passed a judgement. In his petition for retrial, the offender challenged this judgement.

During the first stage of interrogation of the retrial the offender denied that he had in fact committed fornication with the internee, who was his cousin, although he had formerly acknowledged the offence directly after the arrest. Another bond servant convict who had arrested the fornicating couple testified that he had in fact arrested both offenders *in flagrante* and that they had also confessed. In addition, he informed the judicial officials about bribes that had been offered to him by relatives of the woman. The objective of this offer had been to get him as an eyewitness to amend his statement insofar that he did not arrest the couple *in flagrante*. He first accepted the bribes but later gave them back, fearing that the authorities could find out about this without reporting the incident. The official in charge of the internees in the government workshop admitted that the couple had been arrested by his order and that he had obtained the confessions of the accused without resorting to torture. The offender still claimed that he had not been arrested *in flagrante*, as it was required by a special provision for prosecuting fornicators, but he was unable to explain the contradictions between his statements and those of his sexual partner and witnesses.

In the finding of fact, the judicial officials pointed out the differences in the statements and drew the conclusion that the petition of the offender was unfounded. However, they added that this offence would be covered by an amnesty.

The officials of the agency of the minister of trials notified the responsible prefect of the results of their investigation. They decided that the offender should by law be placed under detention among the earth pounder convicts for twelve years. This cumulative sentence consisted of six years detention for an offence punishable with penal labour of the category *nai* committed by bond servant convicts and of an additional six years of detention for the unfounded petition for retrial. However, the offender was exempted from this detention due to the amnesty and was simply made a bond servant convict again.

 | DOI 10.1163/9789004315655_020

Diplomatic Edition

⧄□隸臣□負斧質气鞫曰□⧄$_{189}$
今訊田=曰市田姑姊子雖與和奸與叚子⧄$_{190}$不奸毋智捕田=仁奸其實未奸辤丞詔謁更治詔不許它如气鞫書$_{191}$
•毋智曰□史□□□□□□□□□□□□□□□□□□□□□□□候旦田來與市臥上□□□$_{192}$捕詣田市服仁奸未論市弟夫=驩親走馬路後請貨毋智錢四千曰更言吏不捕田市校上毋智⧄$_{193}$受錢恐吏智不敢自言環錢它如故獄•相曰主治瓣市聞田數從市奸毄所令毋智捕弗治諒田市仁$_{194}$奸它如毋智•驩路曰市令驩路貨毋智以告田=曰剸爲之它如毋智$_{195}$
⧄田妻曰□□□□□□⧄$_{196}$⧄田市言如毋智$_{197}$
•田曰毋智不捕田校上捕田時田不奸驩路以市言告田貨毋智錢田狌除毋辠即弗止不智市□□$_{198}$云故它如驩路及前•爨等言如故獄•詔曰論□田=謁更治詔謂巳服仁奸今獄夬乃曰不奸田嘗□$_{199}$毋智令轉□且有□辠田即受令它如爨等•以言不同詣訊言各如前$_{200}$
詰相令毋智捕田市可解_相曰怒田市奸官府毋它解$_{201}$
•詰田_夏陽吏不治諒田市仁奸_今覆吏訊市=言如故獄田云未奸可解_田曰未奸而毋以解市言$_{202}$
•問驩路以赦前貨毋智以後遝它如辤$_{203}$
•鞫之田與市和奸毋智捕校上田雖不服而毋以解驩路毋智市言田負斧質气鞫不審□□□□$_{204}$它爲後發覺皆審•謂㲋嗇夫重泉隸臣田負斧質气鞫曰不與女子市奸夏陽論耐田爲隸$_{205}$臣不當•覆之市□與田和奸隸臣毋智捕校上田不服而毋以解市毋智言其气鞫不審田毄子縣$_{206}$當毄城旦十二歲遝己巳赦其赦除田復爲隸臣□□重泉夏陽$_{207}$

Edition and Translation

Retrial – Petition for a New Finding of Fact

⧄□隸臣【田】負斧質气（乞）鞫曰：□⧄$_{189}$
[…] The bond servant convict[1241] [Tian] who bore executioner's axe and block,[1242] petitioned for a [new] finding of fact[1243] stating: "[…]."

1241 For *li chen* convicts see footnote 751.

1242 *Fu* 斧 "executioner's axe" and *zhi* 質 "executioner's block" were the implements of execution (see commentary of Yan Shigu in *Hanshu* 31, 1806; Cang Xiuliang 1996, 399). These implements were used in symbolic acts before carrying out death penalties or mutilation punishments in public. In the Spring and Autumn period, criminals were burdened with these implements (*Zuo* Zhao 4,593,18: 王[…]負之斧鉞，以徇於諸侯，使言曰：無或如齊慶封弒其君，弱其孤，以盟其大夫！ "The king […] put the

Retrial – First Stage of Interrogation

今訊田，田曰：
市田姑姊子。雖與和奸，與叚（假）子☐$_{190}$不奸。毋智捕田，田仁奸，其實未奸。辤（辭）丞祒謁更治，祒不許。
它如气（乞）鞫書。$_{191}$

Now, when we interrogated Tian [in the course of the review], he stated: "Shi is the child of my paternal aunt.[1244] Even if I committed fornication[1245]

---

executioner's axe on his (Qing Feng's) shoulder, made him go round [the encampments of] the various states, and ordered him to say: 'Let no one follow the example of Qing Feng of Qi, who murdered his ruler, despised the weakness of his young successor, and imposed a covenant on the great officers.'"). In another version of the story, the king made Qing Feng carry both, the executioner's axe as well as the executioner's block (*Lü* 22, 287). There is also an example from Han times where axe and block were shouldered in order to take the blame and apologise for offences (*Hanshu* 98, 4025). Instead of *fu fu zhi* 負斧質 the expression *fu fu zhi* 伏斧質 meaning "to submit oneself to axe and block" is mostly used for this symbolic act in the dynastic histories (*Shiji* 81, 2440 [cf. Nienhauser VII (1994), 263]: 君不如肉袒伏斧質請罪。"For you, my lord, it would be better to expose the shoulder/upper part of the body, submit to axe and chopping block, and ask for punishment."; *Shiji* 58, 2085 [cf. Watson 1993, vol. I, 384]: 於是梁王伏斧質於闕下謝罪。"Then the king of Liang submitted to axe and chopping block before the palace gate, apologising for his offences.").

Often the above expressions obviously refer to the capital punishment (e.g. *Shiji* 103, 2768 [cf. Nienhauser VIII (2008), 381–382]=*Hanshu* 46, 2198: 罪當伏斧質。"For [this] offence, I, by law, should submit myself to axe and chopping block."; cf. *Hanfei* 33, 225). In the present case, however, the expression appears to refer to a more lenient punishment, which is not mentioned. In Qin times, fornicators (who had sex by mutual consent) were punished with being shaved and penal labour as bond servant convicts (*ZYS* 182) as in the present case. Only in cases involving close relatives, capital punishment was to be used (*FLDW* 172). It is uncertain whether the usage of *fu fu zhi* in the present case means that the sentence had already been imposed but not yet executed, or if it refers to a symbolic act, which confirms Tian's willingness to submit to the jurisdiction of the authorities.

1243 For *qi ju* see footnote 390.

1244 *Gu zi* 姑姊 "elder sister of the father=paternal aunt" (*Shiji* 120, 3111 [cf. Watson 1993, vol. II, 315]: 黯姑姊子司馬安亦少與黯爲太子洗馬。"Sima An, the cross-cousin (son of the paternal aunt) of [Ji] An, in his youth had served as a mounted guard to the heir apparent together with [Ji] An."; *Zuo* Xiang 21,487,2: 季武子以公姑姊妻之。"Ji Wuzi gave him the paternal aunt of the duke as a wife." [for an explanation of *gu zi* 姑姊 in this passage see Lu Deming quoted in *Chunqiu Zuozhuan zhengyi* 34, 1970a-b, Kong Yingda on *Zuo* Xiang 12,454,13 quoted in *Chunqiu Zuozhuan zhengyi* 31, 1952a as well as the commentary in Yang Bojun 1981, 1056]). Cf. however *Zuo* Zhao 25,704,12: 爲父子、兄弟、姑姊、甥舅、昏媾、姻亞。"There were father and son, elder and younger brother, paternal aunt and elder sister, sister's son and maternal uncle, father-in-law and son-in-law and

with her by mutual consent,[1246] with a foster child[1247] [...] I did not commit fornication. [When] Wuzhi arrested me, I acknowledged[1248] to have committed fornication, but in fact[1249] I had not [yet] committed fornication. I lodged a complaint[1250] [against the unjustified verdict] to vice prefect[1251] Shao and

---

brothers-in-law.", where *gu* and *zi* seem to refer to different persons, as well as Krjukov 1972, 192–193.

1245 For *jian* see footnote 1203.

1246 For *he* see footnote 1205.

1247 *Jia zi* 叚（假）子 "foster/adopted child" (*FLDW* 19=*RCL* D 17: 父盜子，不爲盜。今叚（假）父盜叚（假）子，可（何）論？當爲盜。 "A father stealing from his child is not a case of theft. Now a foster father steals from his foster child. How is he to be sentenced? By law it is to be considered a case of theft."; *ENLL* 340; *Hanshu* 76, 3227). According to the explanation of the editors Tian argues that Shi grew up in his family as foster child and his marriage with her might have already been planned. Therefore sexual intercourse between them could not be considered illicit (Zhu and Chen 2013, 205 with footnote 5). It should however be noted that Tian is apparently already married to someone else (*Yuelu WYZ* 196).

1248 *Ren* 仁 (*GSR* 388f [OC rhyme class *zhen* 真 according to Zhou Zumo 1966, 263]) *nin (Baxter and Sagart: *niŋ/Zhengzhang Shangfang and Pan Wuyun: *njin) according to the editors is used as loan graph for *ren* 認 (*GSR* 456j [OC rhyme class *wen* 文 according to Zhou Zumo 1966, 265]) *nən-s (Zhengzhang Shangfang: *njɯŋs/Pan Wuyun: njins) in the sense of "to acknowledge" (Zhu and Chen 2013, 205 and 308) as in *QLSZ* 95–96=*RCL* A 50: 亡、不仁其主及官者 "those who have absconded and did not acknowledge their superior/master or their office". Although both characters belong to different OC rhyme classes, there are a number of reasons that indicate that such a loan writing was possible. Both words share the same MC rhyme class as well as the same MC initial consonant. In addition, there are rhyme contacts between OC rhyme classes *zhen* and *wen* (in *Odes* 192,12 and *Odes* 263,4 according to Fang Xiaoyue 1956, 41; in *Chuci* Tianwen, Yuanyou, Gao Tangfu and *Zhuang* according to Zhao Tong 2003, 119; in *Lao* 4 and 15 according to Starostin 1989, 600). Furthermore, there is sufficient evidence for similar loan writings in early Chinese manuscripts (Wang Hui 2008, 669). For example, *ren* 仁 was used to write *ren* 仞 in the meaning "length measure" (*Yinqueshan Shoufa shouling* 768–769; *Mawangdui Lao* A 57) or in a figurative sense "to measure out (the layout of a town)" (*Yinqueshan Shoufa shouling* 898; cf. *Hanfei* 33, 226). Also, *ren shi* 仁矢 (*Yinqueshan Weiliaozi* 507) is probably used to write *ren shi* 韌矢 "tough/strong arrows". However, in received literature *ren* 認 in the legal sense "to acknowledge" first appeared in a source from Tang times (*Zhoushu* 27, 455), and there is no evidence for a compound *fu ren* 服認.

1249 For *shi* see footnote 533.

1250 For *ci* see footnote 765.

1251 For *cheng* see footnote 488. Here, it obviously refers to the vice prefect of the prefecture of Xiayang, who passed the first judgement on Tian (*Yuelu WYZ* 205).

requested a retrial,[1252] but Shao did not grant this."
Everything else corresponded to the document with the petition for a [new] finding of fact.

毋智曰：
□史□□□□□□□□□□□□□□□□□□□□□□□候。旦田來，與市臥上□□□$_{192}$捕詣田、市。服仁奸，未論。市弟大夫驩、親走馬路後請貨毋智錢四千，曰：更言吏不捕田、市校上。毋智【□】$_{193}$受錢，恐吏智（知），不敢自言。環（還）錢。
它如故獄。

Wuzhi stated:
"[…]. At dawn Tian came and lay down together with Shi […] arrested Tian and Shi and presented them [to the authorities]. They confessed and acknowledged that they had committed fornication, [but] the judgement was not yet passed on them. The younger brother of Shi and holder of the fifth rank, Huan, and her relative[1253] and holder of the third rank, Lu, afterwards were requested to offer me bribes[1254] to the amount of 4,000 cash saying: 'Amend your state-

---

1252 *Geng zhi* 更治 (*Liye* 8–1832+8–1418+8–1133 [cf. Chen Wei 2012a, 281]: 令曰：諸有吏治已决而更治者，其罪節（即）重若益輕，吏前治者皆當以縱、不直論。"The ordinances say: When cases – after having been tried and already decided [by the officials] – have to be tried anew, if it turns out that the punishment [previously] imposed was too severe or much too lenient, judgement is by law to be passed on all officials who previously tried the case for [intentionally] 'leaving [an offender] unpunished' or for 'perversion of justice'."). For *zhi* see footnote 1079. Cf. *fu zhi* 覆治 "retrial, try a case in a review/once again" (*ZYS* 138, 144; *ENLL* 113, 116–117; *Hanshu* 60, 2662; 76, 3204; 77, 3261; 86, 3499), which is the aim of the petition (*qi ju* 乞鞫), as well as *geng lun* 更論 (footnote 548).

1253 *Qin* 親 "(close) relatives" in contrast to *suo zhi* 所知 "acquaintances, friends" (*FLDW* 125=*RCL* D 105: 將司人而亡，能自捕及親、所智（知）爲捕，除毋（無）罪。"If somebody leads and supervises remand prisoners/convicts and they abscond, [but] he is able to personally arrest them or his relatives, or acquaintances arrest them for him, [then] he is exempted from punishment."; *ENLL* 160: 奴婢亡，自歸主，主親、所智（知），及主、主父母、子若同居求自得之，其當論畀主，或欲勿詣吏論者，皆許之。"Supposing slaves or slave women abscond, but then, on their own accord, return to their owner, his close relatives or acquaintances, or if their owner, his parents, children or members of his household search for [the slaves] and catch them on their own, [and these slaves] are by law to be sentenced and given back to their owner, [if their owner] wishes that [the slaves] are not presented [to the authorities] for judgement to be passed, this is granted.").

1254 For *huo* see footnote 586.

ment to the officials[1255] [insofar] that you did not arrest Tian and Shi while they were having sexual intercourse.'[1256] After I [...] had received the cash, I was afraid that the officials could get to know about this, [but] I did not dare to report it myself.[1257] [So] I gave back the cash."
Everything else corresponded to the original case.

相曰：
主治瓣（辨）市。聞田數從市奸𣪠（繫）所。令毋智捕。弗治（笞）諒（掠），田、市仁$_{194}$奸。
它如毋智。

Xiang stated:
"I was responsible for the supervision[1258] of [the internee] Shi. I heard that Tian was after Shi several times to commit fornication at her place of deten-

1255 Wuzhi was a *li chen* 隸臣 (*Yuelu* WYZ 206) and therefore had the legal status of a convict. Therefore, it was most likely not him, who was referred to by the word *li* 吏 "official" in this statement.

1256 *Jiao shang* 校上 "to perform/be in the act of having sexual intercourse with each other" (*FZS* 95=*RCL* E 25: 某里士五（伍）甲詣男子乙、女子丙，告曰：乙、丙相與奸，自晝見某所，捕校上來詣之。"A, rank-and-file man from quarter X, presented the man B and the woman C to the authorities. His report ran: 'B and C had illicit sexual intercourse/fornicated with each other. In the daytime, I just happened to see them at the place X. I arrested them while they were having sexual intercourse and come to present them to the authorities."; *ZYS* 182–183: 捕奸者必案之校上。"Whoever arrests fornicating persons needs to ascertain [at the scene] that they had sexual intercourse."; *ZYS* 188, 194, 195). Cf. McLeod and Yates 1981, 162 as well as Lau and Lüdke 2012, footnote 1470.

1257 For *zi yan* see footnote 755.

1258 *Zhi ban* 治瓣 probably stands for *zhi bian* 治辨 "to be in control of sth./have control over sb., to administer/manage" (*Shiji* 122, 3152 [cf. Watson 1993, vol. II, 404]: 居官數年，一切郡中爲小治辨。"During his several years in office every affair in the province, down to the most trifling, was administered."; *Xun* 19, 248 [cf. Knoblock III (1994), 70]: 君之喪所以取三年，何也？曰：君者，治辨之主也。"Why was a period of three years chosen for the mourning of one's lord? I say that the lord is the head of the administration."; *Xun* 11, 137 [cf. Knoblock II (1990), 156]: 萬乘之國可謂廣大富厚矣，加有治辨彊固之道焉，若是則恬愉無患難矣。"A country of ten thousand chariots can properly be called 'vast and large', 'rich and substantial'. If in addition, it possesses a way that has order and management, power and defensive strength, there will be contentment and enjoyment without any misfortune or difficulty.").

tion.[1259] I ordered Wuzhi to arrest [them]. Without being subjected to torture by caning,[1260] Tian and Shi acknowledged to have committed fornication." Everything else corresponded to [the statement of] Wuzhi.

驩、路曰：
市令驩、路貨毋智。以告田，田曰：剸（專）爲之。
它如毋智。 195

Huan and Lu stated:
"Shi induced us to offer Wuzhi a bribe. [When] we informed Tian about this, he said: 'Do it on your own.'"[1261]
Everything else corresponded to [the statement of] Wuzhi.

☒田妻曰：□□□□□□☒ 196

[...] The wife of Tian stated: "[...]."

☒田、市言如毋智。 197

[...] The statements of Tian and Shi corresponded to [the statement of] Wuzhi.

田曰：
毋智不捕田校上。捕田時，田不奸。驩、路以市言告田，貨毋智錢。田䍧（幸）除毋（無）皋（罪），即弗止。不智（知）市、【毋智】 198云故。
它如驩、路及前。

1259 The *xi suo* 繫所 "place of detention", where Shi is kept, is also called *guan fu* 官府 "government workshop" (*Yuelu* WYZ 201). Therefore it is unlikely that she was in a remand prison as a suspect. More likely, she had to work off debts or fines in a workshop.

1260 *Zhi liang* 治諒 for *chi lüe* 笞掠 "to subject sb. to torture (by caning)" (*Shiji* 122, 3153; ZYS 120: 吏笞諒（掠）毛，毛不能支疾痛。"The officials tortured Mao by caning, Mao was not able to endure the pain."; FZS 4=RCL E 2: 更言不服，其律當治（笞）諒（掠）者，乃治（笞）諒（掠）。"When he changes his statement and does not confess, then, where the respective statutes warrant torture, use torture.").

1261 *Zhuan* 剸 for *zhuan* 專 "(to act) on oneself/one's own" (*Xun* 4, 34 [cf. Knoblock I (1988), 187]: 信而不見敬者，好剸行也。 "Though they are trustworthy, they are not respected, because they are fond of acting on their own."; cf. *Zuo* Xiang 19,481,2: 今無故而廢之是專黜諸侯。"Now, to displace him without any cause is to take it on yourself to degrade a prince."; *Lunyu* 13, 285 [cf. Harbsmeier]: 不能專對。"He is not able to reply on his own."). On this loan writing see also Bai Yulan 2012, 791; Wang Hui 2008, 736–737 and Feng and Deng 2006, 141. The following pronoun *zhi* 之 obviously refers to *huo* 貨 "to offer (valuables as a bribe)".

Tian stated:
"Wuzhi did not arrest me while I was having sexual intercourse. When he arrested me, I was not committing fornication. Huan and Lu informed me about what Shi had told them and offered Wuzhi cash as a bribe. I was hoping[1262] to be exempted[1263] without being punished, so I did not stop them. I do not know the reason for Shi's and Wuzhi's statements."
Everything else corresponded to [the statements of] Huan and Lu as well as his previous [statement].

爨等言如故獄。

The statements of Cuan and his colleagues corresponded to the original case.

衵曰：
論□田，田謁更治。衵謂：巳（已）服仁奸。今獄夬（決）乃曰不奸！田嘗□$_{199}$毋智令轉□且有□辠（罪）。田即受令。
它如爨等。

Shao stated:
"After I had passed judgement [...] on Tian, he requested a retrial. I told him: 'You already confessed and acknowledged to have committed fornication. Now that the case is already decided you say that you did not commit fornication! You once [...].' Tian then obeyed the orders."
Everything else corresponded to [the statements of] Cuan and his colleagues.

以言不同，詣訊。言各如前。$_{200}$

Because the statements were not in accord with each other, [the witnesses] were brought [before the judicial officials] and interrogated [again]. The [new] statements all corresponded to the previous ones.

Retrial – Second Stage of Interrogation (*Confrontation*)

詰相：
令毋智捕田、市，可（何）解？

We confronted Xiang:
"You ordered Wuzhi to arrest Tian and Shi, how do you explain this?"

1262 For *xing* see footnotes 897 and 1232.

1263 For *chu* see footnote 845.

相曰：
怒田、市奸官府。毋（無）它解。201

Xiang stated:
"I got angry with Tian and Shi for committing fornication in the government workshop.[1264] I do not have any other explanation."

詰田：
夏陽吏不治（笞）諒（掠），田、市仁奸。今覆吏訊市，市言如故獄。田云未奸，可（何）解？

We confronted Tian:
"The officials of Xiayang[1265] did not subject you to torture by caning, [but still] you and Shi acknowledged to have committed fornication. Now, when the officials instructed with revision [newly] interrogated Shi, her statement corresponded to that in the original case. You [however] stated that you did not commit fornication. How do you explain this?"

田曰：
未奸而毋（無）以解市言。202

Tian stated:
"I did not commit fornication, but I have no means[1266] to explain Shi's statement."

Retrial – Interagency Enquiries

問：
驩、路以赦前貨毋智。以後遝。
它如辭（辭）。203

[Results of the] interagency enquiries:[1267]

1264 *Guan fu* 官府 "government workshop", cf. RCL "addenda et corrigenda" to A 41, footnote 13.

1265 Xiayang 夏陽 was a prefecture (*Hanshu* 28A, 1545; ENLL 447) within the metropolitan province Neishi 內史 (Hou Xiaorong 2009, 143–144) on the western banks of the Yellow River to the south of present Hancheng, Shaanxi (*Lishi dituji* vol. II, 5–6, 7④).

1266 On the indefinite substitution *wu yi* 無以 see footnote 807.

1267 The aim of the interagency enquiries apparently was to find out why the relatives who had bribed the eye witness had not been punished.

Huan and Lu offered Wuzhi bribes before the amnesty.[1268] Afterwards, they were included[1269] [in the amnesty].
Everything else corresponded to the statements.

Retrial – Finding of Fact

鞫之：
田與市和奸，毋智捕校上。田雖不服，而毋（無）以解驩、路、毋智、市言。田負斧質气（乞）鞫不審，【遝己巳赦】。$_{204}$它爲後發覺，皆審。

Finding of fact:
Tian and Shi committed fornication by mutual consent, and Wuzhi arrested them while they were having sexual intercourse. Although Tian did not confess, he had no means to explain the statements of Huan, Lu, Wuzhi and Shi. The petition for a [new] finding of fact by Tian, who bears the executioner's axe and block, is unfounded, [but he is to be included into the *jisi* amnesty]. Everything else was discovered afterwards.[1270] All these are established facts.

Notification of Competent Officials by the Higher Authorities (Judgement)

謂𩲸（魏）嗇夫：
重泉隸臣田負斧質气（乞）鞫曰：不與女子市奸。夏陽論耐田爲隸$_{205}$臣，不當。
覆之：
市【仁】與田和奸，隸臣毋智捕校上。田不服，而毋（無）以解市、毋智言。其气（乞）鞫不審。田毄（繫）子縣。$_{206}$當毄（繫）城旦十二歲。遝己巳赦，其赦除田，復爲隸臣。【騰詣】重泉、夏陽。$_{207}$

Notification[1271] to the overseer of Wei [prefecture]:[1272]

1268 For *she* see footnote 670.

1269 For *ta* in connection with amnesties see footnote 669.

1270 It is unclear which offences were only discovered after the amnesty. Possibly, the bribes offered by the relatives of Shi in order to bend the law are referred to.

1271 For *wei* see footnote 1235. It is not certain whether this notification came from the authorities of the province (of Handan) or from the *ting wei* as in case no. 17 of the *Zou yan shu* (ZYS 121).

1272 Wei 魏 is the name of a prefecture where Tian is held under detention. It is assumed that during the Qin dynasty the prefecture of Wei belonged to the province of Handan (Hou Xiaorong 2009, 347). It can be identified with the prefecture of the same name in Western Han times, which served as residence to the *du wei* of the province of Wei (*Hanshu* 28A,

The bond servant of Chongquan[1273] [prefecture], Tian, who bore the executioner's axe and block, petitioned for a [new] finding of fact stating: "I did not commit fornication with the woman Shi. [That the authorities of] Xiayang [prefecture] sentenced me to be shaved and made a bond servant convict, is not justified."
[We] reviewed [the case]:
Shi [acknowledged] to have committed fornication with Tian by mutual consent, and the bond servant Wuzhi arrested them while they were having sexual intercourse. Tian did not confess, but had no means to explain the statements of Shi and Wuzhi. His petition for a [new] finding of fact was unfounded. Tian is held under detention in your prefecture [Wei]. He was, by law, to be placed under detention among the earth pounder convicts for twelve years.[1274] [Because] he was included in the *jisi* amnesty, he is to be amnestied and exempted [from this detention] and to be made a bond servant convict again. [A copy of this response shall be forwarded to the prefectures] Chongquan and Xiayang.

1573) and was located south of present Daming in southern Hebei (*Lishi dituji* vol. II, 26, 3④). For the kingdom of Wei cf. footnote 1154.

1273 Chongquan 重泉 was a prefecture (*Hanshu* 28A, 1545; *ENLL* 448) within the metropolitan province Neishi (Hou Xiaorong 2009, 126) with its administrative seat to the west of present Dali in central Shaanxi (*Lishi dituji* vol. II, 5–6, 6④).

1274 In the notification by the higher authorities Tian is mentioned as a bond servant convict. According to Qin law, offenders who committed fornication by mutual consent were to be punished with being shaved (*nai*) and made bond servant convicts (*ZYS* 182). In early Han times, bond servant convicts who committed an offence punishable by penal labour of the category *nai* were to be placed under detention among the earth pounder convicts for six years (*ENLL* 90). This rule appears to have been applied in the present case as well. Tian was furthermore to be sentenced to six additional years of detention among the earth pounder convicts, because his petition for a retrial was unfounded. For such an unfounded petition, the previous conviction of the requesting person would have to be increased by one degree according to Han stipulations (*ENLL* 114). Cf. footnotes 1196 and 1237.

Case II.13

The following case appears to be the most fragmented of all 15 cases. As only parts of two slips are extant, few things can be gathered regarding the actual content of the case. From what remains it is probable that the accused are four persons named Shan, Ding, Liang and Huo. Apparently, these four were conscripts or convicts who did labour service in a government park and, for an unknown reason, illegally left their place of work, returning only several days later. Although it is not stated, this might have been regarded as a case of "vagrancy" (*jiang yang* 將陽) by the authorities.[1275]

Diplomatic Edition

▨□之楊臺苑中除芝徒所聞士五善公士定公卒良▨ $_{208}$ ▨中去作所數日復作•問善⌞定⌞良⌞獲⌞去作▨ $_{209}$

Edition and Translation

Initiation of Criminal Proceedings

▨□之楊臺苑中除芝（芃）徒所。聞士五（伍）善、公士定、公卒良▨ $_{208}$ ▨中去作所，數日復作。

"[...] went to the place in the Yangtai park[1276] where the conscripts/convicts were removing weeds.[1277] I heard that the rank-and-file man[1278] Shan, the holder of the first rank[1279] Ding, the *gong zu*[1280] Liang [...] in [...] left their place of work. After several days they returned to work."[1281]

1275 For *jiang yang* see footnote 858. Cf. footnote 612 on "absconding" (*wang* 亡).

1276 *Yuan* 苑 "park" (*QLSZ* 117, 119, 190=*RCL* A 64, 100; *XL* 55=*RCL* B 27) can probably be identified with *jin yuan* 禁苑 "forbidden park" (*QLSZ* 5–7, 117, 119, 193=*RCL* A 2, 64, 103; *Longgang* 6, 7, 11, 13, 15, 18, 23, 25, 27, etc.). The "Yangtai park" mentioned in this case also occurs on a Qin clay seal (Chen and Zhou 2005, 314; cf. Wang Wei 2014).

1277 For *fan* see footnote 1056.

1278 For *shi wu* see footnote 495.

1279 For *gong shi* see footnote 856.

1280 For *gong zu* see footnote 723.

1281 As a technical term *fu zuo* 復作 apparently referred to a kind of labour service which was applied to convicts who had been exempted from penal labour by an amnesty, but were

 | DOI 10.1163/9789004315655_021

Interagency Enquiries

問：
善、定、良、獲去作〼$_{209}$

[Results of the] interagency enquiries:[1282]
Shan, Ding, Liang and Huo left their [place of] work […].

---

still to fulfil their days of service under less strict circumstances (cf. commentary by Meng Kang to *Hanshu* 8, 235 [cf. Dubs II (1944), 200, footnote 1.4; Hulsewé 1955, 240]: 謂弛刑徒也，有赦令詔書去其鉗釱赭衣。[…]不從徒加，與民爲例，故當復爲官作，滿其本罪年月日，律名爲復作也。 "It means that they are convicts who are exempted from punishment. When there was an imperial edict granting amnesty, their iron collars, leg irons, and their red [convict] garments were taken off. They […] no longer were treated as convicts, but as a rule they were added to the common people. Hence they were to be exempted [from punishment] and they must work for the government to fully serve the years, months and days of their original punishment. In the statutes their name is *fu zuo*."; *Hanshu* 8, 257 [63 BC]; 15A, 452 [122 BC]; 24A, 1135 [155 BC]; 49, 2286; *Shiji* 12, 476 [110 BC]; 12, 479 [109 BC]; *Juyan* 34.9; *Juyan xinjian* EPT56:281; *Xuanquan* 141; for the interpretation of *fu zuo* see Hulsewé 1955, 240–41; Wu Rongzeng 1995, 267–270; Zhang Jianguo 2006, 603–606; Hafner 2013b; cf. the case of a private slave who was obliged to work in a government workshop after being manumitted in *ZYS* 49; Lau and Lüdke 2012, footnote 795). *Fu zuo* was not reserved for female convicts as claimed by Li Qi in his *Hanshu* commentary (*Hanshu* 8, 235 [cf. Dubs II (1944), 200, footnote 1.4]), because several male ex-convicts who perfomed *fu zuo* in government workshops occur in administrative manuscripts of the Eastern Han dynasty (*Juyan* 37.33; 60.2).
The meaning of *fu* in the compound *fu zuo* is disputed. It may be interpreted as "to continue (working)" (cf. the translation "those who still [have to] work" in Hulsewé 1955, 240) or as "to exempt (from punishment)" (cf. the translation "those who have been exempted and are serving [their sentences]" in Dubs 1944, 200, footnote 1.4). There are several examples for *fu* in the sense of "to exempt (from taxes and statute labour)" (*Mo* 70, 351; *Xun* 15, 180; *Hanfei* 17, 84; *ENLL* 162; *Hanshu* 1A, 33).
In the present case, it is unclear whether *tu* 徒 actually refers to convicts or rather to conscripts (as in case I.1 above, see especially footnote 553), and it is furthermore doubtful if *fu zuo* refers to a group of persons. A translation in a "non-technical" sense as "to return to/resume work (after having left the respective place of work)" appears also possible.

1282 For *wen* see footnote 562.

Case III.14

In this case from 225 BC, an underage scribe from the prefecture of Xinye pretended to be the son of a famous general and wrote a private letter to the head of the treasury of the neighbouring prefecture of Huyang in his name, in which he requested to receive a loan of 20,000 cash and seeds and provisions for one year to cultivate fields. In fact, the scribe wanted to use these to buy clothes and weapons to abscond from the state of Qin. The head of the treasury became suspicious after he had opened and read the letter and placed the scribe under detention without granting his request. While under detention, the scribe wrote a second letter, this time to the prefect of Huyang, in which he repeated his request, claiming that a similar request had been granted to him in the neighbouring prefecture of Xinye. Furthermore, he complained about the head of the treasury, extolled his own virtues and asked the prefect to reprimand his subordinate officials.

The interagency enquiries revealed that the accused was a minor, who was aged 15 and had not yet been called up for military service. Additionally, the general, whose name he had used when he forged the letter, held the ninth rank.

The reasons for the judicial officials of Huyang prefecture to submit this case to the higher authorities for decision are not stated. However, as the forged letter is referred to as a "private letter" (*si shu*) several times, it might be the case that the offence of drafting a forged letter (*wei wei shu*) found in Qin and early Han statutes merely refers to official documents. This could also explain that both votes for punishment by the prefecture are rather lenient. The majority voted to punish the offender with penal labour of the category *nai* as a bond servant convict, even though the punishment for forging a letter was the most severe form of penal labour as tattooed earth pounder convict, at least according to early Han statutes. A minority voted for an even less severe punishment, namely to sentence the accused to pay the fee for redemption from penal labour of the category *nai*. Therefore, one might assume that forging a private letter was a less severe offence than forging an official letter. Another mitigating circumstance might be the young age of the offender. At the age of 15, he had already reached the age of criminal liability, but he was still a minor, since the offender had not yet performed military service and was probably not registered for it yet. It seems that during the Qin dynasty, minors who had not committed capital offences were not sentenced to the most severe form of penal labour until they were adults.

 | DOI 10.1163/9789004315655_022

In their response, the leading officials of the province reproved the prefecture for falsely reporting the status of the general in whose name the offender had drawn up the forged private letter as too low. For this, the responsible officials were fined one shield each. Although the provincial authorities demanded the strict application of law by its subordinates, they remained curiously silent on the lawful punishment for the accused. It is of course possible that there is a slip missing at the end of the manuscript.

Diplomatic Edition

廿二年八月癸卯朔辛亥胡陽丞唐敢讞之四月乙丑丞矰曰君子=癸詣私$_{210}$書矰所自謂馮將軍毋擇子與舍人來田南陽毋擇⍁$_{211}$萬及糧食胡陽以田發書=類僞縠官有撟爲私書□□⍁$_{212}$即獄治求請•癸曰馮將軍毋擇叚⍁毋擇舍妻毋擇令癸　⍁$_{213}$⍁糧食以田不爲僞書⌞⍁$_{214}$叚子它如矰•視癸私書曰五夫=馮毋擇敢多問胡陽丞主聞南陽$_{215}$地利田令爲公產臣老癸與人出田不齎錢種顚丞主叚錢二萬貣$_{216}$食支卒歲稼孰倍賞勿環=之毋擇不得爲丞主臣走丞主與胡$_{217}$陽公共憂毋擇爲報敢以聞寄封廷史利⌞有曰馮將軍子臣癸$_{218}$敢昧死謁胡陽公丈人詔令癸出田南陽因糧食錢貣以爲私⌞癸田$_{219}$新=壄=丞主徉叚癸錢食一歲少吏莫敢訶癸今胡⍁$_{220}$謂癸非馮將軍子癸居秦中名聞以爲不⍁$_{221}$□癸糧姓雖賤能權任人有能下人顚公詔少吏勿令環•今$_{222}$⍁□召舍人興來□⍁曰君子=定名學居新壄非五夫=馮將軍毋擇子$_{223}$毆學=史有私印□□□□□馮將□毋擇□□□□□□□□□□$_{224}$害聲聞⌞學父秦居貲吏治秦以故數爲學怒苦姐之歸居室心不$_{225}$樂即獨撟自以爲五夫=馮毋擇子以名爲僞私書問矰欲貣錢$_{226}$胡陽少內以私印封起室把詣于矰徉其肯以威貣學錢即盜以買$_{227}$金衣被兵去邦亡荊矰發讀書未許學⌞令人縠守學=恐欲去亡$_{228}$有撟爲私書自言胡陽固所詑曰學實馮毋擇子新壄丞主巳$_{229}$**[Missing slip]**學吏節不智學爲僞書不許貣學錢退去學=即道胡陽$_{230}$行邦亡且不⌞辭曰吏節不智學爲僞不貣學錢毋以爲衣被$_{231}$資用去環歸有衣資用乃行邦亡•問學撟爵爲僞書時馮$_{232}$毋擇爵五夫=將軍學不從軍年十五歲它如辭$_{233}$

•鞫之學撟自以五夫=將軍馮毋擇子以名爲僞私書詣矰以欲$_{234}$盜去邦亡未得=審縠敢讞之•吏議耐學隸臣或令贖耐$_{235}$讞報毋擇巳爲卿貲某=各一盾謹窮以灋論之$_{236}$

Edition and Translation

Submission by Huyang Prefecture – Introductory Formula

廿二年八月癸卯朔辛亥，胡陽丞唐敢灋（讞）之：

In the 22nd year, on day *xinhai*[1283] of the 8th month with the first day *guimao*, vice prefect[1284] Tang of Huyang[1285] [prefecture] ventures to submit [the following case] for decision:[1286]

Initiation of Criminal Proceedings

四月乙丑，丞矰曰：
君子子癸詣私$_{210}$書矰所，自謂馮將軍毋擇子，與舍人來田南陽。毋擇【□□□叚（假）錢二】$_{211}$萬及穜（種）食胡陽，以田。發書，書類僞。毄（繫）官。有（又）撟（矯）爲私書□□☑$_{212}$

On day *yichou*[1287] of the fourth month the assistant head [of the prefectural treasury][1288] Zeng stated:
"Gui, the son[1289] of a *jun zi*,[1290] presented[1291] a private letter[1292] to me[1293]

1283 This was the ninth day of the eighth month in the 22nd year of the reign of King Zheng of Qin (cf. Zhang Peiyu 2007, 73; Li Zhonglin 2012, 65), i.e. 13/09/225 BC (Xu Xiqi 1997, 1234).

1284 For *cheng* see footnote 488.

1285 In early Han times, Huyang 胡陽 was a prefecture (*ENLL* 457; *Shiji* 8, 360) in the province of Nanyang (*Hanshu* 28A, 1564, where the name of this prefecture appears as 湖陽). Its administrative seat was located to the south of present Tanghe, Henan (*Lishi dituji* vol. II, 7/8, 3⑦; 22/23, 6③). Because the province of Nanyang is also mentioned in the present case, Huyang must already have been a part of this province during the Qin dynasty. It was probably established by the kingdom of Chu in late Warring States times (Hou Xiaorong 2009, 272–273) and needs to be distinguished from the marquisate Huyang (*Shiji* 18, 901), which was located in modern Zhejiang (Wang Guowei cited in Cang Xiuliang 1991, 653).

1286 For *yan* and the phrase *gan yan zhi* see footnote 489.

1287 This was the 21st day of the fourth month in the 22nd year of the reign of King Zheng of Qin (cf. Zhang Peiyu 2007, 73; Li Zhonglin 2012, 65), i.e. 30/05/225 BC (Xu Xiqi 1997, 1234).

1288 *Cheng* 丞 "assistant" could be combined with different titles (see note 3 to *RCL* C 11, note 2 to *RCL* C 13 and note 2 to *RCL* A 42). Here, it perhaps refers to the *cheng* of the *shao nei* 少內 (cf. *Yuelu WYZ* 226–227). For *shao nei* see footnote 1351.

1289 *Jun zi zi* 君子子 can probably be interpreted as the "son of a *jun zi*" (cf. *Yuelu WYZ* 223). The same designation also occurs in Qin administrative documents from the prefecture of Qianling (*Liye* 8–178r [cf. Chen Wei 2012a, 106]: 君子子廢戍。"A son of a *jun zi* was dismissed(?) from military service."; *Liye* 8–1198 [cf. Chen Wei 2012a, 290]: 傳〈傅〉律曰：□爲君子子有故不□ "The statutes on enrolment/registration [for labour and military service] state: [...] for sons of *jun zi* there exists a reason to not [...]."). It is not clear whether the status of *jun zi* as a commander of a unit of conscripts (see footnote 1290) and the military position of *jiang jun* 將軍 "commander of the army/general" are connected in some way. The editors interpret *jun zi zi* as "children from good/respectable families" (cf. *liang jia zi* 良家子 in *Shiji* 109, 2867; Zhu and Chen 2013, 223 with footnote 5).

in which he called himself[1294] son of general[1295] Feng Wuze,[1296] who came with his clients[1297] to cultivate fields[1298] at Nanyang[1299] [province]. Wuze [… to

---

1290 *Jun zi* 君子 "noble/gentleman" occurs in the Shuihudi manuscripts (*QLSZ* 116, 161=*RCL* A 64, 81; *QLZC* 34, 40=*RCL* C 21, 26), where Hulsewé translates the term as "master" and defines it as the title of a local official (with reference to *jun* 君 in *Hanshu* 96A, 3875 and 3880; see note 11 to *RCL* A 64). With regard to the context of these passages, *jun zi* more likely was the commander of a unit of conscripts who were assigned to pound earth walls (*QLSZ* 116=*RCL* A 64). He was responsible for the work of the conscripts under his command in a certain section of the wall (*QLZC* 40=*RCL* C 26) or for mounting guard of these conscripts (*QLZC* 34=*RCL* C 21). The editors (Zhu and Chen 2013, 223 with footnote 5) refer to the elite bodyguard (*si zu jun zi* 私卒君子) of six thousand warriors who constituted the "middle army" (*zhong jun* 中軍) under King Goujian of Yue during the late Spring and Autumn period (*Guoyu* 7.9/119/1; cf. *Houhanshu* 35, 1208) as predecessors of the *jun zi* in Qin.

1291 For *yi* see footnote 496.

1292 *Si shu* 私書 "private/secret letter" (*Shiji* 122, 3133 [cf. Watson 1993, vol. II, 381]: 都[…]公廉，不發私書。"[Zhi] Du was impartial and honest. He never opened private letters."; *Hanshu* 7, 226–227 [cf. Dubs II (1944), 165]: 交通私書，共謀令長公主置酒，伏兵殺大將軍光，徵立燕王爲天子。"They interchanged secret letters and plotted together to have the elder princess [of Eyi] hold a feast [at which] soldiers should be ambushed, [with the purpose of] murdering the general-in-chief, [He] Guang, and summoning and setting up the king of Yan, [Liu Dan], as the son of heaven."; *Mo* 70, 357 [cf. Johnston 2010, 881]: 挾私書行請謁及爲行書者釋守事而治私家事 […] 皆斷無赦。"Those who carry private letters, make requests, or bear letters for others, or who set aside defensive matters to attend private matters […] are all to be executed without pardon.").

1293 For *suo* 所 as postposition that marks the recipient or giver as object after verbs of transmitting see footnote 681.

1294 *Zi wei* 自謂 "to call oneself" (*Shiji* 6, 257 [cf. Nienhauser I (1994), 149]: 於是始皇曰：吾慕真人，自謂真人，不稱朕。"Thus the First Emperor said: 'I long to meet the Perfected. I will call myself the Perfected, no more *zhen*, when referring to myself!"; *Shiji* 33, 1543; 41, 1752; *Hanshu* 60, 2683; 63, 2756).

1295 For *jiang* see footnotes 509 and 529.

1296 Feng Wuze 馮毋擇 must have been elevated to a lord (*lun hou* 倫侯, which corresponds to [*guan*] *nei hou* [關]內侯 according to *Liye* 8–461r [cf. Chen Wei 2012a, 156 with note 13]) of Wuxin 武信 some time before 219 BC when he is mentioned in a message of congratulation to the First Emperor after the unification of the empire (*Shiji* 6, 246; Loewe 2001, 101; cf. *Hanshu* 1A, 39; 79, 3293). For Feng Wuze see also Chen Wei 2009, 86–87; for his son Feng Jing 馮敬 see Loewe 2001, 99. The editors prefer the reading *yi* 亦 for 擇 (Zhu and Chen 2013, 223 with footnote 6).

1297 For *she ren* see footnote 968.

1298 For *tian* see footnote 857.

1299 Nanyang 南陽, an old settlement area of the descendants of Xia (*Shiji* 129, 3269) since the Qin dynasty, was the name of a province with its administrative seat in Wan (*Hanshu* 28A,

borrow 20,000 cash] as well as seeds[1300] and provisions from Huyang in order to cultivate fields. When I opened[1301] the letter it seemed to be forged.[1302] [Gui] was placed under detention[1303] in the office. [There he] again[1304] drew up a private letter under false pretences[1305] [...]."

1563) near present Nanyang in southern Henan (*Lishi dituji* vol. II, 7/8, 3⑦). The province of Nanyang was established by the Qin in 272 BC after the defeated state of Wei had ceded this area to Qin to sue for peace (*Shiji* 5, 213). See also Hou Xiaorong 2009, 266–267.

1300 *Zhong* 種 as noun "seeds" (*Yuelu Wei li* 77.3: 貣（貸）穜（種）食 "to borrow seeds and provisions"; *Hanfei* 31, 180: 黍種貴。"The broomcorn millet seeds are expensive."; *Hanshu* 4, 117 [cf. Dubs I (1938), 242–243]: 民讁作縣官及貸種食未入、入未備者，皆赦之。 "Those people who are punished [and made to] work in the prefectural offices as well as those who have borrowed seeds and food/provisions, and have not paid it back or not fully paid it back, [let] them all be pardoned."; *QLSZ* 40=*RCL* A 28: 縣遺麥以爲種用者。"The prefecture gives barley to be used as seeds."; *Zhuang* 1, 5: 魏王貽我大瓠之種我樹之。"The king of Wei gave me seeds of big gourds, and I planted them.").

1301 *Fa* 發 "to open (a document)" (*FLDW* 53=*RCL* D 43: 有投書，勿發，見輒燔之。 "When there are anonymous letters, these are not to be opened; as soon as they are discovered, they are to be burnt immediately."; *FLDW* 57=*RCL* D 46: 發僞書，弗智（知），貲二甲。 "To open a forged document and not to become aware [that it is forged] is fined two suits of armour."; *Liye* 8–152v, 8–155, etc.; *Yushu* 13; *ZYS* 7, 15, 47; *Zhanguoce* 138/69/13; *Juyan* 136.43, 158.8, 180.39, 506.9B; *Juyan xinjian* E.T.P51:81; *Shiji* 33, 1516; 84, 2497; 87, 2551; *Hanshu* 68, 2933). Cf. Lau and Lüdke 2012, footnote 614 with many further references, as well as Zhu Xiangrong 2012, 187–191.

1302 For the statutory offence of *wei wei shu* 爲僞書 "drawing up a forged document", which was punished with being tattooed and the most severe form of penal labour as an earth or grain pounder (*ENLL* 13; *ZYS* 55, 57, 59, 60; cf. *FLDW* 57=*RCL* D 46; *Shiji* 28, 1388; 129, 3271), see Lau and Lüdke 2012, footnote 844.

1303 For *ji/xi* see footnote 569.

1304 *You* 有 here for *you* 又 in the sense "(once) again".

1305 *Jiao* 撟 (*GSR* 1138j) for the homophonous *jiao* 矯 (*GSR* 1138l) "to pretend, arrogate/presume" (*ENLL* 11: 撟（矯）制害者，棄市。不害，罰金四兩。 "For pretending to execute an imperial order/decision [Giele 2006, 221], one is to be executed in public, if harm was caused; if no harm was caused, one is fined four ounces of gold."; *ENLL* 66: 橋（矯）相以爲吏、自以爲吏以盜，皆磔。"Those who pose an accomplice/assistant as official or pretend to be officials in order to commit theft are without exception executed by quartering."; cf. *FLDW* 55=*RCL* D 44: 僑（矯）丞令可（何）殹（也）？爲有秩僞寫其印爲大嗇夫。 "What is 'to forge an order of the vice prefect'? This is a case of a rank-holder counterfeiting his seal to be [that of] a great overseer."; Wang Hui 2008, 159; Bai Yulan 2012, 139). Cf. *jiao ming/ling* 矯命/令 (*Zuo* Zhao 27,721,9; *Shiji* 7, 298; 48, 1957; 77, 2382; *Hanshu* 73, 3108), *jiao zhi* 矯制 (*Shiji* 9, 407; 19, 1012; 20, 1037; 120, 3105; *Hanshu* 50, 2316; 64B, 2817–2818; 77, 3258; 79, 3294, 3300–3301) and *jiao zhao* 矯詔 (*Shiji* 107, 2853; *Hanshu* 52, 2392; 93, 3728). *Jiao* could also be followed by the verb *wei* 爲 (*Hanfei* 30, 177 [cf. Harbsmeier]: 乃矯爲秦使以知之。"He pretended to be an envoy from Qin in order

即獄治求請（情）。

Thereupon, we tried [the matter] in a criminal case[1306] and sought for the motives [of the accused].[1307]

First Stage of Interrogation – Part 1

癸曰：
馮將軍毋擇叚（假）【子。母】毋擇舍（捨）妻。毋擇令癸☐ $_{213}$☐種（種）食以田。不爲僞書。☐ $_{214}$叚（假）子。
它如贈。

Gui stated:
"I am a foster child of general Feng Wuze. [My mother is] a disowned wife[1308]

---

to ascertain the facts.") or could be used adverbially (*Hanfei* 12, 65 [cf. Harbsmeier]: 彌子矯駕君車以出。"Mi Zi under false pretences let yoke the ruler's carriage in order to go out for a drive.").

1306 *Yu zhi* 獄治 "to try sth. in a criminal case/remand prison" (ZYS 50: 已獄治，不當爲昌錯告不孝。"We tried [the matter] in a criminal case/remand prison; it was not lawful/justified that [Xiangru] was under false pretences reported for having committed impiety by Chang."; *Liye* 8–1562r: 謁上獄治，當論，論。"We request to submit the case to the higher authorities and to bring it to trial. If by law [the offender] is to be sentenced, sentence him."). Cf. *zhi yu* 治獄 (footnote 1079) as well as Lau and Lüdke 2012, footnote 798.

It should be noted that in some passages from received literature *yu* definitely referred to the remand prison as the place where the trial (*zhi*) took place (*Hanshu* 48, 2260: 人有告勃謀反，逮繫長安獄治。"Sb. reported [Zhou] Bo for planning a rebellion, he was arrested and placed under detention in the remand prison of Chang'an for trial."; *Hanshu* 70, 3025: 下獄治。"He was thrown into remand prison for trial."; *Hanshu* 75, 3192: 下獄治服，未斷病死。"He was thrown into remand prison for trial and confessed his guilt, but died of an illness before the case had been decided."; *Hanshu* 99C, 4167 [cf. Dubs III (1955), 409]: 莽遣使者即捕焉，獄治皆死。"[Wang] Mang sent a commissioner immediately to arrest [Li] Yan [and his confederates]; they were imprisoned for trial and all died.").

1307 *Qiu qing* 求請 for *qiu qing* 求情 "to seek after/look for the emotions (as motives/driving force for the action)" (see commentary of Zhang Fei on the Jin code quoted in *Jinshu* 30, 930: 夫刑者，司理之官；理者，求情之機；情者，心神之使。"Punishments are the organs of the overseer of jurisdiction, jurisdiction is the device which seeks after the emotions/motives, emotions/motives are the envoys of heart and mind/spirit."). Cf. Huang Jie (2013) who reads the expression *qiu qing* 求請 in the sense *qing qiu* 請求 "to request for, request".

of Wuze. Wuze ordered me [...] seeds and provisions in order to cultivate fields. I did not draw up a forged letter. [...] a foster child."[1309]
Everything else corresponded to [the statement of] Zeng.

Inspection of Pieces of Evidence

視癸私書，曰：
五大夫馮毋擇敢多問胡陽丞主。聞南陽$_{215}$地利田，令爲公產。臣老，癸與人出田。不齎錢種（種），顯（願）丞主叚（假）錢二萬，貣（貸）$_{216}$食支卒歲。稼孰（熟）倍賞（償）。勿環（還）。環（還）之，毋擇不得爲丞主臣。走丞主與胡$_{217}$陽公共憂毋擇爲報。敢以聞。寄封廷史利。

We inspected[1310] Gui's private letters. [The first] read:
"I, Feng Wuze, holder of the ninth rank,[1311] venture to address a salute[1312] to the vice prefect in charge[1313] of Huyang. I heard that the land of Nanyang [prov-

1308 *She* 舍 (*GSR* 48a) for *she* 捨 (*GSR* 48c) (cf. Feng and Deng 2006, 730–731). *She qi* 捨妻, which does not occur in received literature from Han times or earlier periods, can probably be identified with *qi qi* 棄妻 "disowned wife" (cf. footnote 1043).

1309 For *jia zi* see footnote 1247.

1310 *Shi* 視 here "to closely view/take a close look at (pieces of evidence)" (*ZYS* 167: 臣有（又）診視媚臥莞席。 "For forensic examination I inspected the rush mat on which Mei sleeps."; *ZYS* 202: 視刀 "they took a close look at the knife"; *ZYS* 204). *Shi* was also used in the sense "(in a review) examine/inspect (a former criminal case)" (*ZYS* 99; *Yuelu WYZ* 173; *Yuelu WYZ* 047; *Yuelu WYZ* 064). For *shi* in the meaning "to check up on a suspect" see footnote 1123.

1311 *Wu da fu* 五大夫 is the ninth of twenty ranks (*Hanshu* 19A, 739). Officials were punished severely when they treated holders of this or higher ranks in a degrading way in the exercise of their duties (*ENLL* 46: 吏以縣官事毆詈五大夫以上，皆黥爲城旦舂。 "Officials who hit or curse a holder of the ninth or higher rank because of official matters, in all cases are tattooed and made earth or grain pounder convicts.").

1312 *Duo wen* 多問 was a polite form of salutation in written communication enquiring about the addressee's health (*Liye* 8–650v, 8–659r, 8–1909, 8–1997r; *Shuihudi mudu* 6r=*Sanjian* 1009v, 11v; *Juyan* 157.25A, 乙附 51, *Dunhuang* 904).

1313 In Qin legal manuscripts, *zhu* 主 often means "to be (the official) in charge" (*QLSZ* 116=*RCL* A 64: 君子主堵者 "masters in charge of a wall section"; *XL* 17=*RCL* B 7: 同官而各有主殹（也），各坐其所主。 "[Although serving in] the same office, each [official] is in charge [of a particular area], each one is prosecuted for [misdemeanours of those] under his supervision."). According to the editors (Zhu and Chen 2013, 224 with footnote 15), *zhu* here is a polite form of address to a colleague of the same (*Liye* 8–158r, where both sender and addresse are vice prefects) or of a slightly lower rank (*FZS* 43=*RCL* E 16; *Liye* 16–9v, where a vice prefect addresses the head of a subordinate district). However, this seems unlikely because there are examples where a non-official person submits a report to the *zhu* as the head of a prefecture (*FZS* 6, 13=*RCL* E 4,5). It is uncertain whether *zhu* refers to

ince] is profitable[1314] for cultivation. Let [the land] produce[1315] [grain] for the government. I, your subject,[1316] am old, [so my son] Gui and his men went off to cultivate fields. As they are not provided[1317] with money and seeds, I wish[1318] that the vice prefect in charge loans[1319] them 20,000 cash and lends[1320] them

---

the vice prefect in all references as proposed by McLeod and Yates (1981, 133 footnote 62). Wu Wenling (2013, 163) considers *zhu* to be a polite form of address generally used in (official) documents.

1314 For *li* in the sense "to yield (financial) profit" see footnote 693.

1315 *Chan* 產 "(agricultural) produce" (*Lü* 26, 332 [cf. Knoblock and Riegel 2000, 651]: 以教民尊地產也。"In this way the people are taught to esteem the produce of the land.").

1316 For *chen* 臣 "your servant/subject" as a polite form of address to a superior see Giele 2006, 136 and 193.

1317 *Ji* 齎 (GSR 593u) [probably a character variant of *zi* 資 (GSR 555h), cf. examples in Wang Hui 2008, 533; Bai Yulan 2012, 339 and Feng and Deng 2006, 1084–1085] "to be provided/supplied/equipped with" (*Zhanguoce* 73A/31/5 [cf. Crump 1970, 106]: 藉賊兵而齎盜食 "to lend weapons to bandits and provide robbers with food"; *Lunheng* 45, 150: 孔子出使子路齎雨具。"Confucius went out, having Zilu provide him with rain gear. "; *Shiji* 6, 263 [cf. Nienhauser I (1994), 154]: 乃令入海者齎捕巨魚具。 "Then the emperor ordered those who would enter the sea to equip themselves with tools for catching a huge fish."]; QLSZ 45=RCL A 32: 齎食，毋以傳貣（貸）縣。"If they are provided with food, they must not use their passports to borrow [rations] from the prefectures."; QLSZ 103=RCL A 56: 齎律 "statutes on equipment" with note 6; QLSZ 105=RCL A 57) or nominally in the sense "means, funds" (ENLL 289: 欲受齎者 "those who want to receive funds").

1318 For *yuan* 願 "I wish" or "would it that" as a part of formal speech see Giele 2006, 103–104.

1319 *Jia* 叚 (GSR 33a) for *jia* 假 (GSR 33c) "to loan/lend, to borrow" (ENLL 78: 諸有叚（假）於縣道官，事已，叚（假）當歸。弗歸，盈廿日，以私自叚（假）律論。"For all cases of having borrowed sth. from the offices of prefectures and marches, the borrowed items by law are to be returned after the service has been finished. Those who fail to return them for twenty whole days will be sentenced according to the statutes on illegal borrowing."; QLSZ 101=RCL A 55: 邦中之繇（徭）及公事官（館）舍，其叚（假）公 "when someone borrows government [tools] for statute labour in the capital area as well as for public work in government buildings"). It was common practice that conscripts who were called up for statute labour had to borrow tools required for their work from the government (*jia gong qi* 假公器, QLSZ 77, 104=RCL A 77, 104). Recruits performing military service also had to borrow weapons from the government armoury (ZYS 131; QLSZ 102=RCL A 56). Furthermore, it was possible to borrow balances, weights and measures (QLSZ 100, 194=RCL A 54, 104), clothes (ENLL 286), carriages and horses (FLDW 159=RCL D 139), carts and oxen (QLSZ 126=RCL A 74; *Liye* 8–677r) or boats (*Liye* 6–4, 8–135r) from the government.

1320 *Te* 貣 (GSR 918h) here for the homeophonous *dai* 貸 (GSR 918p) "to borrow" (QLSZ 45=RCL A 32; FLDW 32=RCL D 26: 府中公金錢私貣（貸）用之，與盜同法。 "For secretly borrowing government money in a storehouse and using it the same rules as for theft apply."; QLSZ 44=RCL A 31; QLSZ 142=RCL A 65: 人奴妾毄（繫）城旦舂，

provisions to supply them[1321] for a full year. When the grain is ripe, the double amount will be paid back. Do not reject[1322] [my request]. If you reject it, I am not able to rush about[1323] serving[1324] you, the vice prefect in charge. May you and the chief of Huyang [prefecture] jointly be concerned[1325] about me, Wuze, and give a response[1326] [with a decision]. I venture to bring [this request] to

---

貣（貸）衣食公。"When private male and female slaves are detained among the earth and grain pounder convicts, they are to be loaned clothing and fed by the government."; *ENLL* 184; *Yuelu Shu* 143: 貣（貸）人百錢息八錢 "to lend sb. 100 cash and to earn 8 cash as interest"). *Dai* is also used nominally in the sense "credit/loan" in combination with its synonym *jia* 假 (*Shiji* 112, 2953 [cf. Nienhauser IX (2011), 373]: 家貧，假貸無所得。"His family was poor and did not get a loan from anyone."). The editors interpret *dai* in the present passage as noun and object of *jia* (Zhu and Chen 2013, 225 with footnote 18). However, because of the parallel structure of the two closely linked phrases following *jia* and *dai*, it seems more reasonable to understand *dai* as a verb here.

1321 *Zhi* 支 "to support, sustain", but also "to supply so. with sth." (*Hanshu* 24A, 1135 [cf. Swann 1950, 171]: 足支一歲以上 "enough [cereal] to supply them for one year and more"; *Hanshu* 69, 2986: 足支萬人一歲食 "enough [cereal] to supply 10,000 men with food for one year"; *Shiji* 69, 2259 [cf. Nienhauser VII (1994), 107: 粟支十年 "with cereals you are supplied for ten years").

1322 *Huan* 環 (*GSR* 256n) "refuse/reject (a request/report)" (*FLDW* 102=*RCL* D 85: 免老告人以爲不孝，謁殺，當三環之不？"[A man] relieved [from statutory duties because of] age reports sb. for unfilial behaviour and requests that he be killed. Is [his request] by law to be rejected three times or not?"; *FLDW* 147=*RCL* D 125: 甲徙居，徙數謁吏，吏環，弗爲更籍。"A moves his residence. He requests the official to transfer the [population] registration, but the official refuses and does not change the register."; *ENLL* 36, 482). Cf. the explanation of *huan* as *que* 卻 by Zheng Xuan (*Zhouli* 28, 831a, 844b) as well as the homophonous *huan* 還 (*GSR* 256k) "to withdraw/retreat" (*Hanfei* 21, 118; *Hanshu* 42, 2095).

1323 *Zou* 走 "to run" figuratively for "to hurry while serving sb., serve to the point of exhaustion" referring to subordinates who render service (*Shu* Duoshi §22: 奔走臣我 "to hasten about and serve us"; Duofang §24: 今爾奔走臣我監五祀。"Now you have hastened about and served our inspectors for five years."; *Chuci* 1/1/12: 忽奔走以先後兮。"Instantly I hasten about to be in front and rear.", cf. *Odes* 237,9: 予曰有先後，予曰有奔奏。"We had such who were before and behind us, we had such who hastened forward to us."). For *zou* as "messenger/runner" see footnote 865.

1324 *Chen* 臣 also occurs verbally in the sense "be at sb.'s service, to serve sb." (*Zuo* Xuan 12,311,10; Cheng 2,342,5; Xi 15,166,12; Wen 18,280,8; *Shiji* 23, 1164).

1325 This hardly visible character, which was originally identified as *fu* 复 (Zhu and Chen 2013, 225), is rather the character for *you* 憂 (Chen Songchang 2013; compare the forms of this character in Fang Yong 2012, 157) in the sense "to be worried/concerned about sb./sth." (*Yuelu Wei li* 31.2; *Wei li zhi dao* 40.4).

1326 For *bao* see footnote 581.

your attention.[1327] Send[1328] the letter[1329] [with the response] to court secretary[1330] Li."

有（又）曰：
馮將軍子臣癸$_{218}$敢昧死謁胡陽公：丈人詔令癸出田南陽，因穜（種）食錢貣（貸），以爲私。癸田$_{219}$新壄（野），新壄（野）丞主羘（幸）叚（假）癸錢食一歲。少吏莫敢訶癸。
今胡【陽少内丞矰】$_{220}$謂癸非馮將軍子。癸居秦中，名聞，以爲不▨$_{221}$□。癸穜（種）姓雖賤，能權任人，有（又）能下人。顲（願）公詔少吏，勿令環（還）。

Furthermore it was said [in a second letter]:
"I, the son of general Feng and your subject, venture to risk my life[1331] with [the following] request[1332] to the chief[1333] of Huyang [prefecture]: My father[1334]

1327 *Yi wen* 以聞 means "to bring sth. to sb.'s attention". In legal manuscripts it often occurs in the phrase *ting yi wen* 廷以聞 "the court brought (the case) to (His Majesty's) attention" (ZYS 26, 47, cf. ZYS 68). See Lau and Lüdke 2012, footnote 711 and Giele 2006, 97–100. Here *yi wen* does not refer to the ruler, but to the leading officials of a prefecture.

1328 For *ji* 寄 in the meaning "to accommodate/lodge sb.; to find accomodation" see footnote 1151. *Ji* also appears in the sense "to entrust/deposit" (*FLDW* 11=*RCL* D 10: 甲盜錢以買絲，寄乙，乙受，弗智（知）盜。"A steals money and uses it to buy silk. He entrusts [the silk] to B, and B accepts it without knowing about the theft."). In Han times *ji shu* 寄書 meant "to send a letter" (*Shiji* 100, 2731; *Juyan* 140.4B, 502.14B; *Juyan xinjian* EPT44:8A, EPT53:19; *Dunhuang* 749). This meaning of *ji* also makes sense in the present context.

1329 *Feng* 封 was used as a measure word for letters in the construction *shu mou feng* 書某封 "letters, X items" in Qin administrative documents (*Liye* 8–728r, 8–1119, 8–1225, 8–1533, 8–1886). Here *feng* obviously means "letter".

1330 For *ting shi* see footnote 1212.

1331 *Mei si* 昧死 "to risk one's life" (*Shiji* 43, 1823; *Hanfei* 1, 8), a polite phrase expressing the respect of a subordinate. See Giele 2006, 92–93, 122–125. *Mei* 昧 (GSR 531n) *mˤut-s (Pan Wuyun: *muuds) in this combination was interpreted as loan graph for *mao* 冒 (GSR 1062a) *mˤuk-s "to take a risk, to expose oneself (to danger)" (Feng and Deng 2006, 425), which belongs to a quite different OC rhyme class.

1332 For *ye* see footnote 882.

1333 *Gong* 公, probably an honourable form of address for superiors, was also used to refer to the head of a prefecture (*Liye* 8–135r, 8–472, 8–2196, 8–1430).

1334 *Zhang ren* 丈人 "mature/experienced man" is used as a designation for a man of the older generation (*Lunyu* 18, 393; *Hanshu* 38, 1995; 54, 2460; *Liye* 8–659+8–2088) or the own father (*Shuihudi mudu* 11v=*Sanjian* 1008v, cf. *liang lao* 兩老 on *mudu* 6r), as in the present

instructed[1335] and ordered me to go off and cultivate fields at Nanyang [province], to rely on provisions and money which are lent to me, and make a private [farm][1336] out of it. [When] I cultivated fields at Xinye[1337] [prefecture], the vice prefect in charge of Xinye fortunately loaned me money and provisions [to suffice for] one year. None of the minor officials[1338] dared to bother me with questions[1339] [about this].

---

case. Cf. *jia zhang ren* 家丈人 as a designation for the head of the household (*Shiji* 86, 2537).

1335 From the Qin dynasty onwards, *zhao* 詔 is normally used for orders of the emperor (*Shiji* 6, 236 [cf. Nienhauser I (1994), 136]: 王爲泰皇。命爲制、令爲詔、天子自稱曰朕。"The king is to be called 'His Primeval Majesty'. His orders are to be called 'decrees', and his ordinances 'edicts'; the Son of Heaven should use *zhen* ('the secluded one') when referring to himself."; *Liye* 8–461r). However, as the present case can be dated to pre-imperial Qin times (*Yuelu* WYZ 210 with footnote 1283), this might hint to a less terminological use of *zhao* (not restricted to the ruler) with the meaning "to order" or "to instruct" (*Zhuang* 29, 195: 夫爲人父者，必能詔其子；爲人兄者，必能教其弟。"Now, those who are fathers must be able to instruct their sons; those who are older brothers must be able to teach their younger brothers.").

1336 *Si* 私 perhaps refers to private farmland or privately cultivated fields (*Odes* 212,3: 雨我公田，遂及我私。"It rains on our public field, and then reaches our private ones."; *Hanshu* 24A, 1119 [cf. Swann 1950, 117]: 井方一里，是爲九夫。八家共之，各受私田百晦，公田十晦。"A *jing* was one *li* square and composed of nine *fu* (small squares). It was held in trust by eight families; each [family] received a private field of one hundred *mu*, and [cultivated] ten *mu* of the royal domain (the central square of the *jing*)."). The editors add the word *shu* 書 after *si* (Zhu and Chen 2013, 226). To accept this would of course lead to a different translation: "My father instructed and ordered me to go off and cultivate fields at Nanyang [province]. [As I would have to] rely on provisions and money which are lent to me [he] drew up a private [letter]."

1337 Xinye 新壄（野）was a prefecture (ENLL 448) in the province of Nanyang (*Hanshu* 28A, 1564) during Han times. Its administrative seat was located near present Xinye in southern Henan (*Lishi dituji* vol. II, 22/23, 6③). Xinye already was a prefecture during Qin times (Hou Xiaorong 2009, 274–275).

1338 *Shao li* 少吏 "minor/junior officials" in contrast to *zhang li* 長吏 "superior/senior officials" (ENLL 46: 長吏以縣官事詈少吏 "superior officials who curse minor officials because of official matters"; *Hanshu* 19A, 742: 秩四百石至二百石，是爲長吏。百石以下有斗食、佐史之秩，是爲少吏。"If their salary ranges between 400 and 200 *shi*, they are superior officials. If it is 100 *shi* or less, they are minor officials.").

1339 For *he* 訶 and its variant *ke* 苛 in the meaning "to cross-examine sb., take sb. to task, bother sb. with questions" see footnote 1122.

Now, [the assistant Zeng of the treasury of] Huyang said that I am not the son of general Feng. [As] I live in [the state of] Qin[1340] and I am well-known [there], to consider me not to be [...]. Although my clan[1341] is of low status, I am able to assign tasks to others[1342] in weighing [their pros and cons].[1343] Futhermore, I am able to subdue[1344] others. I wish that you, chief [of Huyang prefecture], instruct the minor officials not to reject me."

1340 Here, the editors refer to the commentary of Yan Shigu on *Hanshu* 31, 1807 (as well as *Hanshu* 1B, 59), where *Qin zhong* 秦中 is explained as Guanzhong 關中, the core area of Qin inside the passes (Zhu and Chen 2013, 226 with footnote 26).

1341 *Zhong xing* 種姓 "clan, lineage" (*Shiji* 110, 2900 [cf. Nienhauser IX (2011), 276]: 惡種姓之失也。"[The Xiongnu] dislike the loss of their clan/lineage."; see Cang Xiuliang 1991, 645).

1342 For *ren* 任 in the meaning "to recommend and guarantee for a person who should be appointed, to stand surety for sb." see footnote 1086. In the present context, *ren* means "to give responsibilities to sb., assign sb. a task, put sb. in charge, to employ sb." (*Zuo* Min 2,128,16: 任能 "to employ the capable ones"; *Hanfei* 32, 208 [cf. Harbsmeier]: 舉賢而任之 "to elevate the talented to high positions and employ them"; *Hanfei* 47, 325 [cf. Harbsmeier]: 任人以事 "employing people according to their public service"; *Xun* 2, 17 [cf. Knoblock I (1988), 155]: 人莫不任。"Everyone would be willing to employ [you]."; *Huai* 9, 135 [cf. Major et al. 2010, 310]: 所任者得其人則國家治[...]所任非其人則國家危。"If he has got the right man for the task he assigns him, then the state will be in order [...] if he has got the wrong man for the task he assigns him, then the state will be in danger."; *Zhanguoce* 384/185/13 [cf. Crump 1970, 277]: 其任官置吏必曰廉潔勝任。"When they assign an office and appoint an official they must say: 'He is honest and can fulfil his duties.'").

1343 *Quan* 權 is used here as an adverb "weighing (pros and cons)" (*Lü* 19, 254: 權而用其長者 "weigh [his abilities] and use his strong points"; *Lunyu* 9, 193 [cf. Harbsmeier]: 可與立，未可與權。"Someone with whom one may get firmly established is not necessarily someone with whom one may weigh pros and cons."; *Zuo* Xiang 23,497,13: 夫克亂在權。"Disorder is best repressed by [acting] as the occasion requires.").
Alternatively, *quan* 權 (GSR 1580) might be used for the homeophonous cognate *quan* 勸 (GSR 158s) "to exhort, motivate sb." (*Huai* 9, 132: 任輕者易權（勸）。"Those who are entrusted with light tasks are easily motivated." [cf. *Wen* 9/48/22–23: 任輕易勸也]; Feng and Deng 2006, 373; *Shu* Duofang §4: 不克終日勸于帝之迪。"He could not be motivated by God's guidance for a whole day."; *Shu* Duofang §29: 爾不克勸忱我命 "if you cannot be exhorted to faithfully observe my commands"). Cf. *quan* in the sense "to persuade, advise" (*Zuo* Xi 5,143,7: 故勸之城其賜邑 "therefore advised him to wall the town, which Qi had conferred upon him").

1344 *Xia* 下 "to subdue, cause to surrender" (*Shiji* 6, 230 [cf. Nienhauser I (1994), 131]: 於是使斯下韓。"Thereupon he sent [Li] Si to subdue Han."). Cf. *xia ren* as "to yield to others/give precedence to others" (*Hanshu* 62, 2729; *Shiji* 40, 1702).

First Stage of Interrogation – Part II

今$_{222}$⍁□召舍人興來。□⍁

Now [...] summoned the client Xing to come. [...]

⍁【癸】曰：
君子子，定名學，居新壄（野）。非五大夫馮將軍毋擇子$_{223}$殹（也）。學學史，有私印□□□□□馮將【軍】毋擇□□□□□□□□□$_{224}$害聲聞。學父秦居貲。吏治（笞）秦，以故數爲學怒。苦𦕅（恥）之。歸居室，心不$_{225}$樂，即獨撟（矯）自以爲五大夫馮毋擇子。以名爲僞私書，問矰，欲貣（貸）錢$_{226}$胡陽少内。以私印封，起室把詣于矰。狌（幸）其肯以威貣（貸）學錢。即盜以買$_{227}$金（錦）衣被兵，去邦亡荊。矰發讀書，未許學，令人毄（繫）守學。學恐，欲去亡，$_{228}$有（又）撟（矯）爲私書，自言胡陽固所。詑曰：學實馮毋擇子。新壄（野）丞主巳（已）⍁$_{229}$

[Gui] stated:
"I am the son of a *jun zi*, my registered name[1345] is Xue and I live at Xinye [prefecture]. I am not the son of the holder of the ninth rank and general Feng Wuze. I studied the profession of a scribe and have a private seal [stamp]. [...] General Feng Wuze [...] harmed the reputation[1346] of [...]. My father Qin[1347] had to work off a fine.[1348] The officials caned[1349] him and this made me angry

1345 For *ding ming* see footnote 685.

1346 *Sheng wen* 聲聞/問 "reputation" (*Xun* 27, 333 [cf. Knoblock III (1994), 226]: 德至者色澤洽，行盡而聲問遠。"When inner power has been perfected in a person, it penetrates into and imbues his countenance. When his conduct fully realises it, his reputation will be far-reaching."; *Hanfei* 30, 169: 子聞寡人之聲聞。"You have heard about my reputation."; *Meng* 8, 334: 故聲聞過情，君子恥之。"Thus, a gentleman is ashamed of a reputation which exaggerates the truth."; see also *Shiji* 75, 2353 [cf. Nienhauser VII (1994), 192]: 名聲聞於諸侯。"His reputation became well-known to the feudal lords.").

1347 Qin 秦 appears to be the given name (*ming* 名) of Xue's father. Liu Zhao (2012) cites some examples of the name "Qin".

1348 *Ju* 居 "to work off (fines/debts)" (QLSZ 78=RCL A 39: 終歲衣食不足以稍賞（償），令居之。"If at the end of the year the food and clothing [deducted] are insufficient to repay the losses completely, orders are to be given to work these off." with note 8; QLSZ 133–134=RCL A 68: 其弗能入及賞（償），以令日居之，日居八錢；公食者，日居六錢。居官府公食者，男子參，女子駟（四）。"Those who are unable to repay or to refund are to work off [their obligations] as from the day the order is given. Per day they work off eight cash; those fed by the government work off six cash per day. For those who work off [their debts] in government workshops and are fed by the government, [the rations are] for men one third [of a *tou* for the morning meal and again for the evening meal]; for women one quarter."; QLSZ 141=RCL A 65; QLSZ 144=RCL A 67: 居貲贖責（債）者歸田農，種時、治苗時各二旬。"Persons who work off fines, redemp-

several times. I suffered pain and was ashamed of this. When I returned home, my heart [felt] sad,[1350] so I, by myself, pretended to be the son of the holder of the ninth rank, Feng Wuze. In his name, I drew up a forged private letter, [in which] I extended my regards to Zeng, [and wrote that I] wanted to borrow money from the treasury[1351] of Huyang [prefecture]. I sealed [the letter] with a private seal [stamp], left home grasping [the letter] and presented it to Zeng. I hoped[1352] that he would be willing to use his authority[1353] to lend money to

---

tion fees or debts [are allowed to] return home for agricultural work at the time of sowing and at the time of weeding for 20 days each."; QLSZ 145=RCL A 69; *Liye* 6–22, 8–145r, 8–197v, 8–284, 8–985, 8–1014, 8–1095, 8–1328, 8–1381, 8–1566, 8–1641, 8–2035r).

1349 *Zhi* 治 (GSR 976z) here for *chi* 笞 (GSR 976b') "to cane" (QLSZ 14, 148–149=RCL A 7, 70; QLZC 6, 19–20=RCL C 4, 12; FLDW 13, 74, 79, 132, 163=RCL D 12, 62, 64, 110, 143; FZS 1, 4–5=RCL E 1, 2; ZYS 107, 109, 110, 113, 114, 115, 117, 118).

1350 *Bu le* 不樂 "uneasy, sad" (*Shiji* 6, 273 [cf. Nienhauser I (1994), 161]: 二世夢白虎齧其左驂馬，殺之，心不樂，怪問占夢。 "The Second Emperor saw in his dream a white tiger bite the horse on the left side of his [carriage] team and kill it. He was uneasy and consulted dream interpreters."; *Shiji* 9, 404 [cf. Nienhauser II (2002), 124]: 心懷不樂。 "In his heart he harboured sadness.").

1351 *Shao nei* 少内 was a treasury at the level of the prefecture, the head of which was in charge of receiving and disbursing money as well as fixing the regular market prices (FLDW 32=RCL D 26: 府中公金錢私貣用之，與盜同法。可（何）謂府中？唯縣少內爲府中。"For secretly borrowing government money in a storehouse and using it the same rules as for theft apply. What is the meaning of 'in a storehouse'? Only the prefectural treasury is 'in a storehouse'."; QLSZ 80=RCL A 40: 縣、都官坐效、計以負賞（償）者，已論，嗇夫即以其直（值）錢分負其官長及冗吏，而人與參辨券，以效少內，少內以收責之。"When prefectures and government offices are prosecuted [for irregularities when] checking and accounting, and they have been charged with repayment, after sentence has been pronounced the overseer immediately proportionally charges [the irregularities] to the accounts of the chief of the office concerned as well as the assigned officials according to the value in cash, and the persons concerned are [each] given one part of a tripartite tally to be presented to the treasury. The treasury uses this to collect the money and to demand the payment of it."; FZS 39=RCL E 15: 令少內某、佐某以市正賈（價）賈丙丞某前。"An order was given to the treasurer X and his assistant Y to fix a price for C according to the correct market price before the vice prefect."; *Liye* 8–75r, 8–155, 8–378, 8–409, 8–893, 8–1593, 8–1783). For descriptions of the functions of the *shao nei* cf. Hulsewé 1985, 50, note 9 to RCL A 40 and the commentary of Yan Shigu on *Hanshu* 74, 3149.

1352 For *xing* in the meaning "to hope for" see footnote 1232.

1353 *Yi wei* 以威 "using authority" (*Shiji* 87, 2559 [cf. Bodde 1938, 47/Nienhauser VII (1994), 352]: 昔者司城子罕相宋，身行刑罰，以威行之。"In ancient times when Zi Han, minister of the city, became prime minister of [the state of] Song, he personally handled punishments and penalties; using his authority he carried them out."; *Shiji* 92, 2612 [cf. Nienhauser VIII (2008), 77]: 今楚彊以威王此三人，秦民莫愛也。"Now Chu

me. Then I would have misappropriated[1354] it to buy brocade[1355] clothes[1356] and weapons, [and then] would have left and absconded from the state[1357] to Jing.[1358] [When] Zeng opened and read[1359] the letter, he ordered to place me under detention and guard,[1360] without granting[1361] my [request]. I was afraid[1362] and wanted to abscond, [so] I again drew up a private letter under

---

enthroned these three persons through its authority; but none of the Qin people love them."; *Hanfei* 9, 38 [cf. Harbsmeier]: 而用其威求誘其君。"And they will use their authority to misguide their ruler.").

1354 For *dao* see footnotes 541, 557 and 795.

1355 According to Chen Songchang (2013a) *jin* 金 (GSR 652a) *k(r)əm is used here for the homophonous *jin* 衿 (GSR 651g) "to tie; string for fastening garments" (cf. Wang Hui 2008, 779). With regard to the context *jin* 金 should rather be interpreted as to stand for the homeophonous *jin* 錦 (GSR 652e) * k(r)əmʔ "brocade" (*Odes* 130,1: 錦衣狐裘 "a robe of brocade and fox fur"; *Odes* 124,3: 錦衾爛兮。"The brocade coverlet so bright!").

1356 *Yi bei* 衣被, literally "robes and coverlets", seems to be a generic term for clothing (*Xun* 18, 222 [cf. Knoblock III (1994), 41]: 衣被則服五采，雜間色，重文繡，加飾之以珠玉。"The clothes and garments he wears are of five basic colours with every gradation of shade in between. They are covered with repeated patterns and embroidered designs with ornaments of pearl and jade."; *Huai* 18, 321; *Lü* 10, 97 [cf. Knoblock and Riegel 2000, 229]: 輦馬、衣被、戈劍，不可勝其數 "carriages and horses, robes and coverlets, halberds and swords, all too numerous to count"; *Shiji* 93, 2637 [cf. Nienhauser VIII (2008), 120]: 以太尉常從，出入臥內，衣被飲食賞賜，群臣莫敢望。 "As chief of staff, [Lu Wan] followed [Gaozu] constantly, [and was permitted] in and out of the [imperial] bedchamber. He was rewarded with clothing, food, and drink, [in a manner for which] none of the other ministers dared to hope.").

1357 For *bang wang* see footnote 512.

1358 For Jing as old name for Chu see footnote 608.

1359 The general word for reading was *du* 讀 (*Hanfei* 31, 184 [cf. Harbsmeier]: 大夫種受書讀之。"Grandee Zhong received the letter and read it."; *Hanfei* 32, 212 [cf. Harbsmeier]: 昭王讀法十餘簡而睡臥矣。"When King Zhao [of Wei] had read ten odd bamboo slips of the law he fell asleep."; *Zhanguoce* 40/14/3 [cf. Crump 1970, 57]: 讀書欲睡引錐自刺其股血流至足。"If while reading he felt a desire to sleep, he drew a gimlet and stabbed his thigh till the blood ran down to his feet."; *Li* 20, 1405a; *Odes* 46,3; *Meng* 10, 428; *Guliang* 8, 2396a; *Mo* 31, 144; *Lunyu* 11, 251; *Shiji* 67, 2212; *Li* 40, 1551b).

1360 *Shou* 守 "to keep guard over the relatives of an offender" (FZS 7, 8, 11–12, 41=RCL E 4, 3, 15).

1361 *Xu* 許 "to grant sb.'s request, comply with sb.'s request" (*Yan* 1, 6: 三請不見許。"He requested it three times [of his duke], but the request was not granted."; *Shiji* 63, 2145 [cf. Nienhauser VII (1994), 24]: 楚威王聞莊周賢使使厚幣迎之許以爲相。"King Wei of Chu heard that Zhuang Zhou was efficient and sent a messenger to invite him with lavish gifts, granting him an appointment as prime minister."; *Zhanguoce* 32/11/7 [cf. Crump 1970, 32]: 魏王因使孟卯致溫囿於周君而許之戍也。 "The king of Wei thereupon sent Meng Mao to present Wenyou to Zhoujun and granted him guard.").

1362 For *kong* without object see footnote 935.

false pretences, in which I myself submitted a request[1363] to [prefect] Gu of Huyang. I lied[1364] saying: 'I am in fact[1365] the son of Feng Wuze. The vice prefect of Xinye in charge has already […].'"

[Missing slip]

Second Stage of Interrogation(?) (Confrontation)

【詰】學：
吏節（即）不智（知）學爲僞書，不許貣（貸）學錢，退去學，學即道胡陽$_{230}$行邦亡，且不？

[We confronted] Xue:[1366]
"If the officials had not realised that you drew up a forged letter, [but still] had not granted [the request] to lend you money and had [instead] sent you away,[1367] you would still have marched off from[1368] Huyang [prefecture] and have absconded from the state, wouldn't you?"

辤（辭）曰：
吏節（即）不智（知）學爲僞【書】，不貣（貸）學錢，毋（無）以爲衣被$_{231}$資用。去環（還）歸。有衣資用，乃行邦亡。

[Gui] explained himself[1369] stating:
"If the officials had not realised that I drew up a forged letter, [but still] had not lent me money, I would have had no means[1370] to procure clothes and resources.[1371] [In that case] I would have left and returned home. If I had had

1363 For *zi yan* see footnote 755.

1364 For *tuo* see footnote 772.

1365 For *shi* see footnote 533.

1366 The following sequence appears to be the beginning of a confrontation (*jie* 詰) as the second stage of interrogation, for this see footnote 792.

1367 *Tui qu* 退去 "to reject, dismiss, send away" (*Hanshu* 36, 1932; *Hanshu* 81, 3360).

1368 *Dao* 道 (GSR 1048a) *lˤuʔ for the homeophonous *you* 由 (GSR 1079a) *lu (Pan Wuyun: *liw) (FLDW 196=RCL D 176; FZS 67, 70=RCL E 21; *Liye* 8–547, 8–1562r; ENLL 404; ZYS 54, 110, 114, 118, 172, 198; *Hanshu* 44, 2148). See Lau and Lüdke 2012, footnote 824.

1369 *Ci* 辤（辭） here as "to explain oneself, apologise" (*Zuo* Xi 4,140,8/10). For the usage as "statement" and "to lodge a complaint" see footnotes 564 and 765, respectively.

1370 On the indefinite substitution *wu yi* 無以 see footnote 807.

1371 *Zi yong* 資用 "resources" (*Guoyu* 1.29/21/3: 資用乏匱。"The resources were lacking and deficient."; *Shiji* 112, 2953 [cf. Nienhauser IX (2011), 374]: 資用乏。"He lacked resources."; *Shiji* 121, 3125 [cf. Watson 1993, vol. II, 366]: 兒寬貧無資用。"Ni Kuan was poor and had no resources."). In the present passage, it may also refer to other supplies such as provisions for the journey.

clothes and resources, then I would have marched off and absconded from the state."

Interagency Enquiries

問：
學撟（矯）爵爲僞書時，馮$_{232}$毋擇爵五大夫，將軍。學不從軍，年十五歲。
它如辤（辭）。$_{233}$

[Results of the] interagency enquiries:[1372]
At the time when Xue arrogated a rank[1373] to himself and drew up a forged letter, Feng Wuze had the ninth rank and was a general. Xue has not done military service [yet], and he is 15 years old.
Everything else corresponded to the statements.

Finding of Fact

鞫之：
學撟（矯）自以五大夫將軍馮毋擇子，以名爲僞私書。詣𢅽，以欲$_{234}$盜去邦亡。未得，得。審。

Finding of fact:[1374]
Xue arrogated to himself to be the son of Feng Wuze, holder of the ninth rank and general, and in his name drew up a forged private letter. He presented it to Zeng, and by this means wanted to commit theft and abscond from the state. Before he succeeded, he was caught. [All these] are established facts.

Submission by Huyang Prefecture – Concluding Formula

毄（繫）。敢讞（讞）之。

[Xue] is held under detention.[1375] We venture to submit [this case] for decision.[1376]

1372 For *wen* see footnote 562. Here, the arrogated rank, the age of the accused (he was a minor) and the fact that he had not performed military service (he had probably not been registered for services at this point) were taken into account as sentencing-relevant particulars.

1373 For *jue* see footnote 834.

1374 For *ju* see footnote 565.

1375 For *ji*/*xi* see footnote 569.

1376 For *yan* and the phrase *gan yan zhi* see footnote 489.

Alternative Votes for Judgement

吏議：
耐學隸臣。
或：
令贖耐。235

The [responsible] officials deliver [the following] legal opinion:[1377]
"Xue is to be shaved and made a bond servant convict."
Some say:[1378]
"Let him pay the fee for redemption from shaving."[1379]

Response to the Submission by the Province (Decision)

瀻（讞）報：
毋擇巳（已）爲卿。貲某、某各一盾。謹窮以灋（法）論之。236

Response to the submission:
Wuze already has the rank of a *qing*.[1380] [Officials] X and Y shall each be fined one shield.[1381] Make a careful and exhaustive[1382] [investigation] and sentence[1383] him (Xue) according to the law.[1384]

1377 For *li yi* see footnote 572.

1378 For *huo yue* see footnote 573.

1379 *Shu nai* 贖耐 "to redeem oneself from penal labour of the category *nai*" (*Liye* 8–149, 8–811, 8–1461r, 8–1734; QLZC 32=RCL C 20; FLDW 64–65, 185=RCL D 136, 52, 164; *Longgang* 109, 121, 234; ZYS 53; ENLL 6, 42, 89, 97, 119, 120, 129, 158, 171, 398). For *shu* cf. footnote 541.

1380 *Qing* 卿 refers to holders of the 18th to the 10th rank as a social stratum. This is evidenced by early Han statutes concerning food rations for holders of passports, burial allowances, registration for labour and military service and appointment as heir, where *qing* ranks above the holder of the ninth rank *wu da fu* 五大夫 (ENLL 236, 289) or between *wu da fu* and the holder of the 19th rank *guan nei hou* 關內侯 (ENLL 291, 359, 367). This classification is in accordance with the *Jue zhi* 爵制 of Liu Shao 劉劭 (third century AD, cited in the commentary to *Houhanshu* 28, 3631). In their response (*bao* 報), the higher authorities state that Wuze's rank in fact is (at least) one degree higher than assumed by the subordinate officials who submitted the case for decision (*Yuelu* WYZ 234).

1381 For *zi* see footnotes 558 and 594. During the Qin dynasty one shield (*yi dun* 一盾) was equivalent to 384 cash (*Yuelu Shu* 82–83; Yu Zhenbo 2010, 38).

1382 Cf. *qiong* 窮 "exhaustively" in the context of investigating crimes (ENLL 93: 鞫獄故縱、不直，及診、報、辟故弗窮審者，死罪，斬左止爲城旦。"Those who, when finding the facts in a criminal case, intentionally leave [the accused] unpunished or pervert justice as well as those who intentionally do not fully establish the facts when gathering evidence by inspection, when giving a response [to requests for information] or when notifying [another office], have their left foot cut off and are made earth pounder convicts if the case involves an offence punishable by death."; *Liye* 8–970; *Hanshu*

67, 2912; cf. *qiong xun* 窮訊 in ZYS 76, 77; *qiong zhi* 窮治 in ZYS 84; *Shiji* 30, 1424; 118, 3088; 122, 3150; 124, 3188).

1383 For *lun* see footnote 540.

1384 For *fa* see footnote 559.

Case IV.15

In this case, two groups of soldiers were prosecuted for having retreated out of cowardice during a military campaign against rebel forces, thus causing some members of their group to be killed.

Although only small parts of the interrogation are preserved, it becomes clear that the two groups of soldiers ran back different distances during their retreat, the first of them about 17 m, the second almost 65 m. In the following part, which can probably be attributed to the second stage of interrogation, the judicial officials confronted the first group of accused soldiers with the fact that other soldiers, who had formed a unit or units of five as prescribed, did not sustain any casualties. In their reply, the soldiers of this group pleaded guilty to the charge of retreating out of cowardice.

Instead of the usual interagency enquiries the next part of the record contains the results of measurements carried out for the different distances the two groups of soldiers ran back during their retreat as well as the height and width of fortifications such as walls and trenches probably belonging to the military camp of the accused soldiers.

In the fragments of the finding of fact it is stated that the members of the second group did not form units of five, enabling the rebels to kill members of the group with crossbows and short-range weapons, which in turn caused the soldiers to retreat out of cowardice. The occurrence of the note that "in all other matters the prefecture has passed judgement" points to the fact that there remained certain legal doubts concerning the punishment of (some of) the accused soldiers.

As in this case the law did apparently not provide a clear basis for judgement, a judicial official submitted a proposal for judgement to be approved by the higher authorities. The proposed sentences differed according to the roles the soldiers played during the cowardly retreat. The soldiers who ran away first were to be punished most severely; the punishments for those who followed them gradually decreased depending on the order in which they retreated. However, it seems that this proposal for judgement was connected to the request to enact a corresponding ordinance. At least, this is suggested by the typical final note of approval by the ruler and the fact that the directly preceding part does not contain the personal names of the accused. The enactment of an ordinance would ensure that in the future similar cases could be tried without submission to the higher authorities for approval.

 | DOI 10.1163/9789004315655_023

Diplomatic Edition[1385]

⧄□六年九月□□□⧄$_{237}$⧄□不敢獨前畏耎與偕環走十二步反寇來追者少皆止□□□⧄$_{238}$⧄走可卌六□□□□□□□⧄$_{239}$積=秥=等伍束符卒毋死傷者⧄$_{240}$敢獨前誠畏耎而與偕環走可十二步反寇來追者少皆□□射反=寇=敗入峇中皋毋解•診丈問得$_{241}$等環走卌六步獿等十二步術廣十二步垣高丈忌等死時得綰等去之遠者百步他如辤•鞫之$_{242}$得文芻慶綰等與反寇戰不伍束符忌以射死卒喜等⧄短兵死畏耎去環走卌六步逢包$_{243}$⧄□轂它縣論⧄$_{245}$⧄□臣□請取□⧄$_{243(3)}$皆致灋焉⌞有取卒畏耎最先去先者次十二人完以爲城旦鬼薪⌞有取其次十四人耐以$_{244}$爲隸臣其餘皆奪爵以爲士五其故上造以上有令戍四歲公士六歲公卒以下八歲□$_{244(2)}$臣昧死請•制曰可$_{244(3)}$

Edition and Translation

Submission by the Prefecture – Introductory Formula

⧄□六年九月□□□⧄$_{237}$

[In the ...]sixth year, in the ninth month [...]

First Stage of Interrogation

【獿等曰：…】
⧄□不敢獨前。畏耎（愞），與偕環（還）走十二步。反寇來追者少，皆止□□□⧄$_{238}$

[Qiao and his comrades stated:][1386]
"[...] we did not venture to advance alone. We were cowardly,[1387] turned around

1385 The arrangement of the slips of this case follows the corrections in Hafner 2014a. Only the tentatively placed fragment 243(2) carrying illegible writing has been left out here due to the lack of evidence as to where it belongs.

1386 The following passage is probably part of the statement of Qiao and his comrades because they were the ones who ran back twelve paces (see *Yuelu* WYZ 242). This would correspond with this statement (cf. Zhu and Chen 2013, 280).

1387 *Wei nuo* 畏耎（愞）"cowardice" was an offence in military penal law (*ENLL* 142–143: 與盜賊遇而去北及力足以追逮捕之而官□□□□□逗留畏耎（愞）弗敢就，奪其將爵一絡〈級〉，免之，毋爵者戍邊二歲；而罰其所將吏徒以卒戍邊各一歲。興吏徒追盜賊，已受令而逋，以畏耎論之。"Running away when confronting bandits as well as, when the strength is sufficient to pursue and arrest them, [...] to halt out of cowardice and not dare to attack [is punished in the following way:] the commander is deprived of one degree of his rank and relieved from his command; those without a rank have to perform two years of [additional] military service at the frontier; the officers

and ran back[1388] twelve paces[1389] together[1390] with them (i.e. De and his comrades). The rebellious bandits[1391] who came to pursue[1392] us were only a few, so we all stopped [...]."

【得等曰：…】
□走可卌六□□□□□□□ 239

[De and his comrades stated:][1393]
"[...] we ran [back] about 46 [paces[1394] ...]."

---

and conscripts commanded by him are each fined one year of [additional] military service at the frontier as [normal] soldiers. If officers and conscripts are drafted by the local authorities for the purpose of pursuing bandits, and they evade service after already having received their [draft] order, judgement is passed on them for 'cowardice'."; *Hanshu* 6, 204 [cf. Dubs II (1944), 107–108]: 匈奴入鴈門，太守坐畏愞棄市。 "The Xiongnu entered Yanmen [province] and its governor was prosecuted for cowardice and publicly executed."). For the variant *wei nuo* 畏懦 see also Ru Chun's commentary on *Hanshu* 6, 204, which cites Han military law: 行逗留畏懦者，要斬。 "Those who halt out of cowardice during an expedition will be cut in two at the waist."; *Shiji* 114, 2982=*Hanshu* 95, 3862; *Hanshu* 98, 4013; *Shiji* 20, 1034=*Hanshu* 17, 645; *Shiji* 20, 1037–1038=*Hanshu* 17, 646; *Hanshu* 17, 655. Cf. the similar offence *dan fa bu dou* 儋乏不鬥, which was punished with *zhan* 斬 during the Qin dynasty (ZYS 157–158).

1388 *Huan zou* 還走 "to turn around and run back/beat a hasty retreat" (*Shiji* 8, 368 [cf. Nienhauser II (2002), 46]: 雍兵敗，還走。"The soldiers of Yong suffered a defeat and beat a hasty retreat."; *Shiji* 106, 2834 [cf. Nienhauser IX (2011), 121]: 又敗梁兩將，士卒皆還走梁。"[Wu] again defeated two commanders of Liang, whose soldiers all beat a hasty retreat to Liang."; *Shiji* 7, 308; 115, 2987).

1389 During the reign of Qin Shihuang, one (double) pace (*bu* 步) as length measure (FLDW 101=RCL D 84; FZS 59, 61, 79=RCL E 20, 22; ENLL 246) was equal to six feet (*chi* 尺) (*Shiji* 6, 238), which equals approximately 1.40 m (cf. Qiu Guangming 1992, 11, 56). Twelve (double) paces amounted to about 16.8 m.

1390 For *xie* see footnote 1223.

1391 *Fan kou* 反寇 are "rebellious bandits, rebels" (*Shiji* 8, 385 [cf. Nienhauser II (2002), 74]: 高祖東擊韓王信餘反寇於東垣。 "Gaozu moved east to strike at the bandits remaining from the rebellion of the king of Han, Xin, at Dongyuan."; *Hanshu* 1B, 70 [cf. Dubs I (1938), 128]: 諸縣堅守不降反寇者，復租賦三歲。 "Those prefectures which had been firmly defended and not surrendered to the rebellious bandits were exempted from the land tax and poll taxes for three years.").

1392 For *zhui* see footnote 510.

1393 The following passage is probably part of the statement of De and his comrades because they were the ones who ran back 46 paces (see *Yuelu* WYZ 241–242), which would be in accordance with this statement (cf. Zhu and Chen 2013, 280).

1394 Ca. 64.4 m, cf. footnote 1389.

Second Stage of Interrogation (Confrontation)

【詰膠等：…】
穨、秙。穨、秙等伍、束符，卒毋（無）死傷者。☐$_{240}$

[We confronted Qiao and his comrades:][1395]
"[…] Tui and Ku. Tui, Ku and their comrades formed a unit of five[1396] and were bound by[1397]

1395 With regard to the following response by Qiao and his comrades (see *Yuelu* WYZ 241 with footnote 1399 below), this passage is probably part of the preceding confrontation (*jie* 詰), cf. Zhu and Chen 2013, 280.

1396 *Wu* 伍 referred to a military "unit (consisting) of five soldiers", which was deployed on campaigns (*ENLL* 141–142: 吏將徒，追求盜賊，必伍之，盜賊以短兵殺傷其將及伍人，而弗能捕得，皆戍邊二歲。卅日中能得其半以上，盡除其罪；得不能半，得者獨除。 "Officials leading conscripts to pursue and search for bandits must organise them into units of five. When they (the units) are not able to arrest the bandits, although these killed or injured their commander or a member of their unit with short-range weapons (i.e. daggers, swords or pikes), they are all to perform two years of [additional] military service at the frontier. If they are able to catch half of the bandits or more within 30 days, they will completely be exempted from punishment; if they are not able to catch half of them, only those who caught bandits will be exempted."). The system of units of five is explained in *Weiliaozi* B 14/28/5–6: 軍中之制，五人爲伍，伍相保也；[…]伍有干令犯禁者，揭之，免於罪；知而弗揭，全伍有誅。 "According to the regulations within the army, five men constitute a unit of five; [the members of] a unit of five stand surety for each other. […] When there is somebody in the unit who disobeys orders or violates prohibitions, [and someone from his unit] exposes him, [the other members] will be exempted from punishment. When [the other members] know about it but do not expose [the offender], the entire unit will be punished."
Wu were also basic units within the rural communities created during the reforms of Shang Yang in Qin around 350 BC (*Shiji* 68, 2230 [cf. Duyvendak 1928, 15]: 令民爲什伍，而相牧司連坐。 "He ordered the people to form units of ten or five, and ordered them to supervise and to watch each other, and made them collectively liable to prosecution [for offences of members in their units]."). This system remained intact and was still maintained at the beginning of Han times (*ENLL* 305: 自五大夫以下，比地爲伍，以辨□爲信，居處相察，出入相司。 "Among [the households of] the holders of the ninth and lower ranks, those with adjoining land form a group of five. They divide [a tally] as evidence [for their collective liability]. When staying at home they watch each other, when going out and coming in, they supervise each other."). The system was also applied to the agricultural garrisons near the Edsin Gol in Eastern Han times (*Juyan* 29.8: 五家相證任。"Five families stand surety for each other."). See also Yates 2009.

1397 The meaning of *shu fu* 束符 is not entirely clear. The editors translate "(the soldiers) received the controlling/restraining credentials" (Zhu and Chen 2013, 314) and quote an obscure passage from *Shangjunshu* (19, 34: 五人來簿爲伍) as reference, which was

the credentials[1398] [noting their collective liability for disobeying orders], so

emended by Sun Yirang as: 五人束簿爲伍 (cf. Duyvendak 1928, 296–297: "five men are organised into a squad"). According to their opinion, *shu fu* 束符 has to be understood in a similar way as *shu bu* 束簿 (Zhu and Chen 2013, 240 with footnote 6). However, the above emendation, which implies a scribal mistake, is problematic for mainly two reasons: First, the character *lai* 來 (Zhang Shouzhong 1994, 81; Chen Songchang 2001a, 218; Fang Yong 2012, 156) was clearly distinct from *shu* 束 (Zhang Shouzhong 1994, 92; Chen Songchang 2001a, 255; Fang Yong 2012, 180), at least until the mid-second century BC. Second, there is no other evidence for the expression *shu bu*. Therefore, although the alternative *lai bu* 來簿 is equally odd, interpretations which rely on this emendation – e.g. Gao Heng (1974, 412), who translates *shu bu* 束簿 as "to be entered/noted in one register" – should be considered tentative. Cf. Zhang Boyuan (2014c), who considers *wu shu fu* 伍束符 to be an abbreviation of *shu wu zhi fu* 束伍之符 with *shu* 束 meaning "to note, enter", as well as Zhu Honglin (2014), who interprets *wu shu fu* 伍束符 as a noun with a similar meaning as *wu ji* 伍籍 or *wu fu* 伍符 found in other sources.

In sources from pre-imperial and early imperial China, there can only be found one other occurrence of the expression *shu fu* 束符 (*Liu tao* 3.13/28/27 [cf. Strätz 1979, 91]: 田里相伍，其約束符信也。"[Those who in times of peace form] units of five with each other in the rural quarters, [in times of war are those who] are controlled/bound by a credential."). In this passage, the two words obviously belong to two separate terms (*yue shu* "control/bind" vs. *fu xin* "credential"), but *shu fu* could be interpreted as an abbreviation of this four-character-phrase.

A second passage from another military text provides further clues for the interpretation, as it not only mentions *shu* 束 and *fu* 符, but also *wu* 伍, which immediately precedes the former two words in the present context: *Weiliaozi* B 16/28/30–31: 束伍之令曰：五人爲伍，共一符，收於將吏之所。亡伍而得伍，當之；得伍而不亡，有賞；亡伍不得伍，身死家殘。"The ordinances for controlling the units of five read: Five men constitute a unit of five and share one credential [of collective liability], which is gathered [and kept] by the leading officers. Losing [a member of] the unit of five but catching [a member of an enemy] unit of five compensates each other; catching [a member of an enemy] unit of five without losing [a member of one's own] unit of five will be rewarded; those who lose [a member of one's own] unit of five without catching [a member of an enemy] unit of five will be put to death and their families will be exterminated."

According to the above passage, the shared credential (*fu*) appears to be the means by which each unit of five (*wu*) is controlled (*shu*). This would correspond with the interpretation of *shu fu* 束符 as "to be controlled/bound by a credential" (see the above passage from *Liu tao*). To explain the passive voice, *shu fu* 束符 would have to be read as *shu yu fu* 束於符 (cf. *Zhuang* 17, 100: 曲士不可以語於道者，束於教也。"A narrow-minded scholar cannot be talked to about the Way because he is bound by his doctrines.").

1398 *Fu* 符 refers to tallies or credentials made of bronze, jade, bamboo or wood serving different purposes (Chen Zhi 1986, 40–44). They certified an authorisation or obligation and were pieces of evidence (*xin* 信 as in *Mo* 70, 348) that were used for verification (*yan*

驗 in *Shiji* 52, 2001). They were introduced in order to "cause the common people not to cheat each other" (*Hanfei* 26, 151). Many references show that *fu* were used as passports for crossing the checkpoints at passes and fords, see received literature (*Mo* 70, 355), legal manuscripts from Qin (*FLDW* 184=*RCL* D 163) and early Han times (*ENLL* 74–75, 488–491, 496) as well as documents from the frontier garrisons at the Edsin Gol (Li Junming 2009, 432–433: *Juyan* 11.8, 11.26, 65.7, 65.9–10, 274.10; cf. Li Junming 1983; Ôba 1992, 159–177). These tallies, mostly made of bamboo or wood, were split into two parts that showed the same notches, thereby proving that the parts belong together. Sometimes such *fu*, which served as official passports, recorded the name and function of the bearer as well as the name and the age of members of his family that travelled with him (e.g. wife, children, siblings and concubines) (Li Junming 2009, 434: *Juyan* 29.2).

In the present context, *fu* must have served military purposes, as in some other references in excavated manuscipts or received literature (*QLZC* 4–5=*RCL* C 3: 游士在，亡符，居縣貲一甲；卒歲，責之。"When wandering warriors are staying [somewhere] without credentials, the prefecture where they dwell will be fined one suit of armour; at the end of the year [the prefecture] will be charged."; *Mo* 70, 348 [cf. Johnston 2010, 861]: 吏從卒四人以上有分〔守〕者，大將必與爲信符。大將使人行守，操信符，信不合及號不相應者，伯長以上輒止之，以聞大將。"Officers from the four assistants upwards who have defensive responsibilities must be given reliable credentials by the commander-in-chief, and when he sends men out on defensive business, they should carry these reliable credentials. In case reliable [credentials] do not correspond or calls do not elicit a matching response, [military officers] from the leaders of a hundred men upward immediately stop them and bring the matter to the commander-in-chief's attention.").

In Qin times, bronze credentials were used to mobilise troops. Some extant examples carry inscriptions, which demonstrate that the right part was kept by the ruler as issuer, while the left one was delivered to the prefecture as the authorised agency (Wang Xueli et al. 1994, 170–171: *Jinwen* 18.12108/12109). An account in received literature further shows that the second part of such credentials could also be handed out to military commanders (*Shiji* 77, 2381).

So-called "bronze tiger credentials" (*tong hu fu* 銅虎符) were first made for the governors of the provinces by the Han Emperor Wen (*Shiji* 10, 424=*Hanshu* 4, 118 with explanations by Ying Shao and Ôba 1991, 216–226; *Shiji* 52, 2001 [cf. Watson 1993, vol. I, 350]: 王欲發兵，非有漢虎符驗也。"Even though the king wants to mobilise the troops, he does not have the tiger credentials of the Han court, which would give him the authority to do so."; *Shiji* 114, 2980 [cf. Watson 1993, vol. II, 220]: 不欲出虎符發兵郡國。"I do not wish to issue the tiger credentials and mobilise the troops of [all] the provinces and kingdoms."; *Shiji* 122, 3151).

Wu fu 伍符 "credentials of the unit of five", which appear to be meant in the present case, are only scarcely mentioned in other sources (*Shiji* 102, 2759 [cf. Nienhauser VII (1994), 366]=*Hanshu* 50, 2314: 夫士卒盡家人子，起田中從軍，安知尺籍伍符。"Now, his officers and soldiers are all sons of [common] families who rose from their fields to join the army. They certainly do not know anything about registers of the length of one foot

among these conscripts there was nobody who died or was injured. [...].”

【獿等曰：…】
敢獨前。誠畏耎（愞）而與偕環（還）走可十二步。反寇來追者少，皆□□射反寇，反寇敗入笿中。辠（罪）。毋（無）解。

[Qiao and his comrades stated:][1399]
“[...] We did [not] venture to advance alone. We were in fact[1400] cowardly, turned around and ran back about twelve paces together with them (i.e. De and his comrades). The rebellious bandits who came to pursue us were only few, so we all [stopped ...] and shot at the rebellious bandits, who [however] defeated us and invaded [our camp's] tiger palisades.[1401] We are liable to punishment. We do not have [any other] explanation.”[1402]

Forensic Examination, Measuring and Interagency Enquiries

診、丈、問：
得₂₄₁等環（還）走卌六步，獿等十二步，術廣十二步，垣高丈。忌等死時，得、綰等去之遠者百步。
他如辤（辭）。

[recording severed heads of enemies] or about the credentials of a group of five [soldiers liable for each other's offences].”; *Weiliaozi* B 16/28/30: 束伍之令曰：五人爲伍，共一符，收於將吏之所。 “The ordinances for controlling the units of five read: Five men constitute a unit of five and share one credential [of collective liability], which is gathered [and kept] by the leading officers.”). Obviously, these *wu fu* were tokens representing the collective liability for any offences committed by any member of a unit of five, which all members had promised to observe. For lack of any archaeological evidence, it remains uncertain whether the credentials of the unit of five were inscribed with the names of the unit's members or an order to stand surety for one another.

1399 The following passage is probably part of a statement of Qiao and his comrades as the response to a confrontation (*jie* 詰), because they were the ones who ran back 12 paces (see *Yuelu* WYZ 241–242), and the formula *zui wu jie* 罪無解 typically occurs in the final part of such a response, see footnotes 800 and 985.

1400 For *cheng* see footnote 801.

1401 *Luo* 笿 according to the editors for *hu luo* 虎落 “tiger palisades” (Zhu and Chen 2013, 240 with footnote 9), a barrier made of lashed bamboo pickets for the protection of a military camp (*Hanshu* 47, 2286; *Liu tao* 4.1/30/26; *Liu tao* 4.1/31/8; according to an emendation by Strätz [1979, 107 with footnote 12] also in *Liu tao* 4.5/33/26).

1402 For the implications of *wu jie* in the reply of the accused see footnote 800. In the present as well as in other criminal cases (*Yuelu* WYZ 130, 165; ZYS 22, 31, 87, 150), the concluding statement *wu jie* is preceded or followed by the confession of guilt *zui* 辠（罪） “I am liable to punishment”.

[Results of] forensic examination,[1403] measuring[1404] and interagency enquiries:[1405]
De and his comrades turned around and ran back 46 paces, Qiao and his comrades 12 paces; the width of the trench[1406] was 12 paces, the height of the wall was one *zhang*.[1407] When Ji and his comrades died, De, Wan and their comrades were 100 paces[1408] away from them.
Everything else corresponded to the statements.

Finding of Fact

鞫之：$_{242}$
得、文、芻、慶、綰等與反寇戰，不伍、束符。忌以射死，卒喜等☐短兵死，畏耎（愞），去環（還）走卌六步。逢包$_{243}$

Finding of fact:[1409]
When De, Wen, Chu, Qing, Wan and their comrades fought against the rebellious bandits, they had not formed units of five and [therefore] they were not

1403 For *zhen* see footnote 1095.

1404 *Zhang* 丈 "to measure out (a length)" (*Zuo* Xiang 9,426,5–6: 巡丈城 "he went around the wall and measured it out"; *FLDW* 6=*RCL* D 5: 甲盜牛，盜牛時高六尺，毄（繫）一歲，復丈，高六尺七寸。"A stole an ox; at the time he stole the ox, he was six feet tall. Having been held under detention for one year, he was measured again; he was six feet and seven inches tall.").

1405 For *wen* see footnote 562.

1406 *Shu* 術 (*GSR* 497d) *m-lut (Baxter and Sagart: *Cə-lut, Pan Wuyun: *Gljud) were "ditches" or "trenches" serving as field boundaries (*Lü* 1, 2=*Li* 14, 1356c: 王布農事，命[…]皆修封疆，審端徑術。"The king distributes the agricultural activities and commands that […] all are to repair the boundary hills and lines and carefully correct the pathways and ditches between the fields."). Based on divergent glosses, *shu* was translated in the cited passage as "canals" (Couvreur 1950, vol. I, 336 based on Zheng Xuan) or "small pathways" (Knoblock and Riegel 2000, 60 based on Gao You). The difference between *jing* 徑 and *shu* 術 is made clear in a description of the system of field demarcation (*Zhouli* 15, 740c: 凡治野〔田〕，夫間有遂，遂上有徑；十夫有溝，溝上有畛；百夫有洫，洫上有涂；千夫有澮，澮上有道；萬（大）〔夫〕有川，川上有路，以達于畿。). Here, its cognate *sui* 遂 (*GSR* 526d) *s-lut-s (Baxter and Sagart: *sə-lut-s, Pan Wuyun: *sGluds; cf. Sagart 1999, 42, 114; Jin Lixin 2006, 299–300; Feng and Deng 2006, 252) is used instead of *shu*. *Sui* is listed among other types of ditches and canals between fields, while *jing* is located above the ditch *sui*. In the present context, *shu* probably means a trench or ditch serving as fortification of a military camp.

1407 A *zhang* 丈 as a measure of length or distance (*FZS* 68, 79=*RCL* E 21, 22) was equal to ten feet (*chi* 尺) and close to 2.30 m.

1408 Ca. 140 m, cf. footnote 1389.

1409 For *ju* see footnote 565.

bound by a certificate [noting their collective liability for disobeying orders]. When Ji was killed by a crossbow bolt and the conscript Xi and his comrades [...] were killed by short-range weapons,[1410] they (i.e. De and his comrades) became cowardly, turned around and ran back 46 paces. They got into an encirclement(?)[1411] [...].

Submission by the Prefecture – Concluding Formula

☒□毄（繫）。它縣論。☒$_{245}$

[...] held under detention.[1412] In all other matters the prefecture has passed judgement.[1413] [...]

Request (For Enactment of an Ordinance)

☒□臣□請：
取□☒$_{243(3)}$[1414]皆致灋（法）焉。有（又）取卒畏耎（愞）最先去、先者次十二人，完以爲城旦、鬼薪。有（又）取其次十四人耐以$_{244}$爲隸臣。其餘皆奪爵以爲士五（伍），其故上造以上有（又）令戍四歲，公士六歲，公卒以下八歲。□$_{244(2)}$[1415]
臣昧死請。

[...] I, your subject [...], request[1416] [the following]:

1410 *Duan bing* 短兵 "short-range weapons" (i.e. daggers, swords or pikes) (*Shiji* 110, 2879 [cf. Nienhauser IX (2011), 241]: 其長兵則弓矢，短兵則刀鋋。"Their long-range weapons are bows and arrows, their short-range weapons are the dagger and pike.").

1411 *Bao* 包 "to encircle" (*Zhanguoce* 33/11/12 [cf. Crump 1970, 30]: 且魏有南陽、鄭地、三川而包二周。"Wei holds Nanyang, the lands of Zheng, and the Three Rivers, thus encircling the two Zhou.").

1412 For *ji*/*xi* see footnote 569.

1413 For the phrase *ta xian lun* 它縣論, which is otherwise used in submissions of doubtful criminal cases to the higher authorities, where it indicates that the prefecture has fulfilled its duties see footnote 635. Due to the occurrence of this phrase as well as the preceding *xi* 繫, this case probably required a decision by the higher authorities.

1414 For photos and a transcription of slip 243(3), which was discovered after publication of Zhu and Chen 2013, see Hafner 2013a.

1415 For photos and a transcription of slip 244(2), which was discovered after publication of Zhu and Chen 2013, see Hafner 2013a.

1416 As a general administrative term, *qing* 請 referred to a written request for imperial approval of measures of different types. In legal contexts, two types of such *qing*-requests are important:

1) Requests for approval of a draft ordinance (*ling* 令) for promulgation. Such requests were made by two senior officials of the imperial government, the chancellor (*xiang guo*

"Select [...] and without exception apply the law[1417] to them. Single out[1418] the conscript who, out of cowardice, ran away first, [as well as the] twelve [conscripts] next in line after him, and make them unmutilated[1419] earth pounder[1420]

相國/*cheng xiang* 丞相) and/or the chief prosecutor (*yu shi da fu* 御史大夫) (*ENLL* 488, 494, 496, 498, 508, 513). In some cases, draft ordinances were submitted to one of these officials by ministers of the imperial government or leading officials of the provinces and were then forwarded to the emperor (*ENLL* 504, 516, 518, 519, 520, 521, 522, 523). Lower-ranking authorities were also permitted to propose edicts and request imperial approval for them, but such requests had first to be submitted to the relevant provincial (*jun*) authority, which then passed them on to the imperial court. To circumvent this procedure was punishable by a fine (*ENLL* 219).

2) Requests for approval of punishment in certain cases in which the fact that an offence had been committed and the applicable laws were not in doubt (*ZYS* 98; *Hanshu* 1B, 63; 4, 122; 8, 251; 8, 274; 23, 1106; *zou qing* 奏請 in *Shiji* 90, 2594; 96, 2684–2685). Imperial approval was necessary for punishment of members of certain privileged groups and for punishment of certain serious offences.

In the present case, a legal basis stipulating different punishments for the different groups of conscripts who had retreated out of cowardice was apparently lacking. Therefore, the case is submitted to the higher authorities by the prefecture, while at least some of the accused persons remained under detention. It seems that here *qing* does not refer to a request for approval of punishment but rather to a request for approval of a draft ordinance that contained differentiated punishments and could also be used for analogous future cases. The concluding formula *zhi yue ke* 制曰可 suggests that the submission that was approved contained a draft ordinance.

1417 *Zhi fa* 致法 "to apply the law" (*Shiji* 10, 426 [cf. Nienhauser II (2002), 169]: 群臣議，皆曰：長當棄市。帝不忍致法於王，赦其罪。"All ministers delivered their legal opinion saying: '[King] Chang [of Huainan] by law is to be executed in public.' The emperor could not bear to apply the law to a titular king and remitted his punishment."; cf. *FLDW* 177=*RCL* D 157: 真臣邦君公有罪，致耐罪以上，令贖。"When princes and leaders of genuine vassal states commit offences to which one should apply punishments of the category *nai* or higher, let them pay the fee for redemption [from the respective punishment]."; *ZYS* 187–188: 致次不孝、䝟（傲）悍之律二章。"Apply to it the two sections on secondary unfilial behaviour and impertinence and insubordination in the statutes.").

1418 *Qu* 取 here in the sense "to choose, select" (*Meng* 8, 342 [cf. Lau 1984, 167]: 其取友必端矣。"When he chooses friends, they must be upright."; *Meng* 12, 497 [cf. Lau 1984, 255]: 取士必得。"The selection of gentlemen should be appropriate.").

1419 For *wan* see footnote 1003.

1420 For *cheng dan* see footnotes 668 and 1003.

or firewood gatherer[1421] convicts, respectively.[1422] Furthermore single out the fourteen conscripts next in line [after the already mentioned thirteen], have them shaved[1423] and make them bond servant convicts.[1424] The remaining [conscripts] are to be deprived of their ranks and made rank-and-file men; those who formerly were holders of the second or a higher rank are furthermore to be ordered to perform [additional] military service[1425] for four years, [those who were] holders of the first rank [are to be ordered to] perform [additional] military service for six years, [those who were] *gong zu*[1426] or of lower [status are to be ordered to] perform [additional] military service for eight years. [...]
I, your subject, risk my life with this request."

Decision by the Ruler

制曰：
可。244(3)[1427]

The decision [by the ruler] read:
"Approved."[1428]

1421 For *gui xin* see footnote 667.

1422 This obviously means that some of the conscripts who ran away first were made unmutilated earth pounder convicts, whereas others were punished less severely due to their rank.

1423 For *nai* see footnote 574.

1424 For *li chen* convicts see footnote 751.

1425 For *shu* as an additional punishment see footnote 542.

1426 For *gong zu* see footnote 723.

1427 For photos and a transcription of slip 244(3), which was discovered after publication of Zhu and Chen 2013, see Hafner 2014a.

1428 The phrase *zhi yue ke* 制曰可 "The decision read: 'Approved.'" (*ENLL* 491, 499, 503, 505, 508, 511, 512, 515, 517, 520, 521, 522, 524; *Shiji* 6, 236; 6, 255; 6, 267; 28, 1380; 60, 2110; 121, 3119; *Hanshu* 23, 1099; 86, 3485; *Juyan* 82.3, 185.2, 206.5, 311.22, 322.26; *Xuanquan* 1; Giele 2006, 245–246, 221) refers to the approval of draft ordinances by the ruler. *Zhi* 制 became the standard term for decisions of the emperor after the Qin unification in 221 BC (*Shiji* 6, 236; cf. *Liye* 8–461r). Its occurrence points to the possibility that at least the final decision by the ruler at the end of this case has to be dated to the imperial Qin period.

APPENDIX I

Stages of Criminal Procedure as Reflected in Legal Manuscripts of the Qin and Early Han Period[1429]

Report and Arrest of an Offender

committing sb. for trial as a non-official or official	*yi* 詣
reporting sb. to the judicial authorities as a non-official	*gao* 告
or as an official (bring an *ex-officio* charge against sb.)	*he* 劾
searching for an offender and catching him	*qiu de* 求得
arrest of sb. suspected of having committed an offence based on a report or an *ex-officio* charge	*bu* 捕

Trial at the Court of First Instance (Prefecture/*xian* 縣)

accused (sometimes also witnesses) are placed under detention	*xi* 繫

First Stage of Interrogation

statement of the accused	*yue* 曰
comment on the statement	*ta ru mou ren/he/shu* 它如某人/劾/書
statement of witnesses or others involved	*yue* 曰
comment on these statements	*ta ru mou ren* 它如某人

Second Stage of Interrogation

confrontation of the accused with the letter of law/different statements of witnesses/his own contradictory statements	*jie* 詰
questioning about exculpatory evidence	*he* (*yi*) *jie* (*zhi*) 何（以）解（之）

1429 Cf. Lau and Lüdke 2012, 351–352: Appendix I.

 | DOI 10.1163/9789004315655_024

reply of the offender	
– if he pleads not guilty	*wu ta jie* 毋它解
– if he pleads guilty	*zui, wu jie* 罪，毋解
– if he pleads guilty on the premise that the official's interpretation is in accordance with the law	*cun li* (*dang, zui*), *wu jie* 存吏（當，罪），毋解

Forensic Examination and Interagency Enquiries

forensic inspection (wounds, pieces of evidence)	*zhen* 診
comment on the inspection	*ru ci* 如辭
interagency enquiries on sentencing-relevant particulars (amount of haul, age, rank, previous convictions)	*wen* 問
comment on the enquiries	*ta ru ci* 它如辭

Finding of Fact

summary of the finding of fact	*ju* 鞫
assurance that the result of investigation is true to the facts	*shen* 審

Decision of the Prefecture

– judgement	*lun* 論
– proposal for judgement (requiring ruler's approval)	*dang* 當
– doubts about the appropriate legal decision	*yi* 疑
in case of doubts about the correct judgement:	
assurance that judgement was passed in all other matters	*ta xian lun* 它縣論
submission to the higher authorities for decision	*gan yan zhi* 敢讞之
request for a response containing a decision	*ye bao* 謁報
comment on the addressee who is authorised to open the response	*shu mou guan fa* 署某官發
statutes/ordinances/precedents which are applicable to the case	*lü/ling/bi yi ci dang* 律/令/比以此當
different legal opinions in case of doubts	
– proposed judgement of the majority	*li dang/yi* 吏當/議
– alternative proposal of the minority	*huo yue* 或曰

Trial at the Court of Second Instance (Province/*jun* 郡)

trial of the case by provincial authorities	*zhi* 治
response by the province	*bao* 報

Decision at the Highest Instance (Agency of *ting wei* 廷尉)

response by the court	*ting bao* 廷報
submission to the ruler for decision	*ting yi wen* 廷以聞

APPENDIX II

Qin Official Titles Mentioned in the *Wei yu deng zhuang* and/or the Qin Cases of the *Zou yan shu*

Local Authorities

xiang (*se fu*) 鄉(嗇夫)	*Yuelu* WYZ 126
xiang zuo 鄉佐	*Yuelu* WYZ 126
xiao zhang 校長	*Yuelu* WYZ 001–002, 004, 025
ting (*zhang*) 亭(長)	*Yuelu* WYZ 068; *ZYS* 100
ting zuo 亭佐	*Yuelu* WYZ 066
qiu dao 求盜	*Yuelu* WYZ 001–002, 032, 040
li dian 里典	*ZYS* 197

Prefectural Authorities

(*shou*) *xian ling* (守)縣令	*Yuelu* WYZ 001, 003, 004, 013, 025, 031, 040, 061, 068; *ZYS* 143
xian se fu 縣嗇夫	*Yuelu* WYZ 186, 205; *ZYS* 121
xian ling cheng 縣令丞	*Yuelu* WYZ 001, 013, 025, 031, 040, 044, 055, 061, 064, 174, 191, 210; *ZYS* 106, 135
ling zuo 令佐	*Yuelu* WYZ 004
ling shi 令史	*Yuelu* WYZ 169; *ZYS* 135
yu shi 獄史	*Yuelu* WYZ 047, 051, 084, 142, 147, 151, 154, 168; *ZYS* 130, 197, 203, 227
shi 史	*Yuelu* WYZ 013, 061, 097, 140, 141, 168
shao nei 少內	*Yuelu* WYZ 227

Provincial Authorities

(*jun*) *shou* (郡)守/*tai shou* 太守	*Yuelu* WYZ 025, 040, 063; *ZYS* 125, 129, 154
zu shi 卒史	*Yuelu* WYZ 149, 170; *ZYS* 124, 128
(*du*) *wei* (都)尉	*ZYS* 129
jian yu shi 監御史	*Yuelu* WYZ 014

 | DOI 10.1163/9789004315655_025

Dependent States

bang wei 邦尉	*Yuelu* WYZ 094(2)
bang hou 邦侯	*Yuelu* WYZ 094(2)

Royal/Imperial Court

ting wei 廷尉	ZYS 184, 190, 192, 194
(*ting wei*) *zheng* (廷尉)正	ZYS 184
(*ting wei*) *jian* (廷尉)監	ZYS 184
ting shi 廷史	*Yuelu* WYZ 175, 218; ZYS 184, 189
yu shi (*da fu*) 御史(大夫)	ZYS 125, 131

APPENDIX III

Overview of the *Wei yu deng zhuang* Cases

MS	Case	Category	Year
I	1	doubtful legal decision (*yan* 讞)	222 BC
	2	doubtful legal decision (*yan* 讞)	222 BC
	3	request for approval (*yan* 讞)	224 BC
	4	request for approval (*yan* 讞)	225 or 226 BC(?)
	5	doubtful legal decision (*yan* 讞)	221 or 225 BC(?)
	6	doubtful legal decision (*yan* 讞)	226 BC
	7	doubtful legal decision (*yan* 讞)	229 BC
II	8	?	246 BC(?)
	9	letter of recommendation	?
	10	letter of recommendation	242 BC
	11	petition for retrial (*qi ju* 乞鞫)	246 BC
	12	petition for retrial (*qi ju* 乞鞫)	?
	13	?	?
III	14	doubtful legal decision (*yan* 讞)	225 BC
IV	15	?	?

 | DOI 10.1163/9789004315655_026

APPENDIX IV

Legal Terms Mentioned in the *Wei yu deng zhuang*[1430]

bang wang	邦亡	to abscond from the state (of Qin) →fn. 512 (005, 009, 027, 033, 038, 041, 088–089, 092, 228, 231–232, 235)
bao	報	to give a response (to the submitting authorities containing a legal decision) →fn. 581 (025, 040, 064, 177, 218, 236)
bi	辟	to inflict punishment on sb., to call sb. to account →fn. 1062 (144) punishment →fn. 501 (003)
bu	捕	to arrest (a suspect) →fn. 505 (003, 005, 008, 015, 018, 026, 032, 036, 037, 039, 040, 145, 191–194, 198, 201, 204, 206)
cheng dan	城旦	earth pounder convict, male convict performing the most severe form of penal labour →fn. 668 and 1003 (045, 061, 087, 094, 136, 152, 153, 161, 162, 166, 177, 187, 207, 244[1])
chi	笞	to cane (a suspect during interrogation) →fn. 1260, **1349** (194, 202, 225)

1430 The following list contains all legal terms that are mentioned in the *Wei yu deng zhuang*. The entries are based on Lau and Lüdke (forthcoming). Most of the translations contained in this list follow the English equivalents selected by Michael Lüdke for the unpublished English version of that work. The entries are sorted alphabetically according to their Hanyu Pinyin transcription. Beside the modern standard character and an English translation of the respective term, an entry also provides references to footnotes ("→fn. X") in which the term is discussed. If more than one footnote is cited and one of them is especially devoted to the term in question, that footnote number is highlighted in bold. The numbers of all slips of the *Wei yu deng zhuang* where the term in question occurs are provided in parentheses.

DOI 10.1163/9789004315655_027

chu	除	to exempt sb. from punishment →fn. 845 (094, 198, 207)
ci	辭	statement (before an authority) →fn. 564 (017, 035, 060, 085, 091, 131, 141, 166, 185, 187, 203, 231, 233, 242)
		to lodge a complaint against (a decision) →fn. 765 (068, 070, 071, 191)
dai/ta she	逮/遝赦	to be included in an amnesty →fn. 669 (045, 061)
dai	紿	to talk sb. into making a deal, to deceive sb. →fn. 555 (015, 019, 020, 081, 082, 083)
dang	當	to be lawful, justified, legitimate →fn. 546 (014, 024, 097, 100, 105, 187, 206)
		to correspond to, to comply with (the law) → fn. 546 (013)
		to be entitled (065, 080, 096, 108, 117, 128, 130)
		(by law) should, is to, has to →fn. 588 (014, 024, 029, 030, 043, 045, 060, 207)
dao	盜	to steal (goods) from sb., to rob sb. →fn. 541, 557 (002, 004, 006, 015–016, 018–019, 022, 025, 030, 031, 033, 035, 037, 041–042, 141, 160, 162, 164, 166–167, 227, 235)
		thief (149, 154)
		during theft, in the act of committing theft →fn. 795 (045, 163)
		illegally →fn. 795 (081–082, 084)
dao mai gong di	盜賣公地	to illegally sell government land (084)

dao sha ren	盜殺人	to kill sb. in the act of committing theft →fn. 499, 1144 (002–003, 141, 164, 166–167)
de	得	to catch sb. (in the act of committing a criminal offence) →fn. **524**, 714 (007, 011, 015, 021, 028, 045, 048, 050, 059–060, 087, 092, 134, 148, 155, 160, 164, 168, 235)
duan	端	intentionally →fn. 898 (102, 166)
duan	斷	to decide (a criminal case) →fn. 501 (003, 021, 087)
fa	灋/法	the law →fn. **559**, 587, 899 (014, 103)
fan	反	to stage a rebellion →fn. 829, 1391 (238, 241, 243)
fu	服	to make a confession (193, 199, 204, 206)
fu	覆/復	to review (a criminal case) →fn. **1039**, 1133 (140v, 172, 173, 175, 187, 202, 206)
gai	改	to amend, change (a statement) →fn. 1057 (143, 158, 176, 183)
gao	告	to report (a person/an offence to the authorities) →fn. 498 (002, 006, 007, 010, 015, 017, 020, 021, 025, 026, 028, 031, 033, 035, 037, 041, 083, 108, 110, 111, 118, 120, 122, 124, 128, 129, 132, 134, 141, 142, 173)
gou	購	reward (for arresting robbers and bandits) →fn. **502**, 519, 563, 624, 646, 647 (003, 006, 007, 009–011, 015, 016, 019–022, 027–029, 036, 037, 039, 042, 043)
gui xin	鬼薪	firewood gatherer convict, male convict performing the most severe penal labour in a privileged form →fn. 494, **667** (045, 061, 244)

han	悍	insubordinate →fn. 1167 (167)
he	和	by mutual consent →fn. 1221 (175, 177, 190, 204, 206)
he	劾	to bring an *ex-officio* charge (against a person) →fn. 545, 872 (014, 097–099)
		ex-officio charge →fn. 758 (016, 044, 064, 067, 097, 105)
hou	候	watchman convict, male convict performing the most lenient form of penal labour →fn. 574 (024)
hou	後	heir →fn. 959 (115, 128, 132)
jian	奸/姦	to have illicit sexual intercourse →fn. 1187, **1203**, 1205, 1221 (171, 173–179, 181, 183, 184, 186, 190, 191, 193–195, 198, 199, 201, 202, 204–206)
jie	劫	to blackmail sb. →fn. **933**, 1003 (110, 111, 122, 123, 129, 130, 133)
jie	詰	to confront (an accused with incriminating evidence during interrogation) →fn. 792 (080, 102, 127, 184, 201, 202)
jie	解	to offer an explanation (justifying one's actions) →fn. 800 (082, 084, 102, 103, 129, 130, 165, 201, 202, 204, 206, 241)
ju	鞫	to find the facts (in a case) →fn. 565 (018, 037, 045, 060, 064, 085, 092, 105, 131, 172, 174,204, 234, 242)
		finding of fact (139v, 140r, 141, 172, 174, 175, 176, 178, 184–187, 189, 191, 204-206)
jue	爵	(meritorious) rank →fn. 494, 724, 825, 833, **834** (091–092, 115, 232–233, 244[2])

lei lun	纍/累論	to pass a judgement based on the accumulation (of sentences) →fn. 876 (095, 102, 106)
li	吏	officials (of all ranks) →fn. 138, section 4.2 of the introduction (015, 022, 024, 034, 038-039, 062, 064, 094, 107, 109, 136, 144–145, 148–149, 160, 166, 169-170, 184, 193–194, 202, 220, 222, 225, 230–231, 235)
li tu	吏徒	officers and conscripts →fn. 553 (014–015)
li	隸	private menial, maidservant →fn. 963 (115, 119, 133)
li chen	隸臣	bond servant convict, male convict performing a less severe form of penal labour →fn. 751 (065, 141, 143, 158, 172, 174, 186, 189, 205–207, 235, 244[2])
ling	令	ordinance →fn. **556**, 1085 (022, 029, 030, 043, 102, 103, 105, 147)
lu	錄	to inspect (criminal cases/remand prisoners, records) →fn. **655**, 863 (044, 096)
lü	律	statute →fn. 556 (015, 022, 029, 030, 036, 039)
lüe	掠	to subject (a suspect) to torture (during interrogation) →fn. 1215, **1260** (194, 202)
lun	論	to pass judgement (on an accused for a criminal offence) →fn. 540 (013, 014, 016, 022, 024, 039, 061, 063–065, 082, 093, 095, 099, 102, 105, 106, 135, 140r, 141, 147, 166, 171, 174, 186, 187, 193, 199, 205, 236, 245)
		judgement (024)

mian	免	to relieve/release/manumit (a person from an office; slavery; penal labour; punishment; an obligation) →fn. 947 (113, 119, 126, 131, 132)
mou	謀	to conspire with sb. (to commit a criminal offence), to plan (an offence) →fn. 522, **829** (007, 028, 034, 053, 054, 059, 060, 069, 089, 092)
nai	耐	to shave off (a criminal offender's beard) as humiliating mark →fn. 574, 666, 751, 1116 (024, 045, 061, 171, 174, 186, 205, 235, 244)
ni	匿	to conceal (a criminal offender, illegally acquired goods), to evade (taxes) →fn. 928 (109, 110, 118, 122, 129, 130, 132, 134)
qi ju	乞鞫	to petition for a retrial/new finding of fact →fn. 390 (139v, 172, 175, 176, 178, 184–187, 189, 191, 204–206)
qiang	強	by force →fn. 1205 (171, 174, 176, 178, 183, 184, 186)
qie	妾	female slave →fn. 941 (112, 119, 126, 131–132)
qing	情	truth →fn. 1142 (160, 184)
qing	黥	to tattoo (a criminal offender) on the forehead →fn. 668 (013, 045, 060, 087, 094)
qiu	求	to search for (a suspect) →fn. 1081 (148, 154, 168)
quan	券	tally (divided in two or three parts and being used as certificate of a contract) →fn. 535 (029, 109, 111, 125)
		to make a contract on a tally, to agree on a tally, to certify by a tally (011, 020, 124)

qun dao	群盜	member(s) of a robber gang →fn. 500 (002, 004, 006, 010, 016, 018, 019, 022, 025, 027, 033, 036-039, 041)
sha	殺	to commit homicide, to kill sb. →fn. 499, 1144 (002–004, 006, 016, 018, 019, 022, 026, 031, 033, 035–037, 041, 042, 140r, 141, 151, 155, 161, 163, 164, 166, 167)
shan	擅	on one's own authority →fn. 769 (070, 071, 085)
shang	傷	to injure sb. →fn. 1009, 1216 (031, 033, 035–037, 041, 147)
she	赦	to grant an amnesty, to pardon sb. →fn. 670 (045, 061, 203, 204, 207)
shen	審	to establish the facts (in a matter), to be firmly established →fn. 584, **633**, 714, 1195 (029, 039, 042, 046, 061, 064, 092, 105, 134, 140r, 141, 172, 174, 176, 185, 186, 204–206, 235)
shi	失	to commit a judicial error (when passing judgement or imposing a punishment) →fn. 186, 549, 594 (014, 095, 102)
shi	實	in fact →fn. 533 (010, 130, 191, 229)
shi wu	士伍	rank-and-file man, commoner without rank →fn. 495 (002–004, 008, 044, 047, 049, 051, 062, 074, 091–092, 096, 109, 137r, 150, 208, 244[2])
shou ren huo cai yi wang lü ling	受人貨財以枉律令	to accept valuables offered by sb. to the effect of bending the statutes and ordinances →fn. 587 (029–030)
shu	贖	to pay a fee for redemption (from a certain punishment) →fn. 541 (013–014, 140r, 235)
shu	戍	to perform military service as punishment →fn. 542, 558, 559 (015, 022, 096, 244[2])

shu ren	庶人	released person (former slave or convict) →fn. 671 (045, 061, 113, 126, 131, 135–146)
si kou	司寇	robber guard convict, male convict performing lenient penal labour →fn. 574, **1116** (155)
ting	廷	court (of justice) →fn. 1193, section 4.2 of the introduction (172, 177, 187)
wan	完	without mutilation →fn. 1003 (136, 244)
wang	亡	to abscond →fn. 612 (051–052, 059, 138, 153, 158–159, 187)
wei shi	未蝕	to have not yet carried out (a planned criminal offence) →fn. 1155, 1187 (164, 171, 174, 176, 183, 184, 186)
wei wei shu	爲僞書	to draw up a forged document →fn. 1302 (212, 214, 226, 230–231, 232, 234)
wen	問	to make enquiries (with competent authorities) →fn. 562 (016, 035, 091, 104, 130, 140r, 141, 166, 185, 203, 209, 232, 241)
xi	繫	to place (a suspect) under detention →fn. 569 (023, 092, 135, 144, 194, 212, 228, 235, 245)
xi cheng dan chong	繫城旦舂	to place (an offending bond servant) under detention among the earth and grain pounder convicts (for a limited period of time) →fn. 1196, 1218 (172, 177, 187–188, 206, 207)
xiang ta/dai	相遝/逮	to be connected with each other fn. 881 (095, 099–100, 105)
xing	刑	to injure/mutilate sb. (not as punishment) →fn. 1009 (137r, 139r, 140r, 151, 163)
xun	訊	to interrogate (a suspect or witness) →fn. 830 (090, 125, 143–144, 153, 154, 157–159, 177, 190, 200, 202)

yan	讞	to submit (a criminal case) for decision (to the appropriate higher authority) →fn. 489, 582 (001, 023, 025, 028, 030, 031, 039–040, 042, 044, 046, 061, 062, 064, 088, 093, 094[2], 095, 106, 135, 210, 235–236)
yi	疑	to be in doubt about the lawful decision (on the punishment/punishability, the amount of rewards, etc.) →fn. 582, 633 (028, 039, 042, 092, 105, 134, 140r)
yi	議	to deliver a legal opinion, to propose a judgement →fn. 572 (024, 039, 094, 107, 136, 235)
yi	詣	to present (a person or goods) to the authorities →fn. 496, 773 (002, 006–007, 009, 011, 019, 021, 025, 027–028, 032, 034, 038, 047, 051, 141, 193, 200, 207, 210, 212, 227, 234)
yu	獄	criminal case →fn. 568, 655, 674, 690 (021, 044, 047, 051, 064, 084, 087, 137v, 142, 147, 151, 154, 168, 173, 175, 179, 192, 194, 199, 202, 213)
yue	約	to reach an agreement →fn. 532 (009, 010, 019, 021)
zang	贓	misappropriated goods →fn. 592 (030, 045, 059–060, 086, 130, 166)
zhe	磔	to execute (an offender) by quartering →fn. 1032 (141, 147, 166, 168)
zhen	診	to gather evidence by inspection, examine forensically (a person's body or things) →fn. 562, **1095** (016, 035, 140r, 151, 241)
zheng	爭	to contest sb.'s claim to something →fn. 109 (066, 068–071, 073)
zheng wu	徵物	piece of evidence →fn. 305 (148)

zhi	知	to know about (an offence) →fn. 537, 659 (005, 010, 019, 021, 027, 045, 073, 080, 118, 122, 126, 145, 151–152, 154, 160, 180, 182, 194, 198, 230–231)
zhi	治	to try (a person or a criminal case) →fn. 1079 (148, 168, 191, 199, 213)
zhuang	狀	correct/proper behavior →fn. 741, 1124, 1129 (064, 155, 157)
		charge report/document →fn. 1036 (137v, 139v, 140v)
		circumstances (of a case) → fn. 741 (143)
zhui	追	to pursue (a suspect) →fn. 510 (004, 015, 018, 026, 032, 238, 241)
zi	貲	to fine (a transgressor) →fn. 558, 594 (015, 022, 030, 107, 136, 236)
		fine (225)
zou	奏	to submit (a matter) in writing to the ruler →fn. 1037 (139v, 140v, 148, 169)
zui	辠/罪	punishment →fn. 501, **514**, 582 (010–011, 016, 019–021, 027–029, 092, 135, 168)
	有罪	to be liable to punishment (034, 076, 200)
	罪	to be liable to punishment →fn. 985 (005, 010, 027, 130, 164–165, 185, 198, 241)
		to hold sb. liable to punishment/to punish sb. (084, 130)
zuo	坐	to be prosecuted for (a criminal offence) →fn. **528**, 880 (009, 030, 095, 099, 102, 105, 145)

Bibliography

An Zuozhang 安作璋 and Xiong Tieji 熊鐵基. 2007. *Qin Han guanzhi shi gao* 秦漢官制史稿. 2nd edition. Jinan: Qi Lu shushe.

Bai Yulan 白於藍. 2012. *Zhanguo Qin Han jianbo gushu tongjiazi huizuan* 戰國秦漢簡帛古書通假字彙纂. Fuzhou: Fujian renmin.

Baoshan 包山 see Hubei sheng Jing Sha tielu kaogudui 1991

Barbieri-Low, Anthony. 2011. "Model Legal and Administrative Forms from the Qin, Han, and Tang and their Role in the Facilitation of Bureaucracy and Literacy." *Oriens Extremus* 50: 125–156.

Barbieri-Low, Anthony J. and Robin D. S. Yates. 2015. *Law, State, and Society in Early Imperial China: A Study with Critical Edition and Translation of the Legal Texts from Zhangjiashan Tomb no. 247*. Leiden: Brill.

Baxter, William H. and Laurent Sagart. 2014a. *Old Chinese: A New Reconstruction*. New York: Oxford University Press.

———. 2014b. *Baxter-Sagart Old Chinese Reconstruction, Version 1.1 (20 September 2014)*. <http://ocbaxtersagart.lsait.lsa.umich.edu/BaxterSagartOCbyMandarinMC2014-09-20.pdf>, accessed March 27, 2015.

Biannianji 編年記 see Shuihudi Qinmu zhujian zhengli xiaozu 1990

Bielenstein, Hans. 1980. *The Bureaucracy of Han Times*. Cambridge: Cambridge University Press.

Bodde, Derk. 1938. *China's First Unifier: A Study of the Ch'in Dynasty as Seen in the Life of Li Ssŭ* 李斯 *(280?-208 B.C.)*. Leiden: Brill.

———. 1940. *Statesman, Patriot, and General in Ancient China: Three Shi Chi Biographies of the Ch'in Dynasty (255–206 B.C.)*. New Haven, Connecticut: American Oriental Society.

———. 1982. "Forensic Medicine in Pre-Imperial China." *Journal of the American Oriental Society* 102: 1–15.

———. 1986. "The State and Empire of Ch'in." In *The Cambridge History of China. Volume 1: The Ch'in and Han Empires, 221 B.C.–A.D. 220*, edited by Denis Crispin Twitchett and Michael Loewe, 20–102. Cambridge: Cambridge University Press.

Bohutong 白虎通 see Lau D. C. and Chen Fong Ching 1995

Bu Xianqun 卜憲群 and Liu Yang 劉楊. 2013. "Qin Han richang zhixu zhong de shehui yu xingzheng guanxi chutan – Guanyu 'zi yan' yi ci de jiedu" 秦漢日常秩序中的社會與行政關系初探——關於"自言"一詞的解讀. *Wen shi zhe* 2013.4: 81–92.

Cai Wanjin 蔡萬進. 2006. *Zhangjiashan Hanjian* Zou yan shu *yanjiu* 張家山漢簡《奏讞書》研究. Guilin: Guangxi shifan daxue.

Caldwell, Ernest. 2014. "Social Change and Written Law in Early Chinese Legal Thought." *Law and History Review* 32.1: 1–30.

Cang Xiuliang 倉修良, ed. 1991. *Shiji cidian* 史記辭典. Jinan: Shandong jiaoyu.

———, ed. 1996. *Hanshu cidian* 漢書辭典. Jinan: Shandong jiaoyu.

Cao Lüning 曹旅寧. 2002. *Qinlü xintan* 秦律新探. Beijing: Zhongguo shehui kexue.

———. 2005. *Zhangjiashan Hanlü yanjiu* 張家山漢律研究. Beijing: Zhonghua.

Changsha shi wenwu kaogu yanjiusuo 長沙市文物考古研究所. 2013. "Hunan Changsha Wuyi guangchang Donghan jiandu fajue jianbao" 湖南長沙五一廣場東漢簡牘發掘簡報. *Wenwu* 2013.6: 4–26.

Changsha shi wenwu kaogu yanjiusuo 長沙市文物考古研究所, Qinghua daxue chutu wenxian yanjiu yu baohu zhongxin 清華大學出土文獻研究與保護中心, Zhongguo wenhua yichan yanjiuyuan 中國文化遺產研究院 and Hunan daxue Yuelu shuyuan 湖南大學嶽麓書院. 2015. *Changsha Wuyi guangchang Donghan jiandu xuanshi* 長沙五一廣場東漢簡牘選釋. Shanghai: Zhongxi shuju.

Chemla, Karine and Guo Shuchun. 2004. *Les Neuf Chapitres: Le classique mathématique de la Chine ancienne et ses commentaires*. Paris: Dunod.

Chen Jian 陳劍. 2013. "Guanyu *Yuelu jian* (*san*) de 'Yan cheng'" 關於《嶽麓簡（叁）》的"燕城". <http://www.gwz.fudan.edu.cn/SrcShow.asp?Src_ID=2122>, accessed February 20, 2014.

Chen Pan 陳槃. 1975. *Han Jin yijian shi xiao qi zhong* 漢晉遺簡識小七種. Zhongyang yanjiuyuan lishi yuyan yanjiusuo zhuankan 中央研究院歷史語言研究所專刊 63. Taibei: Zhongyang yanjiuyuan lishi yuyan yanjiusuo.

Chen Songchang 陳松長, ed. 2001a. *Mawangdui jianbo wenzibian* 馬王堆簡帛文子編. Beijing: Wenwu.

———, ed. 2001b. *Xianggang Zhongwen daxue wenwuguan cang jiandu* 香港中文大學文物館藏簡牘. Xianggang: Xianggang Zhongwen daxue wenwuguan.

———. 2004. "*Xiangxi Liye Qindai jiandu xuanshi* jiaodu (ba ze)" 《湘西里耶秦代簡牘選釋》校讀（八則）. *Jianduxue yanjiu* 4: 17–21.

———. 2009a. "Yuelu shuyuan suo cang Qinjian zongshu" 嶽麓書院所藏秦簡綜述. *Wenwu* 2009.3: 75–88.

———. 2009b. "Yuelu shuyuan cang Qinjian zhong de xingshu lüling chulun" 嶽麓書院藏秦簡中的行書律令初論. *Zhongguo shi yanjiu* 2009.3: 31–38.

———. 2009c. "Yuelu shuyuan cang Qinjian zhong de junming kaolüe" 嶽麓書院藏秦簡中的郡名考略. *Hunan daxue xuebao* (*shehui kexue ban*) 23, no. 2: 5–10.

———. 2010a. "Yuelu shuyuan cang Qinjian *Wei li zhi guan ji qianshou* lüeshuo" 嶽麓書院藏秦簡《爲吏治官及黔首》略說. *Chutu wenxian yanjiu* 9: 30–36.

———. 2010b. "Shuihudi Qinjian 'Guan shi lü' bianzheng" 睡虎地秦簡"關市律"辨正. *Shixue jikan* 2010.4: 16–20.

———. 2012a. "Shuihudi Qinjian zhong de 'jiang yang' xiao kao" 睡虎地秦簡中的"將陽"小考. *Hunan daxue xuebao* (*shehui kexue ban*) 26, no. 5: 5–7.

———. 2012b. "Yuelu shuyuan cang Qinjian zhong de yaolü lishuo" 嶽麓書院藏秦簡中的傜律例說. *Chutu wenxian yanjiu* 11: 162–166.

———. 2013. "Yuelu Qinjian 'wei wei si shu' anli ji xiangguan wenti" 嶽麓秦簡"爲僞私書"案例及相關問題. *Wenwu* 2013.5: 84–89.

———. 2014a. "*Yuelu shuyuan cang Qinjian* (san) 'Gui, Suo xiang yi mou gou an' de xiangguan wenti suoyi" 《嶽麓書院藏秦簡》（叁）"癸、瑣相移謀購案"的相關問題瑣議. In Wang Pei 2014, 1–12.

———, ed. 2014b. *Yuelu shuyuan cang Qinjian de zhengli yu yanjiu* 嶽麓書院藏秦簡的整理與研究. Shanghai: Zhongxi shuju.

———. 2015. "Yuelu Qinjian zhong de ji ge guanming kaolüe" 嶽麓秦簡中的幾個官名考略. *Hunan daxue xuebao (shehui kexue ban)* 29, no. 3: 8–11.

Chen Songchang and Zhang Yijing 張以靜. 2014. "*Yuelu shuyuan cang Qinjian (san)* de shushou bianxi yu shuti tezheng" 《嶽麓書院藏秦簡（叁）》的書手辨析與書體特徵. *Chutu wenxian yanjiu* 13: 140–150.

Chen Wei 陳偉. 1996. *Baoshan Chujian chutan* 包山楚簡初探. Wuhan: Wuhan daxue.

———. 2009. "Yuelu shuyuan Qinjian kaojiao" 嶽麓書院秦簡考校. *Wenwu* 2009.10: 85–87.

———. 2010. *Xinchu Chujian yandu* 新出楚簡研讀. Wuhan: Wuhan daxue.

———. 2011. "'Jianghu' yu 'Zhouling' – Yuelu shuyuan cang Qinjian zhong de liang ge diming chukao" "江胡"與"州陵"——嶽麓書院藏秦簡中的兩個地名初考. <http://www.bsm.org.cn/show_article.php?id=1469>, accessed February 20, 2014.

———, ed. 2012a. *Liye Qin jiandu jiaoshi (yi)* 里耶秦簡牘校釋（一）. Wuchang: Wuhan daxue.

———. 2012b. "Yuelu shuyuan Qinjian *Zhiri* chubu yanjiu" 嶽麓書院秦簡"質日"初步研究. <http://www.bsm.org.cn/show_article.php?id=1755>, accessed October 23, 2015.

———. 2013a. "'Dao wei you qu li zi fa shu lü ling' shi jie" "盜未有取吏貲灋戍律令"試解. <http://www.bsm.org.cn/show_article.php?id=1892>, accessed February 20, 2014.

———. 2013b. "Shi deng bu dao gou jin shu shi shuo" 尸等捕盜購金數試說. <http://www.bsm.org.cn/show_article.php?id=1894>, accessed February 20, 2014.

———. 2013c. "Liye Qinjian zhong de 'guai'" 里耶秦簡中的"夬". <http://www.bsm.org.cn/show_article.php?id=1916>, accessed February 20, 2014.

——— et al. 2009. *Chudi chutu Zhanguo jiance (shisi zhong)* 楚地出土戰國簡冊〔十四種〕. Beijing: Jingji kexue.

——— et al. 2014. *Qin jiandu heji* 秦簡牘合集. 6 vols. Wuhan: Wuhan daxue.

Chen Xiaojie 陳曉捷 and Zhou Xiaolu 周曉陸. 2005. "Xin jian Qin fengni wushi li kaolüe – Wei Qin fengni faxian shi zhounian er zuo" 新見秦封泥五十例考略——爲秦封泥發現十周年而作. *Beilin jikan* 11: 311–321.

Chen Zhi 陳直. 1986. *Juyan Hanjian yanjiu* 居延漢簡研究. Tianjin: Tianjin guji.

Cheng Shude 程樹德. 1955. *Jiuchao lü kao* 九朝律考. First published 1927. Shanghai: Shangwu.

Ch'ü T'ung-tsu. 1972. *Han Social Structure*. Seattle: University of Washington Press.

Chuci 楚辭 see Lau D. C. and Chen Fong Ching 2000

Chunqiu 春秋 see Legge 1960

Chunqiu fanlu 春秋繁露 see Lau D. C. and Chen Fong Ching 1994c

Chunqiu Zuozhuan zhengyi 春秋左傳正義 see Ruan Yuan 1980

Cikoski, John. 2011. *Notes for a Lexicon of Classical Chinese*. 3 vols. Vol. 1: Vocabulary. Saint Mary's, Georgia: The Coprolite Press. <http://www.umass.edu/wsp/resources/books/cikoski/Cikoski-v1.pdf>, accessed February 20, 2014.

Couvreur, Séraphin. 1950. *Li-Ki, Mémoires sur les bienséances et les cérémonies*. 2 vols. Reprint, Paris: Cathasia.

Crump, James Irving Jr. 1970. *Chan-Kuo Ts'e*. Oxford: Clarendon Press.

Cullen, Christopher. 2004. *The Suàn shù shū* 筭數書 *'Writings on Reckoning': A Translation of a Chinese Mathematical Collection of the Second Century BC, with Explanatory Commentary*. Needham Research Institute, Cambridge. <http://www.nri.org.uk/SuanshushuC.Cullen2004.pdf>, accessed February 20, 2014.

Dadai liji 大戴禮記 see Lau D. C. and Chen Fong Ching 1992b

Dong Tonghe 董同龢. 1948. "Shanggu yinyun biao gao" 上古音韻表稿. *Zhongyang yanjiuyuan lishi yuyan yanjiusuo jikan* 18: 1–249.

Dongguan Hanji 東觀漢記 see Wu Shuping 1987

Duan Yucai 段玉裁. 1981. *Shuowen jiezi zhu* 說文解字注. Shanghai: Shanghai guji.

Dubs, Homer H. 1938–55. *The History of the Former Han Dynasty*. 3 vols. Baltimore: Waverly Press.

Dunhuang 敦煌 see Gansu sheng wenwu kaogu yanjiusuo 1991

Duyvendak, Jan J. L. 1928. *The Book of Lord Shang: A Classic of the Chinese School of Law*. London: Probsthain.

ENLL=*Ernian lüling* 二年律令 see Zhangjiashan er si qi hao Hanmu zhujian zhengli xiaozu 2001 (B/W-photos) as well as Peng Hao et al. 2007 (IR-photos/shiwen)

Fang Xiaoyue 方孝岳. 1956. "Guanyu Xianqin yunbu de 'heyun' wenti" 關於先秦韻部的"合韻"問題. *Zhongshan daxue xuebao* 1956.4: 28–48.

Fang Yong 方勇. 2012. *Qin jiandu wenzibian* 秦簡牘文字編. Fuzhou: Fuzhou renmin.

Fangmatan Rishu A 放馬灘日書甲 see Gansu sheng wenwu kaogu yanjiusuo 2009

Fangyan 方言 see Zhou Zumo 1993

Feng Qiyong 馮其庸 and Deng Ansheng 鄧安生. 2006. *Tongjiazi huishi* 通假字彙釋. Beijing: Beijing daxue.

FLDW=*Falü dawen* 法律答問 see Shuihudi Qinmu zhujian zhengli xiaozu 1990

Fu Jiayi 傅嘉儀, ed. 2007. *Qin fengni huikao* 秦封泥彙攷. Shanghai: Shanghai shudian.

FZS=*Fengzhen shi* 封診式 see Shuihudi Qinmu zhujian zhengli xiaozu 1990

Gakushûin daigaku Kankan kenkyûkai 学習院大学漢簡研究会. 2002. "Kansho kon'in jiken – Kôryô Chôkasan Kankan *Sôgensho* wo yomu" 漢初婚姻事件——江陵張家山漢簡「奏讞書」を讀む. *Gakushûin shigaku* 40: 111–119.

Gansu jiandu baohu yanjiu zhongxin 甘肅簡牘保護研究中心, Gansu sheng wenwu kaogu yanjiusuo 甘肅省文物考古研究所, Gansu sheng bowuguan 甘肅省博物館, Zhongguo wenhua yichan yanjiuyuan gu wenxian yanjiushi 中國文化遺產研究院古文獻研究室 and Zhongguo shehui kexueyuan jianbo yanjiu zhongxin 中國社會科學院簡帛研究中心, ed. 2011. *Jianshui Jinguan Hanjian (yi)* 肩水金關漢簡（壹）. 3 vols. Shanghai: Zhongxi shuju.

Gansu sheng bowuguan 甘肅省博物館 and Wuwei xian wenhuaguan 武威縣文化館, ed. 1975. *Wuwei Handai yijian* 武威漢代醫簡. Beijing: Wenwu.

Gansu sheng wenwu kaogu yanjiusuo 甘肅省文物考古研究所, ed. 1991. *Dunhuang Hanjian* 敦煌漢簡. 2 vols. Beijing: Zhonghua.

———, ed. 2009. *Tianshui Fangmatan Qinjian* 天水放馬灘秦簡. Beijing: Zhonghua.

Gansu sheng wenwu kaogu yanjiusuo, Gansu sheng bowuguan 甘肅省博物館, Zhongguo wenwu yanjiusuo 中國文物研究所 and Zhongguo shehui kexueyuan lishi yanjiusuo 中國社會科學院歷史研究所, ed. 1994. *Juyan xinjian* 居延新簡. 2 vols. Beijing: Zhonghua.

Gao Heng 高亨. 1974. *Shangjunshu zhuyi* 商君书注譯. 4 vols. Beijing: Zhonghua.

———. 1980. *Shijing jinzhu* 詩經今注. Shanghai: Shanghai guji.

Gao Heng and Dong Zhi'an 董治安. 1997. *Guzi tongjia huidian* 古字通假會典. Jinan: Qi Lu shushe.

Gao Heng 高恒. 1994. *Qin Han fazhi lunkao* 秦漢法制論考. Xiamen: Xiamen daxue.

———. 2008. *Qin Han jiandu zhong fazhi wenshu jikao* 秦漢簡牘中法制文書輯考. Beijing: Shehui kexue wenxian.

Gao Min 高敏. 1979. *Yunmeng Qinjian chutan* 雲夢秦簡初探. N.p.: Henan renmin.

———. 1981. "Qin Han shi de ting" 秦漢時的亭. In *Yunmeng Qinjian yanjiu* 雲夢秦簡研究, edited by Zhonghua shuju bianjibu 中華書局編輯部, 302–315. Beijing: Zhonghua.

———. 1998. *Qin Han shi tantao* 秦漢史探討. Zhengzhou: Zhongzhou guji.

Gassmann, Robert. 1997. *Grundstrukturen der antikchinesischen Syntax: Eine erklärende Grammatik*. Bern: Lang.

Giele, Enno (=Ji Annuo 紀安諾). 2001. "Yinwan xin chutu xingzheng wenshu de xingzhi yu Handai difang xingzheng" 尹灣新出土行政文書的性質與漢代地方行政. In *Jianbo yanjiu* 2001 簡帛研究二〇〇一, edited by Li Xueqin 李學勤 and Xie Guihua 謝桂華, 786–811. 2 vols. Guilin: Guangxi shifan daxue.

———. 2003. "New Glimpses of the Early Chinese Postal System." Paper presented at the 17th Warring States Working Goup Conference, Leiden, NL, September 18, 2003.

———. 2005. "Signatures of 'Scribes' in Early Imperial China." *Asiatische Studien/Études Asiatiques* 59, no. 1: 353–387.

———. 2006. *Imperial Decision-Making and Communication in Early China: A Study of Cai Yong's* Duduan. Wiesbaden: Harrassowitz.

———. 2010. "Excavated Manuscripts: Context and Methodology." In *China's Early Empires: A Re-appraisal*, edited by Michael Nylan and Michael Loewe, 114–134. Cambridge: Cambridge University Press.

Goldin, Paul R. 2013. "*Heng Xian* and the Problem of Studying Looted Artifacts." *Dao: A Journal of Comparative Philosophy* 12, no. 2: 153–160.

Gongyang(zhuan) 公羊傳 see Ruan Yuan 1980 (*Chunqiu Gongyangzhuan zhushu* 春秋公羊傳注疏)

GSR see Karlgren 1957

Guan(zi) 管子 see *Zhuzi jicheng*, vol. 5 (Dai Wang 戴望, *Guanzi jiaozheng* 管子校正)

Guangyun 廣韻 see Shen Jianshi 1985

Guliang(zhuan) 穀梁傳 see Ruan Yuan 1980 (*Chunqiu Guliangzhuan zhushu* 春秋穀梁傳注疏)

Gulienüzhuan 古列女傳 see Lau D. C. and Chen Fong Ching 1993a

Guo Chengwei 郭成偉. 1992. *Zongguo fa'an da cidian* 中國法案大辭典. Beijing: Zhongguo guji guangbo.

Guo Shuchun 郭書春. 1990. Jiu zhang suanshu *huijiao ben* 《九章算術》匯校本. Shenyang: Liaoning jiaoyu.

Guodian Lao(zi) A 郭店老子甲 see Jingmen shi bowuguan 1998

Guodian Tang Yu zhi dao 郭店唐虞之道 see Jingmen shi bowuguan 1998

Guodian Wuxing 郭店五行 see Jingmen shi bowuguan 1998

Guodian Ziyi 郭店緇衣 see Jingmen shi bowuguan 1998

Guojia wenwuju gu wenxian yanjiushi 國家文物局古文獻研究室, ed. 1980. *Mawangdui Hanmu boshu (yi)* 馬王堆漢墓帛書（壹）. Beijing: Wenwu.

Guoyu 國語 see Lau D. C. and Chen Fong Ching 1999

Hafner, Arnd Helmut (=Sueyasu Ando 陶安あんど). 2009. *Shin Kan keibatsu taikei no kenkyû* 秦漢刑罰體系の研究. Tôkyô: Tôkyô gaikokugo daigaku.

——— (=Tao An 陶安). 2012. "Qin Han lü 'shuren' gainian bianzheng" 秦漢律"庶人"概念辯正. *Jianbo* 7: 265–276.

——— (=Tao An 陶安). 2013a. "*Yuelu shuyuan cang Qinjian (san)* jiaokan ji" 《嶽麓書院藏秦簡（叁）》校勘記. <http://www.gwz.fudan.edu.cn/SrcShow.asp?Src_ID=2098>, accessed February 20, 2014.

——— (=Tao An 陶安). 2013b. "Fuzuo kao – *Hanshu* Xingfazhi Wendi gaige zhao xinjie" 復作考——《漢書》刑法志文帝改革詔新解. *Fazhi shi yanjiu* 24: 159–180.

——— (=Tao An 陶安). 2014a. "*Yuelu shuyuan cang Qinjian (san)* jiaokan ji (xu)" 《嶽麓書院藏秦簡（叁）》校勘記（續）.<http://www.gwz.fudan.edu.cn/SrcShow.asp?Src_ID=2309>, accessed March 30, 2015.

——— (=Tao An 陶安). 2014b. "*Wei yu deng zhuang si zhong* biaoti jian 'zou' zi zijie dingzheng – Jianlun Zhangjiashan Hanjian *Zou yan shu* timing wenti" 《爲獄等狀

四種》標題簡"奏"字字解訂正——兼論張家山漢簡《奏讞書》題名問題. *Zhongguo gudai falü wenxian yanjiu* 8: 22–48.

——— (=Tao An 陶安). 2014c. "Zhongguo chuantong 'gongfan' gainian de ji ze sikao" 中國傳統"共犯"概念的幾則思考. In Wang Pei 2014, 207–219.

Han Shufeng 韓樹峰. 2003. "Qin Han lüling zhong de wan xing" 秦漢律令中的完刑. *Zhongguo shi yanjiu* 2003.4: 49–55.

———. 2005. "Qin Han xingtu sanlun" 秦漢刑徒散論. *Lishi yanjiu* 2005.3: 37–52.

Hanfei(zi) 韓非子 see *Zhuzi jicheng*, vol. 5 (Wang Xianshen 王先慎, *Hanfeizi jijie* 韓非子集解)

Hanguan liu zhong 漢官六種 see Lau D. C. and Chen Fong Ching 1993b

Hanshi waizhuan 韓詩外傳 see Lau D. C. and Chen Fong Ching 1992c

Hanshu 漢書. 12 vols. Beijing: Zhonghua, 1962.

Harbsmeier, Christoph, ed. *Thesaurus Linguae Sericae – An Historical and Comparative Encyclopaedia of Chinese Conceptual Schemes.* University of Oslo/University of Heidelberg. <http://tls.uni-hd.de/>, accessed February 20, 2014.

———. "Translation of *Hanfeizi*." In *Thesaurus Linguae Sericae – An Historical and Comparative Encyclopaedia of Chinese Conceptual Schemes*, edited by Christoph Harbsmeier. University of Oslo/University of Heidelberg. <http://tls.uni-hd.de/>, accessed February 20, 2014.

———. "Translation of *Lunyu*." In *Thesaurus Linguae Sericae – An Historical and Comparative Encyclopaedia of Chinese Conceptual Schemes*, edited by Christoph Harbsmeier. University of Oslo/University of Heidelberg. <http://tls.uni-hd.de/>, accessed February 20, 2014.

———. 1993. "*Fú* in the Mawangdui Manuscripts of the *Laozi* and in the *Remnants of Qin Law*." In *From Classical Fú to Three Inches High: Studies in Honor of Erik Zürcher*, edited by J. C. P. Liang and R. P. E. Sybesma, 1–59. Leuven: Garant.

He Leshi 何樂士. 2006. *Gudai Hanyu xuci cidian* 古代漢語虛詞詞典. Beijing: Yuwen.

He Linyi 何琳儀. 1998. *Zhanguo guwen zidian: Zhanguo wenzi shengxi* 戰國古文字典：戰國文字聲系. 2 vols. Beijing: Zhonghua.

Hedijian 河隄簡 see Chen Songchang 2001b

Heuser, Robert. 1987. *Das Rechtskapitel im Jin-Shu: ein Beitrag zur Kenntnis des Rechts im frühen chinesischen Kaiserreich.* München: Schweitzer.

Hightower, James Robert. 1952. *Han Shih Wai Chuan: Han Ying's Illustrations of the Didactic Application of the Classic of Songs.* Cambridge: Harvard University Press.

Hiranaka Reiji 平中苓次. 1967. *Chûgoku kodai no densei to zeihô* 中國古代の田制と税法. Kyôto: Tôyôshi kenkyûkai.

Hou Xiaorong 后曉榮. 2009. *Qindai zhengqu dili* 秦代政區地理. Beijing: Shehui kexue wenxian.

Houhanshu 後漢書. 12 vols. Beijing: Zhonghua, 1965.

Hsing I-tien. 2014. "Qin-Han Census and Tax and Corvée Administration: Notes on Newly Discovered Materials." In *Birth of an Empire: The State of Qin Revisited*, edited by Yuri

Pines, Lothar von Falkenhausen, Gideon Shelach and Robin D. S. Yates, 155–186. Berkeley, Los Angeles, London: University of California Press.

Hu Pingsheng 胡平生. 1995. "Juyan Hanjian zhong de 'gong' yu 'lao'" 居延漢簡中的"功"與"勞". *Wenwu* 1995.4: 51–55.

Hu Pingsheng and Zhang Defang 張德芳. 2001. *Dunhuang Xuanquan Hanjian shicui* 敦煌懸泉漢簡釋粹. Shanghai: Shanghai guji.

Huai(nanzi) 淮南子 see *Zhuzi jicheng*, vol. 7 (Gao You 高誘, *Huainanzi zhu* 淮南子注)

Huang Dekuan 黃德寬, ed. 2007. *Guwenzi puxi shuzheng* 古文字譜系疏證. 4 vols. Beijing: Shangwu.

Huang Jie 黃傑. 2013. "Yuelu Qinjian 'Xue wei wei shu an' zai bu" 嶽麓秦簡"學爲僞書案"再補. <http://www.bsm.org.cn/show_article.php?id=1898>, accessed February 20, 2014.

Huang Jinyan 黃今言. 1988. *Qin Han fuyi zhidu yanjiu* 秦漢賦役制度研究. Nanchang: Jiangxi jiaoyu.

Hubei sheng Jing Sha tielu kaogudui 湖北省荊沙鐵路考古隊. 1991. *Baoshan Chujian* 包山楚簡. Beijing: Wenwu.

Hubei sheng Jingzhou shi Zhouliangyuqiao yizhi bowuguan 湖北省荊州市周梁玉橋遺址博物館, ed. 2001. *Guanju Qin Hanmu jiandu* 關沮秦漢墓簡牘. Beijing: Zhonghua.

Hubei sheng wenwu kaogu yanjiusuo 湖北省文物考古研究所 and Beijing daxue zhongwenxi 北京大學中文系. 2000. *Jiudian Chujian* 九店楚簡. Beijing: Zhonghua.

Hubei sheng wenwu kaogu yanjiusuo and Suizhou shi kaogudui 隨州市考古隊, ed. 2006. *Suizhou Kongjiapo Hanmu jiandu* 隨州孔家坡漢墓簡牘. Beijing: Wenwu.

Hubei sheng wenwu kaogu yanjiusuo and Xiangxi Tujiazu Miaozu zizhi zhou wenwu chu 湘西土家族苗族自治州文物処. 2003. "Xiangxi Liye Qindai jiandu xuanshi" 湘西里耶秦代簡牘選釋. *Zhongguo lishi wenwu* 2003.1: 8–25.

Hubei sheng wenwu kaogu yanjiusuo and Yunmeng xian bowuguan 雲夢縣博物館. 2008. "Hubei Yunmeng Shuihudi M77 fajue jianbao" 湖北雲夢睡虎地M77發掘簡報. *Jiang Han kaogu* 2008.4: 31–37.

Hulsewé, A. F. P. 1955. *Remnants of Han Law. Vol. I: Introductory Studies and Annotated Translation of Chapters 22 and 23 of the History of the Former Han Dynasty*. Leiden: Brill.

———. 1978. "The Ch'in Documents Discovered in Hu-pei in 1975." *T'oung Pao* 64, no. 4–5: 175–217+338.

———. 1985. *Remnants of Ch'in Law: An Annotated Translation of the Ch'in Legal and Administrative Rules of the 3rd century B.C. Discovered in Yün-meng Prefecture, Hu-pei Province, in 1975*. Leiden: Brill.

———. 1987. "The Functions of the Commandant of Justice during the Han Period." In *Chinese Ideas about Nature and Society: Studies in Honour of Derk Bodde*, edited by Charles LeBlanc and Susan Blader, 249–264. Hong Kong: Hong Kong University Press.

———. 1988. "The Wide Scope of Tao 盜, 'Theft', in Ch'in-Han Law." *Early China* 13: 166–200.

———. 1997. "Qin and Han Legal Manuscripts." In *New Sources of Early Chinese History: An Introduction to the Reading of Inscriptions and Manuscripts*, edited by Edward L. Shaughnessy, 193–221. Berkeley: The Society for the Study of Early China and the Institute of East Asian Studies, University of California, Berkeley.

Hunan sheng wenwu kaogu yanjiusuo 湖南省文物考古研究所. 2006. *Liye fajue baogao* 里耶發掘報告. Changsha: Yuelu shushe.

———. 2012. *Liye Qinjian* (*yi*) 里耶秦簡〔壹〕. Beijing: Wenwu.

———. 2013. "Er shi nian fengyun jidang, liang qian nian chenji hou xian zhenrong: Yiyang Tuzishan yizhi jiandu zaixian Yiyang gudai lishi" 二十年風雲激蕩兩千年沉寂后顯真容：益陽兔子山遺址簡牘再現益陽古代歷史. *Zhongguo wenwu bao* 06/12/2013, 6–7.

Ikeda Yûichi 池田雄一. 1997. "Shindai no ritsuryô ni tsuite" 秦代の律令について. *Chûô daigaku bungakubu kiyô shigakuka* 42: 49–85.

———. 2002. *Sôgensho – Chûgoku kodai no saiban kiroku* 奏讞書 — 中國古代の裁判記錄. Tôkyô: Tôsui shobô.

———, ed. 2015. *Kandai wo sakanoboru sôgen – Chûgoku kodai no saiban kiroku* 漢代を遡る奏讞 — 中國古代の裁判記錄. Tôkyô: Kyûko shoin.

Ji Annuo 紀安諾 see Giele, Enno

Jiang Feifei 蔣非非. 2004. "*Shiji* zhong 'yin gong tu xing' ying wei 'yin guan, tu xing' ji 'yin guan' yuanyi bian" 《史記》中"隱宮徒刑"應爲"隱官、徒刑"及"隱官"原義辯. *Chutu wenxian yanjiu* 6: 136–139.

Jianshui Jinguan Hanjian 肩水金關漢簡 see Gansu jiandu baohu yanjiu zhongxin et al. 2011

Jijiupian 急就篇 see Wang Yunwu 1936

Jin Lixin 金理新. 2006. *Shanggu Hanyu xingtai yanjiu* 上古漢語形態研究. Hefei: Huangshan.

Jingmen shi bowuguan 荊門市博物館, ed. 1998. *Guodian Chumu zhujian* 郭店楚墓竹簡. Beijing: Wenwu.

Jingzhou bowuguan 荊州博物館. 2008. "Hubei Jingzhou Jinan Songbai Hanmu fajue jianbao" 湖北荊州紀南松柏漢墓發掘簡報. *Wenwu* 2008.4: 24–32.

Jingzhou diqu bowuguan 荊州地區博物館. 1992. "Jiangling Zhangjiashan liang zuo Hanmu chutu da pi zhujian" 江陵張家山兩座漢墓出土大批竹簡. *Wenwu* 1992.9: 1–11.

Jinshu 晉書. 10 vols. Beijing: Zhonghua, 1974.

Jinwen 金文 see Zhongguo shehui kexueyuan kaogu yanjiusuo 2007

Jinwen lu 金文錄 see Rong Geng 2011

Jiudian 九店 see Hubei sheng wenwu kaogu yanjiusuo and Beijing daxue zhongwenxi 2000

Jiuzhang suanshu 九章算術 see Guo Shuchun 1990.

Johnson, Wallace. 1979. *The T'ang Code: Vol. 1, General Principles*. Princeton: Princeton University Press.

———. 1997. *The T'ang Code: Vol. 2, Specific Articles*. Princeton: Princeton University Press.

Johnston, Ian. 2010. *The Mozi: A Complete Translation*. New York: Columbia University Press.

Juyan 居延 see Zhongguo shehui kexueyuan kaogu yanjiusuo 1980 (photos) as well as Xie Guihua et al. 1987 (shiwen)

Juyan xinjian 居延新簡 see Gansu sheng wenwu kaogu yanjiusuo et al. 1994

Karlgren, Bernhard. 1933. "Word Families in Chinese." *Bulletin of the Museum of Far Eastern Antiquities* 5: 9–120.

———. 1950a. *The Book of Odes*. Stockholm: Museum of Far Eastern Antiquities.

———. 1950b. "The Book of Documents." *Bulletin of the Museum of Far Eastern Antiquities* 22: 1–81.

———. 1957. "Grammata Serica Recensa." *Bulletin of the Museum of Far Eastern Antiquities* 29: 1–332.

Knoblock, John. 1988–94. *Xunzi: A Translation and Study of the Complete Works*. 3 vols. Stanford: Stanford University Press.

Knoblock, John and Jeffrey Riegel. 2000. *The Annals of Lü Buwei: A Complete Translation and Study*. Stanford: Stanford University Press.

Kongjiapo Rishu 孔家坡日書 see Hubei sheng wenwu kaogu yanjiusuo and Suizhou shi kaogudui 2006

Korolkov, Maxim. 2011. "Arguing about Law: Interrogation Procedure under the Qin and Former Han Dynasties." *Études chinoises* 30: 37–71.

———. 2013. *Czoujan'šu: Sbornik sudebnych zaprosov*. Moskau: Nauka Vostočnaja literature.

Krjukov, Michail V. 1972. *Sistema rodstva kitajcev*. Moskau: Nauka.

Kroll, J. L. 1990. "Notes on Ch'in and Han Law." In *Thought and Law in Qin and Han China: Studies Dedicated to Anthony Hulsewé on the Occasion of his Eightieth Birthday*, edited by Wilt L. Idema and Erik Zürcher, 63–78. Leiden: Brill.

Kuhn, Dieter. 1988. *Textile Technology: Spinning and Reeling*. Vol. 5, part IX of *Science and Civilisation in China*, edited by Joseph Needham. Cambridge: Cambridge University Press.

Kyôto daigaku jinbun kagaku kenkyûjo kandoku kenkyûhan 京都大学人文科学研究所簡牘研究班, ed. 2015. *Kankan goi – Chûgoku kodai mokkan jiten* 漢簡語彙—中國古代木簡辭典. Tôkyô: Iwanami shoten.

Lao(zi) 老子 see *Zhuzi jicheng*, vol. 3 (Wang Bi 王弼, *Laozi zhu* 老子注)

Lao Gan 勞榦. 1951. "Handai de guyong zhidu" 漢代的雇傭制度. *Zhongyang yanjiuyuan lishi yuyan yanjiusuo jikan* 23: 77–87.

———. 1982. "Zai lun Handai de tingzhi" 再論漢代的亭制. *Zhongyang yanjiuyuan lishi yuyan yanjiusuo jikan* 53: 1–20.

Lau D. C. 1984. *Mencius*. Revised edition. 2 vols. Hong Kong: Chinese University Press.

Lau D. C. 劉殿爵 and Chen Fong Ching 陳方正, ed. 1992a. *Bingshu si zhong (Sunzi, Weiliaozi, Wuzi, Sima fa) zhuzi suoyin* 兵書四種（孫子、尉繚子、吳子、司馬法）逐字索引. The Chinese University of Hong Kong, Institute of Chinese Studies Ancient Chinese Texts Concordance Series. Hong Kong: Commercial Press.

———, ed. 1992b. *Dadai liji zhuzi suoyin* 大戴禮記逐字索引. The Chinese University of Hong Kong, Institute of Chinese Studies Ancient Chinese Texts Concordance Series. Hong Kong: Commercial Press.

———, ed. 1992c. *Hanshi waizhuan zhuzi suoyin* 韓詩外傳逐字索引. The Chinese University of Hong Kong, Institute of Chinese Studies Ancient Chinese Texts Concordance Series. Hong Kong: Commercial Press.

———, ed. 1992d. *Wenzi zhuzi suoyin* 文子逐字索引. The Chinese University of Hong Kong, Institute of Chinese Studies Ancient Chinese Texts Concordance Series. Hong Kong: Commercial Press.

———, ed. 1992e. *Zhanguoce zhuzi suoyin* 戰國策逐字索引. The Chinese University of Hong Kong, Institute of Chinese Studies Ancient Chinese Texts Concordance Series. Hong Kong: Commercial Press.

———, ed. 1993a. *Gulienüzhuan zhuzi suoyin* 古列女傳逐字索引. The Chinese University of Hong Kong, Institute of Chinese Studies Ancient Chinese Texts Concordance Series. Hong Kong: Commercial Press.

———, ed. 1993b. *Hanguan liu zhong zhuzi suoyin* 漢官六種逐字索引. The Chinese University of Hong Kong, Institute of Chinese Studies Ancient Chinese Texts Concordance Series. Hong Kong: Commercial Press.

———, ed. 1994a. *Shangshu dazhuan zhuzi suoyin* 尚書大傳逐字索引. The Chinese University of Hong Kong, Institute of Chinese Studies Ancient Chinese Texts Concordance Series. Hong Kong: Commercial Press.

———, ed. 1994b. *Jia Yi Xinshu zhuzi suoyin* 賈誼新書逐字索引. The Chinese University of Hong Kong, Institute of Chinese Studies Ancient Chinese Texts Concordance Series. Hong Kong: Commercial Press.

———, ed. 1994c. *Chunqiu fanlu zhuzi suoyin* 春秋繁露逐字索引. The Chinese University of Hong Kong, Institute of Chinese Studies Ancient Chinese Texts Concordance Series. Hong Kong: Commercial Press.

———, ed. 1995. *Bohutong zhuzi suoyin* 白虎通逐字索引. The Chinese University of Hong Kong, Institute of Chinese Studies Ancient Chinese Texts Concordance Series. Hong Kong: Commercial Press.

———, ed. 1997. *Liu tao zhuzi suoyin* 六韜逐字索引. The Chinese University of Hong Kong, Institute of Chinese Studies Ancient Chinese Texts Concordance Series. Hong Kong: Commercial Press.

———, ed. 1999. *Guoyu zhuzi suoyin* 國語逐字索引. The Chinese University of Hong Kong, Institute of Chinese Studies Ancient Chinese Texts Concordance Series. Hong Kong: Commercial Press.

———, ed. 2000. *Chuci zhuzi suoyin* 楚辭逐字索引. The Chinese University of Hong Kong, Institute of Chinese Studies Ancient Chinese Texts Concordance Series. Hong Kong: Commercial Press.

Lau, Ulrich. 1999. *Quellenstudien zur Landvergabe und Bodenübertragung in der westlichen Zhou-Dynastie (1045?–771 v. Chr.)*. Nettetal: Steyler-Verlag.

———. 2002. "Die Rekonstruktion des Strafprozesses und die Prinzipien der Strafzumessung zu Beginn der Han-Zeit im Lichte des *Zou yan shu*." In *Und folge nun dem, was mein Herz begehrt: Festschrift für Ulrich Unger zum 70. Geburtstag*, edited by Roland Emmerich and Hans Stumpfeldt, 343–395. Hamburg: Hamburger Sinologische Gesellschaft.

———. 2005. "The Scope of Private Jurisdiction in Early Imperial China: The Evidence of Newly Excavated Legal Documents." *Asiatische Studien/Études Asiatiques* 59, no. 1: 333–352.

——— (=Lao Wuli 勞武利). 2013. "Zhangjiashan Hanjian *Zou yan shu* yu Yuelu shuyuan Qinjian *Wei yu deng zhuang si zhong* de chubu bijiao" 張家山漢簡《奏讞書》與嶽麓書院秦簡《爲獄等狀四種》的初步比較. *Hunan daxue xuebao (shehui kexue ban)* 27, no. 3: 5–9.

———. 2014. "Qin Criminal Case Records of the Collection *Wei yu deng zhuang*." *Oriens Extremus* 53: 139–192.

———. Forthcoming. "First Results of the Comparison between the *Zouyanshu* from Zhangjiashan and the Yuelu Academy Collection of Criminal Cases from Pre-imperial Qin." In *Proceedings of the Fourth EASCM Workshop in Paris 2012*, edited by Enno Giele and Olivier Venture.

Lau, Ulrich and Michael Lüdke. 2012. *Exemplarische Rechtsfälle vom Beginn der Han-Dynastie: Eine kommentierte Übersetzung des* Zouyanshu *aus Zhangjiashan/Provinz Hubei*. Tokyo: Research Institute for Languages and Cultures of Asia and Africa (ILCAA), Tokyo University of Foreign Studies.

———. Forthcoming. *Frühchinesische Rechtsterminologie: Ein Lexikon auf der Grundlage qin- und westhanzeitlicher Manuskripte*. Gossenberg: Ostasien Verlag.

Legge, James. 1960. *The Chinese Classics with a Translation, Critical and Exegetical Notes, Prolegomena, and Copious Indexes. Vol. 5: The Ch'un Ts'ew with the Tso Chuen*. 2nd edition, with minor text corrections and a concordance table. Hong Kong: Hong Kong University Press.

Li(ji) 禮記 see Ruan Yuan 1980 (*Liji zhengyi* 禮記正義)

Li Chao 李超. 2009. "Ye tan Qindai 'yin guan'" 也談秦代 "隱官". <http://www.bsm.org.cn/show_article.php?id=1182>, accessed September 1, 2014.

Li Jing 栗勁. 1985. *Qinlü tonglun* 秦律通論. Jinan: Shandong renmin.

——— 李靜. 2009. "Qin jiandu yanjiu lunzhu mulu" 秦簡牘研究論著目錄. *Jianbo* 4: 73–122.

Li Junming 李均明. 1983. "Hanjian suo jian churu fu, zhuan yu churu mingji" 漢簡所見出入符、傳與出入名籍. *Wenshi* 19: 27–35.

———. 2005. "Ejina Hanjian fazhi shiliao kao" 額濟納漢簡法制史料考. In *Ejina Hanjian* 額濟納漢簡, edited by Wei Jian 魏堅, 54–70. Guilin: Guangxi shifan daxue.

———. 2009. *Qin Han jiandu wenshu fenlei jijie* 秦漢簡牘文書分類輯解. Beijing: Wenwu.

———. 2011. *Jiandu fazhi lungao* 簡牘法制論稿. Guilin: Guangxi shifan daxue.

Li Junming and He Shuangquan 何雙全. 1990. *Sanjian jiandu heji* 散見簡牘合輯. Beijing: Wenwu.

Li Junming and Liu Jun 劉軍, eds. 1994. *Handai tunshu yidian falü zhi* 漢代屯戍遺典法律志. Zhongguo zhenxi falü dianji jicheng 中國珍稀法律典籍集成 2. Beijing: Kexue.

Li Konghuai 李孔懷. 2007. "Shangpin jiage 商品價格." In *Zhongguo jingji tongshi: Qin Han jingji juan (shang, xia)* 中國經濟通史：秦漢經濟卷（上，下）, edited by Lin Ganquan 林甘泉, 565–589. 2nd edition. Beijing: Zhongguo shehui kexue.

Li Li 李力. 2007. *Lichenqie shenfen zai yanjiu* 隸臣妾身份再研究. Beijing: Zhongguo fazhi.

Li Mingxiao 李明曉, Hu Bo 胡波 and Zhang Guoyan 張國豔. 2011. *Zhanguo Qin Han jiandu xuci yanjiu* 戰國秦漢簡牘虛詞研究. Chengdu: Sichuan cishu.

Li Mingxiao and Zhao Jiuxiang 趙久湘. 2011. *Sanjian Zhanguo Qin Han jianbo falü wenxian zhengli yu yanjiu* 散見戰國秦漢簡帛法律文獻整理與研究. Chongqing: Xinan shifan daxue.

Li Mingzhao 黎明釗. 2009. "Liye Qinjian: Huji dang'an de tantao" 里耶秦簡：戶籍檔案的探討. *Zhongguo shi yanjiu* 2009.2: 5–23.

Li Shoukui 李守奎, Qu Bing 曲冰 and Sun Weilong 孫偉龍. 2007. *Shanghai bowuguan cang Zhanguo Chu zhushu (yi – wu) wenzibian* 上海博物館藏戰國楚竹書（一～五）文字編. Beijing: Zuojia.

Li Xueqin 李學勤, ed. 2010. *Qinghua daxue cang Zhanguo zhujian* (*yi*) 清華大學藏戰國竹簡（壹）. Shanghai: Zhongxi shuju.

Li Yufu 李玉福. 2002. *Qin Han zhidushi lun* 秦漢制度史論. Jinan: Shandong daxue.

Li Zhenhong 李振宏. 1988. "Juyan Hanjian de laoji zhidu" 居延漢簡中的勞績制度. *Zhongguo shi yanjiu* 1988.2: 57–90.

Li Zhonglin 李忠林. 2012. "Qin zhi Hanchu (qian 246 zhi qian 104) lifa yanjiu – Yi chutu lijian wei zhongxin" 秦至漢初（前246至前104）曆法研究——以出土曆簡爲中心. *Zhongguo shi yanjiu* 2012.2: 17–69.

Lian Shaoming 連劭名. 1988. "Xiyu mujian suo jian *Hanlü*" 西域木簡所見《漢律》. *Wenshi* 29: 131–141.

Lianyungang shi bowuguan 連雲港市博物館, Donghai xian bowuguan 東海縣博物館, Zhongguo shehui kexueyuan jianbo yanjiu zhongxin 中國社會科學院簡帛研究中心 and Zhongguo wenwu yanjiusuo 中國文物研究所, ed. 1997. *Yinwan Hanmu jiandu* 尹灣漢墓簡牘. Beijing: Zhonghua.

Lidai qiyue 歷代契約 see Zhang Chuanxi 1995

Lin Ganquan 林甘泉, ed. 2007. *Zhongguo jingji tongshi: Qin Han jingji juan* (*shang, xia*) 中國經濟通史：秦漢經濟卷（上，下）. 2nd edition. Beijing: Zhongguo shehui kexue.

Lin Jianming 林劍鳴. 2009. *Qin shi gao* 秦史稿. Beijing: Zhongguo renmin daxue.

Lipu 曆譜 see Zhangjiashan er si qi hao Hanmu zhujian zhengli xiaozu 2001 (photos/shiwen) as well as 2006 (shiwen)

Lishi dituji 歷史地圖集 see Tan Qixiang 1982

Liu Hainian 劉海年. 2006. *Zhanguo Qindai fazhi guankui* 戰國秦代法制管窺. Beijing: Falü.

Liu Junwen 劉俊文 [點校]; Zhangsun Wuji 長孫無忌 [等撰]. 1983. *Tanglü shuyi* 唐律疏議. Beijing: Zhonghua.

Liu tao 六韬 see Lau D. C. and Chen Fong Ching 1997

Liu Xinfang 劉信芳 and Liang Zhu 梁柱. 1997. *Yunmeng Longgang Qinjian* 雲夢龍崗秦簡. Beijing: Kexue.

Liu Zhao 劉釗. 2010. "Guanyu Qinyin xingming de chubu kaocha" 關於秦印姓名的初步考察. In *Chutu wenxian yu chuanshi dianji de zhushi – Jinian Tan Pusen xiansheng shishi liang zhounian guoji xueshu yantaohui lunwenji* 出土文獻與傳世典籍的註釋——紀年譚樸森先生逝世兩週年國際學術研討會論文集, edited by Fudan daxue chutu wenxian yu gu wenzi yanjiu zhongxin 復旦大學出土文獻與古文字研究中心, 361–385. Shanghai: Shanghai guji.

Liye 里耶 5–, 6–, 8– see Hunan sheng wenwu kaogu yanjiusuo 2012

Liye 里耶 16– see Hunan sheng wenwu kaogu yanjiusuo 2006

Liye huji 里耶戶籍 see Hunan sheng wenwu kaogu yanjiusuo 2006

Liye Qin jiandu jiaoshi xiaozu 里耶秦簡牘校釋小組. 2014. "Xin jian Liye Qin jiandu ziliao xuanjiao (yi)" 新見里耶秦簡牘資料選校（一）. <http://www.bsm.org.cn/show_article.php?id=2068>, accessed October 21, 2015.

Loewe, Michael. 1960. "The Orders of Aristocratic Rank of Han China." *T'oung Pao* 49, no. 1–3: 97–174.

———. 1967. *Records of Han Administration*. 2 vols. Cambridge: Cambridge University Press.

———. 1986. "The Former Han Dynasty." In *The Cambridge History of China. Volume 1: The Ch'in and Han Empires, 221 B.C.–A.D. 220*, edited by Denis Crispin Twitchett and Michael Loewe, 103–222. Cambridge: Cambridge University Press.

———. 2000. *A Biographical Dictionary of the Qin, Former Han and Xin Periods* (*221 BC – AD 24*). Leiden: Brill.

———. 2004. *The Men who Governed Han China. Companion to* A Biographical Dictionary of the Qin, Former Han and Xin Periods. Leiden: Brill.

———. 2008. "The Organs of Han Imperial Government: *zhong duguan, duguan, xianguan and xiandao guan*." *Bulletin of the School of Oriental and African Studies* 71, no. 3: 509–528.

Loewe, Michael and Edward L. Shaughnessy, ed. 1999. *The Cambridge History of Ancient China: From the Origins of Civilisation to 221 B.C.* Cambridge: Cambridge University Press.

Longgang 龍崗 see Zhongguo wenwu yanjiusuo and Hubei sheng wenwu kaogu yanjiusuo 2001

Longgang mudu 龍崗木牘 see Zhongguo wenwu yanjiusuo and Hubei sheng wenwu kaogu yanjiusuo 2001

Lü(*shi chunqiu*) 呂氏春秋 see *Zhuzi jicheng*, vol. 6

Lüdke, Michael. 2003. "Professional Practice: Law in Qin and Han China." PhD diss. University of Heidelberg.

Lunheng 論衡 see *Zhuzi jicheng*, vol. 7

Lunyu 論語 see *Zhuzi jicheng*, vol. 1 (Liu Baonan 劉寶楠, *Lunyu zhengyi* 論語正義)

Luo Fuyi 羅福頤, ed. 1978. *Hanyin wenzi zheng* 漢印文字徵. Beijing: Wenwu.

———, ed. 1987. *Qin Han Nanbei chao guanyin zhengcun* 秦漢南北朝官印徵存. Beijing: Wenwu.

Ma Chengyuan 馬承源, ed. 2002. *Shanghai bowuguan cang Zhanguo Chu zhushu* (*er*) 上海博物館藏戰國楚竹書（二）. Shanghai: Shanghai guji.

———, ed. 2003. *Shanghai bowuguan cang Zhanguo Chu zhushu* (*san*) 上海博物館藏戰國楚竹書（三）. Shanghai: Shanghai guji.

Ma Yi 馬怡. 2007. "Fushui" 賦稅. In *Zhongguo jingji tongshi: Qin Han jingji juan* (*shang, xia*) 中國經濟通史：秦漢經濟卷（上，下）, edited by Lin Ganquan 林甘泉, 647–699. 2nd edition. Beijing: Zhongguo shehui kexue.

Major, John S., Sarah A. Queen, Andrew Seth Meyer and Harold D. Roth, ed. 2010. *The Huainanzi: A Guide to the Theory and Practice of Government in Early Han China, by Liu An, King of Huainan*. New York: Columbia University Press.

Mawangdui Hanmu boshu zhengli xiaozu 馬王堆漢墓帛書整理小組. 1983. *Mawangdui Hanmu boshu (san)* 馬王堆漢墓帛書（叁）. Beijing: Wenwu.

———. 1984. "Mawangdui boshu *Liushisi gua* shiwen" 馬王堆帛書《六十四卦》釋文. *Wenwu* 1984.3: 1–8.

———. 1985. *Mawangdui Hanmu boshu (si)* 馬王堆漢墓帛書（肆）. Beijing: Wenwu.

Mawangdui Lao(zi) A 馬王堆老子甲 see Guojia wenwuju gu wenxian yanjiushi 1980

Mawangdui Lao(zi) B 馬王堆老子乙 see Guojia wenwuju gu wenxian yanjiushi 1980

Mawangdui Wushier bingfang 馬王堆五十二病方 see Mawangdui Hanmu boshu zhengli xiaozu 1985

Mawangdui Zaliao fang 馬王堆雜療方 see Mawangdui Hanmu boshu zhengli xiaozu 1985

Mawangdui Zhanguo zongheng jiashu 馬王堆戰國縱橫家書 see Mawangdui Hanmu boshu zhengli xiaozu 1983

Mawangdui Zhouyi 馬王堆周易 see Mawangdui Hanmu boshu zhengli xiaozu 1984

McLeod, Katrina and Robin D. S. Yates. 1981. "Forms of Ch'in Law: An Annotated Translation of the *Feng-chen shih*." *Harvard Journal of Asiatic Studies* 41: 111–163.

Meng(zi) 孟子 see *Zhuzi jicheng*, vol. 1 (Jiao Xun 焦循, *Mengzi zhengyi* 孟子正義)

Miyake Kiyoshi 宮宅潔. 1998. "Shin Kan jidai no saiban seido" 秦漢時代の裁判制度. *Shirin* 81: 167–200.

———. 2011. *Chûgoku kodai keiseishi no kenkyû* 中國古代刑制史の研究. Kyôto: Kyôto daigaku gakujutsu shuppankai.

Mizuma Daisuke 水間大輔. 2012. "Qin Han shiqi chengdan fuyu de jiguan yu guanli" 秦漢時期承擔覆獄的機關與官吏. *Jianbo* 7: 277–295.

———. 2014. "*Yuelu shuyuan cang Qinjian* (san) suo jian de gongfan chufa" 《嶽麓書院藏秦簡》（叁）所見的共犯處罰. In Wang Pei 2014, 19–43.

Mo(zi) 墨子 see *Zhuzi jicheng*, vol. 4 (Sun Yirang 孫詒讓, *Mozi jiangu* 墨子閒詁)

Momiyama Akira 籾山明. 2006. *Chûgoku kodai soshô seido no kenkyû* 中國古代訴訟制度の研究. Kyôto: Kyôto daigaku gakujutsu shuppankai.

Nagata Hidemasa 永田英正. 1989. *Kyoen Kankan no kenkyû* 居延漢簡の研究. Kyôto: Dôhôsha.

Nan Yuquan 南玉泉. 1999. "Qinchao de xingfa tixi" 秦朝的刑罰體系. In *Zhongguo fazhi tongshi, di er juan: Zhanguo Qin Han* 中國法制通史，第二卷：戰國秦漢, edited by Xu Shihong 徐世虹, 127–171. Beijing: Falü.

Nienhauser, William H. Jr., ed. 1994–. *The Grand Scribe's Records*. Vols. I (1994), II (2002), V.1 (2006), VII (1994), VIII (2008), IX (2011). Bloomington: Indiana University Press.

Nishijima Sadao 西島定生. 1961. *Chûgoku kodai teikoku no keisei to kôzô: Nijûtô shakusei no kenkyû* 中國古代帝國の形成と構造：二十等爵制の研究. Tôkyô: Tôkyô daigaku.

———. 1986. "The Economic and Social History of Former Han." In *The Cambridge History of China. Volume 1: The Ch'in and Han Empires, 221 B.C.–A.D. 220*, edited by Denis Crispin Twitchett and Michael Loewe, 545–607. Cambridge: Cambridge University Press.

Nylan, Michael. 2005–06. "Notes on a Case of Illicit Sex from Zhangjiashan: A Translation and Commentary." *Early China* 30: 25–45.

Ôba Osamu 大庭脩. 1982. *Shin Kan hôseishi no kenkyû* 秦漢法制史の研究. Tôkyô: Sôbunsha.

———. 1991. *Qin Han fazhi shi yanjiu* 秦漢法制史研究. Shanghai: Shanghai renmin.

———. 1992. *Kankan kenkyû* 漢簡研究. Kyôto: Dôhôsha.

———. 1995. *Kyoen Kankan sakuin* 居延漢簡索引. Suita: Kansai daigaku.

Odes=Shijing 詩經 see Karlgren 1950a

Ou Yang 歐揚. 2015. "Yuelu Qinjian 'wu duo tian shi ling' tanxi" 嶽麓秦簡"毋奪田時令" 探析. *Hunan daxue xuebao (shehui kexue ban)* 29, no. 3: 25–30.

Peng Hao 彭浩, Chen Wei 陳偉 and Kudô Motoo 工藤元男, ed. 2007. *Ernian lüling yu Zou yan shu – Zhangjiashan er si qi hao Hanmu chutu falü wenxian shidu* 二年律令與奏讞書一張家山二四七號漢墓出土法律文獻釋讀. Shanghai: Shanghai guji.

Pian Yuqian 駢宇騫, ed. 2001. *Yinqueshan Hanjian wenzibian* 銀雀山漢簡文子編. Beijing: Wenwu.

Pulleyblank, Edwin G. 1995. *Outline of Classical Chinese Grammar*. Vancouver: University of British Columbia Press.

Qingchuan mudu 青川木牘 see Li Junming and He Shuangquan 1990

Qinghua Baoxun 清華保訓 see Li Xueqin 2010

Qinghua Huangmen 清華黃門 see Li Xueqin 2010

Qiu Guangming 丘光明. 1992. *Zhongguo lidai duliangheng kao* 中國歷代度量衡考. Beijing: Kexue.

Qiu Xigui 裘錫圭. 1981. "Se fu chutan" 嗇夫初探. In *Yunmeng Qinjian yanjiu* 雲夢秦簡研究, edited by Zhonghua shuju bianjibu 中華書局編輯部, 226–302. Beijing: Zhonghua.

———. 1992. *Guwenzi lunji* 古文字論集. Beijing: Zhonghua.

QLSZ=*Qinlü shiba zhong* 秦律十八種 see Shuihudi Qinmu zhujian zhengli xiaozu 1990

QLZC=*Qinlü zachao* 秦律雜抄 see Shuihudi Qinmu zhujian zhengli xiaozu 1990

Quan Hanwen 全漢文 see Yan Kejun 1958

Rao Zongyi 饒宗頤 and Zeng Xiantong 曾憲通. 1993. *Chudi chutu wenxian san zhong yanjiu* 楚地出土文獻三種研究. Beijing: Zhonghua.

RCL see Hulsewé 1985

Richter, Matthias L. 2006. "Tentative Criteria for Discerning Individual Hands in the Guodian Manuscripts." In *Rethinking Confucianism: Selected Papers from the Third International Conference on Excavated Manuscripts, Mount Holyoke College, April 2004*, edited by Xing Wen, 132–147. San Antonio: Trinity University.

Rickett, W. Allyn. 1985/98. *Kuan-tzu. Political, Economical and Philosophical Essays from Early China*. 2 vols. Princeton: Princeton University Press.

Rong Geng 容庚. 2011. *Qin Han jinwen lu* 秦漢金文錄. Beijing: Zhonghua.

Ruan Yuan 阮元, ed. 1980. *Shisanjing zhushu fu jiaokanji* 十三經注疏附校勘記. First published 1815. Reprint in 2 vols. Beijing: Zhonghua.

Sagart, Laurent. 1999. *The Roots of Old Chinese*. Amsterdam and Philadelphia: Benjamins.

Sanjian 散見 see Li Junming and He Shuangquan 1990

Schuessler, Axel. 1987. *A Dictionary of Early Zhou Chinese*. Honolulu: University of Hawai'i Press.

———. 2007. *ABC Etymological Dictionary of Old Chinese*. Honolulu: University of Hawai'i Press.

Shanghai bowuguan Hengxian 上海博物館恆先 see Ma Chengyuan 2003

Shanghai bowuguan Rongchengshi 上海博物館容成氏 see Ma Chengyuan 2002

Shanghai bowuguan Xizhe junlao 上海博物館昔者君老 see Ma Chengyuan 2002

Shangjunshu 商君書 see *Zhuzi jicheng*, vol. 5

Shangshu dazhuan 尚書大傳 see Lau D. C. and Chen Fong Ching 1994a

Shen Gang 沈剛. 2004. "Handai tingwei kaoshu" 漢代廷尉考述. *Qin Han shi luncong* 9: 186–199.

———. 2008. *Juyan Hanjian yuci huishi* 居延漢簡語詞彙釋. Beijing: Kexue.

Shen Jiaben 沈家本. 1985. *Lidai xingfa kao* 歷代刑法考. First published 1913–29. Punctuated and edited by Deng Jingyuan 鄧經元 and Pian Yuqian 駢宇騫. 4 vols. Beijing: Zhonghua 1985.

Shen Jianshi 沈兼士. 1985. *Guangyun shengxi* 廣韻聲系. 2 vols. Reprint, Beijing: Zhonghua.

Shiji 史記. 10 vols. Beijing: Zhonghua, 1959.

Shu=Shangshu 尚書 see Karlgren 1950b

Shuihudi mudu 睡虎地木牘 see Li Junming and He Shuangquan 1990

Shuihudi Qinmu zhujian zhengli xiaozu 睡虎地秦墓竹簡整理小組. 1978. *Shuihudi Qinmu zhujian* 睡虎地秦墓竹簡. Beijing: Wenwu 1978.

———. 1990. *Shuihudi Qinmu zhujian* 睡虎地秦墓竹簡. Beijing: Wenwu 1990.

Shuihudi Rishu B 睡虎地日書乙種 see Shuihudi Qinmu zhujian zhengli xiaozu 1990

Shuowen (*jiezi*) 說文解字 see Duan Yucai 1981

Songbai mudu 松柏木牘 see Jingzhou bowuguan 2008

Staack, Thies (=Shi Da 史達). 2013. "Yuelu Qinjian *Wei yu deng zhuang si zhong* juance yi de bianlian – Yiju jianbei huaxian he jianbei fanyin ziji fuyuan juanzhou yuanmao"

嶽麓秦簡《爲獄等狀四種》卷冊一的編聯——依據簡背劃綫和簡背反印字跡復原卷軸原貌. Translated by Li Jingrong 李婧嶸. *Hunan daxue xuebao (shehui kexue ban)* 27, no. 3: 20–25.

——— (=Shi Da 史達). 2014a. “Yuelu Qinjian *Wei yu deng zhuang si zhong* xin jian de yi mei loujian yu anli liu de bianlian” 嶽麓秦簡《爲獄等狀四種》新見的一枚漏簡與案例六的編聯. *Hunan daxue xuebao (shehui kexue ban)* 28, no. 4: 7–10.

——— (=Shi Da 史達). 2014b. “*Yuelu shuyuan cang Qin jian Wei li zhi guan ji qianshou* de bianlian xiuding – Yi jianbei huaxian yu fanyin ziji wei yiju” 《嶽麓書院藏秦簡・爲吏治官及黔首》的編聯修訂——以簡背劃綫與反印字跡爲依據. Translated by Huang Hai 黄海. In Wang Pei 2014, 73–99.

———. Forthcoming. “The Neglected ‘Backyard’ of Early Chinese Manuscripts – How an Analysis of the Verso of Bamboo Slips can Enable the Reconstruction of a Manuscript Roll.” In *Proceedings of the Fourth EASCM Workshop in Paris 2012*, edited by Enno Giele and Olivier Venture.

Starostin, Sergej A. 1989. *Rekonstrukcija drevnekitajskoj fonologičeskoj sistemy*. Moskau: Nauka.

———. 2006. Database “Chinese characters.” *The Tower of Babel: Evolution of Human Language Project*. <http://starling.rinet.ru/>, accessed February 20, 2014.

Strätz, Volker. 1979. *Luh-T’ao: Ein spätantiker Text zur Kriegskunst*. Bad Honnef: Bock u. Herchen.

Suanshushu 算數書 see Zhangjiashan er si qi hao Hanmu zhujian zhengli xiaozu 2001 (photos/shiwen) as well as 2006 (shiwen)

Su Junlin 蘇俊林. 2014a. “Yuelu Qinjian *Wei yu deng zhuang si zhong* mingming wenti tantao” 嶽麓秦簡《爲獄等狀四種》命名問題探討. *Jianduxue yanjiu* 5: 9–14.

———. 2014b. “Qin Han shiqi de ‘zhuang’ lei sifa wenshu” 秦漢時期的“狀”類司法文書. *Jianbo* 9: 301–310.

Sueyasu Ando 陶安あんど see Hafner, Arnd Helmut

Sun Ji 孫機. 2011. *Handai wuzhi wenhua ziliao tushuo (zengdingben)* 漢代物質文化資料圖說（增訂本）. Shanghai: Shanghai guji.

Sun Kai 孫楷. 2004. *Qin huiyao ershiqi juan* 秦會要二十七卷. Shanghai: Shanghai guji.

Sun Peiyang 孫沛陽. 2011. “Jiance bei huaxian chutan” 簡冊背劃綫初探. *Chutu wenxian yu gu wenzi yanjiu* 4: 449–462.

Sun Wenbo 孫聞博. 2014. “Liye Qinjian ‘shou’, ‘shou cheng’ xin kao – Jian tan Qin Han de shouguan zhidu” 里耶秦簡“守”、“守丞”新考——兼談秦漢的守官制度. <http://www.bsm.org.cn/show_article.php?id=2022>, accessed February 9, 2015.

Swann, Nancy Lee. 1950. *Food & Money in Ancient China: The Earliest Economic History of China to A.D. 25*. Princeton: Princeton University Press.

Takamura Takeyuki 高村武幸. 2008. *Kandai no chihô kanri to chiiki shakai* 漢代の地方官吏と地域社會. Tôkyô: Kyûko shoin.

Tan Qixiang 1982 譚其驤, ed. 1982. *Zhongguo lishi dituji* 中國歷史地圖集. Vols. I, II. Shanghai: Ditu.

Tanglü shuyi 唐律疏議 see Liu Junwen 1983

Teng Rensheng 滕王生. 2008. *Chuxi jianbo wenzibian* (*zengdingben*) 楚系簡帛文字編（增訂本）. Wuhan: Hubei jiaoyu.

Tjan Tjoe Som. 1949/52. *Po Hu T'ung: The Comprehensive Discussions in the White Tiger Hall*. 2 vols. Leiden: Brill.

TLS (=Thesaurus Linguae Sericae) see Harbsmeier, Christoph

Tomiya Itaru 冨谷至. 1998. *Shin Kan keibatsu seido no kenkyû* 秦漢刑罰制度の研究. Kyôto: Dôhôsha.

———. 2003. "Teisei ni kansuru ikkôsatsu – Kankan ni mieru tei no bunseki" 亭制に關する一考察—漢簡に見える亭の分析. In *Henkyô shutsudo mokkan kenkyû* 邊境出土木簡研究, edited by Tomiya Itaru, 367–409. Kyôto: Hôyû shoten.

———, ed. 2006. *Kôryô Chôkasan nihyaku yonjû nana gô bo shutsudo Kan ritsuryô no kenkyû* 江陵張家山二四七號墓出土漢律令の研究. 2 vols. Kyôto: Hôyû shoten.

———, ed. 2015. *Kankan goi kôshô* 漢簡語彙考証. Tôkyô: Iwanami shoten.

Twitchett, Denis Crispin and Michael Loewe, ed. 1986. *The Cambridge History of China. Volume 1: The Ch'in and Han Empires, 221 B.C.–A.D. 220*. Cambridge: Cambridge University Press.

Unger, Ulrich. 1987–97. *Grammatik des Klassischen Chinesisch*. 8 vols. Münster: privately printed.

Wang Huanlin 王煥林. 2007. *Liye Qinjian jiaogu* 里耶秦簡校詁. Beijing: Zhongguo wenlian.

Wang Hui 王輝. 2000. *Qin chutu wenxian biannian* 秦出土文獻編年. Taibei: Xinwenfeng.

———. 2008. *Gu wenzi tongjia zidian* 古文字通假字典. Beijing: Zhonghua.

Wang Li 王力. 1982. *Tongyuan zidian* 同源字典. Beijing: Shangwu.

———. 2000. *Wang Li gu hanyu zidian* 王力古漢語字典. Beijing: Zhonghua.

Wang Liqi 王利器. 1988. *Shiji zhuyi* 史記注譯. 4 vols. Xi'an: Sanqin.

Wang Pei 王沛, ed. 2014. *Chutu wenxian yu falü shi yanjiu* (*di san ji*) 出土文獻與法律史研究（第三輯）. Shanghai: Shanghai renmin chubanshe.

Wang Shumin 王叔岷. 1990. *Guji xuzi guangyi* 古籍虛字廣義. Taibei: Huazheng.

Wang Wei 王偉. 2013. "Du *Yuelu shuyuan cang Qinjian* (*san*) zhaji yi ze" 讀《嶽麓書院藏秦簡（叁）》劄記一則. <http://www.bsm.org.cn/show_article.php?id=1996>, accessed February 2, 2015.

———. 2014. "Yuelu Qinjian yanjiu zhaji (qi ze)" 嶽麓秦簡研究札記（七則）. Paper presented at the International Conference for Research on Qin manuscripts (Qin jiandu yanjiu guoji xueshu yantaohui 秦簡牘研究國際學術研討會), Changsha, December 6, 2014.

Wang Xueli 王學理, ed. 1994. *Qin wuzhi wenhua shi* 秦物質文化史. Xi'an: Sanqin.

Wang Yanhui 王彥輝. 2004. "Cong Zhangjiashan Hanjian kan Xihan si nubi de shehui diwei" 從張家山漢簡看西漢私奴婢的社會地位. *Qin Han shi luncong* 9: 232–246.

Wang Yong 王勇 and Tang Li 唐俐. 2010. "'Zou ma' wei Qin jue xiao kao" "走馬"爲秦爵小考. *Hunan daxue xuebao (shehui kexue ban)* 24, no. 4: 15–16.

Wang Yunwu 王雲五, ed. 1936. *Congshu jicheng chubian* 叢書集成初編. No. 1052: Jijiupian 急就篇. Shanghai: Shangwu, 1936.

Watson, Burton. 1974. *Courtier and Commoner in Ancient China. Selections from the History of the Former Han by Pan Gu*. New York: Columbia University Press.

———. 1993. *Records of the Grand Historian: Han Dynasty I/II*. Revised edition. 2 vols. Hong Kong, New York: Columbia University Press.

Wei Desheng 魏德勝. 2000. Shuihudi Qinmu zhujian *yufa yanjiu* 《睡虎地秦墓竹簡》語法研究. Beijing: Shoudu shifan daxue.

———. 2003. Shuihudi Qinmu zhujian *cihui yanjiu* 《睡虎地秦墓竹簡》詞匯研究. Beijing: Huaxia.

Wei li zhi dao 爲吏之道 see Shuihudi Qinmu zhujian zhengli xiaozu 1990

Weiliaozi 尉繚子 see Lau D. C. and Chen Fong Ching 1992a

Weld, Susan. 1999. "Chu Law in Action: Legal Documents from Tomb 2 at Baoshan." In *Defining Chu: Image and Reality in Ancient China*, edited by Constance A. Cook and John S. Major, 77–97. Honolulu: University of Hawai'i Press.

———. 2003. "Grave Matters: Warring States Law and Philosophy." In *Understanding China's Legal System: Essays in Honor of Jerome A. Cohen*, edited by Stephen C. Hsu, 122–179. New York: New York University Press.

Wen(zi) 文子 see Lau D. C. and Chen Fong Ching 1992d

Wilbur, Clarence Martin. 1943. *Slavery in China during the Former Han Dynasty 206 B.C.–A.D. 25*. Chicago: Field Museum of Natural History.

Wu Fuzhu 吳福助. 1994. *Shuihudi Qinjian lunkao* 睡虎地秦簡論考. Taibei: Wenjin.

Wu Rongzeng 吳榮曾. 1995. *Xian Qin liang Han shi yanjiu* 先秦兩漢史研究. Beijing: Zhonghua.

Wu Shuping 吳樹平. 1987. *Dongguan Hanji jiaozhu* 東觀漢記校注. 2 vols. N.p.: Zhongzhou guji.

Wu Wenling 鄔文玲. 2013. "'Shou', 'zhu' chengwei yu Qindai guan wenshu yongyu" "守"、"主"稱爲與秦代官文書用語. *Chutu wenxian yanjiu* 12: 152–167.

Wu Xu 鄔勖. 2014. "*Yuelu shuyuan cang Qinjian* (san) 'Gui, Suo xiang yi mou gou an' zhong de falü shiyong" 《嶽麓書院藏秦簡》（叁）"癸、瑣相移謀購案"中的法律適用. In Wang Pei 2014, 167–190.

Wuwei yijian 武威醫簡 see Gansu sheng bowuguan and Wuwei xian wenhuaguan 1975

Xiang Xi 向熹. 1986. *Shijing cidian* 詩經詞典. Chengdu: Sichuan renmin.

Xie Guihua 謝桂華. 1997. "Yinwan Hanmu jiandu he Xihan difang xingzheng zhidu" 尹灣漢墓簡牘和西漢地方行政制度. *Wenwu* 1997.1: 42–48.

Xie Guihua, Li Junming 李均明 and Zhu Guozhao 朱國炤. 1987. *Juyan Hanjian shiwen hejiao* 居延漢簡釋文合校. 2 vols. Beijing: Wenwu.

Xin Ziniu 辛子牛, ed. 1997. *Zhongguo lidai ming'an jicheng* 中國歷代名案集城. 3 vols. Shanghai: Fudan daxue.

Xing Yitian 邢義田. 1993. "Handai biansai jundui de jijia, xiumu yu gonglao zhi" 漢代邊塞軍隊的給假、休沐與功勞制. In *Jianbo yanjiu di yi ji* 簡帛研究第一輯, edited by Li Xueqin 李學勤, 192–205. Beijing: Falü.

———. 2007. "Longshan Liye Qin Qianling xiancheng yizhi chutu mou xiang Nanyang li huji jian shitan" 龍山里耶秦遷陵縣城遺址出土某鄉南陽里戶籍簡試探. <http://www.bsm.org.cn/show_article.php?id=744>, accessed February 20, 2014.

Xinshu 新書 see Lau D. C. and Chen Fong Ching 1994b

XL=Xiao lü 效律 see Shuihudi Qinmu zhujian zhengli xiaozu 1990

Xu Fuchang 徐富昌. 1993. *Shuihudi Qinjian yanjiu* 睡虎地秦簡研究. Taibei: Wenshizhe.

Xu Shihong 徐世虹. 1998. "Juyan Hanjian zhong de 'wu zhuang' yu 'zhuang ci'" 居延漢簡中的"毋狀"與"狀辭". *Chutu wenxian yanjiu* 4: 52–56.

———, ed. 1999. *Zhongguo fazhi tongshi, di er juan: Zhanguo Qin Han* 中國法制通史，第二卷：戰國秦漢. Beijing: Falü.

———. 2004. "'San huan zhi', 'xing fu cheng dan chong', 'xi cheng dan chong mou sui' jie – Du *Ernian lüling* zhaji" "三環之"、"刑復城旦舂"、"繫城旦舂某歲"解——讀《二年律令》札記. *Chutu wenxian yanjiu* 6: 79–89.

Xu Xiqi 徐錫祺. 1997. *Xizhou (Gonghe) zhi Xihan lipu* 西周（共和）至西漢曆譜. 2 vols. Beijing: Beijing kexue jishu.

Xuanquan 懸泉 see Hu Pingsheng and Zhang Defang 2001

Xun(zi) 荀子 see *Zhuzi jicheng*, vol. 2 (Wang Xianqian 王先謙, *Xunzi jijie* 荀子集解)

Yan(zi chunqiu) 晏子春秋 see *Zhuzi jicheng*, vol. 4 (Zhang Chunyi 張純一, *Yanzi chunqiu jiaozhu* 晏子春秋校注)

Yan Gengwang 嚴耕望. 1961. *Qin Han difang xingzheng zhidu* 秦漢地方行政制度. 2 vols. Taibei: Zhongyang yanjiuyuan lishi yuyan yanjiusuo.

Yan Kejun 嚴可均, ed. 1958. *Quan shanggu sandai Qin Han sanguo liuchao wen* 全上古三代秦漢三國六朝文. 5 vols. Beijing: Zhonghua.

Yan Xiaojun 閆曉君. 2012. *Qin Han falü yanjiu* 秦漢法律研究. Beijing: Falü.

Yang Bojun 楊伯峻. 1981. *Chunqiu Zuozhuan zhu (xiuding ben)* 春秋左傳注（修訂本）. 4 vols. Beijing: Zhonghua.

Yang Bojun and He Leshi 何樂士. 2001. *Gu Hanyu yufa ji qi fazhan (xiuding ben)* 古漢語語法及其發展（修訂本）. 2 vols. Beijing: Yuwen.

Yang Hongnian 楊鴻年. 1985. *Han Wei zhidu congkao* 漢魏制度叢考. Wuhan: Wuhan daxue.

Yang Jiping 楊際平. 2007. "Qin Han huji guanli zhidu yanjiu" 秦漢戶籍管理制度研究. *Zhonghua wenshi luncong* 85, no. 1: 1–35.

Yang Zongbing 楊宗兵. 2004. "Liye Qinjian xian 'shou', 'cheng', 'shou cheng' tongyi shuo" 里耶秦簡縣"守"、"丞"、"守丞"同意說. *Beifang luncong* 2004.6: 11–14.

Yantielun 鹽鐵論 see *Zhuzi jicheng*, vol. 7

Yates, Robin D. S. 1987. "Social Status in the Ch'in: Evidence from the Yün-meng Legal Documents. Part I: Commoners." *Harvard Journal of Asiatic Studies* 47: 197–236.

———. 1995. "State Control of Bureaucrats under the Qin: Techniques and Procedures." *Early China* 20: 331–365.

———. 2001. "Slavery in Early China: A Socio-cultural Approach." *Journal of East Asian Archaeology* 3, no. 1–2: 283–331.

———. 2005. "The History of Military Divination in China." *East Asian Science, Technology, and Medicine* 24: 15–43.

———. 2009. "Law and the Military in Early China." In *Military Culture in Imperial China*, edited by Nicola Di Cosmo, 23–44. Cambridge: Harvard University Press.

———. 2011. "Soldiers, Scribes, and Women: Literacy among the Lower Orders in Early China." In *Writing & Literacy in Early China*, edited by Li Feng and David Prager Branner, 339–369. Seattle: University of Washington Press.

———. 2012–13. "The Qin Slips and Boards from Well No. 1, Liye, Hunan: A Brief Introduction to the Qin Qianling County Archives." *Early China* 35–36: 291–330.

———. 2014. "The Changing Status of Slaves in the Qin-Han Transition." In *Birth of an Empire: The State of Qin Revisited*, edited by Yuri Pines, Lothar von Falkenhausen, Gideon Shelach and Robin D. S. Yates, 155–186. Berkeley, Los Angeles, London: University of California Press.

Yi(jing) 易經 see Ruan Yuan 1980 (*Zhouyi zhengyi* 周易正義)

Yinqueshan Hanmu zhujian zhengli xiaozu 銀雀山漢墓竹簡整理小組. 1985. *Yinqueshan Hanmu zhujian (yi)* 銀雀山漢墓竹簡〔壹〕. Beijing: Wenwu.

Yinqueshan Shoufa shouling 銀雀山守法守令 see Yinqueshan Hanmu zhujian zhengli xiaozu 1985

Yinqueshan Weiliaozi 銀雀山尉繚子 see Yinqueshan Hanmu zhujian zhengli xiaozu 1985

Yinwan mudu 尹灣木牘 see Lianyungang shi bowuguan et al. 1997

Yu Haoliang 于豪亮. 1985. *Yu Haoliang xueshu wencun* 于豪亮學術文存. Beijing: Zhonghua.

Yu Minjian 俞敏監 and Xie Jifeng 謝紀鋒, ed. 1993. *Xuci gulin* 虛詞詁林. Ha'erbin: Heilongjiang renmin.

Yu Zhenbo 于振波. 2009. "Qin lüling zhong de 'xin qianshou' yu 'xin di li'" 秦律令中的"新黔首"與"新地吏". *Zhongguo shi yanjiu* 2009.3: 69–78.

———. 2010. "Qinlü zhong de jia dun bijia ji xiangguan wenti" 秦律中的甲盾比價及相關問題. *Shixue jikan* 2010.5: 36–38.

———. 2015. "'Fu zhi' zhi zui yu Qin zhi lifa jingshen" "負志" 之罪與秦之立法精神. *Hunan daxue xuebao (shehui kexue ban)* 29, no. 3: 21–24.

Yuelu 27 nian zhiri 嶽麓廿七年質日 see Zhu Hanmin and Chen Songchang 2010

Yuelu 34 nian zhiri 嶽麓卅四年質日 see Zhu Hanmin and Chen Songchang 2010

Yuelu 35 nian si zhiri 嶽麓卅五年私質日 see Zhu Hanmin and Chen Songchang 2010

Yuelu Lüling 嶽麓律令 see Chen Songchang 2012a and 2014a

Yuelu Shu 嶽麓數 see Zhu Hanmin and Chen Songchang 2011

Yuelu shuyuan cang Qinjian zhengli xiaozu 嶽麓書院藏秦簡整理小組. 2013. "Yuelu shuyuan cang Qinjian *Wei yu deng zhuang si zhong* gaishu" 嶽麓書院藏秦《爲獄等狀四種》概述. *Wenwu* 2013.5: 77–83.

Yuelu Wei li (zhi guan ji qianshou) 嶽麓爲吏治官及黔首 see Zhu Hanmin and Chen Songchang 2010

Yuelu WYZ=*Yuelu Wei yu (deng) zhuang (si zhong)* 嶽麓爲獄等狀四種 see Zhu Hanmin and Chen Songchang 2013

Yushu 語書 see Shuihudi Qinmu zhujian zhengli xiaozu 1990

Zhang Boyuan 張伯元. 2014a. *Baoshan Chujian anli juyu* 包山楚簡案例舉隅. Shanghai: Shanghai renmin.

———. 2014b. "'Lei lun' yu shuzui bingfa" "累論"與數罪並罰. *Zhongguo gudai falü wenxian yanjiu* 8: 49–54.

———. 2014c. "Yuelu Qinjian (san) zici kaoshi san ze" 嶽麓秦簡（三）字詞考釋三則. Paper presented at the International Conference for Research on Qin manuscripts (Qin jiandu yanjiu guoji xueshu yantaohui 秦簡牘研究國際學術研討會), Changsha, December 6, 2014.

———. 2014d. "*Yuelu shuyuan cang Qinjian* (san) de neirong ji falü shi jiazhi" 《嶽麓書院藏秦簡》（叁）的内容及法律史價值. In Wang Pei 2014, 220–233.

Zhang Chuanxi 張傳璽, ed. 1995. *Zhongguo lidai qiyue huibian kaoshi* 中國歷代契約會編考釋. 2 vols. Beijing: Beijing daxue.

Zhang Ji 張積. 1999. "Liang Han shiqi de susong chengxu" 兩漢時期的訴訟程序. In *Zhongguo fazhi tongshi, di er juan: Zhanguo Qin Han* 中國法制通史，第二卷：戰國秦漢, edited by Xu Shihong 徐世虹, 576–625. Beijing: Falü.

Zhang Jianguo 張建國. 1999. *Dizhi shidai de Zhongguo fa* 帝制時代的中國法. Beijing: Falü chubanshe.

———. 2006. "Handai de fazuo, fuzuo yu chixing" 漢代的罰作復作與弛刑. *Zhongwai faxue* 2006.5, 597–609.

Zhang Jinguang 張金光. 2004. *Qinzhi yanjiu* 秦制研究. Shanghai: Shanghai guji.

Zhang Jue 張覺. 2010. *Hanfeizi jiaoshu* 韓非子校疏. 2 vols. Shanghai: Shanghai guji.

Zhang Peiyu 張培瑜. 2007. “Genju xin chu liri jiandu shilun Qin he Hanchu de lifa” 根據新出曆日簡牘試論秦和漢初的曆法. *Zhongyuan wenwu* 2007.5: 62–77.

Zhang Peiyu and Zhang Chunlong 張春龍. 2006. “Qindai lifa he Zhuanxu li” 秦代曆法和顓頊曆. In *Liye fajue baogao* 里耶發掘報告, edited by Hunan sheng wenwu kaogu yanjiusuo 湖南省文物考古研究所, 735–747. Changsha: Yuelu shushe.

Zhang Rongqiang 張榮強. 2008. “Hunan Liye suo chu ‘Qindai Qianling xian Nanyang li huban’ yanjiu” 湖南里耶所出“秦代遷陵縣南陽里戶版”研究. *Beijing shifan daxue xuebao (shehui kexue ban)* 2008.4: 68–80.

Zhang Shichao 張世超 and Zhang Yuchun 張玉春. 1990. *Qinjian wenzibian* 秦簡文字編. Kyôto: Chûbun.

Zhang Shouzhong 張守中, ed. 1994. *Shuihudi Qinjian wenzibian* 睡虎地秦簡文子編. Beijing: Wenwu.

———, ed. 2012. *Zhangjiashan Hanjian wenzibian* 張家山漢簡文字編. Beijing: Wenwu.

Zhang Xiancheng 張顯成, ed. 2010. *Qinjian zhuzi suoyin* 秦簡逐字索引. Chengdu: Sichuan daxue.

Zhang Yanxiu 張彥修. 2011. “Zhanguo sheren” 戰國舍人. *Guji zhengli yanjiu xuekan* 2011.2: 67–73.

Zhang Yanyan 張岩岩 and Zhong Yi 鐘意. 2014. “Shi shi *Yuelu shuyuan cang Qinjian* (*san*) jian 136 ‘hou qi’, jian 158 ‘da guan’” 試釋《嶽麓書院藏秦簡（叁）》簡136“後妻”、簡158“大官”. <http://www.bsm.org.cn/show_article.php?id=2039>, accessed February 6, 2015.

Zhangjiashan er si qi hao Hanmu zhujian zhengli xiaozu 張家山二四七號漢墓竹簡整理小組, ed. 2001. *Zhangjiashan Hanmu zhujian* (*er si qi hao mu*) 張家山漢墓竹簡〔二四七號墓〕. Beijing: Wenwu.

———, ed. 2006. *Zhangjiashan Hanmu zhujian* (*er si qi hao mu*) (*shiwen xiudingben*) 張家山漢墓竹簡〔二四七號墓〕（釋文修訂本）. Beijing: Wenwu.

Zhanguoce 戰國策 see Lau D. C. and Chen Fong Ching 1992e

Zhao Jiuxiang 趙久湘. 2011. “Qin Han jiandu falü yongyu yanjiu” 秦漢簡牘法律用語研究. PhD diss. Xinan daxue.

Zhao Tong 2003 趙彤. 2003. “Zhanguo Chu fangyan yinxi yanjiu” 戰國楚方言音系研究. PhD diss. Beijing daxue.

Zhengzhang Shangfang 鄭張尚方. 2003. *Shanggu yinxi* 上古音系. Shanghai: Shanghai jiaoyu.

Zhongguo shehui kexueyuan kaogu yanjiusu 中國社會科學院考古研究所. 1980. *Juyan Hanjian jia yi bian* 居延漢簡甲乙編. 2 vols. Vol. 1: tuban 圖版. Beijing: Zhonghua.

———. 2007. *Yin Zhou jinwen jicheng* (*xiuding zengbuben*) 殷周金文集成（修訂增補本）. 8 vols. Beijing: Zhonghua.

Zhongguo wenwu yanjiusuo 中國文物研究所 and Hubei sheng wenwu kaogu yanjiusuo 湖北省文物考古研究所, ed. 2001. *Longgang Qinjian* 龍崗秦簡. Beijing: Zhonghua.

Zhonghua shuju bianjibu 中華書局編輯部, ed. 1981. *Yunmeng Qinjian yanjiu* 雲夢秦簡研究. Beijing: Zhonghua.

Zhongyang yanjiuyuan lishi yuyan yanjiusuo 中央研究院歷史語言研究所 (Academia Sinica, Institute of History and Philology). *Jianbo jinshi ziliaoku* 簡帛金石資料庫. <http://saturn.ihp.sinica.edu.tw/~wenwu/search.htm>, accessed February 20, 2014.

Zhou Haifeng 周海鋒. 2014. "*Wei yu deng zhuang si zhong* zhong de 'li yi' yu 'bang wang'" 《爲獄等狀四種》中的"吏議"與"邦亡". In Wang Pei 2014, 56–62.

Zhou Minhua 周敏華. 2012. "*Zou yan shu* 'shou zhishu wei tun, qu wang' an san ge sifa shuyu zaitan" 《奏讞書》"受致書爲屯，去亡"案三個司法術語再探. *Xuchang xueyuan xuebao* 31.1: 83–87.

Zhou Zhenhe 周振鶴. 1987. *Xihan zhengqu dili* 西漢政區地理. Beijing: Renmin.

Zhou Zumo 周祖謨. 1966. *Wenxue ji* 問學集. 2 vols. Beijing: Zhonghua.

———. 1993. *Fangyan jiaoqian* (*fu suoyin*) 方言校淺（附索引）. Beijing: Zhonghua.

Zhoujiatai 周家臺 see Hubei sheng Jingzhou shi Zhouliangyuqiao yizhi bowuguan 2001

Zhouli 周禮 see Ruan Yuan 1980 (*Zhouli zhushu* 周禮注疏)

Zhoushu 周書. 3 vols. Beijing: Zhonghua, 1971.

Zhu Degui 朱德貴. 2014. "Yuelu Qinjian zouyan wenshu shangye wenti xinzheng" 嶽麓秦簡奏讞文書商業文體新証. *Shehui kexue* 2014.11: 154–165.

Zhu Hanmin 朱漢民 and Chen Songchang 陳松長, ed. 2010. *Yuelu shuyuan cang Qinjian* (*yi*) 嶽麓書院藏秦簡（壹）. Shanghai: Shanghai cishu.

———, ed. 2011. *Yuelu shuyuan cang Qinjian* (*er*) 嶽麓書院藏秦簡（貳）. Shanghai: Shanghai cishu.

———, ed. 2013. *Yuelu shuyuan cang Qinjian* (*san*) 嶽麓書院藏秦簡（叁）. Shanghai: Shanghai cishu.

Zhu Honglin 朱紅林. 2005. *Zhangjiashan Hanjian* Ernian lüling *jishi* 張家山漢簡《二年律令》集釋. Beijing: Shehui kexue wenxian.

———. 2008. *Zhangjiashan Hanjian* Ernian lüling *yanjiu* 張家山漢簡《二年律令》研究. Ha'erbin: Heilongjiang renmin.

———. 2014. "Du *Yuelu shuyuan cang Qinjian* (*san*) zhaji" 讀《嶽麓書院藏秦簡（三）》札記. Paper presented at the International Conference for Research on Qin manuscripts (Qin jiandu yanjiu guoji xueshu yantaohui 秦簡牘研究國際學術研討會), Changsha, December 6, 2014.

Zhu Qifeng 朱起鳳. 1934. *Citong* 辭通. 2 vols. Shanghai: Kaiming shudian.

Zhu Shaohou 朱紹侯. 2008. *Jungong juezhi kaolun* 軍功爵制考論. Beijing: Shangwu.

Zhu Xiangrong 朱湘蓉. 2012. *Qinjian cihui chutan* 秦簡詞彙初探. Beijing: Zhongguo shehui kexue.

Zhu Xiaoxue 朱曉雪. 2013. *Baoshan Chujian zongshu* 包山楚簡綜述. Fuzhou: Fujian renmin.

Zhuang(zi) 莊子 see *Zhuzi jicheng*, vol. 3 (Wang Xianqian 王先謙, *Zhuangzi jijie* 莊子集解)

Zhuzi jicheng 諸子集成. 8 vols. Beijing: Zhonghua, 1954.

Zuo(zhuan) 左傳 see Legge 1960

ZYS=*Zou yan shu* 奏讞書 see Zhangjiashan er si qi hao Hanmu zhujian zhengli xiaozu 2001 (B/W-photos) as well as Peng Hao et al. 2007 (IR-photos/shiwen)

Index

Printed in the United States
By Bookmasters